MW00676990

SAP® Database Administration with Oracle

SAP PRESS is a joint initiative of SAP and Galileo Press. The know-how offered by SAP specialists combined with the expertise of the publishing house Galileo Press offers the reader expert books in the field. SAP PRESS features first-hand information and expert advice, and provides useful skills for professional decision-making.

SAP PRESS offers a variety of books on technical and business related topics for the SAP user. For further information, please visit our website: *www.sap-press.com*.

Thomas Schneider
SAP Performance Optimization Guide
2005, 522 pp.
ISBN 978-1-59229-069-7

Thorsten Wewers, Tim Bolte
mySAP CRM Interaction Center
2006, 261 pp.
ISBN 978-1-59229-067-3

Marc O. Schäfer, Matthias Melich
SAP Solution Manager
2007, 490 pp.
ISBN 978-1-59229-091-8

Carsten Bönnen, Mario Herger
SAP NetWeaver Visual Composer
2007, 524 pp.
ISBN 978-1-59229-099-4

Michael Höding, André Faustmann,
Gunnar Klein, Ronny Zimmermann

SAP® Database Administration with Oracle

Bonn • Boston

ISBN 978-1-59229-120-5

1st edition 2008

Acquisitions Editors Mirja Werner, Florian Zimniak
English Edition Editor Jutta VanStean
Copy Editor Ruth Saavreda
Cover Design Silke Braun
Layout Design Vera Brauner
Production Katrin Müller
Typesetting III-satz, Husby
Printed and bound in Germany

German Edition first published 2007 by Galileo Press.

Contents at a Glance

Contents

Who is this book for? For users!

1 Introduction

SAP software plays a central role in many organizations.[1] Besides applications in the Enterprise Resource Planning (ERP) area, there is also an entire range of SAP technology-based applications that cover other areas in enterprises. Important examples are SAP NetWeaver Business Intelligence (SAP NetWeaver BI), and SAP Supply Chain Management (SAP SCM), which supports the Supply Chain Management process. The framework for all of these applications is the SAP NetWeaver stack; and what most of them have in common is the *SAP Basis* (i.e., the architecture of the application server and the database). Although SAP software has an inherently high level of database independence, the database management system (DBMS) from Oracle is nonetheless the system that is installed and used the most, especially in live operations.

Administering ERP systems such as SAP is a complex and mission-critical task in enterprises. The wide range of functions and applications provided by SAP often gives rise to solution landscapes that generally develop in a dynamic, and therefore sometimes unpredictable, way. Thus, it is important that you make the correct strategic decisions so that you can plan for the future and, at the same time, optimize your enterprise's costs. Another aspect of this issue is that administrators have to be able to make decisions quickly and assuredly, often under great time restraints. We have learned that having a fundamental and in-depth understanding of SAP technology is critical in helping you to find the right solutions for these mission-critical tasks.

The goal of this book, therefore, is to provide a detailed explanation of how to run Oracle-based SAP systems. As an administrator or decision-maker, you rarely need to focus exclusively on the underlying Oracle database; as a result, some parts of the book deal with topics that are not directly related to

1 Even enterprises that don't use SAP software often require SAP interfaces so that they can conduct business electronically with their partners.

Oracle. In our experience, this approach supports your understanding of the complexity of the SAP landscape, and therefore the daily work of managing the system. After all, solving problems also means being familiar with alternatives and being able to evaluate them; furthermore, the Oracle-based solution is not always the optimal one.

1.1 Reasons for Owning This Book

When planning and preparing a book, authors must always first ask themselves one important question: Why are we writing this book? Ultimately, all of the possible answers to this question can be summarized as follows: We are writing this book because the reader needs it.[2]

The 10 good reasons why the reader (you) should own this book are:

1. You're a Basis administrator and have a specific problem regarding the administration of an SAP system. This book provides several tips and solutions for a range of problems.
2. Your goal is to structure the operation of your system to achieve higher performance. This book will help you develop the level of understanding required to perform this task. It discusses possible solutions in the areas of system landscape, system architecture, and SAP Basis and Oracle.
3. Your goal is to improve data security and availability. This book explains alternative data backup methods in detail, especially in conjunction with Oracle. It also discusses infrastructural aspects, which are seldom addressed in the literature.
4. You want to simplify and enhance the administration of your SAP system landscape. This book introduces you to tools and techniques that you can use for this purpose, along with application servers and the Oracle database.
5. You plan to install an SAP landscape in your enterprise. This book comprehensively presents the technical knowledge you need to do this, and introduces you to the terminology of information technology.

2 We mean "needs" here in two senses: First, in the sense that the reader needs this book in order to understand and solve problems; and secondly, in the sense that it can be used every day as an accessible source of advice, hopefully with well-thumbed pages and Post-it notes ("post-its") marking important points.

6. You want to upgrade an existing "old" SAP installation to the latest release and install other SAP applications at the same time. This book explains the options and methods available for developing your system landscape and hardware.
7. You're an Oracle expert and would like to use your knowledge in the SAP environment. This book explains how SAP uses the Oracle database software.
8. You have an information technology qualification and are interested in learning more about SAP and Oracle. This book connects information technology knowledge with the SAP world. In doing so, it facilitates first steps in this area and helps you avoid common misunderstandings.
9. You have experience with SAP administration and would like to get an up-to-date overview of SAP Basis technology. The didactic approach of this book will help you to achieve this level of knowledge.
10. You would like to use SAP in information management or information technology education or training. Used as a textbook, this book can help you learn about several software engineering and database technology techniques with SAP.

The goal of this introductory chapter is to give you an initial overview of the content and structure of the book, and to help you determine how you would best like to navigate through the chapters.

At this time, we would like to point out some limitations of this book:

- When we refer to "Oracle" in this book, we mean specifically the database management software made by the Oracle company. In other words, we use the term "Oracle" as a synonym for the Oracle database management system (DBMS).[3]
- This book is not thoroughly "modern." Because it is based on practical experience, it deals with some technologies that are already obsolete and therefore are no longer used in new installations. The reason for this is

3 This makes sense because Oracle is known mainly for its extremely innovative and successful database management system. Of course, this doesn't mean that other Oracle products have not also been successful, partly due to takeovers and merger processes. The Oracle E-Business Suite, for example, is a direct competitor product to SAP application software in some areas. Oracle also has innovations and products in the application server area, in which it competes with IBM and Sun, and the Java and SAP NetWeaver area, where it is again in competition with new SAP solutions. Although doubtless interesting, these products are only marginally relevant to most SAP system administrators and are therefore not addressed in this book.

the existence of numerous live systems with R/3 release levels before 4.7, which are based on older versions of Oracle. New technologies, such as that for Space Management, can be complicated to use in such systems. Therefore, in some parts of this book, we must necessarily refer to "obsolete" technologies.

- When dealing with SAP, our sole focus is the technical area. Topics that involve business aspects are mentioned only in passing.
- In principle, SAP supports various database management systems. However, due to its outstanding suitability, Oracle is used in numerous live SAP systems, and is therefore the focus of this book. Nonetheless, this book contains several sections that will be useful to administrators of other kinds of SAP installations, such as the sections on software logistics and the system lifecycle.
- Because UNIX-based SAP systems are used in the vast majority of live SAP installations, we deal only marginally with the administration of SAP systems on Windows platforms. Consequently, this book has many examples and tips for the UNIX environment.

Despite these limitations, and even if your main interest lies outside the scope of this book, it can still help you develop a comprehensive understanding of the subject matter.

1.2 Tasks of the SAP Basis

The term *SAP Basis* is a typical word from the world of SAP terminology. It refers first to the *Basis software*, that is, roughly speaking, all non-business components of the SAP system. Secondly, SAP Basis is often used to refer to the *area of SAP Basis administration*, which comprises technical administration tasks and the staff members who are responsible for carrying them out.

In IT infrastructures, it is not possible to enclose Basis administration tasks fully and in a stable manner. Of course, there is a range of core tasks that clearly belong to the SAP Basis, and there can be varying degrees of strict or formal specialization within a Basis team. Besides these core tasks, there are also several tasks that require the support of the SAP Basis team. Then there are tasks that clearly should not belong to the SAP Basis, as they deal with business or organizational aspects.

Figure 1.1 shows an example of important tasks that belong to each of these three categories.

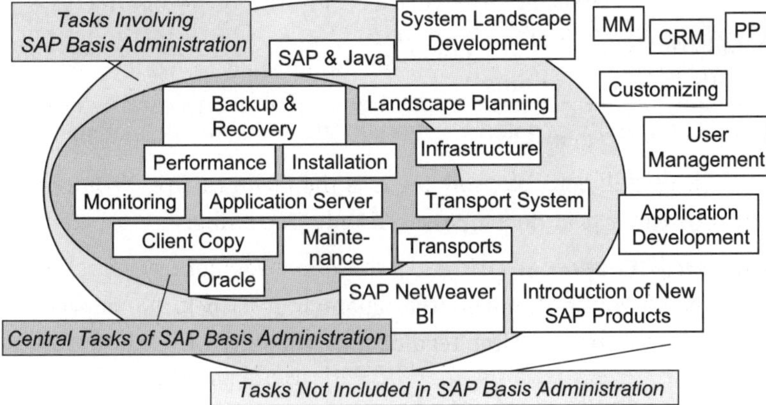

Figure 1.1 Tasks in the SAP Basis Environment

1.3 Structure of This Book

In this section, we present the structure of this book. We describe the content and goal of each individual chapter, and the knowledge and skills that you should possess after reading each chapter.

- **SAP Fundamentals (Chapter 2)**
  This chapter deals with the basic concepts, architectures, and technical foundations of SAP software, with reference to information technology concepts. For many readers, this chapter will seem repetitive; however, it does provide a straightforward way of gaining an understanding of SAP software. This chapter will enable you to do the following:
  - Understand and describe the structure and technology of the SAP system
  - Identify problems and know the part(s) of the software from which they originate
  - Communicate more effectively with users and developers
  - Perform basic monitoring tasks
- **Oracle Fundamentals (Chapter 3)**
  This chapter describes the basic principles of Oracle database technology. Like the previous chapter, this chapter repeats some fundamental points. We present the technical core of Oracle and the relevant administration tools in detail. After reading this chapter and working through the examples, you will be able to do the following:

- Understand and describe the structure and technology of Oracle
- Use and control an Oracle system using the SQL query language and Oracle tools such as sqlplus
- Identify and classify problems, especially those in storage management
- Perform basic monitoring tasks
- Support planners and developers

- **SAP and Oracle (Chapter 4)**
  Based on the previous chapters, this chapter describes the interaction between SAP and Oracle. After reading this chapter, you will know the following:
  - How SAP and Oracle influence and communicate with each other
  - What the prerequisites are for making this interaction problem-free
  - What Oracle characteristics are used by SAP
  - What the main SAP tools are in terms of Oracle administration
- **Planning the System Landscape (Chapter 5)**
  The decisions you need to make in the planning phase of SAP-Oracle installations are complex and far-reaching. This chapter explains both the SAP and the Oracle approaches to this topic. It therefore serves as an aid to the reader in planning system landscapes, for both new and existing planning processes. You can use this chapter in the following ways:
  - As a framework that contains the most important aspects of and basic conditions for planning
  - To evaluate and use SAP strategies to structure system landscapes
  - As a basis for decisions for designing the system landscape
- **SAP Change and Transport Management (Chapter 6)**
  This chapter describes the knowledge you need to work with SAP's change and transport system. It presents the basic concepts and background of software logistics, change management, and transport management in a detailed and systematic way. It will enable you to set up and manage complex transport landscapes, and you will learn how to use the most important tools both in the SAP system and on the operating system level. After reading this chapter, you will be able to do the following:

  - Set up transport systems to interconnect SAP systems
  - Use change management for customizing and development, and use transport management functions
  - Use the available architectures and tools

- **System Lifecycle (Chapter 7)**
  During its lifecycle, an SAP system goes through different phases, which are explained in this chapter. The goal of this chapter is to give you tips and tricks for each individual phase, and it covers everything including installation and post-installation adjustments, software maintenance via patch imports into the mutually influencing GUI, SAP, Oracle and operating system levels, and possible upgrades to new releases. After reading this chapter, you will be able to do the following:
  - Estimate the steps required before and after installation
  - Import system patches
  - Plan an upgrade to your SAP system and the database

- **Performance (Chapter 8)**
  Performance is a central aspect of the usability of a system. For this reason, SAP software provides several analysis and optimization options, covering both administrative aspects and development aspects. This chapter explains the most important of the performance-tuning options. We also elaborate on how to use the performance optimization functions provided by Oracle. This chapter does the following:
  - Helps you identify and classify performance problems
  - Highlights possible solutions on the various levels
  - Supports a fundamental understanding of performance optimization

- **System Operation and Monitoring (Chapter 9)**
  Continuous system monitoring is a necessary task, especially in live systems, so that the system administrator can react preventatively to problems – that is, before an escalation occurs. In this chapter, we use examples to describe the monitoring tools that are available to you. This chapter will help you to do the following:
  - Plan and optimize the administration of SAP landscapes
  - Select and use tools
  - Partially automate the administration task via scripts

- **Backup, Restore, and Recovery (Chapter 10)**
  Data security is one of the most important challenges in business applications. It is implemented mainly through Oracle mechanisms, which are used by SAP Basis. Examples are used in this chapter to explain how to plan a backup strategy. It also presents typical error scenarios and describes the process of systematic restoration. This chapter will help you to do the following:
  - Set up or optimize a backup architecture
  - Plan, execute and automate backups
  - Be aware of alternative tools and technologies
  - Execute any required restoration in a systematic manner
- **Managing the Java Stack (Chapter 11)**
  Currently, SAP requires the use of Java. In this context, many system operators and administrators wonder what implications this has on system operation. The important questions are those related to architecture, software logistics, and use of the Oracle database. This chapter gives you the following:
  - Familiarity with the architecture of the Java core
  - The ability to follow and understand the example of how to use the SAP NetWeaver Development Infrastructure (NWDI)
  - Fundamental knowledge of how to parameterize the J2EE Engine
- **SAP NetWeaver BI and Oracle (Chapter 12)**
  SAP NetWeaver Business Intelligence (SAP NetWeaver BI), SAP's data warehouse, is the most widely used SAP application after the R/3 system. SAP NetWeaver BI is a particular type of database; rather than processing dynamic data, it stores and analyzes historical data. This results in different kinds of requirements of the underlying Oracle software, which has its own data warehousing functionality (from version 9). This chapter provides you with the following information:
  - A concise introduction to the characteristics of data warehousing
  - A description of the SAP NetWeaver BI architecture
  - An introduction to parameterizing Oracle for SAP NetWeaver BI

Although many aspects of SAP system administration cannot be dealt with fully in these chapters, very few readers will be able to read this book in a single sitting. For this reason, most of the chapters are self-contained, although basic SAP knowledge is a prerequisite. For some particular user groups, we would like to recommend the following approaches to using this book:

- **Active Basis administrators whose goal is specific problem-solving**
  Chapters 4, 6, 8, 9, and 10 contain lots of concrete tips for finding quick solutions, and will almost certainly cover any specific problem. It is also a good idea to prepare yourself for potential future situations by honing an understanding of the underlying mechanisms of the system.
- **Active Basis administrators who are interested in new technology**
  New topics that can present challenges to administrators are addressed in Chapters 5, 7, and 11. In this way, administrators can enhance their technical competence in a targeted way and therefore prepare for new challenges that are often presented to them by external parties.
- **Beginners in SAP Basis administration**
  Beginners in this topic with a solid information technology qualification will find a convenient point of access to SAP Basis in Chapters 2, 3, and 4. These chapters make intensive use of the readers' existing knowledge, as building on existing knowledge is integral to understanding SAP technology. This book is therefore suitable for use as a support tool in SAP Basis training.
- **Planners and IT managers**
  Chapters 5, 6, and 7 provide planners and IT managers with a thorough understanding of the technical aspects of SAP landscapes. These chapters will give you a concise and detailed overview of the tasks that need to be performed in your area of responsibility, and will support you in your strategic planning.

If one of these roles applies to you, this book will certainly support you in your daily work.

1.4 Conventions and Other Information

We use the following conventions in this book:

- A path to a specific point in the Easy Access menu is formulated as follows: **Tools • ABAP Workbench • Test • Runtime Analysis**.
- Transaction codes — such as SE30, for example — are given in many cases as a convenient way of directly accessing functions.

- With Oracle 10, the SAP Solution Manager was used in some of the examples. The SAP Solution Manager is based on the SAP core, which you should be familiar with from the R/3 system, and is a comprehensive management tool for SAP landscapes that can be used to roll out SAP solutions. Oracle 10.2 on VMWare and Suse Linux were used for the examples in Chapter 3.
- SAP Notes are an invaluable support for running SAP systems, and are usually very up-to-date and comprehensive. You can access them via the SAP Service Marketplace. At several points throughout the book, we highlight important notes as follows: see *SAP Note 39412*.

Although this book appears to be very comprehensive, not all topics are covered in full. In these cases, we refer you to additional reading, which, in the SAP world, is provided largely by SAP PRESS.

1.5 Acknowledgements

This book was only possible because of the support that we received from many people.

First, we would like to thank our editors at SAP PRESS, Florian Zimniak and Mirja Werner, who guided us through this major project with a gentle hand. We would also like to thank Iris Warkus for resolving many time-consuming problems with the format template, which is a great template. For the translation into English we thank Jutta VanStean, Nancy Etscovitz, and Ruth Saavedra.

The constructive criticism we received from our SAP colleagues on Stefan Kuhlmann's team was particularly valuable. They helped us to keep the content accurate and clearly readable. We must mention two people in particular — Christian Graf and Martin Frauendorfer — for their boundless support. They definitely deserve a heartfelt "thank you."

Another big "thank you" must go to Prof. Dr. Claus Rautenstrauch. In addition to putting us in touch with the publisher, he also provided us with both technical and moral support. Furthermore, as the father of the SAP University Competence Center in Magdeburg, he has created an ideal technical and organizational framework for researching complex SAP landscapes. In this context, we must also thank Heino Schrader and Thomas Habersack (SAP AG), Bernd Herzer and Thomas Alter (HP Deutschland GmbH), and Dr. Wolfgang Schröder (T-Systems Enterprise Services GmbH).

Our eagle-eyed proofreaders, Andrea Diekmann, Hans-Joachim Herzberg, Michael Hoppe, Torsten König, Peter Krüger, Angela Merkel, Norman Meuschke, André Siegling, René Tschiersch, and Stefan Weidner ensured that our awkward expressions, technical errors, and typos were minimal. To them, we give many thanks! Also, our colleagues at T-Systems Magdeburg, SAP UCC Magdeburg, and the Brandenburg University of Applied Sciences all deserve a big "thank you" for their expertise and many ideas and suggestions.

Last, and most importantly, we extend our very sincere thanks to our families and friends, who kept believing in us even in the difficult times. We know it wasn't always easy.

Magdeburg, Germany, January 2008
André Faustmann
Michael Höding
Gunnar Klein
Ronny Zimmermann

What is SAP? What are its capabilities? How does it work? In this chapter, we'll address these questions.

2 SAP Fundamentals

SAP software can be found virtually everywhere. SAP integrates the most diverse departments of an enterprise or even entire enterprises. SAP software is implemented in organizations and public authorities, and, in some cases, connects enterprises and authorities. Numerous views of the complex system require specialists in various areas like applications, Customizing, or SAP Basis administration.

Because the technical view is critical for readers of this book, we begin this chapter with a short categorization of SAP software in the context of information management. Next, we introduce important terminology of the SAP world, and then, we provide you with a detailed look at the fundamental SAP technologies, which primarily include the SAP architecture, which is highly scalable. We will then examine structures and procedures of the SAP application server in detail. Furthermore, we'll present typical administration tasks that will be further illustrated in the following chapters of this book. Using examples, we will briefly describe the ABAP programming language and mention some other concepts that enable the development within and use of SAP systems. You will therefore gain an overview of the basic features of the SAP software.

2.1 Overview of the SAP Software

Although this book clearly focuses on technology, we will still explain some basic terms and concepts that are intended to help you to implement the technical knowledge in larger contexts.

2.1.1 Standard Software versus Individual Software

SAP R/3 is an *integrated* and, above all, *integrating standard business software*. Information management distinguishes between individual software and standard software. *Individual software* is developed for a specific application case. Conversely, *standard software* should be able to be used for many similar application cases. Computer scientists, however, are sometimes confused by the term "standard software" and wonder whether SAP complies with the ISO, DIN, or OSI standards.

2.1.2 Integration

SAP R/3 was developed based on the financial success of and the experience with SAP R/2. The basic business processes were collected, compared, unified (i.e., standardized), and implemented as software. Particularly the identification of processes is a procedure that requires a lot of effort and experience. Vice versa, the introduction of standard software in an enterprise is initially a complex task because it often requires the enterprise to reconsider its operational processes and to optimize them. Therefore, the introduction of standard software always involves investments in the structures and processes of the enterprise.

An important factor that determines success is *integration*. All business-relevant data is stored in a standardized and consistent way. This advantage is significant because on the one hand, you can rely on the data to be complete and correct. On the other hand, complex data and manually driven synchronization can be avoided. For example, once Factory B has been informed that a customer's address has changed, it is no longer possible that Factory A uses the old customer address for delivery.

Users often perceive the restriction of their autonomy and freedom of action as a disadvantage. The reason for these (seeming) disadvantages of integration is, for example, that no actions can be taken which violate the consistency of data. For example, a sales person cannot sell a pump that is not on stock and for which no production capacity is available, if processes have been defined that way. These restrictions are annoying to users but essential for correct business processing. Another disadvantage of integration is that it sometimes rules out better special applications for managing storage locations, for example. However, SAP currently provides powerful technologies for supporting the integration of such systems.

2.1.3 Development of SAP R/3

Since its introduction in 1992, SAP R/3 has been continuously developed. In cooperation with partners, its functionality has been gradually extended according to demand. If an important customer found that new developments were required for essential functional areas, they were directly supported by SAP AG in the form of development partnerships. Successful developments were evaluated and integrated as standard. This is how interesting solutions have been created during the last decade for virtually all general tasks.

The software updates that occur in accordance with changing legal conditions – and that are currently discussed under the keyword *compliance* – is another important aspect to consider. The user of a standard software can be sure that the next tax increase or the next new tax type is correctly mapped in the system via the corresponding support package. The user of individual software probably needs to invest a lot of work and still cannot be sure that the change has really been implemented in all required places.

The SAP technology is continuously enhanced as well. SAP R/3 comes as a *client/server system*. The application of this type of architecture, which is very common today, was a revolution in the late 1980s, when SAP R/3 was developed. Up until then, the integration in business applications was implemented via *one* central mainframe on which all programs were running. There were two different operation types: *stack processing* (derived from the formerly used punchcard stacks) and *dialog mode*. Both concepts have their equivalents in the modern SAP system. The dialog mode presented a special challenge to the mainframe world, because the character-based terminal was usually operated by impatient and erratic users. Therefore, the dialog mode was enabled for only really important tasks to be performed immediately. Operations that didn't need to be urgently processed could later be updated asynchronously.

With the client/server technology used in SAP R/3, the "ignorant" display-only ASCII terminals were replaced with "smart" graphical client computers that were able to solve partial tasks without interacting with the server. The user-friendly presentation was a criterion for success that caused SAP R/3 to be introduced in many companies and application areas.

Another success factor of SAP R/3 is its powerful and scalable architecture that particularly enables a high-performing dialog mode. This powerful and ergonomic architecture led to widespread use of SAP R/3 and enhancement of the standard version for additional task fields. Other SAP products are based on the SAP Basis technology originally developed for SAP R/3. For example, SAP Supply Chain Management (SAP SCM) is available for the administration of supply chains. For strategic support, the products of the

Business Intelligence area, in particular, SAP NetWeaver Business Intelligence (SAP NetWeaver BI), are commonly used. In this respect, the basic knowledge from SAP Basis administration can be directly adapted for other SAP products.

But not all of the operations of an enterprise can be appropriately covered by standard software. In core areas of the enterprise, that is, in the areas contributing considerably to the success and market position of the enterprise, individual software must be used and enhanced. Therefore, there are limits for the integration using standard software.

Of course, individual software refers also to the areas covered by standard software. Integration is necessary to avoid integration gaps, which can lead to additional effort or inconsistencies. For this purpose, SAP offers a wide range of concepts and technologies. Another development of the last decade is the evolution of the Internet into a mass medium. This involves new standard software requirements, for example, E-Commerce or E-Business. Therefore, SAP technologies and solutions were developed to enable a direct connection of external areas to the enterprise-internal standard software.

The SAP NetWeaver architecture bundles these technologies and solutions into a single integration architecture that serves as an overall framework (see Figure 2.1). This involves structuring and homogenizing the architecture as well as developing the technology basis.

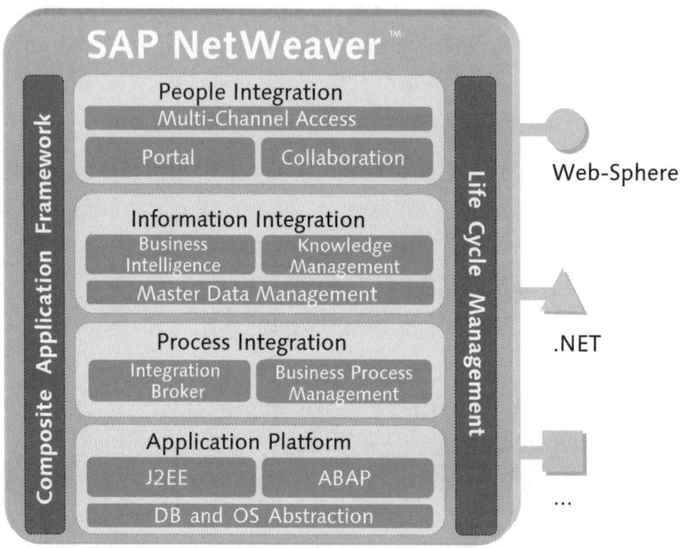

Figure 2.1 SAP NetWeaver as Integration Architecture

For example, the support of Java in the SAP kernel is extensively pushed forward.

Other latest developments focus on supporting flexible business processes, opening the system via *Web Services*, and a *service-oriented architecture*.

Figure 2.2 shows the development of SAP R/3 since Release 4.6C. Up until Release 4.6C, the SAP kernel was presented as a monolith. Release 4.6D separates the application and the SAP Basis, which enables you to enhance the two independently of each other. Since Release 4.7, developments of the original application were offered as *Enterprise Extension Sets (EES)*. In Release 6.10, the *Internet Communication Manager* (ICM) was provided for the first time. But Release 6.10 was used primarily for evaluation projects. Release 6.20 is referred to as the first SAP NetWeaver release; it supports Java. In Release 6.40, the application was restructured and renamed to *Enterprise Core Component (ECC)*. The *Internet Transaction Server* (ITS) was included in the kernel in that version.

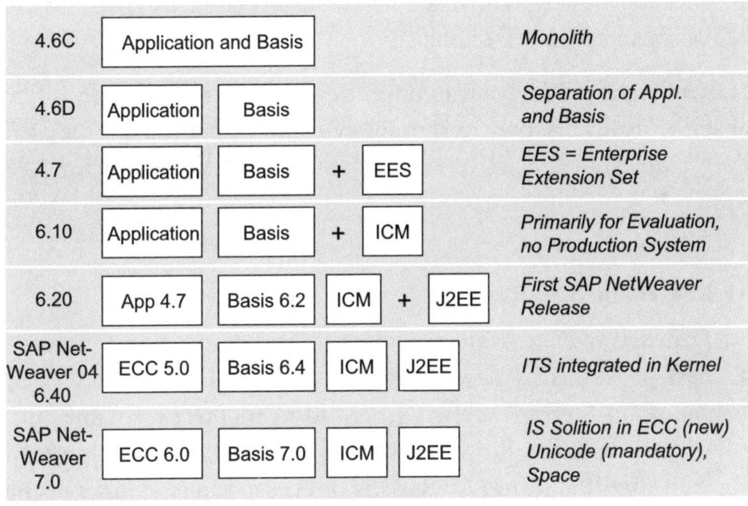

Figure 2.2 SAP History

Release 7.0 provides innovations such as consistent Unicode support, requiring more memory space for the database. Current architectures enable you to set up systems without application components, that is, you can install an SAP Basis without applications; therefore, it's provided with an application server for future installation of applications or any other use.

2.1.4 SAP Terminology

Along with the SAP software, a self-contained terminology has been developed. In this section, we'll explain some of the terms. These include terms that are used in a different sense in computer science. There are also concepts where alternatives have been established in a broader context. There are three objective reasons for this need for alternative concepts, which may be potentially confusing and hard to understand for those who are new to SAP systems:

- SAP R/3 is, among others, based on the standard systems being successfully marketed by SAP. These systems are subject to the mainframe world, which, for example, differentiated between dialog and batch modes. Terms related to it can also be found in the current SAP R/3 system.
- Since its inception, SAP has been strongly characterized by its business application. For this reason, some of the terms refer to this application.
- From a technical point of view, SAP R/3 implemented numerous future-oriented concepts; however, instead of the terms used by SAP, others were established in computer science.

In no way, however, does SAP want to limit the administration to only a few SAP specialists by using its own terminology. Still, you should note that understanding and using special terms and concepts is necessary for SAP administration.

2.1.4.1 SAP Kernel and SAP Basis

The SAP kernel consists of executable programs and programs being executed (processes). These processes are described in detail in Section 2.3.1, *Overview of the SAP Application Server Processes.* In addition to the executable programs, the *SAP Basis* includes the administration transactions programmed in ABAP. Furthermore, the term SAP Basis is often used for the tasks of the fundamental SAP administration, including the database administration and the team responsible for these tasks. With regard to the Java kernel that is now also available, it is more precise to speak of the *ABAP kernel* than of the SAP kernel.

2.1.4.2 Transaction

In the SAP world, the term *transaction* describes a sequence of connected steps for processing an operation, such as the creation of an order. As is the case with the transactions for database systems, the ACID properties (see Section 3.1.2, *Tasks and Functions of Database Systems*) are supposed to be applied, that is, the transaction is executed correctly and without side effects. The term *transaction* has its origin in the business area.

In contrast to typical database transactions, SAP transactions run longer, usually with various user interactions. Moreover, numerous transactions are available for the administration of the SAP system as well. Therefore, transactions could also be described as application programs running on SAP.

In order to solve typical tasks, transaction numbers are often proposed in this book. For example, we recommend using Transaction SM50 later on. SM50 is the transaction number (virtually, the transaction name) calling a respective ABAP program. The numbers are based on a certain system, which is not always entirely clear. All transactions can also be started via the tree structure of the SAP Easy Access Menu, but during practical administration, you have to remember and directly enter the important transaction codes.

If you work with people who are not familiar with SAP, you should keep in mind that the term *transaction* could be confusing or, even worse, lead to misunderstandings.

2.1.4.3 Dynpro

Dynpro stands for dynamic program and describes an SAP screen template with comprehensive functions. This includes the display with value help or screen templates with detailed navigation and so on.

2.1.4.4 ABAP and ABAP/4

ABAP is the programming language of SAP R/3. All programs of the business application and numerous programs for administration are implemented in ABAP. Currently, the description *Advanced Business and Application Programming* is used for ABAP.

The description ABAP/4 stresses that ABAP is understood as a fourth-generation programming language. In fact, it goes beyond the imperative third-generation languages, such as Pascal or C, in many areas. Therefore, the ABAP Framework provides modules to generate surfaces and the respective program codes. Furthermore, object-oriented concepts are also added in

ABAP. Interesting aspects are the direct embedding of SQL in ABAP and some of the extension semantics that are provided.

Those of you who are already familiar with ABAP should not have any problems, although syntax and type concepts are sometimes unusual. For development processes with ABAP, SAP provides a development environment. It includes tools for software management supporting the encapsulation and transport of developments.

In SAP, it is interesting to note that programs are referred to as *reports*. The origin of this is that initially ABAP was used primarily as a flexible tool to generate reports. Therefore, the term *ABAP report* is often used.

2.1.4.5 Customizing

Adjusting a standard system to the precise requirements of an enterprise is called *Customizing*. This concept does not describe how to programmatically set up the system, as computer specialists often erroneously assume. In fact, an initial data basis (e.g., product catalogs, product structures, payment methods, and so on) is maintained or established in the system. The corresponding settings and procedures are already implemented in SAP.

From among the numerous possibilities, the Customizing process chooses those options that must be used for the enterprise. In this context, it may happen that procedures that have not been applied by the enterprise so far but make economic sense can now be used. In very rare cases, SAP has not implemented a procedure being used in the enterprise. Both situations turn Customizing into a process, which involves business and organizational changes that require employee motivation and training.

2.1.4.6 SAP Service Marketplace, SAP Notes, OSS

In the past, SAP offered technical information and help for problem handling via the *Online Service and Support* (OSS). OSS1, a special SAP transaction, was provided for this purpose but has since lost its importance. The term *OSS Note* has been ingrained by SAP administrators and will definitely be referenced often, even if it is viewed as being obsolete. For the past few years, *SAP Service Marketplace* has provided a user-friendly, Internet-based alternative, enabling you to access SAP Notes. Concurrently, the "old" OSS has been disabled and the SAP Service Marketplace has been established as part of the SAP Support Portal.

2.1.4.7 Client and Company Code

Business units often affect the database. In SAP, a *client* is the highest organizational unit and corresponds, for example, to the corporate group. *Company codes* correspond to companies or subsidiaries. SAP contains *client-dependent* and *client-independent* tables. This means that in a client-dependent table, the `MANDT` attribute is always a part of the key for the table. Clients can be copied. In this process, the data sets whose `MANDT` numbers correspond to the `MANDT` number of the source client, are duplicated and the new `MANDT` number is entered at the database level. As an administrator, one of your tasks is to make client copies. In this way, considerable preparations can be made, but creating client copies can significantly strain the system and may be time-consuming.

Only in rare cases do implementations utilize the client concept, that is, usually there is only one company and hence only one client and one company code. If you neglect these structures during application development, this may lead to performance problems (see Chapter 8, *Performance*). The client concept is often used as an alternative. In seminars, client copies are used for trainings to minimize the risk of data losses. Here, the source client is virtually an SAP-internal data backup. Clients can also be used for separating development and testing.

In this section, we explained some of the terms of the SAP terminology that — from our point of view — are sometimes confusing. This book introduces and explains many other terms in detail when specific topics are described.

2.2 Architecture and Scalability

SAP R/3 is provided as a *three-layer client/server architecture*. First, we will briefly describe this architecture:

- The *presentation layer* contains the software needed for communication with the user. In SAP systems, the SAP GUI acts as a fat client that displays the user interface, supports input, and preprocesses and validates input. In general, the presentation layer contains a large number of GUIs.
- Acting as the server, the *application layer* provides data for the SAP GUIs via the SAP GUI protocol and receives orders and input through that protocol. The application server is a unit containing various, synchronized processes that communicate and cooperate via a shared memory. The application layer of an SAP R/3 system can consist of more than one appli-

cation server. These servers are also called *instances*. The instances can run on different servers, thus higher performance and an improved system stability can be achieved.

- As the server for the application servers (as clients), the *database layer* manages the data and is therefore responsible for the secure and quick data storage and recovery. For this purpose, SAP uses relational database management systems (DBMS) such as Oracle. The database layer represents the basic integration platform. Here, the consistent cooperation of different areas of an enterprise is supported via a redundancy-free storage.

By using different configurations, the three-layer architecture provides extensive scalability options (see Figure 2.3):

- The minimal setup consists of one machine. Here, all three levels are located on one machine. This is useful for demo installations (Figure 2.3 a).
- Configurations with an application and database layer installed on one server machine are very common for live systems (Figure 2.3 b).
- If the application and database layers are set up on different machines, a higher performance level can be achieved (Figure 2.3 c).
- By using different application servers each on specific servers, the performance of the application layer can be improved. For this purpose, the filling of the application server caches, which improves the performance, can be optimized by assigning certain application servers to specific business task areas (Figure 2.3 d).

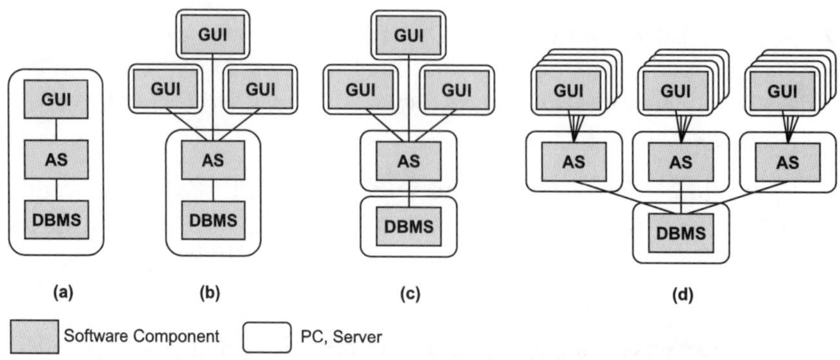

Figure 2.3 Variants of the Three-Layer SAP Architecture

Regarding Oracle, there is another possibility for scaling. The *Oracle Real Application Cluster* (RAC) can be used to distribute the database layer across different servers. On the one hand, this enables you to distribute the database layer to several cost-saving servers. On the other hand, new database performance levels can be achieved by using powerful servers within the cluster. On its website, Oracle promotes its products with the statement that applications using Oracle RAC run "faster than the fastest mainframe." It also improves the availability because the Oracle server as a single point of failure (SpoF) is replaced by a cluster of servers. A disadvantage is its high complexity.

SAP concepts use the current developments in the area of server systems efficiently. Blade servers contain application servers, and powerful servers with a high I/O performance contain the central database layer. Installations used for the purpose of *application service* use such a database server (hardware) to operate different database management systems for different SAP systems (see Figure 2.4).

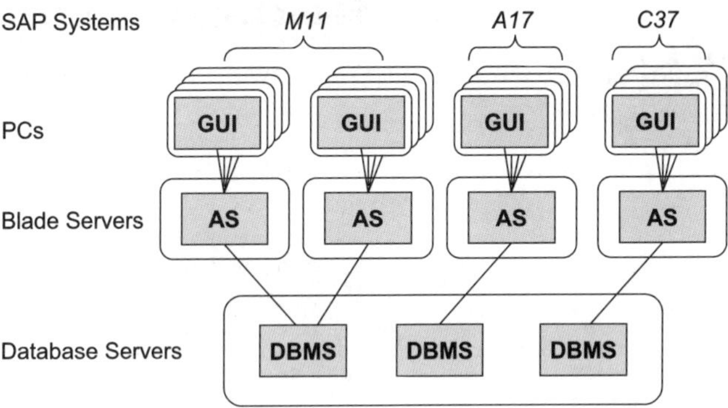

Figure 2.4 Sample Configuration for ASP

For the development, testing, and live operation, SAP proposes a system landscape that consists of separate, self-contained development, testing, and live systems. Therefore, you usually must plan and supervise several different setups of SAP systems. Of course, financially it doesn't make much sense to purchase a similar powerful hardware for the testing and development system, as the one that is being used for the heavily loaded production system. Instead, cheaper configurations are used based on the variants introduced here.

2.3 Application Server

The *application server* is the core of the SAP system. It consists of several processes that communicate with each other, and memory structures. As a *service provider*, it responds to the requests of SAP GUIs. As a *client*, it uses the data service of the database management system via SQL. For this purpose, it uses various database management systems through a standard interface. For administrators, it is essential to understand the concepts and technologies described here. We'll describe the dominating Oracle system in detail in Chapter 3.

2.3.1 Overview of the SAP Application Server Processes

As the active elements of the application server, SAP processes provide services. In UNIX installations, they can be monitored using the `top` or `ps` commands (see Figure 2.5). It is obvious that various processes have their origin in the same executable program (`dw.sap<SID>`). This *Disp+Work program* is the actual kernel of the SAP system and assumes the respective roles.

```
hoeding@servi:~
System: f38                                                Fri Sep 29 11:37:01 2006
Load averages: 0.02, 0.02, 0.03
498 processes: 465 sleeping, 33 running
Cpu states: (avg)
 LOAD    USER    NICE     SYS    IDLE  BLOCK  SWAIT    INTR    SSYS
 0.02    0.0%    0.0%    0.2%   99.8%   0.0%   0.0%    0.0%    0.0%

Memory: 28530644K (5821864K) real, 56380180K (10578288K) virtual, 256488K free  P
Page# 1/36

CPU TTY     PID USERNAME PRI NI    SIZE     RES STATE      TIME %WCPU  %CPU COMMAND
 2    ?   10769 a28adm   155 20   5322M  75448K sleep    134:19  2.49  2.48 dw.sapA28
 5    ?      54 root     152 20   2176K   2176K run      438:34  1.49  1.49 vxfsd
 2    ?   11792 m29adm   155 20   5378M  73664K sleep      0:36  1.30  1.30 dw.sapM29
 1    ?   10775 oraa28   154 20   4523M   5580K sleep     27:25  0.74  0.73 oracleA28
 4 pts/0   7150 hoeding  178 20   5652K   1148K run        0:00  0.63  0.57 top
 2    ?   10080 a08adm   168 20  20316K  11924K sleep    173:32  0.46  0.46 saposcol
 4    ?    1493 root     152 20    261M  44508K run       40:22  0.43  0.43 prm3d
 7    ?   11766 m29adm   155 20   5440M    137M sleep    166:55  0.31  0.31 dw.sapM29
 2    ?     901 root     152 20  17548K   2924K run       26:19  0.26  0.26 ldapclien
 3    ?    4094 a28adm   155 20   5308M  54832K sleep      0:03  0.26  0.26 dw.sapA28
 2    ?   11279 a38adm   155 20   5395M  90392K sleep    143:09  0.26  0.26 dw.sapA38oscol
 4    ?      18 root     191 20    288K    288K run       16:59  0.26  0.26 ksyncer_d
 3    ?   11280 a38adm   155 20   5374M  69580K sleep     18:22  0.24  0.24 dw.sapA3
```

Figure 2.5 SAP Processes Monitored Using top

The following brief overview of the SAP processes should clarify the subsequent detailed description:

- **Dispatcher**
  The central dispatcher process distributes the GUI requests to the dialog work processes.
- **Dialog work process**
  The dialog work processes are the processes that actually work on the application server. They run all ABAP programs belonging to a requested transaction and use the database system for this purpose.

- **Batch work process**
  Batch work processes are provided for more complex transactions without direct user interaction. Their internal function corresponds primarily to that of the dialog work processes.
- **Update process**
  Update processes enable the delayed asynchronous writing of data, which increases performance.
- **Enqueue process**
  The enqueue process manages SAP locks for business objects, which is especially important when two or more application servers execute write operations.
- **Spool process**
  Spool processes are used for outputting data on printers and similar devices.
- **Message server**
  The message server is used for exchanging messages between the instances of an SAP system.
- **Gateway process**
  Gateway processes provide interfaces for the communication with external systems, which can be SAP or non-SAP systems.
- **Internet Communication Manager**
  The Internet Communication Manager is a process availabe from kernel Version 6.10 on. It immediately responds to requests from the Internet by communicating with the Dispatcher and the work processes.

Regarding the database management system, dialog work processes and batch work processes are the most important processes because they directly use the database layer.

2.3.2 Memory Structures

The processes communicate mainly via the shared memory areas. The correct dimensioning and filling of these *buffers* is important for high performance.

The *SAP R/3 table buffer* stores the data of used tables temporarily. If data is required by a work process, the system first checks whether this data already exists in the table buffer. If a process has already retrieved this data from the database system, it can be re-used, which increases overall performance.

The database also stores ABAP programs. The programs are provided as source code and compiled using the ABAP processor. The translated ABAP programs are stored temporarily in the *ABAP buffer*.

The ABAP buffer and the table buffers are automatically set according to the special SAP application requirements. After an appropriate period of time (days, weeks), the filling of the buffers should be optimized. This means that, on the one hand, nearly all required ABAP programs are pre-translated and buffered. On the other hand, data that is required daily by the SAP system is stored in the buffers. The buffers are lost when you shut down the system, for instance, to perform an offline backup. SAP Basis provides transactions for monitoring filling levels and hit ratios. In Chapter 9, *System Operation and Monitoring*, we'll describe these transactions in detail.

The roll buffer stores the user contexts of the user sessions. These contexts can be used by different dialog work processes.

2.3.3 Dispatcher

The *dispatcher process*, provided exactly once for each instance, is responsible for distributing the requests of SAP GUIs to the work processes of an instance. For this purpose, the first available dialog work process is selected. This means that the transaction steps of one transaction may be performed by different dialog work processes of an instance while exchanging the data via the roll buffer. This concept is called *work process multiplexing*. If required, the GUI requests are stored temporarily in a queue called the *Dispatcher Queue* (see Figure 2.6).

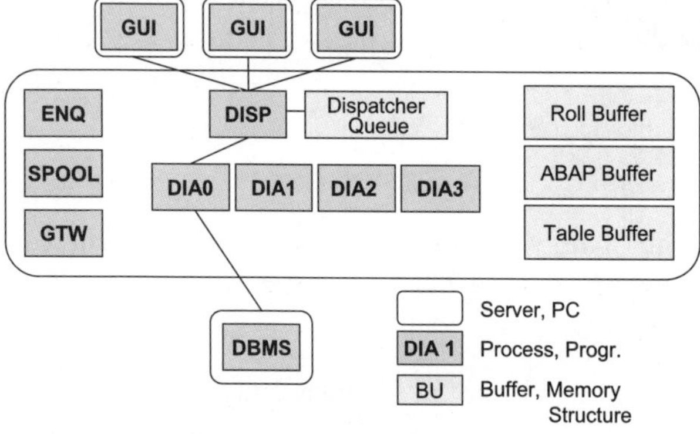

Figure 2.6 Central Role of the Dispatcher

Another consequence of the dispatcher distribution strategy is the significant distribution of the CPU time across the individual dialog work processes (see Figure 2.7). In general, the first *dialog work processes* (DIAs) are working to full capacity, whereas the last processes require hardly any time. If the last processes reach their full capacity, the system may be overloaded; however, these problems should already have been reported by users at that point.

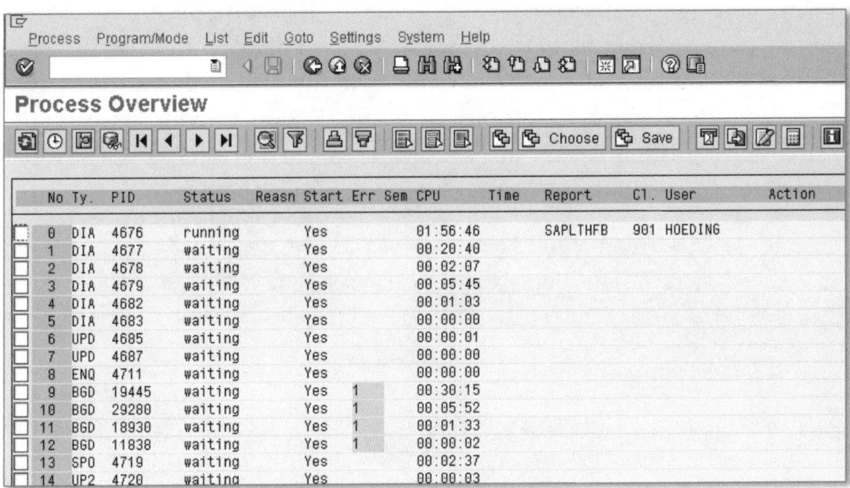

Figure 2.7 Process Overview with Transaction SM50

Figure 2.8 illustrates the work process multiplexing concept from the point of view of an SAP transaction, here shown as an SAP Logical Unit of Work (SAP LUW). The transaction is started on DIA1 and user input values are set via Screen 1. Because DIA1 is occupied by another transaction after completing the data entry, the transaction is processed on DIA2. Then, more user input values are set via Screen 2. Now, both DIA1 and DIA2 are occupied, so the Dispatcher allocates DIA3 for processing. DIA1 and DIA2 are still occupied after the inputs have been completed, so DIA3 is used again. In the respective ABAP program, `COMMIT WORK` successfully concludes the transaction.

The Dispatcher also starts and monitors all other work processes. If an error state has been detected for a work process and the process is locked, the Dispatcher restarts the process. Based on the process numbers listed in Transaction SM50, you can determine whether a process has already been restarted.

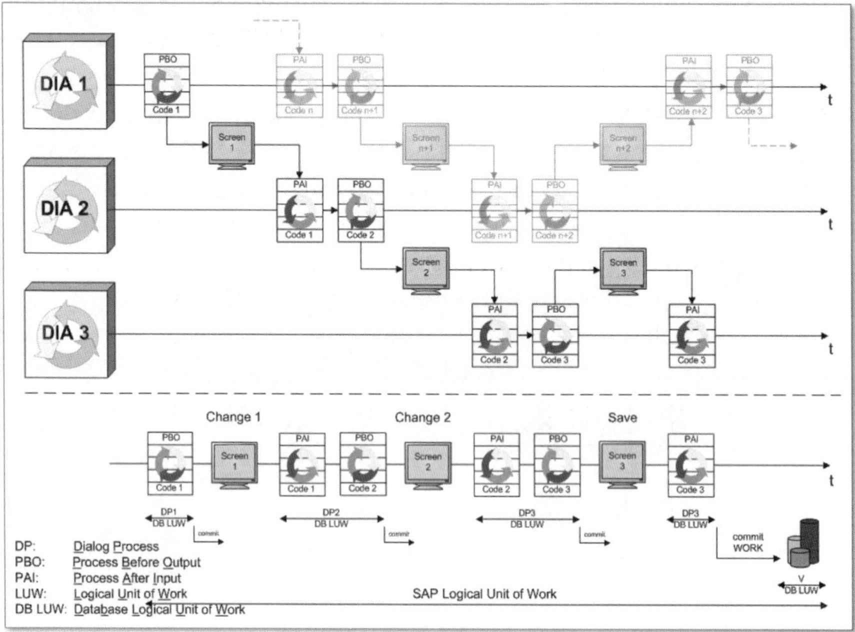

Figure 2.8 Work Process Multiplexing

If you have a demo system based on UNIX, you can carry out the following test:

- Start Transaction SM50 via the process overview, and determine the process ID (Pid) of the last DIA process.
- Stop the Disp+ Work process at the operating system level using `kill -9 Pid`.
- Refresh Transaction SM50 to be able to observe the restart of the work process with a new process ID.

Of course, you shouldn't stop the dispatcher process.

2.3.4 Dialog Work Process

Dialog work processes carry out most of the visible work of an SAP system. They consist of three layers (see Figure 2.9):

- **Dynpro processor**
  The Dynpro processor extracts the data of the GUI requests (transaction steps) assigned by the Dispatcher, writes the data to the respective memory structures (PAI area, *Process After Input*), and calls the corresponding

ABAP programs. After completing one transaction step, the Dynpro processor prepares the results for presentation and provides them to the GUI (PBO area, *Process Before Output*). SAP transactions contain several transaction steps that are usually separate screens.

- **ABAP processor**
  The ABAP processor executes ABAP programs. If an ABAP program cannot be found in the ABAP buffer, the ABAP processor downloads the program via the database interface from the database, translates the program (if necessary into an executable program), and writes it to the ABAP buffer and to the database. The translated ABAP program is executed, that is, calculations, value checks, and database operations are usually performed. This process leads to performing write operations to the database through the database interface, as well as to the output of data to the GUI via the Dynpro processor.

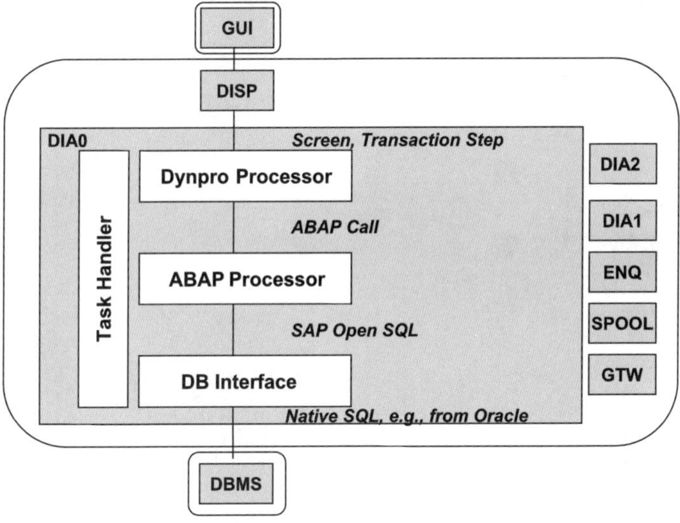

Figure 2.9 Internal Structure of a Dialog Work Process

- **Database interface**
  The database interface retains data for the work processes. It has two primary tasks: On the one hand, it manages the table buffer for enabling a fast data access. On the other hand, it translates requests and results between Open SQL and Native SQL. SAP developed Open SQL, which is a general SQL dialect, in order to use database management systems by different manufacturers. Native SQL is the individual SQL dialect of database management systems.

The layers cooperate via the Task Handler. Exactly one database server process — also referred to as a *shadow process* in SAP terminology — is assigned to each dialog work process (and each batch work process).

We'll now list the steps involved in processing a GUI request in detail. In the processes described in Figure 2.10, the direction of the arrows indicates the data flow direction.

- **Step ❶**: A GUI sends a request to the SAP system.
- **Step ❷**: If necessary, the Dispatcher places the request in the Dispatcher Queue.

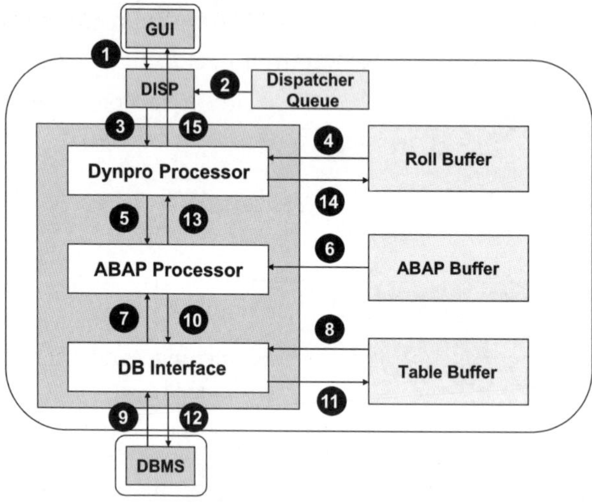

Figure 2.10 Processing a Dialog Step

- **Step ❸**: The Dispatcher assigns the request to a dialog work process and transfers the data.
- **Step ❹**: The Dynpro processor rolls in the respective user context.
- **Step ❺**: The Dynpro processor transfers the extracted data and the respective ABAP program to the ABAP processor.
- **Step ❻**: Assuming that the ABAP program is already contained in the ABAP buffer, the ABAP interpreter reads the ABAP program from the ABAP buffer and executes it.
- **Step ❼**: When processing the ABAP program, data is queried from the database. For this purpose, a request is sent to the database interface.

- **Step ❽**: The database interface detects that the data is partly contained in the table buffer. From there, the data is loaded and returned to the ABAP interpreter.
- **Step ❾**: Data that is not contained in the table buffer is requested from the DBMS via the database interface. For this purpose, the Query is translated from Open SQL into Native SQL. After being properly formatted, the results from the DBMS are forwarded to the ABAP interpreter via the database interface.
- **Step ❿**: The ABAP program also contains write operations, which are transferred to the database interface.
- **Step ⓫**: The database interface checks whether the data to be written is in the table buffer, and invalidates it respectively.
- **Step ⓬**: The database interface transfers the write operation translated into Native SQL to the DBMS which executes the corresponding operations.
- **Step ⓭**: The ABAP processor transfers results to be displayed to the Dynpro processor.
- **Step ⓮**: The Dynpro processor rolls out the user context.
- **Step ⓯**: The Dynpro processor prepares the next screen and sends it to the GUI.

Understanding these processes helps you to recognize, find, and solve problems. Not all of the performance problems during data acquisition originate in the database. Insufficiently dimensioned buffers in the application server may also slow down the data acquisition process.

2.3.5 Batch Work Process (BTC)

Batch or *background work processes* process requests that are not linked to a specific user input. These requests often represent long processes such as comprehensive analyses. In this way, dialog work processes can be kept available for dialog mode. The historical background of this is batch processing where mainframes worked with punchcard batches and printed out the results. Today, a request is created and the process result is checked later. Regarding the code, BTC processes are identical to DIA processes. It is even possible to switch a process from dialog to batch mode (and vice versa), which is referred to as *operation mode switching*.

Consequently, the internal processes are very similar to those described in Figure 2.10. The difference is that no user interaction takes place. In order to use transactions in the batch mode that actually require a user interaction, *batch input sessions* are provided. Here, the user input is logged in dialog mode. The log file is the basis for executing the transactions in the batch mode.

Administrators can draw on a number of transactions that have been specifically developed for the batch mode. They perform regular audit and maintenance tasks, for example.

Figure 2.11 shows jobs that were for the DDIC user on a sample system.[1] These are hourly scheduled jobs. Usually, these jobs collect and aggregate data. For the `SAP_CCMS_MONI_BATCH_DP` job, this may take several minutes, for example.

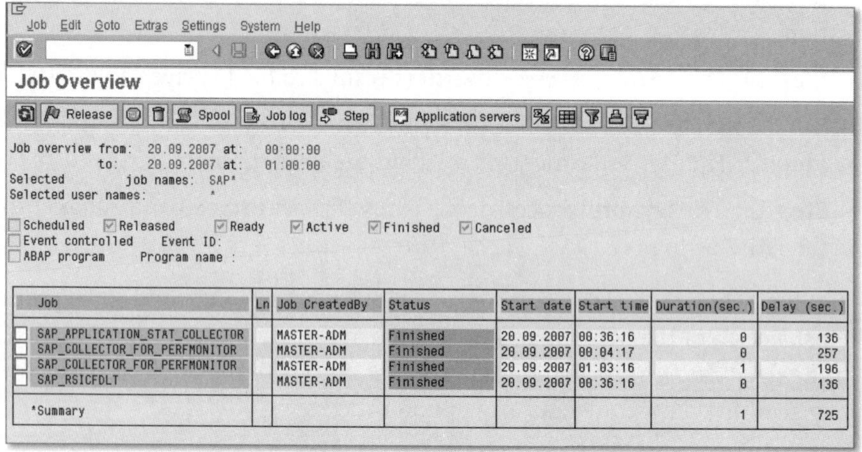

Figure 2.11 Display of DDIC Jobs with SM37

Figure 2.12 describes the scheduling of standard jobs with Transaction SM36, **Goto • Standard Jobs** (see also *SAP Note 16083*).

1 DDIC and SAP* are the traditional two administrative users of an SAP R/3 system. DDIC (which originates from "Data Dictionary") refers to database usage, while SAP* manages the application server. However, there are also limitations to DDIC and SAP.* For example, you cannot use them for development purposes.

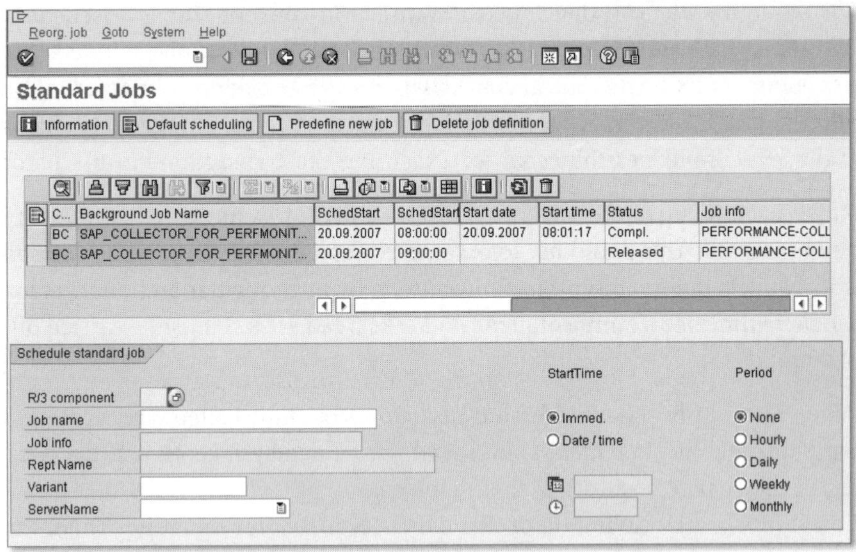

Figure 2.12 Transaction SM36 — Scheduling Standard Jobs

2.3.6 Update Process (UPD)

Usually, numerous database objects are assigned in several tables to one SAP transaction. This quantity of objects is also referred to as SAP LUW (see Figure 2.13). Due to several user inputs, SAP transactions are often complex and therefore the transaction concepts (also called DB LUW) provided by the database management system cannot be used immediately. Furthermore, because of long database locks, users would interfere with each other, or ACID properties would be not be adhered to. Writing many data sets in numerous tables is also relatively time-consuming.

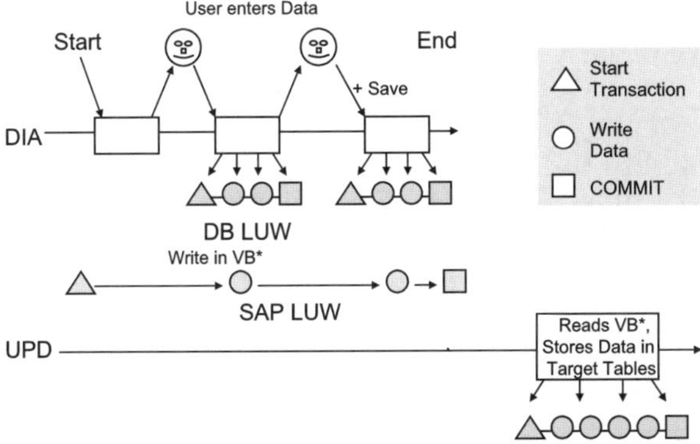

Figure 2.13 Relationship Between SAP LUW and DB LUW

For this purpose, SAP developed a transaction concept that is based on a delayed asynchronous update. On the one hand, application knowledge is used by regarding data-critical conflicts as being not business-critical. On the other hand, SAP-internal mechanisms are used, such as a lock management at the level of business objects.

Objects can be updated at a later point in time, for example, when they are newly created. This could be, for example, a sales order that can be entered exactly once, due to the application context, by only one transactional user at the same time. However, uniqueness checks (read access) must be carried out promptly.

When a work process executes a transaction step, the changes are written to temporary tables (*VB* tables*) and saved with a database `COMMIT`. If the writing of the change requests to these tables is completed and the SAP transaction is finished by saving them, the data is available for updating. Then, the asynchronous update process is activated and writes the changes to the target tables, which is usually done within a few seconds. The inconsistencies[2] emerging in the meantime are not business-critical. Transaction SM13 enables the administrator to detect and solve problems that arise during the update process.

SAP systems contain two types of update processes, namely, update process type 1 and update process type 2. An update process type 1 (UPD) should always exist. To increase the performance, the update process type 1 determined by the developer can forward some of the updates to update process type 2 (UPD2), which runs with a lower priority and whose main task is to update less time-critical data. If UPD2 does not exist, all updates are carried out by the UPD process.

2.3.7 Lock Management with the Enqueue Process (ENQ)

When describing work processes, we dealt with the buffering of data in the application server. During this process, you must ensure that the work processes don't overwrite each other's data. To avoid this, a central enqueue process contains a *lock table*. The locks provided by the database system don't meet the requirements of the SAP architecture. Some advantages of the SAP-internal locking mechanism are:

2 For example, the actual total number of requests does not correspond to the number of requests in the order table for a short period of time.

- Locks are also kept if the dialog work process changes
- Locks are maintained according to the LUW concept
- You can lock several tables at the same time
- Locks can be managed in the entire system across all application servers

The lock management function is particularly important for SAP systems with more than one instance. For this purpose, the dialog work processes communicate with the enqueue process of the central instance via the message server process.

From SAP Basis Release 7.0 onward, you can run the enqueue process on a specific instance for central services, the *SAP Central Service Instance* (SCS). If you make the SCS instance highly available, the entire system will become highly available.

2.3.8 Message Server Process

The *message server process* is responsible for the communication within an SAP system and exists exactly once. It receives the user login data and, if required, assigns an application server and can also support load balancing. In addition, it supports the message exchange between application servers, for example, for starting the update, managing the locks, or starting the batch orders. Furthermore, application servers log in to the message server. To ensure high availability, message services also run on the SCS instance.

2.3.9 Gateway Process

In contrast to the message server process, *gateway processes* are responsible for the external communication. They can communicate with other SAP systems, such as SAP NetWeaver BI, other SAP R/3 systems, SAP R/2 systems, or third-party systems. For this purpose, application systems or old systems provided for special tasks used to be integrated in the past. In this context, the data volume to be transferred is significantly larger than the volume to be transferred if the message server is used.

2.3.10 Variants of an Instance

The exact number of processes of an instance depends on the actual installation requirements and is limited by the hardware resources available. Each instance contains exactly one dispatcher. The ENQ process of the system runs on the central instance. The number of dialog and batch work processes is essential for scaling the system. At least two dialog work processes must exist. The number of dialog and batch work processes also controls the number of the database server processes. All processes of an instance are started simultaneously.

According to SAP conventions, the types of processes to be started for an instance are encoded in the instance name. For example, Instance DVEBMGS28 contains dialog work processes, update processes, one enqueue process, one message server process, as well as gateway and spool processes. Therefore, it can be recognized as a central instance. The number encodes the system number corresponding to the port number, which provides access to the SAP system. For example, an instance named DB38 contains only dialog and batch work processes and can only work with a central instance.

At a minimum, two dialog work processes must run on an instance. For a central system, at least four dialog work processes, one update process, one batch process, one enqueue process, and one spool process must exist (see *SAP Note 39412*). However, restricted demo systems run also with further downsized configurations.

SAP Note 9942 describes the maximum number of work processes. It is often more efficient to install several instances than to configure one central instance with many work processes, for example, to avoid bottlenecks by using different dispatchers.

As of SAP Kernel Version 7.0, you can set up SAP Central Service Instances, which, as high availability solutions, ensure the availability and performance for critical services and don't contain work processes.

2.4 SAP Administration

SAP provides several transactions and tools for the administration of application servers and databases. You can only execute a few tasks at the operating system level. In the following section, we describe some mechanisms as an example and deal with the impact on the database. More detailed explanations can be found in the subsequent chapters.

2.4.1 Profile Files and System Startup

You can start and shut down SAP systems and the database at the operating system level using a script. The required parameters are read from profile files that can also be edited. In this way, you can correct incorrect configurations, which prevent the system from starting up successfully. The profile files also control the database.

There are three types of profile files located in the following path: */sapmnt/<SID>/profile/*. Examples are:

- `DEFAULT.PFL`: The default profile stores parameters that are identical in all instances of an SAP system, such as system names or database names.
- `A28_DVEBMGS28_F38.PFL`: The instance profile stores the specific instance parameters. For example, the instance profile contains the line `rdisp/wp_no_dia = 6`, which defines the number of dialog work processes and thus affects the number of Oracle server processes directly (see Figure 2.14).
- `START_DVEBMGS28_f38`: The start profile determines the start sequence for individual processes of an instance and creates virtual structures in the file system.

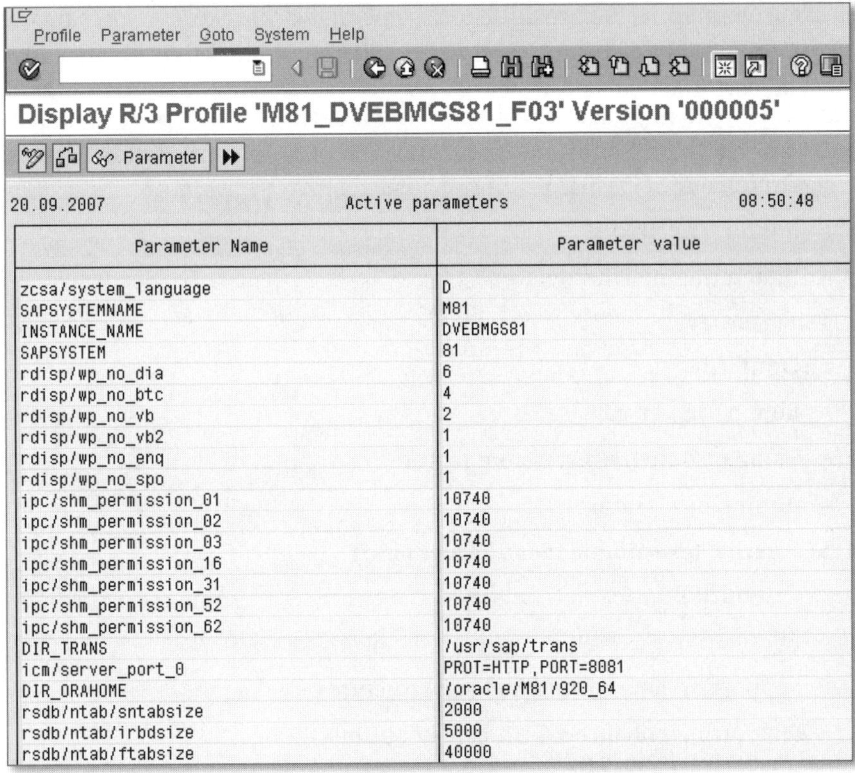

Parameter Name	Parameter value
zcsa/system_language	D
SAPSYSTEMNAME	M81
INSTANCE_NAME	DVEBMGS81
SAPSYSTEM	81
rdisp/wp_no_dia	6
rdisp/wp_no_btc	4
rdisp/wp_no_vb	2
rdisp/wp_no_vb2	1
rdisp/wp_no_enq	1
rdisp/wp_no_spo	1
ipc/shm_permission_01	10740
ipc/shm_permission_02	10740
ipc/shm_permission_03	10740
ipc/shm_permission_16	10740
ipc/shm_permission_31	10740
ipc/shm_permission_52	10740
ipc/shm_permission_62	10740
DIR_TRANS	/usr/sap/trans
icm/server_port_0	PROT=HTTP,PORT=8081
DIR_ORAHOME	/oracle/M81/920_64
rsdb/ntab/sntabsize	2000
rsdb/ntab/irbdsize	5000
rsdb/ntab/ftabsize	40000

Figure 2.14 Instance Profile

The profile parameters should be maintained via the SAP GUI using Transaction RZ10. This transaction includes notes for appropriate parameter values. You can edit the parameter files directly, for example, if an SAP system cannot start successfully due to the number of dialog work processes being set too high. However, afterwards, the file parameters should be reread and rewritten to the database with Transaction RZ10 via **Profile • Import.** Changes only become valid after a restart of the instance.

You can start the system as operating system user *<sid>adm* (see Figure 2.5) using the `sapstart` script. Error messages are recorded in different log files.

2.4.2 Software Maintenance

It is necessary to update a system. The rule "never touch a running system" does not apply to systems that are subject to a changing reality. For example, the application must take into account new legal conditions, such as new tax types, or other changes, such as the new formation of states or new currencies. Furthermore, it is unrealistic to assume that a complex system is free of errors or cannot be further optimized. Therefore, software maintenance must be performed at various levels:

- **Operating system level**
  - Optimizing
  - Eliminating errors
  - Integrating new hardware
- **Database level**
  - Optimizing
  - Eliminating errors
  - Using new operating system features
  - Adding new features
- **SAP kernel (executable files), kernel patch**
  - Optimizing
  - Eliminating errors
  - Supporting new ABAP language structures
  - Supporting enhanced GUI display options
  - Adjusting the database layer to the database system enhancements

- **Application level**
  - Adjusting business-relevant functions to reality
  - Eliminating errors
  - Optimizing
  - Improved administration transactions

All levels are related to the database. In particular, you should consider that changes at the application level are stored immediately in the database. All ABAP programs that represent the basis for SAP transactions are stored in rows within the database. The import of support packages is controlled via SAP GUI and the application server, but the actual work consists of adding the datasets to the database, which is carried out by the SAP Transport Tool that has direct access to the database. Therefore, this topic is described in detail in Chapter 6, *SAP Change and Transport Management.*

2.4.3 Database Administration

As a potential single point of failure, the central database of an SAP system is of particular importance. Therefore, it is imperative that you monitor the database and react appropriately when problems occur. As an SAP administrator, you are responsible for these tasks.

SAP supports various database management systems. Although the basic technology of the relational databases is the same, there are differences in the implementation by different vendors. You can migrate an SAP system from an Oracle database to another DBMS without functional restrictions, but the administrators must familiarize themselves with new concepts and technologies. This book is intended to provide you with useful fundamental knowledge. But sometimes the valuable special knowledge of a database system often gained through years of practice, for example, in areas such as performance optimization or space management, can only be partially used. However, many technologies are similar. For instance, a database space of the database system DB2 roughly corresponds to an Oracle tablespace.

The SAP GUI supports you to a large extent in the administration of the database. The administration transactions for the different database systems used by SAP differ slightly, but the SAP GUI encapsulates the access to the internally differing dictionary tables of the database systems. Thus, the display for the administrator is standardized. The data preparation and representation in the SAP GUI allows for a simple and detailed monitoring of the database.

You can also control the database. For this purpose, BR*Tools[3] are used that can also be controlled at the operating system level.

As an example, Figure 2.15 shows Transaction DB02 as an appropriate point of entry into database administration. Here, various analyses can be started and evaluated.

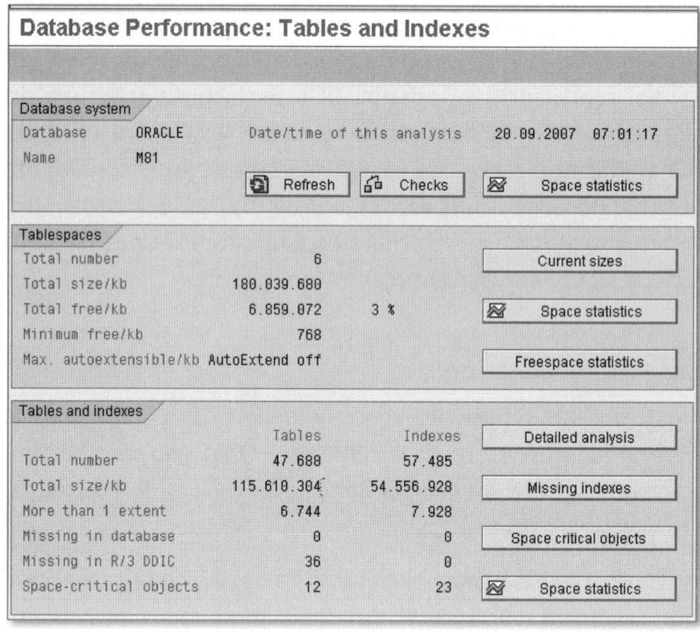

Figure 2.15 DB02 — Database Administration

Chapter 3, *Oracle Fundamentals*, describes technical basics of database systems and the administration of Oracle databases in great detail. This chapter also considers basic Oracle structures. Chapter 4, *SAP and Oracle*, discusses the interaction between SAP and Oracle, as well as their joint administration, in greater detail.

2.4.4 Data Backup

With regard to the assets managed by SAP systems in real life, data backups are essential. You must be able to completely and consistently restore the database when problems occur. This process must be executed quickly, and

3 BR stands for Backup and Recovery, but the BR*Tools offer a large number of other functions as well.

technical and organizational measures must prevent further damage caused by human error.

The topic of data backups focuses mainly on the backup of the database, which contains user data and application programs. Furthermore, the entire system environment, including configuration files, executables, and the operating system, should also be backed up.

For data backups, SAP provides the BR*Tools, which can be controlled via Transaction DB13 (see Figure 2.16).

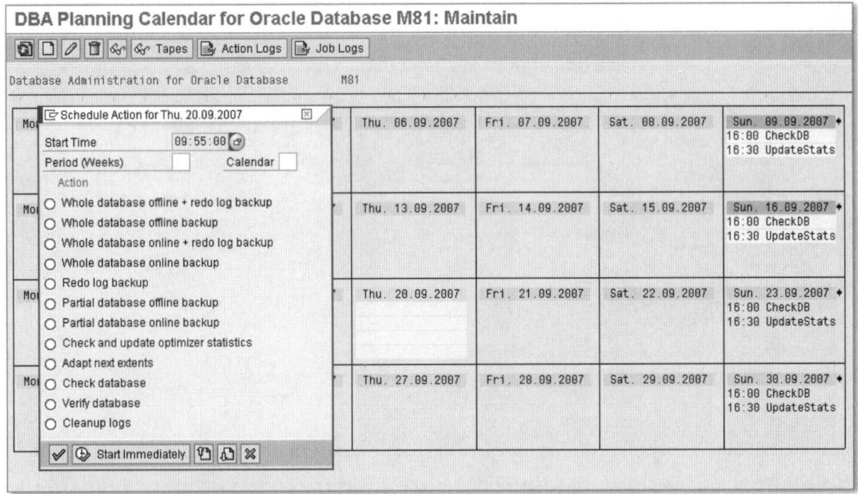

Figure 2.16 Transaction DB13 — Scheduling Backups

There are other mechanisms to back up your data as well. Manufacturers of database management systems offer their own tools, for example, RMAN by Oracle. Vendors of special hardware for data backups also offer their own software that specializes in backing up multiple systems and is often tailored for SAP and Oracle. In many cases, you can control third-party solutions with the BR*Tools.

Data backups, which are essential for every SAP installation, are discussed in greater detail in the context of Oracle in Section 3.4, *Oracle Kernel*. Chapter 10, *Backup, Restore, and Recovery*, contains a comprehensive description of data backups.

2.4.5 Performance Optimization

Performance is important for the usability of an application system. From the point of view of individual users, the response time behavior is essential in this context. The response time for simple transactions should be less than one second. Figure 2.17 shows how Transaction ST03 can be used to display the response time behavior. The values for Dialog mode are highlighted. The response time behavior should only be categorized as critical in a few instances. The reason might be that numerous programs were called for the first time and therefore had to be compiled. But there are also more complex transactions that run comparably longer. This is generally accepted by users.

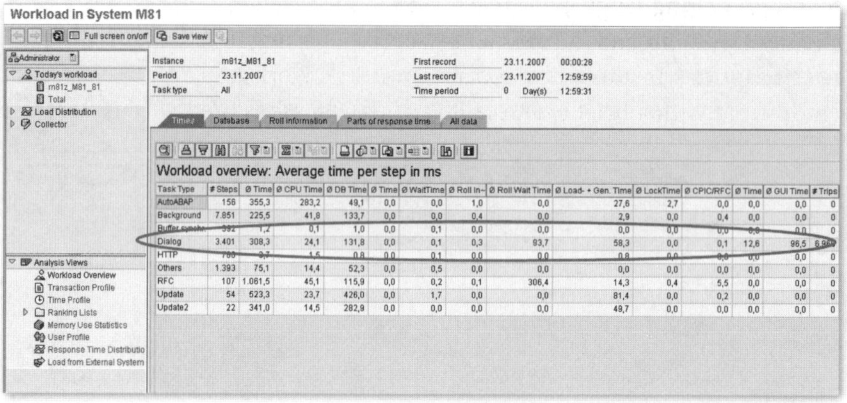

Figure 2.17 Transaction ST03 — Analysis of Response Time Behavior

However, if the response time behavior changes considerably, users will complain about a slow system. There are numerous parameters available to reveal these bottlenecks. Performance must always be considered in the context of hardware, database, parameterization of the application server, and application program.

As the administrator, you will have to monitor and, if necessary, correct the parameters. For this purpose, Chapter 8, *Performance*, describes useful approaches, tools, and techniques in greater detail.

2.5 SAP and Software Development

In this section, we'll discuss basic concepts and terms that pertain to SAP software development and SAP usage via external systems. This overview includes historically developed concepts that will constitute the basis for any SAP system for a long time. In addition, we'll take a closer look at specific current concepts, particularly in the context of Java. The knowledge you'll gain in this section will enable you to understand application programs and give you the necessary know-how to converse with developers. Lastly, you'll be able to assess possible effects of using your SAP system with external software and to submit proposals.

2.5.1 ABAP Framework

As we already explained in Section 2.1.4, *SAP Terminology*, and Section 2.3.4, *Dialog Work Process*, programs written in ABAP play an integral role for SAP. The programming language is connected to a framework that supports software development and deployment (technical publishing). By no means can the descriptions in this book replace an ABAP workshop. We just want to demonstrate with a brief example how the database is used with Open SQL.

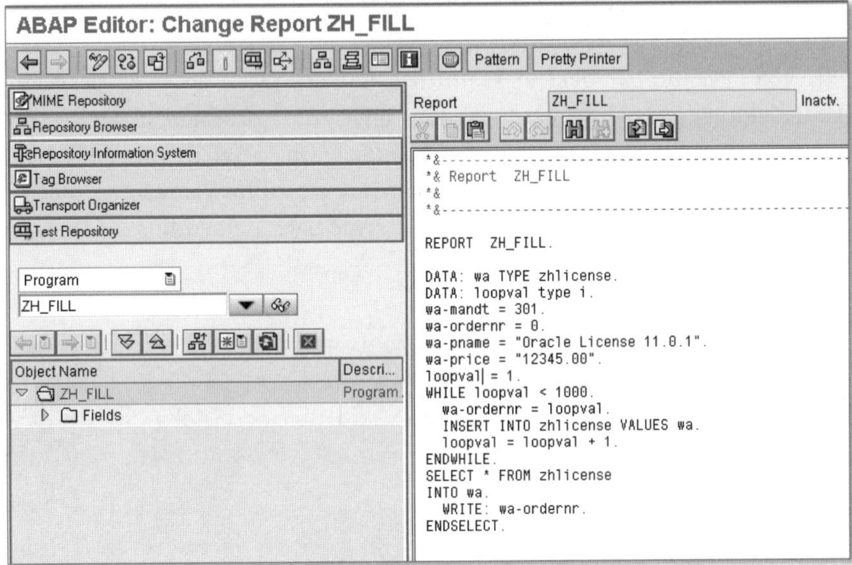

Figure 2.18 Transaction SE80 — Object

Transaction SE80 (**Tools • ABAP Workbench • Overview • Object Navigator**) is used for developing in the SAP environment. As a framework, it includes a range of tools (see Figure 2.18). To create a simple ABAP program, you have to overcome some obstacles:

- Only users who are registered as developers can develop. The respective developer key must be requested via the SAP Service Marketplace.
- Generally, users can only work in the customer namespace, that is, their programs must start with Z or Y. All other names are assigned to other purposes by SAP. To implement changes in the standard SAP system, it is

necessary to communicate with a server at the SAP Service Marketplace. This server logs the change request and provides a respective object key.

- A package (previously referred to as a development class) and a transport request must be created for each development. They are needed for summarizing all objects connected with the development, namely, programs, tables, and values, and preparing them for transport, that is, transfer to other SAP systems. You can also develop local objects.

First, these mechanisms may seem complicated and hinder fast creative working. But they are very useful for avoiding creative chaos. Particularly in complex systems, such as the SAP system, it can be difficult to find the reason for problems. Therefore, the restriction and retraceability of developments is absolutely necessary. As an administrator, you especially will appreciate these mechanisms.

Once you have jumped over these hurdles, you can create an ABAP program. The development environment provides you with a program structure. We won't explain the ABAP programming language in detail at this point, but the following example of creating datasets in a table illustrates some specific characteristics of ABAP, such as the intermediate embedding of SQL in ABAP:

```
*&---------------------------------------------*
*& Report ZH_FILL
*&---------------------------------------------*
REPORT zh_fill.
DATA: wa TYPE zhlicense.
DATA: loopval TYPE i.
wa-mandt = 301.
wa-ordernr = 0.
wa-pname = "Oracle License 10.1.2".
wa-price = "1273.00".
loopval = 1.
WHILE loopval < 1000.
 wa-orderr = loopval.
 INSERT INTO zhlicense VALUES wa.
 loopval = loopval + 1.
ENDWHILE.
SELECT * FROM zhlicense
INTO wa.
 WRITE: wa-ordernr.
ENDSELECT.
```

The program inserts 999 datasets to a table called `zhlicense`. The record structure `wa` is created according to the structure of the database table `zhlicense`. A sample dataset is inserted in the `while` loop with the Open SQL statement, `insert`. The `select` statement defines a cursor, `wa`, which is used to iterate across the entire table.

With the development environment, you can check the syntax (F5), activate the program (F6), and test the execution of the program (F8).

But the program cannot be executed properly because the `zhlicense` table does not yet exist in the system. To create the table, Transaction SE80 provides an option to go to the ABAP Dictionary (see Figure 2.19). The ABAP Dictionary can also be called via **Tools • ABAP Workbench • Development • Dictionary** or directly using Transaction SE11. Here, you can create the table `zhlicense`. In Chapter 8, we'll describe this topic in greater detail in the context of performance optimization. Here, only the following note is provided for your understanding. SAP contains a large number of predefined data types (data elements), for example, for currencies. You can also directly use elementary data types, as proposed for table `zhlicense`.

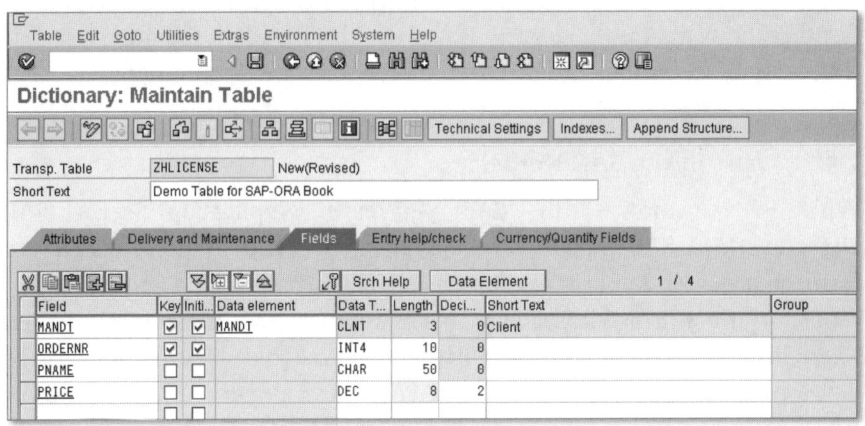

Figure 2.19 Transaction SE11 — Creating a Database Table

Table `zhlicense` is a *transparent* table. Tables are called transparent if there is a corresponding table in the database and if they can be also used immediately from within an ABAP program. The ABAP concept of internal tables is interesting because it enables you to use quantities in ABAP in conjunction with SQL-like language structures.

The Object Navigator is connected to the ABAP source code written by you. In this way, interactive structures are analyzed, and a corresponding navigation structure is set up. For this simple example, the `wa` data structures are already listed as data fields (se also Figure 2.18). This enables you to more easily find and use the structure elements in larger ABAP programs. The Object Navigator can also be used to access other object types. For example, function groups, classes, or BSP applications can be developed:

- BSP stands for Business Server Pages. The BSP Framework allows for the simple development of Internet applications closely coupled to ABAP. As with Active Server Pages, the program source code is embedded in HTML. ABAP is available as embedded programming language. Therefore, you can immediately access SAP functions and data. The framework also provides functions that support the design and an event-driven flow control.
- BAPI stands for Business Application Programming Interface. It combines basic transactions or ABAP programs for important business objects in such a way that an object-oriented access is possible. These BAPIs, in turn, can be used in ABAP programs or BSPs. You can also use them externally. An overview of the existing BAPIs can be found in the BAPI repository.

The ABAP Framework is still the essential basis for SAP business functions but also for essential administration tools. On the one hand, this is due to the fact that the structures have grown over the years; and on the other hand, it is because of the strict and safe structure for software distribution.

2.5.2 Java in the SAP Kernel

With the transition to the SAP NetWeaver Application Server (SAP NetWeaver AS), SAP implemented the repeatedly claimed use of Java in the form of the Java Application Server. A Java kernel with a self-contained repository for storing classes and objects supports the initial ABAP kernel. Therefore, it contains a correspondingly larger database. For the purpose of developing, SAP provides the SAP NetWeaver Developer Studio. Here, tools based on the Java development environment Eclipse are supplied for developing Java applications.

In this way, SAP NetWeaver AS can be used similarly to other application servers, such as BEA Weblogic or IBM WebSphere, for developing any Java application. The business area can be accessed via the respective interface classes. Because the developed Java applications are contained in the SAP kernel, they have better performance compared to other application servers.

The applications are set up in a component-oriented manner. In this context, components are *Enterprise Java Beans*. The components are separated according to the *Model View Controller concept* (MVC concept). MVC is a classic design pattern with the areas of presentation (View), data storage (Model), and flow logic (Controller) encapsulated in specific classes. For this process, some predefined Java Beans are provided. You can easily derive Web services from Java Beans.

For developing and testing Java applications, the SAP system must meet special requirements. It is not efficient when too many developers work on one system, because for deployment a dedicated instance is needed for each developer. That is, you can develop but not deploy simultaneously. As an option, standalone systems are provided with the development environment running with an SAP NetWeaver AS on a PC.

Due to the strategic SAP design and the high popularity of Java, we expect that many new developments in Java will follow, especially, when the technology development enters a less dynamic phase. In Chapter 11, we describe the usage of Java in detail, particularly the aspects that are relevant for administration.

2.5.3 Internet Transaction Server

In addition to the currently and dynamically developed technologies regarding the areas of the Web and Java, numerous applications based on older technologies can be used with SAP. Since these applications are widely used, we will briefly describe them here even though they're not very useful for new developments.

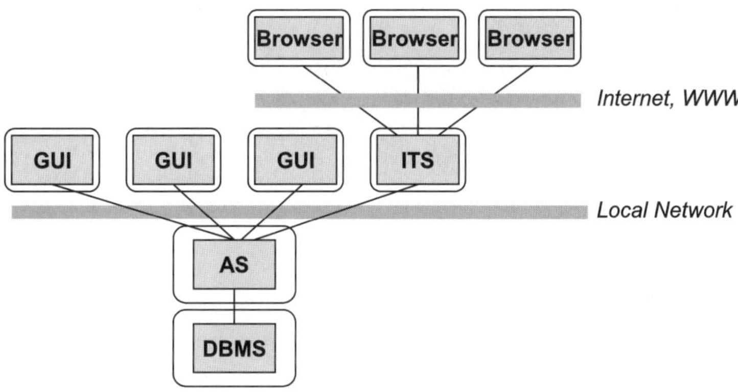

Figure 2.20 Four-Layer Architecture with the Internet Transaction Server

The *Internet Transaction Server* (ITS) was developed by SAP to enable SAP transactions for Internet use. It acts as a wrapper that converts operations and structures of the SAP GUI protocol into HTML (see Figure 2.20). From the point of view of the SAP system, the ITS behaves like a SAP GUI. It uses a Web browser as a client. Of course, there are restrictions because the display capabilities of a real SAP GUI exceed the capabilities of a Web browser. Therefore, not all SAP transactions can be used via the ITS.

However, an ITS provides several components in order to implement web applications as a web shop. Numerous applications were developed based on the ITS; however, we believe that the importance of ITS-based applications will decrease in the future.

2.5.4 Remote Function Call

The *Remote Function Call* (RFC) implements the Remote Procedure Call concept for SAP. In addition to the local call of functions using the ABAP statement `CALL FUNCTION`, you can call functions on remote computers via RFC. For this purpose, the `DESTINATION` parameter is added to the `CALL FUNCTION` call. The required communication via the network, which includes addressing external services and formatting transferred data, is performed by the RFC interface.

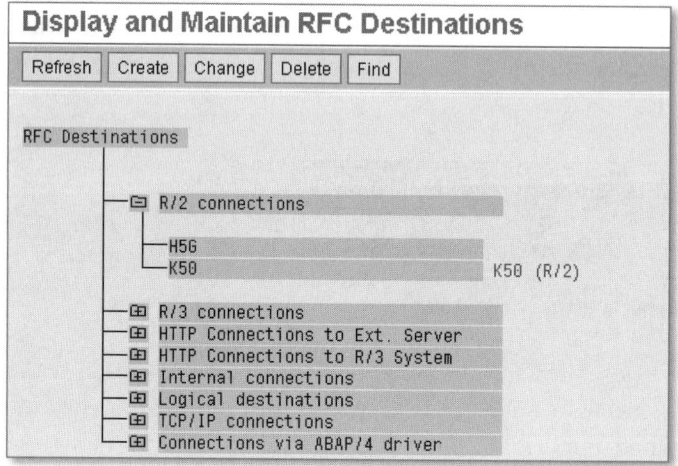

Figure 2.21 Configuration of RFC Destinations

You must make external systems known via Transaction SM59 (see Figure 2.21). After that, you can call functions that are available in these systems. This process supports asynchronous and synchronous coupling.

External systems can access the SAP system via the RFC interface. For this purpose, libraries are provided, for example, for the C programming language. Therefore, you can use SAP data and functions from within a C program. Conversely, application systems implement RFC interfaces that allow you to call their functions from ABAP programs.

The *SAP Java Connector* enables you to use SAP systems from within Java programs. It is part of the SAP Business Connector and has been available since the early versions of SAP. Therefore, it is often employed for special applications that use only a very limited number of SAP functions. The SAP Java Connector enables you to use external Java programs from SAP systems and to access SAP systems from Java programs (see Figure 2.22). Due to Java's object-oriented approach, BAPIs are usually used to implement object-oriented interfaces to SAP data and functions. *Intermediate Documents* (IDocs), which can also be used with other external interfaces, are the containers for data exchange.

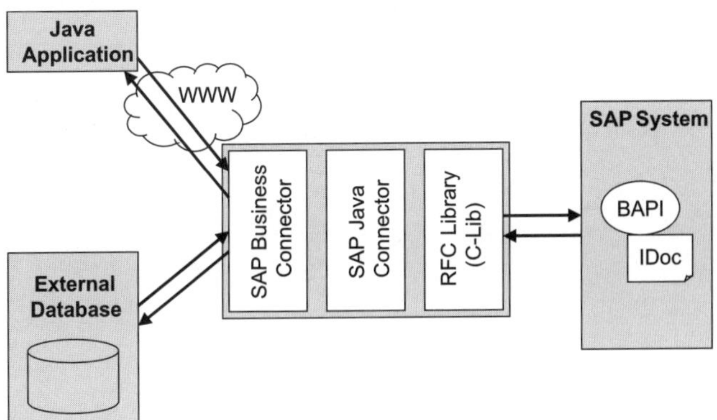

Figure 2.22 Connecting External Systems to the Java Connector

2.6 Summary

In this chapter, we described the fundamental concepts and technologies of SAP. We first classified SAP software in the context of information systems in general, explained important concepts, and examined the SAP system with regard to its historical development. We described the different setups of the client/server architecture in detail, and we also introduced the structure and function of the application server. We explained basic principles of important administrative tasks and of developing applications in the SAP environment. In Chapter 8, we'll use the ABAP knowledge that you have gained in this chapter for some examples and tests. The administrative tasks are explained in detail in the respective chapters. You should now be able to understand the structure and technology of the SAP system and to impart this knowledge. Therefore, you should be able to recognize problems and assign them to the corresponding software layers.

It seems easy to store data, but harder to store data safely. Usually, it takes a lot of effort to search stored data. Modern database management systems provide easy storage, quick research, security, and other functions, even in multiuser mode.

3 Oracle Fundamentals

In this chapter, we'll introduce you to the fundamentals and the technology of the Oracle database management software. But, before we do, we'll summarize the basics of database technology. A sound knowledge of the requirements, architecture and concepts will help you to support your ideas when communicating with colleagues and partners, and also deepen your understanding of the Oracle kernel. The section on SQL is useful as a reference for everyday administration tasks. After we give you a brief history of Oracle, we'll introduce you to some tools that will be important to you in your daily administration work. Then, we'll describe the Oracle kernel in detail. Additionally, we'll discuss the Oracle Net and authorization management, and will touch upon monitoring as well. Throughout our discussion of the Oracle database management software, we'll use examples to show you the aspects and actions relevant to administration.

3.1 Basics of Database Technology

This section summarizes important basic knowledge for administering Oracle and SAP.

3.1.1 Motivation and History

Data is integral to business transactions in every enterprise, not just IT. And data management didn't only start in 1980 with the success of relational databases. As early as 6,000 years ago, the Sumerians methodically collected and used information, and created technologies and methodologies for handling this data. The first data record was a clay tablet; the first data model was a number system; and the first schema was a clay form in which beer recipes were noted.

Therefore, many problems and concepts have their equivalent and motivation in history. For example, the loss of such a collection of clay tablets due to flooding was certainly just as threatening to a Sumerian brewery, as would be the loss of production plans or material BOMs due to a fire in the computer center to a mechanical engineering company today. Therefore, there is a great demand for data security.

Naturally, modern databases and application systems exceed the possibilities of their ancient archetypes by far. Important aspects are speed and multiuser capability. Analyses, like counting the existing beer recipes when selling a brewery, are done within fractions of a second nowadays. Advanced applications, such as determining rarely-used ingredients (ABC analysis), were feasible but very laborious for the Sumerians. In Sumer, these tasks were performed by writers who were respected and well-paid, because of their special abilities (reading, calculating, and possessing structural and intellectual skills in addition to writing) and their important role.

This shows parallels to database management systems (DBMS) as well. They are extremely expensive to procure and operate, and play a central role in the software landscape of an enterprise. A central database management system provides different types of applications with data and services for data usage. Figure 3.1 shows a two-level client/server architecture where the application programs are executed on client computers. In SAP, however, a three-level architecture is used where the SAP application server is the only application based on the DBMS (see Chapter 2, *SAP Fundamentals*).

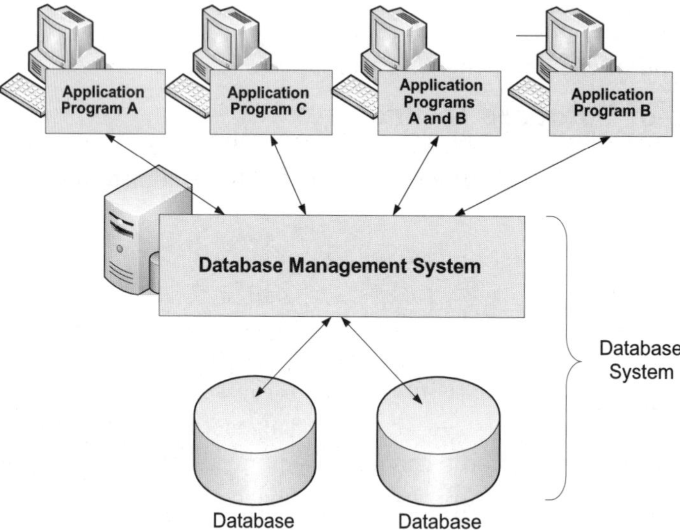

Figure 3.1 DBMS as a Central Data Disk

Edgar F. Codd, one of the pioneers of relational database technology (*Codd's rules*), provided a very good overview of the tasks and functions to be performed by a database system. The list he created is relevant to this book in two ways. On the one hand, we can systematically analyze which points are required from the application layer point of view. On the other hand, it introduces concepts that are implemented also by the SAP application server and, even better, using the knowledge of the business context. For example, transaction management at the application server level enables many users to work more effortlessly because locks are managed for business objects, and the more restrictive locking mechanisms of the database don't always take effect.

The following list contains the database system tasks (*Codd's rules*) along with a short outline of their meaning to the SAP system:

- **Integration**
  The database system enables an integrated, consistent management of all data required by the applications. This helps to prevent multiple storage (redundancy). Related error sources are thus eliminated. Integration is one of the core requests of the SAP software. Work processes are accelerated, because it is no longer necessary to explicitly transfer data and to check whether the data is really up-to-date. This means that there is an improvement in data quality.
- **Operations**
  The database system provides basic operations for manipulating and using (searching) data. These basic operations, like inserting a record, are used by the SAP application server and, in simple terms, merged into business operations like creating an order. SQL is implemented at the database system level. As an SAP and Oracle administrator, you will frequently use SQL, and having a sound understanding of SQL will help you with performance tuning as well.
- **Data Dictionary - Catalog**
  The catalog is used for managing information via the database structure. This includes information that is important for the application (like tables and attribute names). Information on the physical characteristics of the database, like actual file names and created indexes, are included in the catalog as well. SAP uses the database catalog. The SAP application server includes a catalog that contains and provides structures of the application server. Fast access to the catalog data is essential to ensure good system performance. For the special dictionary caches (i.e., the buffers providing

quick access to catalog information), you should aim for high hit ratios by optimizing the cache size, for example.

- **Views**
  Views provide a specific, limited section of the database to different applications. On the one hand, this reduces complexity. The application developer only sees those database sections that are relevant to his project. On the other hand, views can be used to protect data against unauthorized access. In older SAP versions, you'll discover views for calculating faster joins using database mechanisms.

- **Integrity check**
  The DBMS monitors the semantic correctness of the database, which means only those changes are permitted that don't conflict with the data description. This includes a simple check for the correct data types, but also a monitoring of referential integrity. These concepts are implemented in parallel by the SAP application server. SAP has its own type system. Referential integrity finds its equivalent in the concept of check tables, which are additionally implemented in SAP in the input help of the GUI. The integrity check prevents applications from performing actions that violate the correctness of the data set. This may initially be irritating to an individual transactional user, but is nevertheless necessary and the importance of this integrity check must be imparted to users.

- **Access control**
  Access control protects the database from unauthorized access. Database management systems provide very detailed mechanisms that make access control scalable in several dimensions. The database object dimension enables access control for entire database schemas, individual tables, or specific table columns. In the rights dimension type, there is a distinction between administrator rights (like create table and drop), write authority (insert, alter, delete), and read authority (select), which are individually assigned to database objects.

  Modern database management systems like Oracle additionally provide mechanisms to support a comfortable rights management using roles or groups. Like many database applications, SAP rarely uses the rights system. The reason is that, on the one hand, not all database management systems provide a sufficient access control system; and on the other hand, an access control system within the application permits more complex access rights at business object level, for example. In SAP R/3, from the DBMS point of view, there is one main user who is logged on to the database management system several times in parallel. As an administrator, using this user you have access to all SAP data at DBMS level. Therefore, you need to be careful.

- **Transactions**
  A sequence of related database operations is called a *transaction*. A transaction should meet the ACID properties:
  - **A**
    It should be atomic (i.e., be run either as a whole or not at all).
  - **C**
    It should ensure consistency.
  - **I**
    It should run separately.
  - **D**
    It should store its result permanently in the database.

  These properties could be implemented easily with concepts like immediate file storage and locking the entire database. However, this would be in stark contrast to the important requirements of multiuser mode and high performance. Therefore, the developers of database management systems have developed a number of concepts for creating fast transactions. For example, these include log files and very restrictive locks. These concepts have an immediate impact on the installation and the operation of an SAP system.

Attention!

In the SAP context, the term *transaction* is used for dialog programs consisting of several steps. There are indeed similarities to the ACID concept. Still, or probably because of these similarities, the homonymous use of the term causes problems in the communication between SAP administrators and database experts. Therefore, you should be aware of these problems to avoid potential misunderstandings.

SAP has a proprietary transaction mechanism following the ACID concept. A transaction is denoted as a *Logical Unit of Work* (LUW, see Section 2.3, *Application Server*). An SAP LUW regards objects at a business level. The application knowledge used in this context helps you to avoid conflicts between the SAP transactions triggered by different SAP users.

3.1.1.1 Synchronization

By *synchronization*, the DBMS tries to achieve conflict-free multiuser operations. For this purpose, the execution plans of simultaneous transactions are nested so that it is impossible to mutually overwrite data. Sometimes, a transaction is halted until another transaction has released the data. As an administrator, you should be aware that synchronization conflicts can occur as an error source, but could seldom be reproduced or analyzed.

3.1.1.2 Data Backup

It is imperative that you protect data against loss. Database management systems provide a number of mechanisms for restoring data after media or system errors. These comprise concepts (like log files) that need to be regarded in context with fast transaction processing. For a long-term data backup, backup mechanisms are used where the dataset of a database is copied to an inexpensive external storage (tertiary memory, usually magnetic tapes). Depending on the database size and the implemented method, this can take between a few minutes and several hours.

For very large databases as they are used for the SAP system, advanced techniques like an online backup may be used during which the application system is still usable. These DBMS techniques are used intensively by SAP and can be managed via the SAP application server. Data security will be one of your main tasks as an administrator. To disregard this non-productive part of your work would be grossly negligent.

In addition to the database level, data security also concerns the technical infrastructure, the security of the building and the organization of the data center operation. This topic is central to Chapter 5, *Planning the System Landscape*.

Table 3.1 shows that Oracle meets the requirements specified by Codd without restrictions. However, not all of the functions are used by SAP. From the SAP point of view, the complex rights management via DBMS is redundant. The very powerful SQL dialect of Oracle is only used partially as well. Therefore, the obvious thing to do here is to create (tailor) an alternative slimmed-down version of DBMS for SAP. The resulting systems like MaxDB are technically successful. However, they still couldn't outdo Oracle as an SAP database. Oracle enjoys a very good reputation with regard to stability and performance. Additionally, many administrators are familiar with Oracle.

Criterion	Oracle	SAP	Remark
Integration	Yes	Yes	Basic request
Operations	SQL	Uses SQL	Open SQL only uses general parts of the SQL standard

Table 3.1 Codd's Rules Regarding Oracle and SAP

Criterion	Oracle	SAP	Remark
System catalog	Yes	Proprietary dictionary, Oracle dictionary is intensely used	Important: hit ratios in dictionary buffers
Views	Yes	Joins by views	
Integrity check	Yes, manifold mechanisms	Check tables, type system	
Access control	Yes, at a very detailed level	Unused, proprietary mechanisms	Only one DBMS user (or only a few OPS$ users)
Transactions	Yes	Partially used, additional mechanisms	Attention: Term has different meanings
Synchronization	Yes	Used	
Data backup	Yes, numerous concepts	Heavily used	Essential for business applications

Table 3.1 Codd's Rules Regarding Oracle and SAP (Cont.)

3.1.2 Relational Data Model and SQL

The purpose of this subsection is to repeat basic knowledge from the data modeling area. We will disregard the mathematical formalisms. Instead, we'll focus on the ER model (discussed a little later in the text), which is often used in database design and which can be very useful as a common language when communicating with developers, for example. The same applies to the less understandable SQL. In addition, SQL can be important for administration and help you with performance tuning.

According to the literature, data models are tools for describing data. They can exist in both graphical and textual format. A well-known data model for designing databases is the *Entity Relationship model* (ER model). This model is used to illustrate the part of real life to be mapped in the database and therefore represents an important connection between users and database developers. Language elements are *entities* (things from the world to be mapped), their quantifiable *attributes*, and the *relationships* among entities. Using these language elements, you can now model actual parts of real life. Modeling takes place at the type level. Entities of the same kind are grouped to entity types, and homogeneous relationships to relationship types. For every type, properties are defined as attributes. Every type has its (possibly empty) set of entities. As an alternative to ER modeling, the UML class diagram can be used, which has similar and some advanced elements.

The result of ER modeling is an *ER diagram* or *ER schema*. In layman's language, schemas are often referred to as *data models*. Because there are no database management systems that use the ER model as an internal data model, a transfer to the relational data model is necessary. There are mathematically funded methods that can ensure a correct mapping from ER to the relational model.

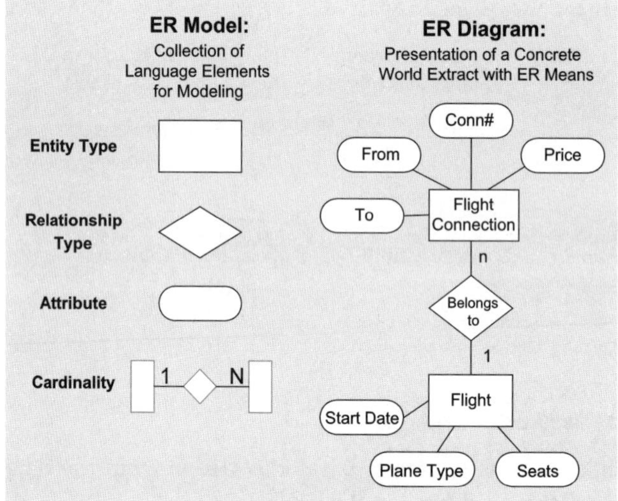

Figure 3.2 ER Model and ER Diagram

Figure 3.2 illustrates the relationship between the ER model and the ER diagram. Using the concepts of the ER model, a schema (ER diagram) is designed that describes data about flight connections and actual flights based on the SAP flight data model. As an example, some attributes are specified for the entity types *Flight Connection* and *Flight*. Particularly interesting is the relationship type that contains the cardinalities. According to the diagram, a flight belongs to exactly one flight connection and many flights can be assigned to one flight connection. The essential restriction, which can be specified or seen from the ER diagram, is hard to determine at the level of the relational data model. This is reason enough for not designing in SQL right from the start.

Figure 3.3 shows the structures used in the flight data model, which we'll use in the following text. The model is quite simple; there are only 1:n relationships.

Current database systems use the relational database model as an implementation data model. Essential language elements of the relational model are relations with attributes and keys. Relations are similar to tables. The table structures created from an ER diagram are less clear than the ER diagram itself. During the following design process, the derived tables are *normalized.* This means the tables are further split in order to ensure a widely redundancy-free database. This is necessary to avoid the risk of redundancy and to later ensure database consistency. However, the clarity of the database structures is further diminished.

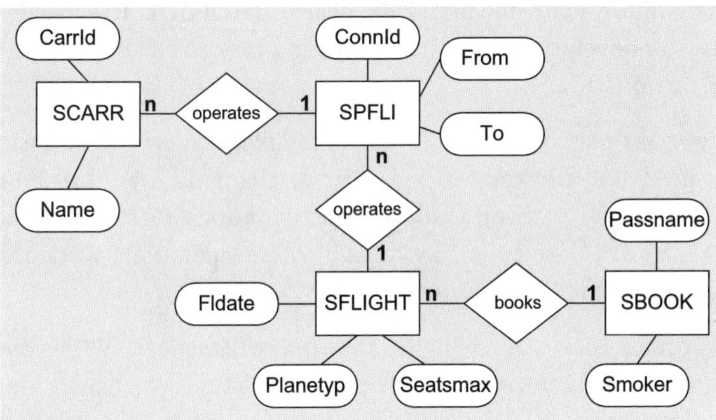

Figure 3.3 ER Diagram of the Flight Data Model

The following structures would result for the flight data model:

- `SCARR(CARRID, CARRNAME)`
  The airlines: `CARRID` is the key attribute of the table.
- `SPFLIGHT(CARRID, CONNID, FROM, TO)`
  The flight connections: `CARRID` is a foreign key referencing `SCARR`. `CONNID` is the key of the table.
- `SFLIGHT (CONNID, FLDATE, PLANETYP, SEATSMAX)`
  The actual flights: `CONNID` is a foreign key to the `SPFLI` table. The primary key consists of `CONNID` and `FLDATE`.
- `SBOOK (CONNID, FLDATE, BOOKID, PASSNAME, SMOKER)`
  The booking: Together, `CONNID` and `FLDATE` form a foreign key to the `SFLIGHT` table. An additional artificial `BOOKID` key is inserted and used as a primary key.

Database structures are implemented via the data definition language (DDL). It is part of the SQL standard. The basic operations are for creating (`create table`), removing (`drop table`), and changing (`alter table`) table structures. Additionally, basic data types are part of the SQL standard. Particularly in the field of data types, however, the DBMS vendors have their own ways and additionally provide additional, very functional data types that help to bind the database developer to the specific DBMS.

SAP implements proprietary data types that are transferred to the data types of the respective DBMS via Open SQL. Key conditions for implementing uniqueness conditions and referential integrity are part of the DDL. Additionally, you can also assign *triggers* (integrity rules) and indexes to the DDL. As an SAP administrator, you will very rarely deal with the DDL. It is usually accessed via the SAP development environments in order to ensure the consistency of SAP dictionaries.

The second important part of SQL is the *data manipulation language*. Basic operations are used for inserting (`insert into`), changing (`update`), and deleting (`delete`) records in combination with operations for transaction control (`commit, abort, rollback`). By default, these operations work for entire sets and not for individual records.

The third important part of SQL is the *query language* with the `select from where` statements. This very powerful language enables the specification of descriptive queries, that is, instead of specifying the detailed way of calculating the query result as in programming, you describe the properties of the desired results. Queries can therefore be optimized via the DBMS.

In specific database systems, the performance of SQL varies. For example, some (pseudo) database management systems don't (or didn't) offer any subqueries and *join* operations, which therefore have to be simulated in the application by program code. In previous R/3 versions, this was done for DBMS independence. You may encounter such constructions in older ABAP, particularly in proprietary developments.

Table 3.2 summarizes the parts of SQL.

Description	Tasks	Sample Statement
DDL – Data Definition Language	Creating and managing database structures like tables	`create table`
DML – Data Manipulation Language	Inserting, changing, and deleting data	`delete from`
IQL – Interactive Query Language	Query language, the actual SQL	`select from where group by order by`

Table 3.2 Sublanguages of SQL

3.1.3 Short Overview of SQL

In the following text, some examples will illustrate the syntax of essential SQL queries. For some tasks, you (as the administrator) will have to specify some SQL queries. Therefore, the following examples will serve as a reference to simplify the specification of queries, which is not always logical.

3.1.3.1 DDL – Data Definition

The DDL part of SQL includes the clauses for creating, managing, and deleting database structures. The following example shows the creation of a table from the flight data model:

```
create table scarr (
  carrid char(3) primary key,
  carrname varchar(20),
  url varchar(255)
)
```

The attribute `carrid` is selected as the primary key, which is the airline code. It is referenced by the `spfli` table. The following shortened example illustrates this foreign key definition:

```
create table spfli (
  carrid char(3),
  connid number(8) primary key,
  countryfr char(3),
  cityfrom varchar(20),
  foreign key (carrid) references scarr (carrid)
)
```

The statement `drop table spfli` removes a table. Please note that the DBMS monitors dependencies. For example, you can only remove a table without problems if it isn't referenced by any data records via foreign keys.

The changing of table structures using the `alter table` statement is restricted. Basically, only extensions like new attributes or larger value ranges (increasing the number of digits in a numeric attribute) make sense.

Numerous other database objects are important for the administrator. They are often related to the internal database structures and the specific possibilities of DBMS software. Typical applications, for tablespace administration, for example, will be discussed later in this chapter. Other structures are relevant for performance optimization and will be described in Chapter 8.

3.1.3.2 DML – Data Manipulation

The DML part of SQL enables you to insert, change, and delete data records (not database structures). The following examples show the typical syntax of important DML operations. If you want to insert a data record with all attributes, you don't need to specify an attribute name list:

```
insert into scarr values ('LTU', 'Lufttransport GmbH','www.ltu.de')
```

If not all attribute values are populated or known, you can specify NULL as a value. However, this is rather unmanageable for very "broad" tables. In this case, you should extend the statement by an attribute name list, as shown in the following example.

```
insert into scarr (carrid, carrname) values ('ORA', 'Oracle Air')
```

Data records are changed as follows:

```
update scarr set ulr = 'www.ora-air.de' where carrid= 'ORA'
```

You can change several attribute values simultaneously. The assignment operations are specified after set using commas. Please note that this is a set operation. The update statement manipulates all data records of a table that meet the where condition. However, if you forget the where condition, all data records will be changed. This also applies to the deletion of tuples:

```
delete from scarr where carrid = 'ORA'
```

In the context of DML statements, the DBMS checks whether consistency is maintained. This is how uniqueness and referential integrity are verified. Operations violating integrity are refused.

3.1.3.3 SQL IDL – Query Language

As the most powerful part of SQL, the query language enables you to specify research queries in a relatively easy and flexible way. The goal of a query is to select a result set from one or several tables that meets specific conditions. At the same time, interim results must be summarized, for example, grouped and aggregated.

The following query returns the entire contents of the `scarr` table:

```
select * from scarr.
```

For large tables, the result is generally not suitable for immediate use. Therefore, it is more beneficial to first gain an overview of the number of data records using the following statement:

```
select count(*) from scarr
```

As an administrator, you often have empirical knowledge of the right values and can immediately determine whether a table is populated "correctly."

In many cases, only specific attributes are relevant for the result set. For this purpose, a *projection list* is used for specifying the attributes to be included in the result. The following example only lists the names of the airlines:

```
select carrname from scarr
select carrname AIRLINE from scarr
```

The second example also demonstrates the renaming of an attribute, which may be relevant for further processing.

The set of specific data records (i.e. of specific rows in a table) is called a *selection*. Only data records that match the conditions after the `where` keyword are further processed. The following query outputs the names of the airlines that have ".de" in their web address:

```
select carrname from scarr where url like '%.de'
```

The query also demonstrates that fuzzy matching with placeholders is available for strings.

Quite frequently, records must be merged from several tables that are linked via foreign key relationships. This operation is called a *join*. For this purpose, you can list the relevant tables after `from`, separated by commas, and add the equivalence of keys as a condition:

```
select cityfrom, carrname
from scarr c, sflight f
where c.carrid = f.carrid
```

The query returns the names of the airlines together with the departure locations. Because this data resides in different tables, it must be linked. The aliases C and F were used for the scarr and sflight tables. In large queries, this can improve clarity. As the following example demonstrates, this is necessary in queries where a table is linked to itself:

```
select f1.carrid, f2. carrid, f1.to
from sflight f1, sflight f2
where f1.from='TXL' and f2.to='JFK' and f1.to=f2.from;
```

The query determines the flight connections from Berlin-Tegel to New York with changing planes once. The sflight table is joined to itself (*auto-join*).

When evaluating large amounts of data, interim results can be grouped in SQL queries, and these groups can then be evaluated. The following example shows a group created by departure location and calculates the number of flight connections to every departure location:

```
select cityfrom, count(connid) from spfli group by cityfrom
```

More aggregate functions are:

- *Average creation* using avg – only makes sense for numeric attributes like the price, for example
- *Sum function* using sum – only makes sense for numeric attributes like the price, for example
- *Maximum value of a group* using max – makes sense for numeric attributes, but also for date values or strings
- *Minimum value of a group* using min – makes sense for numeric attributes, but also for date values or strings

Note that the attribute list may only contain attributes that have been used for grouping or aggregate functions. The having clause enables you to specify additional conditions for groups.

SQL also enables you to sort results. Several sort criteria are available. By explicitly specifying desc, data is sorted in descending order; otherwise, it is sorted in ascending order. The sorting via the DBMS is especially useful for specific data types like date and time because a programmed sorting can be rather complex in this case.

```
select * from spfli order by from city desc
```

Current SQL dialects also support numerous additional options for specifying queries. For example, wherever there is a table, you should be able to place a query that returns a table. However, this is not supported by every database management software.

SQL is a powerful tool for database developers and administrators. Because the information on database structures is stored in database tables as well, it can be used with SQL. In this regard, SQL is important for you as an administrator of an SAP system.

3.1.4 Implementation Techniques for DBMS

The demands on database management systems described in Section 3.1.1, *Motivation and History*, are not easy to meet in this combination. On the one hand, there is a quantitative requirement for a high number of users to be served simultaneously, or in other words, there is a requirement for high performance. On the other hand, they must meet qualitative requirements for transaction security, easy handling using SQL, and semantic-oriented data model concepts. Only if both aspects are equally fulfilled can the DBMS assume an integral role in integrating the IT architecture.

In order to meet these requirements, IT deals with database implementation techniques. Based on a modular layer architecture, solutions are developed for a number of partial problems that are often implemented immediately in commercial database systems. Based on our experience, understanding the concepts can directly help you with your administration tasks. Therefore, at this point, we'd like to introduce important concepts and techniques.

The five-layer architecture shown in Figure 3.4 according to Senko and Härder illustrates the implementation of database management systems and also formed the basis of *System-R*, the first relational DBMS that was developed by IBM in the 1970s. The application program submits SQL queries to the set-oriented interface. Accordingly, results are sets of data records. File management at the lowest level uses the operating system functions for storing data in the secondary memory, on disks, for example.

In this context, we would like to remind you of the term *memory gap*. In the database area, this denotes the access speed ratio between a fast (and expensive and volatile) main memory and a slow (but cheap and stable) disk storage. This is usually around 10^5 (i.e., 100,000). In real life, this means that, for example, a query that can be answered within a thousandth of a second using main memory structures would take 100 seconds by exclusively accessing disks. Therefore, the goal must be to fill the existing main memory with data as effectively and providently as possible, without restricting transaction security.

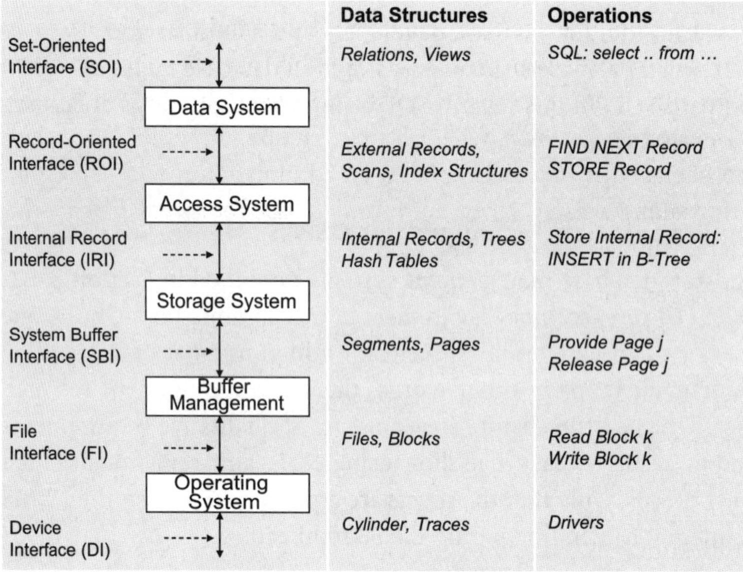

Figure 3.4 Five-Layer Architecture According to Senko and Härder

Numerous optimization procedures were developed for this purpose and are included in the five-layer architecture. Understanding this architecture can support a database or SAP administrator in his or her daily work. Therefore, we'll discuss the five-layer architecture in more detail:.

- **Data System**
  The data system provides the set-oriented interface on which the application software, i.e. the R/3 system in this case, is based. Basically, this layer fulfills three tasks. At first, a cost-efficient plan is created by optimizing the query. This software layer then selects the access paths (Indexes) to be used. The third task is to evaluate all query expressions, i.e. to calculate the result set for which various algorithms are available. You will observe this layer in context with performance optimization.

- **Access System**
  Via the record-oriented interface, the access system provides logical data records, which means that the relations and attributes are named. A relation corresponds to a logical file, and the same applies to the indexes. Therefore, the data dictionary is included here as well. Operations are

scans on logical files that go through the file via a cursor. To enable the access to specific data records via scans there are various file organization procedures, like B-tree or hash procedures.

- **Storage System**
  The storage system manages internal data records and files. Problems are caused by data records that exceed one memory page, incoherent blocks and the growth of data records, which then have to be migrated to other blocks. The storage system is where the transaction log resides and where locks are managed for transactions. As an administrator, you have some options for taking action. For example, a database reorganization merges the scattered storage structures again.
- **Buffer Management**
  The objective of buffer management is to optimally and safely store memory pages (blocks) in the computer's main memory. In general, only a part of the data records fits into the main memory. Therefore, strategies for relocating pages play an important role. With regard to a high-performing SAP system, you should pay special attention to buffer management. SAP implements many techniques that help to ensure a good buffer quality. As an administrator, you'll observe the buffers' hit rates and filling levels and take control, if necessary.
- **Operating System**
  The operating system provides physical files. Mechanisms for increasing performance or improving data security (RAID), management of logical volumes beyond disk limits, or a fragment-free storage are important for very large databases like those used for SAP. Techniques used in this context depend primarily on the actual operating system and the hardware.

The aforementioned architecture can be found with Oracle and is also relevant to administering SAP based on Oracle.

3.2 Development of Oracle

The success story of Oracle started at the beginning of the 1980s. In 1979, Oracle was introduced to the market as one of the first relational database systems and quickly became very popular. The reasons were and still are:

- The easy application development via SQL
- The consequent usage of the results of latest research
- The strategy of providing the DBMS on all important platforms

The last item led to a high degree of portability regarding hardware and operating system, which means that you can operate your Oracle-based system on very different platforms. However, a decision in favor of Oracle leads to a very strong and therefore often long-term commitment. Although Oracle is essentially based on the SQL standard and also contributed to its design, the usage of specific very innovative Oracle concepts often results in software that can only be ported with a great deal of effort. The resulting bonding to the DBMS strengthens the Oracle enterprise and can also be listed as a success factor.

For users, this strong bond to a DBMS vendor is still not critical, because Oracle has proven to be stable and innovative during the past decades. The following overview shows some features of the last Oracle versions:

- **Version 7:** "The semantic database" concepts like *constraints* and *triggers* enable a better integration of semantics in the database.
- **Versions 8 and 8i:** Oracle was consequently positioned as a server database and adapted to the spreading structures of the Internet. The first object-oriented concepts were implemented.
- **Version 9i:** Version 9 also emphasized the strong focus on the Internet. What is quite striking about this version is that the DBMS was renamed from Oracle Server to Oracle Database. This must be viewed in context with the other (also server-based) products in the field of business applications, e-commerce, and application servers. The extended object-oriented concepts that can turn Oracle into an object-relational database are another noteworthy feature. Another notable point is the integration of XML. From the administrator's point of view, the concept of parameter dynamization and the automatic management of DBMS parameters should also be mentioned.
- **Version 10g:** Version 10g has been available since 2004 and is focused on grid computing. The DBMS is spread across several servers as it was partially possible in the previous versions via the Oracle Parallel Server or the real application cluster architecture. This is of particular interest for very large SAP systems and can help you to extend the architecture presented in Section 2.2, "Architecture and Scalability." Equally interesting to administration is the proprietary file system management ASM (Automatic Storage Management).

In addition to these outstanding innovations, new versions are characterized by improvements that could optimally use developing hardware resources.

From the point of view of a standard application like SAP, many Oracle enhancements are not necessary or useful. Therefore, it is common practice to use caution when working with new Oracle versions. Stability and compatibility are the essential criteria. A new version is only implemented if it is more stable and better supported. However, production systems often keep running on an old Oracle version for many years.

Figure 3.5 shows you how to learn more about the Oracle version used in an SAP system. In the SAP GUI, go to **System • Status** (steps ❶ and ❷). Here, you will find information on the implemented DBMS, the version and the user (A). Via the inconspicuous **Kernel Information** button (❸), you will obtain more information on the DBMS (B), for example, on the version of the used client library and on compatible database versions. The **DB releases** field (❹) enables you to navigate to the right; in the sample system, the full entry reads:

```
ORACLE 9.2.0.*.*, ORACLE 10.1.0.*.*, ORACLE 10.2.0.*.*
```

The SAP Basis thus already supports Oracle 10, although Oracle 9.2 is used in this case.

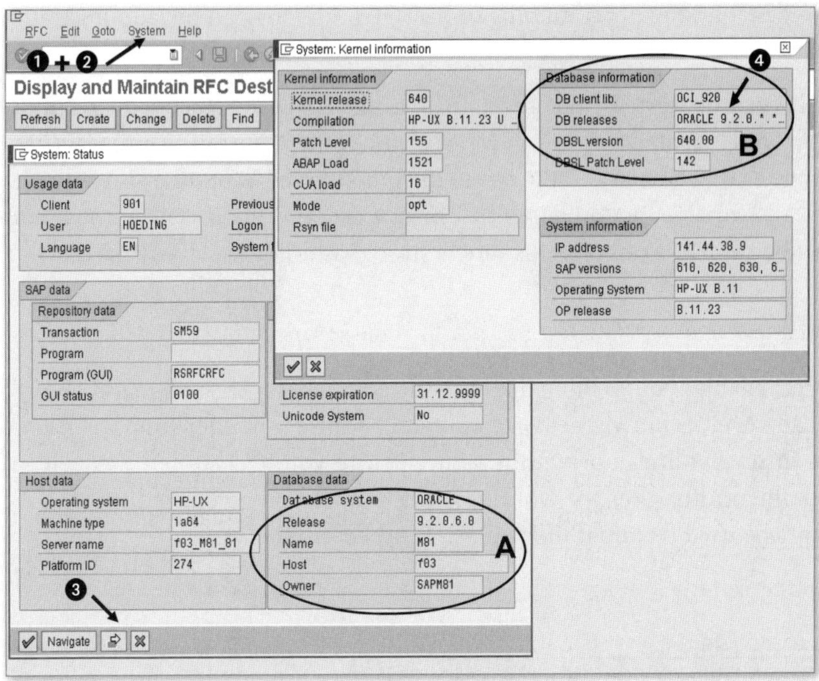

Figure 3.5 Oracle Information under SAP

Libraries, versions, and patches are very important to administration. The five-digit Oracle version number is composed as follows: The first two digits refer to the version and the release and are regarded as "marketing-relevant." In addition to bug fixes, a release also includes new functionalities. The third digit stands for the maintenance release, the fourth for the platform-independent patch set, and the fifth for platform-specific patches.

The "marketing-loaded" version names like Oracle 10g correspond to the first release. Therefore, Oracle 10g is 10.1. Accordingly, Oracle 10g release 2 corresponds to number 10.2.

3.3 Tools for the Oracle Administrator

This section introduces some essential administration tools provided for Oracle. These tools will also help you to reproduce the examples presented in later sections.

3.3.1 sqlplus

sqlplus is Oracle's command line interface. In addition to normal SQL queries, it enables the programming of PL/SQL functions and the administration of Oracle.

sqlplus can be started from a terminal window. The screenshots used in this book were created in Windows via the "putty" terminal program. We assume that you have a UNIX access to your system. As another prerequisite, the `PATH` variable `ORACLE_HOME/bin` must exist, and the `ORACLE_SID` variable must be set. For example, this tool is started as follows:

```
sqlplus fdm_user@orcl
```

sqlplus enables you to immediately issue commands. The command line editor, however, is not very easy to operate, because it neither supports navigation in several lines nor within a line. Before you overburden yourself, we recommend that you try working with a more convenient editor that can simply be used from within sqlplus.[1] Proceed as follows:

1 Kalosi, D.: Vimming with SQL*Plus. Oracle Technology Network 2007; http://www.oracle.com/technology/pub/articles/kalosi_vim.html

```
SQL> select * from scarr;
SQL> define _editor=vi
SQL> edit
```

The editor `vi` is started and enables you to conveniently edit the SQL statement. After you quit `vi`, the SQL buffer is listed in sqlplus:

```
SQL> edit
Wrote file afiedt.buf
  1  select * from scarr
  2* where carrid = 'LTU'
SQL> /
```

The / now runs the SQL statement contained in the buffer. sqlplus uses the editor set in the `EDITOR` environment variable:

```
export EDITOR=vi
```

Note

Editing is only possible if there is something in the SQL buffer of sqlplus. If you try to start the editor to enter the first statement, you will receive an error message. Even if you don't have the writing permission for the directory in which you reside during the startup of sqlplus, you will receive an error message because the *afiedt.buf* cannot be written to.

In many cases, it can be useful to log the sqlplus session. On the one hand, it is important for administration to reproduce what you did so far. On the other hand, logging enables a further processing of query results using an editor. Particularly for large tables, it is often hard to handle the display in a sqlplus window. The following example demonstrates how to use logging:

```
SQL> spool sql01-july-hoeding.txt
SQL> select * from scarr where carrid='LTU';
. . . This is the query result . . .
SQL> spool off
```

sqlplus is particularly important to system administration. It can be used for starting and stopping databases. For this purpose, you need to log on with a system user and the addition AS SYSDBA (see Figure 3.6).

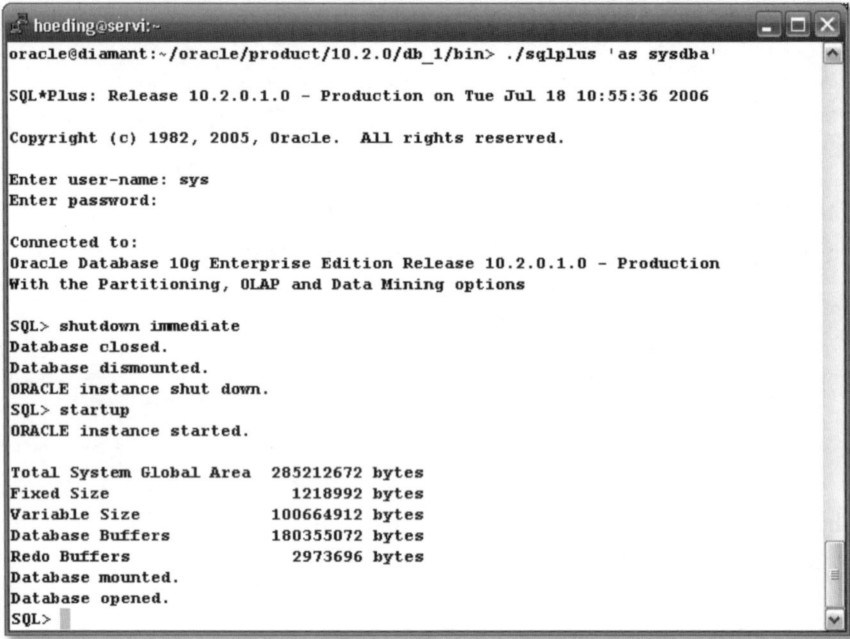

Figure 3.6 Administration Using SQLPlus

It is remarkable that sqlplus can even connect to an Oracle instance that has not been started (*Connected to an Idle Instance*) and then initiate the startup of the database processes during startup.

3.3.2 isqlplus

A comfortable alternative to sqlplus is the web frontend isqlplus. It enables you to use the database via a browser. Only one database user is required; there is no logon at the operating system level. SQL statements are edited intuitively; there is a history function. Via HTML, wide tables are displayed in a clearly more user-friendly way than in sqlplus.

A disadvantage of isqlplus is its limited usability for administration. By default, you are prohibited from establishing a connection to AS SYSDBA. This restriction does make sense because, on the one hand, such an access can be a security gap, and on the other hand, the Oracle Enterprise Manager provides you with an alternative.

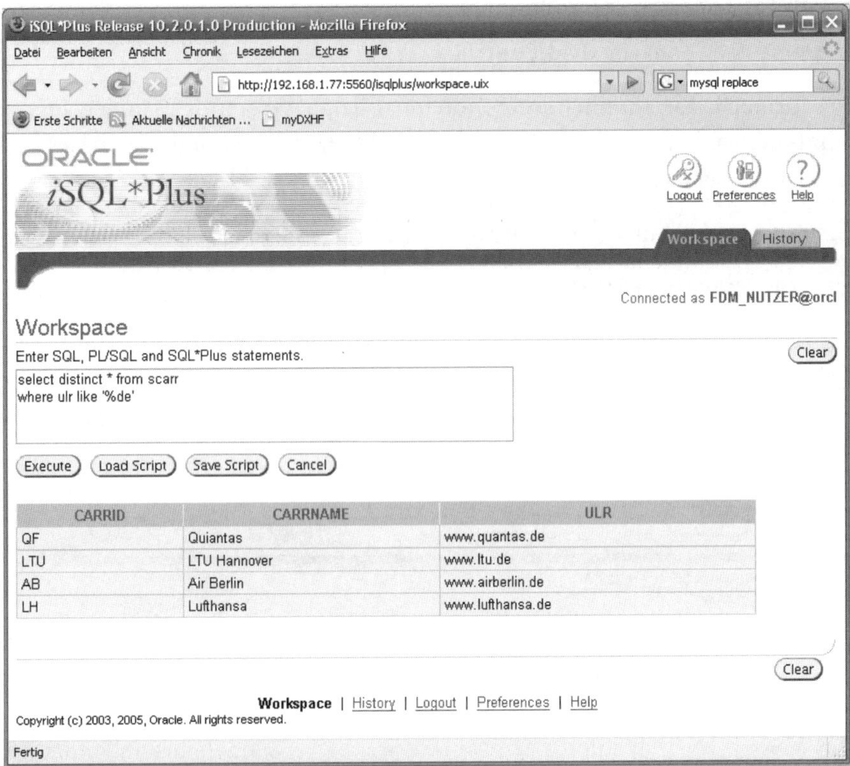

Figure 3.7 Browser-Based SQL Access via isqlplus

By default, isqlplus is addressed via port 5560:

http://servername:5560/isqlplus/

As a prerequisite, an isqlplus server must be started on the server computer that has successfully established a connection to the database. The isqlplus server is a service of the Java-based Oracle application server. It can be started manually as follows:

```
oracle@diamant:~/> ./isqlplusctl start
```

3.3.3 Oracle Enterprise Manager

The *Oracle Enterprise Manager* provides you with a convenient interface for administering Oracle databases. In older Oracle releases, it was implemented as a Java application. Currently, it is only offered as a web application. You need to distinguish between the following:

- Enterprise Manager Database Control and
- Enterprise Manager Grid Control

The former is for administering individual databases and is included in any standard installation. The latter enables you to manage various databases and application servers.

The Enterprise Manager is addressed via port 1158:

http://servername:1158/em/

For logon, you need a database user with administration rights. The Enterprise Manager provides a lot of information and a multitude of functions for administering an Oracle database that are presented in a user-friendly way (see Figure 3.8).

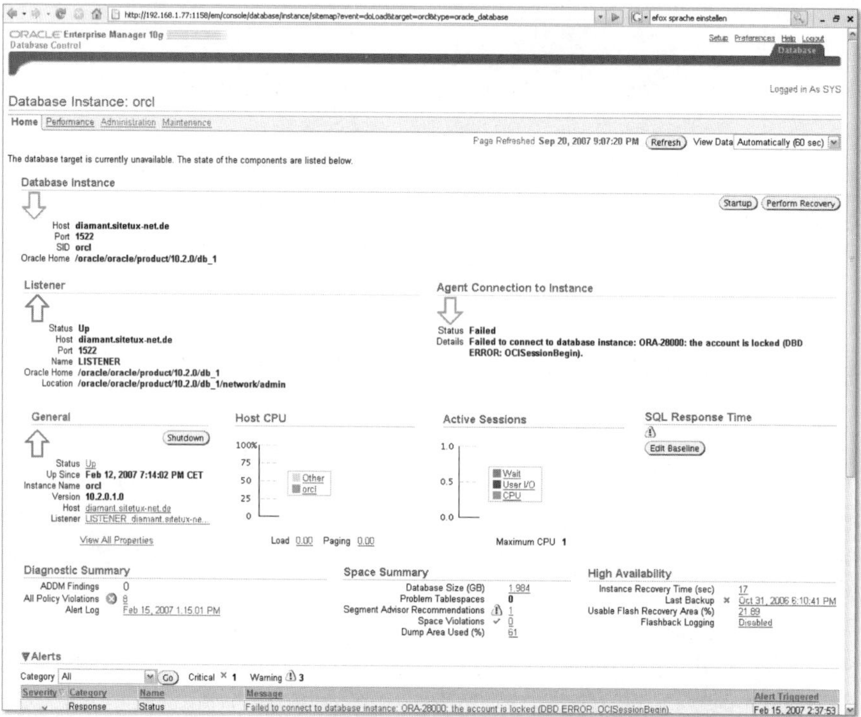

Figure 3.8 Initial View of the Enterprise Manager

Numerous functions support performance optimization or the backup and restoration of databases. The Enterprise Manager can also connect to an idle instance and start the database. Similar to isqlplus, it is started or stopped via a control script:

```
oracle@diamant:~/> ./emctl start dbconsole
```

In this book we will use the Enterprise Manager to illustrate some concepts and administrative tasks.

3.3.3.1 More Tools

Numerous tools are provided with the Oracle DBMS, partially directly from Oracle and partially from third-parties. On the one hand, the purpose is to provide solutions for specific areas. On the other hand, these tools often provide interfaces that simplify the usage of the very powerful Oracle functionality via graphical interfaces or script interfaces. We will mention only a few tools:

- The *Recovery Manager* (RMAN) is an Oracle product used for creating backups and recovering the database, if necessary.
- The *Oracle Database Creation Assistant* (DBCA) supports the creation of databases. The *Oracle Net Configuration Assistant* and the *Oracle Net Manager* enable you to easily configure and oversee the management of Oracle Net.
- The *BR*Tools* are provided by SAP and, in addition to backup and recovery, also support other database-related administration tasks that should be performed at the operating system level.

The BR*Tools, in particular, are relevant to SAP administration.

3.4 Oracle Kernel

As a database management system, Oracle's primary task is to provide database application programs with data. The functionality to be fulfilled is also referred to as OLTP (*Online Transaction Processing*). Transactions are performed online, which means immediately. For a quick execution of a large number of transactions, Oracle implements essential concepts that were introduced in Section 3.1.4, *Implementation Techniques for DBMS*. In the following sections, we will describe the Oracle concepts relevant to administration.

For this purpose, we need to consider the processes and storage structures. *Processes* are running programs that render services either when requested or autonomously. From the application program's point of view, it is primarily the server process that should be mentioned, because it executes the entire SQL processing for a SQL query and provides the data. Storage structures are implemented for communication and data storage. As mentioned previously, this is about the interaction between a very large but slow disk storage and a smaller but very fast main memory.

Along with the use of SAP, the configuration of the main memory, the file structures, and the auxiliary processes are critical to data backup. This will be discussed in Chapter 4, *SAP and Oracle*.

3.4.1 Oracle Processes

The active elements of an Oracle system are the Oracle processes. In UNIX, they correspond to operating system processes and can be regarded using the `top` or `ps` UNIX commands:

- For an SAP system with the SID A38, `ps -u a38adm | grep ora_` provides information on the Oracle processes belonging to the SAP user at the operating system level (see Figure 3.9).
- `ps -u oraa38` provides a list of server processes for the A38 system.

The Oracle instance in Figure 3.9 consists of:

- Several server processes (`oracleA38`) that belong to the SAP user a38adm
- A PMON process (Process Monitor)
- A DBWR process (Database Writer)
- A LGWR process (Log-Writer)
- A CKPT process (Checkpointer)
- A SMON process (System Monitor)
- A RECO process (Recovery)
- Two ARCH processes (Archiver)

Except for the server processes, all Oracle processes belong to the user ora<SID>.

Additionally, Oracle provides the following processes:

- LCK processes (Lock Process) for managing locks
- SNPn processes (Snapshot Process) for managing snapshots

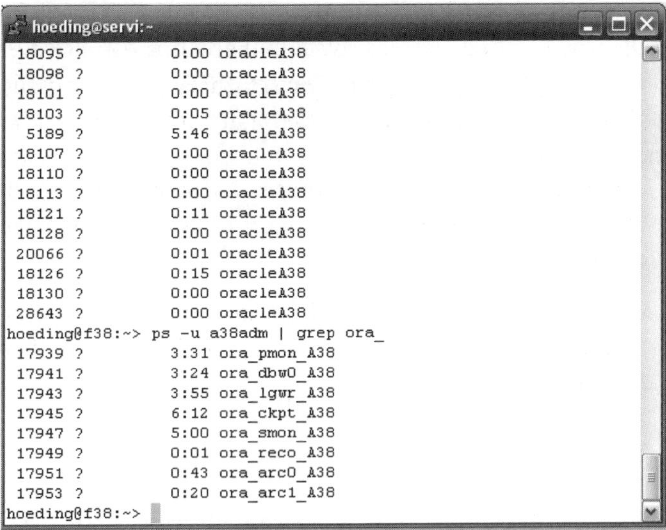
hoeding@servi:~
18095 ? 0:00 oracleA38
18098 ? 0:00 oracleA38
18101 ? 0:00 oracleA38
18103 ? 0:05 oracleA38
5189 ? 5:46 oracleA38
18107 ? 0:00 oracleA38
18110 ? 0:00 oracleA38
18113 ? 0:00 oracleA38
18121 ? 0:11 oracleA38
18128 ? 0:00 oracleA38
20066 ? 0:01 oracleA38
18126 ? 0:15 oracleA38
18130 ? 0:00 oracleA38
28643 ? 0:00 oracleA38
hoeding@f38:~> ps -u a38adm | grep ora_
17939 ? 3:31 ora_pmon_A38
17941 ? 3:24 ora_dbw0_A38
17943 ? 3:55 ora_lgwr_A38
17945 ? 6:12 ora_ckpt_A38
17947 ? 5:00 ora_smon_A38
17949 ? 0:01 ora_reco_A38
17951 ? 0:43 ora_arc0_A38
17953 ? 0:20 ora_arc1_A38
hoeding@f38:~>

Figure 3.9 Oracle Processes under UNIX

- Dispatcher processes for distributing user requests to the server processes in shared server operation
- the MMON process (since Oracle 10), which periodically writes statistical data to the workload repository
- the MMAN process (Memory Manager Process, since Oracle 10), which now flexibly manages the shared memory of the SGA
- the RKWR process (Recovery Writer Process, since Oracle 10) for managing flash backup
- The PSPO process (Process Spawner Process, since Oracle 10), which is now responsible for starting processes

The objective of the interaction of these processes is to ensure a high transaction throughput while maintaining data security. In the following text, we will show you the essential processes and illustrate their interaction. As an administrator, understanding this interaction helps you to correctly assess problems and to find solutions. Additionally, this interaction is the basis for performance optimization as well as for backup and recovery.

3.4.1.1 Server Processes

Server processes are the actual service providers from the application software point of view. The server process speaks SQL and communicates with the application process via Oracle Net (see Section 3.4.7, *Accessing Oracle with Oracle Net*). Internally, the server process is structured according to the five-layer architecture. Accordingly, it performs the entire query processing and optimization, index management, access to buffers and main memory as well as transaction management.

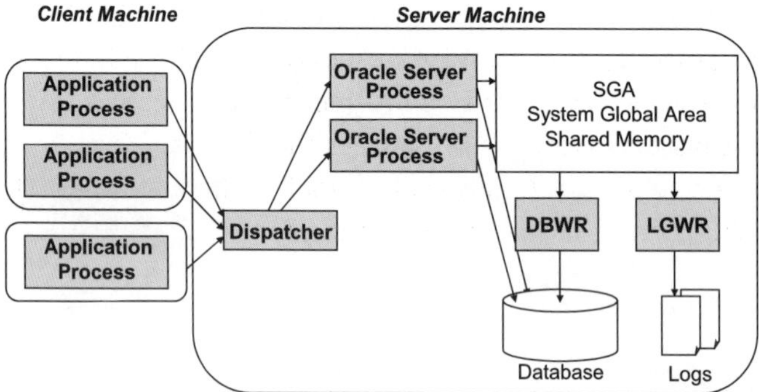

Figure 3.10 Shared Server Configuration in Oracle

Oracle provides two types of server processes. On the one hand, there are shared server processes that can mutually serve a large number of user processes (see Figure 3.10). On the other hand, there are dedicated server processes (see Figure 3.11). Such a process is available to exactly one dedicated application process. This process type is used by the SAP software as well, where every SAP work process is assigned one Oracle server process as a *shadow process*.

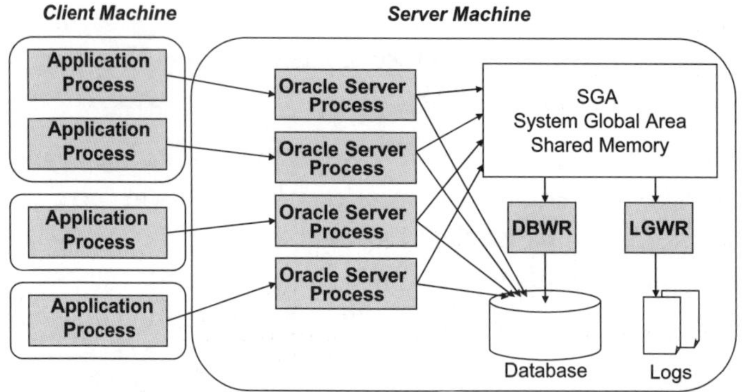

Figure 3.11 Dedicated Server Configuration in Oracle

The concept of shared server processes finds its equivalent in the work processes of your SAP system, which can serve a large number of users (in SAP, these are mainly GUI requests) in a similarly flexible way. The way in which the server process works is explained in more detail in Section 3.4.6, *Interaction of Processes and Storage Structures*.

3.4.1.2 Database Writer

As an asynchronously working background process, the function of the *Database Writer* is to write modified pages from the buffer to the hard disk. The buffer should be as free as possible from such pages, which are indicated as *dirty*. This is where the LRU algorithm is implemented. LRU refers to *Least Recently Used* and means that those memory pages that have not been used for the longest time are relocated. Additionally, data is written at the checkpoint or after a DBWR timeout (every three seconds, for example).

3.4.1.3 Log Writer

The *Log Writer process* is responsible for managing the redo log buffer and the redo log file and thus enables a fast `COMMIT`. If a transaction is completed via `COMMIT`, the LGWR process writes the corresponding log entries to the redo log files. The data is thus permanently stored and can be restored, even if the data files still contain obsolete data records. Writing data sequentially to a file can be much faster than writing changes to various places in many data files. Furthermore, the LGWR process becomes active when a timeout occurs (every three seconds).

3.4.1.4 Archiver

The *Archiver process* is responsible for archiving written redo logs to the archive directory. The archiving of logs enables you to restore the database in order to close the interruption, if necessary.

3.4.1.5 Checkpointer

The *Checkpointer process* creates backup points. For this purpose, it updates the headers of the data files and causes the DBWR process to write all data blocks that are marked as *dirty*. The data files thus represent a consistent state.

3.4.2 Oracle Main Memory Structures

For administering Oracle-based software system, it is important that you know the main memory structures used by Oracle. Only then can a system be configured and optimized for specific requirements. The main memory presents a very fast possibility of exchanging data between processes and for communication. For a database system, the function as a cache is important to work around the memory gap (see Section 3.1.5, *Implementation Techniques for DBMS*). The Oracle main memory is divided into the *System Global Area* (SGA) and the *Program Global Area* (PGA).

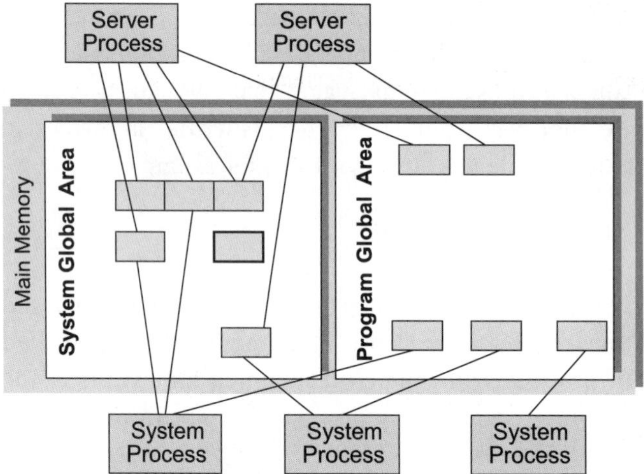

Figure 3.12 Main Memory Access to SGA and PGA

The SGA contains the database data and is for the communication of Oracle processes (see Figure 3.12). The PGA provides the memory area for the individual Oracle processes and, among other things, contains temporary process variables and internal arrays.

The SGA is divided into the following areas (see also Figure 3.13):

- **Database Buffer Cache**
  Database data is cached via server processes and is then available to all processes. For a high DBMS performance, it is important to have all frequently requested data available in the cache, if possible. Therefore, the database buffer cache should be large enough to accommodate all the data. Sizes of up to several gigabytes are desirable. For test installations and demo systems, sizes of under 512 megabytes are reasonable. Experience with SAP systems shows, however, that buffer sizes in the gigabyte region rarely are justified, albeit there are SAP installations with very large buffer pools. In general, only data that should be contained in the buffer is really necessary. Otherwise, it may make more sense to use the main

memory for other purposes. If the buffer is too full, rarely used memory pages are removed according to the LRU procedure. If necessary, they are saved to data files by a DBWR process.

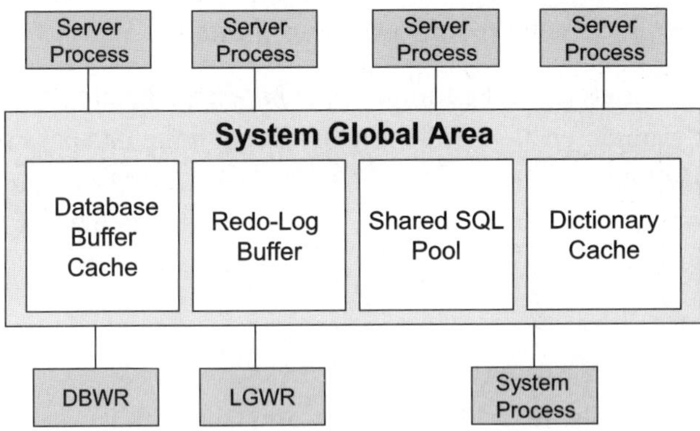

Figure 3.13 Division of the SGA

- **Redo Log Buffer**
  All change operations, via a SQL update, for example, are performed simultaneously in the database buffer cache and in the redo log cache. In the database buffer, the corresponding memory pages are addressed. In the redo log, however, the changes are written sequentially. If a transaction is successfully completed via a `COMMIT`, the LGWR process writes the corresponding section to the redo log files. This sequential writing is considerably faster than writing to the scattered blocks of database files.
- **Shared SQL Pool**
  By buffering SQL statements, functions, and procedures in the shared SQL pool, Oracle can respond faster to a recurring SQL query. For this purpose, parse trees and execution plans are stored so that they don't have to be calculated from scratch again and again. The LRU procedure is also implemented for managing the shared pool.
- **Dictionary Cache**
  Frequently required information on the database structure is stored to the dictionary cache. This includes tables and field names, but the mapping information corresponds to the five-layer architecture. Additionally, the dictionary cache contains user and authorization information. This information is required for parsing SQL queries, creating execution plans, and for the authorization check, which is always performed in Oracle.

On UNIX systems, the SGA is instantiated as a shared memory. Accordingly, all Oracle processes can access this memory. Therefore, the ability of the operating system to manage very large shared memory segments is highly significant. The corresponding kernel parameters also need to be set (e.g., `shmmax` under Linux, and partial patches need to be installed).

Important database parameters can be found in the *init<sid>.ora* file or, as of Oracle 9i, in a server parameter file (SPFile) that is stored in the database system path under *$ORACLE_HOME/dbs* (UNIX) or *%ORACLE_HOME%/database* (Windows).[2] Parameters can be changed in the parameter file via the SQL level using

```
alter system set parameter=value;
```

or using administration tools. Note that changes don't take effect immediately in all cases and might be overwritten. We recommend that you look at the parameter files. Some specifications will already be understandable to you; other parameters will become clear as you read on.

In conjunction with older Oracle versions, the individual buffers and areas in the SGA were firmly defined using parameters. Meanwhile, the storage sizes in the SGA have been *dynamized*, which means that Oracle itself can adapt the sizes at runtime according to the requirements.

In theory, 32-bit operating systems are able to address four gigabytes of main memory. For a large database application like a productive SAP system, this is a desirable dimension. Because in real life, the four-gigabyte limit cannot be used by many 32-bit operating systems and because hardware and databases continue to grow, you should always implement only 64-bit systems. Appropriate processors, architectures, and adequate Oracle installations enable a more stable operation. Meanwhile, 32-bit SAP systems are only supported for Windows and Linux 32. This is another reason for recommending the use of a 64-bit system.

3.4.3 Oracle File System

In most Oracle installations, persistent data storage is performed using files of the operating system. This can be a local file system, that is, hard disks that are physically connected to the server computer. During the past years, how-

2 In SAP installations, the parameter file name is complemented with the SAP SID in the following form: *init<sid>.ora*.

ever, numerous solutions have been established where external storage systems provide logical volumes. Due to the flexible configuration of hard disks and the hardware-side usage of RAID technologies, storage systems have advantages over local hard disks. Usually, they are faster, safer, and more flexible. For example, a logical volume can be enlarged transparently, if necessary, which means that the database administrator does not have to make changes to file management.

The implementation of Oracle based on files provides benefits regarding administration. Files can be copied and analyzed via the operating system. This produces additional possibilities in problematic situations.

Disadvantages of using file systems can be found in caching mechanisms, which are usually implemented in the operating system. First, the file cache unnecessarily consumes storage space because Oracle buffers as well. In worst-case scenarios, the caching algorithms of the operating system and the database management system can even work against each other. Therefore, since early Oracle versions, it is possible to use raw devices under UNIX. In this case, Oracle immediately accesses the hard disk. This improves the I/O performance. However, the administration of raw devices is a bit more complicated. The administration of the Logical Volume Management of modern operating systems and of storage solutions is more flexible and secure.

As of Oracle 9i, *Oracle Managed Files* (OMF) provide a solution that uses default settings to simplify and standardize the naming of Oracle files. You need to specify a mount point using which Oracle consequently and consistently categorizes and names files. In the corresponding statements for creating a tablespace, for example, the clause for specifying the file path can then be omitted. This simplifies administration and prevents configuration errors. However, the possibilities for an optimized distribution of tablespaces to different devices, which are described later in this section, are not available. In this sense the literature recommends OMF rather for test and development systems. With Oracle 10g, Oracle has introduced the *Automatic Storage Management* (ASM) as a proprietary file system that is to present the optimum implementation for operating an Oracle database irrespective of the operating system. Unformatted devices are managed via a specific ASM instance and the OCSS process (*Oracle Cluster Synchronization Service*), and a separate file system is created that also contains control and log files in addition to the data files. ASM performs a striping and mirroring process across all devices. The devices are no longer available to the operating system and cannot be destroyed inadvertently.

In the following text, we will focus on the most common usage of a file system. With regard to the database system requirements, Oracle tries to optimally use the storage space provided by files. Performance ranks first, then the effective usage of the storage space. Knowing these Oracle mechanisms is essential for administering Oracle-based SAP systems. Space management is probably one of your most important tasks.

3.4.4 Oracle Tablespace Concept

Significant performance losses are caused by heavy data fragmentation. From the database system point of view, it would be ideal if the data of a table were sequentially stored on the disks as one coherent area. To make this happen, the database system must roughly know the data requirements of every table. While this seems feasible for master data, a safe forecast is impossible for variable data. There will inevitably be wasted, that is, unused, areas in files. Unused disk space costs money and time.

As a central construct for managing databases and files, Oracle has introduced the *tablespace*. On the one hand, specific tables or other database structures are assigned to a tablespace. On the other hand, it has a flexible number of very large files that store the data. In this context, essential tasks are:

- **Controlling Storage Allocation**
  New areas are requested for data like growing tables. The available storage space is monitored.
- **Storage Allocation Across Several Disk Drives**
  In some operating systems, files cannot grow beyond disk boundaries. A tablespace, however, can bundle files from various disks. If you're running out of disk space, a new drive can be added without having to copy existing files. This can even be done at runtime.
- **Structuring the Database According to Conceptual Aspects**
  Data can be structured according to conceptual aspects and thus achieve a better administrability or performance. It therefore makes sense to separate variable data and master data. While the former probably grows continuously and must be intensely observed and secured, the latter can be optimally configured during the installation.
- **Optimization According to Physical Aspects**
  Using specific tablespace types for indexes and tables, for example, in combination with the distribution of files to different disks, you can enable a parallel access.

- **Performing Partial Backups**
  With regard to the time-consuming backups for large databases, the tablespace concept provides specific techniques for fast backup.

Detailed information on the tablespaces available in an Oracle system is provided by the Data Dictionary via the `dba_tablespaces` or `user_tablespace` tables (or views), for example (see Figure 3.14). The following query produces comprehensive information:

```
Select * from user_tablespaces
```

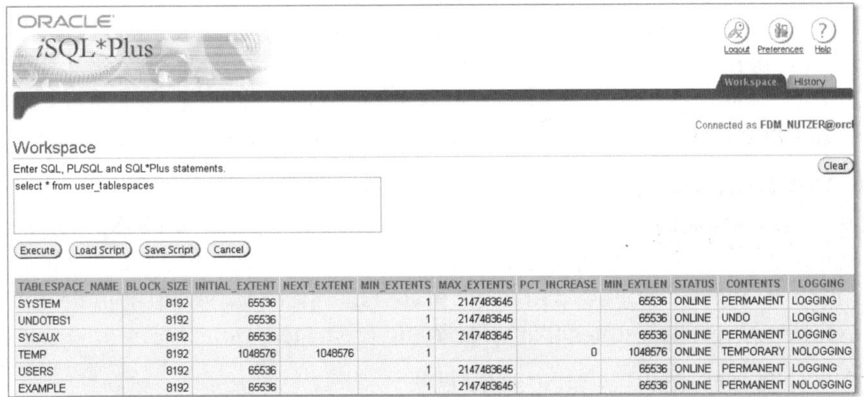

TABLESPACE_NAME	BLOCK_SIZE	INITIAL_EXTENT	NEXT_EXTENT	MIN_EXTENTS	MAX_EXTENTS	PCT_INCREASE	MIN_EXTLEN	STATUS	CONTENTS	LOGGING
SYSTEM	8192	65536		1	2147483645		65536	ONLINE	PERMANENT	LOGGING
UNDOTBS1	8192	65536		1	2147483645		65536	ONLINE	UNDO	LOGGING
SYSAUX	8192	65536		1	2147483645		65536	ONLINE	PERMANENT	LOGGING
TEMP	8192	1048576	1048576	1		0	1048576	ONLINE	TEMPORARY	NOLOGGING
USERS	8192	65536		1	2147483645		65536	ONLINE	PERMANENT	LOGGING
EXAMPLE	8192	65536		1	2147483645		65536	ONLINE	PERMANENT	NOLOGGING

Figure 3.14 Tablespace Information of a Demo Installation

If you look at the Oracle storage structures (see Figure 3.15), the tablespace concept represents the interface between physical and logical database structures. Physically, a tablespace consists of 1 to n data files. Each of these data files is stored on a specific disk across the file structure of the operating system.

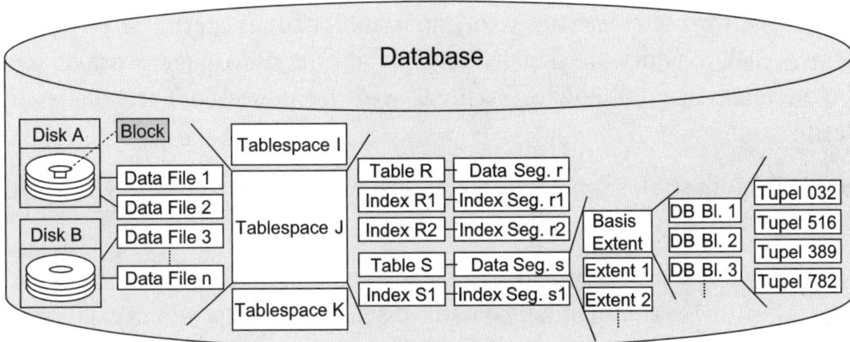

Figure 3.15 Oracle Storage Structures

The following query lists data files together with the assigned tablespace and the filling data. The example shows a demo database where only an initial file exists per tablespace (executable as SYSDBA only):

```
select file_name, tablespace_name, bytes, blocks
from   dba_data_files;
FILE_NAME             TABLESPACE_NAME        BYTES
--------------------- ---------------------- -----------
/orcl/users01.dbf     USERS                  5242880
/orcl/sysaux01.dbf    SYSAUX                 283115520
/orcl/undotbs01.dbf..UNDOTBS1                        435159040
```

3.4.4.1 Types of Tablespaces

For tablespace management, Oracle provides two alternative mechanisms:

- **Dictionary-Managed Tablespaces (DMTS)**
  The management of the tablespace is controlled by the administrator via the Data Dictionary. Up to Oracle version 9, this was the prevalent mechanism, which is still used in many productive systems. When administrating such systems, it helps to understand the concepts.
- **Locally Managed Tablespaces (LMTS)**
  The tablespace is managed by the Oracle instance via a bitmap at the beginning of every data file. This enables an efficient tablespace management that requires the monitoring of critical storage limits, though. Additionally, LMTS performs better because changes to database structures do not recursively cause changes to the dictionary tables. LMTS have been available since Oracle 8.1. Since Oracle 9, they are the preferred standard setting.

Understanding both mechanisms is important for administering SAP systems because DMTS, which are actually obsolete, are still used in many productive SAP systems. In the following sections, we'll introduce both techniques in detail.

Figure 3.14 illustrates some of the tablespace types available with Oracle. In the following text, we will demonstrate several types of tablespaces.

The *system tablespace* contains the database catalog and is created via the `create database` command. It contains essential metadata and management information of the database and is therefore particularly important. As of Oracle 9.2, the system tablespace can be created as an LMTS tablespace.

However, you need to set this explicitly. The Data Dictionary tables are not manipulated explicitly via DML operations, but implicitly via DDL operations. Read access to the catalog is enabled via the Oracle catalog views. They can roughly be divided into the following groups:

- virtual views: `v$, gv$`
- DBA views: `dba_`
- views for all users: `all_`
- views for the local user: `user_`

The views of the external data dictionary can be restored via the `catalog.sql` script.

The *SYSAUX tablespace* was introduced in Oracle 10g. It stores system-level management information that does not really belong to the catalog and has increasingly strained the SYS tablespace in the past. This includes schemas for the workspace manager or the persistent performance data of the AWR (Automatic Workload Repository). The `v$sysaux_occupants` view enables you to retrieve information on the components that use the SYSAUX tablespace.

Temporary tablespaces are used for storing interim results that occur during sorting, hash operations, or grouping and for which the corresponding main memory areas are too small. They are only internally addressed by Oracle and are not explicitly usable by the user. Because they are not imposed on any Oracle block structure, temporary tablespaces are relatively fast. They should be neglected during a file backup because their content only contains interim results that are not of permanent significance. Temporary tablespaces can be newly created without problems, if necessary:

```
create temporary tablespace temp2
  datafile '/orcl/temptbs02.dbf' size 1000M
  autoextend on next 100M maxsize = 5000M.
```

Every Oracle user is assigned a temporary tablespace where temporary segments are created and appropriate interim results are stored. As of Oracle 10g, several temporary tablespaces can be merged into one group that is then assigned to the user. According to internal optimization criteria for the respective operation, Oracle performs the distribution to the various temporary tablespaces of the group.

When processing DML operations, Oracle uses an *optimistic approach*, which means that the changed data is written even before a `COMMIT`. This makes sense because the vast majority of transactions are successful. For changing transactions, the undo tablespace stores the values before the operation. On the one hand, these values enable the data to be reset after a transaction has been cancelled (via *abort*, for example), and on the other hand, they enable reading consistency. Before a `COMMIT`, other transactions do not yet see the changed data but only the previous data, which may still be reconstructed using the undo tablespace. From Oracle 8 to Oracle 9, the management of the undo information has changed. In Oracle 8, there were rollback segments that were included in normal tablespaces. As of Oracle 9, there are specific undo tablespaces where undo segments are independently created via an automatic undo management function by Oracle (`undo_management = AUTO`). An undo tablespace can be created as follows:

```
create undo tablespace undotbs2
  datafile '/orcl/undotbs02.dbf' size 2000M
  autoextend on next 100M maxsize = 5000M.
```

This will create an undo tablespace of an initial size of 2,000 MB that can automatically increase to up to 5,000 MB.

You can define a tablespace as read-only. In that case, it is no longer possible to issue new writing statements. The writing statements that are still open, however, can still be processed. Read-only tablespaces can be used for static data-like pictures or historical data and don't need to be included in the continuous data backup.

3.4.4.2 Dictionary-Managed Tablespaces (DMTS)

Up to Oracle 8.0, Oracle tablespaces were managed using the Data Dictionary. The information on the tablespace characteristics (i.e., on segments, extents, and files) is stored in the Oracle catalog. The administrator must monitor these characteristics and intervene when necessary in order to avoid potential problems.

If a database, and therefore a tablespace, grows, there are several possibilities for extension:

1. First, a data file can be enlarged by the administrator.

   ```
   alter database datafile 'user01.dbf' resize 1000M;
   ```

2. Additionally, the related file can be increased by the DBMS itself. This is enabled using the `autoextend` clause in the following format, for example:

```
alter database datafile 'user01.dbf' autoextend on;
alter database datafile 'user01.dbf' autoextend unlimited;
alter database datafile 'user01.dbf'autoextend maxsize(10M);
```

   The autoextent function may cause a problem with regard to the usually limited disk space. Therefore, you should watch the disk filling level attentively if you use `autoextend`.

3. A third option for enlarging a tablespace is to assign additional data files to the tablespace.

```
alter tablespace users
add datafile 'user02.dbf' size 500M;
```

   This file can be stored physically on a different medium.

As with SAP, operations for storage extension are usually supported by tools. Monitoring the corresponding filling levels is an important task in basic administration.

Logically, a tablespace is assigned 0 to m tables. The assignment takes place during the creation of database tables (`create table`), or generally for an Oracle schema or an Oracle user (`default tablespace`).

Every table has a data segment. The segment consists of 1 to k *extents* (similar to characteristics). The extents consist of several blocks that are physically connected. Their size is often identical to the blocks of the file system. However, the various extents of a table can be scattered across the different files of the tablespace. An excellent extent is the *basis extent*. Ideally, a table only has this basis extent, which means that when you create a table you know its exact storage requirement. This can hardly be applied to dynamically growing data, unless you accept a very large amount of waste. The other extents are also referred to as *next extents* (see also Figure 3.14).

The characteristics of a segment can be specified during the creation of the table via a `storage` clause that is added to the `create table` statement. The following `storage` clause creates a basis extent of 10 megabytes for a table; the size of the first next extent is five megabytes:

```
storage (
  initial 10M
  next 5M
  pctincrease 10
)
```

For managing growing tables and extents, Oracle provides an option for automatic extension. The example uses `pctincrease` to specify that each next extent is 10% larger than its predecessor. This prevents the data of a table from being excessively fragmented with too many small extents. This mechanism is not used in the SAP environment.

Naturally, not only tables are managed in tablespaces, but also other database objects like indexes, for example. Specific tablespaces contain redo data or temporary data. The excellent system tablespace stores the Data Dictionary.

Segments consist of several blocks that are defined by the segment size. The blocks contain a header and a data area with the data records. Often, a block is not fully filled in order to keep some space *within the block* for change operations that require additional space. A complex relocation beyond block boundaries is therefore prevented. This is controlled via the `pctfree` and `pctused` parameters that can be specified in the `storage` clause. As long as a block is not filled up to the limit defined by `pctfree`, it is available for insertions (see Figure 3.16). For this purpose, it is listed in a *free list*. If the limit is exceeded, the block is removed from the free list. If the filling of the block is reduced below the limit defined via `pctused`, it is added to the free list again. You should select different values for the two parameters in order to prevent blocks from being continuously added to or removed from the free list whenever there are marginal changes to the filling level.

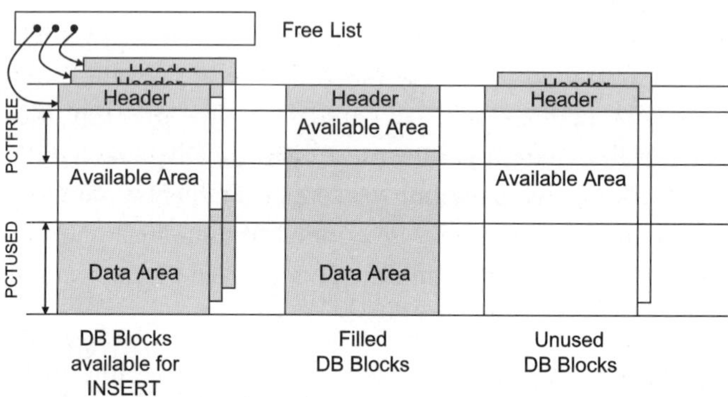

Figure 3.16 Oracle Blocks and Free List

The administrator must now provide a sufficient amount of storage to ensure a smooth operation:

- When operating the system without using `autoextend`, the administrator must observe the storage consumption in the tablespaces and enlarge these by enlarging a file or adding more files, if necessary.

- When operating the system without `pctincrease`, a segment can be heavily split, because many small extents are generated. Alternatively, you can use external tools for observing the growth of a table and for calculating the optimum size for the next extent based on the captured data. This method is also supported by SAP.

The administrator must ensure that there is enough disk space. This topic will be discussed in more detail in Chapter 9, *System Operation and Monitoring*.

3.4.4.3 Locally Managed Tablespaces (LMTS)

Since the introduction of Oracle 8.1 you can use *locally managed tablespaces* as an alternative to DMTS. In this context, the data about the internal use of the tablespace is stored locally in the data files of the tablespace. Each data file begins with a section that contains the allocation information for the data file in the form of a bitmap. For this reason, LMTS were also referred to as bitmap tablespaces in the past.

Using LMTS reduces the load that's placed on the Data Dictionary. Performance increases can be achieved in such a way that allocation operations are no longer linked to other DML operations in the Data Dictionary due to the use of insert statements.

In addition, locally managed tablespaces can be administrated much more easily. You can automate the entire internal management of a tablespace. The main task of an administrator consists of making available sufficient free hard disk space for the automatic extension of the tablespaces (when `autoextend = on`), or of manually providing a sufficient amount of memory to the tablespace (when `autoextend = off`).

Soon after its implementation, the LMTS concept proved to be advantageous and stable so that, as of Oracle 9, tablespaces are locally managed by default.

Oracle provides three different options to allocate extents in a tablespace:

- **User:** This method continues to use the options that are already familiar from the DMTS. The advantage is that the extents are now managed locally and no more load is placed on the Data Dictionary. A disadvantage of this method is that the size of different extents may still vary considerably, which means that the administrator must control the allocation of extents in a reasonable way.

- **System:** Oracle is responsible for space management. Based on a specific algorithm, extent sizes are used that can be handled by the Oracle system. In this context, the use of different extent sizes may entail a waste of storage space.
- **Uniform:** In this method, all extents have the same size. In this way, you can virtually avoid a fragmentation of space in the data files, which, in turn, avoids a waste of storage space.

The following SQL statement illustrates the creation of an LMTS using the *user_m0l.dbf* file, which is initially generated with a size of 100 MB and may increase to a maximum total of 500 MB. The extent management process is carried out using the `autoallocate` method and is managed variably by the system:

```
create tablespace user_m
datafile 'user_m01.dbf' size 100M
autoextend on maxsize 500M
extent management local autoallocate
```

Since Oracle 10g, you can manage very large quantities of data using the `BIGFILE` clause for LMTS and ASSM (Automatic Segment Space Management). Up to and including Oracle 9, the size of a file was limited to a total of 4 million blocks. Based on a block size of 8,192 bytes, this means that the maximum size of a file was 32 GB. Oracle 10 is able to manage 4 billion blocks, which enables a file size of up to 32 terabytes based on a block size of 8k. This reduces the amount of administration work, particularly if a logical volume management process can provide very large files. In that case, a tablespace simply constitutes a file.

As of Oracle 9, ASSM has been available, which allows the LMTS to omit free lists, which could cause a bottleneck under a high transaction load. In this context, a multi-stage process is used to manage the available space within individual blocks via bitmaps. Bitmapped blocks are located at the beginning of a segment, which are checked in DML operations. The only exceptions are segments that contain LOB data, that is, *large objects*.

Several different database views are available for monitoring the free space. The following request provides the free space for the LMTS of the sample system in terms of megabytes:

```
select name, (sum(a.blocks * 8192))/1024/1024  "size MB"
from   dba_lmt_free_space a, v$tablespace b
where  a.tablespace_id = b.ts# group by name
. . . . . . . . . . . .
NAME                              size MB
------------------------------ ----------
UNDOTBS1                          474.625
SYSAUX                            24.0625
USER_M                            99.9375
USERS                              1.9375
SYSTEM                              5.875
EXAMPLE                               .75
```

The conversion of DMTS to LMTS is possible and recommended. The package `DBMS_SPACE_ADMIN` provides useful help on this:

```
EXECUTE DBMS_SPACE_ADMIN.TABLESPACE_MIGRATE_
FROM_LOCAL(tablespace_name => 'USERS01');
```

However, the conversion does not provide all the advantages offered by the locally managed tablespaces. For example, the allocation method used here is USER. A reorganization, for instance via export/import, can represent a viable alternative.

In general, the locally managed tablespaces are a stable, convenient, and powerful mechanism that simplifies the work of an administrator in modern system landscapes.

3.4.4.4 Fragmentation

As mentioned, the problem concerning the tablespaces in an Oracle database is that they are fragmented. You probably know this problem from the area of file systems. *Fragmentation* means that, for various reasons, such as technical restrictions, you cannot use available free space, which means that this space is wasted. In a tablespace, fragmentation occurs in two places — between the segments and within the data blocks. Consequently, we refer to *external* and *internal fragmentation*.

External fragmentation is characterized by the fact that you cannot create any additional extent, although the total amount of free space would theoretically allow for that; however, the free space is not available in one coherent segment. The following SQL command enables you to view the free space areas of a tablespace:

```
select blocks, count(*)
from dba_free_space
where tablespace_name = 'USER01'
group by blocks order by blocks
```

However, you should note that the problem of external fragmentation became obsolete with the introduction of the LMTS, because the manual administration of extents, which caused the fragmentation, was automated in this context. If you use the previous SQL command for an LMTS, you probably won't see many large areas of free space.

On the other hand, the problem of internal fragmentation continues to exist. In this process, the storage space within a block is fragmented; in other words, it is the smallest Oracle storage structure that is affected. Figure 3.17 shows the block fragmentation in a segment with three extents.

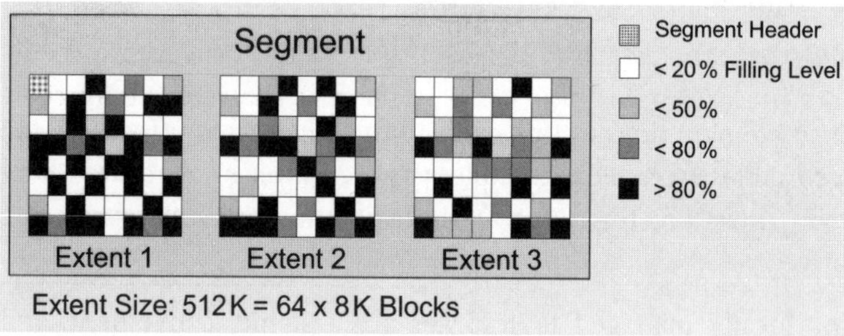

Figure 3.17 Internal Fragmentation

Figure 3.17 also shows that the problem of internal fragmentation has two different dimensions: on the one hand, fragmentation occurs within the single block; and on the other hand, there is fragmentation within the extents of a segment. Both types of fragmentation entail a waste of storage space, which may even reach a problematic dimension under certain circumstances. Block fragmentation involves another problem as the blocks are always imported in their entirety into the Oracle data buffer. With a low filling level of many different blocks, this leads to a corresponding waste of expensive buffer space and thus to a performance decrease.

The internal fragmentation is caused by the insertion and deletion of data records. Consequently, it often occurs in tables that are subject to frequent changes, as well as after mass deletions, for instance, after an archiving run. You can check the internal fragmentation in different ways:

- In the SAP environment, you can use the BR*Tools to generate storage space statistics. Section 4.4.4 provides more information on this topic.
- You can use the SQL script provided in SAP Note 821687 to identify all tables that waste more than 20 MB.
- As of Oracle 10g, you can use the Oracle Segment Advisor (provided you have a license for the Oracle Diagnostics and Tuning Pack). For more information, please refer to the Oracle documentation at the following address: *http://www.oracle.com/pls/db102/homepage*.

To remove existing fragmentations, you can use different reorganization options, depending on the Oracle release you use. Section 4.4.4, *Reorganizing Tables and Tablespaces*, provides detailed information on the reorganization of tablespaces.

3.4.5 Other Important Files

Up to this point, we have primarily dealt with data files. However, in addition to the data files, there are other important files that require an even higher degree of data security. These are the *control files* and *redo log files*, as well as the system files of the Oracle software (see Figure 3.18).

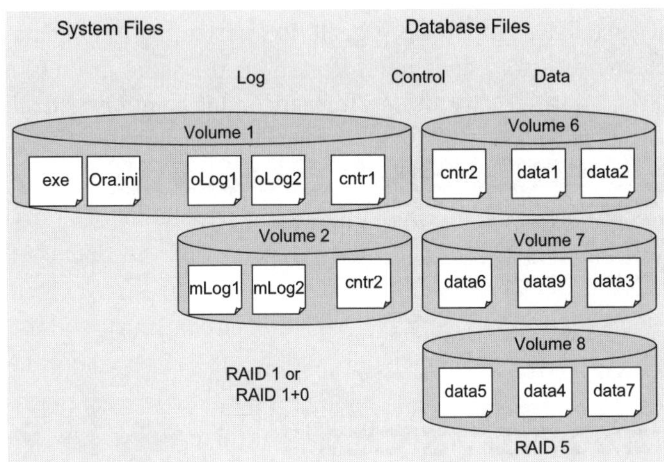

Figure 3.18 Files in Oracle Systems

The following list describes the purpose of these file types as well as their function and usage:

- Control files store control data related to the database, such as the database name, file storage locations, or timestamps. Due to the importance of control files for the database instance, the Oracle system stores three copies of a control file by default. During the installation and planning of the system, you should ensure that these files are physically stored on different media. Chapter 5 describes this in greater detail.

- Similarly, copies are also created for the redo log files (Orig-Log and Mirror-Log), which should be stored on different physical media as well. These files contain the transaction log and are required to enable a fast `COMMIT` during the completion of a transaction. For this reason, you should use disks in a RAID-1 array. Chapter 8 provides more information on this subject.
- System files, which contain, among other things, the executables and basic Oracle configuration data, are less critical regarding system performance and data security. Most of the time, they are only read during the system startup process and aren't changed very often. In problem situations, you can restore them from the installation sources. Note, however, that this involves some work. To avoid this, we strictly recommend that you must include these files in the backup process.

One of the primary tasks to be carried out when planning the installation is that you distribute the files to different media in a way that makes sense. There is useful information available regarding the interaction with SAP systems.

In our simple demo installation of Oracle 10g, all files pertaining to the database are located in one directory and therefore are on the same drive (see Figure 3.19). With regard to security and performance, this layout is critical.

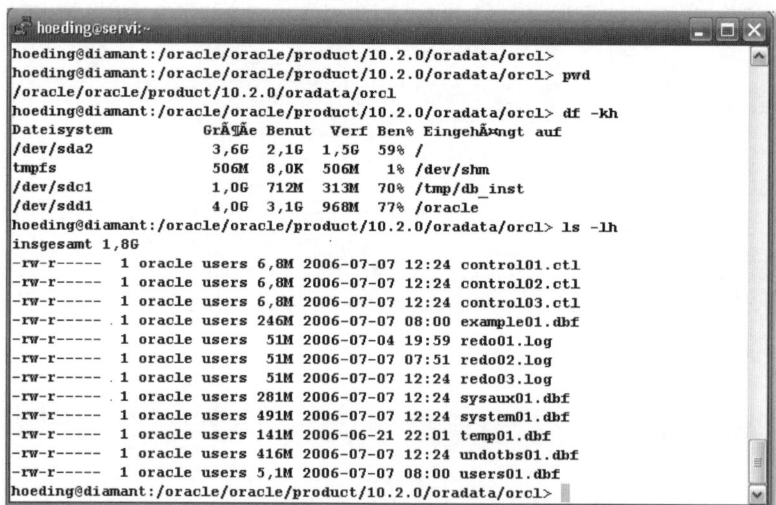

Figure 3.19 Files in a Demo Installation of Oracle 10g

3.4.5.1 System Files

In addition to the executables, which are only modified in the context of a software maintenance process, the system files also comprise the configuration files, which are part of the DBMS rather than part of the database. Examples of configuration files include the *init.ora* file for kernel settings and the *tnsnames.ora* file for configuring the network. These files store important parameters that can be viewed (see Figure 3.20). Note that this is an important characteristic. Whereas in previous versions, the parameters were imported from the files as generic sources, in newer versions, parameters are partly managed in the DBMS and are only saved to the files upon an explicit command or when the instance is shut down.

As of Oracle 9i, parameters are supposed to be managed in the so-called *SPFiles* (server parameter files). To a certain extent, SPFiles are binary files, but they do allow you to read some of the parameters. Changes to these files are not possible, as they would invalidate the parameter file. The *init.ora* file is often overwritten by the *init<SID>.ora* file.

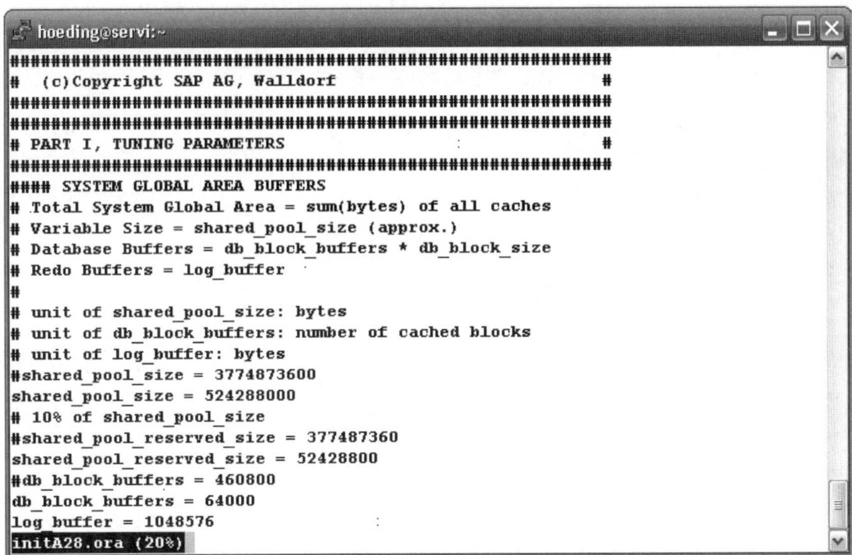


```
############################################################
#   (c)Copyright SAP AG, Walldorf                          #
############################################################
############################################################
# PART I, TUNING PARAMETERS                                #
############################################################
#### SYSTEM GLOBAL AREA BUFFERS
# Total System Global Area = sum(bytes) of all caches
# Variable Size = shared_pool_size (approx.)
# Database Buffers = db_block_buffers * db_block_size
# Redo Buffers = log_buffer
#
# unit of shared_pool_size: bytes
# unit of db_block_buffers: number of cached blocks
# unit of log_buffer: bytes
#shared_pool_size = 3774873600
shared_pool_size = 524288000
# 10% of shared_pool_size
#shared_pool_reserved_size = 377487360
shared_pool_reserved_size = 52428800
#db_block_buffers = 460800
db_block_buffers = 64000
log_buffer = 1048576
initA28.ora (20%)
```

Figure 3.20 Example of an init<SID>.ora File

3.4.5.2 Control Files

In older Oracle versions, the control files are stored in an *init.ora* file, whereas from Oracle 9 on, they are additionally stored in an SPFile. Alternatively, you can view the storage locations using the following SQL request:

```
select name from v$controlfile;
NAME
- - - - - - - - - - -
/oracle/oracle/product/10.2.0/db_1/dbs/control1.ctl
/oracle/oracle/product/10.2.0/db_1/dbs/control2.ctl
/oracle/oracle/product/10.2.0/db_1/dbs/control3.ctl
```

Note that the storage of the three control file copies on the same medium shown in the example is critical. If you want to change the storage location of a control file, you can use the following SQL statement:

```
alter system
        set control_files = '/vol01/control01.ctl',
       'vol02/control2.ctl'
        SCOPE =SPFILE;
```

The change is implemented in the SPFile. After that, you must shut down the database and move the control files to the operating system level.

Sometimes, it may prove useful to generate a trace file for the control files. This may be necessary, for example, for system copies or configuration changes after you have changed the hardware landscape. You can use the following SQL statement to generate a trace file for the control files:

```
alter database backup controlfile to trace;
```

The trace file is stored in the directory, which is addressed using the Oracle parameter, `user_dump_dest`. You can use this file in a SQL script to create new control files for a database. Needless to say, you must first shut down the database to be able to do that.

3.4.5.3 Redo Log Files

Redo log files contain the Oracle transaction log. We'll describe the usage of these files in more detail along with the backup, restore, and recovery processes (see Chapter 10 and Section 3.4.9, *Data Backup and Recovery*). In principle, two groups of redo log files must exist. The groups are written in a cyclical process. Either group should contain at least two redo log files that are written simultaneously. Although the names, Orig-Log and Mirror-Log, may be slightly confusing, they are actually quite descriptive.[3]

The fact that the files are periodically overwritten makes it necessary to archive these so-called online logs. This task is carried out by the archiver process, which copies the files of the group that is currently not used into an archive directory.

The size of the redo log files is fixed and must be defined during the configuration of the system. For example, an SAP production system that is based on Oracle 9.2 uses a log file size of 50 MB, just like our Oracle 10 demo system. You can modify the redo log size at any time (see *SAP Note 79341*).

Very large logs reduce the number of log switches, which always involve a load-intensive checkpoint. This increases the system performance under high transaction loads. The disadvantage of doing this is the long system startup time that occurs if the database wasn't stopped properly prior to reducing the number of logs. Moreover, there is the risk of losing many transactions if you lose all copies of the redo log group.

```
hoeding@servi:~
drwxr-xr-x    4 oraa08      dba              96 Sep  3   2003 saptrace
-rw-rw-rw-    1 oraa08      dba            2154 Apr 28   2004 set_autoextend_off.sql
hoeding@f38:/oracle/A08> ll mirrlogA/
total 204804
-rw-rw----    1 oraa08      dba        52429824 Jul  7  08:12 log_g11m2.dbf
-rw-rw----    1 oraa08      dba        52429824 Jul  7  13:50 log_g13m2.dbf
drwxr-xr-x    2 root        root             96 Jun 22   2005 lost+found
hoeding@f38:/oracle/A08> ll mirrlogB
total 204804
-rw-rw----    1 oraa08      dba        52429824 Jul  7  13:50 log_g12m2.dbf
-rw-rw----    1 oraa08      dba        52429824 Jul  7  01:44 log_g14m2.dbf
drwxr-xr-x    2 root        root             96 Jun 22   2005 lost+found
hoeding@f38:/oracle/A08> ll origlogA/
total 204804
drwxr-xr-x    2 oraa08      dba              96 Jun 22   2005 cntrl
-rw-r-----    1 oraa08      dba        52429824 Jul  7  08:12 log_g11m1.dbf
-rw-r-----    1 oraa08      dba        52429824 Jul  7  13:51 log_g13m1.dbf
drwxr-xr-x    2 root        root             96 Jul 10   2003 lost+found
hoeding@f38:/oracle/A08> ll origlogB/
total 204804
-rw-r-----    1 oraa08      dba        52429824 Jul  7  13:50 log_g12m1.dbf
-rw-r-----    1 oraa08      dba        52429824 Jul  7  01:44 log_g14m1.dbf
drwxr-xr-x    2 root        root             96 Jul 10   2003 lost+found
hoeding@f38:/oracle/A08>
```

Figure 3.21 Redo Log Directory in an SAP System

Figures 3.21 and 3.22 show an intelligent redo log configuration. As you can see, there are four redo log groups containing two files each. The two files of

3 They may be confusing, because of the fact that Orig-Log and Mirror-Log are identical and of equal value.

each redo log group are stored on different system drives. In addition, sequential files are stored on different media. This way you can increase the system performance, as the archiving of a redo log file, which has just been closed, does not interfere with the writing of a redo log file that is currently open.

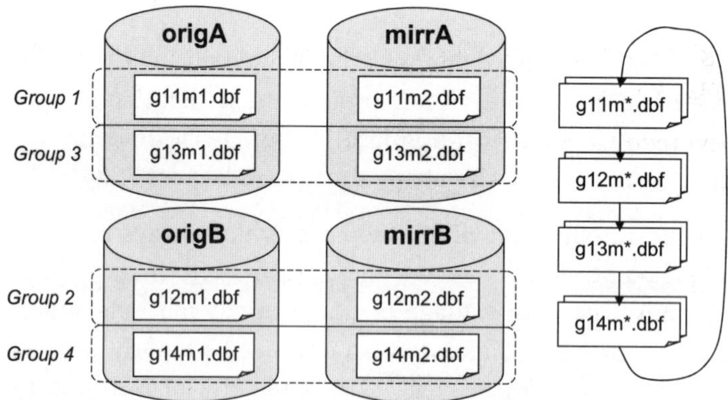

Figure 3.22 Redo Log Files and Groups in an SAP System

Figure 3.23 outlines the interaction between the log writer process (LGWR) and the archiver process (ARCH). The log writer saves the redo information from the redo log buffer of the SGA. After a log switch to the next redo log group, the archiver process becomes active and saves the log file that has just been closed to the archive directory. In this process, the files are marked with the log sequence number.

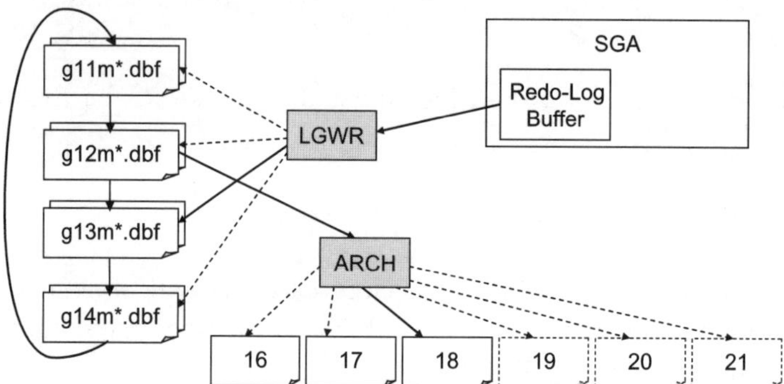

Figure 3.23 Cyclical Use of Redo Logs and Archiving

You can find information about the redo log files in V$ Tables `v$log` and `v$logfile`.

```
select group#, sequence#, bytes,status from v$log;
    GROUP#  SEQUENCE#       BYTES STATUS
---------- ---------- ---------- ----------------
         1         74   52428800 INACTIVE
         2         75   52428800 INACTIVE
         3         76   52428800 CURRENT
```

As you can see, group 3 is currently being used. The `V$logfile` table contains the file storage locations.

You can add a new redo log group as follows:

```
alter database add logfile group 4 '/vol01/redo_4_1.log' SIZE 50M;
```

Moreover, you can also add files to an existing redo log group. To do that, you must enter the following statement:

```
alter database add logfile member '/vol02/redo_4_2.log' to group 4;
```

If you want to define new storage locations for the redo log files, you can rename redo log files in the following manner:

```
alter database rename file '/oracle/oracle/product/10.2.0/oradata/o
rcl/redo01.log' to '/vol01/redo_1_1.log';
```

However, note that you must ensure that this file is not being used at the same time (check for the "current" status in `V$log`). Furthermore, it must be copied at OS level. In this context, you must take into account the access permissions:

You can monitor the usage of the online logs and archiver in the `V$log_history` table.

```
select * from v$log_history;
```

During the installation (initial filling) of a large database with an active archiving mode, redundant archives are created. For this reason, you should disable the archiving mode in this process.

The configuration of log files represents an important task during the planning of a system. The monitoring of redo log files, in particular, their archiving, is one of the most important tasks of an administrator.

3.4.6 Interaction of Processes and Storage Structures

The following sections discuss the interaction between the Oracle components described here in a closer context. Figure 3.24 shows the possible processes involved in processing a reading SQL-Query.

The following steps are carried out when a SQL-Query is processed by an Oracle system:

❶ An application process (an SAP dialog process, for example) sends a query to the Oracle server process.

❷ The server process checks the syntax of the query and performs a prepare (such as a view expansion).

❸ The server process checks whether an execution plan for the query already exists in the buffer. If so, the plan will be loaded.

❹ If no suitable and up-to-date plan is available, the optimizer calculates a new execution plan.

❺ The new plan is stored in the buffer for later use.

❻ We assume that the first step of the plan consists of accessing a secondary index; in the example, that's the `to` attribute. The execution first checks whether the database blocks that contain the index exist in the data buffer.

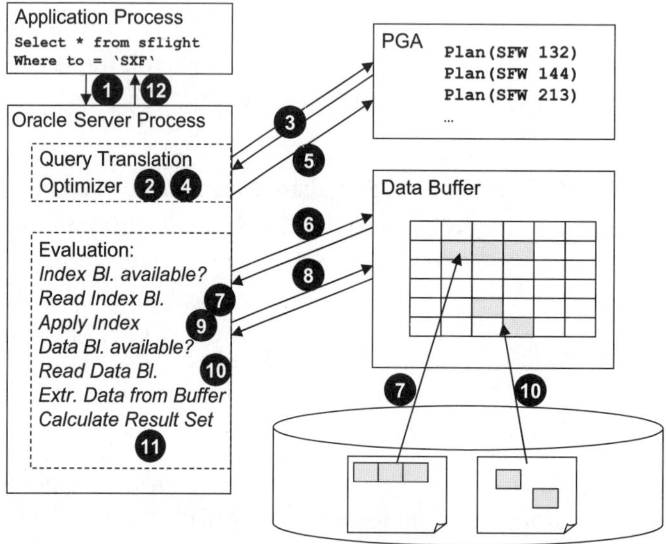

Figure 3.24 Processing a Reading SQL-Query

❼ If these index blocks are not available, the server process reads them from the respective data files in order to store them in the buffer. If there isn't sufficient space available in the data buffer to carry out this process, the DBWR process may have to free up some space (this is not depicted in Figure 3.24).

❽ The evaluation process then uses the index blocks located in the data buffer in order to determine the addresses of the required data blocks.

❾ Analogous to Step ❻, a check is made to determine whether the required data blocks exist in the data buffer.

❿ If not all of the required data blocks are available, the missing blocks are read from the data files and stored in the data buffer, as in Step ❼.

⓫ The evaluation process can now access all required data blocks and data records in the data buffer and compile the result of the request. For special operations, such as sorting large quantities of data, the temporary segment may have to be accessed (not shown in the figure).

⓬ Finally, the Oracle server process transfers the result set to the application process.

With regard to processing a query, the Data Dictionary plays a key role. The Data Dictionary is already involved in the syntax check of the request in order to determine whether tables or fields that are addressed really exist. Another example involves the access to data files where the Data Dictionary provides information as to which tablespace and therefore which files store the blocks that are required for a specific table. Consequently, it is important that you buffer the Data Dictionary.

The processes described here also demonstrate the importance of the data buffer and an optimized database design. Accesses to the hard disks represent essential bottlenecks (❼ and ❽). In this context, you should improve the I/O performance, which provides some potential for optimization. Of course, it would be much better to skip these steps. But that's only possible if the required blocks are already located in the data buffer. A sufficiently large data buffer might be able to help you here.

In the following text, we'll describe the activities of LGWR and DBWR in the context of a write operation. We will look at a sample request, which increases the price for all flights of airline ORA by 120%. For this purpose, the request must be checked and optimized, as in the reading request. The affected index and data blocks must be determined and stored in the data buffer, if necessary.

To process a write request, the system carries out the following steps, which are also shown in Figure 3.25:

1. An application program sends an update statement to the Oracle server process.
2. The server process creates copies of the data blocks to be changed. Reading transactions can continue to use the original block. Furthermore, a write lock is set for the respective blocks or data records.
3. Then, the changes to the data are implemented. In our example, only a numeric value needs to be changed. This doesn't present a problem for the server process. Neither does it need a larger storage area for a data record, or have to check or maintain a key or unique value for an index. Note, however, that data may have to be moved within blocks or across block boundaries. The modified blocks are marked as *dirty*. New data is already available for the writing session.
4. The server process writes the entries into the redo log buffer.
5. If the transaction finishes with a `COMMIT`, the original blocks will be removed (5a) and the transaction log is written to the redo log files by the LGWR process (5b). This makes the change permanent and visible to all involved components.
6. The DBWR writes the blocks that are marked as dirty into the data files in an asynchronous manner, that is, independently of the completed transaction.

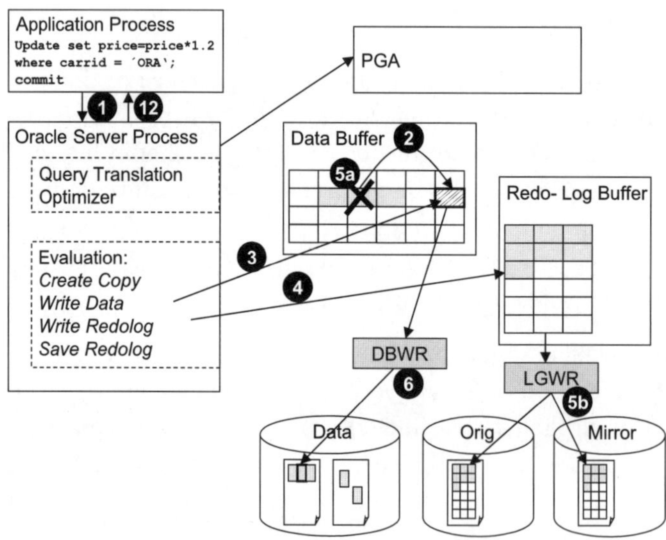

Figure 3.25 Processing a Writing SQL-Query

The processes described here are relatively simple. Conversely, insert operations, change operations to key or index fields, and delete operations on foreign keys are far more complex tasks for the DBMS. Regarding insert operations, the DBMS must check the uniqueness condition and, at the same time, maintain the indexes that were created for the relevant table. If these indexes also contain less frequently used, or rather, redundant ones, it is very likely that those are not contained in the data buffer. Consequently, they don't only cost space in data files and in the buffer, but also require a lot of time during change operations. Similarly, operations that increase the length of character strings represent a particular challenge for the database management system. The mechanism provided by `pctfree/pctused` or Automatic Segment Space Management (ASSM) provides useful results for standard applications.

3.4.7 Accessing Oracle with Oracle Net

Oracle offers a specific communication stack to establish a connection between an application process and the Oracle server process. In previous Oracle versions, this software layer was referred to as *SQL*NetV2*; with the introduction of Oracle 8, it was renamed to *Net 8*, and since Oracle 9, it is called *Oracle Net* or *Oracle Net Services.* Of course, it was not only the name that has changed as fundamental developments in the areas of architecture and functionality were implemented over time. In this section, we'll briefly describe the structure of Oracle Net and discuss the aspects that are relevant for everyday administration tasks. Chapter 4, *SAP and Oracle*, describes the use of Oracle Net along with SAP systems in more detail.

3.4.7.1 Architecture of Oracle Net

Figure 3.26 illustrates the structure of Oracle Net in the dedicated-server variant, which is also relevant for SAP systems. In this variant, each application process is assigned to exactly one Oracle server process. The stack exists as a library that is integrated in the processes both on the server machine, which is where the Oracle server process runs, and on the client machine. On the server side, Oracle Net is usually installed and configured along with the installation of the database software.

On the client side, you must explicitly install Oracle Net. For this purpose, Oracle provides specific packages. For Oracle 10g, the *Instant Client* is a solution that requires the installation of only a few libraries. Regarding Java, you can use the Thin JDBC solution, which doesn't require the installation of an Oracle client on the client machine (e.g., in order to be used by applets or Ajax).

The individual layers of the Oracle Net architecture have been implemented since SQL*Net2. They are described in the following list:

- **Application and server:** The client, that is the application, uses the *Oracle Call Interface* (OCI). The server, in turn, uses the *Oracle Program Interface* (OPI). The server responds to a call from the OCI by calling the OPI.
- **TTC – Two Task Common:** The TTC layer is used to convert character sets and data formats. It corresponds to the presentation layer in the ISO/OSI-seven-layer model.
- **TNS – Transparent Network Substrate:** The TNS layer enables you to monitor the connection between the client and the server as well as the correct establishment and termination of a connection. This layer corresponds to the session layer of the ISO/OSI model.
- **Protocol Support:** The protocol support layer represents the interface between the different network protocols. Oracle Net enables the use of TCP/IP, TCP/IP with SSL, named pipes, and SDP. Also, the very fast communication via shared memory (IPC) is very interesting. The protocol support layer also corresponds to the session layer.
- **Network:** This layer is provided by the operating system and corresponds to the low-level layers of the ISO/OSI model.

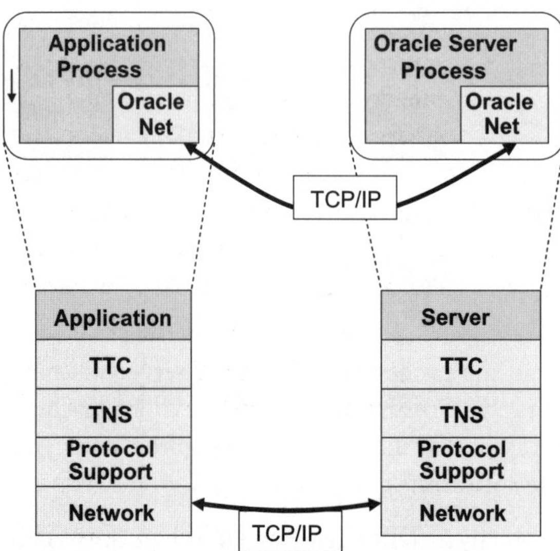

Figure 3.26 Oracle Net Architecture

3.4.7.2 Listener Process

The TNS layer is particularly important for a database system that's typically used on a network. Here, the relevant database services must be named and configured. Based on these definitions the connection parameters must be specified in client programs.

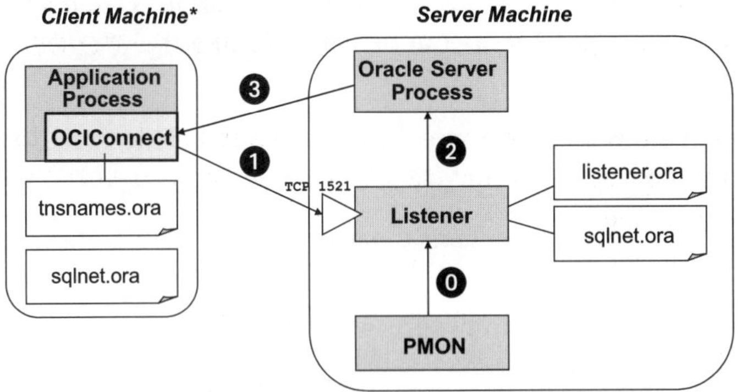

*In SAP systems, this is the machine that runs the application server

Figure 3.27 Role of the Listener in Oracle Net

Setting up a connection represents the central task of the TNS layer. For this purpose, the Oracle system contains a Listener process, which uses a specific port (mostly 1521, in SAP systems: 1527) to wait for connection requests, as shown in Figure 3.27. The Listener process, which doesn't depend on the database instance, checks the connection data transferred from a client on the basis of its configuration files (❶). If the connection data is accurate and the process finds an appropriate service, that is, an appropriate database system, the Listener starts a dedicated server process (❷). It then passes the connection on to the dedicated server process, which, in turn, checks the authentication data and responds to the client (❸). After that, the Listener is no longer involved in the process. As of Oracle 8.1, a database instance can also register automatically in the Listener instead of using the service definition in the *listener.ora* file (⓿). The registration is carried out once in every minute by the PMON process.

As an alternative to this *direct hand-off mechanism*, the *redirect* process can be used in which the Listener returns the connection data of the started server process to the client process. A Listener can serve multiple database systems. In principle, you can also operate multiple Listeners on one server machine.

3.4.7.3 Configuring the Listener

There are comprehensive configuration options available for the Listener, for instance in order to increase security. For example, it is possible to permit connections to specific clients only.

The following sections describe some basic configuration options. The Oracle Net configuration files are located in the *$ORACLE_HOME/network/admin* directory. Alternative storage locations can be defined using the `TNS_ADMIN` environment variable.

The following configuration files play an essential role in Oracle Net (and its predecessors respectively):

- tnsnames.ora on the client side contains the data required for establishing a connection.
- listener.ora on the server side defines the settings for the Listener and for services that may be available.
- sqlnet.ora defines the individual settings of the Oracle Net configuration such as the name resolution methods, the domain name, and the trace level.
- protocol.ora (Oracle <= 8.1) contains protocol-based parameters and has been integrated in sqlnet.ora since Oracle 9.

Let us first consider the server side. The following example describes a simple Listener configuration in the *listener.ora* file:

```
LOG_DIRECTORY_LISTENER = /oracle/network/log
LOG_FILE_LISTENER = listener.log
LISTENER =
  (DESCRIPTION =
    (ADDRESS = (PROTOCOL = TCP)(HOST= diamant)(PORT= 1521))
  )
```

In this case, the name of the Listener is `LISTENER`. This name must also occur in the parameters for the log path and log file. In addition, the protocol, the server, and the socket are defined for this Listener. The previous example uses port 1521, which is the standard port for Oracle Net. Database instances can now log in to the Listener. Alternatively, the services can be explicitly defined here:

```
SID_LIST_LISTENER =
 (SID_LIST =
```

```
  (SID_DESC =
    (SDU = 32768)
    (SID_NAME = DB1)
    (ORACLE_HOME = /oracle/product/db1/10.2.0)
  )
)
```

Here, the SDU parameter (Session Data Unit parameter) is used to specify the SID and the home directory as well as the size of the data packets transferred in the session layer for a specific service.

The counterpart to the *listener.ora* file on the client side is the *tns-names.ora* file. Oracle Net provides several different options for name resolution, *tnsnames.ora* being the most popular of them. This file is also used in the SAP environment. The following example describes a service definition in a *tnsnames.ora* file:

```
DB1.WORLD=
  (DESCRIPTION =
     (SDU = 32768)
     (ADDRESS_LIST =
       (ADDRESS = (PROTOCOL = IPC) (KEY = DB1))
       (ADDRESS = (PROTOCOL = TCP) (HOST = diamant)
                  (PORT = 1521))
     )
     (CONNECT_DATA =
        (SID = DB1)
     )
  )
```

Two possible network addresses are defined for the `DB1.World` service. The connection via IPC can only be used if both the client and server are located on the same machine. Alternatively, you can use the TCP/IP connection. As is the case with the *listener.ora* file, the maximum size of network packets is set to 32768. Regarding the use of an SAP system, SAP Note 562403 provides some useful information.

The use of IPC changed with the introduction of Oracle 8.1. In previous versions, it was possible to use the `AUTOMATIC_IPC` option in order to automatically convert a TCP/IP connection into an IPC connection. In current versions, IPC must be defined explicitly in *tnsnames.ora*.

The creation and maintenance of Oracle Net configuration files is supported by graphical tools provided by Oracle. The *Oracle Net Configuration Assistant*, which can be called via `netca`, enables you to configure the files and services. The *Net Manager*, which can be called via `netmgr`, allows you to enter additional comprehensive settings in the configuration files (see Figure 3.28).

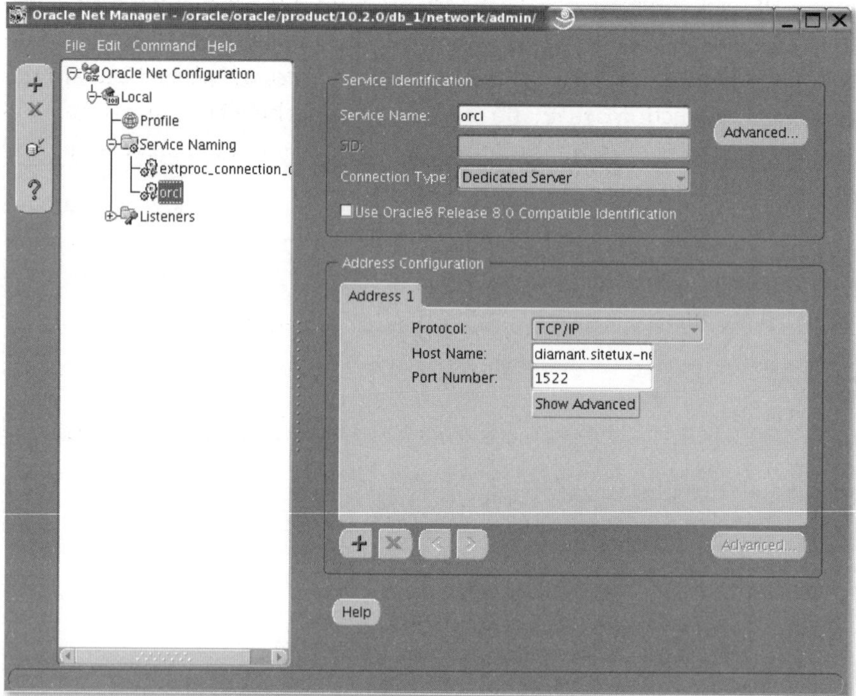

Figure 3.28 Oracle Net Manager for the Definition of Services

The Instant Client provided in Oracle 10g also uses *tnsnames.ora* and *sqlnet.ora*. You can download the Instant Client for different operating systems from the Oracle website. The environment variables must be set. The storage locations of *tnsnames.ora* and *sqlnet.ora* are defined via the `TNS_ADMIN` environment variable.

In addition to the dedicated server variant discussed here, Oracle provides a shared server configuration, which allows the dynamic assignment of server processes via a dispatcher process. This variant is particularly useful for applications in which a large number of application processes initiates rather small SQL requests. In this context, a load distribution process and connection pooling are supported as well. Connection pooling processes considerably reduce the period of time that is typically required to establish a connection. For SAP software, the shared server configuration is not relevant, as an SAP work process connects once to its dedicated Oracle server process during startup and then maintains this connection over a long period of time.

Oracle Real Application Cluster (RAC) is supported by Oracle Net and the Listener. The individual server machines of the RAC propagate their load values to the listeners. This enables the listeners to carry out load balancing. Furthermore, Oracle Net supports *Transparent Application Failover* (TAF). In this process, a connection becomes transparent if a machine fails, that is, the connection continues on a different machine without the client process noticing that this has occurred.

3.4.7.4 Controlling the Listener

At the OS level, the listener process can be started directly or script-based using the `lsnrctl` command.

```
fwil588.fh-brandenburg.de - PuTTY
oracle@fwil588:~/oracle/product/10.2.0/db_2/bin> ./lsnrctl start

LSNRCTL for Linux: Version 10.2.0.1.0 - Production on 11-FEB-2007 14:31:29

Copyright (c) 1991, 2005, Oracle.  All rights reserved.

Starting /home/oracle/oracle/product/10.2.0/db_2/bin/tnslsnr: please wait...

TNSLSNR for Linux: Version 10.2.0.1.0 - Production
System parameter file is /home/oracle/oracle/product/10.2.0/db_2/network/admin/listener.ora
Log messages written to /home/oracle/oracle/product/10.2.0/db_2/network/log/listener.log
Listening on: (DESCRIPTION=(ADDRESS=(PROTOCOL=ipc)(KEY=EXTPROC1)))
Listening on: (DESCRIPTION=(ADDRESS=(PROTOCOL=tcp)(HOST=fwil588.fh-brandenburg.de)(PORT=1521)))

Connecting to (DESCRIPTION=(ADDRESS=(PROTOCOL=IPC)(KEY=EXTPROC1)))
STATUS of the LISTENER
------------------------
Alias                     LISTENER
Version                   TNSLSNR for Linux: Version 10.2.0.1.0 - Production
Start Date                11-FEB-2007 14:31:29
Uptime                    0 days 0 hr. 0 min. 0 sec
Trace Level               off
Security                  ON: Local OS Authentication
SNMP                      OFF
Listener Parameter File   /home/oracle/oracle/product/10.2.0/db_2/network/admin/listener.ora
Listener Log File         /home/oracle/oracle/product/10.2.0/db_2/network/log/listener.log
Listening Endpoints Summary...
  (DESCRIPTION=(ADDRESS=(PROTOCOL=ipc)(KEY=EXTPROC1)))
  (DESCRIPTION=(ADDRESS=(PROTOCOL=tcp)(HOST=fwil588.fh-brandenburg.de)(PORT=1521)))
Services Summary...
Service "PLSExtProc" has 1 instance(s).
  Instance "PLSExtProc", status UNKNOWN, has 1 handler(s) for this service...
The command completed successfully
oracle@fwil588:~/oracle/product/10.2.0/db_2/bin>
```

Figure 3.29 Starting the Listener

Figure 3.29 shows the start of the Listener for a Linux-based Oracle 10g system via the `lsnrctl start` command. The `lsnrctl stop` command enables you to stop the Listener.

If you use `lsnrctl`, you end up in a kind of interactive shell where you can control the Listener. The following list contains some important commands:

- `reload`
  Loads the parameter file and SIDs
- `service`
  Determines the service information for the Listener
- `change_password`
  Sets or changes the Listener password in order to protect the Listener
- `trace`
  Sets the trace level
- `status`
  Displays the current status similar to Figure 3.29

The logs are located either in the directory specified in *sqlnet.ora* or in *$ORACLE_HOME/network/log*. They provide immediate help for problem analysis. At this point, we don't want to go into further detail as Chapter 4 contains a comprehensive description of Oracle Net in relation to SAP systems.

3.4.8 Query Optimization

In the context of query processing (see Section 3.1.2, *Relational Data Model and SQL*, and Section 3.4.6, *Interaction of Processes and Storage Structures*), we have touched on the aspects of execution plans and query optimization several times. A good optimizer is a distinctive feature of a database system. The system can be automatically optimized via the DBMS, since descriptive SQL queries determine only the results set, but not how the result is calculated. When considering the entire knowledge about the structures and data of the database, it can be assumed that the DBMS draws up a better plan than an average developer.

Oracle 10g provides several options for automatic SQL tuning. The *Automatic Tuning Optimizer* (ATO) extends the cost-based optimizer by an expert system with enhanced functions for analyses and proposals. In future, these possibilities will be certainly used by SAP to optimize performance. Chapter 8 describes performance optimization in SAP systems in detail.

Despite the powerful Oracle Optimizer, it is important for the administrator to be familiar with the basic principles of query optimization. The performance of a database application can be improved by various actions, such as creating indexes, maintaining statistics, or supplementing queries with hints. Therefore, this section describes some basic principles and technologies for optimization.

According to the five-layer architecture, the optimization process is contained in the data system. For a declarative SQL query, plans that consist of operations of the record-oriented interfaces are created using access paths (indexes). In this process, among other things, the appropriate indexes must be selected:

- Does an appropriate index exist? To answer this question, the DBMS checks its data dictionary.
- Does the use of the index have any advantages? This is checked by the DBMS on the basis of the data, for example, statistics and metrics.

This approach can be found again in the following optimization phases:

- **Translation and view expansion**
  A SQL query is implemented in an unoptimized plan. Views are replaced by the SQL statements or plans that define the views. Figure 3.30 illustrates the plan creation and view expansion for a join that lists passenger names and the respective airlines booked on September 24, 2006. Here, a view is used that includes all September bookings. For the presentation of the plans, we use a different syntax than the syntax usually used in literature to simplify the diagram.

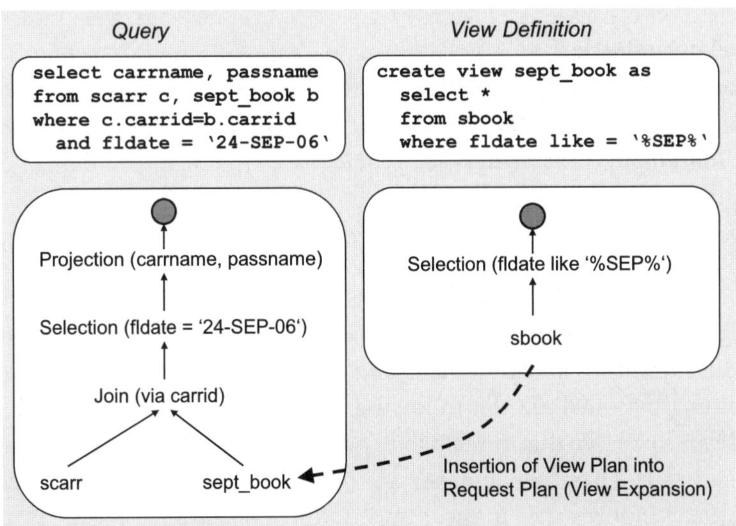

Figure 3.30 Plan Creation and View Expansion

- **Algebraic or logical optimization**
  The query is optimized according to algebraic rules. Here, the main goal is to receive interim results as small as possible. Selections should be performed as soon as possible (Figure 3.31, ❶). This does also apply (but not as strictly) to projections (❷). Moreover, redundant operations should be summarized. For example, the selection by '%SEP%' can be combined with the selection by '24-SEP-06', since the latter is more precise (see Figure 3.31, ❸). The application developer cannot anticipate this step, since he views SEPT_BOOK as a table.

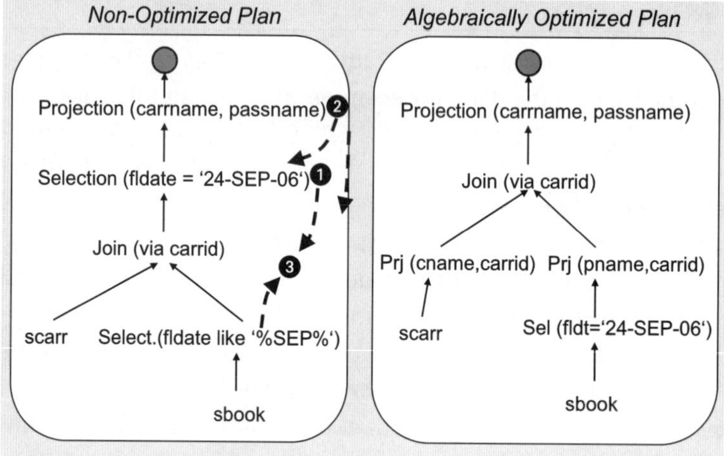

Figure 3.31 Algebraic Optimization of a Plan

- **Internal optimization**
  Here, a specific memory and index structure are used. Additionally, access algorithms are selected, for example, a full table scan or a hash join. Usually, different alternative plans are generated.
- **Cost-based selection**
  A plan is now selected using heuristics. For this purpose, statistic information is used.

Regarding performance optimization, it is important that you as an administrator understand the execution plans and cost-based selection. Some problem situations may include the following: You would waste your time by using indexes in a table that contains only a few entries, for example, that fit into a data block. Therefore, indexes are not used in short tables. For data manipulation, indexes are unnecessarily time-consuming. Also, Oracle doesn't use the index for long tables when the data quantity would be only slightly reduced. We want to demonstrate this with some examples and describe several Oracle optimization technologies.

For this purpose, let's look at the `sbook` table that contains 1.4 million data sets in our sample database. The `smoker` attribute divides the number of bookings into similarly sized parts:

```
SQL> select smoker, count(smoker)
      from sbook group by smoker;
S COUNT(SMOKER)
- -------------
1        853773
0        555306
```

The `smoker` attribute is less selective (selectivity), that is, Oracle would not use an index based on this attribute. For this purpose, an execution plan can be created and displayed:

```
SQL> explain plan
set statement_id = 'splan'
for select smoker, count(smoker)  from sbook group by smoker
SQL> select plan_table_output
from table(dbms_xplan.display('plan_table','splan','basic'))
PLAN_TABLE_OUTPUT
------------------------------------
Plan hash value: 3858586639
------------------------------------
| Id  | Operation            | Name  |
------------------------------------
|   0 | SELECT STATEMENT     |       |
|   1 |  HASH GROUP BY       |       |
|   2 |   TABLE ACCESS FULL| SBOOK |
------------------------------------
9 rows selected.
```

This example demonstrates the use of `explain plan` and the output of a plan via the PL/SQL package, `dbms_xplan`. The plan runs a full table scan and a hash grouping. Please observe the correct position of `statement_id` in `explain`.

Oracle doesn't use an index created in the following way:

```
create index smoker_idx on sbook(smoker).
```

Not only is such an index useless, but it also comes at the expense of performance and memory space.

However, the selection by a specific date is more precise. For September 24, 2006, sbook contains approximately 4,000 bookings. When a respective index is used, Oracle could exclude 99.7% of the data records before processing. Let's look at the plan:

```
SQL> explain plan
set statement_id = 'fplan'
for select * from sbook where fldate = '24-SEP-06'
Explained.
SQL> select plan_table_output
from table(dbms_xplan.display('plan_table','fplan','basic'))
PLAN_TABLE_OUTPUT
-----------------------------------
Plan hash value: 1649697462
-----------------------------------
| Id  | Operation          | Name  |
-----------------------------------
|   0 | SELECT STATEMENT   |       |
|   1 |  TABLE ACCESS FULL| SBOOK |
-----------------------------------
8 rows selected.
```

Here, the very selective index created with

```
create index fldate_idx on sbook(fldate);
```

was not used, because statistics for the sbook table are missing. Because the maintenance of statistics includes complex and extensive analysis functions, it is usually carried out asynchronously from the normal use of the database. A statistic for the sbook table can be created as follows:

```
SQL> analyze table sbook compute statistics;
Table analyzed.
```

Here, the compute keyword determines exactly how the statistic is calculated. The statistic can also be estimated by *sampling* the table, which saves time. In this example, where the data records were created randomly, very good results would be received via estimation. This applies to most real-life applications.

After the next `explain`, the execution plan is structured as follows:

```
SQL>  select plan_table_output from table (dbms_xplan.dis-
play('plan_table', 'smoker_plan2','basic'));
PLAN_TABLE_OUTPUT
---------------------------------------------------
Plan hash value: 77626240
---------------------------------------------------
| Id  | Operation                    | Name       |
---------------------------------------------------
|   0 | SELECT STATEMENT             |            |
|   1 |  TABLE ACCESS BY INDEX ROWID| SBOOK      |
|   2 |   INDEX RANGE SCAN           | FLDATE_IDX |
---------------------------------------------------
9 rows selected.
```

Here, Oracle uses the `fldate` index.

Finally, you find the plan related to Figure 3.31 as follows:

```
SQL> explain plan
set statement_id = 'joinp'
for select carrname, passname
from scarr c, sbook b
where c.carrid = b.carrid and fldate = '24-SEP-06'
Explained.
SQL> select plan_table_output
from table(dbms_xplan.display('plan_table','joinp','basic'))
PLAN_TABLE_OUTPUT
---------------------------------------------------
Plan hash value: 1134128092
---------------------------------------------------
| Id  | Operation                    | Name       |
---------------------------------------------------
|   0 | SELECT STATEMENT             |            |
|   1 |  HASH JOIN                   |            |
|   2 |   TABLE ACCESS FULL          | SCARR      |
|   3 |   TABLE ACCESS BY INDEX ROWID| SBOOK      |
|   4 |    INDEX RANGE SCAN          | FLDATE_IDX |
---------------------------------------------------
11 rows selected.
```

The usage of the index range scan demonstrates that the selection is brought forward.

Generally, statistics should be created with the analyze command only in special cases. Both DBMS_STATS and ANALYZE create statistics for all relevant objects. The application is illustrated by means of the following example:

```
SQL> exec dbms_stats.gather_schema_stats( -
  ownname          => 'FDMUSER', -
  options          => 'GATHER AUTO', -
  estimate_percent => dbms_stats.auto_sample_size, -
  method_opt       => 'for all columns size repeat', -
  degree           => 34 -
   )
PL/SQL procedure successfully completed.
```

In this process, the statistics for the FDMUSER schema are calculated. This is a convenient option, since it also includes newly added tables and indexes.

Oracle 10 logs changes to tables by default. This is controlled via the server parameter, statistic_level, which is set to TYPICAL. The automatic creation of statistics can be switched off using

```
alter system set statistics_level = "BASIC".
```

However, it is highly recommended not to use this option.

In SAP systems based on Oracle 9, the administrator schedules explicitly the maintenance of statistics at low usage times.

In rare cases, it may be necessary that you define a plan creation method for the optimizer, for example, force it to use an index or to carry out a full table scan. The following example illustrates this procedure:

```
SQL> explain plan set statement_id = 'fplan' for
select /*+ full(sbook) */*
from sbook where fldate = '24-SEP-06'
Explained.
. . .
-----------------------------------
| Id  | Operation          | Name  |
-----------------------------------
|   0 | SELECT STATEMENT   |       |
|   1 |  TABLE ACCESS FULL| SBOOK |
-----------------------------------
```

When the `full(sbook)` hint is used, the optimizer doesn't use the index and runs a full table scan.

Other hints refer to parallelization, join processing, or the optimization goal. For the optimization goal, you can, for example, specify whether the DBMS is supposed to deliver the first data set as soon as possible (`FIRST_ROWS`), or whether the complete results set is more important (`ALL_ROWS`).

3.4.9 Data Backup and Recovery

Although data security represents a direct contradiction to the aspects of performance and user-friendliness, it is indispensable with regard to the monetary value of the data assets of an enterprise. Under no circumstances can data be lost. Legal regulations also require secure data retention.

Consequently, you, as an administrator, are responsible for the following tasks:

- Ensuring that backups are carried out properly
- Recovering the database after errors occurred

For the data recovery, you need theoretical knowledge, as well as practical experience, for example, gained at regular recovery trainings.

Modern database management systems provide numerous mechanisms to recover the database in the case of errors. Most of the errors can be assigned to the following categories:

- **Transaction errors**
  Here, transactions are canceled via the application transaction, for example, due to an `abort` statement or after program errors, such as a division by 0.
- **System errors**
  All errors related to the DBMS software, the operating system, and the hardware can be referred to as system errors. These errors often damage the data in the main memory, but not in the secondary memory.
- **Media errors**
  Media errors are errors that involve losses in the stable storage area, such as disk or controller errors. The effects can be minimized by using a redundant layout (RAID). In this context, you must also consider physical catastrophes, such as fire, water, or earthquakes.

Also, operation errors occur very often and require the recovery of backups. In the literature, operation errors are rarely taken into account, since they actually shouldn't occur at all. However, experience draws a different picture. Data can be deleted due to incorrect administration, too far-reaching assignment of privileges, or customer developments that contain errors. SAP concepts, such as development landscapes and transport systems, mostly eliminate such errors. However, it is also time-consuming and may lead to the loss of work results to reset a development or training system used by several users.

The Oracle concepts for data backups are described on the basis of the Oracle structures explained previously. Chapter 10, *Backup, Restore, and Recovery*, specifies the backup aspects of SAP databases. But data security goes beyond technical aspects, and organizational as well as infrastructural aspects must also be considered. Chapter 5 and Chapter 9 describe these aspects in greater detail. In Oracle systems, data is stored at the following levels:

- Main memory
- Secondary memory, mostly hard disks
    - Redo log files
    - Data files
    - Archive directory
- Tertiary memory, mostly tape backups

Figure 3.32 illustrates the involved processes and data structures.

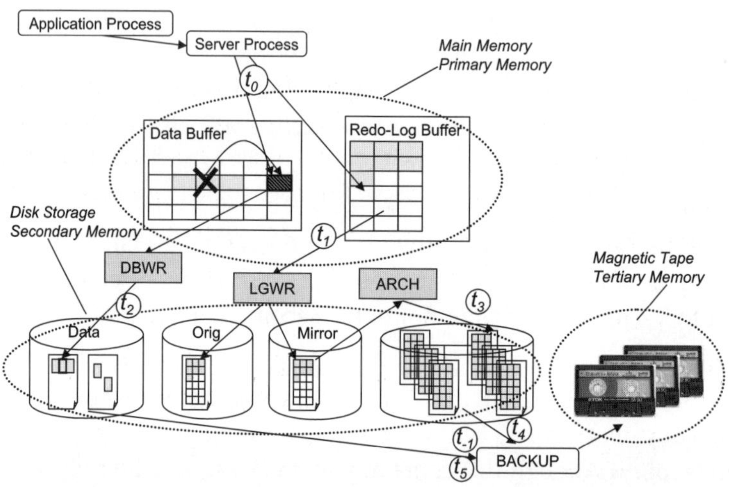

Figure 3.32 Memory Hierarchy in Oracle Systems

A transaction changes the data at the time t0. At t1, a `COMMIT` is run, and the data is permanently written to the disk by writing the redo logs with the log writer. The data files that have not been written yet are inconsistent with the data that has already been written. Later at t2 will the changes be written to the data files. At t3, a completed redo log is copied into the archive directory. At t4, the archived redo logs are stored on tape. Together with the data files copied at t-1 (that is, at a further distant point in time in the past) and the previously archived logs, they constitute the basis for a full recovery.

Transaction errors are managed via the DBMS in a defined way. The respective data is reset via the undo information. According to the ACID properties, there are no side effects.

System errors have the following effects:

- Transactions that are in a status before `COMMIT` (i.e., between t0 and t1) will be lost. This should be transparent to the user or application, that is, an error message that indicates the cancellation of the transaction is displayed.
- Data files are not consistent for transactions in the status between t1 and t2. When restarting the database, the data files must be updated via the redo logs. Such transactions do generally exist; however, it is very unlikely that only transactions exist that are either not completed (before t1), or whose changes have already been written to the data files (after t2). Oracle can determine the status via the timestamps (sequence numbers) in the control files and in the data file headers.
- The tertiary memory, namely, the actual backup, is not required.

Oracle generally recovers the data automatically after a system error. In this case, the database is not available for some time, since, on the one hand, the reason for the system error must be determined, and, on the other hand, the recovery, particularly the redoing of transactions, can take some time. Furthermore, problems may occur, which you must pay attention to.

3.4.9.1 Media Errors

If media errors occur, the administrator must usually take action. Thanks to the Oracle and hardware data backup concepts, not every media error causes the live operation to stop. However, the error should be corrected, since it generally limits the data security.

This section discusses some media errors and their effects, as well as the respective measures as examples. The errors that are caught by RAID technologies are not considered:

- **Loss of the disk with the original logs**
  The DBMS continues to work without restrictions. The administrator must initiate the storage of original logs on a new media.
- **Loss of the disk with a control file**
  The DBMS first continues to work without restrictions. The administrator must initiate the storage of the control file copy on a new media.
- **Loss of a disk with the data files**
  The DBMS cannot continue to work. A backup must be installed.

You can usually avoid the last of these issues by using RAID arrays. Because the failure of a disk within the RAID group can often have a physical cause that also affects other disks, you must be prepared for this possibility.

The following example shows the behavior of Oracle when a control file is lost. In this example, we renamed the respective control file at the operating system level. Figure 3.33 illustrates the behavior of the Oracle instance during the start.

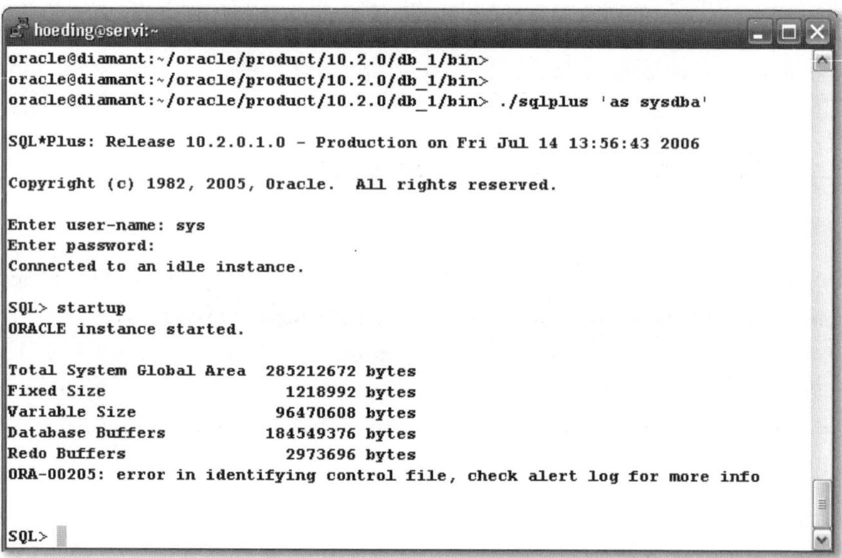

hoeding@servi:~
oracle@diamant:~/oracle/product/10.2.0/db_1/bin>
oracle@diamant:~/oracle/product/10.2.0/db_1/bin>
oracle@diamant:~/oracle/product/10.2.0/db_1/bin> ./sqlplus 'as sysdba'
SQL*Plus: Release 10.2.0.1.0 - Production on Fri Jul 14 13:56:43 2006
Copyright (c) 1982, 2005, Oracle. All rights reserved.
Enter user-name: sys
Enter password:
Connected to an idle instance.
SQL> startup
ORACLE instance started.
Total System Global Area 285212672 bytes
Fixed Size   1218992 bytes
Variable Size   96470608 bytes
Database Buffers   184549376 bytes
Redo Buffers   2973696 bytes
ORA-00205: error in identifying control file, check alert log for more info
SQL>

Figure 3.33 Starting Oracle with SQLPlus

The instance cannot be started, and the error message refers to further information in the alert log. The log can be found in the *bdump* directory or, in SAP systems, under *oracle/<SID>/<VER>/rdbms/log*. Figure 3.34 shows an excerpt of the alert log based on our example.

Now you have different options to solve the problem. You can either remove the control file in a not mounted status using sqlplus or move it to a different location as described in Section 3.4.5, *Other Important Files*. However, it is better to recover the initial status and to position the missing log file at the right place. Of course, you must ensure that the control file is the right one. Therefore, it makes more sense to copy the undamaged version than the possibly obsolete version that we created by renaming the file. Then, Oracle can start without an error (see Figure 3.35).

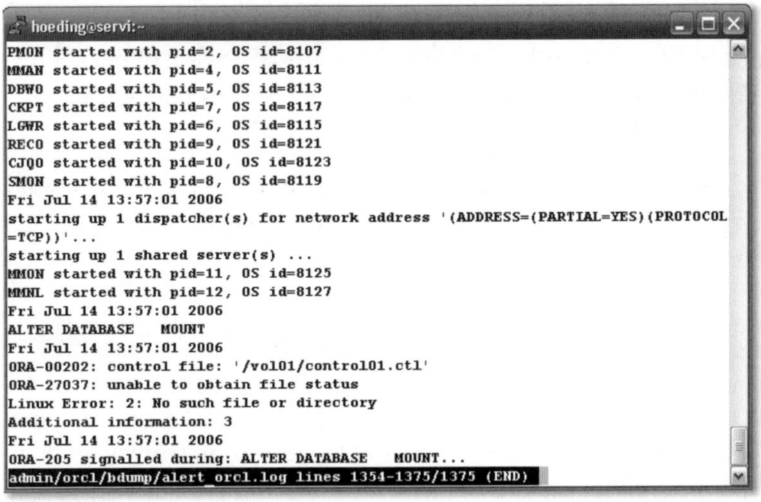

```
hoeding@servi:~
PMON started with pid=2, OS id=8107
MMAN started with pid=4, OS id=8111
DBW0 started with pid=5, OS id=8113
CKPT started with pid=7, OS id=8117
LGWR started with pid=6, OS id=8115
RECO started with pid=9, OS id=8121
CJQ0 started with pid=10, OS id=8123
SMON started with pid=8, OS id=8119
Fri Jul 14 13:57:01 2006
starting up 1 dispatcher(s) for network address '(ADDRESS=(PARTIAL=YES)(PROTOCOL
=TCP))'...
starting up 1 shared server(s) ...
MMON started with pid=11, OS id=8125
MMNL started with pid=12, OS id=8127
Fri Jul 14 13:57:01 2006
ALTER DATABASE   MOUNT
Fri Jul 14 13:57:01 2006
ORA-00202: control file: '/vol01/control01.ctl'
ORA-27037: unable to obtain file status
Linux Error: 2: No such file or directory
Additional information: 3
Fri Jul 14 13:57:01 2006
ORA-205 signalled during: ALTER DATABASE   MOUNT...
admin/orcl/bdump/alert_orcl.log lines 1354-1375/1375 (END)
```

Figure 3.34 Detailed Error Message in the Alert Log

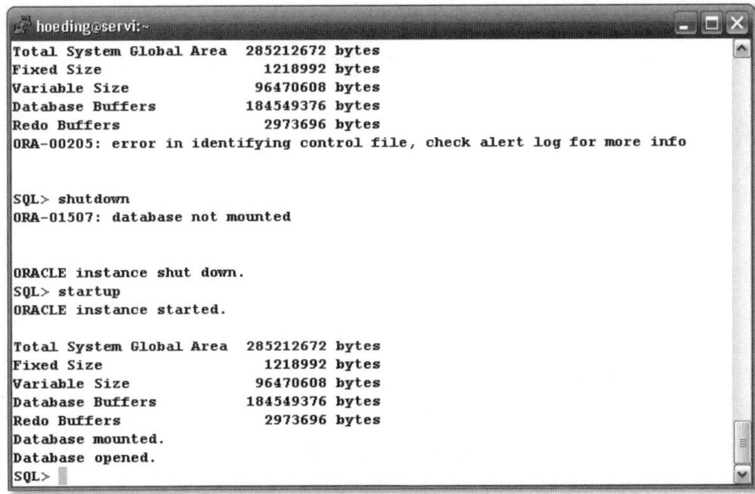

```
hoeding@servi:~
Total System Global Area  285212672 bytes
Fixed Size                  1218992 bytes
Variable Size              96470608 bytes
Database Buffers          184549376 bytes
Redo Buffers                2973696 bytes
ORA-00205: error in identifying control file, check alert log for more info


SQL> shutdown
ORA-01507: database not mounted


ORACLE instance shut down.
SQL> startup
ORACLE instance started.

Total System Global Area  285212672 bytes
Fixed Size                  1218992 bytes
Variable Size              96470608 bytes
Database Buffers          184549376 bytes
Redo Buffers                2973696 bytes
Database mounted.
Database opened.
SQL>
```

Figure 3.35 Successful Start After Solving the Problem

3.4.9.2 Oracle Backup Technologies

When backing up databases, you are caught between the requirements of speed, simplicity, and security. You cannot save large databases within a few seconds. However, large databases set in a global or time-based context of an E-Commerce application should be available 24/7.

The full backup of an offline database is a simple, secure method, but unfortunately, it is also very time-consuming. This method is also referred to as *offline backup*. For this purpose, data and control files are saved. Since the shutting down of the DBMS is linked to a checkpoint, you don't need to save the redo log files. However, the fact that the offline backup requires a lot of time and memory space is certainly a disadvantage. Usually, this limitation is not acceptable for systems as complex as an SAP system.

To solve this problem, Oracle developed *online backups* that are generally used. For this process, files are saved during live operation; however, this means that not all files have the same status. Therefore, you must also save all logs that were written during the backup process. The full online backup is also time-consuming and requires a lot of space on the backup media.

Oracle uses *incremental backups* to save time and space. These backups only save blocks that were changed. Therefore, the backup times and volumes required are considerably reduced in the standard system. However, compared to the offline backup, this method is neither simple nor transparent. For this method, you should definitely use specific tools, particularly the Oracle *Recovery Manager* (RMAN).

The incremental backup process supports various backup levels. In the example, a full backup is performed every Sunday; a level 1 backup is performed every Wednesday; and a level 2 backup is performed on all other days.

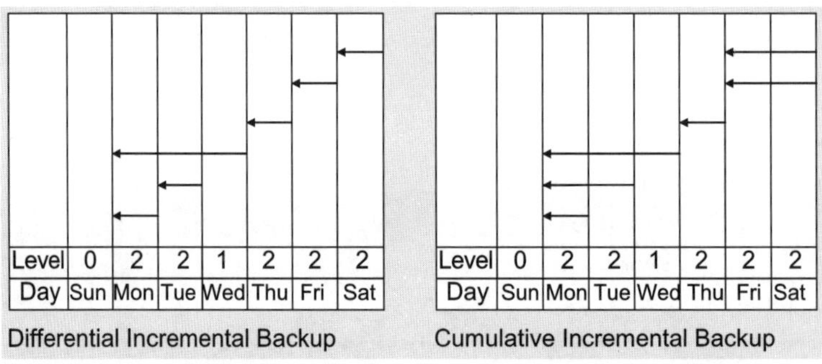

Figure 3.36 Incremental Backup

In this context, you can perform differential or cumulative backups. Differential backups save all blocks that have been changed since the last backup. Cumulative backups save all blocks that have been changed since the last backup at a higher level. If an error occurs on Wednesday, you can recover the database as follows:

- **Differential Incremental Backup**
  You import the full backup made on Sunday. Then, you import the backup from Monday, followed by the one from Tuesday and all redo logs written since then.
- **Cumulative Incremental Backup**
  You import the full backup from Sunday. Then, you import the backup from Tuesday. You don't have to import the backup from Monday, as all changes since Sunday are contained in the Tuesday backup. In addition, you import all redo logs written since the Tuesday backup.

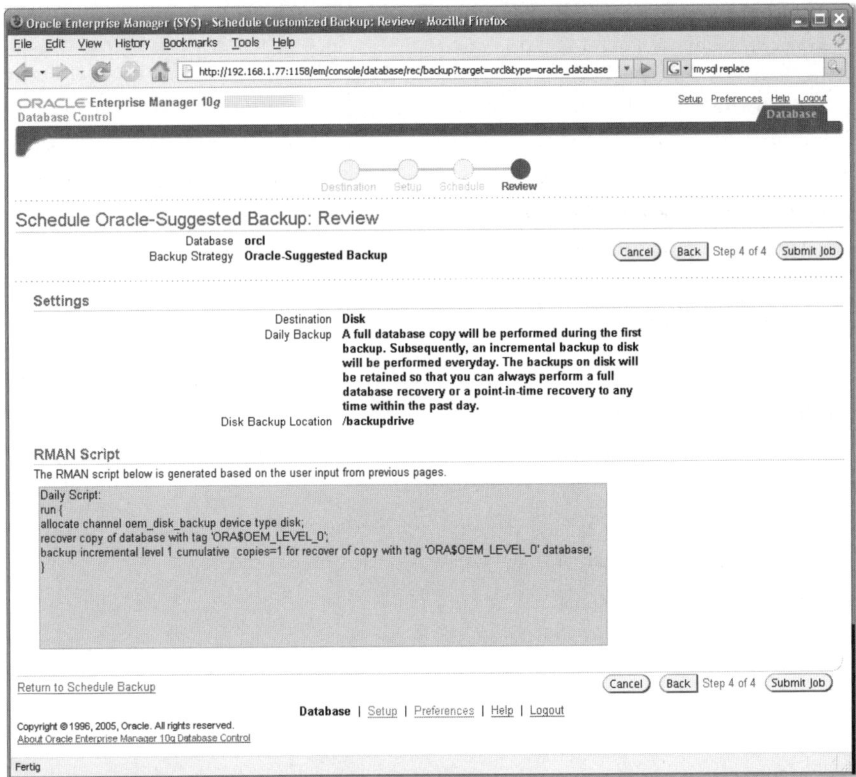

Figure 3.37 Backup Scheduling with the Enterprise Manager

In Oracle systems, backups are usually run using the Recovery Manager. The RMAN can be started from the command prompt, or by using a script. You can find a detailed description in Section 10.5. For a convenient administration, you can control the RMAN via the Enterprise Manager. Figure 3.37 illustrates how a backup is scheduled with the Enterprise Manager and the respective RMAN script. Oracle provides a scheduler for scheduling regular backups. Reports on performed backups can also be analyzed with the Enterprise Manager. The Enterprise Manager also supports database recovery. However, in SAP systems, BR*Tools are usually used. Chapter 10 describes the use of BR*Tools for backup and recovery in greater detail.

Oracle 10 makes the flash backup technology available for entire databases. A specific process, the *recovery writer* (RKWR), writes but does not archive flashback recovery logs. Instead, these logs are deleted after a defined period of time. Similar to the LGWR process, which stores redo information in redo log files, the RKWR process writes the undo information. Thus, you can simply reset the database to any point in time within the flashback interval.

Data security is a main task of the Basis administration. Unfortunately, the quality of the work is only visible in an emergency situation. Try to calculate the costs of an unplanned system downtime for your specific application case, and compare them with the effort involved. The result justifies all measures required. The following notes summarize the measures and technologies described in this section for ensuring data security.

Notes: Data Security Measures

- Organizational and infrastructural measures
- Use of RAID technologies for redundant data storage
- Control files: three copies on different media
- Redo log: two groups on different media
- Archiving redo log files
- Periodic backup: backup of data files, control files, redo logs, DBMS system files, and operating system files
- Emergency plan and recovery training

3.4.10 Users and Privileges

Oracle provides sophisticated mechanisms for data protection. First, there are the users that are known to the system and identify themselves, for example, by entering a password. The use of external authentication services, such as LDAP, is also supported. Secondly, there are database objects, such as tables, views, or tablespaces. Thirdly, there are authorization models, which can include the right to only read data up to the right to manipulate database structures. Roles, as a link, bundle the rights. Roles can be nested to any depth.

In Oracle, the authorization to run a class of SQL statements for specific objects or classes of objects is a privilege. We must distinguish between *system privileges* and *object privileges*:

- System privileges include rights for all objects of a specific type and for general system rights, such as the authorization to log in to the system.
- Object privileges refer to particular objects.

Of course, you can explicitly assign rights to users. In practice, however, you often work with groups of persons with the same importance, and you want to assign the same privileges to them. For this purpose, you can define a role and assign certain users to it. In the following example, we define the role of a weight supervisor for our flight data model with the `create role` statement:

```
create role weightsupervisor
```

With the `grant` statement, we assign special read authorization to the `sbook` table, which also contains the luggage weight:

```
grant select (connid, fldate, luggweight)
on sbook
to weightsupervisor
```

Then, we assign the `weightsupervisor` role to specific persons:

```
grant weightsupervisor to peter
grant weightsupervisor to paul
```

But, it can also be assigned to other roles, that are, in turn, assigned to other users:

```
grant weightsupervisor to shiftsupervisor
grant shiftsupervisor to mary
```

This creates a flexible structure that makes changes of the initial rights for all users involved valid. Additionally, it often happens that real persons assume responsibility for various new tasks over time and therefore change roles in real life and in the database.

```
revoke shiftsupervisor from mary
grant weightsupervisor to mary
```

The following list contains some examples of basic privileges in Oracle:

- `create session`
  basic right to log in to the database
- `create any table`
  very extensive right to create any table
- `drop any table ... with admin option`
  right to delete any table structure and to pass this right on
- `update (luggweight) on sbook`
  right to change the `luggweight` attribute in the `sbook` table

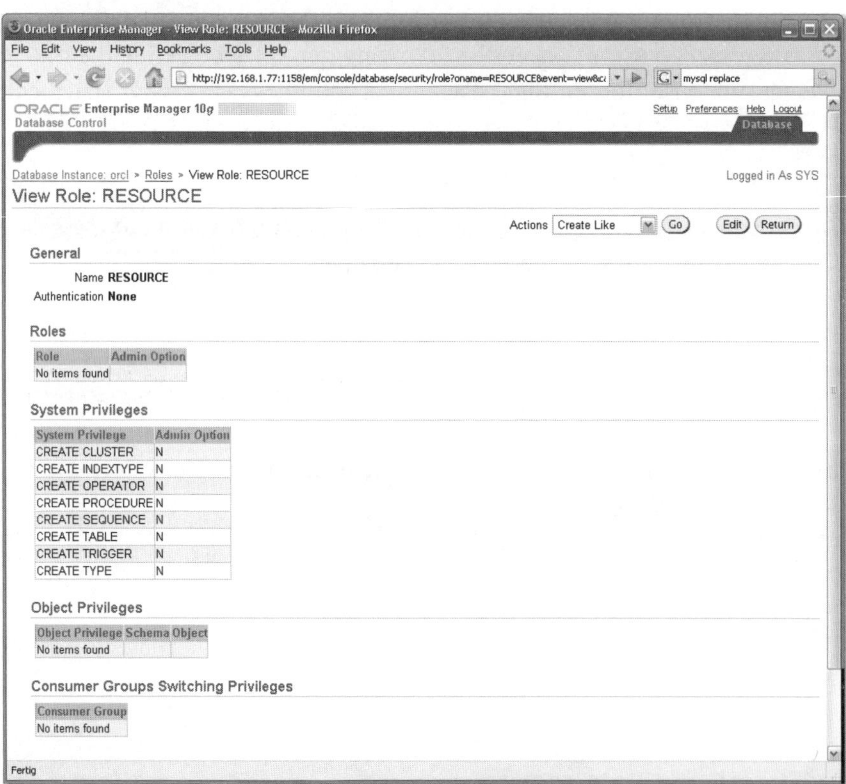

Figure 3.38 Viewing the Resource Role in the Enterprise Manager

Oracle already provides numerous roles that simplify the administration. Some sample roles are listed here:

- CONNECT is based on the session right and allows a user to log on to an Oracle system.
- RESOURCE bundles the major system privileges for creating database objects and is shown in Figure 3.38 via the Enterprise Manager.
- DBA is assigned to the SYS and SYSTEM users along with the admin option (the right to pass on the right), which allows for an administrative access to all database objects. You should view the script that creates the DBA role with the Enterprise Manager via **Administration • Roles • DBA • Generate DDL.**

With the Enterprise Manager, you can easily create users (see Figures 3.39 and 3.40), lock and unlock users, and manage roles.

The Enterprise Manager uses SQL statements for all actions. Therefore, you can also obtain an overview of rights and roles with sqlplus. This is important if you can't use the Enterprise Manager.

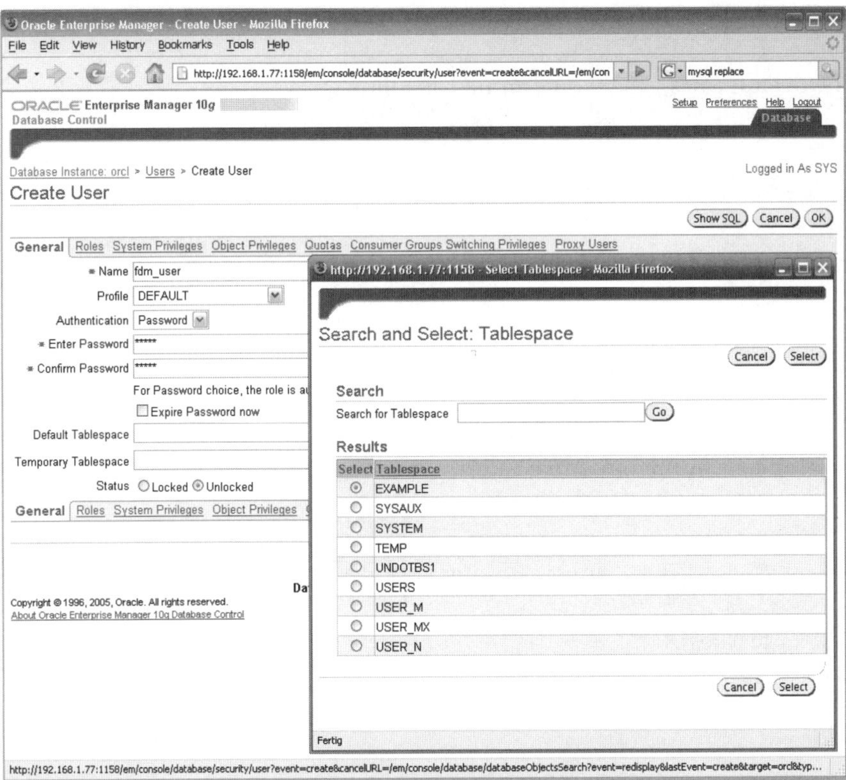

Figure 3.39 Using the Oracle Enterprise Manager: Creating a User

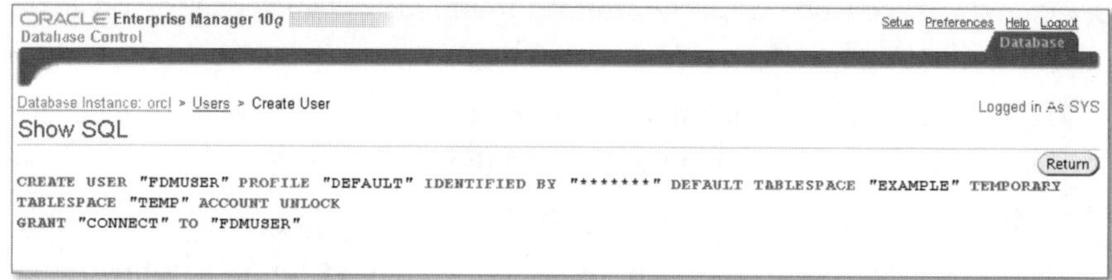

Figure 3.40 SQL Statement for Creating a User, Generated by the Enterprise Manager

The `user_role_privs` view provides information on the roles of the logged-in user:

```
select username, granted_role, admin_option
from user_role_privs
USERNAME                GRANTED_ROLE               ADM
---------------------- -------------------------- ---
FDMUSER                 CONNECT                    NO
FDMUSER                 RESOURCE                   NO
```

The default roles can be determined as follows:

```
select granted_role
from user_role_privs
where default_role= 'YES';

GRANTED_ROLE
------------------------------
CONNECT
RESOURCE
```

You can determine the active roles in the `session_roles` view. Object privileges can be selected as follows:

```
select table_name, privilege, grantable from user_tab_privs
```

System privileges of a user can be found in `user_sys_privs`:

```
select * from user_sys_privs;
USERNAME       PRIVILEGE                                ADM
-------------- ---------------------------------------- ---
FDMUSER        CREATE TABLE                             NO
FDMUSER        UNLIMITED TABLESPACE                     NO
```

Oracle systems contain some users that are created during the installation and whose password must be changed:

- Both administrative users, SYSTEM (initial password MANAGER) and SYS (initial password CHANGE_ON_INSTALL), have extensive rights in the Oracle system. Therefore, the passwords should be changed already during installation. The interactive installation of Oracle 10 prompts you to change the passwords, as follows:
- The task of the DBSNMP user (initial password DBSNMP) is to monitor Oracle via the Simple Network Monitoring Protocol (SNMP). The user is unlocked after the installation. If you don't use SNMP, you should lock the user, as follows:

  ```
  alter user dbsnmp account lock
  ```
- In Oracle systems, the user `scott` with the password `tiger`[4] is a popular point of attack. The user `scott` provides a small training database. Many Oracle examples are based on this database. After an installation of Oracle 10, `scott` is locked. This was not always the case in older versions. Check whether you can connect to an Oracle database via the `scott` account.

As an administrator, you probably won't be involved immediately in the assignment of privileges, since SAP has implemented its own mechanisms to protect data.

3.4.11 Monitoring an Oracle Instance with the Enterprise Manager

One of the main tasks of administrators is to monitor large database applications. This involves monitoring the entire systems, taking counteractions in critical situations, and avoiding critical situations. For this purpose, among others, the basic principles described in this chapter are important. However, for the operation of Oracle-based systems, experience assumes a special role, too.

You can hardly be expected to implement simple and safe mechanisms and procedures that automate the monitoring process, because of the following reasons:

4 Bruce Scott was the first Oracle employee after its foundation in 1977. His cat's name was Tiger.

- The complexity of Oracle
- The different usage scenarios (as is the case in SAP) and
- The continuously enhancing technologies.

As an administrator, you will permanently make a plan/actual comparison. Tools, such as the Enterprise Manager, support you in performing this task. Planned or threshold values are already defined for important parameters. But the adjustment and maintenance of such values for your own system involve a certain amount of extra work. For example, a log often displays error messages that are rated as uncritical by the administrators and can therefore be ignored. In many cases, this is not recorded by the monitoring system.

You can also reduce the complexity by using graphical tools. Figure 3.41 shows how the performance monitor of the Enterprise Manager inserts data records via individual insert statements.

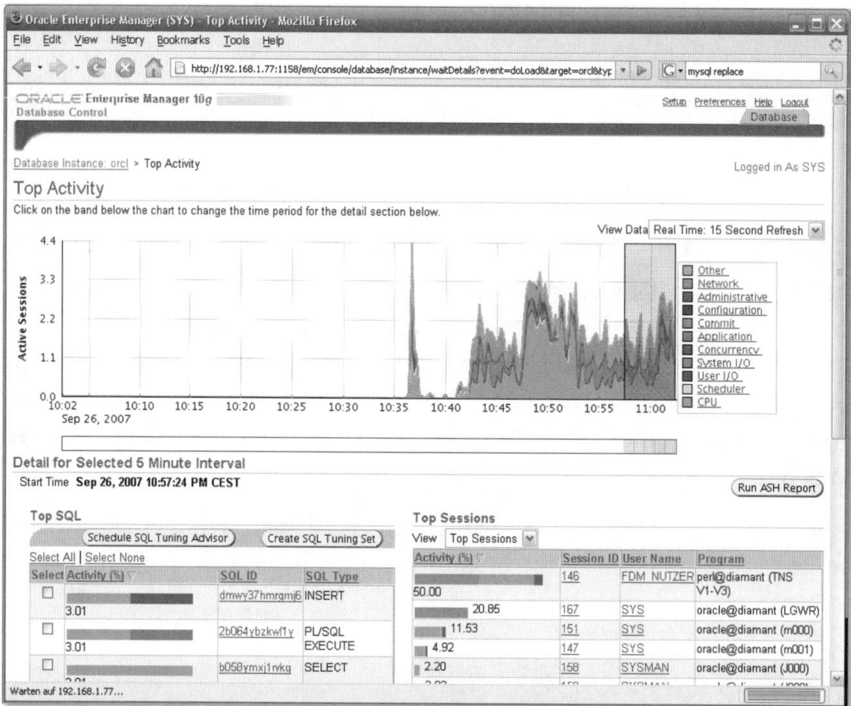

Figure 3.41 Monitoring the Database Load with the Enterprise Manager

Other tools are provided for SAP systems as additional options. SAP provides a wide range of monitoring tools that, for example, can be controlled via Transaction RZ20 and not only monitor the Oracle system, but also monitor the application server and the operating system. Furthermore, third parties develop high-performance tools with some advantages. For example, the PATROL system enables you to monitor large landscapes in the application/hosting area.

3.5 Summary

Oracle is a typical relational database management system that implements this technology in an excellent manner to make it available for live operation. Experience has shown that basic principles in the architecture and generation of relational databases help you to manage Oracle-based systems and support the communication with developers and decision-makers.

This chapter introduced typical Oracle tools, such as sqlplus, that you as an administrator must use very often. In these cases, the tools can help you to maintain the system operation. The difference between a very good administrator and a good administrator is, among other things, the administrator's ability to manage such tools in critical situations.

We introduced the core of the Oracle system in this chapter with our objective being to give you a basic understanding of Oracle systems. We tried to clearly illustrate the interaction between Oracle processes and memory structures on the basis of simple examples. The following chapters will describe the aspects that are important for SAP administration in greater detail.

Seventy percent of all installed SAP production systems run on Oracle databases. This chapter describes the interaction between SAP and Oracle products.

4 SAP and Oracle

This chapter combines the SAP and Oracle architectures described in the previous chapters (Chapter 2, *SAP Fundamentals*, and Chapter 3, *Oracle Fundamentals*) into a complete SAP system. Starting with a description of the processes and the system startup, the chapter continues by describing the interactions between the Oracle database and the SAP instance. Furthermore, it discusses the communication between the two, as well as aspects related to security.

Regarding a successful system operation, the implementation of a corresponding SAP- and Oracle-based environment is equally important. Therefore, we'll describe the various relevant aspects, such as operating system users, environment variables, and Oracle clients, in greater detail. The section on the SAP Tablespace Layout describes how the SAP system stores applications and data in the database.

Moreover, this chapter includes a comprehensive description of the *BR*Tools* toolset provided by SAP for administering Oracle databases.

Notes

All descriptions in this chapter are based on the assumption that a UNIX operating system is used. Consequently, in some instances, you'll see that there are significant differences to operating SAP and Oracle systems on a Windows operating system. We won't describe these differences in greater detail, but notify you about them wherever distinguishing them is relevant.

The following sections refer exclusively to a pure SAP-ABAP instance, that is, a pure ABAP system. For details on the interaction between an SAP-Java system and an Oracle database, you should refer to Chapter 11.

4.1 Processes of SAP and Oracle Systems

At this point, we'll take another look at the processes of Oracle and SAP systems (see Tables 4.1 and 4.2) and their primary functions.

The tables list all SAP and Oracle processes that run permanently during system operations. Other SAP processes that interact with the Oracle database, but run for only specific purposes, such as R3trans, are described separately at the respective places in this chapter. In addition, the tables don't list processes that aren't relevant for the interaction between SAP and Oracle, such as the *Internet Graphics Server* (IGS).

SAP Process	Description	Representation in the Operating System (UNIX)
Work Process	Maps the individual SAP work processes and their tasks (dialog, batch, spool, etc.). The dispatcher of an instance is one such work process.	dw.sap<SID>_<Instance Name>; example: dw.SAPM05_DVEBMGS05
Message Server	Handles the communication between the instances of an SAP system and distributes the users when logon groups are used.	ms.sap<SID>_<Instance Name>; example: ms.SAPM05_DVEBMGS05
Syslog Sender	Sends the SAP syslog messages to the central syslog collector, if central logging is enabled.	se.sap<SID>_<Instance Name>; example: se.SAPM05_DVEBMGS05
Syslog Collector	Collects the SAP syslog messages of individual syslog senders and writes them to a file, if central logging is enabled.	co.sap<SID>_<Instance Name>; example: co.SAPM05_DVEBMGS05
Internet Communication Manager	Receives HTTP requests and redirects these to the work processes or to the J2EE server.	icman; example: icman -attach -pf...
Sapstart	Initiates the start of the SAP system (see Section 4.1.1, *System Startup*).	sapstart; example: /usr/sap/M05/SYS/exe/run/sapstart
Gateway Process	Handles all RFC connections to the SAP system, with the exception of SAP GUI.	gwrd; example: gwrd -dp -pf...

Table 4.1 Overview of Key SAP Processes

Oracle Process	Description	Representation in the Operating System (UNIX)
DB Writer (DBWn)	Writes changes into the database files.	`ora_dbw(n)_<DBSID>`; example: `ora_dbw0_M05`
DB Work Process	This process is connected with the SAP work processes and processes their requests.	`oracle<DBSID>`; example: `oracleM05`
PMON	Monitors the processes and is responsible for "cleaning up" in case of a termination.	`ora_pmon_<DBSID>`; example: `ora_pmon_M05`
SMON	Monitors the system and performs a crash recovery in emergency situations.	`ora_smon_<DBSID>`; example: `ora_smon_M05`
RECO	Handles the failure of distributed transactions.	`ora_reco_<DBSID>`; example: `ora_reco_M05`
CKPT	Controls and executes the checkpoints that put the Oracle database into a defined and consistent state.	`ora_ckpt_<DBSID>`; example: `ora_ckpt_M05`
ARC Process (ARCn)	Moves the full Redo Log files into a defined archive.	`ora_arc(n)_<DBSID>`; example: `ora_arc0_M05`
LGWR	Writes the Redo Log files from the Redo Log buffer.	`ora_lgwr_<DBSID>`; example: `ora_lgwr_M05`
Listener	Receives the initial connects from Oracle clients. For SAP, this includes the initial connects of the SAP work processes.	`tnslsnr`; example: `/oracle/M05/102_64/bin/tnslsnr LISTENER -inherit`

Table 4.2 Overview of Key Oracle Processes

Note

The dedicated work processes of the Oracle database are often referred to as *Oracle shadow processes*. Consequently, we will use both terms (i.e., *work processes* and *shadow processes*) as synonyms in this book.

From a technical point of view, you should note that (almost) all processes of the SAP and Oracle software (that is, the ABAP world and the standard Oracle database system) are "classic" processes. Therefore, they don't use multiple threads because they consist of only one thread to carry out activities. Consequently, a process can utilize only one CPU. However, in modern software development, it has become standard to use multi-threaded processes, particularly because of the significantly faster switching of CPUs between different threads compared to the switching of CPUs between processes (factor 5 to 10). For this reason, it is hardly surprising that the recent SAP developments are primarily based on the multi-threaded concept, such as the *Internet Communication Manager* (ICM) or the entire J2EE Engine.

A Windows-based Oracle system is an exception to that. Here, you only "see" one big Oracle process in the Task Manager. All other processes, such as background and shadow processes, are executed as threads in this process.

4.1.1 System Startup

To better understand the interaction between the different processes, it is useful to begin with the process of the system startup. Here, you will see a first indication of the relationships between processes.

Note

The following sections refer to SAP Basis Release 6.40 and the Oracle 9i database. The subsequent versions of the SAP Basis contain some additional steps as part of the system startup, such as the synchronization of local instance executables (see also Section 7.2.2, *SAP Support Packages, Patches, and Corrections*). Similarly, Oracle 10g also has some new server processes. However, the basic process with all the different interactions, as described here, is not affected by these differences.

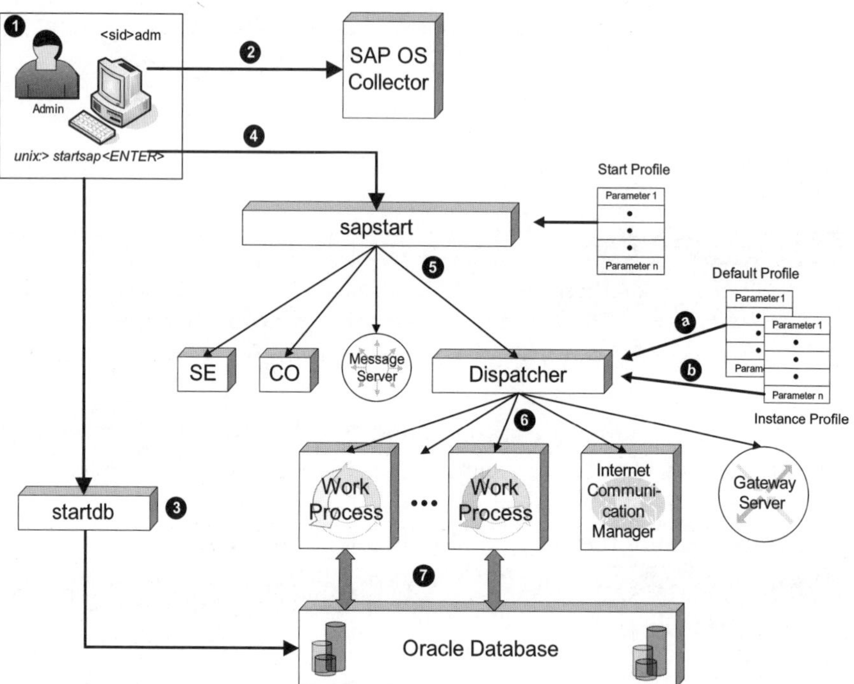

Figure 4.1 Starting an SAP System

We want to begin with a rough description of the process of starting an SAP system, followed by a detailed description of how the Oracle database and SAP instance are involved in that process. Figure 4.1 shows the system start on a UNIX system with a database and central instance.

The process is carried out in the following sequence:

❶ The *<sid>adm* user is the UNIX user of the SAP system. This user is used to call the `startsap` script, which is part of the SAP kernel.

❷ First the SAP OS Collector (`saposcol`) starts, provided it isn't running yet. Only one SAP OS Collector is started per host, irrespective of how many SAP systems or instances are running on a host.

❸ Then, the `R3trans` program is used to test whether the database is available. If it isn't, the `startdb` script is called to start the database. If the Oracle database is located on a different host than the instance to be started and the database test (`R3trans`) fails, the system startup process terminates. `R3trans` and `startdb` are also part of the SAP kernel (see Section 4.3.2, *Login Processes*).

❹ To start the SAP system, the `sapstart` program is called. This program reads the *start profile* of the instance to be started.

❺ The start profile contains the components and services to be started:

- In a central instance, the following services are started: Message Server, Dispatcher, Collector, Sender, and Gateway Server.
- In a dialog instance, the following services are started: Dispatcher, Sender, and Gateway Server.

❻ The Dispatcher reads the *default profile* (ⓐ) and the *instance profile* (ⓑ) and starts the individual kernel processes (dialog, background, spool, etc.) according to the parameterization using the `fork()` function.

❼ Once the individual work processes have started, the processes connect to the Oracle database, and the system is "online."

This "rough" process is identical in all SAP systems without a Java stack. On Windows, the system startup does not occur within a shell, but through the Microsoft Management Console (MMC) and an integrated snap-in adapter. As of SAP Basis Release 7.0, you can also start and stop SAP systems on UNIX via the GUI of the SAP Start Service. You can find additional information on this subject in SAP Note 936273; however, the individual phases of the startup process are the same as those described previously.

Of course, there are differences, for instance, if the central instance and the Oracle database don't run on the same server, or if another instance, such as a dialog instance, is started separately. In contrast to the previous scenario, those cases don't allow for an automatic start of the database, that is, the system merely checks whether the database is running. If the database is not running, the startup process terminates. You cannot use the SAP start scripts to start the Oracle database remotely. Therefore, your administrator must start the database manually prior to the system startup. All other start phases of an SAP instance are identical to those described previously.

The process already makes clear what types of relationships exist between the SAP processes. Figure 4.2 shows an excerpt of the list of system processes with SID M05 (without Oracle processes), which has been generated using the following UNIX command:

```
"ps -ef | grep <SID> | grep -v ora"
```

```
File  Edit  View  Window  Help
m05adm 12183     1  0 13:32:19 ?        0:00 /usr/sap/M05/SYS/exe/run/sapstart
m05adm 12214 12183  0 13:32:19 ?        0:00 se.sapM05_DVEBMGS05 -F pf=/usr/sap
m05adm 12213 12183  0 13:32:19 ?        0:00 co.sapM05_DVEBMGS05 -F pf=/usr/sap
m05adm 12211 12183  0 13:32:19 ?        0:00 ms.sapM05_DVEBMGS05 pf=/usr/sap/M0
m05adm 12212 12183  0 13:32:19 ?        0:02 dw.sapM05_DVEBMGS05 pf=/usr/sap/M0
m05adm 12216 12212  0 13:32:25 ?        0:02 icman -attach pf=/usr/sap/M05/SYS/
m05adm 12215 12212  0 13:32:24 ?        0:00 gwrd -dp pf=/usr/sap/M05/SYS/profi
m05adm 12233 12212  0 13:32:25 ?        0:00 dw.sapM05_DVEBMGS05 pf=/usr/sap/M0
m05adm 12229 12212  0 13:32:25 ?        0:00 dw.sapM05_DVEBMGS05 pf=/usr/sap/M0
m05adm 12230 12212  0 13:32:25 ?        0:24 dw.sapM05_DVEBMGS05 pf=/usr/sap/M0
m05adm 12225 12212  0 13:32:25 ?        0:00 dw.sapM05_DVEBMGS05 pf=/usr/sap/M0
m05adm 12231 12212  0 13:32:25 ?        0:30 dw.sapM05_DVEBMGS05 pf=/usr/sap/M0
m05adm 12219 12212  0 13:32:25 ?        0:04 dw.sapM05_DVEBMGS05 pf=/usr/sap/M0
m05adm 12217 12212  0 13:32:25 ?        1:33 dw.sapM05_DVEBMGS05 pf=/usr/sap/M0
m05adm 12223 12212  0 13:32:25 ?        0:00 dw.sapM05_DVEBMGS05 pf=/usr/sap/M0
smaragd:~#
```

Figure 4.2 Processes of SAP System M05

The `sapstart` process is the parent process of all service processes (syslog, Message Server, and Dispatcher), and it must run during the entire duration of the system operation, as a termination of this process automatically terminates the SAP instance as well. You can determine this on the basis of the process ID (PID) of sapstart (12183), which, in turn, is the parent process ID (PPID) of the other processes listed.

The Dispatcher (process ID 12212) is a child process of `sapstart`; at the same time, it is a parent process as well, which starts the ICM, the gateway, and all work processes (parent process ID 12212 for all). This enables the dispatcher to monitor and, if necessary, stop and start all its child processes.

The SAP system administrator can start the Oracle database in several different ways. At this point, we list only those methods that can be used in the SAP environment, that is, we won't describe any external or Oracle-specific tools such as the Oracle Enterprise Manager here:

- To start the database with the `startsap` and `startdb` scripts, the operating system user of the SAP system, <sid>adm (example: C-shell and system ID M05), must enter the following command:

  ```
  f05:m05adm 1>startsap db
  ```

  or

  ```
  f05:m05adm 1>startdb
  ```

  These scripts write a log file — startdb.log — into the home directory of user <sid>adm.

- The second option to start the database is to launch the Oracle instance directly as an Oracle operating system user (ora<sid>) using the corresponding SQL commands (example: C-shell and system ID M05):

  ```
  f05:oram05 1>sqlplus „/as sysdba"
  ... Connected to an idle instance.
  SQL> startup
  ```

- In addition, the operating system user of the SAP system — <sid>adm — can also start the Oracle database using the BR*Tools (example: C-shell and system ID M05):

  ```
  f05:m05adm 1>brtools
  ```

  This can also be done via the following menu path in `BRTOOLS`: **Instance management • Start up database**

There's one process that we should take a closer look at. To start the SAP instance, it is not sufficient to have the Oracle database up and running. To enable the SAP work processes to connect to each other, you must also launch the Oracle Listener. But when exactly do you need to start the Oracle Listener? This depends on the startup method you select. To start the system through the scripts, the Oracle Listener must be running, because the scripts test the functionality of the Listener explicitly and terminate the startup process in case of a failure. `sqlplus` and `BRTOOLS` allow you to start the database without the Listener running.

Note

None of the three methods described here starts the Oracle Listener. That must be done by the administrator as an Oracle operating system user, ora<sid> (example: C-shell and system ID M05):

```
f05:oram05 1>lsnrctl start
```

On another note, you shouldn't be surprised that the Oracle background processes run either under the <sid>adm user (SAP scripts and BR*Tools) or under the ora<sid> user (sqlplus), depending on the startup method. This doesn't affect the functionality of the database in any way. Why this occurs and how this works is described in greater detail in Sections 4.2.1, *Users, Groups, and Environment Variables (UNIX)*, and 4.3, *Authentication Between SAP and Oracle*.

If you examine the `startdb` script and the process of the `BRTOOLS` further, you will see that these methods ultimately call sqlplus as well to start the database. Consequently, the actual database startup process is identical in all methods, irrespective of which method you select. Figure 4.3 illustrates the startup process of an Oracle database.

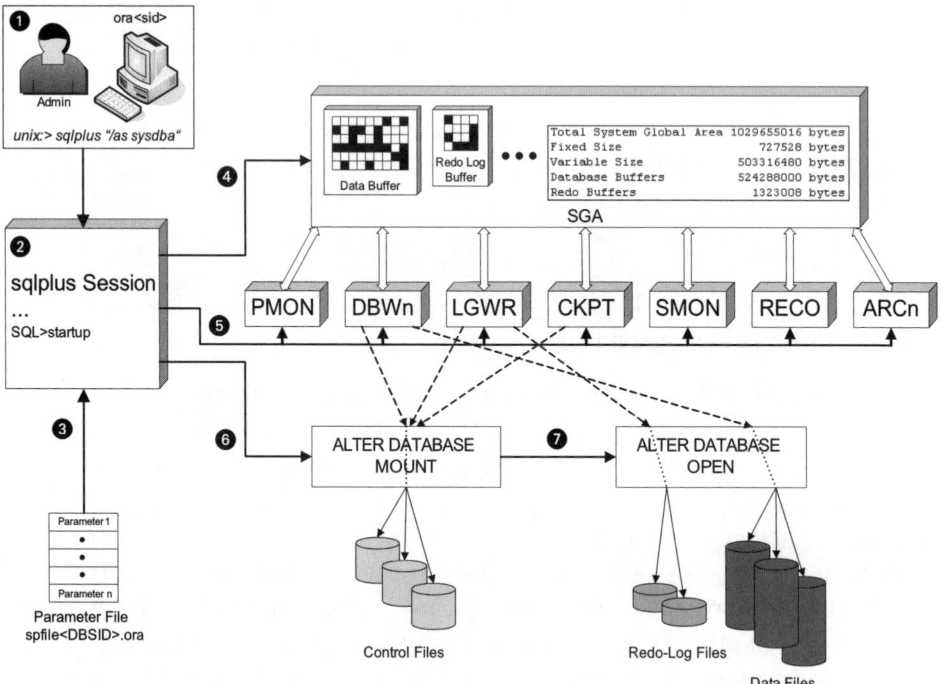

Figure 4.3 Start of an Oracle Database

The process is carried out in the following sequence:

❶ The UNIX user of the Oracle database (ora<sid>) starts an `sqlplus` session.

❷ In the `sqlplus` session, the `startup` command is used to initiate the start-up process for the database.

❸ The server parameter file (*spfile<DBSID>.ora*) is read to determine the database configuration.

❹ Then, the System Global Area (SGA) is created including all storage and buffer areas. This step can be identified by the output of corresponding size values in the `sqlplus` session.

❺ The Oracle background processes start. Figure 4.3 shows the sequence in which these processes are started. Then, the Oracle database is in the NOMOUNT status.

❻ Finally, the database is set into a usable state. In the first step, the `ALTER DATABASE MOUNT` command is used to set the database into the MOUNT state, that is, Oracle opens the control files and imports all the required information about the database. This process is also described in such a way that the Oracle instance is assigned a database, that is, the data files. Once the Oracle process `CKPT` is open, it exclusively locks all control files against write access. At that stage, the `DBWn` and `LGWR` processes also open the control files in read-only mode due to the lock mechanism.

❼ In the final step, the `ALTER DATABASE OPEN` command is used to change the status of the database to OPEN. For this purpose, the `DBWn` process (or processes respectively) opens all data files that belong to the database, while the `LGWR` process opens the Redo Log files. At that point, the `SMON` process can detect that a database hasn't been closed accurately, for instance because of a system crash, and can initiate an instance recovery process, if necessary. Thus, the database is brought into a consistent state via the Redo Log files. Once the OPEN status has been established, a corresponding message displays in the `sqlplus` session, and the database can be used.

Contrary to SAP processes, Oracle processes don't have a parent process. Figure 4.4 shows the Oracle background processes after the database startup (including the Listener but without an SAP system).

Because the sqlplus session, which starts the database processes, is stopped when the user logs off, it cannot act as a parent process. For this reason, a "trick" is used to make the processes orphans and to attach them to the central UNIX process, `init` (PID=1). The Listener process is also a child process of `init`.

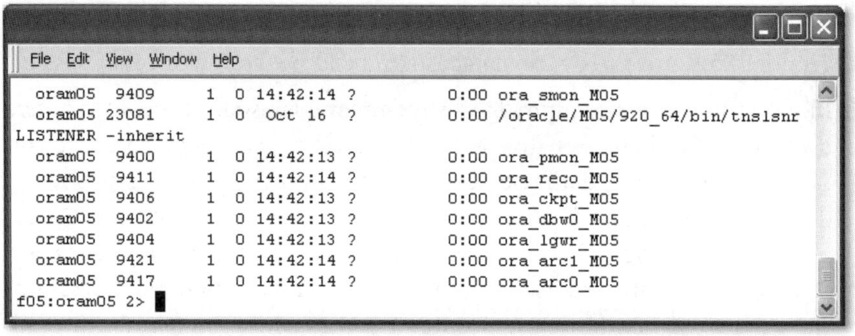

```
File  Edit  View  Window  Help
  oram05  9409     1  0 14:42:14 ?          0:00 ora_smon_M05
  oram05 23081     1  0  Oct 16  ?          0:00 /oracle/M05/920_64/bin/tnslsnr
LISTENER -inherit
  oram05  9400     1  0 14:42:13 ?          0:00 ora_pmon_M05
  oram05  9411     1  0 14:42:14 ?          0:00 ora_reco_M05
  oram05  9406     1  0 14:42:13 ?          0:00 ora_ckpt_M05
  oram05  9402     1  0 14:42:13 ?          0:00 ora_dbw0_M05
  oram05  9404     1  0 14:42:13 ?          0:00 ora_lgwr_M05
  oram05  9421     1  0 14:42:14 ?          0:00 ora_arc1_M05
  oram05  9417     1  0 14:42:14 ?          0:00 ora_arc0_M05
f05:oram05 2>
```

Figure 4.4 Oracle Background Processes after Database Startup (Oracle 9i)

Now that the Oracle database has been started, we'll demonstrate in a second step how the SAP instance connects to it. Figure 4.5 shows the process of establishing the connection and underlines the important role of the Oracle Listener during this process.

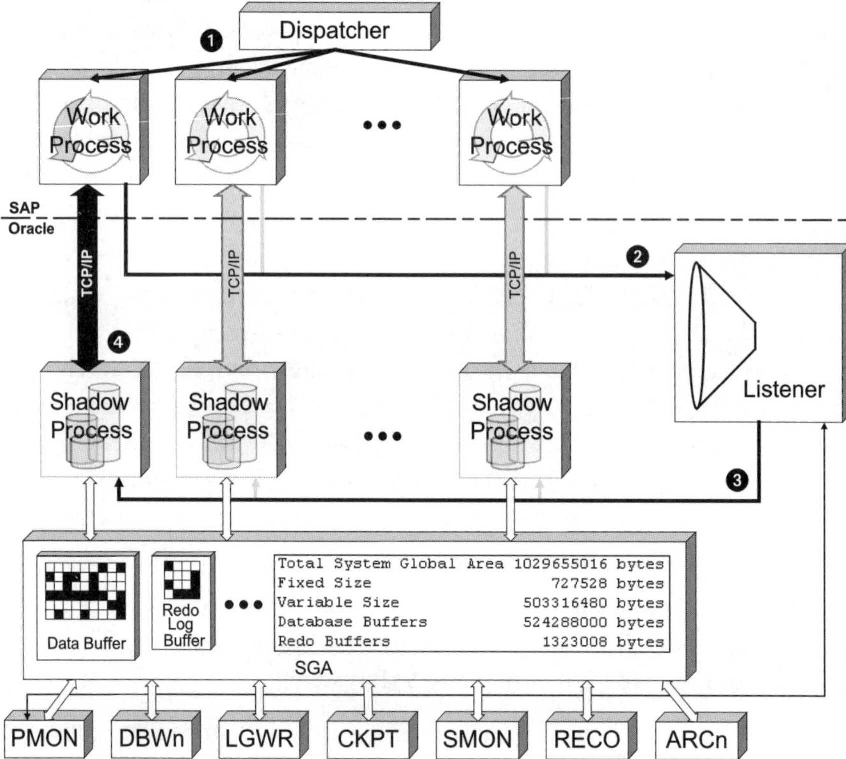

Figure 4.5 Establishing a Connection Between the SAP Instance and Oracle

The process is based on the following sequence:

❶ As described previously, the Dispatcher starts the SAP work processes.

❷ The first step of a work process always consists of establishing the connection to the database. For this purpose, the work process receives the connection data to the database server from the SAP DEFAULT profile (or rather, it inherits this data from the Dispatcher). After that, it starts the `db_connect()` function. Then, the work process connects to the Oracle Listener and authenticates itself in the database (you can find more details on the topic of authentication in Section 4.3, *Authentication Between SAP and Oracle*). Note: Only the work processes connect to the database, ***not*** the Dispatcher, the ICM, or any other process of an SAP instance.

❸ Once the connection has been established, the Listener starts an Oracle shadow process and passes the connection with the SAP work process on to the shadow process. Then the shadow process "becomes an orphan" and is attached to the central UNIX process, `init` (PID=1), like the background processes. The Listener is always connected to the `PMON` process from which it receives information on the database.

❹ Once the shadow process has started, the SAP work process completes the connection setup. From that point onward, the work process (that is, its database interface) and the shadow process are linked to each other via a TCP/IP connection. Then, the work process carries out additional internal startup steps, such as building up the memory and carrying out connection tests.

You can trace the establishment of the connection between the processes in detail in various log and trace files. For more information, please read Section 4.1.4, *Log and Trace Files*. This knowledge of the startup process between Oracle and SAP helps you to understand the following sections on the interaction between the two. We want to conclude this section by providing a list of the five most frequently occurring startup problems related to the interplay between SAP and the Oracle database, including a description of the possible causes and solutions. This list is based on our past experience:

- **Problems with the Oracle client**
  This problem can have many different causes. Actually, there are too many possibilities here to mention them all. The best point of entry for analyzing the cause of the problem is to call the following SAP command as a <sid>adm user:

  ```
  f05:m05adm 1>R3trans -d
  ```

This command initiates a test connection to the database, which works in exactly the same way as the connection setup between an SAP work process and Oracle. After that, you can find a file called trans.log in the home directory of <sid>adm. This file contains comprehensive trace information. The Oracle error codes in the file will definitely help you to find a solution in the SAP Notes. You can find basic information about related topics in Sections 4.2.2, *Oracle Client*, and 4.3.2, *Login Processes*.

- **Oracle Listener doesn't run**
  The Oracle Listener must be started manually before the SAP instance can log in to the Oracle database. However, the SAP start script shows that the Oracle Listener is missing so that this error cause is usually quickly detected.
- **Problems with Oracle parameters**
  You can configure almost every parameter in such a way that it prevents the database from starting. Consequently, the possible causes of errors are manifold in this context. Therefore, we can only provide two brief examples here: typos in the Oracle memory parameters (all of which are specified in terms of bytes) entail incorrect size values and may thus prevent the system startup. The paths to an important file or directory, such as the control files or the archive directory, are no longer correct because they have been moved. You can find detailed information on using Oracle parameters in Section 4.5.6, *Maintaining Oracle Parameters*.
- **Problems with the operating system**
  Basically, there are two primary causes for this type of startup problems: insufficient swap memory or incorrect parameters in the operating system kernel. The kernel parameters in particular can vary significantly, depending on the operating system (e.g., Shared Memory, Max Open Files, and so on) and must be set in accordance with the SAP recommendations (see SAP Notes). However, even then, there is still no guarantee that it works because the recommendations refer to "normal" systems. For example, in particularly large systems, you will usually have to adjust the operating system parameters as well. SAP Note 546006 contains a list of the most frequently occurring Oracle problems that are caused by operating system errors or incorrectly configured operating system parameters.
- **SAP database user**
  The password is incorrect or the user is locked. Let's look at an example from our own experience. It is not unusual that the operating system users are administered centrally in a server landscape, for instance, via NIS or

LDAP. If this central administration function fails, for example, because of a network problem, the SAP work processes cannot connect to the Oracle database, as the authentication based on the user name fails (see Section 4.3.2.2, *OPS$ Process*). Once the user administration is available again, the login process should also work. Note that a new type of behavior can be detected under Oracle 10g if you use it after a standard SAP installation process. The specific characteristic of this problem is that it only occurs from Oracle 10g onward as in this database, theFAILED_LOGIN_ATTEMPTS resource in the DEFAULT user profile is set to 10, which means that a user is automatically locked after 10 failed login attempts. In Oracle 9i, this resource was set to UNLIMITED. You can unlock and lock a user by using the following SQL command:

```
alter user <Oracle user> account [lock|unlock];
```

Section 4.3.1, *Database Users*, describes how you can change a user's password.

4.1.2 Relationships Between Processes

As described, SAP work processes establish a direct relationship with the Oracle shadow processes, but how can an administrator determine which work process belongs to which shadow process and vice versa? This question primarily arises when you search for performance problems, for instance, when you need to clarify which ABAP program causes a specific database lock or executes a complex SQL statement.

First, you must determine the process IDs of Oracle and SAP processes. The corresponding UNIX commands have already been described in Section 4.1.1, *System Startup*. In Windows, you use the Task Manager for this purpose. You can also determine the process IDs from within the SAP system. Regarding SAP work processes, you must use the process overview (Transaction SM50) to do that, whereas the Oracle shadow processes can be found in Transaction ST04N or by going to **Resource Consumption • Oracle Session Monitor** (**ORA proc** column, see Figure 4.6).

Also, the Oracle Session Monitor provides you with the first option to assign the processes of SAP and Oracle to each other. Figure 4.6 highlights the columns for the IDs of Oracle processes and client processes, that is, the SAP work processes, are highlighted.

Oracle Session Monitor

In...	Inst...	SID	ORA proc.	SAP Instanc...	Cl...	Clnt proc.	Status	Event	SQL text
1	A22	1	7734		f42	Shadow	ACTIVE	pmon timer	
1	A22	2	7736		f42	Shadow	ACTIVE	rdbms ipc message	
1	A22	3	7738		f42	Shadow	ACTIVE	rdbms ipc message	
1	A22	4	7740		f42	Shadow	ACTIVE	rdbms ipc message	
1	A22	5	7742		f42	Shadow	ACTIVE	smon timer	select from fet$ f, ts$ t where t.ts#=f.ts# and t.
1	A22	6	7744		f42	Shadow	ACTIVE	rdbms ipc message	select from pending_trans$ where session_
1	A22	7	7746		f42	Shadow	ACTIVE	rdbms ipc message	
1	A22	8	7748		f42	Shadow	ACTIVE	rdbms ipc message	
1	A22	9	7845	f42_A22_22	f42	7840	ACTIVE	SQL*Net message from...	SELECT FROM GV$SESSION T1, GV$PROC
1	A22	10	7848	f42_A22_22	f42	7841	INACTIVE	SQL*Net message from...	
1	A22	12	7850	f42_A22_22	f42	7842	INACTIVE	SQL*Net message from...	
1	A22	13	7854	f42_A22_22	f42	7843	INACTIVE	SQL*Net message from...	
1	A22	14	7857	f42_A22_22	f42	7846	INACTIVE	SQL*Net message from...	
1	A22	15	7861	f42_A22_22	f42	7851	INACTIVE	SQL*Net message from...	
1	A22	16	7870	f42_A22_22	f42	7858	INACTIVE	SQL*Net message from...	
1	A22	17	7864	f42_A22_22	f42	7852	INACTIVE	SQL*Net message from...	
1	A22	18	7867	f42_A22_22	f42	7855	INACTIVE	SQL*Net message from...	
1	A22	19	7873	f42_A22_22	f42	7860	INACTIVE	SQL*Net message from...	
1	A22	20	7879	f42_A22_22	f42	7865	INACTIVE	SQL*Net message from...	
1	A22	21	7876	f42_A22_22	f42	7862	INACTIVE	SQL*Net message from...	

Figure 4.6 Oracle Session Monitor

The Session Monitor provides additional useful information. For example, the **SQL text** column contains the SQL statement that's currently being executed by the respective Oracle process. Of course, that's the native SQL statement from Oracle, in other words, the Open SQL statement that has already been translated by the SAP database interface and that is therefore not included in the ABAP source code. The **SAP Instance** column indicates the instance that belongs to a specific process in systems that contain multiple instances. The **Client system** column next to it indicates the host of the SAP instance.

By right-clicking on a row in the Session Monitor, you can obtain other details related to a specific Oracle process, such as the PGA memory consumption, for example.

The Oracle V$ views queried in the Session Monitor can also be directly read by the administrator by means of an SQL command. The following command provides you with the most important details about Oracle processes and their clients:

```
SELECT a.SPID, b.PROCESS, b.PROGRAM, b.SCHEMANAME,    b.OSUSER
from V$PROCESS a, V$SESSION b
where a.ADDR = b.PADDR;
```

(SPID = PID of the Oracle process, PROCESS = PID of the SAP work process).

The assignment between the Oracle and SAP processes changes during system operation only if an SAP work process is terminated and restarted. This may happen if an internal error occurs or if the administrator terminates the process manually. The new connection with the database then generates a new shadow process as well because the old one was "done away with" by PMON after the previous connection terminated. However, in case of a short dump or if the type of operation of an SAP work process changes, the connection is kept.

4.1.3 Communication Between SAP Instances and Oracle Processes

The communication between Oracle and SAP is carried out only through the TCP/IP family of protocols, irrespective of whether the SAP instance is installed on the same host as the Oracle database. The option to establish a local communication via *inter process communication* (IPC) is not used in the default settings but can be activated (see SAP Note 562403). Regarding performance, the IPC provides some advantages in a local connection between Oracle and the SAP instance; however, these advantages are not often significant due to various reasons. On the one hand, the data volume is not very big, and on the other, the most important pieces of information that are frequently required by the SAP system are buffered on the individual instances (see Chapter 8, *Performance*).

The fact that the SAP instances are distributed across different hosts makes the network a critical infrastructure component for the entire system, particularly with regard to availability and performance. For security reasons, it is common practice to install the central components, that is, the Oracle database and the central SAP instance (including message server and enqueue process), on one host, which enables the communication to be carried out via the internal TCP/IP stack of the operating system and no longer through the physical network components. It is also possible to use a redundant network connection to the database for the distributed instances. In this type of connection, two network cards would be bundled into one virtual network card on both the database and the instance hosts, and the virtual network cards would be assigned the host ID. In that case, the physical network cards are connected to their counterparts via two independent networks.

To ensure and restore system availability, you can use an internal mechanism of the SAP work processes. If a work process loses the connection to the Oracle shadow process, it switches to the so-called *reconnect status*; that is, the process tries to reconnect via the Listener. This enables you to restart the database if an error occurs in one of the SAP instances. Note that this option should only be used in cases of emergency because it is not possible to work in the system for the entire period during which the database is not available. Moreover, this type of situation may entail some rework in the SAP system, such as unlocking locks or restarting update processes.

The greatest advantage of the reconnect mechanism is that the SAP buffers of the individual instances keep their established and synchronized state, as the synchronization of buffers in particular can take several hours in large SAP installations. SAP Note 98051 describes the functionality and setup of the DB Reconnect mechanism in greater detail.

Regarding performance, the network plays an important role as well, as the time required by the network directly affects the database response time. All implementation guides for SAP software contain the note that a 100-MBit network must be installed between the database and SAP instances. This is more than sufficient for connections within an overall SAP system; however, if multiple SAP systems and their database communicate over the network, for instance, in a server farm, a changeover to a gigabit network is recommended. This type of network is standard in modern data centers. Previously, the use of separate networks was recommended for communication between the database and SAP instances as well as between frontends and SAP instances. Even SAP made this recommendation. With the modern, high-performance networks that are available today, separation is no longer necessary.

However, even a modern, high-performing network will reach its limits if the data quantity to be transferred between the database and an SAP instance is increased unnecessarily. Usually, these volume increases are caused by problematic SQL statements that call an unnecessarily high number of data rows. Also, an incorrect buffering of tables in the SAP instances could represent another source of such a problem (see Chapter 8). As a reference value, you can say that the average quantity of data transferred per SQL query is 10 KB. The total number of user calls of the database (provided by Transaction ST04N) enables you to assess the network load during normal operation. Note, however, that peak loads, such as data loads in SAP NetWeaver BI, must be taken into account as well.

At this point, we want to mention another characteristic of the Oracle Listener: Because the Oracle Listener is only responsible for establishing the connection and is not involved in the communication process, you can stop or start it during live operation, for instance, to implement changes to the configuration. However, you shouldn't do that too often or for too long for several reasons. On the one hand, connection problems could then cause you trouble and require a reconnect, and on the other hand, other SAP tools, such as `R3trans` and `BRTOOLS`, also require the Listener for the initial connection to the database.

4.1.4 Log and Trace Files

Now we will again list all relevant log and trace files from Oracle and SAP and describe what kind of information they contain in order to document the interaction between Oracle and SAP. Table 4.3 provides a list of the most important files and a brief description of their purpose.

Name	Meaning
Listener Log	The log file of the Oracle Listener logs the setting up of connections by clients. Path: `/oracle/<DBSID>/<ora_release>/network/log/listener.log`
Listener Trace	Depending on the trace level, the trace file represents the operations of the Listener. Path: `/oracle/<DBSID>/<ora_release>/network/trace/listerner.trc`
Oracle Alert Log	This file contains the most important output information of the Oracle background processes (`PMON`, `SMON`, `ARCn`, etc.) as well as information about serious errors that occurred. Path: `/oracle/<DBSID>/saptrace/background/alert_<DBSID>.log`
Session Traces	These files contain detailed information about Oracle background and shadow processes in case of an error. Path: `/oracle/<DBSID>/saptrace/usertrace/<dbsid>_ora_<pid>.trc` or `/oracle/<DBSID>/<ora_release>/rdbms/log/<dbsid>_ora_<pid>.trc`
SAP Work Process Trace	Depending on the trace level, the trace files of the SAP work processes contain information about running operations. Path: `/usr/sap/<DBSID>/<InstanceName>/work/dev_w<WP_number>`
Oracle start and stop logs	These files log the operations of the `startdb` and `stopdb` scripts, which belong to the SAP kernel. Path: `/home/<sidadm>/startdb.log` and `/home/<sidadm>/stopdb.log`
SAP start and stop logs	These files log the operations of the `startsap` and `stopsap` scripts, which belong to the SAP kernel. Path: `/home/<sidadm>/startsap_<InstanceName>.log` and `/home/<sidadm>/stopsap_<InstanceName>.log`

Table 4.3 Important Log and Trace Files for Oracle and the SAP Instance

The `startsap`, `stopsap`, `startdb`, and `stopdb` scripts that belong to the SAP kernel each write a log file into the home directory of the <sid>adm user. These files log the individual steps of the scripts as well as the returns of the individual programs that are called. For example, the log file for the database start (*startdb.log*) contains information about how the environment variables are checked at the start or how the Listener functionality is tested via TNSPING.

The logs of the four scripts are primarily used to determine at which point during the startup or stop process a problem occurs, which may ultimately lead to a complete termination of the process. Based on a corresponding message, the administrator can the search for the cause of the problem in the right place, that is, in one of the log or trace files for the SAP system and the Oracle database described in a moment.

The start and stop scripts also generate a simple output on the console that contains status information about the individual steps. By setting the $TRACE environment variable, in the C-shell, for example, this output becomes much more detailed:

```
f05:m05adm 1>setenv TRACE TRUE
```

The sequence of the following descriptions of the other log files is oriented toward the sequence of processes during the system startup, as described in Section 4.1.1.

When the Listener starts up, the console already contains comprehensive information about

- Ports to which the Listener "listens "
- Protocols that are supported (TCP, IPC, etc.)
- Storage locations of log and trace files
- Terminal points, that is, databases to which the Listener can establish a connection (several are possible)

This information is also stored in a Listener log file. Details about the processing of the Listener configuration file, for example, can be found in the trace file.

The next step, the start of the Oracle database, involves the Oracle alert log. This file logs the details of the startup process. This includes the following data:

- License information
- All nondefault parameters
- Start information about the functionality of the archiver and the log writer
- Messages about an instance recovery that may be required or has been carried out already

All messages are grouped into the different startup phases of the database, which are marked by the following entries:

```
ALTER DATABASE [MOUNT|OPEN]
Completed: ALTER DATABASE [MOUNT|OPEN]
```

The most important messages are constantly written to the Oracle alert log during database operation. These messages include:

- Oracle errors that may occur (ORA-XXXXX)
- All log switches that have been carried out
- Backup operations of the BR*Tools

Consequently, this file is the first thing the administrator of the Oracle database needs to examine in case of an error.

If the SAP work processes connect to the database, this is logged in the Listener log. The corresponding entry looks as follows:

```
25-OCT-2006 21:34:47 * (CONNECT_DATA=(SID=M05) \ (GLOBAL_
NAME=M05.WORLD) (CID=(PROGRAM=disp+work@f05) \
 (HOST=f05)(USER=m05adm))) * (ADDRESS=(PROTOCOL=tcp) \
 (HOST=141.44.38.13)(PORT=49269)) * establish * M05 * 0
```

Such a log record contains information about who (USER) established a connection to the Oracle database when (time stamp) and from where (HOST), using which client program (PROGRAM) through which address and which port (HOST, PORT). The Listener log contains similar entries for other SAP kernel programs, such as `R3trans` or `tp`, but *not* for the BR*Tools.

During the operation of the Oracle database, you may have to log the details of specific processes that are carried out in the database. This can be done using the `ORADEBUG` tool that is integrated in sqlplus. The major options provided by `ORADEBUG` are as follows:

- Trace of an Oracle session (SQL execution plan, bind variables, wait events with times)

- Dump of different Oracle system areas:
  - System state dump
  - Process heaps and library caches
  - Control files, data files, and redo logs
  - Communication data (semaphores, shared memories, etc.)

You can only call the ORADEBUG tool as a sysdba user of the database:

```
f05:oram05 1>sqlplus "/as sysdba"
SQL> oradebug <options>
```

Depending on the options and trace level used, the trace files generated by ORADEBUG can become rather large; consequently, you should ensure that sufficient storage space is available in the respective directories (see Table 4.3). For more detailed information about using ORADEBUG, please refer to SAP Note 613872. The analysis of the comprehensive trace information is supported by the Oracle tool, TKPROF. Based on several different parameters, the program "translates" a trace file into a readable version. SAP Note 654176 contains more information and specific usage examples for this program.

We conclude this section by describing the trace files of the SAP work processes. Of course, system trace files are available for all other processes of an SAP instance as well, for the Dispatcher (dev_disp) or gateway (dev_rd), for example. All relevant output of the work processes during system operation is stored in those files, whereby the level of detail depends on the trace level you configure. The trace is controlled via the work process overview (Transaction SM50). The path is as follows: **Process • Trace • Active Components** (see Figure 4.7). Another option to activate or change the trace functions is to use the rdisp/TRACE =<trace level> and rdisp/TRACE_COMPS = <component> profile parameters.

The settings for specific work process types can be made separately (see Figure 4.7). You can even activate individual trace options for one or several work processes by checking the relevant checkboxes in the process monitor. Processes whose trace behavior has changed are highlighted in yellow in the process monitor. As is the case with the Oracle traces, the file size increases rapidly here, particularly with trace level 3. For this reason, you should activate the default trace level 1 again once the analysis has finished.

If you want to record a trace over a longer period of time, you can use the rdisp/TRACE_LOGGING=<options> profile parameter to configure trace files to be copied and reset once they reach a specific size.

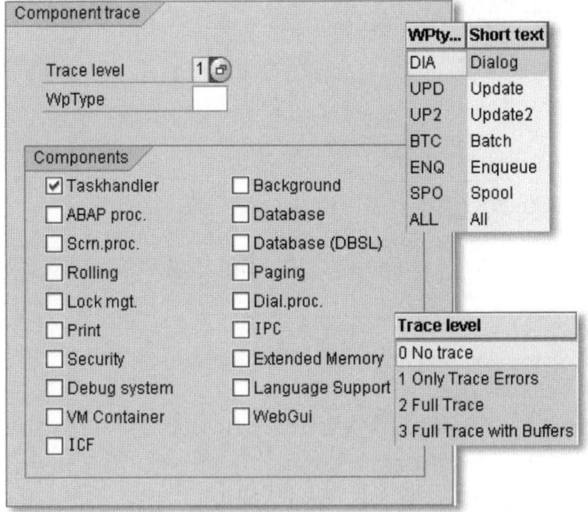

Figure 4.7 Trace Options of the SAP Work Processes

Another very useful option is that you can analyze individual components or aspects of a work process, such as the communication with the database, for example. Within the trace file, the first letter of each trace record indicates the source of the entry. Table 4.4 contains a list of letters used for the work processes.

Letter	Work Process Component/Function
M	Task Handler
A	ABAP process
Y	Dynpro procedure
R	Rolling
E	Lock management
S	Print
N	Security
H	ICF
J	VM container
T	Debug system
B	Database (DBSL)
C	Database
L	Background

Table 4.4 Indicators for SAP Work Process Components in the Trace File

Letter	Work Process Component/Function
P	Paging
D	Dialog procedure
I	IPC
X	Extended memory
G	Language support
W	Web GUI

Table 4.4 Indicators for SAP Work Process Components in the Trace File (Cont.)

Once the described startup process of an SAP instance has completed, the start section of each trace file must contain corresponding entries that begin with a C and document the establishment of a connection to the Oracle server. Figure 4.8 shows an excerpt of this type of entry.

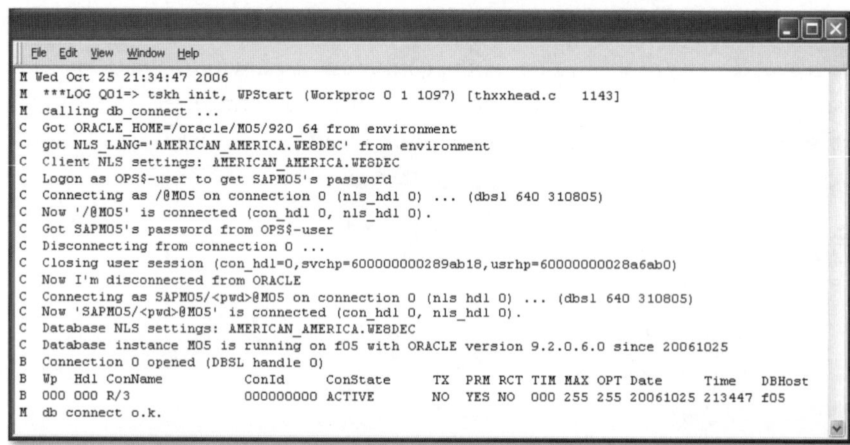


```
M Wed Oct 25 21:34:47 2006
M  ***LOG Q01=> tskh_init, WPStart (Workproc 0 1 1097) [thxxhead.c   1143]
M  calling db_connect ...
C  Got ORACLE_HOME=/oracle/M05/920_64 from environment
C  got NLS_LANG='AMERICAN_AMERICA.WE8DEC' from environment
C  Client NLS settings: AMERICAN_AMERICA.WE8DEC
C  Logon as OPS$-user to get SAPM05's password
C  Connecting as /@M05 on connection 0 (nls_hdl 0) ... (dbsl 640 310805)
C  Now '/@M05' is connected (con_hdl 0, nls_hdl 0).
C  Got SAPM05's password from OPS$-user
C  Disconnecting from connection 0 ...
C  Closing user session (con_hdl=0,svchp=600000000289ab18,usrhp=60000000028a6ab0)
C  Now I'm disconnected from ORACLE
C  Connecting as SAPM05/<pwd>@M05 on connection 0 (nls hdl 0) ... (dbsl 640 310805)
C  Now 'SAPM05/<pwd>@M05' is connected (con_hdl 0, nls_hdl 0).
C  Database NLS settings: AMERICAN_AMERICA.WE8DEC
C  Database instance M05 is running on f05 with ORACLE version 9.2.0.6.0 since 20061025
B  Connection 0 opened (DBSL handle 0)
B  Wp  Hdl ConName          ConId     ConState     TX  PRM RCT TIM MAX OPT Date     Time   DBHost
B  000 000 R/3              000000000 ACTIVE       NO  YES NO  000 255 255 20061025 213447 f05
M  db connect o.k.
```

Figure 4.8 Excerpt from an SAP Work Process Trace File (Connection to the Oracle Database)

Tracing the SAP processes enables you to analyze the operations in the kernel of the system or instance in great detail. Moreover, in case of an error that affects the SAP Basis or the communication, the trace files usually contain the decisive information needed to solve the problem. SAP Note 112 ("Fire Brigade Note") contains valuable information about getting started with the trace file analysis.

The start and stop log files of the SAP scripts are newly generated for each start or stop. The corresponding predecessor files are deleted in this context. During a restart of the database, all Oracle log files and Oracle trace files are either preserved (such as the session traces) or continue to be used (such as the Listener log file and trace file and the Oracle alert log). If you restart the SAP instance, the trace files of the SAP work processes are assigned the ending *old*, whereby all previous *old* files are deleted during the restart process.

4.1.5 System Stop

Prior to stopping an SAP system, you should check the following items:

- Check the status of updates using Transaction SM13.
- Check which users are still logged on to the system using Transaction SM04 (if necessary, send a system message using Transaction SM02).
- Check if background jobs are scheduled or still running using Transaction SM37.

If an SAP system has multiple instances, you must stop all dialog instances before you stop the central instance.

We will now describe the system stop process, which is similar to starting up an SAP system with an Oracle database. The process is illustrated in Figure 4.9 and is described step by step in this section (like the example in Section 4.1.1, the example used here also has the central instance and database instance installed on one host).

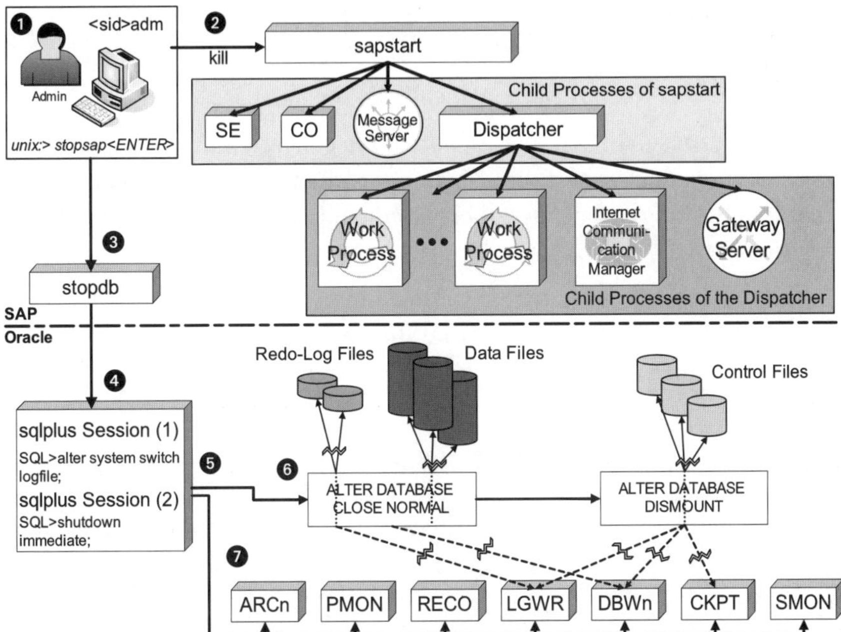

Figure 4.9 Process of Stopping an SAP System with an Oracle Database

As is the case with the system startup, there are differences if the central instance and the Oracle database don't run on the same server, or if another instance, such as a dialog instance, is stopped separately. Here, too, no automatic function is available to stop the database. Moreover, the Oracle database cannot be stopped remotely via the SAP start scripts. For this reason, the database must be stopped "manually," that is, on the database host, after the SAP central instance has been stopped. All other stop phases of an SAP instance are identical to those described next.

The process of stopping an SAP system occurs as follows:

❶ The `stopsap` script is called as the <sid>adm user.

❷ First the script stops the `SAPSTART` process. To do that, it calls the following command:

```
kill -2 <sapstartPID>
```

This command is stored in the kill.sap file, which is located in the following directory after the instance has been started:

/usr/sap/<SID>/<InstanceName>/work/kill.sap

Because all SAP processes are child processes of `sapstart`, these processes are stopped as well. The `-2` option ensures a "soft shutdown"; that is, it ensures that the SAP processes are stopped in a controlled manner. Of course, when the SAP work processes are stopped, the associated Oracle shadow processes stop as well.

❸ Then, the `stopdb` script starts, which halts the database.

❹ For this purpose, an SQL file (*stopdb.sql*) is generated in the home directory of the <sid>adm user. This file contains all Oracle commands required to stop the database; these commands are executed in the following two `sqlplus` sessions.

❺ In the first session, a log switch is forced in order to be able to archive all relevant changes that originate from the SAP system. (In the process, the last active online redo log is written to the archive directory.)

❻ In the second session, the database is shut down using the `shutdown immediate` command. First, this initiates the `ALTER DATABASE CLOSE NORMAL` process, which closes the online redo logs and data files. That process is followed by a `ALTERvDATABASEvDISMOUNT` process, which closes the control files and thus terminates all connections that exist between the processes and files.

❼ The last step stops the Oracle background processes. This sequence corresponds to the sequence illustrated in Figure 4.9. Finally, the `sqlplus` session stops.

The individual phases of stopping an SAP system with an Oracle database can be identified in detail in the corresponding trace files (see Tables 4.3 and 4.4).

You can also stop the SAP system or single instances from within the system using the CCMS Control Panel from **SAP Menu • Tools • CCMS • Control Panel**.

Notes

The SAP OS Collector is not stopped by the `stopsap` script. If necessary, the administrator must stop it manually. To do that, the <sid>adm user must enter the following command:

```
f05:m05adm 1>saposcol -k
```

The Oracle Listener isn't stopped either.

4.2 Requirements at the Operating System Level

To enable proper interaction between the SAP instance and the Oracle database, several requirements must be met. In this section we'll describe the requirements that must be met at the level of the operating system. These descriptions focus on UNIX-based environments. The requirements are related to the following three areas:

1. Users, groups, and environment variables
2. Oracle client
3. SAP kernel

Let us first take a look at some general considerations regarding the operating system requirements.

SAP supports the installation of SAP software with the different versions of Oracle databases on different combinations of hardware and operating systems. For further details on this topic, please visit the following page in the SAP Service Marketplace: *http://service.sap.com/pam*.

Because of this large number of variants, it is all the more important for you to know the specifics of your own system. The following aspects should help you in this respect:

- **Operating system kernel**
  For each operating system, the SAP Notes contain recommendations and guidelines regarding the configuration of the operating system kernel parameters (just search for "kernel parameters <name_of_operating_system>"). However, these parameters do not only affect the SAP instance; there are also specific settings to be made for operating an Oracle database. If problems occur or if you use a particular installation variant (multiple SAP systems on one host, for example), contact SAP or your hardware or operating system partner.
- **Version of the operating system or important components**
  SAP also provides notes regarding the extent to which the different versions of operating systems are supported and which of these versions have been released. In this context, you must pay particular attention to Linux because — due to the open source-driven development — significant changes may "sneak" into subversions of the kernel and glibc. Therefore, only specific combinations of the kernel and glibc versions of the two major Linux enterprise distributions from SUSE and Red Hat are supported by SAP.
- **Operating system patches**
  Usually you must not only use a specific operating system version, but also install specific patches or corrections for that version.
- **OS-level application software**
  In addition to the actual operating system, other software components are also required for the installation of an SAP system. Let's look at two examples here: You need the saplocales package for the SAP system code pages on Linux, and you need the different Java versions, which are required for the use of SAPinst and for using a J2EE server.

You can find the necessary information about these aspects for your specific platform in the SAP Notes as well as in the respective installation guides for SAP systems.

The second aspect of our general considerations involves the directory structures in which the installations of an SAP system and an Oracle database are located. Figure 4.10 shows the directories of an SAP system (without Java stack), which consists of a central instance (**C11**) and a dialog instance (**D01**), on a UNIX operating system. Table 4.5 lists the most important directories (indicated by a bold frame in the figure) and their meanings.

Because you can install the SAP instances separately from the Oracle database, the directories are also separated from each other. This also holds true if they are installed on the same host. SAP provides an installer tool for the installation of the Oracle database in the context of an SAP installation. This installer defines the directory structure, as shown in Figure 4.11. However, some of the structures, such as the location of the data files, can be changed by the administrator during the installation process.

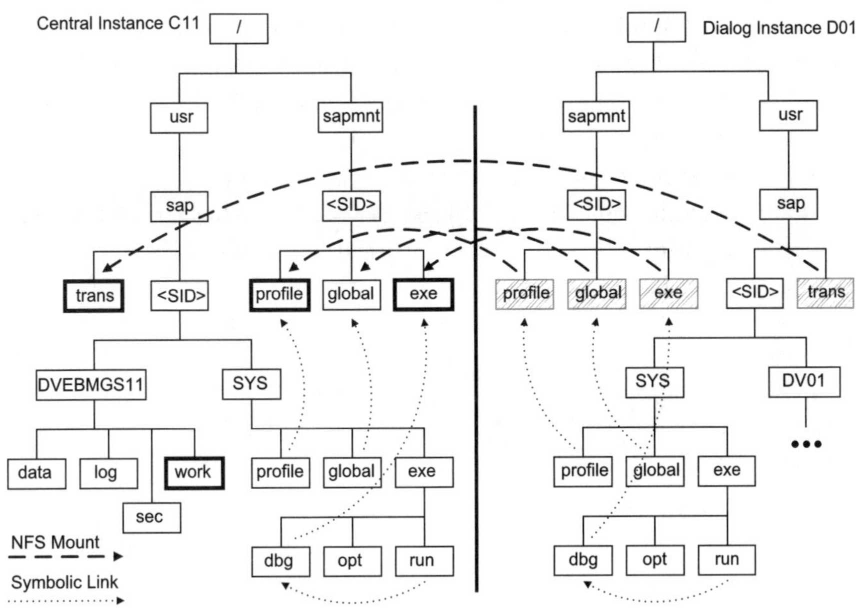

Figure 4.10 Directory Structure of an SAP System on UNIX (SAP Basis 6.40)

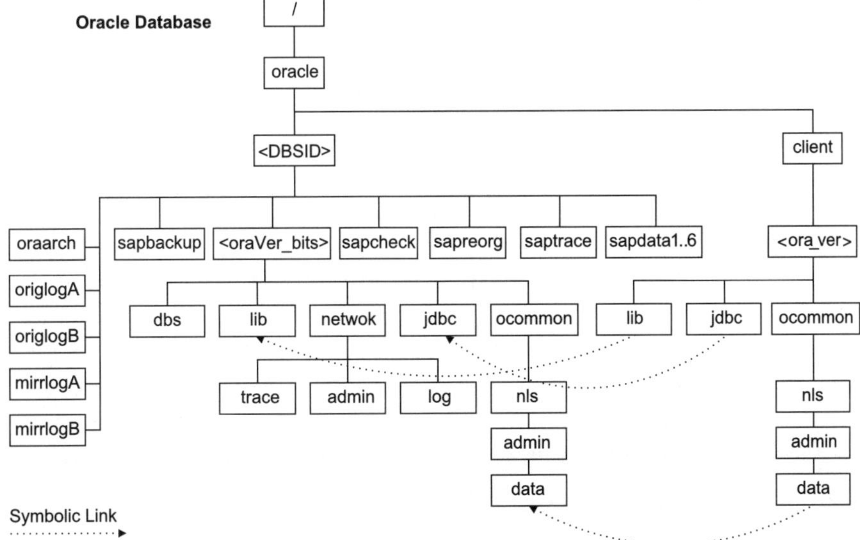

Figure 4.11 Directory Structure of an Oracle Database under SAP

Figure 4.11 shows an Oracle database Version 9i. The client directory is linked (as shown in the figure) only if the client is installed on the same server as the Oracle database. Again, there are significant differences concerning the client if you use Oracle 10g. You can find more details on the Oracle client in Section 4.2.2, *Oracle Client*. Furthermore, Figure 4.11 does not show all subdirectories of `$ORACLE_HOME` (see Section 4.2.1, *Users, Groups, and Environment Variables (UNIX)*), but only those that are most relevant to the reader. Table 4.5 provides an overview of the most important directories for the Oracle database and the SAP system.

Directory	Meaning
/sapmnt/<SID>/profile	Directory for all SAP profiles
/sapmnt/<SID>/exe	Kernel files of the SAP instance
/sapmnt/<SID>/work	Work directory of the SAP kernel processes and storage location for the traces
/usr/sap/trans	Directory for transport management
oraarch	Directory for offline redo log files, which are generated by the archiver
origlogA|B and mirrlogA|B	Directories for the Oracle redo log files, divided into four redo log groups with two files each
sapbackup	Log and trace files of `BRARCHIVE` and `BRBACKUP` (see Chapter 10, *Backup, Restore, and Recovery*)
sapcheck	Log files of the different actions from the DBA scheduling calendar, Transaction DB13 (e.g., Adapt Next Extents or Database Check)
sapreorg	Work directory for reorganizations and log directory for specific `BRSPACE` operations
saptrace	Traces of the Oracle background processes and specific Oracle user sessions
sapdata1...6	Data files of tablespaces
<oraVer_bits>	Main directory for the installation of the Oracle DBMS (`$ORACLE_HOME`)
dbs	Parameter files for the Oracle database (see Section 4.5.1, *Development and Content*)
network	Main directory for the Oracle Listener (see Chapter 3, *Oracle Fundamentals*)
client	Directory for the Oracle client (see Section 4.2.2)

Table 4.5 Important Directories for the SAP System and the Oracle Database

Note

The acronym SID exists both in SAP systems (SAP system ID) and in Oracle systems (Oracle system ID). From now on, we will use SID to refer to the SAP SID, whereas we'll use DBSID to describe the Oracle SID. The simple convention SID = DBSID is often used, as that's also proposed by default in a standard installation. This method makes sense, simply for reasons of clarity; however, it is not *mandatory*, that is, you can also choose the DBSID independently of the SID.

A different DBSID would be conceivable in MCOD (Multiple Components in One Database) (systems, for example, as those systems contain only one DBSID but many SIDs. The use of a different SID and DBSID is primarily reflected in the file names and directory paths. For this reason, you should be aware of the difference between the SID and DBSID.

4.2.1 Users, Groups, and Environment Variables (UNIX)

This section examines the users and groups at the level of the operating system, which are required to operate an SAP system on an Oracle database.

First, you need the <sid>adm user as the operating system user of the SAP system. This user is created during the installation if it doesn't exist yet. The user has write access to all directories of the SAP system (see Figure 4.10), and all SAP processes run under its name or ID.

Warning

The background processes of the Oracle database run under <sid>adm as well if the database is started using the SAP start script. The operating system user is the same for all instances of an SAP system even if these instances are distributed across several machines.

The same holds true for the operating system user of the Oracle database, ora<sid>, which must also be made known to all machines that run an SAP instance. Due to the distribution of users across different machines, it makes sense to implement a central user management for the operating system users, particularly in larger SAP landscapes. Another aspect involves the uniqueness of operating system users within an SAP transport domain, as this type of domain allows users to access the transport directory (usually */usr/sap/trans*) from different systems. There are different modern solutions on LDAP basis available for this kind of task, such as Microsoft Active Directory or Netscape iPlanet, but you can even use `nis` or `nis+`. Note, however, that the latter two are outdated and insecure.

The Oracle user has write permission for all directories below `$SAPDATA_HOME` (usually */oracle/<DBSID>*; see Table 4.7). Moreover, the Oracle Listener and all Oracle shadow processes connected to the SAP work processes run under the Oracle user, as these are started by that user. The user ID behind the user names can be freely chosen for both ora<sid> and sid<adm>.

In addition to the users, the UNIX groups play a major role in the interaction between the SAP system and the Oracle database. These groups include the following: sapsys, oper, dba, and — since SAP Basis 7.00 (SAP NetWeaver 7.0) — sapinst. Table 4.6 shows which users are assigned to which group.

User	Primary Group	Secondary Group	Home Directory
<sid>adm	sapsys	oper, dba, sapinst	*/home/<sid>adm*
ora<sid>	dba	oper, sapinst	*/oracle/<DBSID>*

Table 4.6 Operating System Users and Their Groups

These groups and the assignment of the users are important for the following reasons:

- **sapsys**
  This primary group of the SAP user must be identical within the SAP transport domain because it controls the shared write permission in the transport directory.
- **dba**
  The primary group of ora<sid> is also the owner of the */oracle/<DBSID>* directory. Therefore, <sid>adm must be a member of this group to enable the Oracle background processes to write data into the Oracle directories, such as sapdata or origlog and mirrlog.
- **oper**
  This group controls or enables the SYSOPER login in the Oracle database; consequently, the <sid>adm and ora<sid> users must be members of this group (see Section 4.3).

The groups are also created during the installation process if they don't exist yet; the group ID can be freely chosen as long as it is unique.

Thus, the users and groups control permissions and access mechanisms in the interaction between an SAP system and an Oracle database as well as between different SAP systems and a transport domain. The second important aspect in this context deals with the environment variables of the operating system users, <sid>adm and ora<sid>.

The environment variables depend on many different factors, so no universally valid overview is available. The two primary factors are the version of the Oracle database and the release of the SAP kernel. The overview in Table 4.7 contains brief descriptions of the most commonly used ones. The default values that are configured during a standard installation are provided in parentheses.

Environment Variable	Description
ORACLE_BASE	Path to the Oracle Inventory (*/oracle*)
ORACLE_HOME	Path to the Oracle software (*/oracle/<DBSID>/<oraVer_bits>*)
ORACLE_SID	Name of the Oracle instance (<DBSID>)
SAPDATA_HOME	Main directory of the SAP-specific Oracle directories such as saptrace, sapdata, and so on (*/oracle/<DBSID>*)
SAPSYSTEMNAME	SAP system ID (<SID>)
dbs_ora_schema	Database schema for the SAP system (see Section 4.4.1)

Table 4.7 Environment Variables

The variables described in Table 4.7 are valid for both the <sid>adm and the ora<sid> users. In addition, various other variables are either set for only one of the two operating system users or differently for both of them. You will get to know some of those environment variables in Sections 4.2.2 and 4.3.

Another aspect of user environments involves the login shells used and thus the configuration files. Basically, SAP recommends using the C-shells and the Bourne shell and provides the necessary configuration files for these. You can tell to which shell a file belongs by its ending: *.csh* (C-shell) and *.sh* (Bourne shell). The following files are located in the home directories of the SAP and Oracle users:

- **.profile, .login, .cshrc**
  These are configuration files for the respective shells: C-shell (.cshrc, .login) and Bourne shell (.profile). The most important content of these files consists of instructions for loading the following configuration files for the environment variables.
- **.dbenv_<hostname>.[sh|csh]**
  Here you can find all variables related to the database, such as all variables contained in Table 4.7, with the exception of SAPSYSTEMNAME.
- **.sapenv_<hostname>.[sh|csh]**
  In this file, all other environment variables are set or customized, which are needed by the SAP user or Oracle user, such as SAPSYSTEMNAME or — depending on the operating system — the path to the libraries.

For various SAP systems, such as SAP NetWeaver Exchange Infrastructure (XI) or SAP Supply Chain Management (SCM), other configuration files are available for specific environment variables. The variables that are valid for both <sid>adm and <ora>sid must be maintained "synchronously" in the respective files if you make adjustments.

Please refer to SAP Note 602843 for further information on environment variables and configuration files in the context of SAP with Oracle databases, for instance, regarding release dependencies.

4.2.2 Oracle Client

The Oracle client software will certainly keep any administrator of SAP systems on Oracle databases busy. Unfortunately, many aspects related to the Oracle client and its usage with the different SAP kernel releases have often been changed in the past. Therefore, we want to focus on the current clients, Oracle 9i and 10g, in the following sections.

What exactly is an Oracle client, and how is it used by the SAP kernel? The Oracle client implements the Oracle Call Interface (OCI), that is, it provides libraries, which are loaded into applications to access the Oracle database. The OCI is an Oracle-specific (proprietary) API that enables access to Oracle databases and is available for the programming languages C (OCI), C++ (OCCI), and Java (JDBC-OCI). SAP uses this interface for accessing the database in such a way that the SAP kernel loads the Oracle client. Figure 4.12 illustrates the relationship between the SAP kernel and the Oracle client. The implementation of this link (static versus dynamic linking) depends on the SAP kernel release being used. All kernels from Release 6.10 on use the dynamic linking method, as shown in Figure 4.12.

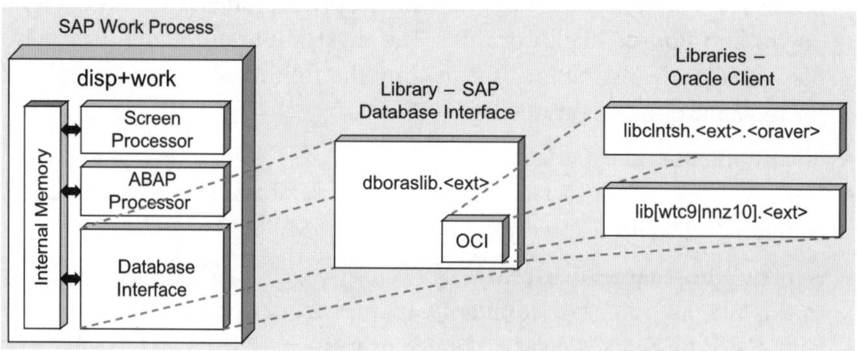

Figure 4.12 Relationship Between SAP Work Process and Oracle Client

The SAP database interface is implemented in a library (*dboraslib.<ext>*) that's separated from the SAP work process executable (Disp+Work) and loaded dynamically at runtime at the first database function call. The library, in turn, has dynamically established links to the corresponding libraries of the Oracle client. Depending on the releases status, these are the following:

- For Oracle Client 9i: libclntsh.<ext>.9.0 (Oracle client) and libwtc9.<ext> from the directory */oracle/client/92x_64/lib*
- For Oracle Instant Client 10g: libclntsh.<ext>.10.0 (Oracle client) and libnnz10.<ext> from the directory */oracle/client/10x_64/instantclient*

The criterion the decides which Oracle client must be used is the version of the SAP kernel. Only one rule must be adhered to regarding the interaction between the Oracle client and the Oracle database: The version of the client must be smaller or identical to the version of the database. From this point onward, we will differentiate between Oracle Client 9i and Oracle Instant Client (10g).

4.2.2.1 Oracle Client 9i

Oracle Client 9i, or to be more exact, 9.2.0, is used for the following SAP kernel releases:

- Release 6.20 UNICODE
- Release 6.40
- All 64-bit kernels up to and including Version 6.40

All earlier kernel releases use Client 8.1.7 or older. Figure 4.13 shows the structure of an installed Oracle Client 9i on an application server.

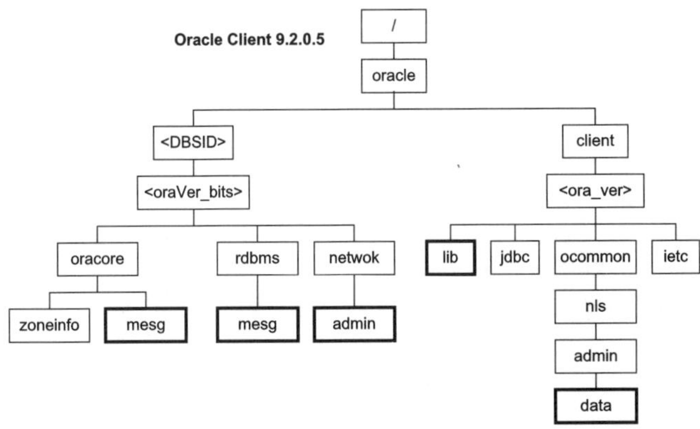

Figure 4.13 Structure of Oracle Client 9.2.0.5

Table 4.8 provides information about the meaning and contents of the major directories of the client (these are depicted with a bolded frame in Figure 4.13).

Directory	Description/Content
../lib	This directory stores the libraries, *libclntsh.<ext>.9.0* etc.
../data	This directory contains the file for the National Language Support (NLS) (see the following text on NLS).
../mesg	Files are stored here that contain the texts for all Oracle error codes.
../admin	This directory stores the configuration files for the Oracle Net Services (such as listener.ora and tnsnames.ora). The services are needed so that the client and hence the SAP kernel knows the required data for connecting to the database.

Table 4.8 Important Directories of Oracle Client 9i and their Contents

Now, we want to address a special case that occurs rather often. If an Oracle 9i database is installed on a server, and a client is installed there as well, all important subdirectories of */oracle/client* are only linked. Figure 4.11 shows this situation.

A critical and sometimes even tricky feature of Oracle Client 9i is its *NLS files*. Basically, the files contain the *Oracle character sets* (code pages) for the conversion of characters. These character sets allow the Oracle database to support different languages and different ways of formatting — of dates, for example. However, in the SAP environment, these features are not used because the SAP system has its own code page administration. Therefore, to be able to use an SAP system on an Oracle database, it is essential that data that is written to or read from the database must not be converted. This can be achieved by synchronizing the NLS environment of the database and client. This synchronicity is checked during the system startup process, which immediately terminates if an error exists.

In a non-Unicode environment, the eight-bit character set WE8DEC is used for all Oracle databases with Release 8 or higher. You can check this setting by using the following SQL command:

```
select VALUE from V$NLS_PARAMETERS
where PARAMETER='NLS_CHARACTERSET';
```

In Unicode environments, the UTF8 character set is used exclusively. The code page of the Oracle client is set through environment variable `NLS_LANG`.

For non-Unicode systems, its value must be AMERICAN_AMERICA.WE8DEC, whereas the value for Unicode systems must be AMERICAN_AMERICA.UTF8. This variable must be set for both the SAP user, <sid>adm, and the Oracle user, ora<sid>.

The second environment variable for NLS is ORA_NLS33. This variable defines the location at which the Oracle client can find the code page files and must be set to the following values for <sid>adm and ora<sid> in the file for the environment variables (.dbenv_<hostname>.[sh|csh]):

- **<sid>adm**

  ```
  ORA_NLS33=/oracle/client/<oraVer_bits>/ocommon/nls/admin/data
  ```

- **ora<sid>**

  ```
  ORA_NLS33=$ORACLE_HOME/ocommon/nls/admin/data
  ```

The exception to this is that if only the database is installed on the host, ORA_NLS33 for <sid>adm is set to the same path as for ora<sid>.

It is very important that you set the NLS variable accurately to ensure a smooth interplay between the SAP instance and the Oracle database, as otherwise several errors would occur, the causes of which are hard to trace. For more information on this topic, please refer to SAP Notes 393620 and 592657.

Finally, the following question arises: How can the SAP kernel find the Oracle client? Well, it can easily find the client because the path is hard-coded in the *dboraslib.<ext>* library. All SAP kernels from Version 6.x onward load Oracle Client 8.1 or 9i (depending on the SAP kernel version) from the fixed path, */oracle/client/ [81x|92x]_<bits>/lib*. If this path doesn't exist, the system uses the operating system-specific environment variable for the library path (see Section 4.2.3, *SAP Kernel*) and searches for the Oracle client in the directories specified in that variable. In a normal situation, that is, in a standard installation, the Oracle client is not located in any of those directories, which is why we won't go into further detail about the search path at this point.

4.2.2.2 Oracle Instant Client (10g)

The Oracle Database 10g was introduced along with a new Oracle client. This client is referred to as the Oracle Instant Client, as it consists of only a few files and can be installed very easily. The structure of the new client is much less complex; the only directory it contains is */oracle/client/ 10x_<bits>/instantclient_<ver>* including the files contained in that directory. The most important of these files are as follows:

- libclnstsh.so.10.1: client code library
- libociei.so: OCI Instant Client Data Shared library
- libnnz10.so: security library
- libocijdbc10.so: Instant Client JDBC library
- classes12.jar and ojdbc14.jar: Oracle-JDBC drivers

The relationship between the Oracle client and an SAP J2EE instance is described in greater detail in Chapter 11, *Administrating the Java Stack*.

SAP uses the Oracle Instant Client in the following releases:

- All SAP systems with Kernel 7.00 or higher
- Whenever the BR*Tools 7.00 must be used; for example, after upgrading the database to 10g (the SAP system can continue to use an older kernel release with Oracle Client 9i)

The Oracle Instant Client is always installed in the following directory: */oracle/client/10x_<bits>/instantclient_<ver>*. After the installation, a symbolic link (*instantclient*) is set, which references the client that is currently to be used. In contrast to Oracle Client 9i, it is no longer relevant whether the Oracle Instant Client is installed on a host with database instance. Because the Oracle Instant Client no longer depends on the `$ORACLE_HOME` variable, it doesn't need to be adjusted.

Of course, this affects the environments of the <sid>adm and ora<sid> to some extent. For example, the NLS file no longer plays any role, which makes the `ORA_NLS33` variable redundant. However, you still need to set the character set to be used. In an SAP-Unicode system, `NLS_LANG` must always be set to `AMERICAN_AMERICA.UTF8`.

Because of the independence of $ORACLE_HOME, some important information is not available to the SAP user, <sid>adm, namely, the data for connecting to the Oracle Net Services from the directory */$ORACLE_HOME/ network/admin* (see Figure 4.13 and Table 4.8). For this reason, a new subdirectory exists in the directory tree of the SAP kernel: */sapmnt/<SID>/ profile/oracle*. This subdirectory contains the configuration files of the Oracle Net Services, *sqlnet.ora* and *tnsnames.ora*, to enable the Oracle client to connect to the database. You must make this directory known to the SAP user, <sid>adm, by means of an environment variable (`TNS_ADMIN=/usr/sap/<SID>/SYS/profile/oracle`).

The difference from SAP kernel releases lower than 7.00 is that the path is no longer hard-coded to a fixed position; instead, the libraries are searched for in different locations and in the following sequence:

1. */oracle/client/10x_<bits>/instantclient*
2. */oracle/client/10x_<bits>/lib*
3. */oracle/db_sw/10x_<bits>/instantclient*
4. /oracle/db_sw/10x_<bits>/lib

You can find a compatibility matrix for the support of different combinations of Oracle databases and Oracle clients in the Oracle Metalink Directory, Note 207303.1 (*https://metalink.oracle.com/*; the user name and password are provided in SAP Note 758563).

4.2.3 SAP Kernel

If you download a completely new SAP kernel from the SAP Service Marketplace, the download always contains two archives. The first archive, which is significantly bigger than the other one, contains the part of the kernel that is independent of the database you use. The name of the archive complies with the following notation method: SAPEXE_<patch_level>-<HW/OS-Code>.SAR. In contrast to the database independence, the files contained in that archive have nevertheless been compiled for a specific combination of hardware and operating system that's supported by SAP. These include:

- All executables of SAP processes, such as work processes (`disp+work`), gateway process (`gwrd`), and Message Server (`msg_server`)
- SAP libraries for the executables
- Start and stop scripts for the SAP system or SAP instance
- Tools for transport management (CTM): `R3trans`, `tp`, etc.

The second archive contains the files that belong to the specific database being used. The name of the archive is based on the following notation: SAPEXEDB_<patch_level>-<HW/OS-Code>.SAR. This archive contains the following files, among others:

- SAP database library db<DB>slib.<ext>
- Start and stop scripts for the database
- SAP tools for importing and exporting the database (`R3ldctl`, `R3load`, `R3szchk`)

SAP provides a third archive specifically for the Oracle database; this archive contains the BR*Tools. In terms of functionality, this archive does not belong to the SAP kernel, but because the tools are also located in the kernel directory, it makes sense to mention it here. The files, which are also referred to as DBA tools, are located in an archive whose name is based on the following notation: DBATL<KernelVer>O<OraVer>_<patch_level>-<HW/OS-Code>.SAR. The BR*Tools are described in greater detail in Section 4.5, *Administrating Oracle with the BR*Tools*.

How does the interaction between the executables of the SAP work processes and the SAP database library work? Section 4.2.2 already described this briefly. Figure 4.14 shows the entire context and the process during the startup phase in greater detail.

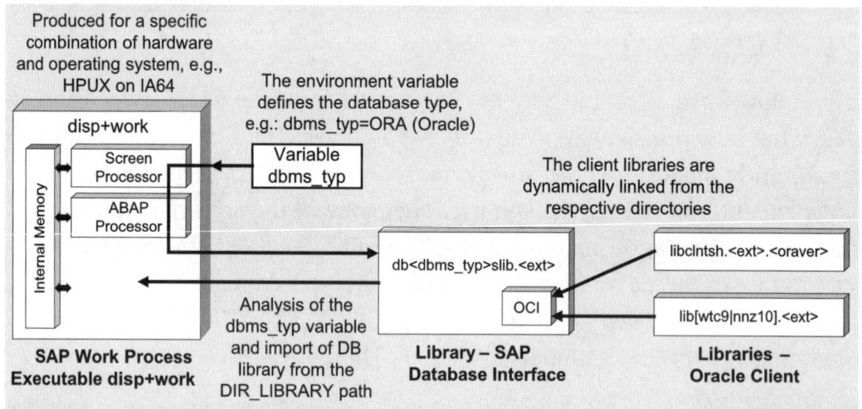

Figure 4.14 Loading the Database Library into the Work Process in a System with an Oracle Database

As shown in the figure, the environment variable, `dbms_type`, decides which database should be loaded. The work process can identify the exact location of the database by means of the `DIR_LIBRARY` variable, which usually references the */usr/sap/<SID>/SYS/exe/run* directory. Whether additional database-dependent libraries are "hidden" behind the database library, as in the case of Oracle, depends on the database platform you use. For example, Informix involves the use of a client (IConnect), whereas an SAP database (MaxDB) doesn't need any.

To show the dependencies between the executables and the different libraries, you can use the UNIX operating system command `ldd`, which stands for *List Dynamic Dependencies*. This command enables you to view all libraries, which are integrated in an executable or another library at runtime. If one of these dependencies cannot be resolved, the system displays an error message. Figure 4.15 shows the dependencies of the SAP database library for Oracle on HP-UX.

The location at which the libraries to be integrated are searched for in the file system depends entirely on the programming. You can specify the different library directories by using a specific environment variable.

```
File  Edit  View  Window  Help
f03:s10adm 4> ldd dboraslib.so
        libnsl.so.1 =>  /usr/lib/hpux64/libnsl.so.1
        libpthread.so.1 =>      /usr/lib/hpux64/libpthread.so.1
        libsapu16.so => /usr/sap/S10/SYS/exe/run/libsapu16.so
        libclntsh.so.10.1 =>    /oracle/client/10x_64/instantclient/libclntsh.so.10.1
        libnnz10.so =>  /oracle/client/10x_64/instantclient/libnnz10.so
        libc.so.1 =>    /usr/lib/hpux64/libc.so.1
        libxti.so.1 =>  /usr/lib/hpux64/libxti.so.1
        libm.so.1 =>    /usr/lib/hpux64/libm.so.1
        libc.so.1 =>    /usr/lib/hpux64/libc.so.1
        libnnz10.so =>  /oracle/client/10x_64/instantclient/libnnz10.so
        librt.so.1 =>   /usr/lib/hpux64/librt.so.1
        libnss_dns.so.1 =>      /usr/lib/hpux64/libnss_dns.so.1
        libdl.so.1 =>   /usr/lib/hpux64/libdl.so.1
        libm.so.1 =>    /usr/lib/hpux64/libm.so.1
        libpthread.so.1 =>      /usr/lib/hpux64/libpthread.so.1
        libunwind.so.1 =>       /usr/lib/hpux64/libunwind.so.1
        libnsl.so.1 =>  /usr/lib/hpux64/libnsl.so.1
        libdl.so.1 =>   /usr/lib/hpux64/libdl.so.1
        libuca.so.1 =>  /usr/lib/hpux64/libuca.so.1
f03:s10adm 5>
```

Figure 4.15 ldd Output of the SAP Database Library for Oracle

This variable has different names on the different operating systems. (Warning: These variables have nothing in common with the `DIR_LIBRARY` variable, as that is an SAP-specific variable.):

- `LIBPATH`: AIX
- `SHLIB_PATH`: HP-UX
- `LD_LIBRARY_PATH`: all others

The SAP database library for Oracle, *dboraslib.<ext>*, doesn't need this library path to find the library of the Oracle client; instead, it searches for it in hard-coded locations. The `disp+work` executable, on the other hand, searches for the SAP-specific libraries in the library path. For this reason, it is mandatory that the corresponding environment variable for the operating system users of SAP (<sid>adm) and Oracle (ora<sid>) contains the SAP kernel directory, */usr/sap/<SID>/SYS/exe/run* (see also Figure 4.10).

> **Note**
>
> When calling `ldd disp+work`, you won't find any link to the SAP database library. This library is loaded by the work processes by means of a different method, as the name of the library to be loaded can change depending on the `dbms_type` environment variable.

As described in Section 4.2.2, the Oracle client version to be used depends on the version of the SAP kernel and is defined by SAP. SAP Note 521230 contains an overview of all kernel releases and the Oracle clients they use. If you want to determine which client the SAP kernel is linked to, you can do that using the "ldd" command described previously. However, it is easier if you call `disp+work -V` as a <sid>adm user. Figure 4.16 shows an excerpt of the result. The `-V` option can be used with almost all SAP executables and tools, such as `R3trans`, `BRSPACE`, `tp`, and so on.

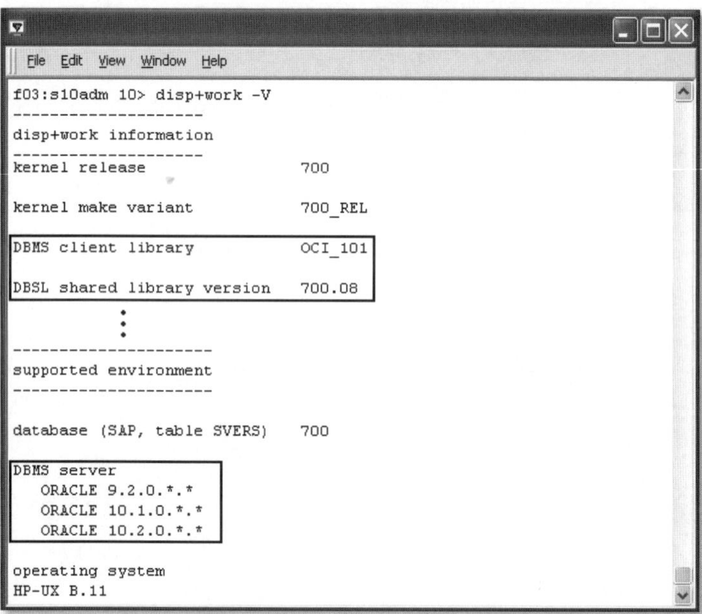

Figure 4.16 Excerpt of the Results Provided by disp+work -V

The two highlighted sections in the figure show the connection between the SAP kernel and the Oracle database. The entries in the upper section have the following meaning:

- **DBSL Client Library**
  Version of the Oracle client that's linked in the SAP database library

- **DBSL Client Library (Version)**
  Version of the SAP database library depending on the kernel release

The lower section that's highlighted in the figure shows the parts of the result, which provide information about the Oracle database server version that may be used with this kernel. The entire output of `disp+work -V` contains additional information about all patch levels including the associated SAP Note for the kernel and database library.

> **Note**
>
> The separation of SAP executables that access the database on the one hand and the database library on the other was implemented in kernel Release 4.5A. Prior to that, various scenarios of the kernel structure existed depending on the release. This could even involve the entirely static linking of all required libraries.

Let us now take a look at the SAP kernel parameters, which are particularly relevant if you use an Oracle database. However, note that almost all of these parameters are used only in specific scenarios or exceptional situations. The two parameters that are always relevant are automatically assigned the value of a corresponding environment variable:

- **dbs/ora/tnsname**
  This parameter must correspond to the name that can be used to connect to the Oracle database via SQL*Net (`tnsnames.ora`). Default value (automatic): $SAPSYSTEMNAME
- **rsdb/oracle_sid**
  This parameter specifies the Oracle SID under which the SAP system is located. Default value (automatic): $SAPSYSTEMNAME

You only need to change these parameters if the database installation does not correspond to the SAP conventions. All other SAP kernel parameters for Oracle are very specific and are used only rarely. Consequently, it doesn't make sense to list them here. Nevertheless, you should note that these parameters can be roughly categorized in two groups: The first group defines the behavior of the SAP instance when using Oracle Parallel Server (see SAP Note 24874).[1] The second group specifies certain types of behavior of the database interface in the SAP kernel toward the Oracle database, for example, whether hints for the Oracle Cot-Based Optimizer (CBO) should be generated.

1 Note that SAP does not officially support Oracle Parallel Server. However, the parameters do exist, and SAP also provides some notes regarding the use of Oracle Parallel Server.

As is the case with all parameters in the SAP system, you can maintain the profile parameters that are relevant for an Oracle environment using Transaction RZ10. You can find all kernel parameters for Oracle by entering "*ora*" und "rsdb/reco*" in the search field in Transaction RZ11. By double-clicking on a displayed parameter, you can open the detail view, which also contains documentation.

4.3 Authentication Between SAP and Oracle

When the SAP work processes log in to the Oracle database, they must authenticate themselves. The same holds true for all other SAP tools that access the database, such as `tp`, BR*Tools, `R3load`, and so on.

4.3.1 Database Users

Using SAP solutions with an Oracle database requires numerous database users. Database users are users that are only defined in the database where they are used for login purposes and for assigning permissions. Consequently, you should not confuse them with the users of the operating system that execute (ora<sid>) or call the database (<sid>adm).

The users of the Oracle database are stored in the SYSTEM tablespace. You can view a list of all user names by entering the following SQL command as ora<sid> user:

```
sqlplus "/ as sysdba"
SQL>select USERNAME from DBA_USERS;
```

Table 4.9 lists the most important Oracle database users in the SAP environment along with their purpose and the corresponding default password.

User	Meaning
▸ SAPR3 ▸ SAP<SID> ▸ SAP<xyz>	These are the standard database users for the SAP NetWeaver Application Server ABAP. SAPR3 was used prior to the introduction of MCOD (SAP Basis 4.6D SR1). After that, the SID became a part of the user name. Since SAP Basis 6.20, you can freely choose the alphanumeric part after SAP. Default password: sap
SYSTEM	This user is created in each installation of an Oracle database and has a wide range of permissions. Default password: manager

Table 4.9 Oracle Database Users for SAP Solutions

User	Meaning
SYS	For this user, the same applies as for SYSTEM. Default password: change_on_install
▸ ESAPR3SHD ▸ SAP<SID>SHD ▸ SAP<xyz>SHD	These users are created temporarily for the shadow database during a system upgrade
▸ SAP<SID>DB ▸ SAP<xyz>DB	These are the standard database users for the SAP NetWeaver Application Server Java (J2EE engine as of Release 6.30). The password must be set during the installation process
OPS$-User	These users are required for the OPS$ login process (see Section 4.2.3, *SAP Kernel*). No password is required here

Table 4.9 Oracle Database Users for SAP Solutions (Cont.)

In current installations, you can also find the user SAPSR3 or SAPSR3DB (Java). This user is proposed by the SAP installation process, whereby the used SID is not taken into consideration. If you don't change this proposed value during the installation, the correspondingly named Oracle users are created by the system.

The default passwords for the first three users in Table 4.8 are only listed for the sake of completeness. When you install current SAP software, you must set the passwords anyway. Of course, you can change them after the installation. To do that, you must enter the following SQL command (again, as user ora<sid>):

```
sqlplus "/ as sysdba"
SQL>alter user <USERNAME> identified by <PASSWORD>;
```

However, if you want to change the password of the SYSTEM user or of the standard SAP database user, you must consider that this will have some significant effects. By default, the SYSTEM user with its default password "manager" was used by BR*Tools Release 6.20 and the predecessor tool, `SAPDBA`. When this password was changed, the new password had to be specified explicitly whenever the tools were supposed to be used. The exception to this rule was the call of these tools by the database scheduler in the SAP system (Transaction DB13), as the scheduler used the OPS$ mechanism for authentication. Since the introduction of Release 6.40 of the BR*Tools, these tools use only the OPS$ login process (see Section 4.3.2), which means the password can be changed without a problem.

If you want to change the password of the standard SAP database user (SAPR3 | SAP<SID> | SAP<xyz>), you do not use the previously mentioned SQL command, but the BR*Tools. Therefore, you must enter the following command as user ora<sid> or <sid>adm:

```
brconnect -f chpass -o <SAP DB-Nutzer> -p <Passwort>
```

The reason for this can be found in the login process for the SAP database user. This process requires that the password for this user be stored in the SAPUSER table, which is exactly what the `BRCONNECT` command does (see Section 4.3.2).

If you want to change the password for the Oracle database users of a J2EE engine, you can do so by using the previously mentioned SQL command. However, this change must be made known to the Java environment. Chapter 11 describes how you can do that.

Note

If you change the password of an Oracle database user, you must ensure that scripts or other applications, such as a backup program, for example, can continue to interact smoothly with the database.

4.3.2 Login Processes

Three methods are available for authenticating with the Oracle database, which will be described in greater detail in this section. The first method, of course, consists of logging in with a user name and password. The command that's used to log in to the SAP database from the command prompt is:

```
sqlplus <user>/<passwort>@<DBSID>
```

In this context, it is important that <DBSID> as the *Oracle Connection Identifier* is resolved in the tnsnames.ora file. In the SAP environment, this type of login is used in two different places: in the second phase of the login process of the standard SAP database user (more on this in Section 4.3.2.2, *OPS$ Process*) and in the login process of the standard database user to the SAP J2EE engine.

The following sections describe the other two login processes in greater detail and tell you where they are used in the system.

4.3.2.1 SYSDBA/SYSOPER-Connect

The login process to the Oracle database with the SYSDBA/SYSOPER authentication almost always occurs on the database server itself. A connection from a different host can only be established with a specific configuration that is not installed in the standard installation. The authentication process is not based on a user name and password, but on the membership in specific operating system groups. For a SYSDBA connection, an operating system user must call `sqlplus` in the following manner:

```
sqlplus "/ as sysdba"
```

Oracle then checks whether the operating system user is a member of the dba group (Windows: ORA_<DBSID>_DBA). If so, the user is assigned comprehensive permissions and is logged in to the database. If the check fails, a password must be entered, which only makes sense if a password file had been created previously, which is rare (see SAP Note 168243). After that, one of the two following Oracle errors displays:

- *ORA-01017: invalid username or password; logon denied*
- *ORA-01031: insufficient privileges*

The same principle applies to the SYSOPER connection that is established with the following command:

```
sqlplus "/ as sysoper"
```

However, in contrast to the SYSDBA connection, here the user must be a member of the oper group (Windows: ORA_<DBSID>_OPER) to be authenticated. In addition, the user has fewer permissions after logging in. For example, SYSOPER cannot create a new database.

Oracle databases with an earlier release than 9i contain the INTERNAL login, which determines the group membership of the operating system user that logs in and then assigns SYSDBA or SYSOPER privileges automatically to that user. This type of login is no longer supported as of Oracle 9i.

The feature that distinguishes the SYSDBA/SYSOPER connection is that the connection works even if the database is offline, because it doesn't need to access the Oracle Data Dictionary. As a result, the areas of application for this login process in the SAP environment are as follows:

- Starting and stopping the Oracle database, either by means of the start and stop scripts of the kernel, via the BR*Tools, or manually (see Section 4.1.1)
- In restore and recovery operations carried out by the BR*Tools

This explains why the operating system users of SAP (<sid>adm) and Oracle (ora<sid>) must be members of the corresponding operating system groups, as shown in Table 4.6.

4.3.2.2 OPS$ Process

The third method for authenticating in the Oracle database is the *OPS$ process* (OPS: *Operating System Specific*). Like the SYSDBA/SYSOPER connection, this process doesn't need a password in the database. It is instead based on the existence of a pair of users, namely, the operating system user and the associated OPS$ user in the Oracle database. The fact that the two belong together results from the symmetry in the naming convention:

- OS user: <sid>adm
- Oracle database user: OPS$<sid>adm

Note that the abbreviation OPS$ is not fixed; it is defined via the Oracle parameter, `os_authent_prefix`. You can establish an OPS$ connection from the operating system as follows (example: SAP OS user of system M05 in the C-shell):

```
f05:m05adm 1>sqlplus /
```

After `sqlplus` is called without user and password, Oracle searches for a corresponding OPS$ user in Table DBA_USERS. In our example, that's OPS$M05ADM. Once the user is found, it is logged in to the database with the privileges of the OPS$ user. Thus, the Oracle database "trusts" the user authentication in the operating system. To enable this process from a different host than the database server, for example, for SAP application instances, you must set the Oracle parameter `remote_os_authent` to `TRUE`. In contrast to the SYSDBA/SYSOPER connection, the OPS$ connection is only possible if the database is up and running.

The following SQL command enables you to view all OPS$ users:

```
select USERNAME from DBA_USERS where USERNAME like 'OPS$%';
```

If the OPS$ users for the <sid>adm and ora<sid> users do not display, you must create them manually. This may be necessary, for example, if you operate an SAP NetWeaver Application Server Java standalone on an Oracle database and want to use the BR*Tools (SAP Note 320457). The following SQL command enables you to create the user:

```
create user „OPS$<OS_USER>„ default tablespace <default_
tablespace> temporary tablespace PSAPTEMP identified externally;
```

Depending on the SAP system type and release, the default tablespace can be determined as follows:

- PSAP<SID>USR: Web AS ABAP as of Release 6.10
- PSAPUSER1D: R\3 prior to Release 6.10
- PSAP<SID>DB: SAP NetWeaver AS Java

After you have created the OPS$ user, you still need to assign the corresponding permissions to it so that it can carry out its tasks (see Section 4.3.3, *Privileges in the Database*).

In the SAP environment, the "simple" OPS$ login is primarily used by the BR*Tools as of Release 6.40 and in each DBA operation that's scheduled via DB13. Because in this case, the privileges of the OPS$ user are used in the database, they must be maintained correspondingly. Section 4.3.3 provides further information on this topic.

Another important aspect of the OPS$ login of the BR*Tools, `BRTOOLS`, `BRBACKUP`, `BRARCHIVE`, and `BRCONNECT` is that the operating system user of these tools is not <sid>adm, but ora<sid>. Consequently, the login to the Oracle database must be carried out with the OPS$ORA<SID> user. There are two reasons for this:

1. The OPS$ users can be assigned different permissions, which are adapted to the respective tasks.
2. The BR*Tools need to have a wide range of permissions, such as the right to delete and write files in the Oracle directories during the different types of operations such as archiving, for example. These permissions are only assigned to an Oracle operating system user.

This can be achieved in such a way that the executables of the BR*Tools are assigned to the ora<sid> user even though they are located in the SAP kernel directory (see Figure 4.17).

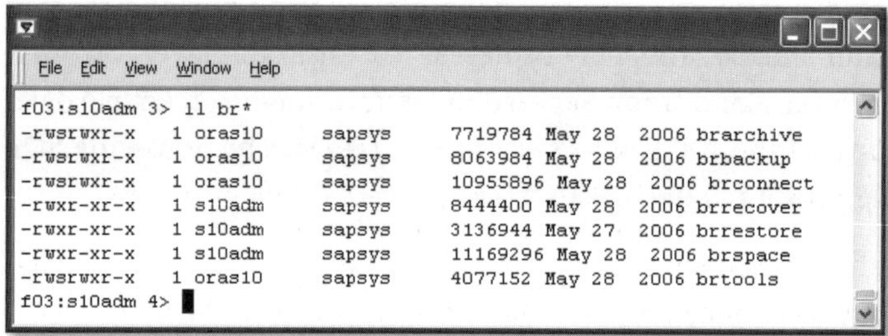

File Edit View Window Help
f03:s10adm 3> ll br*
-rwsrwxr-x 1 oras10 sapsys 7719784 May 28 2006 brarchive
-rwsrwxr-x 1 oras10 sapsys 8063984 May 28 2006 brbackup
-rwsrwxr-x 1 oras10 sapsys 10955896 May 28 2006 brconnect
-rwxr-xr-x 1 s10adm sapsys 8444400 May 28 2006 brrecover
-rwxr-xr-x 1 s10adm sapsys 3136944 May 27 2006 brrestore
-rwxr-xr-x 1 s10adm sapsys 11169296 May 28 2006 brspace
-rwsrwxr-x 1 oras10 sapsys 4077152 May 28 2006 brtools
f03:s10adm 4>

Figure 4.17 Executables of the BR*Tools

The corresponding files are marked with the s-bit so that they automatically assume the process user ID of their owner when they are executed, in this case that's ora<sid>. The `saproot.sh` script is responsible for accurately setting the user and file permissions. This script is located in the SAP kernel directory. It must be executed after each installation of the BR*Tools.

For the login of the SAP work processes to the Oracle database, a two-stage process is used, which is based on the OPS$ mechanism. The login process is shown in Figure 4.18.

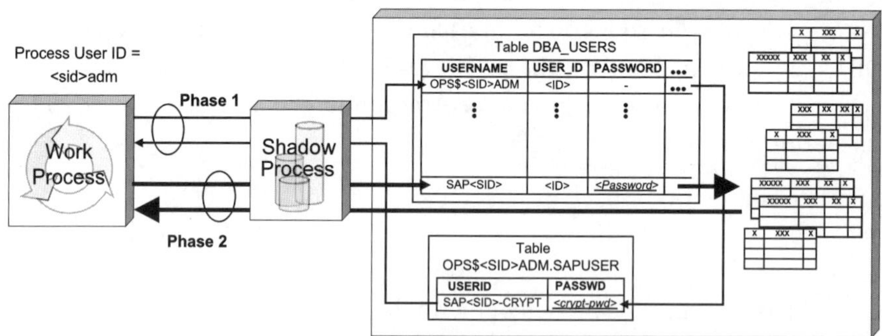

Figure 4.18 Two-Stage Login Process Between SAP and Oracle Database

In the first phase, the work process logs in using the OPS$ process and — as the OPS$<SID>ADM user — reads the password for the standard SAP database user (SAP<SID> or SAPR3) from Table SAPUSER. This table belongs to the OPS$ user and can therefore be connected to in the following manner:

```
select * from OPS$<SID>ADM.SAPUSER;
```

After that, the connection is terminated again. Then, phase 2 starts, in which the work process logs in to the Oracle database using the standard SAP database user and the password read from the SAPUSER table. If the login process fails because the password is incorrect, the work process starts another login attempt using the default password (see Table 4.9). The work process uses this connection until it is terminated or a DB reconnect process needs to be carried out. You can find the flow of this two-stage connection process in the corresponding trace file of the SAP work process (see Figure 4.8).

The SAPUSER table, which contains the password for the standard SAP database user, can only have one entry and may exist only once in the Oracle database. In addition, the table must belong to database user OPS$<SID>ADM. You can check that using the following SQL command:

```
select OWNER from DBA_TABLES where TABLE_NAME =
'SAPUSER';
```

If this query doesn't return OPS$<SID>ADM, you should use the following SQL commands to delete and recreate the table:

```
drop table "<owner>".SAPUSER;
create table "OPS$<sid>ADM".SAPUSER USERID VARCHAR2(256), PASSWD VA
RCHAR2(256));
```

After that, you must set the password again using the BRCONNECT command described in Section 4.3.1, *Database Users*.

4.3.3 Privileges in the Database

Chapter 3 described in detail how the privileges within an Oracle database are structured and organized, and how you can use them. Now, we want to discuss the specifics in relation to SAP systems; the question we have to deal with here is: who needs which privileges and why?

In addition to the roles defined in the Oracle Dictionary, SAP provides another one — and two as of Oracle 10g. The first role that is used in all Oracle releases is SAPDBA. This role is defined to collect all privileges required by the BR*Tools or the predecessor tool, SAPDBA, within the database. If the role in the database is not up-to-date, various errors will occur if you want to use the aforementioned tools, such as the following:

```
BR301W SQL error -1031 at location BrLicCheck-7
ORA-01031: insufficient privileges
BR301W SQL error -942 at location BrbDbLogOpen-1
ORA-00942: table or view does not exist
```

Therefore, the SAPDBA role is always included with the DBA tools. For example, the sapdba_role.sql file is located in the following archive: *DBATL<KernelVer>O<OraVer>_<patch_level>-<HW/OS-Code>.SAR*. Then, the role is installed or updated in the Oracle database in the following manner:

- Oracle 8.1: sqlplus internal @sapdba_role <SAPSCHEMA_ID> [UNIX|NT]
- Oracle 9i and 10g: sqlplus /nolog @sapdba_role <SAPSCHEMA_ID>

You can find more detailed information about the SAP Schema ID in Section 4.4, *SAP Tablespaces*.

The SAPDBA role has different variants depending on the different Oracle releases and must therefore be updated after each database upgrade. In addition to information about the kernel archive, you can find the latest SAPDBA role for each Oracle release in SAP Note 134592.

Since Oracle 10gR2, another SAP-specific Oracle role has been available, which is called SAPCONN. This role became necessary because the standard Oracle roles used previously had either been limited or completely done away with. This is also why the SAPDBA role was significantly enhanced with Oracle 10g. The SAPCONN role is defined in the sapconn_role.sql file, which is also located in the DBA tools archive. Table 4.10 lists the roles and associated system privileges for the most important database users in Oracle 9i and 10g:

Database Users	Roles	System Privileges
SAP database user (SAP<SID>) Oracle 8, 9i, 10gR1	1. CONNECT 2. RESOURCE 3. SELECT_CATA-LOG_ROLE	1. SELECT ANY TABLE 2. UNLIMITED TABLESPACE 3. SELECT ANY DICTIONARY
SAP database user (SAP<SID>) Oracle 10gR2	SAPCONN	UNLIMITED TABLESPACE
OPS$[<SID>ADM| ORA<SID>] Oracle 8, 9i, 10gR1	1. CONNECT 2. RESOURCE 3. SAPDBA	UNLIMITED TABLESPACE
OPS$[<SID>ADM| ORA<SID>] Oracle 10gR2	SAPDBA (enhanced)	UNLIMITED TABLESPACE

Table 4.10 Overview of Roles and System Privileges of Database Users

The old roles, CONNECT and RESOURCE, are still used in Oracle 10gR2 – at least partly – but they will soon be made obsolete. The new SAP-specific roles contain all the necessary privileges to enable an SAP system to use the Oracle database. The advantage of this is that the privileges for all SAP-specific database users do not depend on the standard privileges of current and future Oracle database releases.

4.3.4 Security Aspects

Hardly anyone would deny that security is a major issue in the IT industry, particularly with regard to business-critical applications such as an SAP system or a database. Consequently, a comprehensive discussion of this topic would fill several books. Therefore, we will describe only the security aspects related to an Oracle database in an SAP environment and give you some food for thought and useful tips.

In principle, you must consider two aspects: external security, which involves the security of the operating system, for example, and internal security, that is, the security within the database. Let us first look at some items related to external security. Note, however, that these descriptions are by no means exhaustive. The operating system represents the environment of a database and is therefore critical with regard to security considerations. Typically, ensuring the security of the operating system is not the responsibility of the SAP or Oracle administrator, but of operating system and networking experts. Even so, you should take into account several aspects.

The operating system users introduced in Section 4.2.1, that is, the standard SAP and Oracle users, represent a particularly critical aspect for the Oracle database, as these users can log in to the database without further authentication and with many or even universal privileges. These users should be protected with a password and, if possible, it should be forbidden to log in to the operating system as an administrator. Regarding the login of individual application instances, you must permit remote authentication (`remote_os_authent`). This opens the door to many attack options, but you can limit this risk by explicitly permitting the connections established by the individual application servers. To do that, you must make the following entries in the sqlnet.ora file (`$ORACLE_HOME/network/admin/`):

```
tcp.validnode_checking=yes
tcp.invited_nodes=(IP AppServer_1, IP AppServer_2,...)
```

Furthermore, you must take all necessary action to protect the operating system, while taking into consideration the specifics of the SAP system and Oracle database:

- Protect the network ports (documentation: TCP/IP Ports used by SAP Applications in the SAP Service Marketplace).
- Install the latest security patches for the operating system and the Oracle database.
- Restrict the assignment of file access permissions; this includes the withdrawal of change permissions for the Oracle parameter files for the operating system users – <sid>adm and ora<sid>.
- Protect the Oracle Listener

Now, we want to describe the protection of the Oracle Listener in greater detail. For databases with Oracle Release 9i or smaller, you must assign a password to the Listener to ensure that not every user can execute the administrative functions, such as stopping the database. To do that, you use the following commands as an Oracle user:

```
f05:oram05 22> lsnrctl
LSNRCTL> change_password
Old password:
New password: <new_password>
Reenter new password: <new_password>
LSNRCTL> set password
Password: <new_password>
LSNRCTL> save_config
```

The password is saved in the listener.ora file. Oracle 10g contains the new `ADMIN_RESTRICTIONS_LISTENER` parameter for Listener configuration. By default, this parameter is activated (=`ON`) in an SAP installation. It initiates a check to see whether a user has write access to the listener.ora file and allows access to the Listener configuration only if that's the case.

Another aspect regarding external security concerns the transfer of data between the Oracle and SAP instances. Currently, the data transfer is not encrypted. One of the new features introduced in Oracle 10g is the *Oracle Advanced Security Option*, which enables *network encryption* to tackle this problem. These Oracle features are currently in the pilot phase and if you want to use this feature, you must contact SAP. Please refer to SAP Note 973450 for further information on this topic.

Let us now discuss internal security. Here, the SAP or Oracle administrator has significantly more work, as this area is his responsibility. The rule is: Only the absolutely necessary database users with the fewest required privileges should be activated. You can obtain a first overview of the status of existing database users by entering the following SQL command:

```
sqlplus "/ as sysdba"
SQL>select USERNAME, ACCOUNT_STATUS from DBA_USERS;
```

You will see that most Oracle Default Accounts, such as the famous user SCOTT, no longer exist. This is because the database was installed with the Oracle files preconfigured by SAP. The only users you might still find — depending on the Oracle release you use — are OUTLN, DBSNMP, and DIP. If you haven't done so yet, you can lock these users in the direct SAP environment via the following SQL command:

```
SQL>alter user <USERNAME> account lock password expire;
```

In the SAP environment, this means that SAP applications and tools don't use these users. However, if you monitor the Oracle database using a monitoring system via SNMP, you should, of course, not lock the corresponding users.

The privileges or roles assigned to the database users are listed in Table 4.10. Because these privileges and roles are created and — in part — defined by the SAP system (such as SAPDBA and SAPCONN), it is quite risky to change them. SAP provides two useful hints regarding such changes (SAP Note 926023):

1. Remove superfluous privileges of group PUBLIC (which are automatically assigned to every database user) to execute the following packages: UTL_SMTP, UTL_TCP, UTL_HTTP, UTL_FILE, UTL_INADDR, and DBMS_RANDOM:

   ```
   revoke execute on <PACKAGE> from public;
   ```

2. Remove the CREATE DATABASE LINK privilege from all users and roles:

   ```
   revoke CREATE DATABASE LINK from <CONNECT(9i)|SAPCONN(10g)>
   ```

If the database contains other users, for instance, for backup or monitoring solutions, you must, of course, check their authorization profile for existing superfluous privileges (see Section 3.4.10, *Users and Privileges*).

Finally, we want to provide you with some reference sources that offer additional information so that you can study this topic in more detail:

- Important SAP Notes: 700548 – FAQ: Oracle Privileges and 926023 – Oracle Database Security

- You can find the latest Oracle Database Security Checklist at the following URL:

  www.oracle.com/technology/deploy/security/pdf/twp_security_checklist_db_database.pdf

- The Oracle Security Technology Center (*www.oracle.com/technology/deploy/security/index.html*) provides the latest security information, for instance, regarding critical security patches or specific guidelines.

If you want to implement Oracle security recommendations, you should first refer to the SAP Notes or contact SAP Support to ensure that the respective settings are permitted and supported in the SAP environment.

In its *Configuration Pack*, the Oracle Enterprise Manager (Version 10g) contains the *Policy Manager*. This tool enables you to scan the entire configuration with regard to security-relevant settings.

4.4 SAP Tablespaces

In Chapter 3, we described the Oracle tablespaces and their functionality. In addition, you learned how to manage tablespaces. In this section, we will describe how you can use and implement these concepts in the SAP environment.

4.4.1 Tablespace Layout

First we want to take a look at the historical development of the Oracle tablespace layout in SAP systems, because here, the implementation of the MCOD technology represented a major change. The option to install multiple SAP systems in one database (MCOD: *Multiple Components in One Database*) requires a unique assignment of the tablespace names to the respective systems. For this reason, the SID was integrated in the tablespace name. Along with the development of MCOD, the database and hardware technologies had reached a point at which some of the reasons behind the old tablespace layout became obsolete. Nevertheless, it is advisable to introduce the old tablespace layout as well at this point because you can still find it in many systems with older releases and because it allows us to clearly demonstrate the transition to the new layout. Table 4.11 lists the tablespaces in an SAP system whose Basis release is below SAP Web AS 6.10 (warning: as of SAP Basis Release 4.6C SR2, the new tablespace layout is optionally possible).

Tablespace Name	Meaning
SYSTEM	Tablespace of the Oracle Dictionary
PSAPTEMP	Temporary tablespace, for sort operations, for example
PSAPROLL	Tablespace for Oracle rollback operations; contains the rollback segments
PSAPBTAB[D|I]	Tablespace for data that is changed frequently (transaction data)
PSAPSTAB[D|I]	Tablespace for data that is changed rarely (master data)
PSAPPOOL[D|I]	Tablespace for the pool tables
PSAPPROT[D|I]	Tablespace for the log files collected by the SAP system
PSAPLOAD[D|I]	Tablespace for the compiled ABAP code (loads)
PSAPSOURCE[D|I]	Tablespace for the ABAP source code
PSAPDOCU[D|I]	Tablespace for all documentation tables
PSAPCLU[D|I]	Tablespace for the cluster tables
PSAPDDIC[D|I]	Tablespace for the SAP ABAP Dictionary
PSAPUSER1[D|I]	Tablespace for customer-specific data
PSAPEL<REL>[D|I]	Tablespace for the release-dependent compiled ABAP code (SAP BASIS, for example)
PSAPES<REL>[D|I]	Tablespace for the release-dependent ABAP source code
PSAPFACT[D|I] PSAPDIM[D|I] PSAPODS[D|I]	Tablespace for the fact (FACT), dimension (DIM), and ODS tables in SAP NetWeaver BI (and thus in SAP APO as well)

Table 4.11 Old SAP Tablespace Layout

Note regarding Table 4.11

[D|I] means that for each tablespace purpose, one tablespace existed for the database tables (D) and one for the corresponding indexes (I). Consequently, this type of SAP system used to have 27 (SAP R\3) or 33 (BI or APO) tablespaces.

SAP provides the following reasons for using the old layout:

- Clarity due to the separation of data according to its purpose
- Distribution of tablespaces across different disks according to I/O aspects; this distribution was caused by the respective load to be handled and was

based on the respective purpose of the data (log and transaction data were assigned to fast hard disks, for example)

- Small tablespaces reduce the reorganization requirements significantly

The following technological innovations and organizational reasons led to the new layout:

- Innovations in memory and hard disk technology have moved the I/O optimization primarily into the hardware subsystems. Therefore, the Oracle or system administrator has almost no more influence on this type of optimization. At this point, we refer you to the description of the "virtual" hard disk provided in Section 8.2.2.
- The introduction of locally managed tablespaces (LMTS) in Oracle 8 enabled the efficient use and administration of tables with different change frequencies within one tablespace.
- The introduction of MCOD.
- According to SAP, the assignment of a table to specific purposes and hence to a specific tablespace became increasingly difficult with newer releases. For this reason, the logical separation could no longer be consistently implemented.
- Oracle no longer recommended a separation of the tablespaces by data and indexes as of Release 8.

Table 4.12 describes the current tablespace layout of all SAP systems in an Oracle database:

Tablespace Name	Meaning
SYSTEM	Tablespace of the Oracle Dictionary
SYSAUX	Tablespace for reducing the load on the SYSTEM-TS as of Oracle 10g
PSAPTEMP	Temporary tablespace, for sort operations, for example
PSAPROLL or PSAPUNDO	Tablespace for the Oracle rollback operations: ▸ PSAPROLL: for system installations with Oracle 8 ▸ PSAPUNDO: for system installations with Oracle < = 9i
PSAP<S_ID>	Tablespace for all SAP objects and tables of the ABAP world
PSAP<S_ID>DB	Tablespace for all SAP objects and tables of the Java world
PSAP<S_ID>USR	Tablespace for all customer-specific objects and tables
PSAP<S_ID><REL>	Tablespace for all release-dependent objects and data of the ABAP world

Table 4.12 Current SAP Tablespace Layout

Note regarding Table 4.12: S_ID stands for schema ID. To explain this term, we should first describe what is meant by the term *schema*. In an Oracle database, a schema is always directly assigned to a database user and contains all objects that belong to this user. The name of the schema is always identical to the user name. The access to an object that belongs to a different user and is therefore contained in a different schema is enabled by `<SCHEMA>.<DB_object>`. For example, if you want to access an SAP table as the SYSDBA user, you must enter the following command:

```
sqlplus "/ as sysdba"
SQL>select * from SAP<SID>.<table>;
```

The environment variable, `dbs_ora_schema`, defines which schema the SAP instance uses after connecting to the database. This is necessary, for example, if you want to migrate an SAP Basis 4.6C release to Release 6.20, because in this case, the database user changes from sapr3 to sap<sid>, whereas the tables continue to belong to sapr3 so that the name of the schema is sapr3.

The schema ID is a freely selectable three-digit alphanumeric key figure to identify a schema. Don't confuse the schema ID with the Oracle system ID (DBSID). The schema ID is defined during the installation of a system and can be created independently of the SID. Up to and including Oracle 9i, it was recommended to always create the schema ID independently of the SID. The reason was that in a system copy, for instance, from a production system to a test system, the tablespace names were preserved, which meant that the SID was preserved as well, provided it was used. Form a technical point of view, that's not a problem, but it can lead to some confusion. Table 4.13 shows the difference.

Schema ID = SID (M05)	Schema ID (PRD) ≠ SID (M05)
PSAP**M05**	PSAP**PRD**
PSAP**M05**DB	PSAP**PRD**DB
PSAP**M05**USR	PSAP**PRD**USR
PSAP**M05**<REL>	PSAP**PRD**<REL>

Table 4.13 Different Schema IDs

Oracle 10g allows you to rename the tablespaces. To do that, you must enter the following SQL command:

```
SQL>alter tablespace <name_old> rename to <name_new>;
```

This renders obsolete the old recommendation to select a schema ID independently of the SID.

You can switch from the old to the new tablespace layout by means of a reorganization, which is explicitly recommended by SAP. Please refer to Section 4.4.4, *Reorganizing Tables and Tablespaces*, for more information on reorganization.

The SAP tablespace layouts (both the old and new one) can be enhanced; that is, if necessary, you can move individual tables into separate tablespaces, for instance, if the material table MARA is "dramatically" large (>50 GB). However, if possible, you should stick to the following naming convention: PSAP<S_ID><NAME> (example: PSAPM05 MARA).

Let us conclude this section by taking a look at the SAP conventions for the directory structure and the file names of the Oracle data files. Deviations from these conventions are not supported by SAP and are therefore not permitted. The starting point is always the *SAPDATA_HOME* directory. This directory contains the following subdirectories for the actual data:

- sapdata<n>: These directories contain all Oracle data files based on the conventions described in a moment.
- sapraw: Here, you can find all links to the data-raw devices.

Figure 4.19 shows an example of the SAP conventions. The individual items are explained as follows:

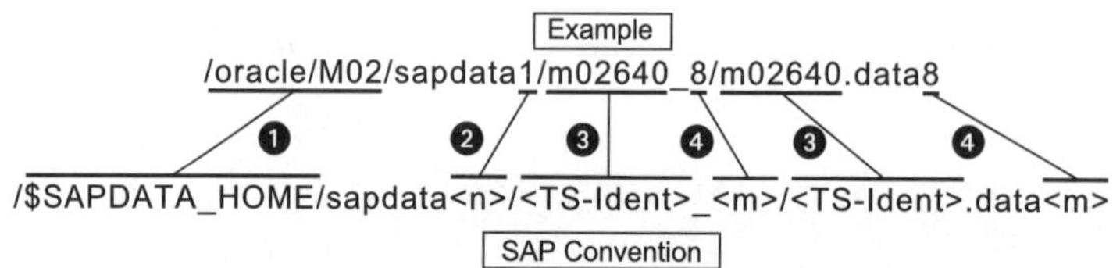

Figure 4.19 SAP Directory and Naming Conventions for Data Files

❶ All data subdirectories are located in the *SAPDATA_HOME* directory.

❷ <n> represents a sequential number for the individual data directories. A typical installation of an SAP system uses the subdirectories 1 through 4. There is no convention that specifies which data from which tablespace must be located in a specific position. Usually, the tablespace files are distributed across the individual directories. Background: SAP assumes that the sapdata<n> directories represent mount points that enable the distribution of data across several storage areas. However, this is not mandatory.

❸ <TS-Ident> describes the tablespace that contains the data file. Theoretically, you can structure this ident as per your requirements, but the standard SAP installation uses the following convention: TS-Ident=lowercase(<SAP TS-Name> – PSAP). For example, the TS-Ident for Tablespace PSAP<SID>USR is <sid>usr. For non-SAP tablespaces (SYSTEM, for example), the following applies: TS-Ident=Tablespace name. There is no reason why you shouldn't use this "meaningful" TS-Ident and choose another one instead. As shown in Figure 4.19, each data file is located in a separate subdirectory, which is why TS-Ident is contained both in the name of the data subdirectory and in the actual file name.

❹ <m> is the sequential number for the data file of a tablespace. This number is also used as part of the name of the respective data subdirectory and of the actual file name.

Regarding raw devices, the convention is almost identical. The *sapraw* directory contains all objects with the name <TS-Ident>_<m>; however, these are not subdirectories, but symbolic links to the respective raw device, for instance if a logical volume manager is used:

```
/oracle/M02/sapraw/m02usr_8 -> /dev/vgM02/lvol8
```

SAP Note 27428 describes the naming conventions for UNIX and Windows in great detail and provides additional information on how you can use symbolic links including the restrictions you must take into consideration.

4.4.2 Tablespace Types

In Chapter 3, we described which types of tablespaces exist in an Oracle database and the differences between them. Table 4.14 repeats this information briefly and can be used as a legend for the following descriptions.

Type	Extent Management	Content	Allocation Management	Segment Management
1	Dictionary	Permanent	USER	MANUAL
2	Dictionary	Temporary	USER	MANUAL
3	LMTS	Permanent	SYSTEM(auto)/ UNIFORM	MANUAL

Table 4.14 Brief Overview of Tablespace Types

Type	Extent Management	Content	Allocation Management	Segment Management
4	LMTS	Permanent	SYSTEM(auto)/ UNIFORM	AUTO
5	LMTS	Temporary	UNIFORM	MANUAL

Table 4.14 Brief Overview of Tablespace Types

The following list describes which SAP software uses or used which tablespace type *initially*, that is, after thc standard installation. The decisive factor in this context is always the SAP Basis release:

- SAP BASIS 4.6D or smaller, installed with Oracle 8.1.7: All tablespaces have type 1.
- SAP BASIS 610–620, installed with Oracle 8.1.7: SYSTEM, PSAPROLL, and PSAPTEMP are type 1. All others are type 3.
- SAP BASIS 620–63, installed with Oracle 9i: SYSTEM and PSAPROLL are type 1. PSAPTEMP is type 5. All others are type 3.
- SAP BASIS 640–700, installed with Oracle 9i or Oracle 10g: SYSTEM and PSAPUNDO are type 3. PSAPTEMP is type 5. All others are type 4.

The following SQL command enables you to check the tablespace types in your Oracle database (as sysdba):

```
SQL>select tablespace_name, extent_management, allocation_
type, segment_space_management from dba_tablespaces;
```

Because SAP production systems tend to have long lifecycles, sometimes the Oracle database is upgraded during that period. Because the tablespace types are not changed during such an upgrade process, numerous combinations of tablespace types in the different Oracle releases are possible. In addition, when SAP supports a new Oracle database release, this does not mean that all new features of this release are also supported at the same time. Such features are usually released for use in a production system at a later point in time, after comprehensive testing.

SAP recommends using LMTS and ASSM for all SAP systems on Oracle Release 9i and higher, and these functions are activated by default on systems using a Basis release higher than Web AS 6.40. Nonetheless, you might hear different recommendations in specific unique cases by SAP's Oracle experts. However, you can only migrate the tablespaces to a newer type by means of a reorganization. A changeover from type 1 to the current type 4 can be performed directly, provided you run Oracle 9i. If necessary, you can also migrate from type 1 to type 3 first and then to type 4; however, this requires an additional reorganization. Note that you cannot migrate all tablespaces to type 4. The following restrictions apply:

- The tablespace for the temporary operations, PSAPTEMP, can only be type 2 (Oracle 8.1.7) or type 5 (Oracle 9i or higher).
- If the SYSTEM tablespace is type 3, the automatic undo management (AUM) must be active, that is, PSAPUNDO is the rollback tablespace instead of PSAPROLL.
- SYSTEM and PSAPUNDO cannot be type 4.

Refer to Section 4.4.4, *Reorganizing Tables and Tablespaces*, for more information on the topic of reorganization.

4.4.3 Object Assignment and Object Parameters

How does the SAP system or the administrator know where a specific object (table or index) is located and how it is parameterized?

Basically, all objects are specified by means of two dimensions:

1. **Data class (TABART)**
   The data class defines the software category to which the object belongs. The software categories are defined in Table DDART. Figure 4.20 shows an excerpt from this table.

TABART	DDCLASS	DARTTEXT
APPL0	STD	Master data, transparent tables
APPL1	STD	Transaction data, transparent tables
APPL2	STD	Organization and customizing
CLUST	CPT	Phys. cluster table
DDIM	STD	
DFACT	STD	
DODS	STD	
POOL	CPT	Phys. pooled table
SAUS	SYS	Exchange tables for upgrades
SDIC	SYS	ABAP Dictionary Table
SDOCU	SYS	Documentation
SLDEF	SYS	Repositoryswitch tablespace 640
SLEXC	SYS	Repositoryswitch tablespace 640
SLOAD	SYS	Screen and report loads
SPROT	SYS	SPOOL and logs

Figure 4.20 Data Classes in an SAP System

2. **Size category (TABKAT)**
   The size category defines the storage parameters (`INITIAL`, `NEXT`, `MIN-` and `MAXEXTENTS`) that are used to initialize the object when it is created. In

Tables TGORA (tables) and IGORA (indexes), the classes from 0 to 15 are defined correspondingly; note that only the classes from 0 to 4 are used by default.

The importance of size categories has significantly decreased since the introduction of the LMTS technology, as the storage parameters are not relevant in this technology. The only exception is the `INITIAL` parameter, which also determines the initial number of extents in a LMTS.

In Table DD09L, all SAP-specific objects with technical parameters are assigned to these two dimensions. Moreover, this table contains additional specifications such as the buffering in the SAP system or the status in the SAP Repository. Figure 4.21 shows an excerpt from this table.

TABNAME	AS4LOCAL	AS4VERS	TABKAT	TABART	PUFFERUNG	SCHFELDANZ	AS4USER	AS4DATE	AS4TIME
B987	A	0000	0	APPL0	X	000	TRIEGER	18.07.2004	20:43:14
BALMP	A	0000	4	APPL1		000	SAP	08.11.2000	20:23:46
BALOBJ	A	0000	0	APPL2	X	000	SAP	08.11.2000	19:46:50
BALOBJT	A	0000	0	APPL2	P	000	SAP	07.11.2003	09:29:36
BALSUB	A	0000	0	APPL2	G	001	SAP	08.11.2000	20:05:23
BALSUBT	A	0000	0	APPL2	P	000	SAP	07.11.2003	09:29:36
BAL_AMODAL	A	0000	2	SPROT		000	SAP	08.11.2000	19:46:51
BAL_INDX	A	0000	2	SPROT		000	SAP	08.11.2000	20:20:53
BAM5RTIME	A	0000	1	APPL2		000	SAP	23.02.1999	20:33:53
BAMGROUPS	A	0000	0	APPL0	X	000	SAP	23.02.1999	22:12:38
BAMGROUPST	A	0000	0	APPL0	G	001	SAP	07.11.2003	09:29:49
BAMUI	A	0000	0	APPL0	X	000	SAP	24.02.1999	00:03:59

Figure 4.21 Excerpt from Table DD09L

To be able to categorize the objects completely, two things are still missing: first, the assignment of the data class and thus of the individual objects to a tablespace. The link is established in Tables TAORA for tables and IAORA for indexes. In these tables, the simple n:1 relationship between the data class and tablespace is mapped. In the old tablespace layout with its many different tablespaces, this assignment was, of course, much more interesting than in the new layout that contains only one primary tablespace for ABAP. The second element that's missing is the mapping between the table tablespace and the index tablespace. This type of assignment has also lost its importance with the new layout; however, it is still maintained in Table TSORA.

In addition to Table DD09L, another table stores technical parameters of tables. The user-specific settings for individual tables are contained in Table DDSTORAGE, irrespective of the defined size categories. You can maintain new data entries in this table via Transaction SE14 by following the path **Storage Parameters • For New Creation**. Entries in Table DDSTORAGE override the corresponding entry in DD09L.

Other information:

- All tables that have "ORA" in their name (TAORA, TGORA, etc.) are also available analogously for the databases MSSQL Server, DB2, and Informix, which are supported by SAP. Their names are, for example, TADB2 for the DB2 database.
- You can also define your own data classes to administrate custom developments separately. SAP Note 46272 contains information about how you can do that and what you need to consider.

Because the storage parameters decreased in importance after the introduction of the LMTS technology, the most frequently occurring task regarding the technical parameters involves the customizing of the buffer function in the SAP NetWeaver Application Server. This buffering and its characteristics are also stored in Table DD09L and maintained via Transaction SE13. You can find additional information on table buffering in Section 8.2.3, *Analyzing the SAP System*.

4.4.4 Reorganizing Tables and Tablespaces

During a reorganization, tables are organized in a different way, that is, they are created from scratch or moved to a different position. You can reorganize individual tables as well as entire tablespaces. In this process, the Oracle administrator can customize the technical parameters of the objects, for example, to better utilize the storage space. Indexes are not reorganized but created from scratch. For this reason, we won't described them any further in this book.

Note

When tables are reorganized, the associated indexes are also always recreated.

The following lists describe when or for what reason a reorganization is necessary or useful. In this context, we make a distinction as to whether a single table or an entire tablespace is supposed to be reorganized. The following situations require the reorganization of tablespaces:

- The main reason for the reorganization of a tablespace is probably the possibility of freeing hard disk space. In this context, you can return space that is no longer needed (for instance, after an archiving process) to the file system by reducing the number of data files. In addition, you could reduce the actual file size, which reduces the number of data files as well.

In a database that has grown over a long period of time, this reduces the amount of administrative work and avoids performance problems (see SAP Notes 793113 and 875477).

In Section 3.4.4.4, *Fragmentation*, we described the theoretical background for the creation of a fragmentation in the Oracle database.

- The second situation has already been mentioned several times. It involves changing the tablespace type to use the new LMTS and ASSM technologies.
- Another cause for a tablespace reorganization is the changeover of an SAP system to the new tablespace layout.

The reasons for reorganizing a single table are as follows:

- As is the case with an entire tablespace, freeing up hard disk space is the main reason here as well. In a newly organized table, the the storage space that has been made available is transferred to the tablespace, not to the file system. For this purpose, the table blocks are filled completely up to the limit PCTFREE during the recreation process (also when ASSM is used), which eliminates the internal fragmentation. You can customize the storage parameters only during the reorganization.
- If you have to move highly frequented tables into a separate tablespace, you must do this by means of a reorganization as well.
- Tables in a DMTS should be reorganized if the number of their extents gets too large (>1000). In this process, you should customize the technical parameters correspondingly (`NEXT` and `PCTINCREASE`, for example).
- Other, less frequent, reasons for a table reorganization include the changeover from LONG to LOB columns (during the migration from Oracle 9i to Oracle 10g). You can find these reasons in SAP Note 541538.

Before we describe the tools that enable you to carry out a reorganization, we need to mention the two basic types of reorganization: online and offline reorganization. In an *online reorganization*, the segments are moved within the database without the occurrence of locks. This way the database object can still be accessed so that the SAP system can continue to run. That's not possible in an *offline reorganization*, as this type of reorganization requires you to export the corresponding object from the database, then delete it, and finally re-import it. Table 4.15 shows which Oracle database version supports which type of reorganization.

Version	Offline	Online
8.1	Yes, with: `ALTER TABLE ... MOVE TABLESPACE` or via `EXP / IMP`	No
9i	Yes, with: `ALTER TABLE ... MOVE TABLESPACE` or via `EXP / IMP`	Yes, with package DBMS_REDEFINITION. Exceptions: no tables with FILE or LONG columns and not the tables of the SYS or SYSTEM schema.
10g	Yes, with: `ALTER TABLE ... MOVE TABLESPACE`, via `EXP / IMP` or with Data Pump (new export/import function of 10g)	Yes, with package DBMS_REDEFINITION (enhanced in 10g). FILE or LONG columns must be converted to LOB. Exception: not the tables of the SYS or SYSTEM schema.

Table 4.15 Reorganization Options of the Different Oracle Database Releases

Despite the advantages of an online reorganization, you should note two significant disadvantages:

- **Increased space requirement**
  During an online reorganization, the currently processed object exists virtually twice — as the original and the copy. In addition, there's a temporary table, which records the changes to the original table during the reorganization period to ultimately duplicate these changes in the copy table.
- **Change of the tablespace name**
  In Oracle 9i, you cannot rename a tablespace, which is why the online reorganization of a tablespace always creates a tablespace with a different name, which may lead to confusion. This problem no longer exists in Oracle 10g.

Moreover, the online reorganization as of Oracle 9i enables you to redefine tables, that is, to make structural changes, such as adding columns or partitioning the table. However, SAP does not recommend carrying out this type of change during an online reorganization.

The recommended tool for a reorganization is the SAP tool, `BRSPACE` (part of the BR*Tools), or its predecessor, `SAPDBA`, for older SAP and Oracle releases. The tools provide the administrator with comprehensive configuration options and issue warnings against risks that may occur in different operations. The `BRSPACE` tool uses the Oracle database package DBMS_REDEFINI-

TION, which defines all procedures as of Oracle 9i in order to reorganize tables online.

Another reason for using BRSPACE is the necessary changes to the table types (TABART) during the creation of a new tablespace. These changes are automatically carried out by `BRSPACE` if parameter `-l` is set.

Although SAP permits the direct use of the Oracle commands listed in Table 4.15, it does not provide any support in the case of problems or subsequent damage. The same applies to the use of third-party tools for reorganization purposes. If problems occur, the third-party provider must provide support.

It doesn't make much sense to describe all steps involved in a reorganization with `BRSPACE`, as that would go into too much detail in order to be completely accurate. For this reason, you should refer to the additional sources of information provided at the end of this section. Nevertheless, in the following steps, we will describe the basic process of an online reorganization for a better understanding:

1. First, a check is made to determine whether the table meets all the requirements of an online reorganization.
2. For performance reasons, parameter `DB_FILE_MULTIBLOCK_READ_COUNT` is increased to `128`.
3. Then, the metadata required for the reorganization is determined (Step a in Figure 4.22). This metadata includes:
   - The `CREATE` statements for creating the table and index
   - All objects depending on the table, such as triggers, grants, and constraints
4. After that, the target table is created. This table may be located in the same tablespace as the source table or in a different one.
5. The statistics of the source table are exported to restore them after the reorganization.
6. Now the actual start of the reorganization occurs with the following steps (see Figure 4.22):

   ⓐ Refer to the steps described under 3.

   ⓑ Copy the table entries and — at the same time — log the current changes to the source table in Table MLOG$.

   ⓒ Restore the depending objects.

   ⓓ Generate the indexes for the new table.

   ⓔ Reproduce the changes to the source table in the target table.

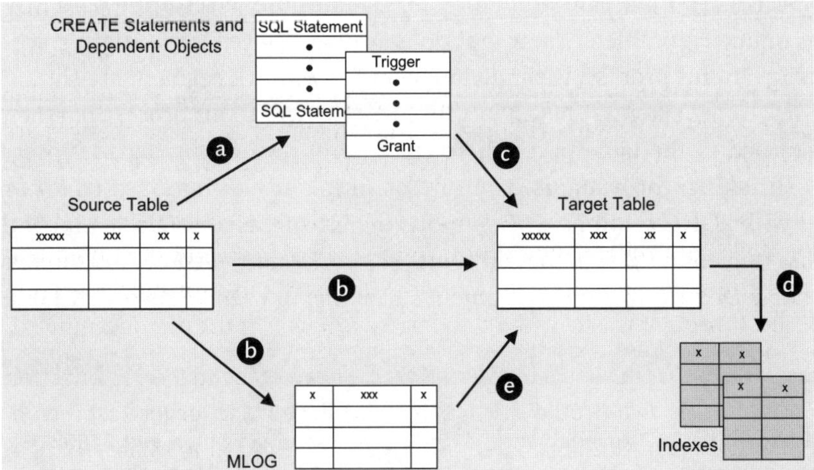

Figure 4.22 Online Reorganization of a Table

7. Then, the source table is replaced by the target table so that the original source table can be deleted. In addition, the index name is adapted.
8. Finally, the statistics exported in Step 5 are re-imported.

All these steps are controlled and monitored by BRSPACE. As otherwise you would have to carry out each step separately using SQL commands, you can imagine the amount of work saved by this tool for the Oracle database administrator.

A reorganization, whether online or offline, places high requirements on performance. The administrator should take this into account and include it in his plans. Although you can carry out online reorganizations during live operations, you should at least do that in periods of low system load. The I/O capacities, in particular, are greatly impacted by a reorganization, and it is the I/O that predominantly determines the runtime of a reorganization. However, this doesn't enable us to make a universal statement about the runtime. You need to consider two major aspects:

- Ensure that no archiver stuck occurs because of the high I/O rate (you can find additional information on the archiver stuck in Chapter 10, *Backup, Restore, and Recovery*).
- Ensure that sufficient hard disk space is available:
  - Online: in the target tablespace for the table to be reorganized and in the default tablespace of the executing database user for the MLOG table
  - Offline: in the file system for the export or in the target tablespace

If you carry out a reorganization only for the purpose of restoring hard disk space, another, completely new, option is available since Oracle 10g: *segment shrinking*. In this process, the individual entries within a segment are shifted into the "front" extents. The extents that are released in this process can then be returned to the tablespace. There are several restrictions regarding segment shrinking; for example, you cannot shrink any compressed tables or tables with LONG columns. SAP supports the use of this new Oracle function and has implemented it in the BR*Tools (`BRSPACE`) from Version 7.00 on. For more detailed information on segment shrinking, refer to SAP Note 910389.

Note

SAP provides two important SAP Notes regarding the reorganization of an Oracle database in the SAP environment: 541538 – FAQ: Reorganization and 646681 – Reorganizing tables with BRSPACE. If you want to perform a reorganization, you should read these SAP Notes as well as the other SAP Notes mentioned in this section. These notes describe almost all of the pitfalls and provide help for errors.

4.5 Administrating Oracle with the BR*Tools

SAP provides its customers with specifically developed tools for administrating an Oracle database: the BR*Tools. But why does SAP do that, when there are numerous tools and scripts available for the widely used Oracle database, both from Oracle and from many third-party providers? That's probably the reason. There is probably nothing more critical for the support of an Oracle database in an SAP production system than the uncontrolled use of different tools "puttering about" in the database without taking into consideration SAP-specific facts.

Oracle is probably the database that provides the most functions and options. However, a lot of them are not used in the SAP environment. There are two reasons for this:

- In principle, SAP software is supposed to be independent of a database, which is why many different databases are supported. However, if you delve too deeply into the features of a database, this would contradict the SAP principle and increase support requirements significantly.
- In a business-critical environment, the focus of a software landscape clearly lies on the aspects of stability and continuity. For this reason, using a new software function only makes sense if the associated cost-benefit

ratio justifies the effort. Consequently, SAP supports new Oracle features only with the appropriate care and after extensive testing.

The great advantage of the BR*Tools for Oracle administrators is that the SAP strategy is reflected in the tool. That is, those who use the BR*Tools, use only the Oracle features supported by SAP including the recommended procedures. Thus, errors are almost impossible. The following sections describe the BR*Tools and demonstrate how the administrator can use them.

Note

SAP Note 105047 contains all main functions of the current Oracle database 10.2 as well as information on the position taken by SAP in this regard: What will be supported when and where, or not at all?

4.5.1 Development and Content

Before we describe the individual tools in detail, we should consider their historical development. In terms of the logic, the BR*Tools are part of the SAP kernel, although they work as independent applications. That's why the names of different versions correspond to the SAP kernel nomenclature. The first release of the BR*Tools was 4.6D. The predecessor of the BR*Tools was SAPDBA, which was maintained up to and including Version 6.20. The transition between the two went smoothly, as the entire functional scope was not implemented until the release of Version 6.40 of the BR*Tools. That's when SAPDBA was finally replaced. Table 4.16 shows an overview of the history of SAP-Oracle tools.

Release	Tool	Special Characteristics
4.6C and earlier	SAPDBA and tools	▸ For Oracle 8.0 and 8.1 ▸ Tools for backup and restore and recovery
4.6D	SAPDBA and BR*Tools	▸ For Oracle 8.0 and 8.1 ▸ No new corrections since 2003; corrections are implemented in Release 6.10/6.20
6.10–6.20	SAPDBA and BR*Tools	▸ For Oracle 8.0, 8.1, and 9i ▸ Equal coexistence ▸ Enhanced downward compatibility for three main SAP releases, up to and including SAP 3.X

Table 4.16 Releases of SAP BR*Tools

Release	Tool	Special Characteristics
6.40	BR*Tools	▸ For Oracle 9i ▸ SAPDBA 6.20 can still be used, except for restore and recovery ▸ Can also be used with some limitations for J2EE-only SAP systems (see SAP Note 320457)
7.00	BR*Tools	▸ For Oracle 10g ▸ Can be used for Oracle 9i if Oracle Client 10g is installed (see SAP Note 849483)

Table 4.16 Releases of SAP BR*Tools

The content, or rather, the functional scope of the BR*Tools, has been enhanced across the different releases, on the one hand, to adopt the functions of SAPDBA and, on the other, to map new Oracle functions. However, the SAPDBA package already contained tools that later became part of the BR*Tools. Figure 4.23 illustrates this.

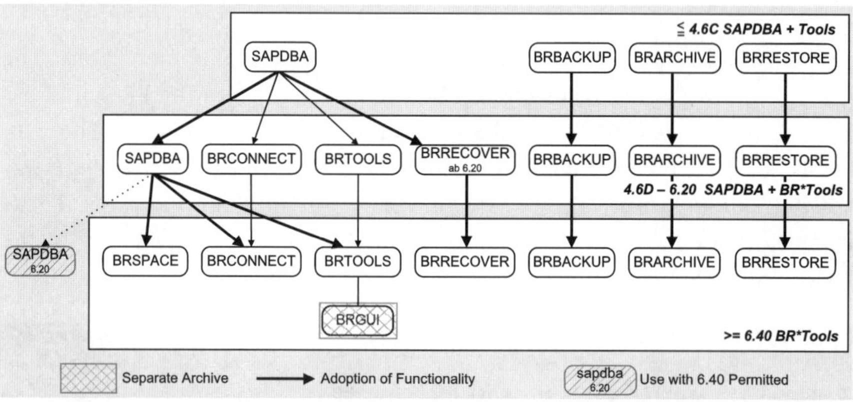

Figure 4.23 Development of the BR*Tools

The figure shows that the tools for backup and restore have been maintained in their previous form, whereas the administration tool SAPDBA was split up into the following components:

- **BRRECOVER**
  Tool for recovery operations.
- **BRCONNECT**
  This tool carries out important administrative tasks, including password changes, start and stop operations, creating statistics, and so on (see Section 4.5.4).

- **BRSPACE**
  This tool enables the administrator to manage all Oracle database objects (tables, indexes, etc.) and the tablespaces. In addition, it allows you to perform various other tasks, such as changing parameters and starting and stopping the database (see Section 4.5.5).
- **BRTOOLS and BRGUI**
  The BRTOOLS program is the text-based menu interface for all other tools. BRGUI is a Java application that's based on the BRTOOLS program and acts as the graphical display of the menu interface.

In the following sections, we'll mainly focus on BRCONNECT, BRSPACE, and the interfaces. The tools for backup and recovery (BRBACKUP, BRARCHIVE, BRRESTORE, BRRECOVER) are described in great detail in Chapter 10.

4.5.2 Environment, Options, and Log Files

Because the BR*Tools belong logically to the SAP kernel, they are located in the kernel directory (*/usr/sap/<SID>/SYS/exe/run*). This also includes the download from the SAP Service Marketplace. Here, as well, the BR*Tools archive (*DBATL<KernelVer>O<OraVer>_<patch_level>-<HW/OS-Code>.SAR*) is located in the SAP kernel folder.

If you need the version number or other information about your BR*Tools, you can call one of the tools with the option -V. Example:

```
f05:m05adm 1>brconnect -V
```

This way you can obtain information about the release and patch status as well as the specific build, including the hardware and software platform and the linked Oracle client.

The operating system user of the BR*Tools is based on the operating system that's used. On Windows, the <sid>adm user carries out all manual calls of the BR*Tools, whereas the sapservice<sid> user is used for all calls from within the SAP system. In a UNIX environment, manual calls are always carried out by the ora<sid> user, whereas automatic calls, for instance, from within Transaction DB13, are made by the <sid>adm user. However, if you set the s-bit, the process user is changed to ora<sid> within the operating system. In Section 4.3.2.2, we described the details and background for this as well as for the login process used.

The BR*Tools as well as the predecessor tool, SAPDBA (including the original BR*Tools), each contain a configuration file. This file contains all parameters for the backup tools (BRBACKUP, BRARCHIVE, BRRESTORE, BRRECOVER) and for the administration tools (BRCONNECT, BRSPACE, BRTOOLS). The names of the configuration files are as follows:

- BR*Tools: init<sid>.sap
- SAPDBA: init<sid>.dba

The files are always located in the configuration directory of the Oracle database: *$ORACLE_HOME/dbs/*. The parameters control all important data backup settings, such as:

- The destination of the archive backups
- The destination of the backups

You will get to know some important backup options in Chapter 10. Furthermore, various options are available for the tasks of the BRCONNECT and BRSPACE tools:

- Compression and parallel processing
- Export directory for dumps and so on

A number of options are identical for all tools of the BR*Tools, or are at least used in an identical manner. To better understand the different calls of BR*Tools you will encounter during the further course of this book, you should take a look at the overview of the most frequently used options, presented in Table 4.17.

Option	Meaning
-c [force]	Determines the *Unattended* mode (see the text following this table).
-l [E|D]	Defines the language: E = English (default) or D = German.
-o <option>	Controls the output to the session log. Possible options: detail, process (default), summary, or time.
-p <profile>	Enables the use of a configuration file other than *$ORACLE_HOME/dbs/init<sid>.sap*.
-s <lines>	Specifies how many lines are output together in one display.
-u <user/pw>	Defines the user with which the BR*Tool logs in to the database. The default value is system/manager. A call with the option -u / forces an OPS$ login process. The BRSPACE program ignores -u, because it always logs in as Oracle-SYSDBA.

Table 4.17 General Options of the BR*Tools

Option	Meaning
-V	Displays the version, patch, and other information.
-f <function>	Always represets the entry point into the actual functions of the called tool. Moreover, -f represents the separation between the general options (this table) and the function-specific options.
-h	Help function. It displays *all* possible options for each program of the BR*Tools.

Table 4.17 General Options of the BR*Tools (Cont.)

All options listed in this table are optional, that is, if you don't set them when calling one of the BR*Tools, the system will use the default value.

Note

Don't get confused by possible duplicate options such as -o. The -o option in front of the function-specific option -f controls the output in the session log (see Table 4.17). However, if it is placed after the -f option, the -o option defines the database user (owner) of the respective database schema. This information is important if you use MCOD systems.

The most important option when calling a BR*Tools program is -c. This option determines whether this tool should be run in *attended* or *unattended mode*. Two types of menus are available: *choice menus* and *input menus*. In a choice menu, you must select a number to navigate to the next submenu, whereas in an input menu, you select a number to fill out an underlying input field. Input menus must always be confirmed using c - cont (see Figure 4.24). Once you have selected the required function, such as "Enhance tablespace," and entered all required and additional input, such as the tablespace name (mandatory field) and new file size (optional), the type of mode (attended or unattended) comes into play. In the attended mode, the administrator obtains a detailed overview about which command will be executed next, which the administrator must confirm by entering c - cont or yes. In the unattended mode, the program execution starts directly after entering c - cont in the input menu.

If you use the -c force option in a direct call of BRCONNECT or BRSPACE, you can further strengthen the unattended mode. Then, the input menus are filled with default values (including the mandatory fields), if that's necessary, that is, if no command prompt parameters were included. The program execution starts immediately. Therefore, you should only use this option if you are an experienced BR*Tools user. However, this option provides one of the greatest advantages of the BR*Tools: the automated processes. For example, you can automatically configure the test system of an SAP landscape from a backup of the production system.

All tools write data into different log files during each start and for each action. On the one hand, a separate session log file exists for each program start, and on the other hand, there is a central file for each tool, which documents all program starts. The environment variables of the sid<adm> and ora<sid> users determine the location of the individual files. Table 4.18 lists variables for the individual tools and their default values and central log file.

BR*Tool	Environment Variable	Default	Central Log File
BRBACKUP	SAPBACKUP	$SAPDATA_HOME/sapbackup	back<DBSID>.log
BRRESTORE	SAPBACKUP	$SAPDATA_HOME/sapbackup	rest<DBSID>.log
BRRECOVER	SAPBACKUP	$SAPDATA_HOME/sapbackup	recov<DBSID>.log
BRARCHIVE	SAPARCH	$SAPDATA_HOME/saparch	arch<DBSID>.log
BRCONNECT	SAPCHECK	$SAPDATA_HOME/sapcheck	conn<DBSID>.log
BRSPACE	SAPREORG	$SAPDATA_HOME/sapreorg	space<SID>.log

Table 4.18 Environment Variables for the Log Files of BR*Tools

The environment variables also define three additional properties of the BR*Tools:

- **BR_LINES**
  Defines the maximum number of lines in the different menu lists.
- **BR_LANG**
  Defines the output language: E = English (default) and D = German.
- **BR_TRACE**
  Enables the tracing of BR*Tools. For more information on this topic, refer to SAP Note 29321.

The naming convention for the individual session logs is as follows: <ToolCode> <timestamp>.<extension>. The tool code is very simple: a = BRARCHIVE, b = BRBACKUP, c = BRCONNECT, and so on. The timestamp is fairly cryptic and contains only letters. Figure 4.24 shows an example. The name of the extension, on the other hand, is mnemonic; that is, it is assigned to a specific primary function of the respective tool. In the SAP Help, the term <ToolCode><timestamp> is referred to as *action ID*, and the <Extension> is called *function ID*. Appendix B contains the extensions (or function IDs) for the primary and secondary functions of each of the BR*Tools.

Figure 4.24 shows the start and end of a log file, which was generated by a BRARCHIVE session. The start of a BR*Tool immediately initiates the output of certain system information. The most interesting piece of information is the **command line** line, as it contains the exact command prompt call of the tool that has been started. This is particularly important, for example, to understand what exactly a BR*Tool does when it is called from within the SAP system or from a third-party application.

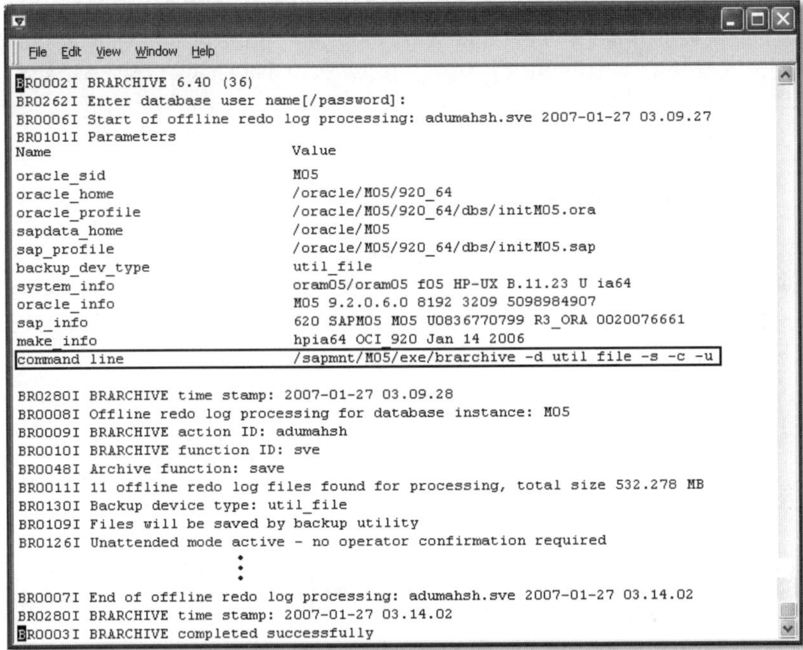

File Edit View Window Help

```
BR0002I BRARCHIVE 6.40 (36)
BR0262I Enter database user name[/password]:
BR0006I Start of offline redo log processing: adumahsh.sve 2007-01-27 03.09.27
BR0101I Parameters
Name                          Value
oracle_sid                    M05
oracle_home                   /oracle/M05/920_64
oracle_profile                /oracle/M05/920_64/dbs/initM05.ora
sapdata_home                  /oracle/M05
sap_profile                   /oracle/M05/920_64/dbs/initM05.sap
backup_dev_type               util_file
system_info                   oram05/oram05 f05 HP-UX B.11.23 U ia64
oracle_info                   M05 9.2.0.6.0 8192 3209 5098984907
sap_info                      620 SAPM05 M05 U0836770799 R3_ORA 0020076661
make_info                     hpia64 OCI_920 Jan 14 2006
command line                  /sapmnt/M05/exe/brarchive -d util_file -s -c -u

BR0280I BRARCHIVE time stamp: 2007-01-27 03.09.28
BR0008I Offline redo log processing for database instance: M05
BR0009I BRARCHIVE action ID: adumahsh
BR0010I BRARCHIVE function ID: sve
BR0048I Archive function: save
BR0011I 11 offline redo log files found for processing, total size 532.278 MB
BR0130I Backup device type: util_file
BR0109I Files will be saved by backup utility
BR0126I Unattended mode active - no operator confirmation required
                    :
BR0007I End of offline redo log processing: adumahsh.sve 2007-01-27 03.14.02
BR0280I BRARCHIVE time stamp: 2007-01-27 03.14.02
BR0003I BRARCHIVE completed successfully
```

Figure 4.24 Log File of a BRARCHIVE Session

As you can see in the figure, the log file contains all actions carried out by the BR*Tool. All log entries begin with a key that's structured as follows: BR[0000 – 9999][I|W|E]. The individual elements have the following meanings:

- **[0000 9999]**
  This is a code for the action that's being executed or for the output of a message. For example, code 0280 always represents the timestamp at various points in the current session. The BR*Tools of Release 6.20 or lower used a three-digit code.
- **[I|W|E]**
  The final letter categorizes the message as information, warning, or error.

This key helps you quickly find important information and solutions in the SAP Service Marketplace if an error occurs.

> **Note**
>
> The log files for BRBACKUP and BRARCHIVE are much more important than other log files, as they are not only used for monitoring purposes. They are actively used during the recovery of an Oracle database to determine information such as how, when, and where a specific file was saved. You cannot perform a database recovery without these logs.
>
> Moreover, note that the BR*Tools (and the old SAPDBA) not only write log files to the file system, but also insert log entries in two database tables: SDBAH and SDBAD.

4.5.3 BRTOOLS and BRGUI

As described, BRTOOLS and BRGUI are the frontends for all other tools. Although you can run all tools directly from the command prompt, SAP generally recommends using the frontends of the BR*Tools whenever you need to perform complex operations, such as a database reorganization or restore. One of the reasons for this is that the frontends provide a much better overview of the possible parameters for an action. Moreover, they offer a step-by-step process that facilitates the overall handling and reduces the potential for errors. Figure 4.25 shows the initial menu after starting BRTOOLS.

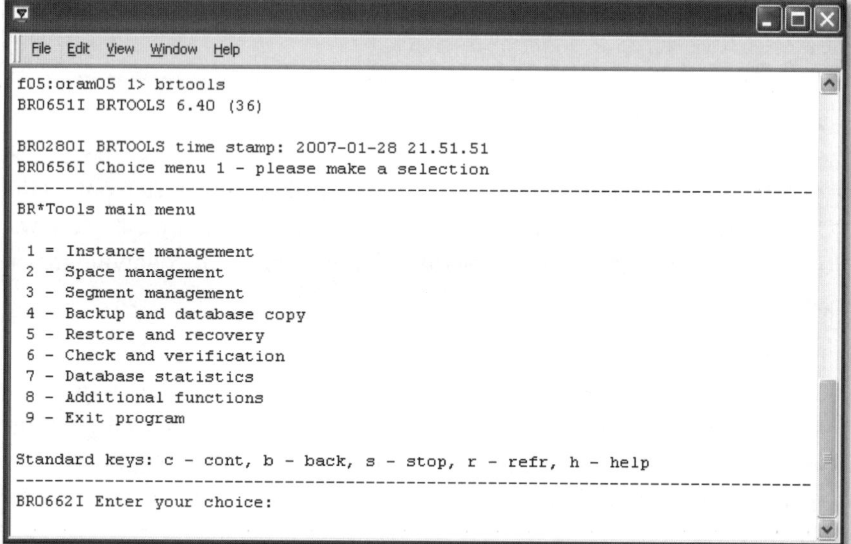

Figure 4.25 Initial Menu of BRTOOLS

Table 4.19 is an overview of the purpose or function behind the primary menu items as well as the tool used for that purpose.

Menu Item	Function	Tool
Instance Manag.	▸ Stop, start, and status of the Oracle database ▸ Oracle parameter maintenance ▸ ALTER INSTANCE functions	BRSPACE
Space Manag.	▸ Create, enhance, and delete tablespaces ▸ ALTER TABLESPACE functions ▸ Administration of data files	BRSPACE
Segment Manag.	▸ Reorganization of tables and tablespaces ▸ Index management (rebuild, ALTER) ▸ Import, export, and ALTER of tables	BRSPACE
Backup and DB Copy	▸ Backup of the database and archive logs, verification of backups ▸ Backup of database disk backups ▸ Database copies ▸ Initialization of backup tapes	BRBACKUP, BRARCHIVE, BRRESTORE
Restore and Recovery	▸ Restore and recovery in the different variants, such as point-in-time recovery, database reset, etc. (see Chapter 10)	BRRESTORE, BRRECOVER
Check and Verification	▸ Database check ▸ Check of the database structure ▸ Verification of database blocks	BRCONNECT, BRBACKUP
Database Statistics	▸ Creation of statistics (for access performance) ▸ Deletion of poor statistics	BRCONNECT
Additional Functions	▸ Display of profiles and logs ▸ Deletion of old logs ▸ Changing passwords for different database users ▸ Customizing Next Extents sizes (for DMTS)	BRCONNECT

Table 4.19 Functions in the Main Menu of BRTOOLS

The only (sub)function that is executed by the BRTOOLS program itself is the displaying of profiles and log files (under **Additional functions**). For all other functions, the program calls the various BR*Tools with the relevant parameters.

Note: You can also start all functions of the individual tools directly from the command prompt. We'll make use of this option quite often in this book. For an experienced administrator, that's the fast way to the goal. For those of you who are not yet very familiar with the administrative tasks, the BRTOOLS menus always provide an option to call the respective function.

The second frontend for the BR*Tools is the Java-based program, BRGUI. This program is not provided with the other programs in one archive but can be downloaded separately via the following URL in the SAP Developer Network (SDN): *www.sdn.sap.com/irj/sdn/ora*. BRGUI is available in German and English and can be executed on all platforms where a Java VM 1.4 is available. For the display of log files, a web browser is required too (Internet Explorer or Mozilla), which runs on the same machine as BRGUI.

The main advantage of BRGUI is that it is remote-enabled, that is, the graphical user interface can run on a different machine than the actual BR*Tools programs, for instance, on the desktop of the administrator. For this purpose, BRGUI connects to the database server in the background and executes the appropriate tools depending on the functions that are called. These connections can be configured in such a way that they are established automatically, that is, without requiring a password. Moreover, they can be encrypted (ssh) or not (rsh). SAP Notes 935240 (ssh) and 898224 (rsh) provide instructions for these configurations.

Of course, each connection to the database server is initiated by an operating system user. Because the operating system user must have the necessary privileges to execute all BR*Tools functions with the Oracle database, the ora<sid> is the one that's typically used in this context.

The configuration itself is carried out in the text-based brgui.properties file. This is where the individual connections are stored, which can then be selected in the login screen. Figure 4.26 shows this login screen in the foreground and the initial screen of BRGUI after a successful connection in the background.

Furthermore, in the configuration file, you must specify which web browser you want to use, and you can activate various trace options.

Although the first version of BRGUI was introduced in 2003, it now represents the first attempt to provide a graphical user interface for the BR*Tools. A successor tool called *BR*Tools-Studio* is about to be released soon. This studio is based on the Web Dynpro technology and can be operated through a web browser.

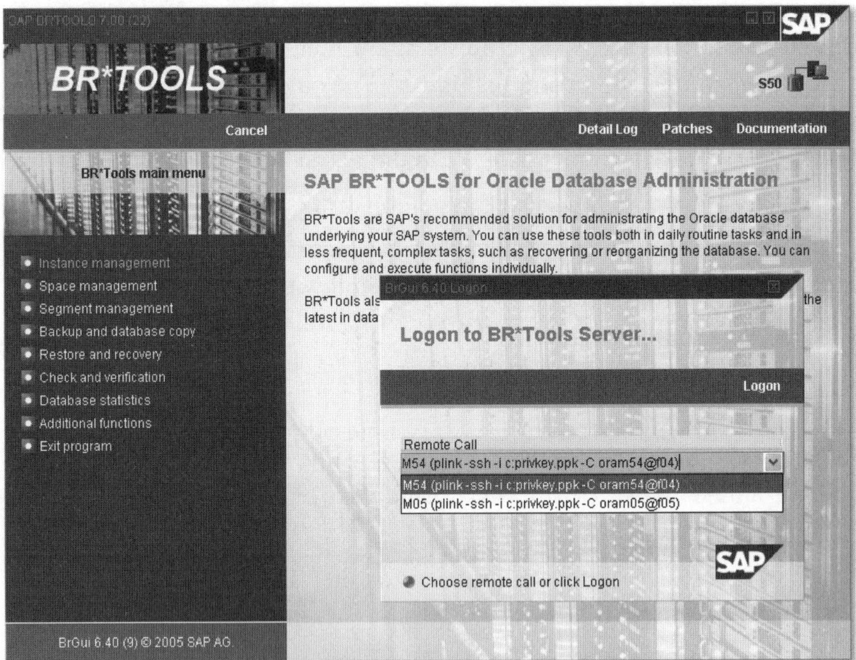

Figure 4.26 BRGUI – Graphical User Interface of the BR*Tools

4.5.4 BRCONNECT

The previous sections have made it clear that the administration tools, `BRCONNECT` and `BRSPACE`, represent the core of the BR*Tools. Consequently, we will take a closer look at these tools in this and the next section. Let us start with the functions of `BRCONNECT`. Some of these functions and their background will be described in greater detail in other chapters, which we'll point out to you in the appropriate places.

> **Note**
>
> We will execute all command prompt calls in these sections as the ora<sid> user. Many of them could also be run as <sid>adm, but with ora<sid> you're always on the safe side.

The database check carried out by `BRCONNECT` is a powerful database monitoring tool. You can start the check using the following command:

```
brconnect -c -u / -f check
```

You already know the -c option; the -u option activates the login via the OPS$ process. All calls of BR*Tools contain the -f option in front of the actual function name — check, in this case. The output appears on the screen and in the generated log file (see Section 4.5.2, *Environment, Options, and Log Files*).

After the start, the database check function examines the status of the redo-log groups or the status of all data files. In a second phase, it checks values and conditions that can be divided into the following four categories:

- **Database administration (DBA)**
  For example, archiver stucks, full tablespace, malign statistics, missing indexes, and so on.
- **Database operation (DBO)**
  For example, last successful backup and archive backup and so on.
- **Database messages (ORA)**
  For example, all registered Oracle error messages ORA-XXXXX such as ORA-00600 (Internal Error).
- **Oracle profile parameters (PROF)**
  For example, all registered Oracle profile parameters such as LOG_BUFFER or LOG_ARCHIVE_START.

The Oracle administrator can configure all these values and conditions. The ORA and PROF categories even allow for the entry of new data, that is, new checks. All database check conditions are stored in Table DBCHECKORA and must be maintained using Transaction DB17 (see Figure 4.27).

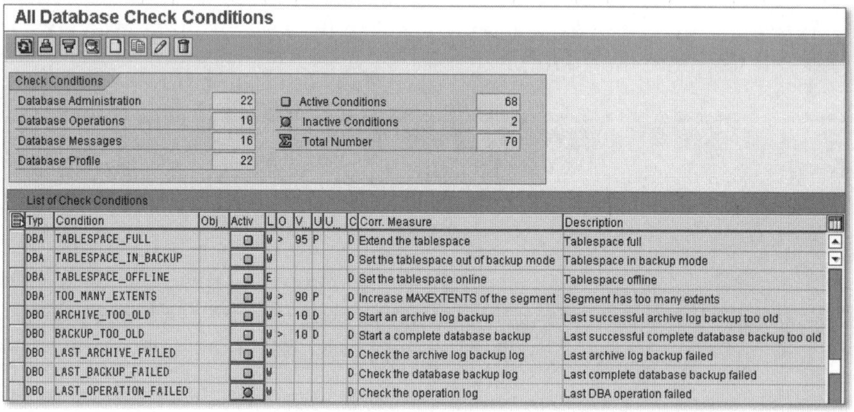

All Database Check Conditions
Check Conditions
Database Administration 22
Database Operations 10
Database Messages 16
Database Profile 22
Active Conditions 68
Inactive Conditions 2
Total Number 70
List of Check Conditions
Typ Condition Obj Activ L O V U U C Corr. Measure Description
DBA TABLESPACE_FULL W > 95 P D Extend the tablespace Tablespace full
DBA TABLESPACE_IN_BACKUP W D Set the tablespace out of backup mode Tablespace in backup mode
DBA TABLESPACE_OFFLINE E D Set the tablespace online Tablespace offline
DBA TOO_MANY_EXTENTS W > 90 P D Increase MAXEXTENTS of the segment Segment has too many extents
DBO ARCHIVE_TOO_OLD W > 10 D D Start an archive log backup Last successful archive log backup too old
DBO BACKUP_TOO_OLD W > 10 D D Start a complete database backup Last successful complete database backup too old
DBO LAST_ARCHIVE_FAILED W D Check the archive log backup log Last archive log backup failed
DBO LAST_BACKUP_FAILED W D Check the database backup log Last complete database backup failed
DBO LAST_OPERATION_FAILED W D Check the operation log Last DBA operation failed

Figure 4.27 Maintaining Database Check Conditions (DB17)

For example, the administrator can define the maximum period of time between two successful backups (BACKUP_TO_OLD) or at which point a tablespace is supposed to be considered full (TABLESPACE_FULL). Chapter 9, *System Operation and Monitoring*, provides further information on the topic of database checks.

Another function of BRCONNECT is that it enables you to determine the size of the next extent for segments in a DMTS; this function is referred to as *Adapt Next Extents*. You can call the function using the following command:

```
brconnect -c -u / -f next -t all
```

The -t option defines for which tables or indexes the next-extents calculation is supposed to be performed. The calculation must include many different factors, such as the entries for a table in DD09L with regard to the size category (see Section 4.4.3, *Object Assignment and Object Parameters*). The exact description of the calculation algorithm would exceed the scope of this section and is not really necessary because it is losing its importance with the gradual disappearance of DMTS. You can find the algorithm in the SAP Online Documentation.

The third function of BRCONNECT, however, is very important for the operation of the Oracle database, or rather, for its performance. In the SAP environment, Oracle usually employs the cost-based access optimization function — the Cost-Based Optimizer (CBO). However, up to and including Oracle 9i, you can find tables that are processed using the RBO, and sometimes even the RULE hint is used as well. The CBO enables the analysis of statistics via table accesses to calculate the costs of different access paths. This is exactly what BRCONNECT does with its *Update Statistics* function, which can be called using the following command:

```
brconnect -u / -c -f stats -t all
```

Because the statistics are important, Chapters 8 and 9 provide a detailed discussion of this topic.

In Section 4.3.1, we described how you can use BRCONNECT to set or change the passwords of the database users. You can call this function as follows:

```
brconnect -f chpass -o <DB_user> -p <password>
```

As mentioned earlier, it is particularly recommended that you use BRCONNECT with the standard SAP database user.

Another useful function of BRCONNECT is that it cleans up different logs and backups both in the file system and in the database. The function is referred to as *cleanup* and must be started as follows:

```
brconnect -u / -c -f cleanup
```

The cleanup task is complex and is composed of the following files and tables:

- Session log files of all BR*Tools
- Disk backups of Oracle data files and offline-redo log files as well as database export dumps
- Oracle trace files
- Log entries in Tables SDBAH, SDBAD, and DBMSGORA as well as in the XDB interface tables

For each individual object, you can specifically define the length of the period after which the individual logs or backups are deleted. To do that, you can either use a command prompt parameter (such as `-s <days>` for the log files of BRSPACE) or the corresponding parameter in the *init<sid>.sap* configuration file of the BR*Tools (such as `cleanup_brspace_log=<days>` for BRSPACE logs). The default values are as follows: 30 days for all logs in the file system and 100 days for the logs in database tables.

Last, the administrator can use BRCONNECT to start and stop the database and to query its status:

- **Start:** `brconnect -u / -f dbstart`
- **Stop:** `brconnect -u / -f dbshut`
- **Status:** `brconnect -u / -f dbstate`

The status request returns the following simple return codes: 0 = open, 1 = stop, 2 = mount or unmount, and 3 = error during status determination. The database can also be started and stopped using BRSPACE (see next section).

4.5.5 BRSPACE

The second primary program in the BR*Tools is BRSPACE, which contains even more functions than BRCONNECT. Again, we will describe some of these functions in detail and refer to other sections in the book that describe those functions that aren't described here.

Let us begin with starting and stopping the database. In BRSPACE, this function contains many more possible parameters, which makes it more powerful. For this reason, BRSPACE is always used in the background when the Oracle database is started or stopped via the BRTOOLS program. The function calls look as follows:

- **Start:** `brspace -f dbstart -m [mode] -s [state]`
  The `-m` option defines the mode in which Oracle is supposed to be started, such as *restrict* for the administration mode. The `-s` option, on the other hand, defines the status of the database, such as open or mount. The default values for the `-m` and `-s` options always correspond to the normal database start.
- **Stop:** `brspace -f dbshut -m [mode]`
  Here, `-m` specifies the option for shutting down the database, such as *immediate* for an immediate shutdown caused by a direct termination of all Oracle sessions and a rollback of open transactions. **Warning**: *immediate* is the default value for `-m`; it is not the normal database stop.

The status function of BRSPACE differs significantly from that of BRCONNECT, as it enables you to retrieve comprehensive information about the database. To do that, you must use the following command:

- **Show:** `brspace -f dbshow -c <parameter>`

Table 4.20 provides an overview of the capabilities of the main option, `-c`.

Main Options of dbshow	Display of
dbstate	Database status
tsinfo	Tablespaces
rfinfo	Redo log files
idinfo	Index information
dvinfo	Database disks or directories
ipinfo	Information about index partitions
seinfo	Segment extents
dbparam	Database parameters
dfindo	Data files

Table 4.20 Display Options with the dbshow Function

Main Options of dbshow	Display of
cfinfo	Control files
tbinfo	Table information
tpinfo	Information about table partitions
sginfo	Segments
feinfo	Free extents

Table 4.20 Display Options with the dbshow Function

In addition, you have the option to limit the display to specific areas:

`-f <file>, -s <tablespace>, -t <table>, or -i <index>.`

The ALTER database function enables you to trigger two basic database actions: a log file switch (`-a switchlog`) or a checkpoint (`-a checkpoint`). Furthermore, it allows you to switch the log file mode of the Oracle database on or off (`-a archlog | noarchlog`). To call these actions, you must enter the following command:

```
brspace -f dbalter -a <action>
```

Note that you must restart the Oracle database after a change to the log file mode, which means the SAP system won't be available for the duration of the restart process.

For the administrator, a constantly recurring task involves the extension of the database and thus the extension of a tablespace. The frequency at which you must carry out this task depends on whether you use the Autoextend function and how quickly the database grows. If you use the Autoextend function, you must define the maximum size to which a data file may grow. Consequently, the total of all maximum size values of the data files of a tablespace determines the maximum size of that tablespace as well. If the tablespace is full and you don't use the Autoextend function, you must extend the tablespace using the following command:

```
brspace -f tsextend -t <tablespace> -s <size>
```

If you do use Autoextend, some more parameters must be added:

```
brspace -f .. -t .. -s .. -a -m <max_size> -i <increase in MB>
```

You can also define a file name (-f ...) for the new file if you don't want to adhere to the SAP naming convention for data files. Some additional parameters are available for this complex BRSPACE function, such as the *target directory* (-r ...). In this context, it is useful to use the menu-controlled user interfaces of BRTOOLS or BRGUI.

You won't often need to create a new tablespace. However, if that does become necessary, for instance, during a reorganization, the BR*Tools, and BRSPACE, in particular, can provide help in this context as well. Because when you create a tablespace, you must define all its properties (DMTS versus LMTS, Autoextend, type, etc.), the BRSPACE function -f tscreate has 19 additional options. Calling the function from the command prompt does not make much sense here, except for complex automations. Therefore, you should use BRTOOLS or BRGUI.

Deleting a tablespace is very easy:

```
brspace -f tsdrop -f -t <tablespace>
```

Caution: The -f option ensures that the tablespace is deleted even if it isn't empty.

Section 4.4.4 already described when and why the administrator should carry out a reorganization. We also described the theoretical process of such a reorganization. The actual work is again carried out by BRSPACE. Here are some examples of calling the reorganization function:

- One or several tables are reorganized:

  ```
  brspace -f tbreorg -t <table1,table2,...>
  ```

- All tables that can be entered via a search pattern ("T*") are reorganized and moved to a new tablespace:

  ```
  brspace -f tbreorg -t "T*" -n <destination_tablespace>
  ```

- All tables of a tablespace are reorganized in three parallel processes:

  ```
  brspace -f tbreorg -s <tablespace> -t "*" -p 3
  ```

As you can see, many possible options are available. In addition, several other alternatives exist for the handling of special cases during a reorganization, such as tables that contain LONG fields. A reorganization for the purpose of freeing up hard disk space is relatively easy to perform with the commands listed previously. However, if you want to migrate the tablespace types or the tablespace layout, a considerable number of additional steps is necessary so that you should use BRTOOLS and BRGUI again. In any case, make sure you use the SAP Notes recommended in Section 4.4.4 with regard to reorganizations.

The last BRSPACE function we want to describe here enables you to rebuild an index. You can call this function as follows:

```
brspace -f idrebuild [-i <index> | -t <table>]
```

This function also contains numerous additional options, most of which work in the same way as with the reorganization function, such as -s ... for all indexes of a tablespace or -n ... for the simultaneous move into a new tablespace. The index rebuild can be performed online, like a reorganization. However, you should ensure that no changes are made to the index during the rebuild process, if that's possible. Otherwise, lock situations can occur under certain circumstances (for instance, with specific Oracle releases or patch statuses; see SAP Note 682926).

BRSPACE contains some more functions that we will only mention briefly here:

- **dbparam:** This function is used to administrate the Oracle parameters. For more information on this topic, refer to the following section, 4.5.6, *Parameter Maintenance for Oracle*.
- **dbcreate:** This function enables the administrator to create a new database. This includes the Oracle Dictionary data and metadata, but not the SAP data, that is, the SYSTEM, SYSAUX (as of 10g), PSAPUNDO, and PSAPTEMP tablespaces. This function enables the following actions:
  - Migrating the SYSTEM tablespace from DTMS to LMTS
  - Removing a fragmentation or eliminating extent problems (such as too many extents) in SYSTEM or SYSAUX tablespace (as of 10g)
  - Removing corruptions in the SYSTEM or SYSAUX tablespace (as of 10g)
- **tsalter:** This function performs the different ALTER TABLESPACE actions, for instance, by setting or disabling the backup mode (see Chapter 10).
- **dfalter:** This function performs the different ALTER TABLESPACE actions, for instance, by setting or disabling the backup mode (see Chapter 10).

- **dfmove:** This function enables you to move or rename Oracle data files. Warning: For moving or renaming data files, the respective tablespace must be set offline.
- **tbexport:** This function enables you to export one or several tables or an entire tablespace.
- **tbimport:** The corresponding counterpart function allows you to import the exported objects.
- **tbalter:** This function performs the different ALTER TABLE actions, such as segment shrinking of table segments as of Oracle 10g (see Section 4.4.4).
- **idalter:** This function performs the different ALTER INDEX actions.

4.5.6 Parameter Maintenance for Oracle

The parameter maintenance for the Oracle database is also carried out using BRSPACE. However, we believe this function is very important because parameter maintenance occurs or must be carried out in almost all areas of Oracle administration. Therefore, we dedicate an entire section to it.

Oracle 9i came with a new type of parameter maintenance. The central component of this new feature is the *Oracle Server Parameter File* (SPFILE). The corresponding file, spfile.ora or spfile<DBSID>.org, replaces the old parameter file, init.ora or init<DBSID>.ora, respectively, which is also referred to as PFILE. In contrast to the old files, SPFILE is stored as a binary file; that is, it can be viewed with any editor (such as vi on UNIX), but you cannot modify it.

Warning

Each manual change to SPFILE destroys it.

The storage location for the parameter file (both old and new) is always *$ORACLE_HOME/dbs* (Windows: *%ORACLE_HOME%\DATABASE*). Theoretically, Oracle also allows other storage locations, but that's not permitted in the SAP environment because the BR*Tools does not support this.

When you start an Oracle database (Version 9i or higher), it searches for a parameter file in the following sequence, and then uses the first file that can be found and ignores all others:

1. *spfile<DBSID>.ora*
2. *spfile.ora*
3. *init<DBSID>.ora*

This sequence shows that the old parameter files can still be used. This becomes necessary if SPFILE is corrupted. In the SAP environment, PFILE (init<DBSID>.ora) is still required because various SAP transactions that interact directly with the Oracle database are based on that file, such as Transactions ST04 or DB02. For this reason, a new version of the init<DBSID>.ora file is generated whenever `BRBACKUP`, `BRARCHIVE`, and `BRCONNECT` ("`–check`" function) are started and a parameter change is carried out using `BRSPACE`; the old version of init<DBSID>.ora is overwritten in this process.

Before we move on to describe the actual parameter management processes, let us first take a look at some basic principles. Three types of parameters are available for an Oracle database:

- **Normal parameters**
  These parameters determine the properties of the database. This is the type of parameter we are going to focus on in this section.
- **Underscore parameters** (beginning with "_")
  These are specific Oracle-internal parameters, which are intended for emergency situations and may be set only if you are explicitly instructed to do so by SAP or Oracle.
- **Events**
  These are Oracle-internal flags that can change a certain behavior, simulate a situation, or collect trace and debug information. Note that you should set these flags only if you are specifically instructed to do so.

The normal parameters can be divided into *dynamic* and *static* parameters. A change to a dynamic parameter can immediately affect the Oracle database if the administrator wants this to happen. In that case, the database becomes active right away. However, the activation of a static parameter always requires a restart of the database. You can use the V$PARAMETER view to determine whether an Oracle parameter is dynamic or static. This view contains two important columns: ISSYS_MODIFIABLE and ISSES_MODIFIABLE. You can use the following command to query the characteristics of an Oracle parameter:

```
SQL>select ISSYS_MODIFIABLE, ISSES_MODIFIABLE
    from V$PARAMETER where NAME='<parameter_name>';
```

The ISSYS_MODIFIABLE column can contain the following three values and thus define the most important parameter properties:

- **FALSE**
  The parameter is static, which means a change cannot take effect until you restart the Oracle instance.
- **IMMEDIATE**
  The parameter is dynamic, which means changes take effect immediately and in all components involved.
- **DEFERRED**
  The parameter is dynamic, but a change affects only new sessions. In that case, the administrator must start the SAP instance or cancel and restart the individual SAP work processes (using Transaction SM50, for example) to rebuild the session. However, only a few parameters have this property.

The second column, ISSES_MODIFIABLE, specifies whether the parameter can be set or activated for a single session using the following SQL command:

```
alter session set <parameter>=<value>
```

However, this measure doesn't occur often in the everyday work of the administrator, as it is used for advanced debugging and tracing purposes. Consequently, the BRSPACE tool doesn't contain the ALTER function for a session.

Let us now take a look at how you must administrate the Oracle parameters. You can set the parameters either using an SQL command or via BRSPACE. Again, you should be aware that a manual entry of a parameter into SPFILE corrupts the file so that you can no longer use it. The syntax of the SQL command is as follows:

```
SQL>alter system set <parameter>=<value>
    comment='<comment>'
    scope=[BOTH|SPFILE|MEMORY]
    SID='[<Oracle instance SID>|*]';
```

The BRSPACE counterpart is structured as follows:

```
brspace -f dbparam -a change -p <parameter> -v <value>
-i <Oracle instance SID> -s [both|spfile|memory]
```

You can use the Oracle instance option for an RAC installation to specify an instance. The scope or -s option plays a particularly important role, as it defines where exactly the parameter is changed. Depending on the value, this can have the following effects:

- **Memory**
  The parameter is modified only in the memory of the running instance and will therefore be reset to its previous value during a restart. This makes sense only with dynamic parameters.
- **Spfile**
  The parameter is modified only in SPFILE and will therefore be valid only after a restart. This is the only possible option for a static parameter.
- **Both**
  The parameter is modified in the memory of the running instance and in SPFILE. This is the default option for a dynamic parameter, as it can be generally assumed that changes are supposed to be valid even after a restart.

A particularly convenient function is the parameter management through the menus of BRTOOLS or BRGUI, as here you can see all important information relating to a specific parameter. Figure 4.28 illustrates this and shows an excerpt from the parameter display in BRTOOLS.

```
File  Edit  View  Window  Help

Pos.  Parameter                        Modif.  Spfile  Inst.   Deft. Value
  1 - active_instance_count            spfile   no      *      yes   <null>
  2 - aq_tm_processes                  both     no      *      yes   0
  3 - archive_lag_target               both     no      *      yes   0
  4 - audit_file_dest                  spfile   no      *      yes   ?/rdbms/audit
  5 - audit_sys_operations             spfile   no      *      yes   FALSE
  6 - audit_trail                      spfile   no      *      yes   NONE
  7 - background_core_dump             spfile   no      *      yes   partial
  8 - background_dump_dest             both     yes     *      no    /oracle/M02/saptrace/back
ound
  9 - backup_tape_io_slaves            both     no      *      yes   FALSE
 10 - bitmap_merge_area_size           spfile   yes     *      yes   1048576 -> 2048000
 11 - blank_trimming                   spfile   no      *      yes   FALSE
 12 - buffer_pool_keep                 spfile   no      *      yes   <null>
 13 - buffer_pool_recycle              spfile   no      *      yes   <null>
 14 - circuits                         spfile   no      *      yes   0
 15 - cluster_database                 spfile   no      *      yes   FALSE
 16 - cluster_database_instances       spfile   no      *      yes   1
 17 - cluster_interconnects            spfile   no      *      yes   <null>
 18 - commit_point_strength            spfile   no      *      yes   1
 19 - compatible                       spfile   yes     *      no    9.2.0
 20 - control file record keep time   both     yes     *      no    30
```

Figure 4.28 Parameter Maintenance with BRSPACE through BRTOOLS

Table 4.21 explains the meaning of the individual columns.

Column	Meaning
Parameter	Name of the parameter (in alphabetical order)
Modif.	Displays where exactly the parameter is changed by default. This means: `both` = the parameter is dynamic and is permanently changed right away; `spfile` = the parameter is static and can only be changed in the parameter file. The `memory` can be used during execution.
Spfile	Displays whether the parameter is set in SPFILE.
Inst.	Displays the valid Oracle instance. * = all
Deft.	Displays whether the value corresponds to the Oracle default value.
Value	Displays the current value *and* the future value if it has already been modified in SPFILE (see Figure 4.28, **bitmap_merge_area_size**, line **10**).

Table 4.21 Explanation of Parameter Display

Note

One of the big advantages of using `BRSPACE` to modify Oracle parameters is that the program stores a change history in the $SAPDATA_HOME/sapreorg/param<DBSID>.log file. This can be very helpful in an error analysis.

We want to conclude this chapter by taking a look at the error case of a destroyed SPFILE, which was mentioned several times in the previous sections. For this purpose, it is useful to know how the parameter files — both old (PFILE) and new (SPFILE) — can be managed and converted. The following SQL command enables the administrator to determine which parameter file is active:

```
SQL>show parameter spfile
```

The result must return the value `?/dbs/spfile@.ora` in the VALUE column if SPFILE is active. If the value is blank, the system uses the old parameter file, init<DBSID>.ora. If you run Oracle 9i or higher, it is generally advisable to use SPFILE. However, a prerequisite for this is that you use BR*Tools Version 6.40 or higher. To migrate the old parameter management to the new one, you merely need to enter the following SQL command, which generates an SPFILE from a PFILE:

```
SQL> create spfile from pfile;
```

After that, you can start the Oracle database. Due to the search sequence described previously, the database then uses SPFILE. Similarly, to convert the parameter files in the opposite direction, you must use the following command:

```
SQL> create pfile from spfile;
```

Then, after removing SPFILE and restarting the database, PFILE will be loaded. You can also specify a path as the source or target of a conversion process, such as the following:

```
SQL> create pfile='/path/pfile.tmp' from
    spfile='/path/backup_spfile';
```

Thus, if you have a corrupt SPFILE, you must generate a new one from the one that was automatically generated or from a backed-up PFILE. If you set a parameter to an incorrect value and the database won't start, you cannot correct the value directly in SPFILE; instead, you must proceed as follows:

1. `create pfile='pfile.tmp' from spfile;`
2. Reset the parameter in file pfile.tmp.
3. `create spfile from pfile='pfile.tmp';`

Because PFILE is generated automatically when you use `BRSPACE`, you must search for the old value in the corresponding session log of `BRSPACE`, provided you haven't memorized it previously.

The automatic creation of PFILE involves an oddity the administrator should be aware of: If SPFILE is corrupt, the Oracle database starts nevertheless, because a current PFILE exists. Consequently, such an error would not be recognized until `BRTOOLS` was used (see Figure 4.28) and displayed `yes` or `no` instead of `spfile` or `both` in the **Modif** column. That would indicate that PFILE is active.

4.6 Summary

This chapter has described the interaction between the SAP system and an Oracle database. The interaction between SAP and Oracle takes place at several different levels in the following areas:

- Operating system: users, groups, and variables
- Processes: SAP work processes and Oracle shadow processes
- SAP kernel: database library and Oracle client

Regarding the administration of Oracle databases, SAP provides a powerful tool that will be continuously maintained and further extended in future releases: the BR*Tools. BR*Tools Studio, which will be released soon, will further increase the convenience and ease-of-use related to that tool.

All administrators who already have experience with Oracle databases should be aware that SAP systems do not use all functions of Oracle databases, for the following reasons:

- A high degree of stability in production systems requires the limitation to features that are technically mature.
- If possible, you should only use functions that are also provided by other databases to ensure that you do not depend too much on a specific database product.
- The SAP-specific BR*Tools must support an Oracle feature to keep the amount of required support services as small as possible.

It is these principles in particular, and the long association between Oracle and SAP systems, that make the combination of SAP systems and Oracle databases so successful.

"Imagine a house. The whole thing must be organized — like a computer. Power, heat, costs, safety. All of its parameters must be optimally tuned to one another. Effectively, and cost-effectively."
Professor Djamshid Tavangarian (University of Rostock)

5 Planning the System Landscape

Every restructuring or rebuilding of a system landscape requires planning or a rethinking of the future location of the hardware. This especially includes appropriately air-conditioned rooms to house the infrastructure, but the safety of a building against natural disasters or break-ins and theft cannot be ignored. An overview of the many aspects to be considered is presented in the following sections.

5.1 From Product to Solution Landscape

Over the course of the past few years, the product range of SAP has continued to expand, divided into many complex products. These, usually starting from a core module or product (often SAP R/3, CRM, ERP, or ECC), handle very specialized tasks, such as up-to-the-minute production planning (APO/SCM) or the analysis of business data (SAP NetWeaver BI). Another result is a change in the product range offered by SAP. Instead of product sales, the focus is increasingly on the sale of solutions. In the context of a solution, different functions and processes in SAP products are woven together into a complex landscape of mutual dependencies. These products are presented to the customer as a complete package. The complexity of this solution, however, must necessarily result in an ever-increasing hardware complexity supporting the installation. Especially for an extension or a release upgrade, the structure of the existing landscape must be analyzed to avoid exceeding the physical limits of the servers in use or even the entire landscape during the software conversion. An example of a typical landscape is shown in Figure 5.1.

In the figure, the central system is SAP ERP 6.0, which uses a connected supply chain management system (SCM system) for production planning and provides data to SAP NetWeaver BI for use in reporting and analysis. To access the data in each system, different paths have been implemented. For the company's internal staff, who work very intensively with the systems, there is a direct SAP GUI access method. For the consolidated provision of information from multiple systems and a graphically sophisticated presentation, an enterprise portal has been installed, allowing browser-based access to enterprise data. Finally, for an internal shop system developed in Java, an SAP NetWeaver Web Application Server Java has been set up, giving customers web-based access to the company's product catalogs.

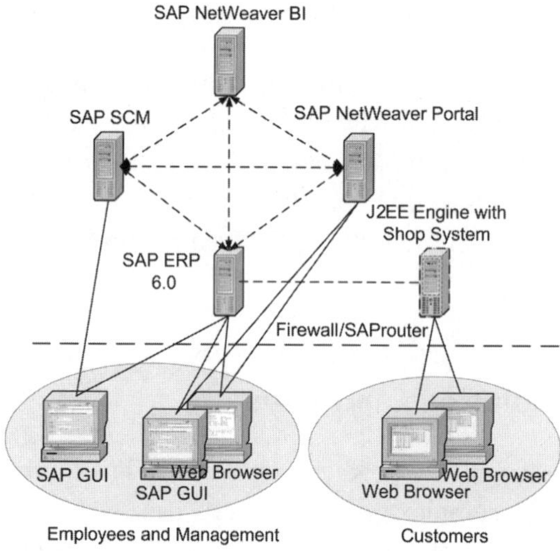

Figure 5.1 Sample Landscape of Multiple Connected Systems and Different Access Methods

This is intended as an example of how different components are affected when building or changing a system landscape. No matter what the size of a landscape, the same questions are almost always asked during the planning phase:

- Where and how are the systems operated?
- How should systems be distributed on servers? Do you want one big server that can handle all of the systems, or should things be distributed across several smaller servers?
- Is a development and test system needed for each system?
- Do the systems need high availability?
- What does the planned backup strategy look like?
- How do employees and customers access the systems?

This chapter will start you on your way to answering these questions, helping you find the simplest possible introduction into system operations.

5.2 Overview of Planning Criteria

After the decision to build a system landscape has been made, the design of the landscape can begin. Starting from the planned size of and future extensions to a system landscape, a decision can often be made relatively early on whether the underlying servers can be located at the company's own facilities or will be operated in an outsourcing mode by an *application service provider* (ASP).

An application service provider handles customers' system operations, hosting servers and systems in their own data center. The customer more or less gets the application system "from an outlet." In the context of this book, however, we will assume that all systems will be operated under your own responsibility. If that's not the case, many of these decisions (room, climate, physical security) will be handled for you by an ASP, because the ASP already has a particular infrastructure.

For the complete construction of a system landscape from scratch, during the construction phase there are already two significant points to keep in mind. These are:

- **Physical planning values**
  The physical planning factors include the location of the server, power supply, climate control, and security against both environmental influences and criminal attacks.
- **Hardware infrastructure**
  This includes the server platform and its operating system, the SAN and LAN infrastructure, and the structure of the backups. You should also consider whether a highly available solution is planned, because that entails special requirements for the hardware.

Both factors influence one another, within certain limits. Thus, one part of this planning should not be considered without the other. Depending on the choice of server platform and the scope of the system, there will be different requirements for climate control, power supply, and space requirements for the hardware. Additional effects on construction planning stem from security requirements and high availability requirements for the landscape or by the enterprise.

5.2.1 Construction Infrastructure

Even during planning and construction or renovation of a building, you must take into account that certain spaces will be reserved for use as server rooms. These are generally equipped with a false floor. These false floors provide about 30 to 40 cm of space above the actual floor, which can be used for climate control and wiring. To compensate for the height difference from the "normal" floor, stairs should *not* be used. Instead, a ramp should be used, allowing heavy hardware to be rolled into the room. Other threats to the delivery of hardware are insufficient load capacities of ceilings, capacity or height of elevators, and insufficiently large doors or stairways. Care must therefore be taken that problem-free transport of hardware from the place of delivery (for instance, the loading ramp) to the computer room will be possible. The load capacities already mentioned and ceiling heights on the way to the computer room, as well as access to the room itself, must all be considered.

Based on the sizing of the landscape (see Section 5.2.2, *Server Technology and Platforms*) and the resulting decision on a platform, you can derive the space requirements for that server. Servers are usually structured in rack systems (racks). These racks are simply cabinets for the storage of the hardware. It is important to note that you don't simply need space for the racks, but also space in front of and behind the racks for access for maintenance. These spaces are also required for climate control for the server. Cool air is generally blown onto servers on one side and then exhausted from the other side. This means that the data center can be divided into warm (exhaust side) and cold (intake side) corridors. The goal is to guide the flow of cold air onto the servers as optimally as possible (for instance, through larger air outlets in the floor plates in front of the servers) and to return the warm air to the air conditioner as quickly and concentrated as possible (for instance, intakes directly behind the servers). Thus, the entire data center may not need to be cooled. Specific introduction and removal of cold and heat may make it possible to save on power costs. When setting up the servers, it is then important to ensure that the air intakes and outlets are facing the same direction. A schematic view of the implementation of warm and cold corridors is shown in Figure 5.2.

To distribute cool air in the data center, the false floors mentioned earlier are used. These serve, on the one hand, to introduce the cool air to the racks and, on the other hand, to lay the cables needed by the servers (power, LAN, SAN). It should be noted that there should be no "cable pile" under the floor to disturb the air flow. Precise adjustment of the outlet openings in the floor plates is necessary, because otherwise there may be islands of heat due to insufficient cold air, particularly for the top servers (the air pressure will be too low). If gaps exist between servers in the rack, dummy plates must be used to maintain the air flow within the rack. Otherwise, the higher servers may take in the hot air from the lower servers.

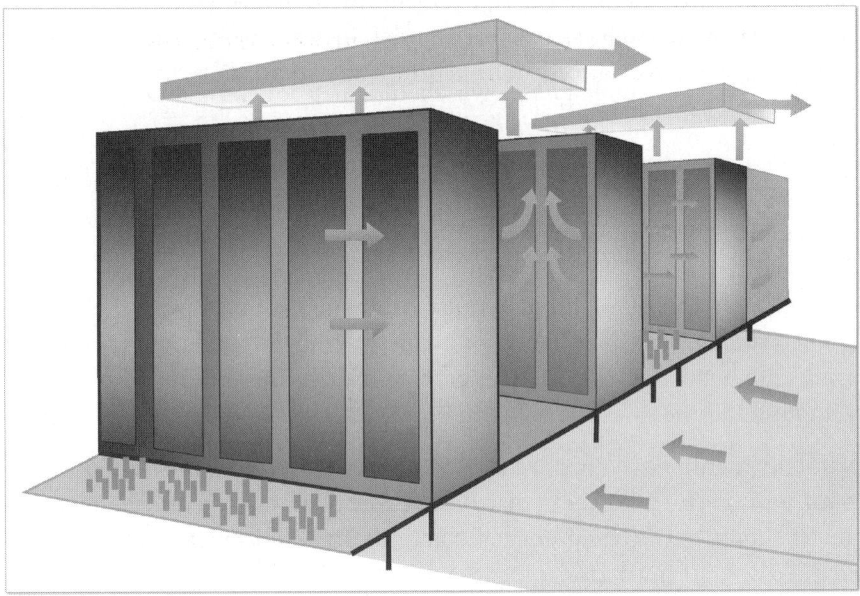

Figure 5.2 Implementation of Warm and Cold Corridors in a Data Center

For a rough estimate of the air conditioning power required, you can assume the following values: A medium-sized server "heats" at an average of 500 to 700 watts, a SAN or LAN switch at about 200 watts, and a storage system at about 1,000 to 1,500 watts. To precisely calculate the power data for your server, check the manufacturer's documentation . When calculating the data, *all* electrical equipment in the infrastructure must be taken into account. This includes, as mentioned earlier, the switches and storage systems, as well as the local uninterruptible power supplies (UPSs) and any additional smaller computers or PCs. Furthermore, you shouldn't just look at current conditions. You should leave room for planned expansions in the landscape. Later expansion during ongoing data center operation can only be done at great expense.

Climate control in the data center is always built with redundancy. Only the exact type of redundant operation differs. Ideally, two air conditioners should be running in alternation, that is, they relieve one another at regular intervals. Continual standby operation of the redundant system should be avoided, because in case of a failure of the primary system, the secondary system may not be able to operate properly if maintenance has been neglected. Errors will only be noticed when the system is used again and is relied upon for continued operation in the server room.

During the construction of the climate control, however, redundancy should not be lost because the second system is needed to ensure sufficient power.

For the sake of completeness, we should mention humidity in the data center. Water may be the enemy of every electrical device, but it is very good heat storage, helping guide heat away. The correct humidity is normally controlled by the air conditioning. If it falls below a threshold of 35%, the air will charge, causing electrostatic discharges. Above a humidity of 62%, equipment starts to rust. Especially in the summer months, high outside temperatures and humidity may cause problems, but otherwise the outside temperature doesn't play much of a role in climate conditioning, because rooms are generally either in the basement or in the interior of buildings, without windows.

Naturally, neither servers nor air conditioners can be operated without electrical power. In the context of construction planning, therefore, adequate power supply to the computer room and the air conditioner must be considered. To operate an IT landscape, the use of UPSs is absolutely mandatory. A UPS is capable of screening out variations in power and protecting equipment from overvoltage (for instance, due to lightning strikes or a defective server power supply). It provides an even voltage to all of the equipment connected to it and can also take over the power supply entirely for a certain period of time. If the power supply fails for a longer time, the UPS can trigger a shutdown of systems and servers in a particular sequence using thresholds defined by load or by time and avoiding data loss. Critical systems may be operated longer if necessary but probably have to be shut down at some point.

When using UPS solutions, however, it must always be taken into consideration that not only servers, but also the entire associated infrastructure, must be supplied with power. This includes the LAN, SAN, and air conditioners. There's not much point in a running IT landscape if nobody can connect to the server or if the room temperature in the data center exceeds the server's limit. If high load means that the entire climate control system cannot be operated, at least the fans of the air conditioners should continue to operate in the data center to circulate the air. Otherwise, hot spots will quickly develop, which can lead to the protective shutdown of the servers.

If a shutdown of systems is impossible, there is still the option of integrating an emergency generator into the landscape. This can be engaged as required, ensuring continual power. You should ensure that the generator can generate more power than is needed in the data center. This is due to both the startup power and to the length of the power lines to the data center. If an emergency generator is in use, its regular maintenance and functional testing is absolutely mandatory so you can rely on it when needed.

In view of the high costs of procurement and provision of such systems, however, you should consider carefully whether that kind of investment is really needed. If a decision is made to procure an emergency power system, this should be taken into consideration during construction planning to implement fuel storage and feed, for instance, as well as ventilation of the exhaust.

The redundant layout of air conditioning systems and power supplies is a factor in ensuring continued operation of an infrastructure, but this still doesn't provide any protection against fire, earthquake, explosions, or other catastrophes that can lead to destruction of the data center or the building itself.

If it is a requirement that the systems in a landscape must be available around the clock and only minimal outages — or none at all — can be tolerated (for instance, for flight safety systems or central control systems), a high-availability solution must be considered. This type of solution can protect against system outages, whether related to hardware or software, and switch to alternate systems. It can even be possible to mirror an entire data center. The systems can then be used for load balancing during normal operation, for instance, and take over full operations in case of a catastrophe. However, it doesn't make much sense to operate alternate systems in the same data center in which the original systems are located. Thus, there should either be strong shielding between the standard systems and the alternative systems, for instance, using fire walls, or a spatial separation should be planned between the two systems. This separation should already be considered during the construction of the data center or the rebuilding of existing rooms.

The problem of shielding or spatial separation comes up again in the context of backup planning. Here, too, it doesn't make sense to keep the backups of the system landscape in the same room where the systems themselves are operated. Two solutions can be imagined:

- Backups are created in the same room but then stored in a safe place.
- Data is backed up and stored in a separate location.

In either case, systems can be restored to working condition in case of a catastrophe, without loss of data.

5.2.2 Server Technology and Platforms

In the context of system planning and the sizing performed along with it, normally together with an SAP consultant, you decide on a particular server platform and the operating system running on it. Oracle is approved for all operating systems for which SAP software is offered.

For basic sizing, you can use the Quick Sizer provided by SAP. You can find the Quick Sizer in the SAP Service Marketplace under the quick links *sizing* and *quicksizer*. Based on information about the number of users expected, working hours, and user profiles, the Quick Sizer allows you to determine rough dimensions for the system landscape required. The so-called *SAP Application Performance Standard* (SAPS) is used as a unit of measure.

Table 5.1 shows the three categories of user profiles based on a large portion of standard users, with a longer period of thinktime between individual transaction steps (low) up to power users (high), who enter and process data very quickly.

User profile	Thinktime	Portion of total users
Low	6 min.	60–70%
Medium	30 sec.	30%
High	10 sec.	5–10%

Table 5.1 User Profiles for Determining SAPS

SAPS reflects the performance of a system configuration for the SAP environment regardless of hardware. This benchmark test was derived from the *Sales and Distribution Benchmark* (SD Benchmark), in which the performance was measured for the entire process of a sales transaction (creation of the order, creation of the delivery document, display of and changes to the order, posting of goods issue, creation of the invoice). One hundred SAPS corresponds to about 2,000 completed transactions per hour. From a technical standpoint, that corresponds to about 6,000 dialog steps, or 2,400 SAP transactions.

Calculation of the SAPS is done without reference to a certain hardware vendor. However, SAP Quick Sizer can suggest suitable hardware for a given SAPS value. Figure 5.3 shows the results of a Quick Sizer session. SAP values of 5,800 were determined for the SAP CRM 4.0 system, and 10,400 SAPS for the SAP ERP system. Moreover, at least 5,540 and 54,692 MB of RAM are required, respectively, to achieve the performance desired.

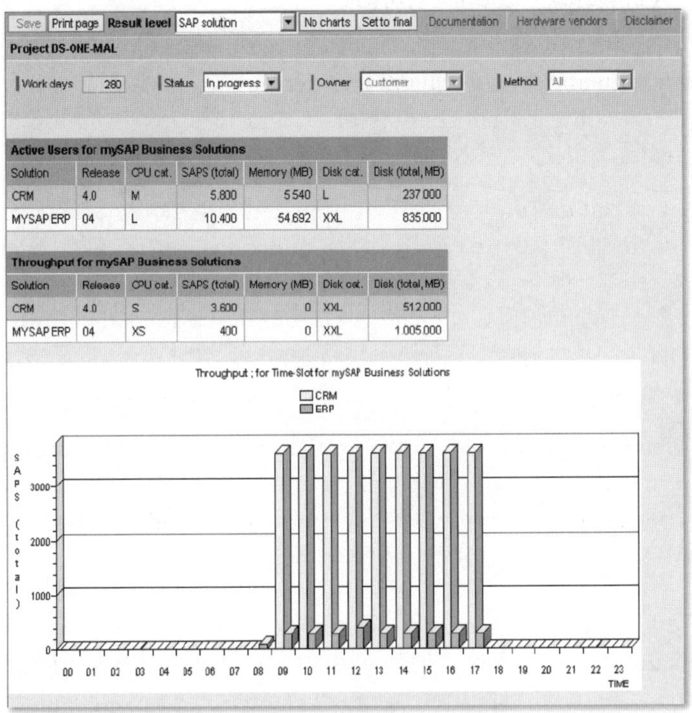

Active Users for mySAP Business Solutions

Solution	Release	CPU cat.	SAPS (total)	Memory (MB)	Disk cat.	Disk (total, MB)
CRM	4.0	M	5.800	5540	L	237000
MYSAP ERP	04	L	10.400	54692	XXL	835000

Throughput for mySAP Business Solutions

Solution	Release	CPU cat.	SAPS (total)	Memory (MB)	Disk cat.	Disk (total, MB)
CRM	4.0	S	3.600	0	XXL	512000
MYSAP ERP	04	XS	400	0	XXL	1005000

Figure 5.3 Sizing Results of the Quick Sizer

Both the products from SAP and the different underlying database systems are available for a variety of operating systems. The decision for or against an operating system or vendor can have entirely different reasons — from an existing strong partnership to a bad experience with a product. More relevant, however, are usually the costs of procurement, extension, and maintenance of the hardware; its future capability; and investment protection and performance forecasts. For particular scenarios, however, you may have to choose solutions from a specialized hardware vendor, for instance, in case of high availability, cluster solutions, and so on.

An overview of the possible hardware and software platforms is provided by the Product Availability Matrix (PAM), which you can find in the SAP Service

Marketplace at the following URL: *http://service.sap.com/pam*. Figure 5.4 shows an excerpt of the PAM, showing the operating system approvals for an SAP liveCache on SAP NetWeaver 7.0.

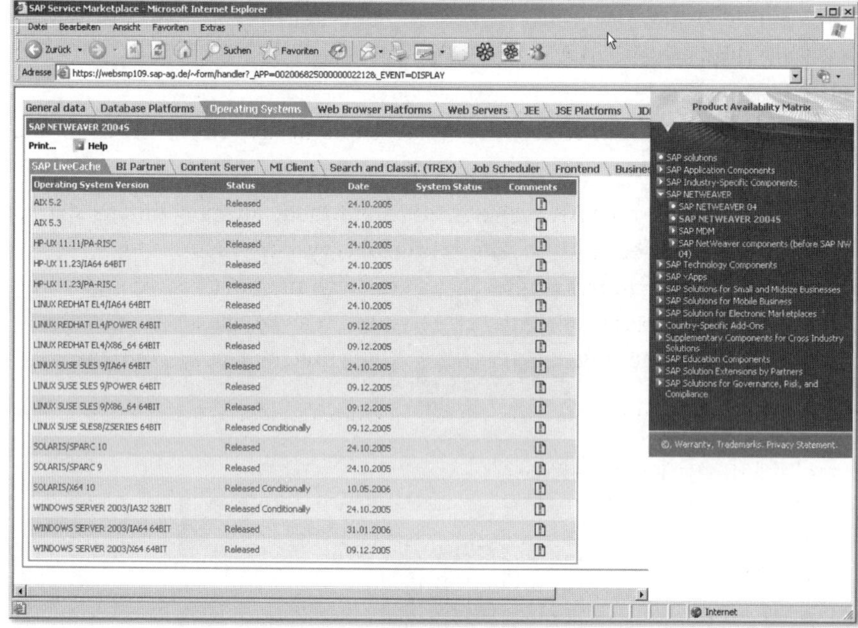

Figure 5.4 Product Availability Matrix for SAP NetWeaver 7.0

When deciding on a platform, it must be noted that the operating system uses 64 bits for addressing memory. This is the only way to operate large systems efficiently. The only real difference between 64-bit software and its 32-bit version is the different method of addressing memory. The 64-bit software uses a 64-bit-long address pointer, which can theoretically address 18 billion gigabytes of memory directly. In real-life, a 64-bit application can usually address significantly less memory on different operating systems and given available hardware, but multiple terabytes (that is, multiple thousands of gigabytes) can still be addressed. This is significantly more than the amount needed for the components of SAP software. For a 32-bit address pointer, the limit on the address space is about 4 gigabytes, but in reality the application often has less available. In some examples, this 4-gigabyte limit can hinder the effective operation of an SAP system.

Since SAP Basis Release 4.0, it has been possible to install the SAP kernel as a 64-bit version. All current releases based on SAP Web AS 6.10 or higher are almost exclusively offered for 64-bit environments. Since January 2007, all new products and versions of SAP systems are only available for 64-bit environments. For old releases, SAP offers upgrade or migration paths.

Here are the advantages of 64-bit technology for SAP solutions:

- The administration of SAP systems is significantly simpler (fewer instances, because more power is available per instance, so the system becomes less complex).
- The SAP software can scale with the available hardware (RAM, CPU) to a much higher degree.
- Because with 64-bit SAP systems there is practically no limit to shared memory, all buffers can be dimensioned very large. Note SAP's recommendations. The addressability of a very large memory requires the configuration of a correspondingly large swap area. To use a 64-bit SAP kernel, therefore, you must have at least 20 gigabytes of swap configured.

The system requirements for the use of 64-bit SAP software are:

- **64-bit-capable hardware**
  A basic prerequisite for the use of 64-bit operating systems and 64-bit applications is 64-bit hardware. In particular, the version of the processors (CPU) used influences the capability of existing hardware. Information about details like the compatibility of hardware with 64-bit operating systems should definitely be requested from your contact at the relevant hardware partner. Nearly all manufacturers now offer suitable hardware and operating systems based on 64 bits (for instance, all operating systems for Intel Itanium CPUs, that is, Windows 64, HP-UX IA64, or 64-bit Linux).
- **64-bit operating system**
  To use 64-bit SAP software, you may need to upgrade to a 64-bit operating system. For approval, see the approval notes available for every database and every SAP kernel release.
- **64-bit database**
  To use SAP software with 64 bits, SAP recommends the combination with a 64-bit database version (RDBMS). Databases from SAP, IBM, Informix, and Oracle are already supported in 64-bit versions since SAP Release 4.0.

Combinations of 32-bit and 64-bit systems within a system landscape are possible. However, you must take a few caveats into consideration. Transports with `tp` or `R3trans` (see Chapter 6, *SAP Change and Transport Management*) between 32-bit and 64-bit SAP systems are possible in principle. However, a number of differences, such as the parameter settings of the operating system kernel and the SAP kernel, don't take a mixed configuration of test and production systems into consideration. All properties and functions that depend on these parameter settings cannot be sufficiently tested in a 32-bit test or development system for a 64-bit production environment. This particularly includes the effects of parameter settings on memory management and the performance of an SAP system. For this reason, SAP recommends that for each existing 64-bit production system, another 64-bit system within the transport path should be available in which the usability of the SAP kernel, operating system, and database can be tested.

5.2.3 Storage and SAN Infrastructure

Due to the ever-increasing memory requirements of databases, it is normally no longer possible to store the data files of databases on local hard disks. Despite the growing storage density of hard disks, it also doesn't make sense to access direct attached storage media. Rather, current practice in a dynamically built and changing landscape is to use so-called storage arrays. These are large hard disk systems that can be accessed directly through a controller or indirectly through a *storage area network* (SAN).

These arrays often provide the capability to implement a certain RAID level right at the controller level. RAID, which used to stand for *redundant array of inexpensive disks*, is now a *redundant array of independent disks*, and ensures that information is retained on the hard disks even if one or several hard disks in the RAID array fail.

Operating a RAID system requires at least two hard disks. The hard disks are operated together and form an array that in at least one aspect is more powerful than either of its component hard disks. With RAID systems, you can achieve the following advantages:

- Increase in failure safety (redundancy)
- Increase in transfer rates (performance)
- Creation of large logical drives
- Exchange of hard disks and increase in storage capacity during system operation
- Cost reduction due to the use of multiple inexpensive hard disks.
- Significant increase in system performance

The exact type of interaction of the hard disks is specified by the *RAID level*. The most frequently used RAID levels are RAID 0, RAID 1, and RAID 5, as well as a series of combinations of these levels (RAID 0+1, RAID 10, RAID 00, and so on.) An overview of the advantages and disadvantages of the RAID levels is shown in Table 5.2.

RAID level	Memory space usable	Error tolerance Redundancy
0 – Striping	n × s	None, because there is no mirroring of data. Writing the data in blocks to the disks merely improves performance, because parallel access to multiple disks is possible.
1 – Mirroring	1/2n × s	Data is synchronized across all disks. Data loss only results when all disks are defective.
3 and 4 – Striping with parity information on a separate disk; precursor to RAID 5; no longer, or rarely, used	1/n × s	Parity information is stored on a special hard disk, but that disk represents a bottleneck, because every operation requires the parity information to be changed there. If a disk in the RAID array fails, the data can be reconstructed from the parity information. If the parity disk fails, the information is simply recalculated.
5 – Combination of performance and redundancy, together with combinations of RAID 0 and 1, one of the most used RAID levels	(n-1) × s	At most one disk may fail. RAID 5 offers both increased performance when reading data and redundancy at relatively low cost and is therefore the most popular RAID variant. In write-intensive environments, RAID 5 is not recommended, because performance falls significantly during both sequential and random write accesses. In that situation, a RAID 0+1 configuration would be recommended. However, RAID 5 is the less expensive option of storing data redundantly on at least three disks. The more disks that are integrated into a RAID 5 array, the longer the rebuild takes, or the worse performance is when there is a hard disk failure.

Table 5.2 Overview of RAID Levels (n = number of disks, s = size of the smallest disk)

Which RAID level should therefore be used on which storage medium in the context of an Oracle installation?

To answer that question, let's take a look at the architecture (see Section 3.4, *Oracle Kernel*). For ongoing access during operation, the data files, redo logs, mirror logs, and control files are especially relevant. Access to the executables in the installation is only required during startup, or only to a negligible extent during operation. Thus, for good performance, it is necessary to distribute the frequently used parts of the database in a sensible way.

In general, be sure to consider the following points:

- Redo logs and data files should be located in different parts of the disks.
- The two copies of the redo log files should be located in different parts of the disks.
- Two sequential redo logs should not be located in the same part of a disk.
- Because write access to the online redo logs is ongoing, these can be a bottleneck at high load. Thus, they should be located on very fast disks and shouldn't be mixed with other change-intensive data. Furthermore, avoid the use of RAID levels that have a negative influence on performance (that is, RAID 5). For logs, RAID 1 should always be used, or storage should take place on a storage array with hardware RAIDs. The use of software RAIDs is not recommended for performance reasons. Alternatively, storage can take place in the form of raw devices. This is SAP's recommendation for high-end systems.
- The data files should be "scattered" over the largest possible number of disks to distribute load evenly.
- Another very change-intensive part of the data files are the rollback, undo, and temporary tablespaces of the database.

The disk layout shown in Figure 5.5 can be derived based on these recommendations.

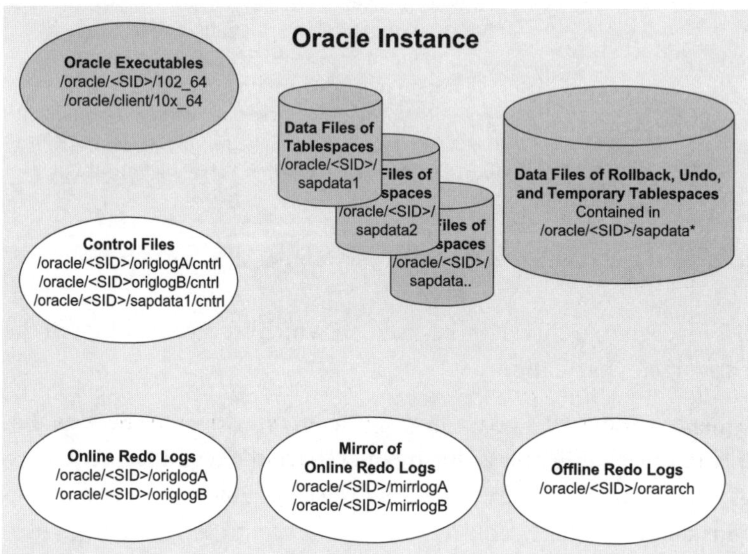

Figure 5.5 Layout of an Oracle Database

All of the dark gray areas in the figure can be maintained in RAID 5 or similar RAID levels. To achieve the best performance possible, the data files in the rollback, undo, and temporary tablespaces are separated from the data files of the *sapdata* directories. To achieve even better performance, these can be further distributed across their own disks or storage arrays.

For the database areas shown in white, RAID 1 is preferred. However, you should avoid a software RAID here, because this degrades performance. The control files can be left in the directories named and attached in the correct places as separate mount points. For the remaining areas of the logs (online, mirror, and offline), separate hard disk sections should be selected.

Modern storage arrays are usually connected using fiber channel interfaces (FC interfaces), which offer transfer rates of up to four gigabytes per second. To avoid losing access to the file systems in case of failure of a fiber channel adapter, thus risking danger to system operation, a redundant layout of the fiber channel connection is strongly recommended. Note as well that a fiber channel switch should also be laid out redundantly. Besides redundancy, such a SAN can contribute to performance increases, by permitting load distribution of the individual file systems across the FC adapters and switches.

5.2.4 Backup

In any electronic processing of data, backup of the data is essential to permit restoration of the system state in case of failure to a given point before the failure. The larger and more complicated the system landscape, the greater the resulting backup volumes. Although initially it may be possible to back up data to tapes that can be manually swapped, as the landscape grows, the backup will also have to grow. Many vendors offer automatic backup systems that handle management of the backup tapes in a tape library and can start and perform the backups automatically.

Even during the planning of a system landscape, the size specifications of SAP AG for tablespaces and for the anticipated monthly data added can be used to create an estimate of the size of the system databases. With that estimate and the backup strategy (see Chapter 10, *Backup, Restore, and Recovery*), the approximate storage volume can be calculated. You should also consider that not only the database must be backed up, but also the executables of the SAP system, the databases, and the operating system files.

The classical backup variants are *online backup* and *offline backup* of a database. In online backup, in contrast to offline backup, the system can continue to be operated. However, in case of failure, after the database is restored, a recovery run is required to complete all of the changes made to the database during the backup. That recovery run requires the offline redo logs, because they contain a description of the changes to be made. The online backup of an Oracle database without backing up the redo log cannot be recovered. In contrast, the restoration of an offline backup can be restarted immediately after the volume is reloaded. If additional changes are made to the data after the backup, they can also be recovered from the redo logs. If those are missing, there is data loss, but the database is still usable. More information on this topic can be found in Section 10.3.

An increasingly important problem is the ever-decreasing time available for backups. Once a normal online backup of a database is started on backup tapes, you can expect performance degradation, because CPU time and access to the hard disks are required to write the backup. Because many companies and their systems are internationally networked or operate globally, this kind of performance decrease, let alone downtime for offline backups, can no longer be tolerated. In SAP system landscapes, with their large volumes of data, this problem is particularly noticeable. One possible solution is an increase in the number of tape drives used. This raises the data throughput during a backup, which reduces the time it takes. However, this also results in additional costs for the procurement of additional drives, and the complexity of the backup environment increases as well. Moreover, additional performance hits result from the higher load during the reading of data. Ultimately, for very large databases, a long backup and recovery time must be planned. Alternative solutions for this dilemma include *virtual tape libraries* (VTL) or the so-called *split-mirror backup procedure*.

Virtual tape libraries provide procedures that enable the provision of a number of virtual drives that act just like normal tape drives for the backup tool. The backup data is buffered on a hard disk cache. By using many virtual tape drives, you may be able to reduce the time required for your online backup. Once the backup has completed, the data can be copied to tapes for storage or be kept in the VTL for restores.

When using the *split-mirror backup procedure*, the running database is completely mirrored, either continually or during the backup period, and that mirror is separated after synchronization. Based on the mirror, a tape backup is then prepared, with no effect on the performance of the production system. This process is now supported by many backup and recovery solutions (such as HP OpenView Storage Data Protector 5.5 and EMC TimeFinder).

The costs of this type of backup are naturally higher than traditional backup methods. For a complete copy of the database, you have to provide sufficient storage space. That can be done either in an additional storage array or by increasing the storage space of existing systems. If an additional array is used, that may be associated with higher costs, but in case of a hardware failure of the production array, there is no effect on the backup array. The system can be remirrored very quickly after repair of the production array and be back to work. Alternatively, the backup array can be used as the production array, saving the time required for the remirroring. If the same array is used for both the production and mirror databases, restore and recovery from tape may be necessary. This requires more time.

You can find more detailed information about backing up an Oracle database in Chapter 10, *Backup, Restore, and Recovery*.

5.2.5 Frontend

Finally, when planning a system landscape, the connection of the user to the application system must be taken into consideration. There are two basic ways to access an SAP system (see also Figure 5.1): access via the SAP GUI or access via a web browser.

For access via the SAP GUI, two versions are offered by SAP: one version is for use on Microsoft Windows operating systems, and the other is a Java version for system-independent use of the SAP GUI. Information about the required operating system versions, as well as current release levels of the SAP GUI, can be found at the *sapgui* quick link in the SAP Service Marketplace (*http://service.sap.com*).

The Java version of the SAP GUI, however, has a few limitations compared with the Windows version, because not all of the graphical tools can be implemented in Java. To find out whether a transaction can run in the Java GUI, you should call the following transaction in the SAP system: **Tools • ABAP Workbench • Development • Other tools • Transactions** (Transaction SE93). There, after entering a transaction code, it can be determined whether that transaction is approved for use in the different GUI versions (see Figure 5.6, which shows that Transaction CJ2B is not suitable for use in the SAP GUI for Java or SAP GUI for HTML).

To make an SAP system accessible through a web browser, a few years ago SAP created the *SAP GUI for HTML*. It uses a middleware package, the so-called *Internet Transaction Server* (ITS), to allow access to the system through a web browser. The ITS is responsible for converting the SAP dynpros to HTML. The continued development of the standalone ITS was concluded in Version 6.20. Support will only be provided as long as SAP is still offering products that use ITS 6.20. That version of ITS should therefore no longer be used, if possible.

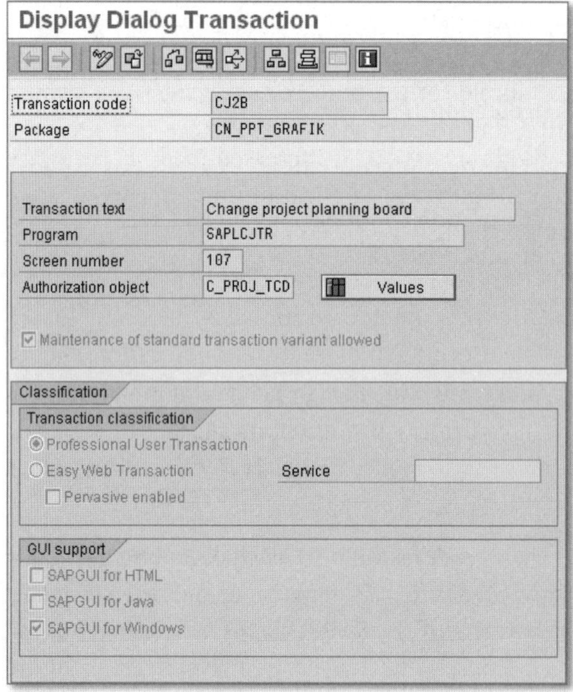

Figure 5.6 Example of GUI Capability (Transaction CJ2B)

As of SAP Web Application Server 6.40, therefore, SAP offers an integrated ITS for all its products. It is now a part of the kernel. This provides some advantages, but also some disadvantages:

- **Advantages**
  - No additional hardware or software is needed to operate it.
  - Installation, maintenance, and administration are performed centrally in the SAP system.
  - No additional web server is needed, because the SAP system's internal web server is used.
  - Load balancing in the SAP system can be used, whereas earlier the ITS was responsible for its own load balancing.

  - The ITS is available for all platforms on which SAP NetWeaver Application Server is available. Previously, ITS was only available for Windows, Linux, and Solaris (WGate only).
- **Disadvantages**
  - The previous separation of the application connection (AGate) and web server connection (WGate) allowed the placement of a firewall between the levels to protect the application system. That is no longer possible with the new ITS. SAP now provides the SAP Web Dispatcher for a front-line access protection.
  - Under heavy load on the integrated ITS, increased load on hardware resources (CPU, RAM) can affect the application server. This must be considered if you plan to use the integrated ITS.
  - Applications created with earlier ITS versions based on SAP FlowLogics, WebRFC, and GuiXT are no longer operational with the integrated ITS. All other applications developed as Internet application components (IACs) are either immediately usable or can easily be customized to the new environment. SAP's recommendation is therefore to convert the applications to newer technologies such as Business Server Pages (BSP) or Web Dynpro (see the next section).

Over the course of later development and the increasing orientation of applications toward web services, SAP has developed new technologies to make applications available for Internet users. *Business Server Pages* (BSPs) were the first to be introduced, with Release 6.20 of the SAP Web Application Server. They function like other server page technologies (Java Server Pages, Microsoft's Active Server Pages), allowing the embedding of programming code in an HTML layout. BSPs also allow the implementation of the *Model-View-Controller pattern* (MVC pattern), which helps break up applications into the three parts: *data view* (model), *program logic* (controller), and *presentation* (view). This allows very simple development and good maintainability, because development work can be performed in separate expert teams.

However, because the capabilities of BSPs are limited, SAP Web Application Server Java 6.40 added a second technology for data presentation, *Web Dynpro for Java*. You can see a simple example in Figure 5.7.

The advantage of Web Dynpros is their simple creation using templates, allowing easy implementation of a uniform look and feel of applications. The creation of your own template makes it easy to extend the object palette.

With the arrival of SAP Basis 7.00 (SAP NetWeaver 2004), this technology was also implemented for ABAP, so that in addition to Web Dynpros for Java you can create Web Dynpros for ABAP. The advantage of Web Dynpros over BSPs is their significantly higher flexibility when creating applications.

The areas of usage of Web Dynpros and BSPs, for instance, are custom-developed web shops or catalog systems that provide customers with direct access to current system data.

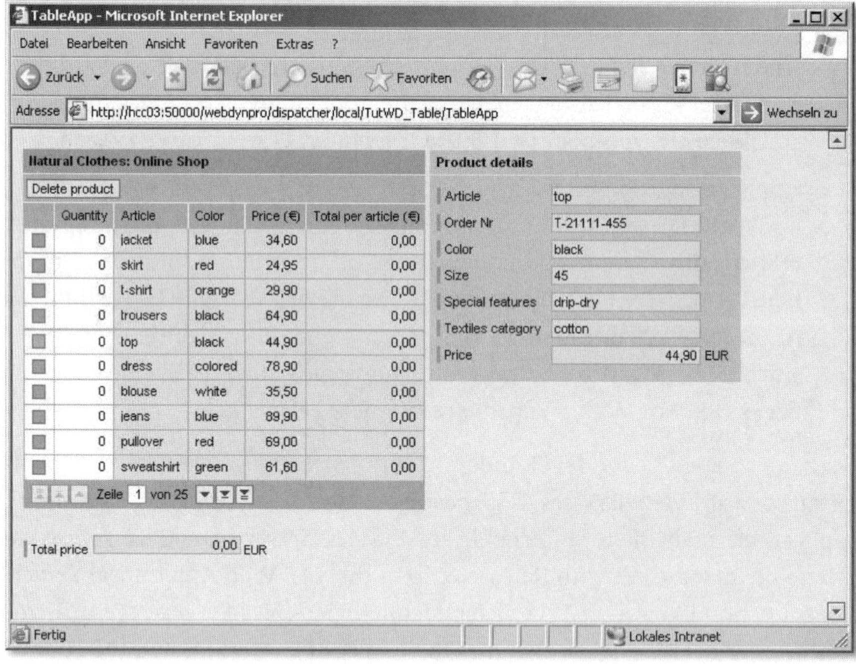

Figure 5.7 Web Dynpro for Java

The final option for data presentation to be described here is the SAP NetWeaver Portal. This application provides web-based, role-oriented access to data in a central location. This makes it possible to use role definitions to adapt the content displayed by the portal to the user's specific tasks. The user also has the option of adapting the information and presentations on offer to fit their personal taste. Moreover, using Portal Knowledge Management, all types of structured (ERP, BI, CRM, etc.) and unstructured (web, intranet, groupware, document management, email) information can be presented within a portal. For searching for particular information, SAP's own search engine TREX can be used.

The representation can embed any of the frontend technologies named above (SAP GUI, ITS, BSP, Web Dynpro).

To handle a variety of tasks, *business packages* are provided that can be used in a portal. A business package contains role-specific content and links for the handling of business processes. This can be the specific preparation of information such as BI reports or a predefined set of transaction calls.

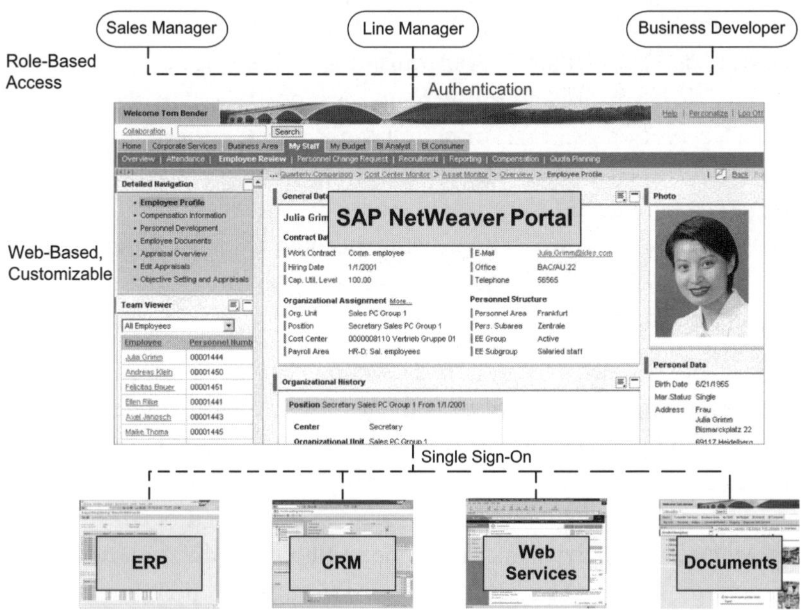

Figure 5.8 SAP NetWeaver Portal

For additional information on Enterprise Portal, see the SAP Service Marketplace under the quick link *nw-ep*.

The possibilities shown here are just a taste of how access to an SAP system can be achieved. This can be limited by existing frontend tools available (thin clients on which an SAP GUI must run) or training costs entailed by switching to a new frontend strategy. On the technical side, however, a number of implementation methods are available.

5.3 High Availability

In today's business environment, almost no company can afford to lose its central application system for several hours. The resulting business damage can be significant and even lead to long-term damage to the company – either due to lost or unpostable orders or production downtime at a facility – but the ongoing global distribution of company locations means ever higher expectations of system availability.

The availability of a system isn't just the fact that a connection can be established, but also that it is possible to work fluidly with the system. A response time of several seconds after every work step will surely be intolerable to users. To be able to meet those high expectations, the technical failure safety of systems must be considered even during the planning of a landscape. Today's available hardware and software makes it possible in many areas, for instance, in a server or a storage array, to lay out a system so robustly that it is available even after the failure of individual components. To do this, redundant components are very often used (for instance, power supplies, FC, or LAN adapters), which also usually permits their exchange during ongoing operation. Because this is no longer possible for all parts, maintenance periods are defined.

This is especially important if system operations are not performed internally but are purchased as a service (from an ASP). In this case, when the contract is concluded, a *service level agreement* (SLA) is defined to specify precisely what percentage of the time over a year or a month a system must be available. These SLAs are increasingly also being concluded between enterprises and their own IT departments. Some examples of the remaining permitted downtimes that can occur over a year for ongoing operation of a system are shown in Table 5.3.

Percent availability	Minimum expected operating time in hours per year (365 days)	Maximum permitted downtime in hours per year
99%	8,672.4	87.6
99.5%	8,716.2	43.8
99.95%	8,755.62	4.38
100%	8,760	0

Table 5.3 Permitted Downtime per Required Availability Level

You can see that the remaining downtimes hardly provide enough time to perform necessary maintenance tasks on the infrastructure. Thus, normally a regular maintenance window is defined that provides the time for this sort of task.

The downtime in case of a failure is composed of four parts:

1. Time to detect that there has been an error
2. Time until the cause of the error has been found
3. Time until the error has been corrected
4. Time until normal system operation is restored

The largest part of that time is normally needed for finding and correcting the error. Many modern server systems have mechanisms for self-diagnostics and can send appropriate messages about failed components to the administrator. As a result, there is still a possibility of minimizing the time needed for repair. There are several approaches to this: cold standby, hot standby, hot standby with load balancing, and the construction of an emergency data center.

In *cold standby*, the redundant system is kept available offline. If the active system fails, any unsaved data, states, or incomplete transactions are lost. After detection of the failure, the passive system is activated. This can be done manually by an employee or automatically. After the replacement system is started, the resources needed, such as data or IP addresses, must be obtained. This can also be manual or automated by the use of scripts. Once these processes are complete, the application can be restarted and is then available again. The duration of the handover, due to the nonautomated detection of errors and startup of the replacement system, can be quite long, usually measured in minutes if no time-consuming restoration of data is required.

A trimmed-down variant of cold standby is simply to keep an extensive stock of replacement parts for the hardware and staff for fast repairs in case of failure. That can be implemented by concluding an appropriate support agreement with the hardware manufacturer or by training your own staff.

In *hot standby*, the redundant system is kept available online. The active system and the redundant one are connected by a crossover cable. Using that connection and special software (for instance, HP MC ServiceGuard or Sun Cluster), the passive system can use a "heartbeat" to check whether the active system is still responding. If the active system fails, any unsaved data, states, or incomplete transactions are lost in this solution, too. If the passive system misses any signs of life from the active system for a longer period of time, the passive system switches service to itself after a predefined time. This is referred to as a *failover*.[1] Because the replacement system is already started up and ready to use, only the resources needed (for instance IP addresses, volume groups, NFS mounts) must be obtained. This switching of resources is typically carried out by scripts started automatically by the failover software. After the scripts are processed, the restart of the application or parts of the application is performed automatically.

Figure 5.9 shows a diagram of the splitting of an SAP system into different failover packages. The three cluster nodes A, B, and C each represent a physical server, which is capable of providing one or more packages with resources. Each package is equipped with a virtual IP address to ensure server-independent communication. If node C fails, as shown, the DI package affected is automatically restarted on one of the nodes still available (in the example, on node B). If another node fails, depending on the resources available to the last server, it may still be possible for it to handle all of the packages, or a package that isn't absolutely necessary, here the second DI package, for instance, may be temporarily deactivated. The division of the system into packages, as well as the number of cluster nodes, can be changed during installation.

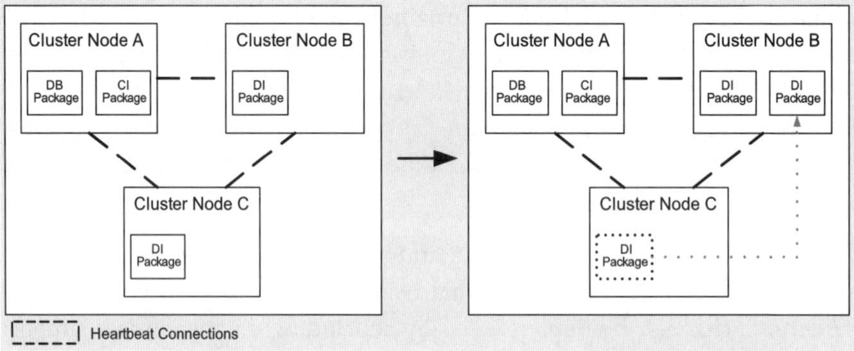

Figure 5.9 Use of a Failover Solution in an SAP System Landscape

The duration until restored availability is significantly less than in the case of cold-standby operation — between a few seconds and a few minutes. The costs for this alternative are higher, because costs for the operation of the

1 The core principle of a failover system is that a secondary system monitors a primary system. If the primary system fails, the secondary system assumes all its tasks to ensure smooth operation. It is absolutely necessary for the secondary system to monitor the primary system to be able to detect the failure. That monitoring shouldn't be done through the primary network connection, but rather through a separate connection. Either a null-modem connection or a separate network connection can be used for this purpose.

normal server, the replacement server (power, air conditioning, maintenance, license, etc.), and the failover software itself all apply. For scenarios like this, changes may be needed to the SAN infrastructure, because both servers must be capable of accessing the storage areas of the application system (database volumes).

Because it is not very cost-effective to operate the passive system in hot-standby mode without using it, there are options for using that server for load balancing. It is appropriate to operate an additional dialog instance of the SAP system on the standby server and thus increase the performance of the system. In case of error, that instance is stopped and the central instance activated on that server. After correction of the error situation, the dialog instance can be activated again.

For a hot-standby system with load balancing, a load balancer provides a virtual server. Requests to the virtual server are forwarded to one of at least two real servers. This real server processes the request and gives a response back to the load balancer, which forwards it back to the appropriate client. If a real server now fails, the load balancer notices that and stops forwarding requests to the failed real server. With this approach, the failure of $n - 1$ real servers can be tolerated, where n is the total number of real servers. If a real server fails, though, we still have the problem that all unsaved data, states, and incomplete transactions are lost.

The most expensive, but the safest, alternative, is to build an emergency data center. Here, a mirror of the entire infrastructure is built, and there is ongoing synchronization of data between storage systems. In normal operation, this mirrored data center can be used for load balancing, or the mirrored arrays can be used for a split-mirror backup. The emergency data center can be operated entirely autonomously in case of failure of the primary data center, so that almost no downtime is detectable.

5.4 IT and System Security

For every centralized data storage and processing system, there must be a security design. Both the physical security of the landscape and the technical security of the data in the software systems must be taken into consideration. Physical security must already be taken into consideration during the construction phase, because fire alarm systems and fire extinguishing systems, for instance, must be involved in the construction planning.

The *German Federal Office for Information Security* (BSI) has prepared an overview of typical risks[2], an excerpt of which is shown in Table 5.4.

▸ **Force majeur** ▸ Failure of the IT system ▸ Lightning ▸ Fire ▸ Water ▸ Cable fire ▸ Excessive temperature and humidity ▸ Dust, contamination ▸ Technical catastrophes in the vicinity ▸ Difficulties due to mass events ▸ Storm
▸ **Organizational failures** ▸ Missing or insufficient regulation ▸ Insufficient knowledge of regulations ▸ Insufficient control of IT security measures ▸ Unauthorized access to secured rooms ▸ Insufficient joist dimensioning ▸ Insufficient documentation of cabling
▸ **Technical failures** ▸ Power failure ▸ Failure of internal power supply grid ▸ Failure of existing security systems
▸ **Deliberate action** ▸ Unauthorized penetration into a building ▸ Theft ▸ Vandalism ▸ Attack ▸ Risk during maintenance/administration work by internal personnel ▸ Risk during maintenance work by external personnel ▸ Unauthorized access to active power components ▸ Sabotage

Table 5.4 Risks According to the BSI

2 The BSI distributes free CD-ROMs that contain the entire basic IT security handbook in PDF, HTML, and DOC formats. Besides the current German version of the basic IT security handbook, these CD-ROMs also include the English translation and other information from the BSI. For more information, see *www.bsi.de*.

Many of the risks listed in Table 5.4 can be countered by structural measures. These include fire detection and fire extinguishing, correct dimensioning of air conditioners, the construction of secure access (security doors and bolts on doors), and the redundant layout of supply lines (power, network). This minimizes the probability of occurrence of some risks.

We already addressed climate control and supply lines in Section 5.2.1, *Construction Infrastructure*, so we won't discuss them again here. In this section, we'll chiefly be concerned with the topics of fire protection, access security, and technical security.

For the detection of fire and smoke, a variety of systems are available that are also suitable for use in data centers. Whereas the selection of a fire alarm system is relatively trivial, when selecting a smoke alarm system, you should ensure that detection of fine particles is possible. Only then can small amounts of smoke be detected early and countermeasures be taken. However, it is important, for instance, when renovating data centers, that large amounts of dust are avoided, because they can trigger false alarms in the smoke sensors. The avoidance of false alarms is particularly important when there is a direct connection from the fire alarm system to the fire department.

If there is a fire in the data center, extinguishing should be carried out with extreme care, so that the expensive, very sensitive equipment is not damaged or destroyed. Extinguishing systems with a gaseous basis are the most suitable. Fire extinguishing gases include natural gases such as argon and CO_2 or chemical gases such as Novek or FM200[3]. The use of argon or CO_2 during fire extinguishing forces the oxygen out of the air in the computer room, reducing its oxygen content to about 15%. This corresponds roughly to the oxygen content at a 4,000 meters' elevation. An advantage of argon is that in low concentrations, it is a component of breathable air and thus is not immediately a health hazard. That means that staff may be able to save data or help fight the fire. By adding perfumes, such as an intensive lemon odor, personnel can be warned before the oxygen content is too low to breathe.

The chemical gases Novek and FM200 are based on a chemical reaction that ensures cooling at the source of the flame. This removes the energy from the flame.

3 FM200 is a partially halogenized hydrocarbon that is also known as HFC227ea. FM200 uses a chemical extinguishing mechanism, meaning that the chain of the combustion process is disrupted or interrupted by reducing or preventing the formation of radicals.

The use of powder extinguishing systems in data centers is not recommended, because in case of fire (and successful extinguishing), the result is a lengthy and costly cleaning of the hardware.

For the introduction of the extinguishing agent to the source of the flame, there are two variants. The fire extinguishing system can be set up for the entire data center, so that the gas flows out at specific places. In addition, rack-based solutions exist for fire extinguishing systems, permitting targeted firefighting at the source of the fire. This solution is particularly effective for smaller data centers with up to four racks.

Another fact to consider when planning the computer room or data center is the possible endangerment from neighboring rooms, whether these are above, below, or next to the computer room. In any case, there is a risk to the IT room itself. A possible problem is a fire above the computer room that must be fought with water. The probability that some of the water might penetrate into the computer room is very high if no specific measures have been taken against that eventuality. Here, too, during planning of the building or room, such risks must be eliminated or limited.

Besides risks from environmental influences and force majeur, a computer room for the processing of sensitive, business-critical data can also be the target of criminal action. On the one hand, the technology used is of significant material value, and on the other hand, the data of the enterprise is of great interest to the competition. For security against theft of equipment and penetration of unauthorized persons into the building, structural measures are possible in the form of access control, video monitoring, and double door arrangements. These must usually be supported by staff in the form of security services or internal security agents. The monitoring of access as well as the surroundings (approach paths, outside areas) must be ensured at all times, depending on the security requirements.

Technical security in the SAP environment must be implemented and monitored on several levels. Figure 5.10 shows the individual layers of the system and how technical security is implemented on each.

Based on access security to the servers, securing of systems starts with the server's operating system. After the operating system, the individual layers of the database, application server, and frontend at the user follow. The network connections between these layers must also be secured.

At the operating system level, access security to all user accounts must be implemented with dedicated authorization in all participating systems. For the sake of convenience, a single master user with all permissions is often used by different people. This allows abuse of the user without the ability to track who is responsible. It is better to assign every authorized administrator his own account with a fixed assignment. This also allows you to assign specific authorizations for certain tasks.

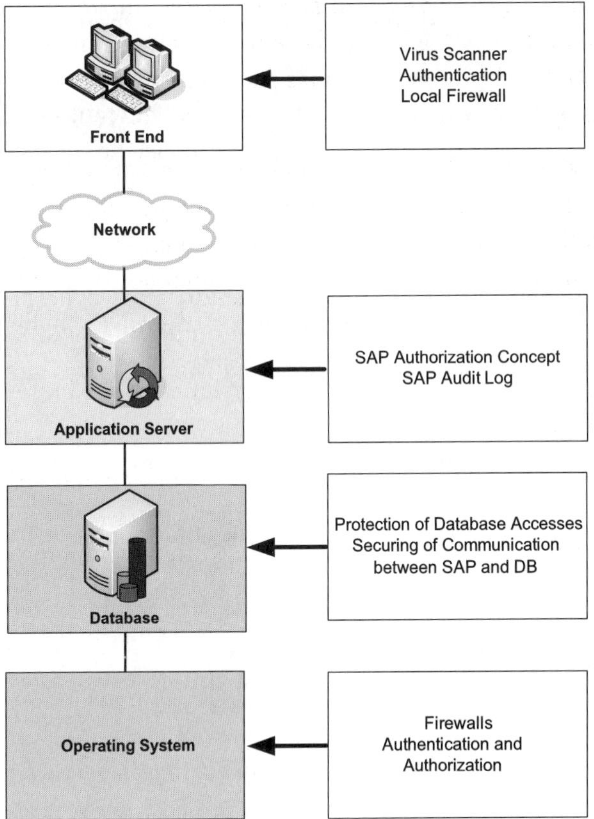

Figure 5.10 Layers of Technical Security

The operating system users of an SAP installation with Oracle were already described in Section 4.2.1, and the Oracle database users were covered in Section 4.3.1. The security-relevant aspects of these two points, such as permissions and groups, were already discussed in Section 4.3.4. This is a very important topic for IT security, which you should in any case consider very carefully.

After the operating system, we next consider the security of the database. On the one hand, it must be secured against access to the data files, which can be implemented using the assignment of permissions in the previous section.

On the other hand, unauthorized login into the database must also be prevented. For this reason, you must absolutely change the default passwords of all standard users of the Oracle database. In early releases, it was partly necessary to do this manually. In current SAP installations, the passwords for the users sap<sid>, sap<sid>db, sys, system, outln, and dbsnmp are already set by the installation routine. The OUTLN and DBSNMP users can be blocked later, because they aren't explicitly used in the SAP environment.

The next layer after the database "on the way to the user" is the SAP system, which has its own user and permission concept. This allows the granting of transaction-specific authorizations and thus the creation of specific profiles for each user. A detailed description of the functionality and instructions for working with the SAP permissions concept is far beyond the scope of this book. At this point, we only want to note the importance of the topic. For more information, consult other works on the SAP authorization concept, such as *SAP Authorization System* by IBM Business Consulting (SAP PRESS 2002) and *Security and Authorizations in SAP Systems* by Mario Linkies and Frank Off (SAP PRESS 2005).

This still leaves the IT security at the user's workplace. Besides the obligatory access control of the computer, for instance, using the authorization systems of the operating system in use, it is often useful to include additional security using key cards. The user account at the corresponding workstation is also only provided with dedicated rights, for instance, which prevent the installation of additional software. The use of virus scanners and local firewalls rounds out frontend security, in order to protect against viruses, trojans, key loggers, and the like.

Now we have established security within the individual system layers. The only thing left is to secure communications between those layers. For communication, TCP/IP connections are used in all cases. If the Oracle database is installed on a single host with the SAP system, only a local connection is in use. Generally, the internal connections between systems should be operated separately from external connections. To do that, two separate networks (for instance, a local network for internal communication and host administration and an external network for customer access) must be used. If this isn't possible, corresponding filter rules should be defined in the intervening firewalls. The use of a firewall is particularly important in the communication between the SAP GUI and the application server. The recommendation here is to use a *demilitarized zone* (DMZ). The systems set up in the DMZ are shielded by filter systems (packet filter, firewall) against other networks (for instance, the Internet or LAN). This isolation can permit access to publicly accessible services and simultaneously protect the internal network from unauthorized access. "Public services" for access to an SAP system include SAProuter from SAP.

SAProuter is software by SAP that can monitor the access between your R/3 server and the frontend. It functions to a certain extent as a gateway at the application level between the SAP system and the outside world. The SAProuter is capable of performing filtration at the IP address level. Without any additional firewall, however, it is impossible to speak of real protection for the system, because SAProuter only represents one of the possible holes in the firewall, controlling the connections coming in and out there. In practice, it makes sense to use a SAProuter, both centrally for all frontends, for instance, as a gateway for a subsidiary, and for server access (e.g., DMZ). Because the SAProuter can use virtual aliases, there are no significant adaptations necessary when changing IP addresses or server names. One possible structure for a SAProuter network is shown in Figure 5.11.

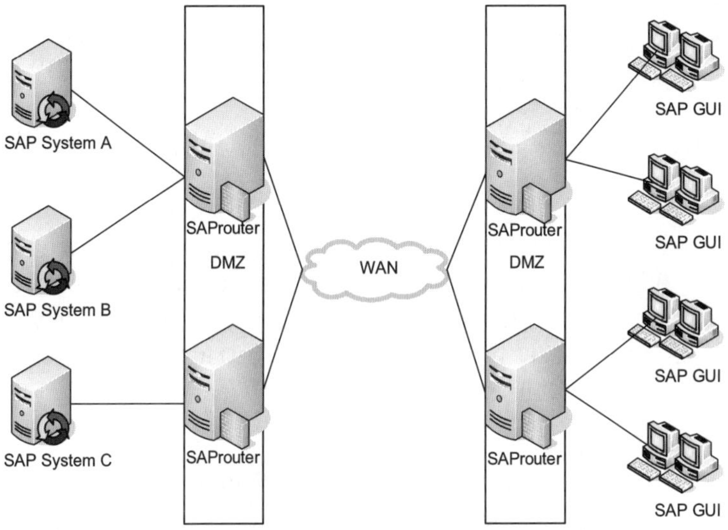

Figure 5.11 Sample Configuration for the Use of SAProuters

The use of a SAProuter makes sense:

- To control and log connections to your SAP system (for instance, from an SAP Service Center)
- To provide an indirect connection when a given partner network cannot be accessed directly (for instance, local private networks)

- To improve network security by using a password to protect your connection and your data against unauthorized access from the outside
- To restrict access only to particular SAProuters or IP addresses
- If only encrypted connections from a known partner are permitted (use of SNC)
- To increase performance and stability by reducing the load on the SAP system within a local area network (LAN) when communicating with a wide area network (WAN).

For a more detailed description of functionality and configuration, you can use the quick link *saprouter* in the SAP Service Marketplace.

For the sake of completeness, the topics of password security and dedicated authentication and authorization on individual server or frontend systems should be mentioned, but to cover those topics here would take far too long, so we refer you to the appropriate literature. You can partly find this, especially for the SAP environment, under the quick link *security* in the SAP Service Marketplace, and the BSI also provides some special manuals for the use of SAP software.

5.5 Extending an Existing Landscape

Very often, before installing an SAP landscape, certain systems (for instance, email or web servers) are already active and occupy some resources within the landscape. While this represents no problems for many applications, for instance, for mail servers or web servers, it can occur that an already existing Oracle database, for instance, may already occupy certain Oracle listener ports or a custom application is using TCP/IP ports from the default SAP space.

Table 5.5 lists all of the ports that can be used in the context of an SAP installation. Depending on the scope of the installation (including the J2EE engine, ICM activated, etc.) all of the given areas may be involved or only some of them. Many of the ports used are determined by the system number. That means that if you are planning to operate several SAP systems on one server, you should be correspondingly careful when granting system numbers, especially when installing on a single server, in order to avoid overlapping systems and therefore ports. The same applies when you are planning to extend the system landscape.

Service name	Default port	Port range	Use in system type	Remark
sapdp<SN>	32xx	3200–3299	ABAP Dispatcher	▸ E3298 default for `niping` ▸ E3299 default for SAProuter
sapdp<SN>s	47xx	4700–4799	Secure ABAP Dispatcher	Connection SNC-secured
sapgw<SN>	33xx	3300–3399	ABAP gateway	
sapgw<SN>s	48xx	4800–4899	Secure ABAP gateway	Connection SNC-secured
sapms<SN>	36xx	3600–3699	ABAP/Java Message Server	
Message Server HTTP	81xx	8100–8199	ABAP/Java Message Server	HTTP access to message server
ICM HTTP	80xx	Any	ABAP HTTP Server	
ICM HTTPS	443xx	Any	ABAP HTTPS Server	
SAProuter	3299	Any	SAProuter	
Oracle Listener	1527	Any	Database	
Java HTTP	5<SN>00	SN from 00 to 99	Java	
Java HTTPS	5<SN>01		Java	
Java P4	5<SN>04		Java	
Java Telnet	5<SN>08		Java	Can be deactivated
Java SDM	5<SN>18		Java	

Table 5.5 Overview of Ports in an SAP Landscape (SN = system number)

Moreover, you should be careful because when installing special instances for central services (for instance, for J2EE systems), separate system numbers will be needed. They may not overlap with other systems on this server.

We recommend that you not use duplicated system numbers, user IDs, or ports, as far as possible. This is particularly difficult in larger landscapes. By sensible planning of system IDs and instance numbers before installation, with a view to existing or future systems, however, you can achieve as small an overlap of installations as possible.

5.6 Summary

The machinery of the IT infrastructure is composed of many different sizes of "gears", which must all work together harmoniously. The topics covered in this chapter should be considered food for thought when planning and make no claim of completeness. When planning your own landscape or infrastructure, always consider the particular features of your environment and your specific requirements for a system or its surroundings.

Similarly, during planning keep in mind where the landscape is expected to grow and whether plans for the future should already be taken into consideration. With the information from the remaining chapters, you'll get a better feeling for what should be a part of a landscape and what effects changes can have.

While production systems have to be stable and highly available, they also have to adjust flexibly to changing realities. SAP has developed an extensive set of techniques and tools for this purpose. They are subsumed under the term transport system and support the maintenance and development of entire system landscapes.

6 SAP Change and Transport Management

The powerful components of the transport system are one of the success factors of SAP technologies. It is the task of the administrator to set them up, manage them, and use them. Knowing and understanding the inherent concepts and techniques will help you keep your systems available and up-to-date.

At first glance, these tasks have little to do with the underlying Oracle database. A more in-depth look at the mechanisms involved, however, reveals that essential actions are closely related to Oracle and have an impact on the Oracle database. Although changes to application programs (such as business transactions, for example) are controlled by basic tools such as the Support Package Manager (Transaction SPAM), the transport tool `tp` is active in the background, writing tuples directly to the Oracle database. In addition, extensive software changes result in an increased memory requirement for the database. As an administrator, you can anticipate this increase and thus avoid problems. In very rare cases, problems can also be solved by accessing the database directly.

This chapter provides the information you need to use the transport system. Basic concepts are introduced systematically and in detail. First, we will describe the basic principles of software logistics in SAP systems. This includes the various data, the definition of a system landscape, and the concept, tools, and management of the Change and Transport System (CTS). We will then introduce you to the change management for Customizing settings and for developments. Finally, you will learn how to set up and manage complex transport landscapes and which tools to use for this.

6.1 Standard Software and Changes to the Standard

As already mentioned in Chapter 2, *SAP Fundamentals*, software can be divided into two categories: individual software and standard software. Individual software includes proprietary developments or software developed by software companies, which are commissioned for particular projects. This type of software is mainly developed for a specific application case in a company. It is customized and specifically tailored to meet the customer's needs. Standard software, on the other hand, refers to software that a company can buy on the market as an off-the-shelf solution and then use without major additional programming.

SAP is a software manufacturer offering standard software for business information processing. This standard software is composed of a complex infrastructure, which usually comes in multiple variants and forms. One of the main tasks when implementing SAP systems is the customization of the system to suit customers' needs so that business processes in customer companies can be optimized. This means changing the system standard.

SAP provides various tools to enhance, modify, or even reduce the default functions to suit a particular environment. Figure 6.1 illustrates the options and tools available to set and modify the processes and functions of the SAP standard. *ABAP Workbench*[1] tools are used for modifications, business add-ins, extensions, and customer developments. Customizing and most of the personalization take place as part of the system implementation according to the *Implementation Guide* (IMG).

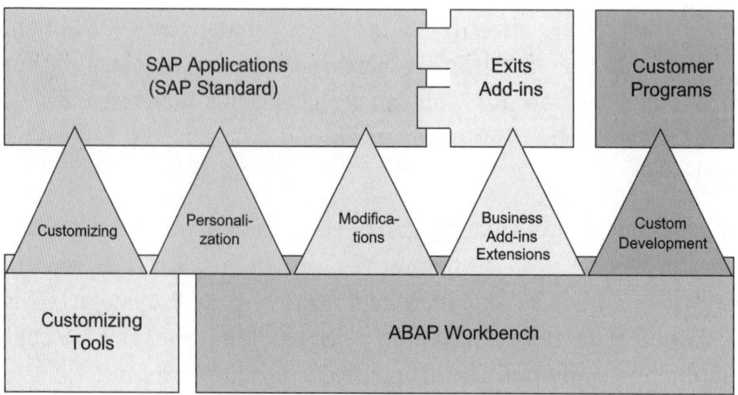

Figure 6.1 Tools and Options for Changes to the SAP Standard (Source: SAP Library, SAP NetWeaver 7.0 SP9)

1 This is the development environment of SAP, where the proprietary programming language ABAP is used for coding.

The figure illustrates the following options for modifying the SAP standard:

- **Customizing**
  Customizing is the setting of system parameters via an interface in the SAP system. Possible changes to the standard have been predefined and organized by SAP. Customizing is required before the system can go live.
- **Personalization**
  Personalization means adjusting the system to meet the work requirements of specific users or user groups. Personalization is aimed at accelerating and simplifying the business transactions that have to be processed by the users. Personalization consists of the two subareas of simplifying navigation and simplifying transactions.
- **Business add-ins (BAdIs) and extensions**
  Business add-ins and extensions are defined places in the source code, where customers can insert appropriately coded logic without having to modify the original SAP object. These places correspond mostly to requirements by partners and customers, which have not been implemented in the standard, but have been anticipated by SAP. The advantage of these extensions is that the call interfaces are retained in future releases, thereby guaranteeing upward compatibility.
- **Modifications**
  Modifications to SAP standard objects should only be implemented if none of the previously mentioned options produce the required changes in the environment. Such modifications require that the person implementing the changes has extensive background knowledge about the application structure and processes. Modifications to SAP objects can be lost when applying corrections or installing an upgrade.
- **Developments**
  Customer developments are performed by the customer in a separate customer namespace. These namespaces ensure that the developed objects are not overwritten by SAP objects when a new development status becomes available for the system.

These tools enable you, the customer, to adapt your SAP system to your own needs by using Customizing or by modifying objects. If all users were allowed to implement changes in the system, the system intended to support the activity output would soon stop working, as would the activity output itself (that is, production).

The following questions arise out of the available changes and the problem mentioned above:

- How can you ensure that these changes work properly in a production environment?
- Who documents these changes?
- Can the changes be tested first?
- What provisions are made for quality assurance?

All of these questions have been considered in a concept developed by SAP. As part of this concept, the system landscape is being enhanced by additional SAP systems, and a release and transport mechanism for changes is being implemented. This allows for Customizing and customer developments to be documented, tested, versioned, released, and transported.

In the following sections, we will explain the concept of managing and transporting changes in more detail. The next section will introduce you to the basic principles of this concept.

6.2 Basic Principles of Software Logistics

This section will describe the various types of data within a system as well as the concept of a system landscape. Next, we will explore the Change and Transport System (CTS) and its tools in more detail, and we will investigate when changes to the standard are allowed and where they will be recorded. Finally, we will discuss the Transport Management System and its tools, which allow you to define transport routes to transport the changes between systems in a system landscape.

6.2.1 Data in the SAP System

We will first describe what data is available in an SAP system and where and how they can be found. To do so, we first have to explore the concept of a *client*.

A client is a unit, which is clearly defined from a technical, organizational, and business point of view. It encompasses master, transaction, user, and Customizing data. From a business point of view, a client is a unit with its own financial accounting, including separate financial statements. Each user in a particular client of an SAP system always logs in with his username and password. A client is defined by its *client number*. The master and transaction data is specific to a particular client in the system and do not impact each other. A client can also assume different roles (see the next section for more information).

Figure 6.2 displays the different data using the example of an SAP ERP ECC system.

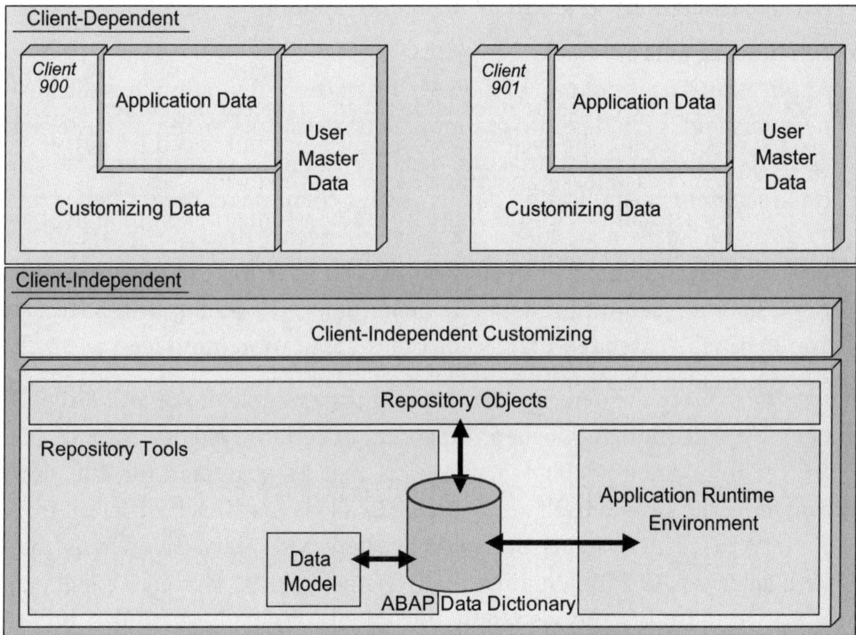

Figure 6.2 Data in an SAP ERP ECC System

Data can be divided into two categories: *client-dependent* data and *client-independent* data. Depending on the type of data to be changed, these are modified throughout the whole system or only in the respective client.

- **Customizing data**
  Customizing data is contained in Customizing tables. This data is created by changes in the Customizing tools. They are evaluated in applications by the runtime system and are used to control business processes and checks. Most Customizing data is client-dependent. Changes to client-dependent Customizing data do not affect the system behavior of another client. Client-independent Customizing data can be accessed by all clients (for example, the factory calendar). This is also called cross-client Customizing. Changes to client-independent Customizing data therefore directly affect all clients in an SAP system.

- **Repository data**
  Changes to the repository, which includes the ABAP programs, function modules, the data model, and the objects of the ABAP Data Dictionary, are stored in the repository tables using the repository tools. The contents of these tables are called repository data or repository objects. Apart from a few exceptions, all repository data is client-independent. Again, all changes directly affect all clients in an SAP system.
- **Application data**
  Application data is not part of the SAP software configuration. It is the business data and is divided into master data (for example, material, customer, and supplier data) and transaction data (for example, sales orders or financial documents). Application data is always client-dependent. Change and Transport Management does not manage changes to this type of data. Other tools enabling the transfer of application data have to be used for this purpose, such as ALE (Application Link Enabling), CATT (Computer Aided Test Tool), eCATT (Extended CATT)[2], or other application interfaces.

Before we explore the delivery clients using the example of the SAP ERP ECC system, we will address the client capability of certain systems. An ERP ECC system is fully client-enabled. This means that all processes and functions provided by the system itself are available in all clients. This is different from SAP NetWeaver BI systems or systems where SAP NetWeaver BI is integrated, such as SAP SCM (Supply Chain Management). Although clients are available in these systems also, only one client (originally client 001 in SAP NetWeaver BI) provides full functionality. Although client copies can be created, they do not provide full functionality. In SAP SCM systems, for example, the functions of SAP SCM are available in the copy. However, once the internal SAP NetWeaver BI system is accessed, errors occur. You can configure an SAP SCM system such that it is client-enabled (as used in the SAP University Competence Centers).[3] It is not yet certain whether SAP NetWeaver BI will be shipped client-enabled in a future release.

Figure 6.3 illustrates the *delivery clients*, using the SAP ERP ECC system as an example. We distinguish between the *standard version* and the *delivery of an IDES system*.[4] Delivery clients are clients that are already present in the sys-

2 eCATT can only be used on systems with SAP Web AS 6.20 and later. It replaces CATT step by step.

3 You will find more information on Release SCM 4.x in SAP Note 522569. The procedure for releases earlier than SCM 4.0 (particularly APO 3.x) is described in SAP Note 384057.

4 IDES is an acronym for Internet Demo and Education System. For more information, see the SAP Service Marketplace at *http://service.sap.com/ides*.

tem after delivery. The standard version of SAP ERP ECC systems contains three clients:

- Original SAP client 000
- Sample SAP client 001
- EarlyWatch client 066

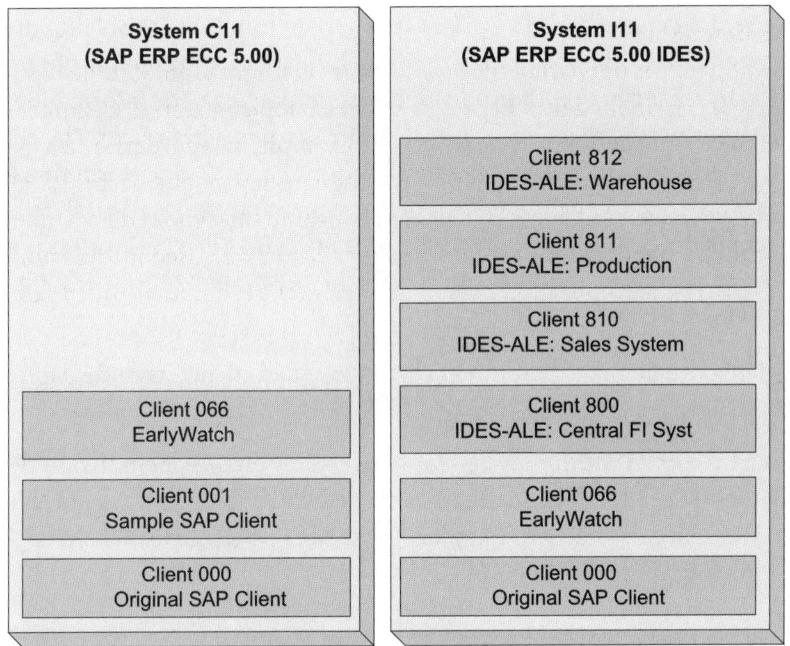

Figure 6.3 Delivery Clients in SAP ERP ECC Systems

The original SAP client with client number 000 is used as a reference client and cannot be changed by customers. This client receives new Customizing through upgrades, legal change packages, support packages, and language imports. This way, it always contains the current reference Customizing.

Client 001 is only a sample client and can be deleted any time. Regarding upgrades, language imports, and new Customizing, it is obsolete. Translations are only imported in client 000. Client 001 only contains German and English. Consequently, the sample client is no longer used as a template for client copies. These should be created exclusively from client 000 (for more information, see SAP Note 550894). An exception to this is SAP Solution Manager prior to Release 4.0. In Basis releases up to and including 4.6C, client 001 was also used as a template for additional clients.

The EarlyWatch client 066 is used to perform *SAP EarlyWatch Checks*, which analyze the components of the SAP systems, of the operating system, and of the database and determine how the performance of the system can be optimized and how the total cost of ownership can be kept to a minimum. These checks are triggered and performed automatically by SAP EarlyWatch Alert. Should a critical situation occur in the system, SAP schedules a check, during which an experienced service engineer performs a detailed analysis of the system via a remote connection and offers appropriate solutions for solving the critical system state. The maintenance contract includes a maximum of two detailed analyses for each SAP production system per year (for information, see the SAP Service Marketplace at *http://service.sap.com/earlywatch*). The client contains a user EARLYWATCH, who is only authorized to perform transactions that are used to analyze system performance and read statistical data. If this client is not present in your system or if the EARLYWATCH user is not authorized to perform service sessions, refer to SAP Note 7312 for troubleshooting information.

IDES systems usually have additional clients installed, which include extensive sample data.

Clients can be copied within a system or between different systems using client copy tools. The more clients that are created and copied in a system, the more database space is needed. Chapter 7, *System Lifecycle*, covers client copies and the available tools.

6.2.2 System Landscape

In Section 6.1, *Standard Software and Changes to the Standard*, we mentioned that SAP has developed a concept to record, document, and test certain changes in the SAP system, before they are implemented in a production environment. As part of this concept, the system is enhanced with dedicated systems. In an SAP environment, this is referred to as the *system landscape*. SAP recommends a landscape consisting of three systems, as illustrated in Figure 6.4. Each system in this group is used for different tasks:

- The development system (DEV) is used for Customizing, parameterization, and all customer developments.
- The quality assurance system (QAS) is used to check if changes from the development system affect the production system. These tests are mainly performed on copies of real data from the production system.
- The production system (PRD) itself is locked for developments and tests. It receives developments that have been checked and released from QAS.

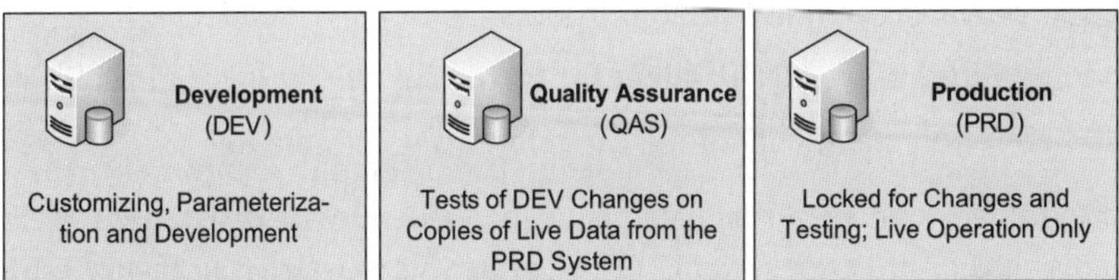

Figure 6.4 Recommended Three-System Landscape

The division into development, test, and production system ensures that the repository objects in the production system are consistent and that the production environment is stable and secure. Moreover, performance in the production client is not affected by development and testing activities in other clients or by Customizing or repository changes. These are first implemented in the development system and tested in the test system. All work on developments and on Customizing can be done simultaneously with the production operation.

When defining clients, we already mentioned that different *client roles* exist. When planning an SAP landscape, you should consider in advance which clients are needed for which activities. A client is given a role by assigning it activities. You can specify these in **Tools • Administration • Administration • Client Administration • Client Maintenance** (Transaction SCC4).

Assigning client roles to a client, however, does not affect its function. Only the client roles Production and SAP Reference prevent client copies from being implemented on these clients. Whereas changes to Customizing can also be implemented in a client marked as a production client, the Customizing objects that can be maintained as current settings (such as posting periods) are excluded from being recorded via the transport system.

Classifying clients in this manner is therefore mainly used for documenting purposes. The assignment of a role to a client can be changed any time. It is important to remember the following: If a system measurement is performed, it is considered production-related if at least one of the clients in the system has the role of a production client.

The following roles can be set in client maintenance in the SAP system:

- Production (PROD): client for productive operation
- Test (TEST): client for testing activities
- Customizing (CUST): client for Customizing, personalization, and development activities

- Demo (DEMO): client for demo purposes
- Training/Education (TRNG): client for providing workshops and trainings
- SAP Reference: client containing the reference Customizing

After defining these client roles, you have to decide how to distribute the clients among the different systems in the system landscape (see Figure 6.5). Remember that cross-client Customizing and changes to repository objects made in a client directly impact all clients in a system. Therefore, all changes to Customizing and repository data are made in the Customizing client (CUST). After the changes have been transported to the test client (TEST) of the quality assurance system (or quality assurance client (QTEST), as it is also known), a check is performed to see if they have arrived at their destination and to verify that the test data yield the required results. If this is the case, the changes are then transported to the production client (PROD), where they are ready for use. Regarding the client-independent data, the quality assurance client and the production client are totally separate from the clients in which the changes are made.

If more clients with additional roles are needed, they can be set up in one of the three systems. Development test clients (TEST) and prototype clients (SAND) can be set up in development systems. Developers can test their changes in development test clients, before transports are released. Prototype clients are used to test the behavior of client-independent Customizing. The training and education clients (TRNG), however, are set up in the quality assurance system and have access to the data there. In SAP systems, the client roles in client maintenance do not provide values for the aforementioned additional client roles or for the quality assurance client. You have to use the values provided earlier. The quality assurance client, for example, can be mapped through the *Test Client* role, and the prototype client through the Customizing role.

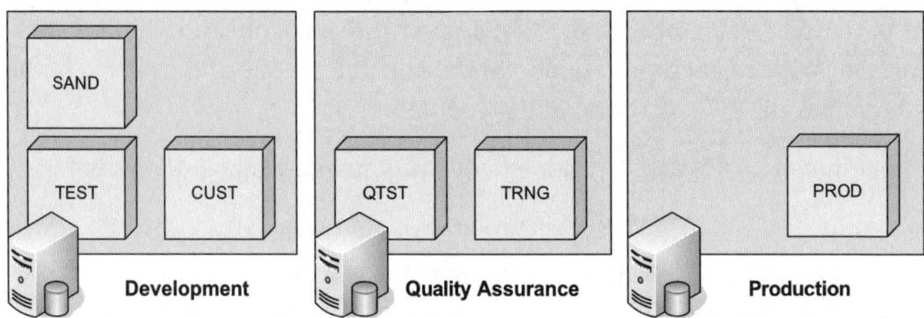

Figure 6.5 Client Roles in a Three-System Landscape

For smaller implementations, where only minor developments are done in ABAP, for example, a two-system landscape represents an alternative to the three-system landscape described earlier. No separate quality assurance system (QAS) is provided in such a landscape. The quality assurance client (QTEST) is located in the development system (DEV). As is the case in the three-system landscape, the production client is fully separated from the other clients and systems (see Figure 6.6).

The disadvantages of the two-system landscape are obvious: Client-independent data are shared in the Customizing and quality assurance client. On the one hand, the changes made to client-independent data in the Customizing client can negatively affect the tests in the quality assurance client. On the other hand, changes cannot be guaranteed to be transported fully. After the final transport to the production client, errors can occur there, although all tests in the quality assurance client passed successfully. This can be caused by changes to client-independent data, which have not yet been transported.

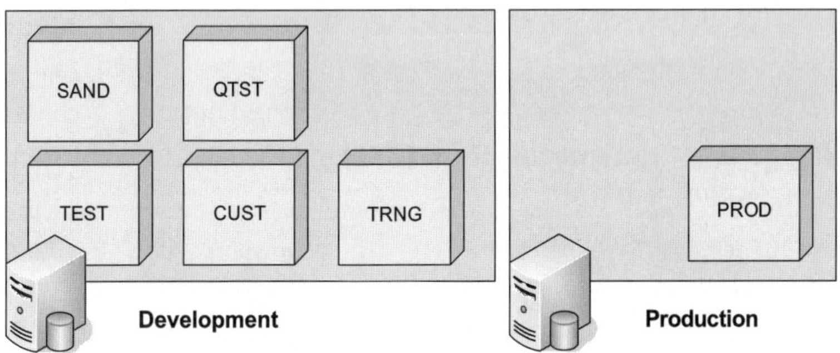

Figure 6.6 Two-System Landscape

In addition to two- and three-system landscapes, landscapes with much more complex systems are possible and can be useful. Such multisystem landscapes, for example, are useful, if locally separate production systems have to be used to separate different locations, which may be located on different continents. The division into development (DEV), quality assurance (QAS), and production system (PRD) is retained in this case. Multiple systems of a particular type can simultaneously exist in a multisystem landscape. Figure 6.7 shows an example of a multisystem landscape.

In this landscape, the central development system *DEV* and the quality assurance system *QAS* can be found at location *A*. It is likely that changes of a more international nature will be made here. The tested changes are transported from the QAS system to the downstream systems of each location (*DEA*, *DEB*, and *DEC*). There, additional regional changes can be made, which have to be tested again (*QAA*, *QAB*, *QAC*) and can then be transported to the separate production systems (*PRA*, *PRB*, *PRC*).

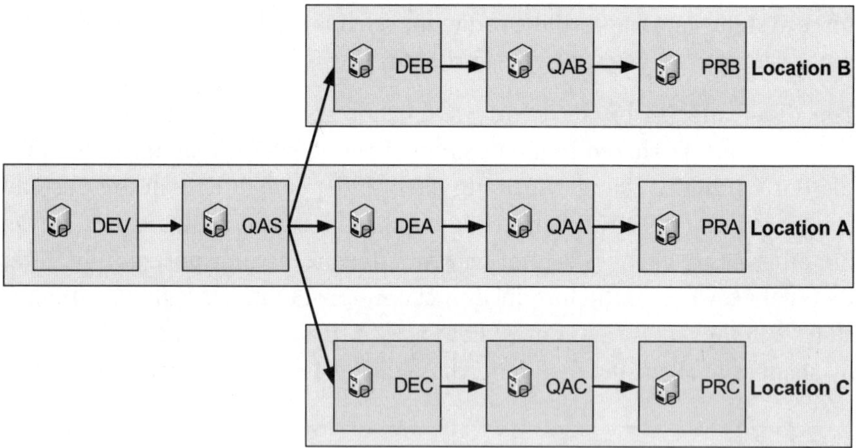

Figure 6.7 Multisystem Landscape

6.2.3 Change and Transport System (CTS)

The *Change and Transport System* consists of the *Transport Organizer*, the *Transport Management System* (TMS) and the *transport tools* (`tp` and `R3trans`). Through the CTS, your changes are recorded in the systems. They are then transported between systems via routes defined by you. It is extremely important to configure the CTS in each newly installed SAP system before you define any settings in the system. Figure 6.8 provides an overview of the tools listed for the CTS. The bottom of the graphic contains a listing of the transport tools used by the CTS.

The Transport Organizer is a powerful tool, which registers and documents all changes to objects in the repository and in Customizing. It is fully integrated into the ABAP Workbench and Customizing tools. Previous releases distinguished between a Customizing Organizer (Transaction SE09), a Workbench Organizer (Transaction SE10), and an extended Transport Organizer (Transaction SE01). Starting from Release 4.6C, all of these tools have been combined in the Transport Organizer in a single interface. You can access it through **Tools • Administration • Transports • Transport Organizer**.

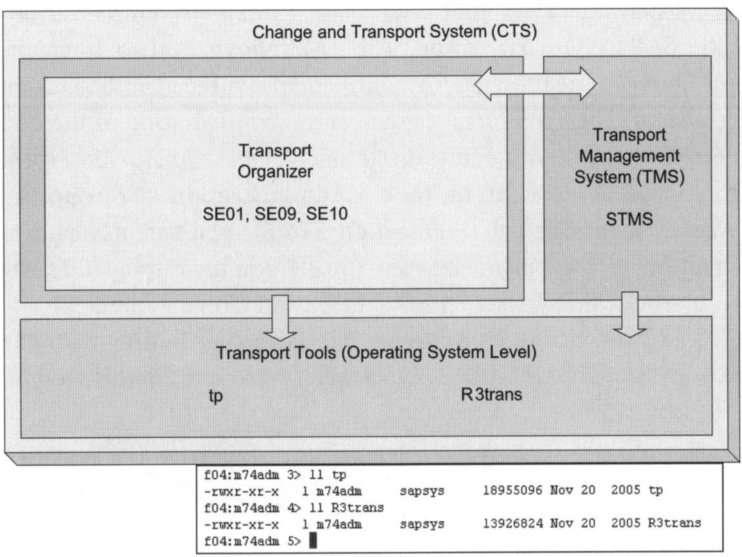

Figure 6.8 Change and Transport System (CTS)

The initial screen (see Figure 6.9) includes many functions that allow you to filter the changes by user name, request type, and request status, and to view and edit them.

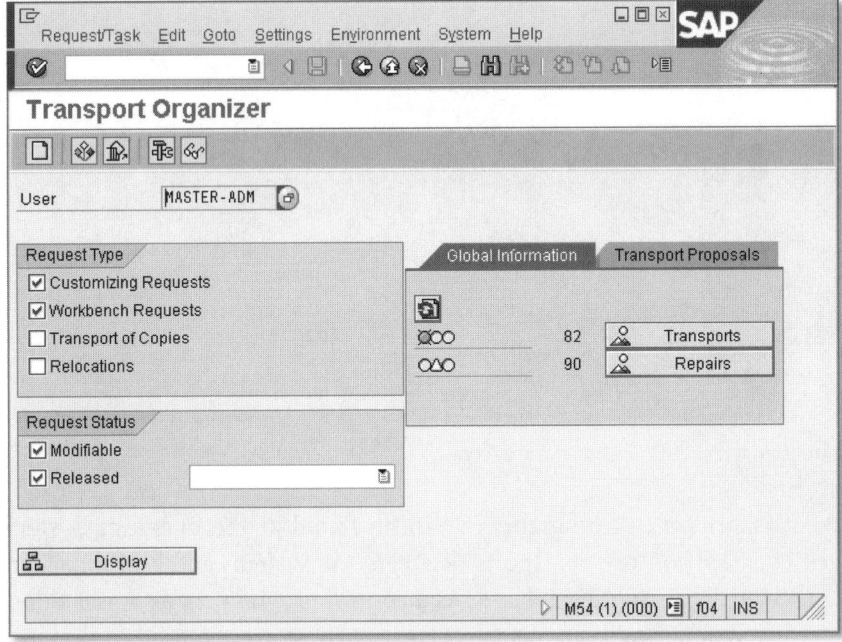

Figure 6.9 Initial Transport Organizer Screen

The Transport Management System (TMS) acts as a link between the various systems in the SAP system landscape. The TMS allows you to transport developments between the individual systems and provides an authorization and tracking system. The TMS includes the central configuration of the CTS for all connected SAP systems. From the initial screen of the TMS (Figure 6.10), which can be accessed from **Tools • Administration • Transports • Transport Management System** (Transaction STMS), you can navigate to three important areas: the *import overview* (in the graphic displayed as the button with the truck), the *system overview* (the button with the hierarchically linked boxes), and the *transport route configuration* (the button with the boxes linked with curved lines). We will look at all three areas in this section.

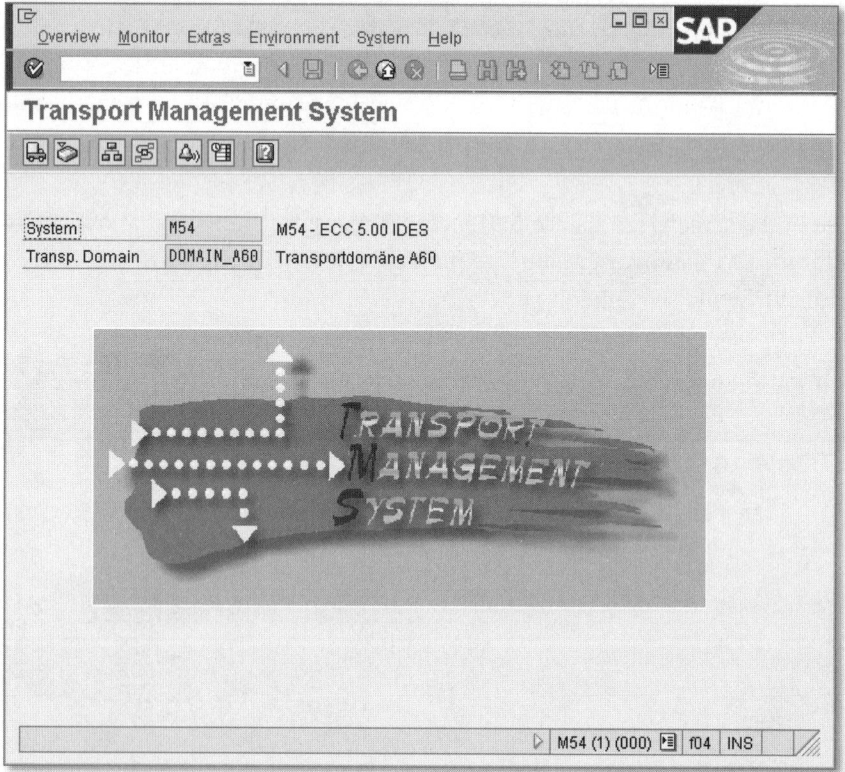

Figure 6.10 Initial TMS Screen

The transport control program `tp` can be found at the operating system level. This tool controls transports between SAP systems and is also needed when changing to another release. As a control program, `tp` also uses other operating system programs such as `R3trans`. These are required to perform complete transports. The transport control program `tp` is usually called from programs in the SAP system. It controls transports and generates control files for `R3trans`. The `R3trans` tool, however, performs the actual task and writes directly to the Oracle database. In certain circumstances, however, such as in emergency situations, it is useful to know the syntax of the `tp` program so that you can use it from the operating system level (see Section 6.5.6, *Using the Transport Control Program*).

6.2.4 Recording Changes

How are changes to Customizing and repository objects recorded?

On the one hand, we have to consider the SAP system change option. Using the **System Change Option Settings** (Transaction SE06), you can control whether client-independent Customizing and repository objects are modifiable or not. You can also specify which software components are modifiable in which namespaces. The production and quality assurance systems (PRD, QAS) should receive a status of "not modifiable," because no original programs are allowed here. All changes to objects need to be made in the development system (DEV), from which they can be transported to the downstream systems.

On the other hand, you specify in **Client Administration** (Transaction SCC4) if these changes will be recorded (provided this is permitted by the system change option). Sometimes, as in the case of the SAP University Competence Center, it can be preferable for certain training, demo, or test clients of the systems not to record or transport any changes. Training participants are neither asked for a transport request in development or Customizing exercises, nor is this information intended for transport to another system.

For each client, the client settings can be used to determine its behavior regarding client-dependent or client-independent changes and changes to the repository.

The following settings can be specified for changes to and transports of *client-dependent* objects:

- Changes without automatic recording
- Automatic recording of changes
- No changes permitted
- Changes without automatic recording, no transports permitted

You have to record all changes in Customizing clients. These are intended for transport to downstream systems at a later time. In this case, the **Automatic recording of changes** setting is recommended. For the production client, you should choose the **No changes permitted** setting.

Separate settings have to be specified in Client Administration to enable changes to *client-independent* objects. The following are valid options:

- Changes to the repository and client-independent Customizing permitted
- No changes to client-independent Customizing objects
- No changes to repository objects
- No changes to repository and client-independent Customizing objects

This division ensures that you can define a single client in the development system (DEV) that can change client-independent Customizing and repository objects as provided in the system change option. You can prevent all other clients in the development system from system-wide changes.

In addition to these two options, you can protect the client from being overwritten, prevent CATT (Computer Aided Test Tool) and eCATT (Extended CATT) from being executed, and protect the client against SAP upgrades. The latter is only possible for clients to which you have assigned the roles Test or SAP Reference.

In addition to these system and client settings, initializing the CTS is an important task once the system has been set up. If a system is installed directly from the DVD shipped with the system, this action does not have to be performed. However, if a system is created as a copy of an already existing system, it needs to be initialized. During initialization, the basic CTS settings are re-generated, and the change requests already present in the system (see next section) are closed. CTS initialization is performed through Transaction SE06 as part of processing after installation. For proper processing after installation to be performed, you have to choose if the SAP system has been installed from an SAP CD or DVD, as a database copy, or through a database migration.

6.2.5 Change Requests

Now that we have explained when a client records changes, we will investigate how the system does this. In the preceding sections, we merely pointed out that changes are transferred or transported between systems.

This is donc through *change requests*. A change request is an information carrier of the Transport Organizer, which records and administers all changes to repository objects and Customizing settings. A change request is queried whenever a change has been made, and the result is saved to the database.

We distinguish between two types of change requests: *Customizing requests* and *Workbench requests* (see Figure 6.11).

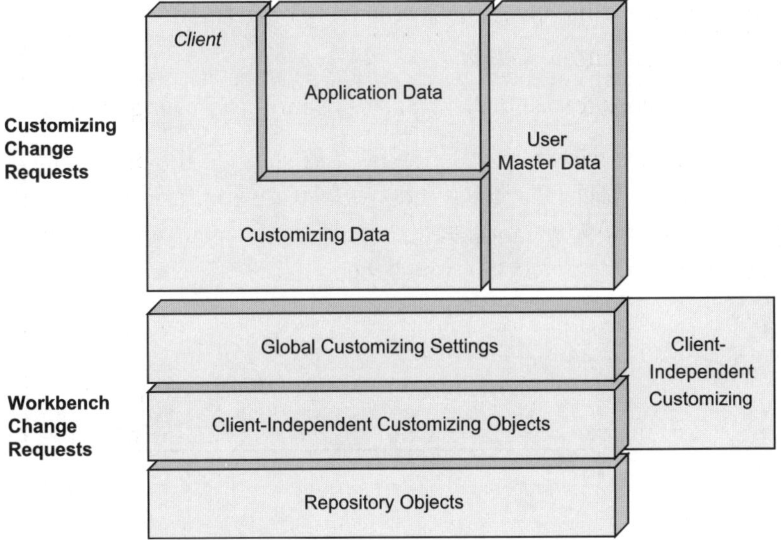

Figure 6.11 Customizing and Workbench Requests

Customizing requests are queried from a single client (the source client of the request) when changes are made to client-dependent Customizing. *Workbench requests* are used to record changes to repository objects and to client-independent Customizing. They can also include client-dependent Customizing, provided that it comes from the source client of the request.

You can recognize these change requests by their unique syntax consisting of letters and numbers. The request consists of a three-digit system-ID (SID), followed by the letter K and a consecutive six-digit number. For example, a request might have the number M54K900034. Each change request has exactly one owner, that is, one user in the SAP system, who is responsible for managing the request and who may be changed as required.

Figure 6.12 shows several dialog boxes that are displayed when a request is queried.

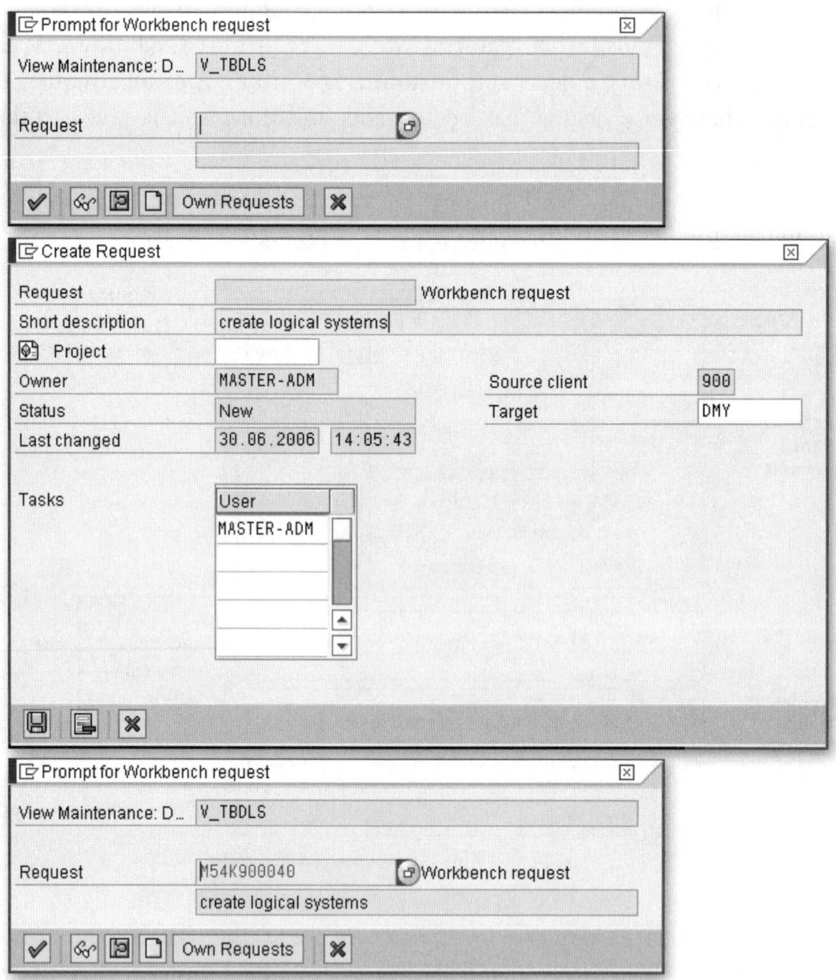

Figure 6.12 Sample Query of a Workbench Request

We use the example of creating a logical system through Transaction BD54, which represents a change to client-independent Customizing. As described earlier, for client-independent Customizing, Workbench requests are queried. The first dialog is displayed when saving the change. In this case, no change request has been specified yet. Using the **Create New** button, user MASTER-ADM creates a new Workbench request in client 900. Because of the transport route configuration, this request will be transported to system DMY. The request is created by clicking on the **Save** button. It is given a unique number, in our example M54K900038, and it is used to record changes.

The currently created transport request is then listed in the Transport Organizer. Figure 6.13 displays all transport requests in all clients of system M54 for user MASTER-ADM. You can see that in client 900, several Workbench and several Customizing requests have been created. All requests have a status of Modifiable. This means that these requests can be used (to record changes) and modified (changes to the request itself). Selection options allow you to collapse or expand the displayed list of change requests.

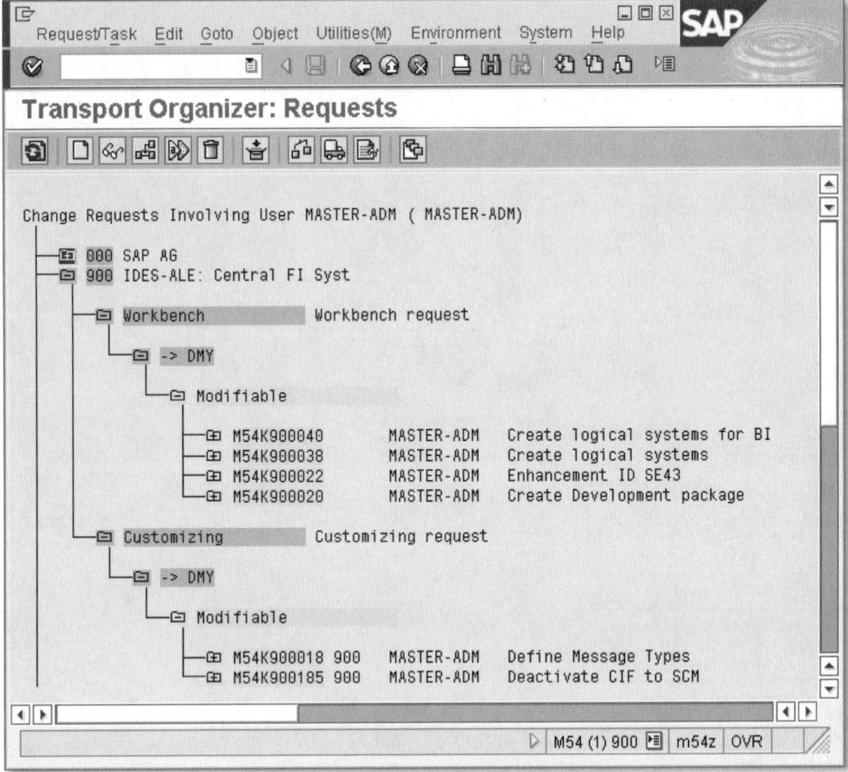

Figure 6.13 Displaying Change Requests in the Transport Organizer

The transportability of these requests and the existence of local change requests that cannot be transported are linked to the configuration of the transport routes in the TMS. We will explore this in more detail in Section 6.2.7, *Transport Routes and Transport Layers.*

Change requests can be assigned one or more tasks. The owners of the tasks can be different from the owners of the change requests. The owner of a change request is a user in the SAP system. Each task is assigned a unique number based on the syntax described earlier. If required, the task can be transferred to a different user. To display the tasks in the Transport Organizer, drill down the hierarchical display (see Figure 6.14). Workbench request M54K900038 has exactly one associated task, M54K900039, whose owner is MASTER-ADM. In this task, the maintenance of the logical system M54CLNT903 has been recorded using maintenance view V_TBDLS. The changed database table is TBDLS, and the associated text table is TBDLST.

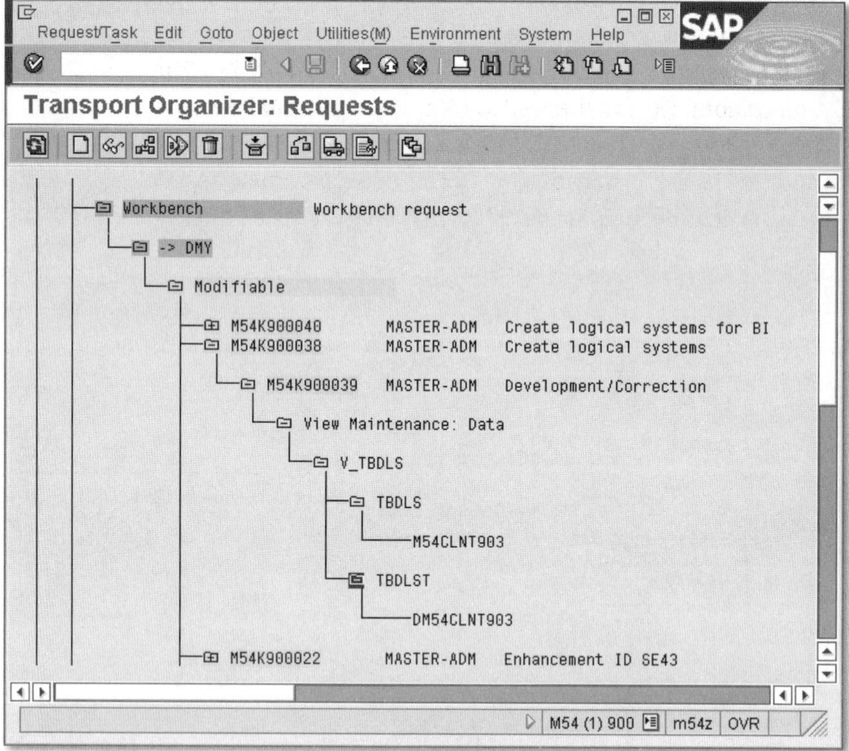

Figure 6.14 Tasks in Change Requests

Thus, tasks are "attached" to change requests. They collect the actual changes to different objects (for information on task types, see Section 6.4, *Change Management for Developments*).

6.2.6 Transport Management System

The TMS acts as a link between the different systems of the SAP system landscape. A central interface allows you to configure all settings of a system landscape's transport system and to monitor, perform, and track all transports between systems (Transaction STMS). In the extended TMS you can configure workflows of authorization steps for transports. Imports are always the responsibility of the administrator. For each change request, a transport log is created automatically during transport. This way, you can track what has been transported when and where. However, the TMS cannot check if developments have been tested.

The TMS always uses a *transport directory*, which stores all required transport files, logs, and configurations. This transport directory and all required subdirectories are generated during system installation and are located at the operating system level. The default value is */usr/sap/trans*. This default value can be customized for the SAP system in **Profile Maintenance** (Transaction RZ10). To do so, change or maintain the `DIR_TRANS` and `DIR_EPS_ROOT` parameters in the instance profile. The latter parameter specifies the directory, in which the support packages and add-on installations are stored.

It makes sense to have all systems in a system landscape access a central transport directory. It is therefore not necessary to create a local directory for each system. From each system, you can access the transport files and configurations from a central directory, which you share using network shares (see Figure 6.15).

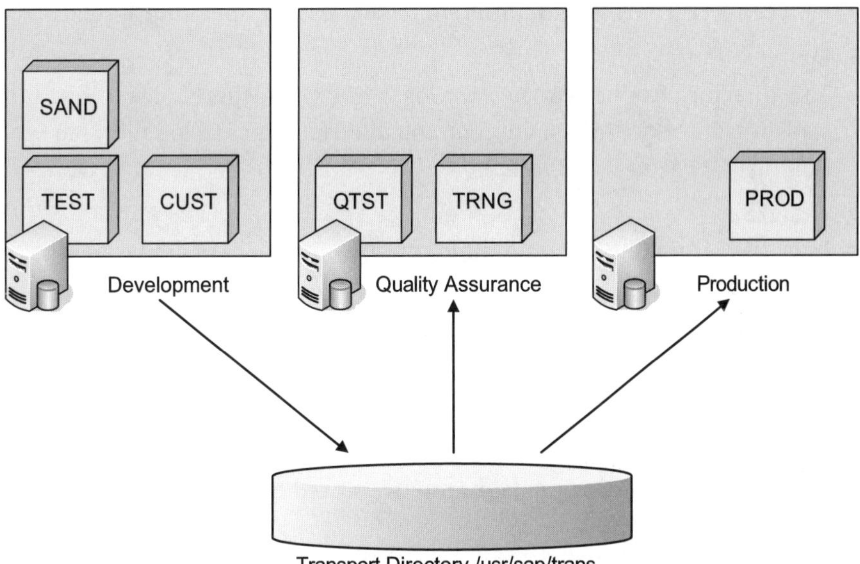

Figure 6.15 Transport Directory in a Three-System Landscape

The transport directory contains several subdirectories:

- **actlog**
  This directory records all actions for the individual transport requests in log files.
- **bin**
  This directory contains the configuration files for the `tp` program (TP_<DOMAINNAME>.PFL) and for the transport domain (DOMAIN.CFG).
- **buffer**
  This directory contains an import buffer for each connected system. This buffer lists all requests that are to be imported or are pending import, including all import steps.
- **cofiles**
  All control files for transport requests are stored here. These files list the transport type, object classes, import steps, return values, and the import status.
- **data**
  This directory contains all data files for transport requests. The format of the data files written by `R3trans` is also known as the `R3trans` format. It is platform- and release-independent and can therefore be exchanged between SAP systems with different databases and operating systems.
- **log**
  This directory can be searched for log files for transports, trace files, and statistics. For more information on the different types of log files, see Section 6.5.7, *Logging Transports*.
- **olddata**
  Data files from the data subdirectory are moved here once they have exceeded a specified storage period.
- **sapnames**
  All information related to transport activities for each user in an SAP system using the CTS is stored here.
- **tmp**
  Temporary log files and semaphores[5] are stored in this directory.

5 Semaphores are used to synchronize processes or threads that need to be coordinated timewise when executed simultaneously. Problems can occur in the transport environment when exporting a request (see SAP Note 132536).

Note

After installing your SAP system, verify that all of the required subdirectories mentioned above have been created. If this is not the case, create the missing directories and note to which user groups they belong and what their write permissions are (depending on the operating system). Additional optional subdirectories include backup and serial.

All SAP systems sharing a central transport directory form a *transport group*. The transport group belongs to a *transport domain*. The TMS supports multiple transport groups within a transport domain. This domain includes all systems that are to be managed jointly. For technical reasons, all system IDs have to be unique (this does not apply to the system numbers in a system landscape). Transports between two different groups of a domain are possible (see also Section 6.5.4, *Transports Between Transport Groups*). However, transports between groups that are located in different domains can only be performed via domain links or external systems (for information, see Section 6.5.5, *Transports Between Transport Domains*).

One SAP system in the domain has to assume the function of *transport domain controller* (TDC). The controller generates and manages the reference configuration for the TMS. All connected systems in the domain receive a copy of this configuration from the TDC. The required settings are always configured in the TDC, from where they are distributed. All communication between the controller and the domain systems takes place via RFC connections. These are generated automatically during TMS configuration. The TDC should be configured on a system with high availability, such as a quality assurance or production system. The load in the SAP system caused by the TMS is minor and does not affect performance. You specify all TMS configuration settings in client 000 of the system hosting the TDC. Figure 6.16 summarizes the concepts of transport domain, transport group, and transport domain controller.

In addition to the TDC, a *backup domain controller* (BDC) can be configured. This is useful so that you can continue to make configuration changes even in the event of a failure of the system running the TDC. The complete TDC configuration can be applied using a BDC. The BDC has to be enabled manually in case of a system failure by following the menu path **Transport Management System • System Overview • Extras • Activate Backup Controller**. In Figure 6.17, production system PR2 takes on the role of BDC in domain A.

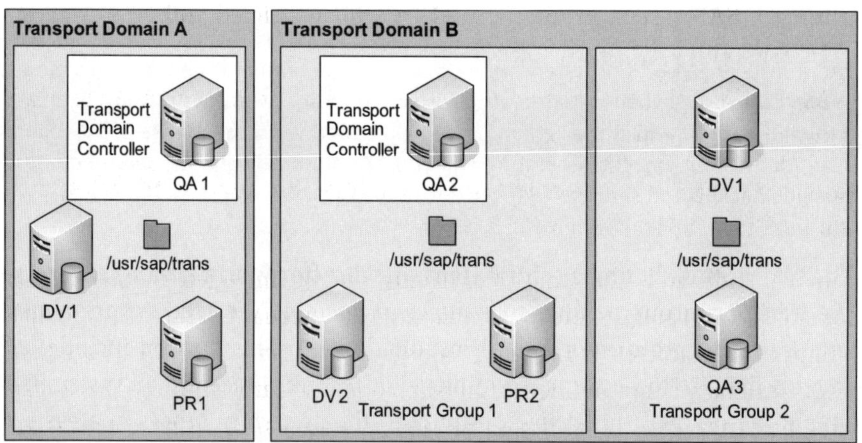

Figure 6.16 Transport Domains and Transport Groups

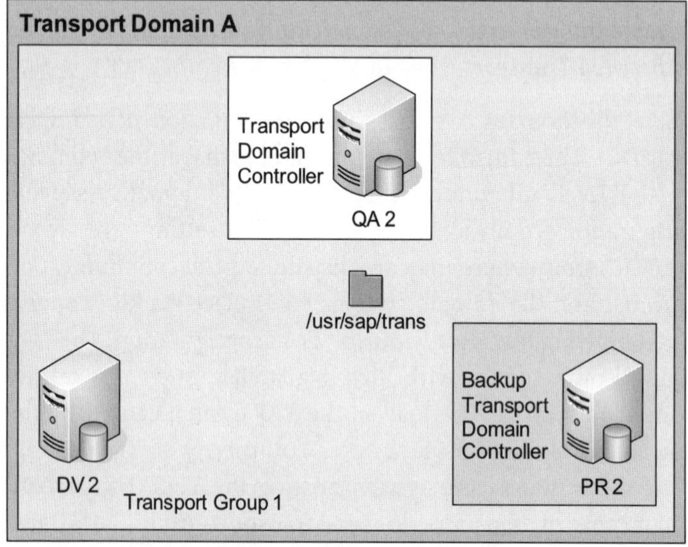

Figure 6.17 Backup Domain Controller

During the definition of the transport domain and when adding additional systems to this domain, several actions are performed automatically in the background. These are required for the proper functioning of the TMS.

- The updated configuration is stored in the database and partly in the DOMAIN.CFG configuration file in the */usr/sap/trans/bin* directory at the operating system level.

- In each SAP system, a user TMSADM with restricted authorizations for TMS activities is created.
- All required RFC connections to the domain and from the domain to other systems are created.

Basis Release 3.1H is the earliest possible release for integrating an SAP system into a transport domain.

Both Unicode and non-Unicode systems can be included in a transport domain and run at the same time. *Unicode* is an international standard, which assigns each character in a language a unique number. Currently, more than 90,000 characters are defined in the Unicode standard, with the possibility of adding more than a million additional characters. By using the Unicode standard, SAP aims at achieving complete internationalization of its software and enhancing the integration of SAP with Internet technology. In Unicode-based systems, characters from practically all languages can be stored in the database. As for the TMS, ensure that you use the most up-to-date release of the TDC, if possible, and at least Web Application Server Release 6.10.[6] You should also import the latest support package. For example, problems with the transport profile in Unicode systems have only been solved as of Basis Package Level 19 for Web Application Server 6.20 (SAP Note 584333). Section 6.5.8, *Transports Between Unicode and Non-Unicode Systems*, deals specifically with problems arising during the transport of changes between Unicode and non-Unicode systems.

As already mentioned, the transport control program `tp` is a utility at the operating system level, which controls transports between SAP systems or when changing to another release. `tp` needs a profile to establish a connection to Oracle databases or to other databases of the SAP systems in the transport domain. This profile is saved in the *TP_<DOMAINNAME>.PFL* file in the */usr/sap/trans/bin* directory. The profile is automatically generated by the TMS during its configuration by the TDC. It should *not* be customized at the operating system level using editors. The parameters included in the profile can be viewed using the TMS. If you do not specify a value for a parameter, the default value is used automatically. Globally defined values overwrite default values, and locally defined values overwrite global values.

Figure 6.18 displays the most important `tp` parameters, which have been defined for system M54: `TRANSDIR` indicates the path to the transport directory, `DBTYPE` the underlying database, in this case Oracle, `DBHOST` the compu-

6 Please check SAP Note 584333 for changes.

ter hosting the database, DBNAME the database name, DBSWPATH the path to the Oracle server software, and DBLIBPATH the path to the SAP database client.

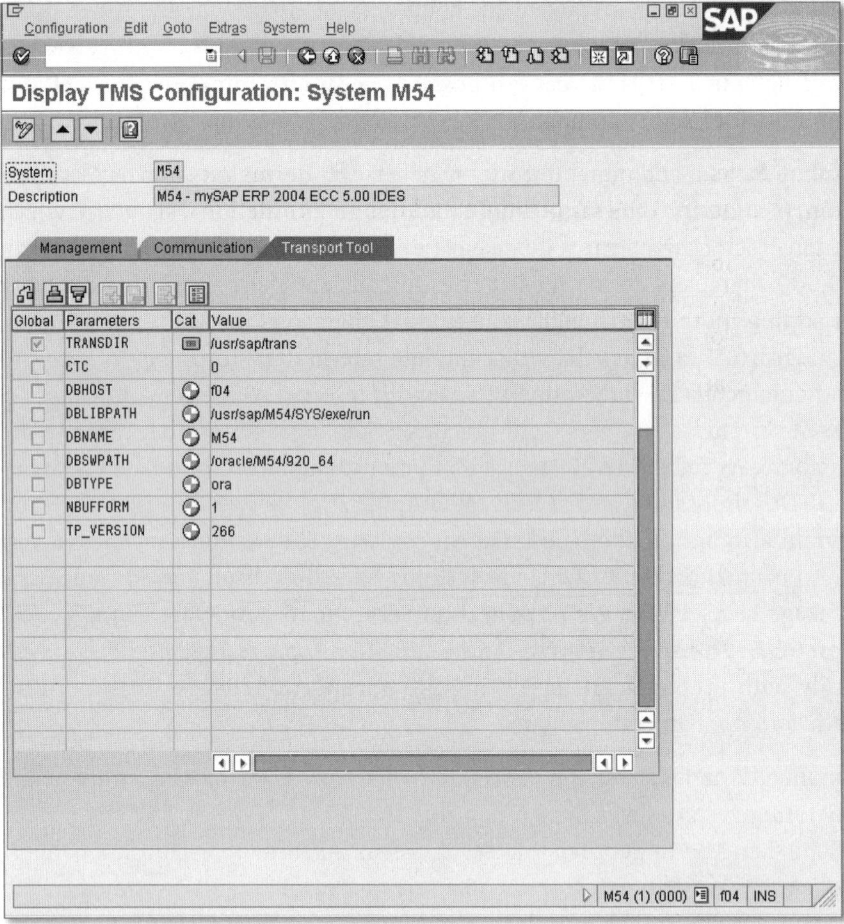

Figure 6.18 Profile of the Transport Control Program tp

6.2.7 Transport Routes and Transport Layers

As already mentioned in Section 6.2.5, *Change Requests*, the transportability of change requests and the existence of local change requests that cannot be transported are linked to the configuration of the transport routes in the TMS.

Transport routes are therefore used to transport change requests between systems that have been defined in the system landscape. There are two different types of routes:

- Consolidation route
- Delivery route

In a three-system landscape, these routes can be defined easily: A consolidation route describes the path followed by changes as they move from a development system to the quality assurance system. The delivery route then connects the quality assurance system with the production system.

In a multisystem landscape, we have to resort to terms used for system operation to describe the consolidation and delivery routes:

- **Integration system**
  The integration system corresponds to the development system. It is used for developments and Customizing.
- **Consolidation system**
  This type corresponds to the quality assurance system. Here, the changes made in the integration system are verified.
- **Recipient system**
  The recipient system is the system receiving the tested changes. It can be a production system, a development system, or a quality assurance system.

Figure 6.19 illustrates the example of a multisystem landscape where the newly introduced terms have been added. The development systems from the local sites are therefore not only recipient systems for changes from the global consolidation system QAS, but also integration systems.

In more general terms, the consolidation route is a path for changes originating from an integration system, whereas the delivery route defines a path for changes originating from a consolidation system.

Note

Because different terminology is used for the system landscape, depending on the point of view, this can lead to some confusion. Integration tests, for example, are not performed in the integration system, but in the consolidation system.

The transport route is defined through a *transport layer*. This transport layer is generated in the TMS. It can be up to four characters long, but must start with the letter Z. For easy understanding, it is recommended that you use the system ID label for the integration system in this layer, for example ZDEV. If this is not possible, because you want to define several transport layers for the integration system to create multiple consolidation routes to the same or to different systems, use meaningful variants (ZDEA, ZDEB, etc.).

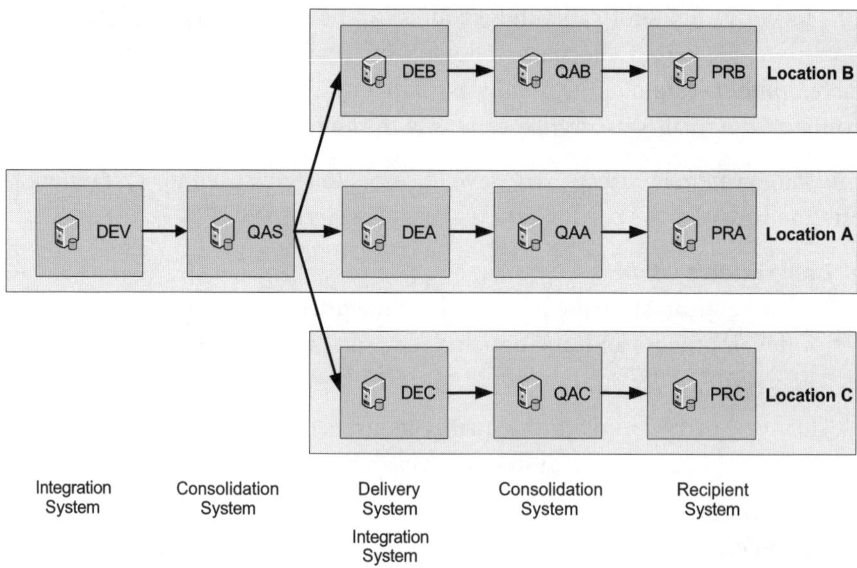

Figure 6.19 System Differentiation from a System Operation Point of View

Assigning the transport layer to Workbench changes is done by assigning the transport layer to packages (previously referred to as development classes). You use *packages* to group together repository objects that form a functional unit. For example, you can group together all programs, ABAP Dictionary objects, and message classes that belong to a transaction. Packages help structure the repository. They also help assign objects to various SAP components. One package can be assigned to one transport layer. Original SAP objects are assigned the SAP transport layer. This transport layer ensures that changes to the objects delivered by SAP can be transported to downstream systems by a transport route that uses this transport layer.

Customizing changes are assigned to the standard transport layer. This layer is stored in the TMS. Using the *transport route editor* in the TMS, you can view the standard transport layer by double-clicking on the system in the dialog that opens (see Figure 6.20). If you are logged on to the TDC, you can even change it.

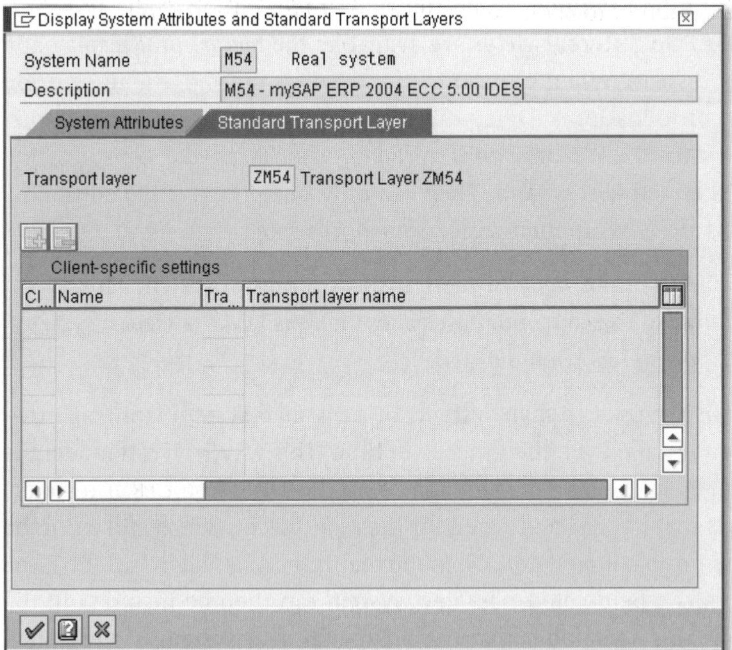

Figure 6.20 Viewing the Standard Transport Layer

Assigning transport layers to objects and defining the standard transport layer, however, does not necessarily mean that a change is transported to other systems. For this to happen, the transport layer needs to be assigned to a transport route.

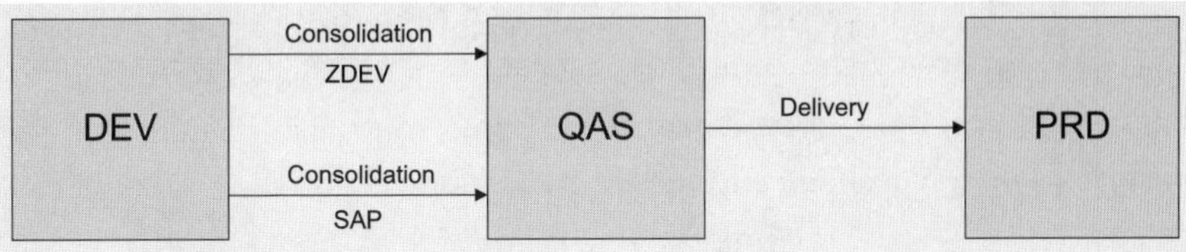

Figure 6.21 Transport Routes in a Three-System Landscape

Figure 6.21 displays the transport routes in a three-system landscape. The ZDEV transport layer is used for proprietary developments and Customizing. Changes to SAP objects are made using the SAP transport layer. Based on these two transport layers, two consolidation routes are defined from the development system to the quality assurance system. The delivery route ensures that the changes transported via the consolidation routes are automatically marked in the production system.

Transport routes are defined in the transport route editor of the transport domain TMS. Two different views are available: the *hierarchical* display and the *graphical* display. When a consolidation route is created, the integration system, the consolidation system, and the transport layer used are all queried. Delivery routes are only configured by specifying the consolidation system and the recipient system. They can only be defined if the consolidation system is already supplied with a transport route.

Figure 6.22 shows an example of the transport routes of system M54 in the hierarchical editor. The consolidation system here is DMY (a virtual system). No recipient system has been defined.

Virtual systems are used to map systems in a planned system landscape that have not been installed yet due to a lack of time. This way, you can model the transport routes in the entire landscape using the TMS. You can also collect the transports that have accumulated for the real system, which still has to be installed, and import them later. Once the real system has been installed, the virtual system can be deleted. The new system can then be included in the transport domain. Remember that the SID of the real system has to match the SID of the virtual system.

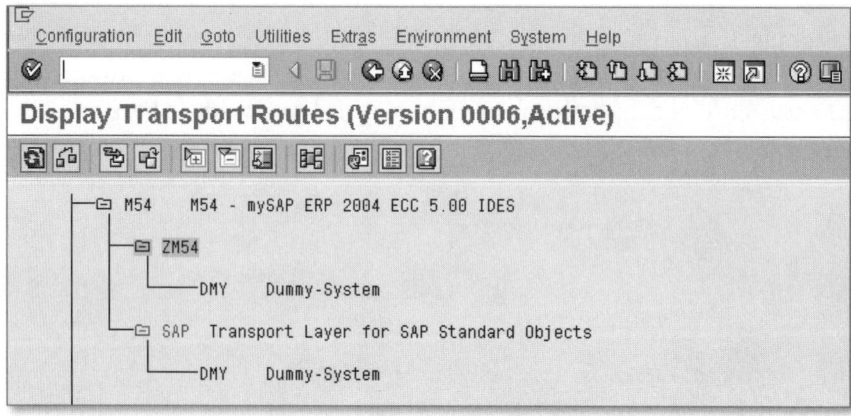

Figure 6.22 Hierarchical View of the Transport Route Editor

In larger system landscapes, delivery routes can be connected serially. You can select not only consolidation systems, but also any SAP systems in the system landscape as a source. This creates a chain of transport routes. In complex system landscapes, particularly in layered development projects that build upon each other, a multilevel delivery can be useful. Figure 6.23

shows a multilevel delivery. Delivery occurs from the QAS system to the DE3 system (another development system) and also to the PRD system, from where delivery to the PR2 system takes place.

In this configuration, neither the QA3 system nor the PR3 system receive objects developed in the DEV system, because no delivery routes from the QAS system to these two systems exist.

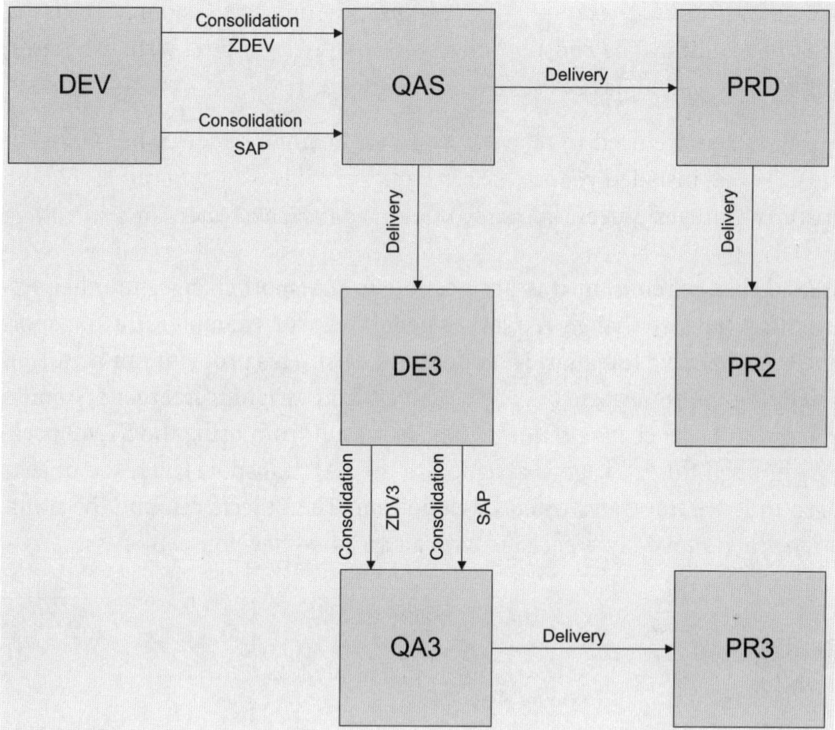

Figure 6.23 Multilevel Transport Routes

Changes to objects and Customizing settings are transported via the consolidation route, which uses the transport layer defined in the objects and Customizing settings (standard transport layer). On the one hand, this means you can use the transport layer and associated transport route to specify to where objects should be transported. On the other hand, objects are not transported unless a transport route has been defined for their transport layer. Figure 6.24 shows that objects from the ZDEV transport layer and SAP objects are transported to the QAS system, and objects from the ZTRN transport layer are transported to the TRN system.

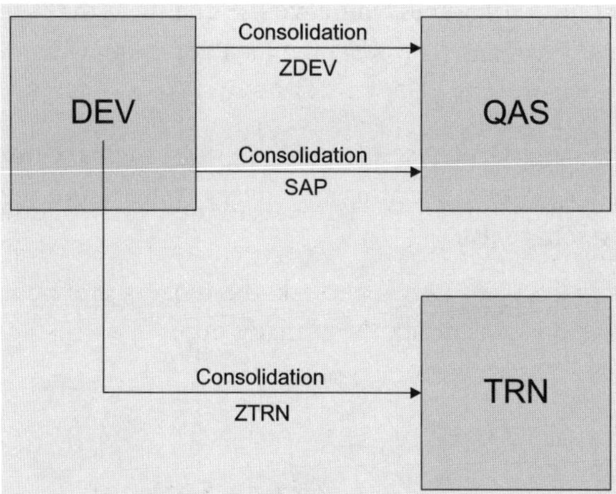

Figure 6.24 Dependency Between Transport Layers and Transport Routes

For *local* change requests, it is not possible to transport changes to other systems. This type of change request is generated, for example, if a transport route to an existing transport layer does not exist. This problem can be solved by defining the transport route retroactively and assigning a target system in the request. Local change requests can also result from using the $TMP package. Although this package is assigned to the SAP transport layer, the objects stored in it are not transported by definition. The objects can only be transported when moved to a package with an assigned development class.

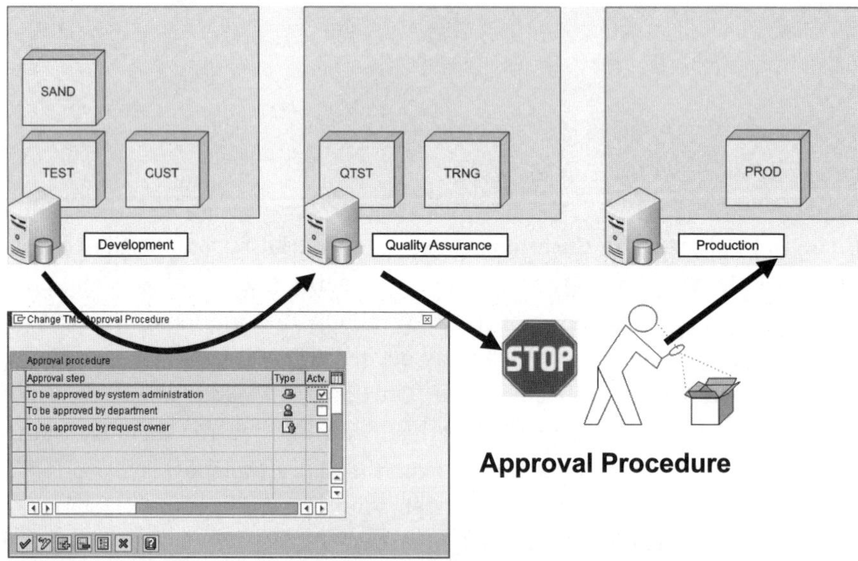

Figure 6.25 QA Approval Procedure

The *quality assurance* (QA) of the TMS helps improve the quality and availability of production systems. You do this by checking requests in the QA system and then delivering them to the recipient systems. The system, for which the QA approval procedure is activated, is also known as the QA system. If the QA approval procedure is activated, your transport requests to the recipient systems are not transported until all approval steps for each request have been processed in the QA system and have been approved by all approvers. If a particular step does not pass the check, the request cannot be approved. During configuration, you define how many approval steps are required for each request (see Figure 6.25).

6.3 Change Management for Customizing Settings

This section provides a detailed description of the aforementioned Implementation Guide (IMG), which allows you to implement changes to client-dependent and client-independent Customizing.

Customizing refers to the setting of system parameters from an interface in the SAP system. Possible changes to the standard (including several variants) have been predefined and organized by SAP. Customizing allows you to select those changes to certain processes scheduled for implementation that best meet customer requirements. The Implementation Guide plays a key role as a tool in this process. All Customizing activities are included in the Implementation Guide. Users can use them to structure and organize the implementation of the system in the company. The Implementation Guide also includes other activities relevant to the administration of the SAP system.

By default, SAP delivers the *SAP Reference Implementation Guide*. This guide includes all Customizing settings that are possible in an SAP system. The SAP Reference Implementation Guide is structured hierarchically by application areas. It contains all of the work steps required for Customizing, together with documentation for each step. You can access the Implementation Guide (see Figure 6.26) from **Tools • Customizing • IMG • Edit Project • SAP Reference IMG** or from Transaction SPRO.

You can significantly reduce the complexity of the configuration steps in the SAP Reference Implementation Guide by defining individual projects. For these projects, only those functions will be selected that are required for the project processes. For example, a single application area can be selected from the different application areas in the Implementation Guide to be edited by a project group during implementation.

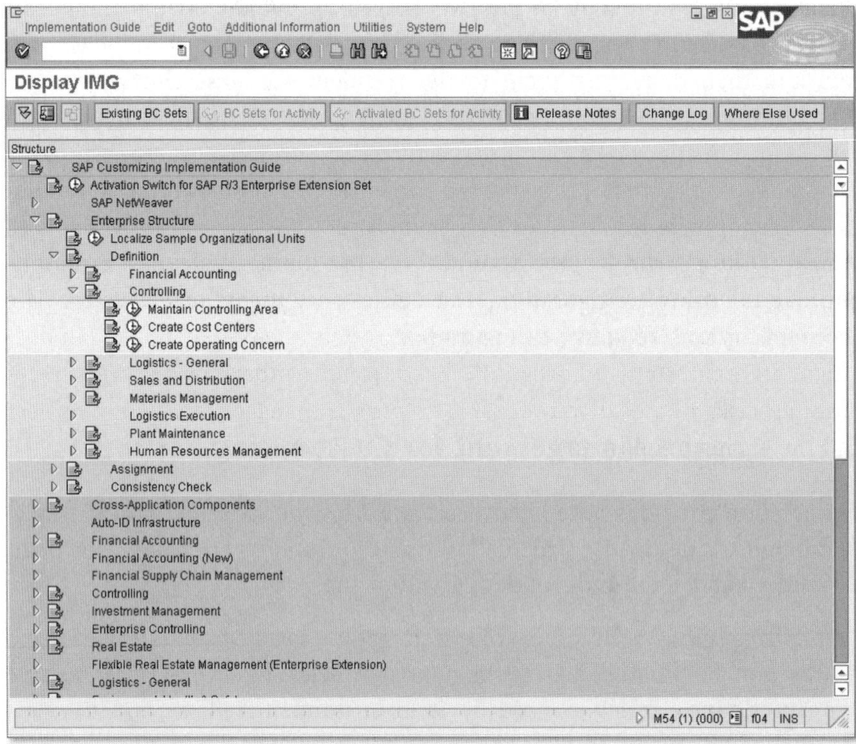

Figure 6.26 Hierarchical Structure of the SAP Reference Implementation Guides

You can generate *project IMGs* to facilitate this. A project IMG is the implementation guide for a particular implementation or Customizing project. It contains all of the Customizing activities that are to be performed for a particular project. The project scope can be limited by countries, components, or individual Customizing activities. A project IMG is always based on the SAP Reference Implementation Guide, which can be reduced by certain activities according to the criteria mentioned above. In addition, several basic administrative functions are available to the users, such as a schedule, the ability to maintain different statuses and assign system-internal and system-external project team members, as well as documentation options.

Projects are client-independent, which means that you can view and use the generated projects from all clients. Project IMGs are also permanently linked to Change and Transport Management. Once the CTS function has been enabled manually, change requests can be assigned to the project. If changed Customizing settings, which have been specified using the project IMG, are subsequently saved, only requests that have been assigned to the project IMG are suggested for recording. In the import overview of the TMS, requests can then be sorted and imported according to which project they are assigned to.

To create projects, use Transaction SPRO_ADMIN. Figure 6.27 illustrates a sample project named CONTRL, whose scope has been reduced to the nodes located below the company structure in the Controlling area, by manually selecting activities from the SAP Reference Implementation Guide.

When working with project IMGs, two clearly defined roles can be distinguished: the role of *project manager* and the role of *project team member*. The latter specify Customizing settings and document the project process in documentation and status information. Each team member can own and create multiple tasks of a change request. The project manager creates the project and the change request and manages both.

In each project, you can also assign *views* to specific activities. Defining a view allows you to further structure and organize the already limited project activities and assign them to individual project team members. In their worklists, individual project team members are therefore presented with precisely the views of the projects in which they are involved.

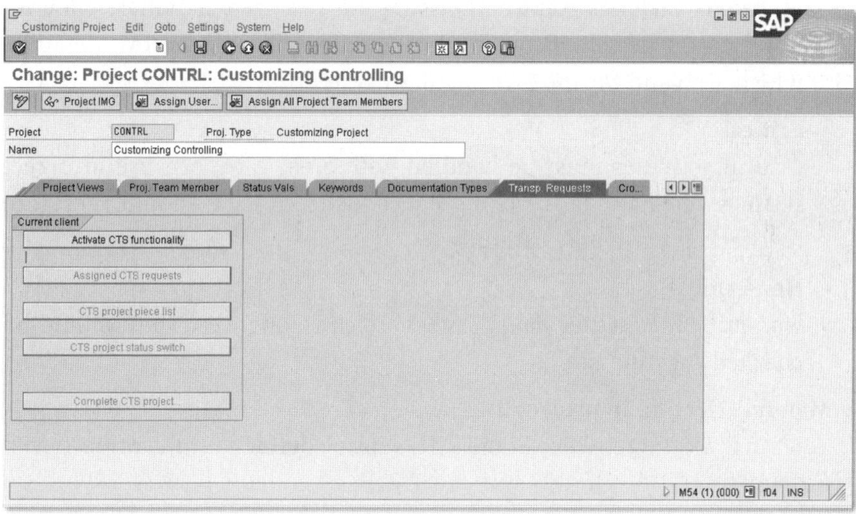

Figure 6.27 Selecting IMG Nodes for a Project IMG

A project view is always based on the project IMG. A view is a reduction of the Implementation Guide by selecting attributes. Creating project views can be useful in the following situations:

- Creating implementation projects
- Changing to another release or upgrading the system
- Legal changes

When you create views, you can choose among the following four options:

- **Activity necessity**
  The activities in the SAP Reference Implementation Guide are assigned flags specifying the urgency of execution. When creating a view, you can combine several of the following flags:
  - **Mandatory**
    Views with this type of activity include steps for which SAP cannot supply a full set of standard settings. Customizing activities must be performed before you can use the SAP standard system.
  - **Optional**
    Optional activity views include steps for which Customizing settings are not necessarily required. They have SAP defaults, but you should check them and change them if necessary.
  - **Not required**
    This view includes steps comprising not required activities. They do not have to be edited or checked, because they have SAP defaults, which are valid for the SAP standard system.
  - **Critical**
    Critical activities must be handled with great care, because incorrect settings can have far-reaching consequences. They should therefore be checked extremely carefully.
  - **Non-critical**
    Non-critical activities have less severe consequences. They should be checked regardless.
- **Manual selection in project IMG**
  You can limit the activities in the IMG subtree defined for the project even further.
- **Release-Customizing**
  Using release-specific flags, you can filter for activities that you need to perform to ensure continued use of the functionality of the old release after an ugrade (upgrade Customizing) or to implement additional functionality from the new release (delta Customizing).

- **Legal changes**
  You can use release-specific flags (LawKeys) to select activities that need to be performed after legal changes have been imported into the system.

This way you can group the specified project IMG into individual structured views and distribute it among the project team members.

6.4 Change Management for Developments

As mentioned at the beginning of this chapter, the standard functions of SAP software can be enhanced or changed. This option should only be used if other configuration options provided for this purpose, such as Customizing, personalization, and extensions using business add-ins, do not adequately meet the requirements for the SAP software. For this purpose, SAP provides the *ABAP Workbench*, a powerful and complete programming environment, including development tools. These include tools

- For defining data structures (Data Dictionary)
- For developing ABAP programs (ABAP Editor)
- For designing user interfaces (Screen Painter and Menu Painter)

The Workbench allows you to develop your own reports or transactions, to modify existing SAP programs, or to implement your own extensions, also known as *customer exits*. This requires in-depth and detailed knowledge of the ABAP Workbench, especially of the proprietary programming language ABAP, and of the application where the implementations take place.

Changes made in the ABAP Workbench are stored in the repository tables in the Oracle database. They are also known as *repository data* or *repository objects*. Apart from a few exceptions, all repository data are client-independent. When changed, they directly affect all clients in the SAP system.

You can access the ABAP Workbench from **Tools • ABAP Workbench • Overview • Object Navigator** or Transaction code SE80. Figure 6.28 shows the initial screen of the ABAP Workbench.

Despite appropriate development authorizations, you cannot simply start developing your own programs and modifying SAP programs in an SAP system. You have to be registered as a developer for the relevant SAP system. A *developer key* is generated in the SAP Service Marketplace (*http://service.sap.com/sscr*). It is associated with the user name and the installation number of the system and therefore remains valid even after an upgrade. This key is requested and entered when you try to create or change an object for the first time. By issuing developer keys, both system administrators and SAP can track the scope of changes users perform in the system.

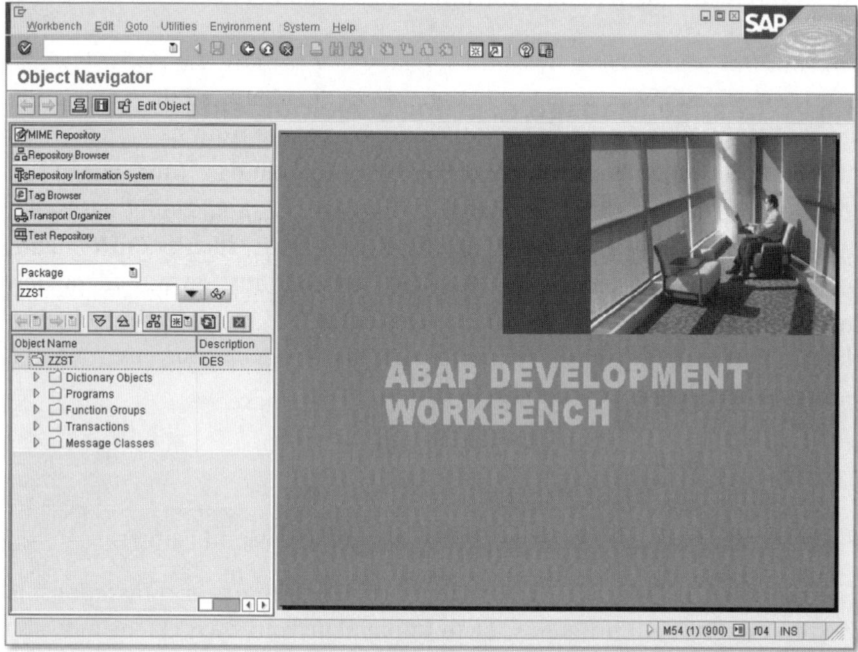

Figure 6.28 ABAP Workbench

SAP Software Change Registration (SSCR) is performed independently of registering as a developer. This registration is required when you perform manual changes to SAP source code and dictionary objects. Tuning measures, such as configuring database indexes and buffers, are excluded from registration. This information is queried once when you first attempt to modify an SAP object. Like the developer key, the object key is registered in the SAP Service Marketplace (*http://service.sap.com/sscr*). The required information includes the object ID, the object type, the name of the object, the installation number, and the Basis release. After a system upgrade, object keys are no longer valid. Logging changes to SAP objects helps to support and accelerate SAP service and support functions and to support customer projects. If problems occur in the system, these changes can be taken into account during troubleshooting.

New developments have to be implemented in the customer namespace. This namespace provided by SAP ensures that objects created by the customer cannot be overwritten by SAP objects when support packages are imported or an upgrade is installed. Using the customer namespace, you can separate your proprietary developments from SAP developments. SAP has reserved the name range between Y and Z for all customer developments. Using the V_TRESN view, you can assign specific name ranges to specific packages in system landscapes with more than one development system. This ensures that even in system landscapes with more than one development system, proprietary objects can be uniquely identified. If these objects are incorporated into one system, they are prevented from having the same name and getting overwritten by accident.

SAP partners or customers with complex customer-specific development projects can ask SAP to reserve a separate namespace. This namespace is implemented by a 5- to 10-digit prefix, which is enclosed by slashes and precedes the object name of the customer development (/xxxx/object name). A license key protects this reserved namespace against unauthorized use. SAP Note 16466 contains a current listing of all namespaces.

Note

Remember that the SAP standard ships with several objects that are included in the customer name range. These objects existed already when the customer name range was extended from YY*/ZZ* to Y*/Z*. You can view the affected objects in the TDKZ table.

In Section 6.2.7, *Transport Routes and Transport Layers*, we have already discussed in some detail the assignment of transport layers to Workbench requests via packages. A package combines all objects that are to be developed, modified, maintained, and transported together. Before you create a new object, you must first create a package in the development system. These packages are objects themselves, which in turn can be transported to other systems. Because all objects of a package have to arrive in a single target system, only the package is assigned a transport layer. The objects are then transported to the appropriate systems via the transport route defined in the layer.

Figure 6.29 shows the properties of a package. In addition to a short description, the name of the person responsible for the package, and the name of the person who created and last changed it, the transport layer is specified in the **Transport Attributes** section. This package and its contents are then transported along the transport route defined by the ZM54 transport layer. We know from Figure 6.22 that this transport route transports the package and its included objects to the virtual system DMY.

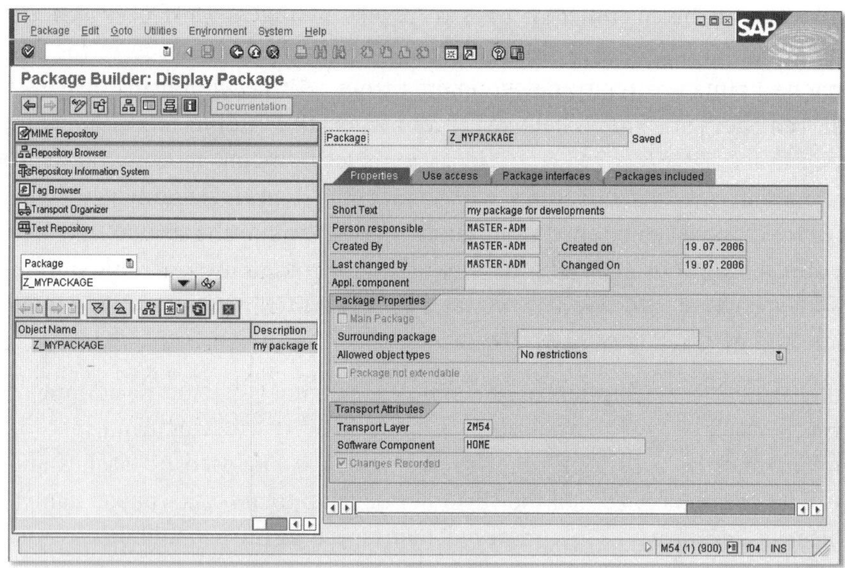

Figure 6.29 Package Properties

Each repository object has an *object directory entry* containing all important information and properties for the object. The object directory is located in the repository and contains all repository objects available in the SAP system. An entry specifies, for example, the person responsible for the object, the underlying package, the original language, the original system, the transport target, the transport layer, and the lock attributes.

In a system landscape, the original system is of particular importance. Generally, each object exists as an original object in only one system. It is an original object in the system in which it was developed. All other systems only contain copies of this object. This helps ensure that changes to objects are only made in the development system.

An integration system therefore contains all originals of proprietary objects. If an object is transported to a downstream system (that is, to the consolidation or recipient system), it is created there as a copy. If this object needs to be modified, you should perform all changes to the original in the development system and then transport the changes to the downstream systems. Changes to original objects are referred to as *corrections*. Copies should only be modified in urgent cases. These changes later have to be made to the originals as well, so twice as much work is involved. The changes to copies are referred to as *repairs*. If the system in which an object has been repaired receives a corrected object, the repaired object is overwritten. However, the repair flag has to be reset first.

SAP objects in all customer systems are copies. Changes to SAP objects in the original systems are corrections, whereas changes to SAP objects in the customer systems are repairs. If you implement correction instructions from SAP Notes in your SAP system, you always change copies of original objects. This means you create repairs. When you import support packages into your system, however, you maintain corrections of SAP objects from the original system. If you have applied preliminary corrections to the system and then import the support packages that contain the corrections, you have to reset the repair flag as described above. You can do this using the Organizer tools (see Section 6.5.1, *Transport Organizer Tools*). For detailed information on support packages and the import tools, see Chapter 7, *System Lifecycle*. Figure 6.30 illustrates when a change to an object is a correction and when it is a repair.

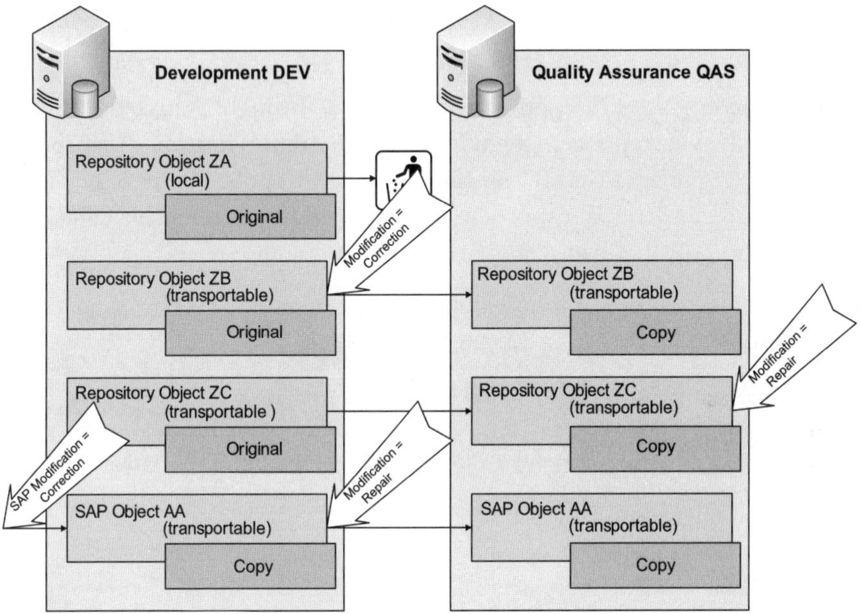

Figure 6.30 Correction and Repair and Originals and Copies

The tasks in change requests can be classified by the objects to be edited. The following task types are available:

- Development/Correction (objects are edited in the original system)
- Repair (objects are edited in a system other than their original system)
- Customizing (client-dependent Customizing objects are edited)
- Unclassified (the type is assigned after the change has been assigned)

You can change the objects in a request only if you are involved in a task of the right type in this request. Unclassified tasks are assigned a specific type only when a change has been assigned.

6.5 Transport Management

In this chapter, we will describe the Transport Organizer Tools and explain the transport strategy using a simple example. We will also explore concepts such as import buffer, transports between different transport groups in the same domain, and transports between different transport domains. We will then describe the manual use of the transport control program `tp` and illustrate this with several examples. Finally, we will discuss the logging of transports and transports between Unicode and non-Unicode systems.

6.5.1 Transport Organizer Tools

You can access the *Transport Organizer Tools* through Transaction SE03. Alternatively, you can access them from **Tools • Administration • Transport • Transport Organizer • Goto • Transport Organizer Tools**. Figure 6.31 shows the initial screen. The Transport Organizer Tools are an extensive collection of powerful tools that help you work with the CTS.

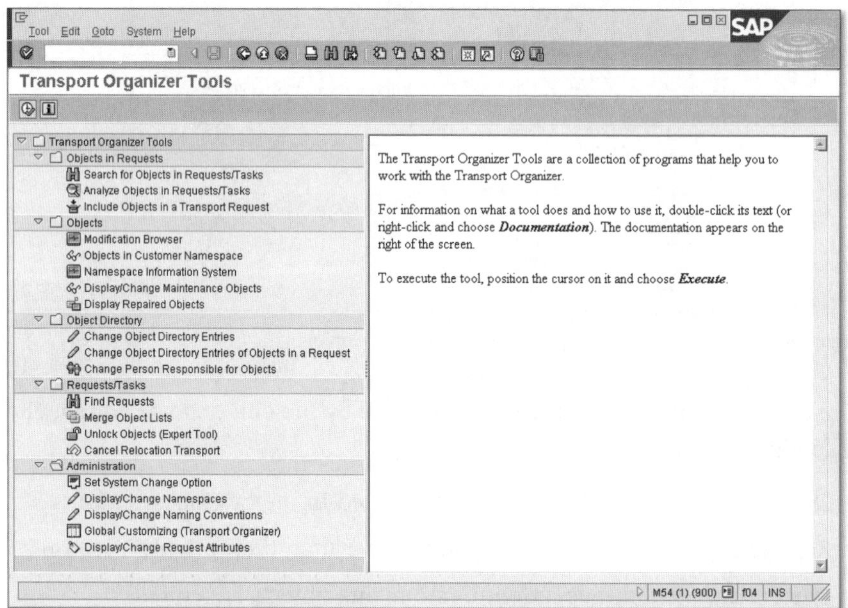

Figure 6.31 Transport Organizer Tools

The tools in the Transport Organizer are subdivided into the following areas: **Objects in Requests**, **Objects**, **Object Directory**, **Requests/Tasks**, and **Administration**. For a detailed description of the function, click on the appropriate tool. To execute a tool, position the cursor over the tool and click on the **Execute** button.

6.5.2 Transport Strategy

In this section, we will discuss the transport strategy. Using a simple example, we will illustrate how changes are transported between the systems in the three-system landscape recommended by SAP.

Figure 6.32 shows an overview of the transport strategy. The changes are released from the development system and exported to the transport directory. We have already seen that these changes are always transported along the transport routes. As a second step, the changes are imported into the quality assurance system. The change requests to be imported are listed in the import queue of the target system and are generally imported into the system via the TMS. Once they have been tested successfully, the changes can be applied to the production system.

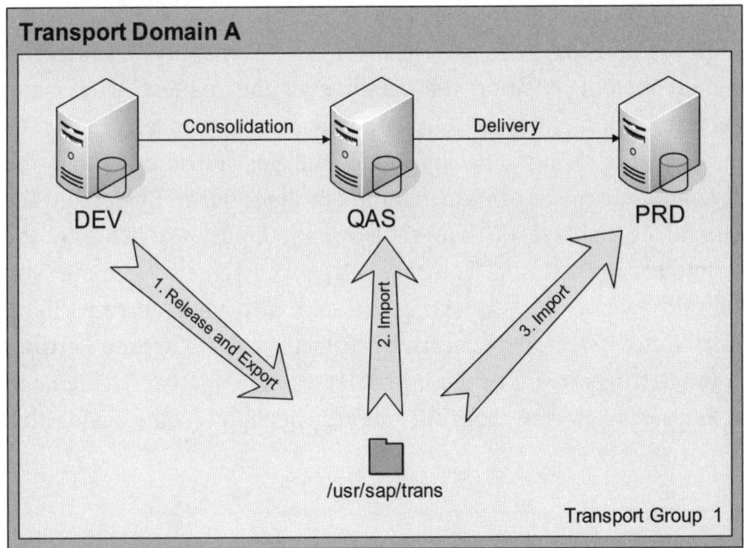

Figure 6.32 Transport Strategy in a Three-System Landscape

For our example, we will keep the naming conventions of the systems in the landscape as we have used them so far. In the development system DEV, changes were made to Customizing and to the repository using the SAP Implementation Guide and the ABAP Workbench. Transport request DEVK00018 is a Workbench request composed of various tasks. These will now be tested and, if successful, imported into the production system.

As we have mentioned several times already, the request first has to be released. Releasing Customizing and Workbench requests happens the same way, and prerequisites and results are identical. However, different processes are involved when releasing Customizing and Workbench requests.

Transport requests can only be released in the following circumstances:

- The person releasing the request is the owner of the transport request.
- All tasks of the request have been documented and released.
- All objects are locked or can be locked.

A basic prerequisite is that all associated tasks have already been released. For this to happen, the person releasing the task has to be the owner of the task, and the objects have to be assigned to the task and must be documented. After tasks have been released, they can no longer be changed or deleted. The same applies to requests: Released requests can no longer be changed or deleted.

Transport requests and tasks are released from the Transport Organizer of the development system. Position the cursor over the request or task and select the **Release** option from the **Request/Task** menu. You can launch the release from the dialog or in the background. Your decision should be based on the number and size of the objects included in the request. By default, the Transport Organizer displays all requests from all clients, restricted by the selection parameters in the initial Transport Organizer screen. Note that you can only edit and release the requests associated with your current client. You can restrict the selected requests by selecting the **Further Settings** option from the **Settings** menu in the initial Transport Organizer screen and clearing the **Requests Selected from All Clients** checkbox in the dialog that opens (see Figure 6.33).

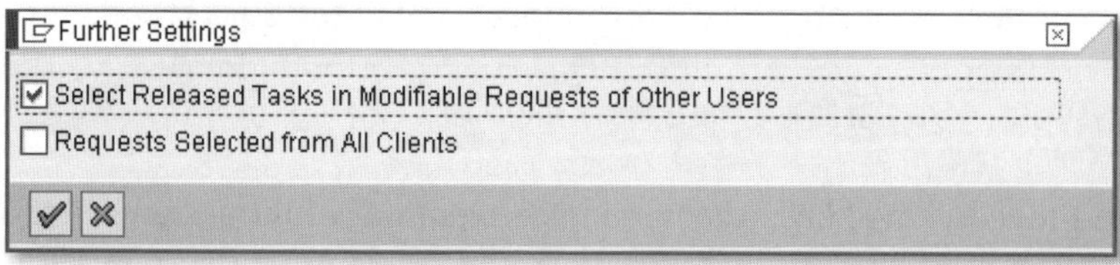

Figure 6.33 Further Settings in Transport Organizer

When a Customizing request is released, the primary key values from the Oracle tables, which have been entered in the change request task, are used to copy the changed table entries from the database and write them into a file in the transport directory.

When a Workbench request is released, the current state of the objects entered in the task is stored in the versioning database. The sequence of change requests, according to which an object is edited, corresponds to the different versions of the object, which are archived in the database. During release, the objects are copied and written to a file in the transport directory. The objects entered in the request are unlocked and can then be modified again.

In both cases, a file is written to the transport directory. More specifically, two files, the transport files, are copied at the operating system level. One file is the data file containing the actual objects. This file is copied to the *data* directory. It has the following syntax: *R9<6-digit number>.<SID>*. The other file is the control file, which is written to the *cofiles* directory. The filename is based on the name of the transport request: *K9<6-digit number>.<SID>*. The request is also marked for import into the target system defined by the transport route. This takes place in the import buffer (which is the representation of the import queue of the SAP system at the operating system level (see Section 6.5.3, *Import Queue and Import Buffer*). When you release local change requests, no file is written. The transport files are stored in a format that is independent of the operating system and the database so they can be used on all available platform combinations.

Requests can also be released into other (already existing or new) requests. This way, multiple requests can be collected, and released and transported as a complete package at a later time.

In our example (see Figure 6.34), the transport request DEVK900018 is released, and the copied objects are copied as data file R900018.DEV to the *data* subdirectory and as control file K900018.DEV to the *cofiles* subdirectory of the transport directory. At the same time, the change request is marked for import in the import buffer of the target system QAS.

In the second step, the change request is transported to the quality assurance system. The import queues of all systems in a transport domain can be viewed and administered from any transport domain system by selecting **Import Overview** in the TMS. This also allows you to start the import of requests. In the import overview of a transport domain, all systems with the number of requests to be transported are displayed. A detailed view of the requests is available by selecting the relevant system.

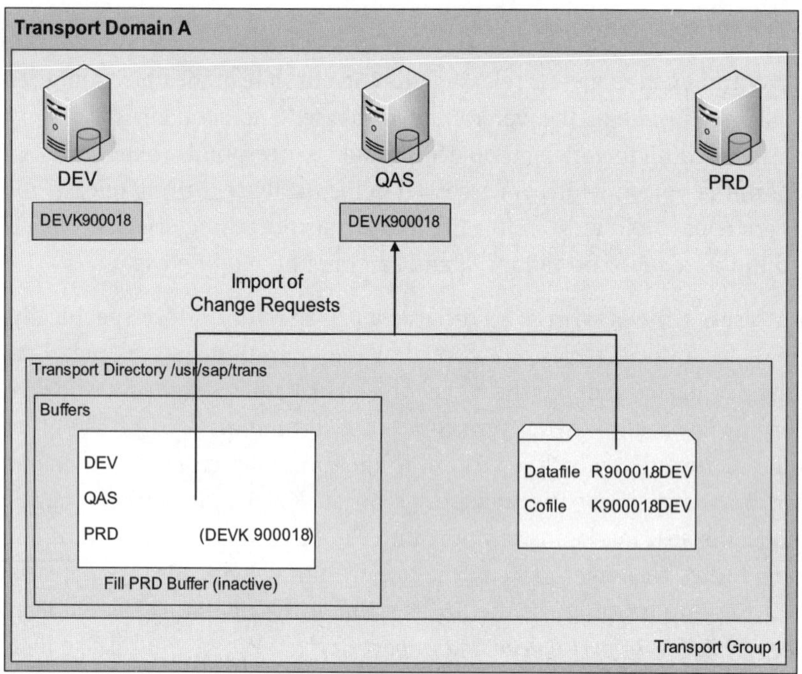

Figure 6.34 Step 1 — Request Release and Export

This overview forms the basis for administrating all pending transports (see also Section 6.5.3, *Import Queue and Import Buffer*). You can start the import into a target system using any subset of the requests waiting in the import queue or using the entire queue. Individual requests in a system's import queue can be combined by selecting **Edit • Select • Select Request** or **Edit • Select • Select Block**. You can start the import of the selected transports from the **Request • Import** menu. You can import the entire queue from the **Queue • Start Import** menu, or you can import individual requests into the system using the **Request • Import** menu. The current import is displayed by a truck icon next to the transport requests. Once the import has completed, this icon is replaced by a green checkmark, or by a yellow triangle if the transport is marked for another import. To reflect the changed status, you have to click on the **Refresh** button.

The progress of the import process can be viewed from the import monitor, which you can access from **Goto • Import Monitor**. Figure 6.35 displays the import monitor of system M54, where an import into client 000 of the system is currently taking place.

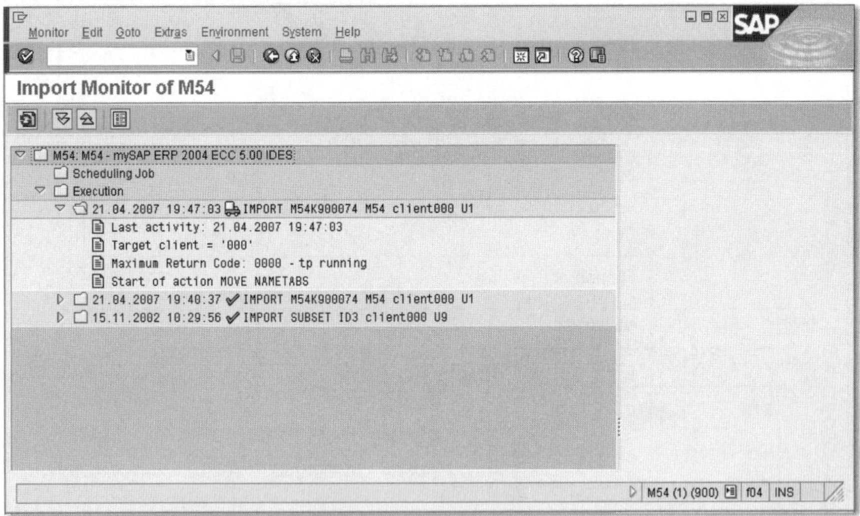

Figure 6.35 TMS Import Monitor

The actual import is executed by the operating system programs `tp` and `R3trans`. In the SAP system, the program `RDDIMPDP` has to run in client 000, and the program `RDDIMPDP_CLIENT_<client>` in all other clients of the target system to enable it to receive imports. The programs in the SAP system run in the background and are controlled by events. They wait for messages issued by the `tp` program to indicate that a transport is ready for processing. For the `RDDIMPDP` programs to function properly, a free background process has to be configured in the system. If a transport hangs during import or export, you should check to see if the program `RDDIMPDP` works properly. Very often, the problem can be found there. Composite Note 71353 suggests solutions for problems with transports and background processing.

Figure 6.36 illustrates the second step, that is, the import of all transport requests in import buffer QAS into the quality assurance system. Because our example only contains one transport request, the single request DEVK900018 is imported into the system. Importing the request inactively fills the buffer of the production system with transport request DEVK900018. *Inactive* means that the request cannot yet be transported to the production system. You can now perform tests in the quality assurance system using data from the production system.

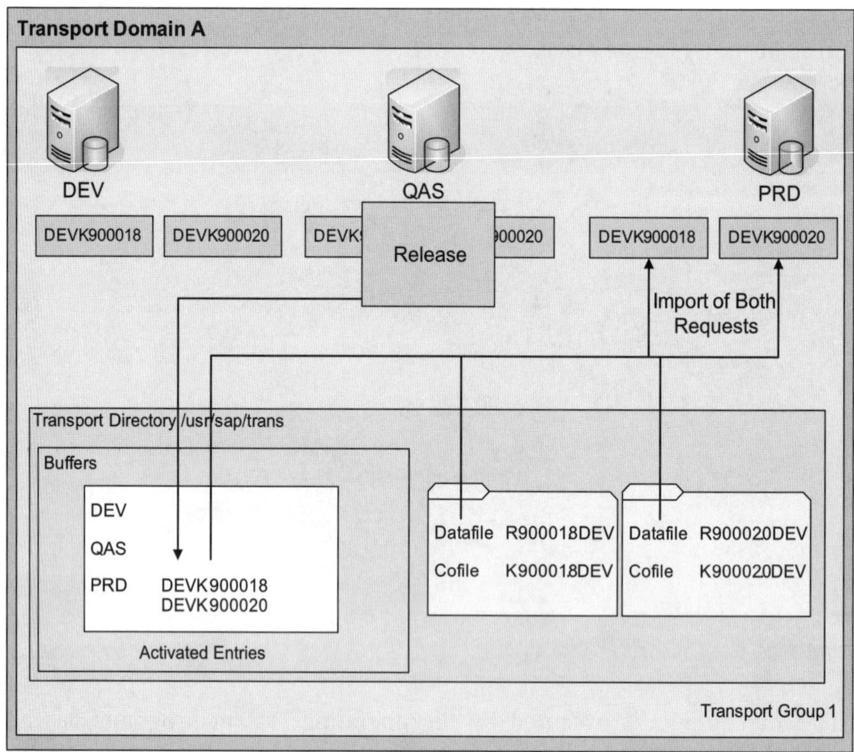

Figure 6.36 Step 2 — Import into the Quality Assurance System

The tests in the quality assurance system show that the changes to the objects, which were performed in the quality assurance system, do not meet expectations and contain errors. This information is communicated back to the development team so that the objects can be adjusted accordingly. This is done in the development system. After all corrections have been made, the underlying transport request can be released and exported (see Figure 6.37).

The correction request in our example is called DEVK900020. As in the first step, one data file and one control file are written to the corresponding subdirectories of the transport directory. The correction request is marked for import in the import buffer of the QAS system.

In the next step, the import of the request containing the corrections into the QAS system can be started. After the import has finished successfully, the correction request DEVK900020 is set to inactive in the import buffer of the production system (Figure 6.38). The tests in the quality assurance system can now be repeated.

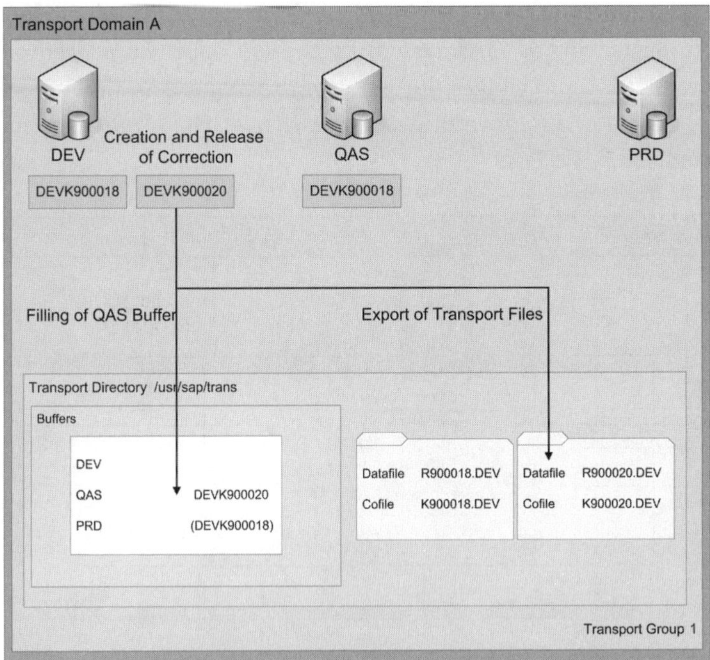

Figure 6.37 Step 3 — Release of Corrections

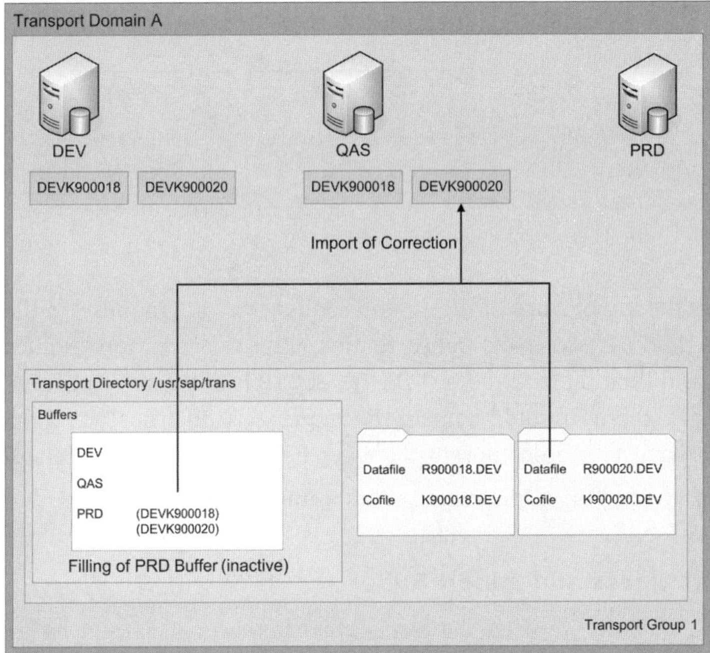

Figure 6.38 Step 4 — Import of Corrections into the QAS System

When all analyses and tests have been successfully completed, the change requests are confirmed in the QAS system by the QA approval procedure (compare Figure 6.39). This changes the status of the requests in the import buffer of the production system from inactive to active. These requests can now be imported using the TMS.

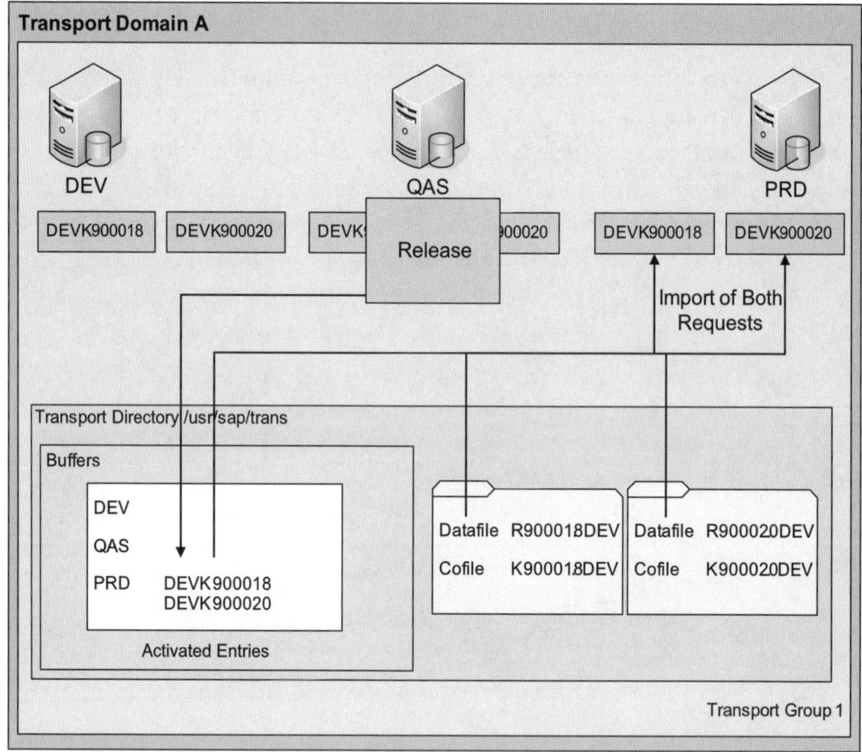

Figure 6.39 Step 5 — QA Release and Import into the PRD System

This also shows the importance of the default sequence of the requests in the import buffer. It does not make sense to first import correction request DEVK900020 and then the bad request DEVK900018 into the system. However, in principle, the user could control the sequence using the TMS functions. Related requests should therefore always be imported in the default sequence.

6.5.3 Import Queue and Import Buffer

In the previous section, we used the terms *import queue* and *import buffer* several times. The import queue, which you can access from the import overview of an individual system in the TMS, is the representation of the import buffer at the operating system level. Technically, when a request is released and the import buffer of the target system is filled, the request control information is stored in a file in the *buffers* subdirectory of the transport directory. The name of the file is the system SID. This directory contains such a file for each system in a transport domain. The assignment in this file determines the import sequence.

In addition to the requests listed in the import queue (see Figure 6.40), an end mark can be specified. The equivalent to an end mark in the import buffer is known as a stop mark. This mark allows you to close the import queue at a specific time and to exclude all subsequent requests added to the queue from transport. This is useful to avoid inconsistencies and to maintain a defined interim state for Customizing and development work. The excluded requests are marked for the next import into the system. The end mark can be set using the **Queue • Close** function. The **Queue • Move End Mark** function allows you to place the mark in the import queue after any request. You can remove an end mark using the **Queue • Open** function.

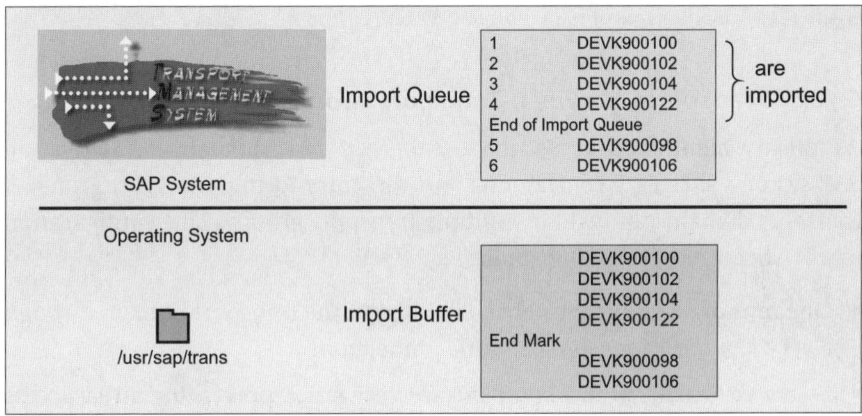

Figure 6.40 Import Queue and Import Buffer

Apart from maintaining the end mark and importing requests into a system, the TMS also allows you to display the status of individual requests and to view associated object lists, documentation, and log entries. Other important functions include deleting and adding requests to the import queue and forwarding requests to other systems. Figure 6.41 shows an example of the import queue of the virtual system DMY including transport requests pending import.

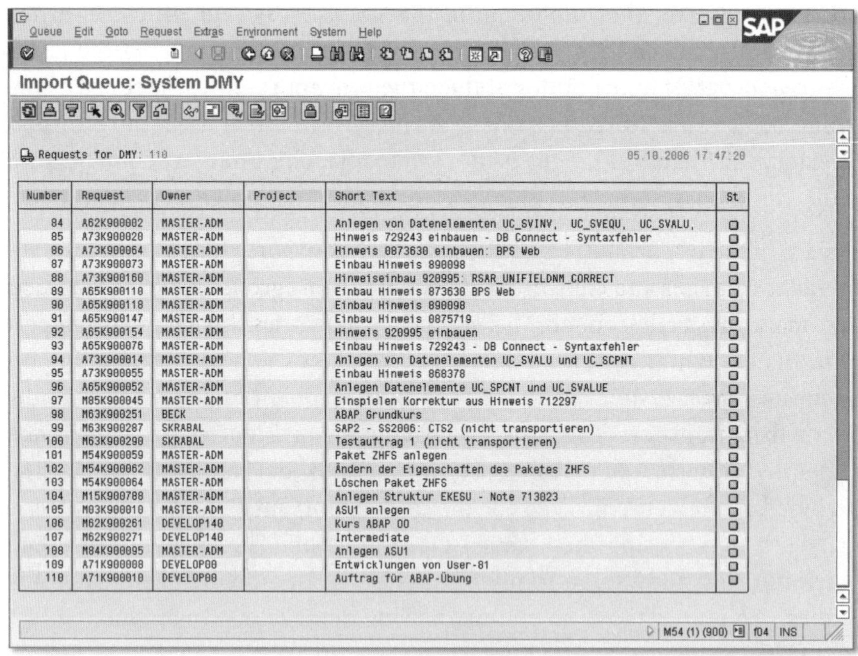

Number	Request	Owner	Project	Short Text	St
84	A62K900002	MASTER-ADM		Anlegen von Datenelementen UC_SVINV, UC_SVEQU, UC_SVALU,	
85	A73K900020	MASTER-ADM		Hinweis 729243 einbauen - DB Connect - Syntaxfehler	
86	A73K900064	MASTER-ADM		Hinweis 0873630 einbauen: BPS Web	
87	A73K900073	MASTER-ADM		Einbau Hinweis 890098	
88	A73K900160	MASTER-ADM		Hinweiseinbau 920995: RSAR_UNIFIELDNM_CORRECT	
89	A65K900110	MASTER-ADM		Einbau Hinweis 873630 BPS Web	
90	A65K900118	MASTER-ADM		Einbau Hinweis 890098	
91	A65K900147	MASTER-ADM		Einbau Hinweis 0875719	
92	A65K900154	MASTER-ADM		Hinweis 920995 einbauen	
93	A65K900076	MASTER-ADM		Einbau Hinweis 729243 - DB Connect - Syntaxfehler	
94	A73K900014	MASTER-ADM		Anlegen von Datenelementen UC_SVALU und UC_SCPNT	
95	A73K900055	MASTER-ADM		Einbau Hinweis 868378	
96	A65K900052	MASTER-ADM		Anlegen Datenelemente UC_SPCNT und UC_SVALUE	
97	M85K900045	MASTER-ADM		Einspielen Korrektur aus Hinweis 712297	
98	M63K900251	BECK		ABAP Grundkurs	
99	M63K900287	SKRABAL		SAP2 - SS2006: CTS2 (nicht transportieren)	
100	M63K900290	SKRABAL		Testauftrag 1 (nicht transportieren)	
101	M54K900059	MASTER-ADM		Paket ZHFS anlegen	
102	M54K900062	MASTER-ADM		Ändern der Eigenschaften des Paketes ZHFS	
103	M54K900064	MASTER-ADM		Löschen Paket ZHFS	
104	M15K900788	MASTER-ADM		Anlegen Struktur EKESU - Note 713023	
105	M03K900010	MASTER-ADM		ASU1 anlegen	
106	M62K900261	DEVELOP140		Kurs ABAP OO	
107	M62K900271	DEVELOP140		Intermediate	
108	M84K900095	MASTER-ADM		Anlegen ASU1	
109	A71K900008	DEVELOP00		Entwicklungen von User-81	
110	A71K900010	DEVELOP00		Auftrag für ABAP-Übung	

Figure 6.41 Import Queue of the Virtual SAP System DMY

6.5.4 Transports Between Transport Groups

As already mentioned in Section 6.2.6, *Transport Management System*, all SAP systems sharing a central transport directory form a transport group. A transport domain can include multiple transport groups. This configuration can be used if the following applies:

- One or more SAP systems are connected to the transport domain through a very slow or expensive network connection.
- Security regulations in a company are very strict, preventing direct access from the system to the domain.
- Different SAP systems run on different hardware platforms, and it is impossible to use a shared transport directory.

The TMS supports the transport between transport groups in a domain. After a change request has been released from the development system DEV, it is entered as an entry in the import buffer of the quality assurance system QAS. This entry is made in the QAS import buffer of the transport group in which the DEV system is located physically. If the development system and the quality assurance system are in different transport groups, the import queue and consequently the import buffer of the QAS system of the transport group, in which the QAS system is located physically, have to be adjusted to the import buffer of the QAS system in the other (already updated) transport group.

You can do this in the TMS from **Extras • Other Requests • Find in Other Groups**. The system then searches all change requests for the selected target system in the import buffers of all connected transport groups and copies the relevant data files and control files to the transport group to which the target system is physically connected. Figure 6.42 illustrates this relationship.

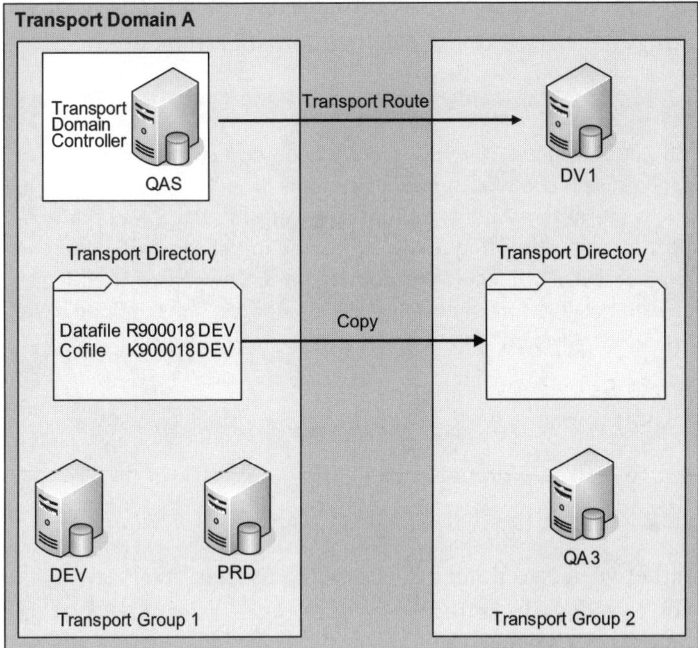

Figure 6.42 Transports Between Transport Groups

6.5.5 Transports Between Transport Domains

Transports between two transport domains can be accomplished in two different ways: via *domain links* and via *external systems*.

It is recommended that you use domain links. This requires a permanent network connection between the systems in different domains, similar to the connection between systems within the same domain. Also, the domain controllers of both domains must use SAP Release 4.6C or higher. The connection via a domain link provides the following functions:

- You can carry out transports between the two domains in the same way as transports between systems in different transport groups. The transport files needed for the transport are transferred via generated RFC connections between the transport directories involved in the transport.
- You can view transport logs from the external domain systems.
- You can compare repository objects in systems in different domains.
- Transport routes are not distributed across domain boundaries. However, you can configure a transport route between systems in different domains. It is important to create this transport route in both domains.
- The workflow engine, if used, can be configured in each domain, or the previously configured engine of the external domain can be used.

Note

You will soon find out that distributing domain configuration changes can be very time-consuming if a domain contains numerous systems (usually more than 50). In these situations, it is useful to establish multiple domains in such a way that systems that transport to each other frequently are placed in the same domain. The individual domains are then connected via domain links. This makes it easier to distribute configuration changes. Domains linked via a domain link continue to be administrated separately. Any configuration changes are made locally.

Linking two transport domains with a domain link involves two steps:

1. Request a link between two domains.
2. Confirm the link between the two domains.

To request a link between two domains, access the **System Overview** in the TMS of one of the two domain controllers. From there, select **SAP System • Create • Domain Link**. The **Request Domain Link** dialog opens. Enter the system name, the host name, and the system number of the domain controller for which you want to request the domain link, and confirm your entries. The domain controller then automatically generates the required RFC connections, and the system data of the domain controller is sent to the controller in the external domain. You can now see that you have requested the domain link to the external domain.

To confirm the link between the two transport domains, access the **System Overview** in the external domain controller. Position the cursor over the domain controller that has requested the domain link, and select **SAP-System • Accept**. Confirm the prompt. You are now ready to distribute the configuration of the TMS. The two domain controllers now exchange all of the required system information for the two domains. This information is distributed to all systems in the domain whose controller you are currently logged on to. A transport profile is generated, which contains all systems in both domains. The information on the systems of the external domain is not automatically distributed to the systems of the domain in which you requested the domain link. This means that you must manually activate the new configuration in these systems. You can now see all systems from both domains in the system overview and the import overview of the TMS.

If no permanent communication can be established between the systems in the two domains using an RFC connection, you can use external systems to perform transports between domains.

External systems are a special type of the virtual systems mentioned earlier (Section 6.2.7, *Transport Routes and Transport Layers*), because they do not physically exist in the transport domain in which they are created. They act as a proxy for systems in an external domain.

External systems can be used if either of the following conditions exist:

- Change requests are to be exchanged between systems in different transport domains.
- Transport data are to be exported from or imported into a disk.

Unlike for virtual systems, which use the standard transport directory, the underlying transport directory can be chosen freely for external systems. You must, however, choose one. This directory, which is used to exchange transport information externally, can reside on a hard disk or on a removable disk accessible from an SAP system in the other domain.

You have to perform the following steps to enable transports between two transport domains using external systems:

1. In each transport domain, define an SAP system that exists as a real system in the other transport domain as an external system (**Transport Management System • System Overview • Systems • SAP System • Create • External System**).
2. As the communications system, choose an SAP system that can access the external transport directory (the default for the communications system is a transport domain controller).
3. For each external system, define the path for the transport directory to this external directory (using the local parameter `TRANS_DIR`, which is main-

tained in the external transport group). You can now route transports to the external system. All necessary files are stored in the external transport directory, and, using the import queue of the external system, you can check which transport requests have already been created.

4. To transfer the transport requests to the other domain, you must adjust the import queue in the relevant target system.

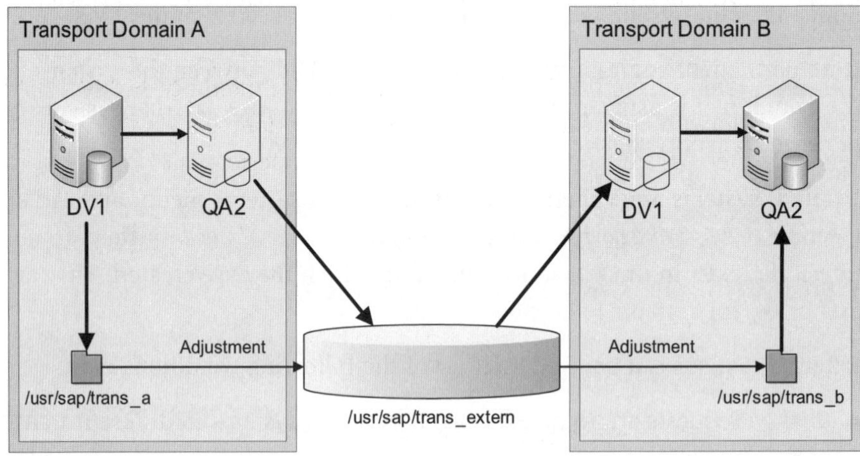

Figure 6.43 Transports Between Domains Using External Systems

Figure 6.43 shows an example of a link between domains using external systems. A route should be defined between system DV1 in domain A and system QA2 in domain B. System DV1 accesses transport directory *trans_a*, and system QA2 accesses *trans_b*. System QA2 is configured as an external system in domain A. A transport route is then created between DV1 and QA2 in domain A. The external system QA2 is assigned the transport directory *trans_extern*. Similarly, system DV1 is configured as an external system with transport directory *trans_extern* in domain B, and the transport route to system QA2 is created.

The transport between the two domains is performed using transport directory *trans_extern*. This transport directory can be accessed from both domains using the external systems. Two adjustment steps are required for transports between DV1 and QA2:

1. All transport data of requests marked for import into system QA2 are copied to the *trans_extern* directory. This adjustment step is performed in the TMS in domain A. The transport requests for system QA2 can now be viewed in systems in domain B.

2. The transport data for system QA2 are now copied from the *trans_extern* directory to the transport directory of the real system QA2. This step is performed in domain B.

System DV1 in domain A is used as the communications system for the external system QA2. The SAP servers of system DV1 therefore have to be configured in such a way that they can access the *trans_extern* transport directory. System QA2 from domain B also needs to have access to this directory.

External systems have the disadvantage that none of the functions described above for domain links can be used for connecting domains via external systems. Connecting domains via domain links (if a permanent network connection exists) is therefore the preferred option.

6.5.6 Using the Transport Control Program

In certain emergency situations, it can be necessary to perform imports at the operating system level. To do so, you need to know the syntax used in `tp` program calls. In this section, we will introduce you to a few important commands.

We will first look at the interaction between the SAP system, `tp`, `R3trans`, and Oracle. When a change request is released and exported, the development system DEV calls the `tp` program. `tp` can read, write, and modify the buffer, logs, and *TP_<DOMAINNAME>.PFL* domain configuration file in the transport directory. It also creates table entries in the control tables (for example, TRBAT and TRJOB) in the Oracle database, which it can also delete and modify. These tables are also used by the ABAP programs of the CTS in the SAP system. The actual export and import process is handled by the `R3trans` program, which is controlled by `tp`. `R3trans` reads the data specified in the requests from the Oracle database and stores it in data and control files in the transport directory. During an import, `tp` communicates with ABAP programs (such as RDDIMPDP) and modifies the above-mentioned control files in the Oracle database. By calling `R3trans`, `tp` can launch and monitor the import of data from the data and control files into the Oracle database. This process is, of course, much more complex than described in this section. However, this description and Figure 6.44 will suffice to provide a brief and basic overview.

As described in Section 6.2.6, *Transport Management System*, the configuration for the `tp` program is saved in the *TP_<DOMAINNAME>.PFL* file. Using this profile, the program can establish a connection to the Oracle database of each SAP system in the domain.

By default, the profile is stored in the */usr/sap/trans/bin* directory and has to be specified whenever `tp` is called manually.

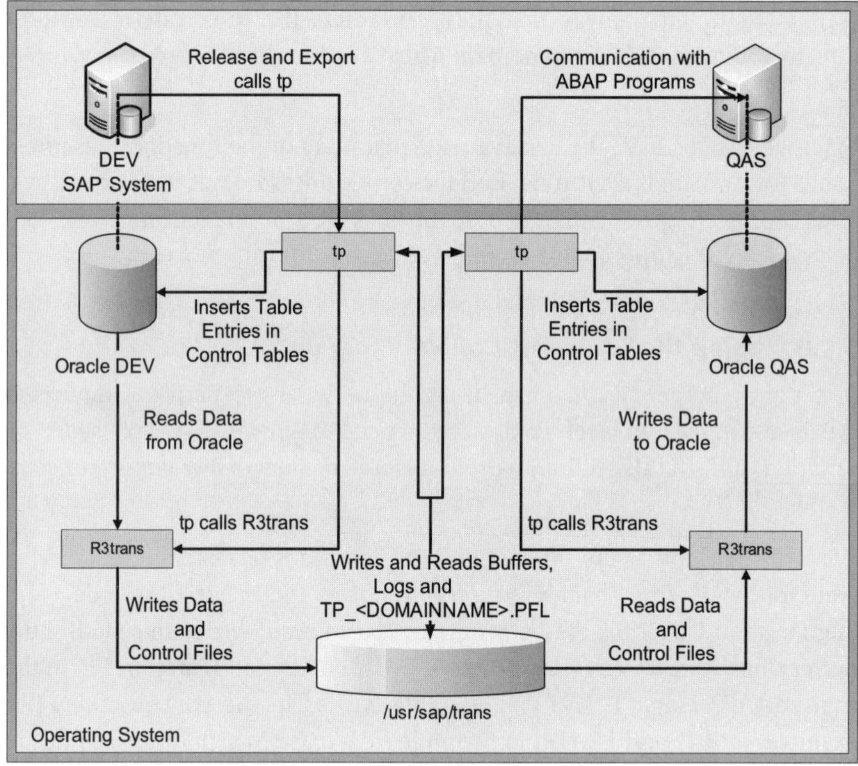

Figure 6.44 Interaction Between tp, R3trans, and Oracle

To test if the `tp` program can establish a connection to the specified system, use the following command as <SID>ADM user:

```
tp connect <SID> pf=<path to TP_<DOMAINNAME>.PFL>
```

The parameter `<SID>` indicates the system ID of the target system, whereas the argument `pf=<...>` indicates the location of the configuration file. The full name of the path has to be entered here.

The command

```
tp showbuffer <SID> pf=<path to TP_<DOMAINNAME>.PFL>
```

lists all transport requests in the import buffer of the system. The command

```
tp addtobuffer <request> <SID> pf=<path to TP_<DOMAINNAME>.PFL>
```

adds transport requests to the import buffer of the system. This requires the data file and the control file to exist in the appropriate subdirectories of the transport directory.

All transport requests available in the import buffer can be imported using the command:

```
tp import all <SID> pf=<path to TP_<DOMAINNAME>.PFL>
```

Selected requests can be imported into the system using the command:

```
tp import <request> <SID> pf=<path to TP_<DOMAINNAME>.PFL>
```

By default, transport requests are always imported into the client from which the data from the source system was exported. If this client does not exist in the target system, the import process is cancelled with an error. For example, if you want to use a different client when importing client-dependent Customizing settings than the one you used for the export from the source client, you can use an additional argument:

```
client=<number of selected client>
```

Many more commands and arguments are available than are presented here. You can view a summary of all commands by entering the following command:

```
tp help
```

To get help for other optional arguments of a command, simply call `tp` with the command name for a detailed explanation:

```
tp <command>
```

6.5.7 Logging Transports

When describing the structure of the transport directory, we already mentioned two subdirectories storing transport log files. Two log types are available.

One type is the *action log*. All activities performed in a transport request are stored in this log. You must first select the transport request to be reviewed before you can view the log in the Transport Organizer. You can access the log from **Goto • Action Log**. The log is stored in the *actlog* subdirectory of the transport directory in the operating system. You can also use specific operating system editors to view the log.

Another type of log is the *transport logs.* Transport logs are created separately for each transport and all included transport steps, and they are stored in the *log* subdirectory. Each import and export is composed of several steps. The transport control program `tp` completes the same import step for all requests before continuing with the next step. In other words, `tp` does not complete all import steps of a single request before moving on to the next request. Each step is completed with a return code, indicating if a transport step has been completed successfully or not. If errors occur, it is recommended to view the logs. The log file syntax includes the system ID of the source system, the transport step completed, the number of the transport request, and the system ID of the source or target system:

```
<source system SID><step><transport request number>.<source or target SID>
```

The individual steps are indicated by the letters listed in Table 6.1.

Letter	Transport steps
A	Activate repository
C	Transport C source text
D	Import application-defined objects
E	Main export
G	Generate programs
H	Import repository
I	Main import
L	Import control file
M	Activate enqueue modules
P	Test import
R	Version adjustment for release upgrades
T	Import table entries
V	Set version flag for imported objects
X	Export application-defined objects

Table 6.1 Transport Steps

As you can see, a number of steps are completed during import and export. You can easily view the log files in the Transport Organizer. To view the log files, select a transport request and then choose **Goto • Transport Logs**. For ease of reading, the individual transport steps are summarized in an overview. This overview can be expanded in several layers to contain a more detailed description. When fully expanded, you can view the entire log as it is saved at the operating system level. You can also view the logs using operating system editors.

As already mentioned, the return codbe at the end of the log indicates if a transport step has been completed successfully or not. There are several different levels, three of which we will mention here:

- **Return code 0**
  Finished successfully
- **Return code 4**
  Finished with a warning
- **Return code ≥ 8**
  Finished with an error, process terminates

If return code 8 or higher is returned, you must check the log files for what might have caused the error, correct the error, and restart the process.

6.5.8 Transports Between Unicode and Non-Unicode Systems

This section explores the problems that might occur if objects are transported between SAP systems with and without Unicode. In Section 6.2.6, we pointed out that technically it is no problem to use both Unicode and non-Unicode systems in a transport domain controller.

Generally, the `R3trans` program associated with the system has to be used for both import and export. Two categories of problems can occur during transports between the two system types:

- Technical transport problems
- Logical transport problems

The direction in which the transports occur also plays a role. More problems occur during transports from non-Unicode systems to Unicode systems than the other way around.

When transporting from Unicode to non-Unicode systems, technical transport problems occur with exotic languages (such as Azerbaijani), with report sources from a Basis release starting from Release 7.10, with exotic characters in table keys, and during direct transports of Unicode to systems with a Basis release earlier than 6.10. Logical transport problems occur with language-dependent character conversions, with special characters, during transports of Customizing objects containing address data, and during dynpro transports from Unicode systems.

So far, there are no known technical problems with transports from non-Unicode to Unicode systems. Logical transport problems occur with language-dependent character conversions and during transports of Customizing objects containing address data.

For more information, refer to SAP Note 638357, which documents all known problems with transports between Unicode and non-Unicode systems. It suggests solutions and refers to additional SAP notes.

6.6 Tips and Tricks

This section provides you with some tips and tricks, which might be of use in your transport management environment:

- **Deleting outdated transport requests**
  Over time, many old transport requests and log files accumulate in the transport directory, which might not be needed anymore. It can be quite time-consuming to determine the status of each request in the Transport Organizer and then delete it manually. This can be achieved more easily using `tp` commands:

  ```
  tp check all pf=<path to TP_<DOMAINNAME>.PFL>
  tp clearold all pf=<path to TP_<DOMAINNAME>.PFL>
  ```

  The first command selects all transport requests and log files, whose retention period has expired, and the second command then moves them to the olddata subdirectory and deletes the control and log files if they are no longer needed. If the second command is called again, the transport requests in the olddata directory are deleted if their retention period in this directory has expired. Times are controlled by the `tp` parameters `datalifetime`, `cofileslifetime`, `loglifetime`, and `olddatalifetime`.

You can schedule these calls to run periodically in the background (Transactions SM36 and SM69). You can use the

```
tp testold all pf=<path to TP_<DOMAINNAME>.PFL>
```

command to simulate the actions performed with the Clearold command.

- **Recreating a missing control file**
  If you have accidentally deleted the control file associated with a data file from the transport directory or if the control file is missing, you can recreate it using the following command:

```
tp pf=<path to TP_<DOMAINNAME>.PFL> createcofile <transport number>
```

6.7 Summary

In this chapter, we have covered the concept, settings, and tools of Change and Transport Management.

You can now distinguish between client-dependent and client-independent data in SAP systems, and you know which tools to use to make changes to the SAP standard. When explaining the basic principles of software logistics, we have discussed important settings that allow you to specify if and how changes are recorded. We have explored the concept of a three-system landscape and investigated which roles clients can assume in this system.

You have also learned how to configure and connect the individual systems in your landscape using the Transport Management System to distribute changes. We have covered topics such as the transport directory, the transport domain, and transport groups and have discussed the domain controller and its configuration. Transport routes show where changes are transported in the system landscape. They are based on transport layers. While Customizing uses the standard transport layer, developments use the transport layers specified by the developer in the development packages.

We have further described transport management and have presented an example of a transport strategy. Finally, you have been introduced to the interaction between the SAP system, the operating system tools `tp` and `R3trans`, and the Oracle database during the transport process.

You will have noticed that in the area of Change and Transport Management, there are few points of contact between the applications in SAP and the Oracle database. Only the operating system programs `tp` and `R3trans` communicate directly with Oracle when data imports and exports have to be performed. The data format of the associated transport files, however, is platform-independent. The system data of Oracle databases (and also of other databases) for the individual systems are summarized in the `tp` parameters, which are maintained in the Transport Management System.

A business application system such as an SAP system can typically be operated for several decades. However, the underlying technological basis, that is, the hardware, operating system, database system, and application server, has a lifecycle of only a few years. Therefore, an SAP installation must be continuously enhanced and further developed.

7 System Lifecycle

This chapter provides an overview of the individual phases of a system lifecycle. From the planning and preparation of an installation to the installation itself and later patches or upgrades, we'll describe the individual stages of the lifecycle and the associated tasks.

7.1 Installation

The lifecycle starts with the installation of a system. In this section, you will learn which tools are involved in this task, and you'll get to know the single phases of the installation. Moreover, we'll provide some useful tips for manipulating the installation.

7.1.1 Installation Tools

The installation of an SAP system with an Oracle database always involves the SAPinst tool for the SAP system and the runInstaller tool for the Oracle database. SAPinst is responsible for controlling the entire installation process, whereas runInstaller is used only for the intermediate step of installing the database.

7.1.1.1 SAPinst

SAPinst is used to start the entire installation process. It is a Java-based program which consists of a client and a server component. The server is started once SAPinst is called on the current host. Prior to that, you should go into a directory that's specifically created for this purpose, such as */usr/sap/<SID>/*

install.<CI|DI|DB|etc.>, where SAPinst extracts several files and stores XML files to document the installation status.

After the start, SAPinst creates a directory called *sapinst_instdir* that contains all executables that are extracted during the start of SAPinst. SAPinst then checks if the environment variables, TEMP, TMP, and TMPDIR, have been set as storage locations for this directory. If none of these variables is set, the */tmp* directory is used by default. On UNIX systems, the installation-specific files are stored in the current directory. On Windows systems, installation-specific data is stored in the following location: *C:\programs\sapinst_instdir\<system_type>\<database>*.

The extracted executables are deleted when you exit SAPinst. However, the installation-specific files are retained in the respective directory in order for the system to be able to continue the installation process in case of an abort and to carry out a deinstallation based on this data at a later stage.

The following code listing shows a possible procedure to start SAPinst on UNIX. To be able to start SAPinst, you must have administrator rights:

```
mkdir -p /usr/sap/<SID>/install.ci
cd /usr/sap/<SID>/install.ci
export SAPINST_JRE_HOME=/opt/java1.4
/<InstallationMaster_DVD>/IM_<OS>/sapinst \
SAPINST_USE_HOSTNAME=<virtual host name>  \
SAPINST_START_GUISERVER=false
```

In this example, we pass on two additional parameters during startup. SAPINST_USE_HOSTNAME ensures that SAPinst doesn't use the current host name for the installation, but the name that's specified here. This is particularly useful for the installation of high-availability systems with virtual host names.

The second parameter, SAPINST_START_GUISERVER, instructs SAPinst not to start any SAPinst GUI on the current host, but to wait for a remote connection through a GUI. This enables you to install the system on servers that have no graphical display option, such as UNIX servers without an installed X-Server. Alternatively, you can also use the short form, -nogui. You can view a list of all parameters by calling sapinst -p.

SAPinst GUI is used to enable a graphical display and interaction during the installation process. It is a self-contained component and can be used for local installations as well as for an installation from a remote machine. If you decide on a remote installation, the connection can be established either directly or via a SAProuter. By default, port 21212 is used for the communication between SAPinst GUI and GUI Server. GUI Server is a component of SAPinst and communicates with it through port 21200.

To start SAPinst GUI, you must use the `startInstGui.sh` or `startinstgui.bat` command respectively. By using the parameters, `–gui -host <SAPinst Server> -port <SAPinst Port>` in the command, you can directly instruct SAP GUI to which server it is supposed to connect. If you don't use any parameters, you have the following two options:

- SAPinst runs locally, and SAP GUI automatically connects to this installation.
- The initial screen displays where you can specify the connection parameters. If you establish the connection via a SAProuter, you can pass the SAProuter string when starting the GUI. To do that, you must use the following key word: `–route <SAProuter-String>`.

If errors occur during the start of SAPinst or SAPinst GUI, you have several options for troubleshooting. Let us take a look at some of them:

- **Errors during extraction of SAPinst files**
  All SAPinst messages created during the extraction of executables to the sapinst_instdir directory are logged in the dev_selfex.out file that is located in the same directory.
- **Errors during the start of SAPinst GUI in local installations**
  On UNIX systems, you must check whether the `DISPLAY` variable is set and, if so, to which value. If this variable is set correctly and the GUI still won't start up, you should check if the communication ports to be used are available.
- **Errors during the start of SAPinst GUI in remote installations**
  You have started SAPinst using the `–nogui` option and want to carry out the installation process from a remote host, but no connection can be established.

  First you should use the `ping` command to check whether a network connection between the two hosts is at all possible. Then check if the specified ports are available. If they aren't, you can adjust these ports as per your requirements using the following SAPinst parameters:

  ```
  SAPINST_DIALOG_PORT=<port for communication from SAPinst to GUI Server>
  GUISERVER_DIALOG_PORT=<port for communication from GUI Server to SAPinst GUI >
  ```

7.1.1.2 runInstaller

The installation of the Oracle software requires the use of a separate installation software: runInstaller. This is a variant of the standard Oracle program, `runinstaller`. The difference from the standard version is that runInstaller allows you to preselect the installation options. For this purpose, a response file is created when SAPinst starts the installation process. This file provides input for most of the selection options during the installation. If you need other Oracle components apart from those provided automatically by runInstaller, you can, of course, select them as well.

As of Oracle 10, you can find runInstaller in the following directory: */oracle/stage/<Release>/database/SAP/RUNINSTALLER*. In previous releases, the path was */oracle/stage/<Release>/DISK1/SAP/RUNINSTALLER*. You must start the installation as the ora<sid> user. Prior to the start, you must set the `umask` parameter to `022` to ensure the correct assignment of permissions during the installation.

runInstaller is based on Java and has a graphical user interface. Therefore, you must set the `DISPLAY` variable correspondingly on UNIX systems. After the start, all required files are extracted in the */tmp* directory, which should have sufficient free space available (approximately 300 MB).

Apart from the installation, runInstaller is used for patching an Oracle installation. For this purpose, either the currently installed runInstaller is used or it is updated through the patch set. Refer to the patch set notes with regard to the method to be used. Section 7.2.3, *Maintaining the Oracle Database*, provides further information about patching Oracle databases.

7.1.2 Phases

The following section provides an overview of the individual installation phases for an SAP system with an Oracle database. However, this is only a rough outline of the process, and depending on the requirements and system configuration, other steps may be required as well. Refer to the implementation guide for your specific combination of operating system, database, product, and release to learn about the individual installation steps to be carried out. Our goal is to give you an understanding of the components you can manipulate at specific points during the installation.

7.1.2.1 Planning and Preparation

Let us start with planning the installation and the necessary preparations. The complete planning of the landscape and the associated infrastructure was described in Chapter 5, *Planning the System Landscape*.

Prior to starting the installation, you should decide on the components you want to install (DB, CI, DI, Java or ABAP system, and so on) and on the instance numbers to be assigned to these components, particularly the SAP components. Furthermore, it is important to know if and how you want to distribute the components across different servers. You can find useful information and support for those considerations in the *Master Guide*, the *Technical Infrastructure Guide*, and in the *Planning Guide* for the product. All planning and installation guides that are available can be found in the SAP Service Marketplace under the *instguides* quicklink.

Once you have made these decisions, you can start preparing the file system of the server or servers. This task includes creating the required mount points for the SAP system (*/usr/sap/<SID>*, */sapmnt*, */usr/sap/trans*). If you want to integrate the system into an existing transport landscape, you must mount the transport directory of that landscape to enable the integration during the installation process. The same holds true for using a high-availability system in which the file systems are supposed to be mounted from a network file system (NFS) server. Again, you should integrate the directories prior to starting the installation.

The following directories are required for the Oracle database:

- */oracle*
- */oracle/client*
- */oracle/stage/102_32|64*
- */oracle/<SID>/102_32|64*
- */oracle/<SID>/mirrlogA|B*
- */oracle/<SID>/origlogA|B*
- */oracle/<SID>/oraarch*
- */oracle/<SID>/sapreorg*
- */oracle/<SID>/sapdata[1-n]*

During the installation process, SAPinst checks if these file systems exist. If a directory does not exist, SAPinst issues a corresponding error message, and you must eliminate this error before you can continue the installation.

Furthermore, you should also check the kernel parameters of the servers before starting the installation. The installation guides contain the parameter sets recommended by SAP. In addition, you can create all required users and user groups before the installation. This is particularly advisable when you use central directory services, such as NIS, LDAP, or ADS, because SAPinst is not always able to write its data into those systems. If you don't create the users and user groups, SAPinst will do that automatically.

To check some of the installation requirements after starting SAPinst, you can select the **Prerequisites Check** item from the menu (see Figure 7.1). You can find this menu item at the following location: **<SAP System> • Additional Software Lifecycle Tasks • Additional Preparation Tasks • Prerequisites Check**. When carrying out this check, note that the storage parameters can be used for development and test systems. Regarding the memory size of the production system, you should refer to the sizing results. However, you can still use the check to perform a general check of the kernel parameters.

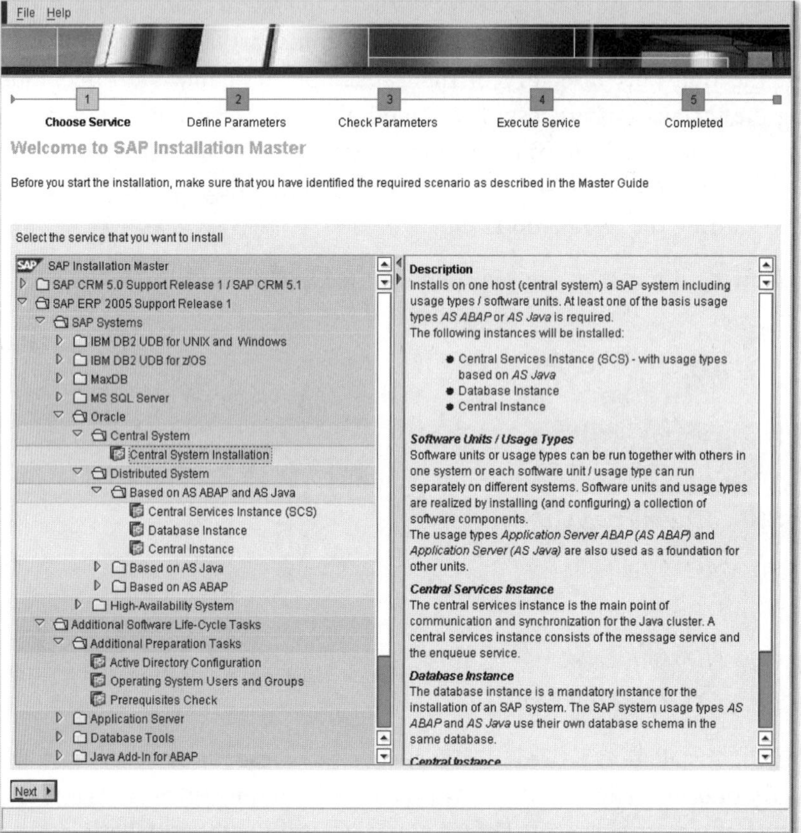

Figure 7.1 Selection Options in SAPinst

Other questions that should be answered during the installation preparations include the following:

- Which SAP components are supposed to be installed and which instance numbers should they be assigned? In this context, you should also note the specific central instances, ACS and SCS, if available, which must also be assigned instance numbers.
- Do you want your system to be Unicode-enabled? In particular, if you plan to use Java components, the use of Unicode is mandatory.
- Do you want to use MCOD for the system? You should first consider the advantages and disadvantages described in Section 4.4.1 and then decide in favor or against using MCOD. If you do want to use MCOD, you need to install the database software only once during the entire installation process. All other systems will then be stored in additional schemas in the same database.

Ultimately, don't forget that you need the complete set of installation DVDs or CDs. If possible, you should provide all media at the same time. The best way to do that is to copy the media into a central directory and carry out the installation from there. Here's a rough overview of which media are needed for which type of installation:

- **Central service instance, central instance, dialog instance**
  - Installation master DVD
  - Kernel DVD
  - NetWeaver-Java DVD
- **Oracle database instance**
  - Installation master DVD
  - Kernel DVD
  - NetWeaver-Java DVD
  - RDBMS DVD, RDBMS client DVD, RDBMS patch
(for MCOD installations you don't need any RDBMS DVDs)
  - Export DVDs

If you don't want to copy the media upfront, you can do that at a later stage using SAPinst. When entering a media location in SAPinst, you can specify where you want the tool to create a copy of the media.

At that point, the largest part of the preparatory consideration has been completed, and you can start SAPinst. For this purpose, you should set the

SAPINST_JRE_HOME or JAVA_HOME variable to a valid Java runtime environment if you haven't done so yet. Then start SAPinst from the installation master, as described earlier in Section *SAPinst*.

7.1.2.2 Entering Basic Data

After starting SAPinst and SAPinst GUI, you must first enter the system type and the type of installation, such as central instance, database instance, dialog instance, add-in-Java installation, Java instance, and so on. We recommended that you start with the central instances and set up the remaining system around these instances. Consequently, you should install an SAP ERP 6.0 installation and the associated Java component in the following sequence:

1. Central instance
2. Database instance
3. Java central instance
4. Dialog instances (ABAP and Java)
5. Web Dispatcher, if necessary

Note

Note that this is only a recommendation, and the order may vary depending on the SAP products you install. The exact installation order is specified in the installation guides.

For each component to be installed, you should start SAPinst in a separate folder to be able to store important information or installation logs at a later stage. If you don't need that, you can always use the same folder.

Once you have selected a component, SAPinst prompts you to enter several parameters that describe the system to be installed. We already dealt with most of the parameters during the preparation so that SAPinst merely checks if they have been configured. All remaining decisions shouldn't pose any problem. These include the following:

1. The master password for all users that are created by SAPinst.
2. For the installation of a Java instance, SAPinst also queries data related to the Java administration, communication, and guest users. In the standard version, these are J2EE_Admin, SAPJSF, and J2EE_GUEST. If necessary, you can change these names. However, the master password is also used as a password for those users as well as for the secure store.

3. When installing a Java add-in into an existing system, you are prompted to enter the connection data for the associated ABAP client. The ABAP client must be coupled with the Java instance. You should know the relevant data here, such as the DDIC password and client number.
4. SAP Solution Manager Key.

The SAP Solution Manager Key plays a special role. To be able to generate the Solution Manager Key, you need SAP Solution Manager 3.2 with Support Package Level 8 or higher or Release 4.0. You cannot continue the installation process if you don't enter the key. If you don't have SAP Solution Manager in your landscape yet, you must first install a Solution Manager system. As an SAP customer, you can obtain the installation CDs and licenses free of charge.[1] For further detailed information about SAP Solution Manager, use the *solutionmanager* quicklink in the SAP Service Marketplace.

Some parts of the installation can be carried out in the expert mode, which provides you with detailed options to manipulate the system setup. This is relevant for the creation of the database and the configuration of data files and redo logs. Figure 7.2 shows an overview of the configurable Oracle options in SAPinst.

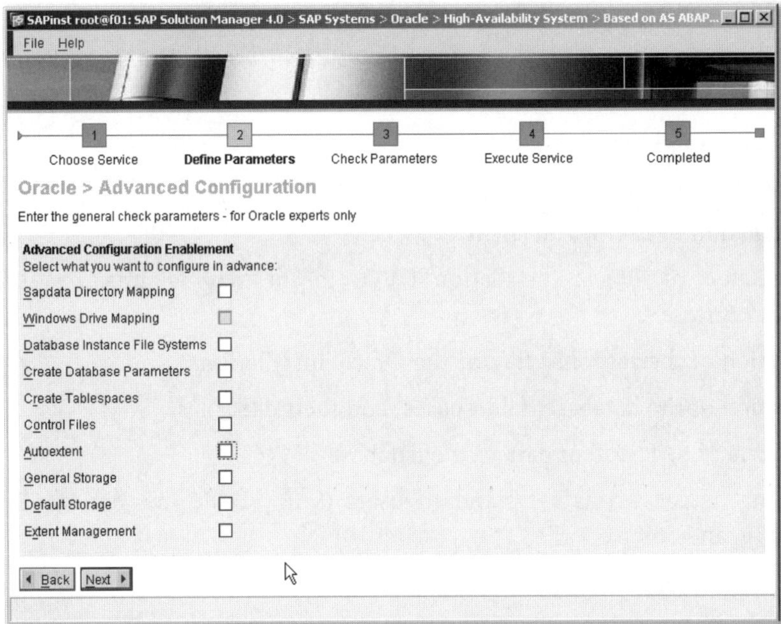

Figure 7.2 Extended Options for Defining the Database Installation

1 This does not include specific agreements, such as the use by third parties. Therefore, you should refer to your SAP consultant if something is unclear.

Once all data has been collected, SAPinst displays an overview of all entries you have specified. You must confirm this list to start installing the selected component. If you detect errors or if changes have occurred in the meantime, you can select the item and click on the **Revise** button to modify the relevant parameter. Click on the **Start** button to start installing the selected components.

7.1.2.3 Installing the Components

After starting the installation, SAPinst begins processing all other installation steps. If no errors occur, no further user interaction is needed until the installation process is finished.

If you use an Oracle database, the interruption needed for installing the Oracle software represents the only exception. For this purpose, SAPinst displays a message that prompts you to install the database software. If this occurs, you can either cancel SAPinst or install the Oracle software in a separate window using runInstaller. After that, you can simply continue the installation process using SAPinst.

In addition, SAPinst carries out the following activities during the installation phase:

1. Creation of users, user groups, and file systems (*/usr/sap/trans*, */usr/sap/<SID>*, */sapmnt/<SID>*)
2. Assignment of permissions
3. Creation of profiles for the individual instances
4. Installation of the Oracle client
5. Extraction of Oracle installation DVDs to the staging area, */oracle/stage/<Release>*
6. Creation of the response file for the Oracle installation
7. Creation of the database, tablespaces, and their data files
8. Loading of SAP system data to the database
9. Setting of passwords for standard users (SAP*, DDIC, system, J2EE_Admin, and so on)
10. Creation of current statistics data

This list of steps represents only a general overview and is by no means complete. Depending on the installed component, some of the steps may be omitted, whereas others might be added.

If errors occur during the installation process and cause an interruption of the process, SAPinst displays a corresponding message. Depending on the type of error, you can directly eliminate the problem and simply continue the installation. However, some errors cause SAPinst to abort. If that happens and you need further information about the errors, you can check various log files in your installation directory. Some of the files are described in detail in the following list:

- **sapinst.log**
  A short log of all installation steps and errors that occurred. This log often contains a reference to another detailed log file or error number. You can use that number to search for troubleshooting advice related to the specific error in the SAP Service Marketplace.
- **sapinst_dev.log**
  This is an extended version of sapinst.log that contains comprehensive information about what exactly was done by SAPinst. For example, in addition to the command lines called, the file stores the associated return codes and, if necessary, the output as well.
- **keydb.xml**
  This file describes the exact status of each installation step and controls the entire installation process. Furthermore, the file stores the input made in the preparation phase. If you search for an error in one of the installation steps, you can identify the error by the XML entry, `CDATA[ERROR]`. Apart from that, you can find a short description of the step in this file (here: `stopSdmServer`), which may be useful when searching for the related message:

  ```
  <fld name="STEPKEY">
  <strval><![CDATA[J2EE_... stopSdmServer]]> </strval>
  </fld> <fld name="STATUS">
  <strval><![CDATA[ERROR]]>
  </strval></fld>
  ```

- **DBSIZE.XML**
  This file contains information about the size of tablespaces and data files to be created. If necessary, you can modify the size in this file. However, we recommend that you do this in SAPinst to avoid problems caused by misspellings or incorrect XML tags in the DBSIZE.XML file.

- **java.exe.<NR>.log**
  This file contains all log information about SDM starts and stops during the installation as well as deployment-related information.
- **callSdmViaSapinst.<NR>.log**
  If the SDM is started and stopped directly through SAPinst, the log data is written to this log file.

Once all installation steps have been completed and SAPinst has displayed a success message, you will find a running SAP system on your server. You can use that system, but if you want to use it in live operations, it is advisable to carry out a number of additional tasks first. The following section describes these tasks and how they can be performed.

7.1.2.4 Post Installation and Additional Tasks

Once SAPinst has completed the installation process for the database software and SAP instances, several additional tasks need to be carried out before you can use the system in live operations. This phase is often referred to as *post installation*. The following sections provide a brief overview of the most important elements of the post installation phase. Again, we refer you to the specific installation guide and recommend that you consider your specific environment, which may require you to perform other important tasks as well.

Before you continue to use the system, you should first carry out a complete stop and start to test the functions. This way you can also activate adjustments to the start and environment profiles that may have been implemented after the installation process was finished.

From this point onward, you should no longer use the standard SAP administration user, SAP*, when using the SAP system. For this reason, it is advisable to create a copy of the user, for instance, master-adm, as early as possible, and to keep the SAP* user only for emergency situations. In current installations, the password of the user is set by SAPinst. If you install older releases, you must change the standard passwords in all clients after the installation. In addition, you should assign separate passwords to the other standard users – DDIC, SAPCPIC, and EARLYWATCH. Regarding DDIC, SAPinst carries out this task as well in current releases.

To be able to use the SAP system, you must install a valid license when the temporary license of 30 days has expired. You can obtain the license in the SAP Service Marketplace under the *licensekey* quicklink. There, you must first enter the relevant information about your operating system and release as well as the hardware-dependent hardware key. To determine this hardware key in your SAP system, follow the menu path **Tools • Administration • Administration • SAP Licenses** (Transaction SLICENSE). This is the location where you also need to install the license once you have received the license key. If the license has expired, you can only log in to the system as the SAP* user. All other login attempts will be refused with a notification about the expiration of the license.

If you cannot access the SAP system or if you prefer using the command prompt, you can use the `saplicense` program as a <sid>adm user. This program enables you to set up, check, and maintain your SAP licenses. You can find the program in the following directory: */usr/sap/<SID>/SYS/exe/run*. Table 7.1 provides an overview of the options provided by `saplicense`.

Option	Meaning
`-delete`	Deletes an installed license
`-get`	Determines the hardware key of the installation
`-help [option]`	Displays the general help or help for a specific option
`-install [ifile= file name]`	Installs an SAP license. The `ifile` option enables you to specify a file that contains the license data.
`-number`	Returns the installation number
`-show`	Displays the installed license data
`-temp`	Installs a temporary license
`-test pf=<profile>`	Tests whether a valid SAP license exists for an installation. The additional `TRACE=2` enables you to force the detailed logging of the test in the *dev_slic* file that will be stored in the current directory.
`-version`	Displays the version of `saplicense`

Table 7.1 Options of saplicense

To install a license using `saplicense`, you must use the `-install` option. If you don't specify any other parameters for the license file path (`ifile=<file name>`), the system requests the required information step by step. When entering the system number, don't forget to enter all leading zeros.

If you use a high-availability system, you must ensure that your system's message server finds valid license data on all hosts that are available. To do that, you must request a separate license for each physical server (usually, there are two of them). You must do that because the physical servers have different hardware keys. If you encounter a problem with the licenses in case of an error, you can use a temporary license for a short period of time.

Up to this point, we haven't implemented any security mechanisms in our system. Thus, it is high time we set up a backup process in the system to avoid having to re-install the entire system if an error occurs in the following steps. Setting up a backup process includes checking whether the ArchiveLog mode is active as well as the further configuration of the system backup. Once you have done that, you should first carry out a full system backup. Chapter 10, *Backup, Restore, and Recovery*, describes how you can set up and execute backups.

To provide system users with support, you must either install the documentation or set up links to the documentation of the respective SAP products. To do that, the following options are available:

1. Install the documentation on a separate web server. SAP provides help CDs and DVDs that contain the relevant help files for this kind of installation.
2. Establish a link to the documentation on the SAP Help server at *http://help.sap.com*.
3. Install the user help locally.

To manage the access to the various help files, you should use the client-independent Transaction SR13. Figure 7.3 shows a sample configuration that provides access to the German and English help versions on a web server (**saphelp.hcc**...).

Change View "Administration: Display of the SAP Library"

New Entries

DynamicHelp | PlainHtmlHttp | PlainHtmlFile | HtmlHelpFile

Variant	Platform	Area	Server Na...	Path	Langua...	Default
Saphelp deutsch	WN32	IWBHELP	saphelp.hcc...	ecc_500/helpdata	DE	☑
Saphelp englisch	WN32	IWBHELP	saphelp.hcc...	ecc_500/helpdata	EN	☐

Figure 7.3 SAP Help Administration

Another major aspect related to the post installation phase involves the *ABAP configuration*. This includes the configuration of operation types under **Tools • CCMS • Configuration • Operation Modes/Instances** (Transaction

RZ04), the definition of logon groups under **Tools • CCMS • Configuration • Logon Groups** (Transaction SMLG), the setup of required printers under **Tools • CCMS • Print • Spool Administration** (Transaction SPAD), as well as the scheduling of all background jobs that are required to purge and reorganize the logs in both the SAP system and the Oracle database. Section 9.3, *Background Jobs in the Scope of Monitoring*, provides a detailed description of those jobs and describes how they can be scheduled.

The patching of the installed systems represents an integral part of the post installation phase. Because the installation media reflect only a specific status of the development and the SAP software is continuously enhanced and improved, you should always update the software to the current status. Section 7.2.2, *SAP Support Packages, Patches, and Corrections*, describes how you can do that for the ABAP part of the system. Section 11.3.3, *Patching Java Instances and Applications*, describes how you can patch a Java-based system.

Once you have finished patching the system, you can start creating clients for your production data and fill these clients with the necessary data. To copy the customizing template to the separate client, you must use client copies.

This concludes all basic steps to be carried out in post installation. Depending on the components used and how you want to use the system in the future, you may still need to carry out additional tasks. For example, you may have to link different systems within a system landscape for the purpose of data exchange. For this purpose, you need to define the corresponding users, RFC connections, and, if necessary, queues. If you have installed a high-availability system, you should check whether your HA solution (high availability) and the SAP system react as expected regarding errors and carry out a system switch, for example.

Refer to the relevant installation guides to determine if those steps are necessary.

7.1.3 Unattended Installation

In addition to the graphically guided installation, SAPinst also allows you to perform an unattended installation. For this purpose, you can configure an installation once and then run it without monitoring it. This way, you can easily install systems of similar types, such as test or development systems.

The procedure described in the following steps can be used for all installations as of SAP NetWeaver 7.0, such as SAP ERP 6.0, SAP CRM 5.0, SAP SRM 5.0, and so on:

1. **Record the input parameters**
   Start SAPinst and enter all required system parameters. SAPinst records these entries in the *inifile.xml* file in the SAPinst installation directory. Terminate the installation process when you reach the point "Parameter Summary." If you install multiple components, such as an additional dialog instance, the information is recorded in the same file.
2. **Customize inifile.xml**
   In the next step, you must customize the new configuration file in accordance with your new installation. To do that, you can edit the XML file using a text editor. Note that you can only modify the specified parameters. You cannot add new parameters or modify the installation sequence.
3. **Create a new installation directory**
   Save the *inifile.xml*, *keydb.dtd*, and *doc.dtd* files in a new installation directory. The two additional files are needed because they describe the XML structure of the *inifile.xml* file and thus ensure the accuracy of its syntax.
4. **Store the CD paths**
   Create a file called *start_dir.cd* in your new installation directory. This file should contain the paths to all required installation media. Each path must be written in a separate line. On UNIX systems, you can simply specify all required mount points. In Windows environments, you can additionally specify network drives. To do that, you must use the following syntax:

   ```
   C:\sapdvds\kernel    # local drive
   \\sapdvdserver\dvds\java  # network drive
   ```

5. **Determine the product ID to be installed**
   Each product that can be installed has a product ID based on which it can be uniquely identified. You can find this ID in the *product.catalog* file on the installation master DVD.

   Open the file and search for "component.id." The description in the following lines can then help you determine which type of system will be installed with the ID:

   ```
   <component id="d0e24327" output-dir="AS" name="NW_Onehost" os-
   type="ind" os="ind" db="ind" product="ind" ppms-component="ind"
   ppms-component-release="ind"
   table="t_NW_Onehost">
   <display-name><![CDATA[Central System Installation]]> </display-name>
   <user-info><![CDATA[<html><B>Description</B><BR>
   ...
   </user-info>
   ```

In this example, the product ID is d0e24327, and it is used for the installation of a central system on a host.

6. **Start SAPinst**

   To start the installation, you must start SAPinst using the parameters `SAPINST_EXECUTE_PRODUCT_ID=<Produkt-ID(s)`, `SAPINST_PARAMETER_CONTAINER_URL=<path to inifile.xml>`, and `SAPINST_SKIP_DIALOGS=true`. A call could then be structured as follows:

```
sapinst SAPINST_PARAMETER_CONTAINER_URL=\usr\sap\S10\install\inifile.xml \
SAPINST_EXECUTE_PRODUCT_ID=d0e24327        \
SAPINST_SKIP_DIALOGS=true
```

   If an error occurs during the installation, SAPinst provides information on the cause of the error. This information is also contained in the sapinst.log and sapinst_dev.log files.

7.2 System Maintenance

This section covers the maintenance of an SAP system and its Oracle database. Over time, an SAP system is provided with error corrections, quality improvements, and even functional extensions by means of support packages. At a certain time, the system is upgraded to a higher release. In addition to installing support packages in the SAP system, the frontends, the Oracle database, and the operating system must be provided with up-to-date fixes. Especially with regard to the operating system, patches are used to fill security gaps. All of these aspects are described in the following sections. However, before that, it makes sense to take a brief look at client copies in the system. After installing a system, you must create client copies. They can be useful as a copy of the production system in the test system or for refreshing the training system.

7.2.1 Client Tools

In Chapter 2, *SAP Fundamentals*, and in Chapter 6, *SAP Change and Transport Management*, we described the client concept from a business and technical point of view. In addition, we provided a comprehensive description of the different types and classes of data as well as the client roles within a three-system landscape.

SAP delivers systems with different clients. For example, the standard version of an SAP ERP system contains an SAP reference client, a sample client, and an EarlyWatch client. To be able to use data from other clients, you need either client copies or client transports. Performing and monitoring client transports is the responsibility of an SAP Basis administrator. Therefore, we want to introduce the important basic principles of this task now. Client copies have an immediate effect on the features and size of the Oracle database. The parameterization of the Oracle system, in particular, with regard to the allocation of secondary memory and undo management, affects the process of creating and handling a client copy.

Let us first take a look at the different types of client copies and transports, as shown in Figure 7.4:

- Local client copy
- Remote client copy
- Remote client copy with client-independent customizing
- Client export and client import
- Client export and client import with client-independent customizing

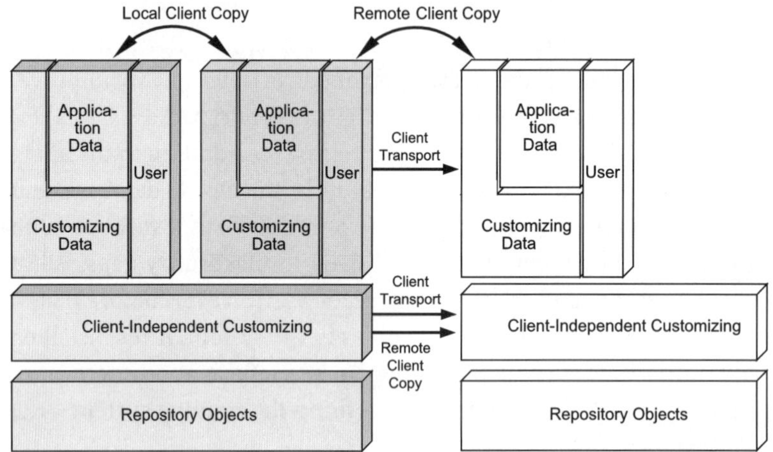

Figure 7.4 Categorization of Client Copies

The different types of client copies can be controlled via transactions and copy profiles. You copy or transport the data that is specified via copy profiles from one client to another within an SAP system or between two clients of two different SAP systems. Simply put, in this process, the SAP application logic first reads the individual data records of a client from the tables of the Oracle database and then writes the records back into the same tables, but with a different client key. This type of activity generates a high load on the database server, and redo log files are created during change operations. For this reason, you should carry out those processes only at times of low system load (when no users are logged in or during maintenance periods). Let us now take a closer look at the individual tools.

The local client copy (Transaction SCCL) copies data between two clients of an SAP system. It is started from within the target client. In this process, copy profiles are used to select the data to be copied (see Figure 7.5). During a copy process, no user should log in to the target and source clients.

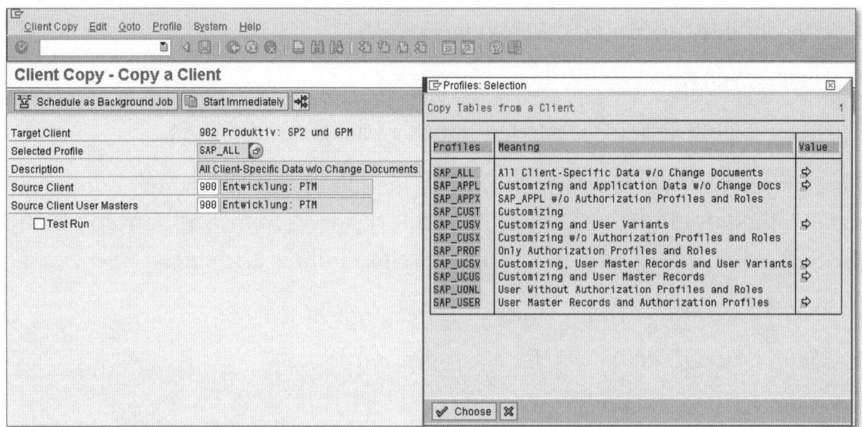

Figure 7.5 Selecting the Copy Profiles

The remote copy copies the data of a client between two SAP systems. The copy process is started from within the target client. In this process, the data is transferred via RFC connections (see Figure 7.6). You should ensure that the repository structures in the source and target systems are identical. Therefore, the system performs a consistency check during the copy process. In addition, a remote copy can include client-independent customizing. In contrast to transports, the remote copy (Transaction SCC9) does not store any files at the operating system level.

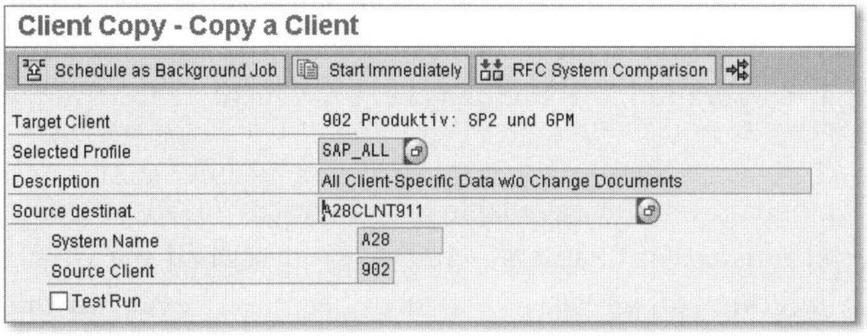

Client Copy - Copy a Client
Schedule as Background Job | Start Immediately | RFC System Comparison
Target Client 902 Produktiv: SP2 und GPM
Selected Profile SAP_ALL
Description All Client-Specific Data w/o Change Documents
Source destinat. A28CLNT911
System Name A28
Source Client 902
Test Run

Figure 7.6 Remote Client Copy

A client export (Transaction SCC8) copies data between SAP systems and does not use any RFC connection. The data must first be exported from the source system before it is imported to the target system. The target system to which the data is exported must be selected, which means it must previously have been created in the transport management system. Depending on the profile you select, the data is stored in specific files at the operating system level during this process:

- Client-dependent data: *RT<number>.SID*
- Client-independent data: *RO<number>.SID*
- Texts: *RX<number>.SID*

The data export should be carried out as a background process.

The counterpart to the client export is the client import, which copies the data to the target system. The client import process must be started via the TMS. The files in the import queues have the following names:

- *<Source SID>KO<number> for client-independent data*
- *<Source SID>KT<number> for client-dependent data*
- *<Source SID>KX<number> for texts*

Client transports must be imported individually, the client-independent data first, followed by the client-dependent data. Once the data has been imported successfully, you must import texts using Transaction SCC7 and carry out additional activities. You can view transport logs using the Transport Organizer. It is useful to perform a repository consistency check between the two systems prior to or during the client import process to detect and eliminate inconsistencies.

When you prepare a client copy process, you must check the system requirements with regard to the storage space, irrespective of whether you are planning a local copy, remote copy, export or import. Figure 7.7 shows the requirements of sample SAP R/3 or SAP ECC clients concerning the storage space requirements after the system has been installed. If you enter data into the system during live operation, the size of a client can increase to terabyte level over time.

If the amount of secondary memory available to a client copy is insufficient, the copy process terminates. In Chapters 3 and 4, we described the Oracle mechanisms for allocating storage space that may become relevant in this context.

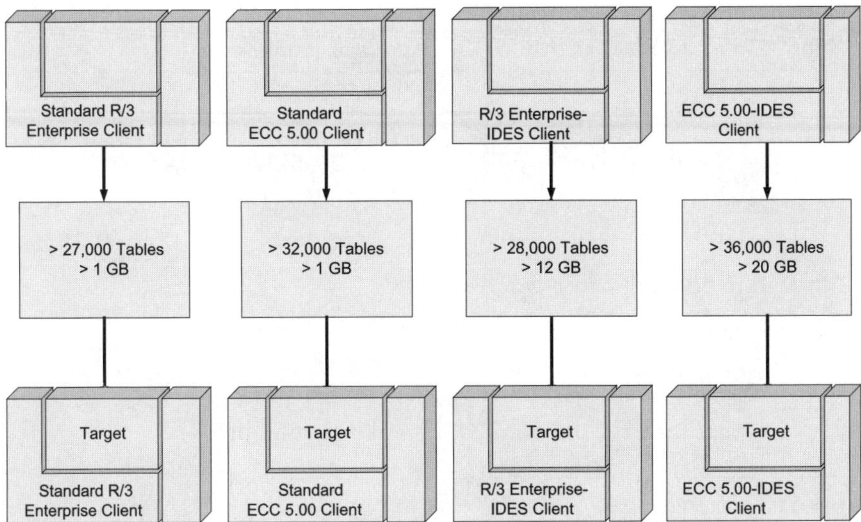

Figure 7.7 Storage Space Requirements of Different Clients

If no storage space is allocated automatically, the administrator must ensure that sufficient space is available in the tablespaces prior to starting the client copy process. The SAP data is distributed to a number of tablespaces, each of which must be increased.

Even the modern mechanisms that can increase files and tablespaces are only useful if sufficient physical storage space is available. Therefore, prior to starting a client copy process, you should check whether sufficient hard disk space is available in the target system.

You can use parallel processes for database-intensive client operations (see Figure 7.8). This way, you can better use all of the options provided by the Oracle database. The number of parallel processes and associated RFC server groups can be defined prior to starting the operation. The reference value recommended by SAP provides for two processes for each available database CPU. Note that the parallel processes can be used only during the actual copy process, but not for analysis and postprocessing purposes.

Because the processes monitor each other, parallel processing is fairly stable. However, note that the client copy process cannot be terminated by simply stopping the running processes.

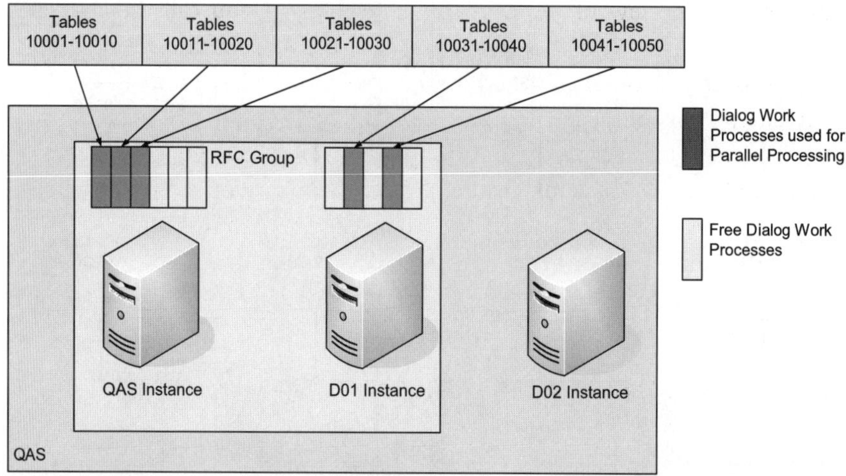

Figure 7.8 Parallel Processing

At this point, we don't want to go into further details regarding client copies in a newly installed system. For further information on this topic, you should refer to SAP Note 550894. This SAP Note describes the creation of a new client in great detail. However, the following three general tools and functions should be briefly mentioned:

1. New clients are created in client table T000. To do that, you must use Transaction SCC4 (**Tools • Administration • Administration • Client Administration • Client Maintenance**). This transaction can be used to define the header data of the new client, some informational data, the role of the client, as well as its changeability. When logging in to this new client, you should use the SAP* user with password pass.[2]
2. Prior to starting a copy process, you can carry out a test run. In this context, you can choose between a fast resource check and a simulation in which all data is read but not written. Notifications about problems and especially the information about the storage space requirement to be expected for the copy in the Oracle database are of specific interest here.
3. You can view the progress of client copy processes using Transaction SCC3 (**Tools • Administration • Administration • Client Administration • Copy Logs**). This transaction enables you to access the copy logs. First, you will

2 You may have to reset the `login/no_automatic_user_sapstar` profile parameter. That is, you may need to set it to 0 and then restart the application server, as otherwise you can't log in with this user ID and password. For more information on this subject, refer to SAP Notes 2383, 2467, and 68048.

obtain an overview of the available copy logs. If you call the overview from within a client that is not client 000, the view of the client you are logged in to will be restricted. You can extend the view by clicking on the **All Clients** button. Each log can be displayed as an overview or in a detailed view (see Figure 7.9). Among other things, the log contains information about the duration of the copy process as well as the number of copied tables and data records. The example shown in the figure describes an IDES client.

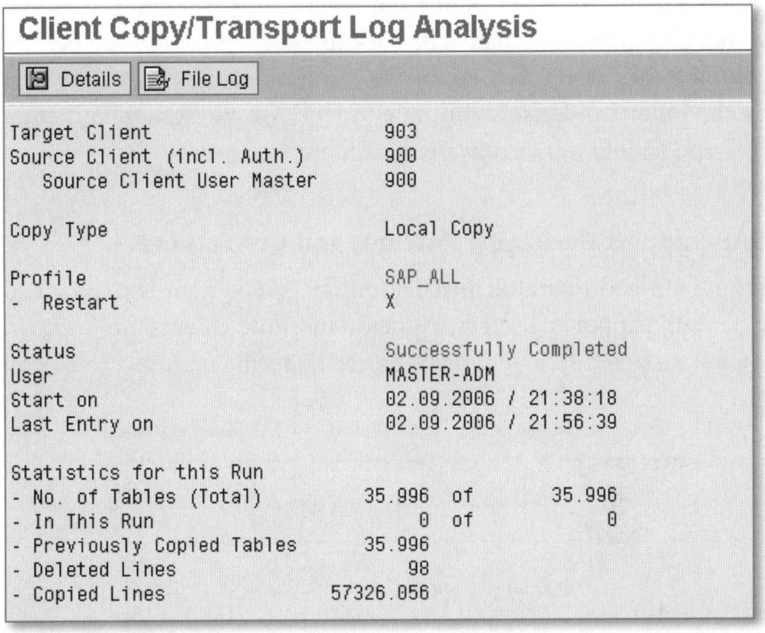

Client Copy/Transport Log Analysis

Details | File Log

```
Target Client                          903
Source Client (incl. Auth.)            900
   Source Client User Master           900

Copy Type                              Local Copy

Profile                                SAP_ALL
-  Restart                             X

Status                                 Successfully Completed
User                                   MASTER-ADM
Start on                               02.09.2006 / 21:38:18
Last Entry on                          02.09.2006 / 21:56:39

Statistics for this Run
- No. of Tables (Total)            35.996  of        35.996
- In This Run                           0  of             0
- Previously Copied Tables         35.996
- Deleted Lines                        98
- Copied Lines                  57326.056
```

Figure 7.9 Client Copy Log

If you add new clients to a system, you should ensure that the required client-dependent standard and reorganization jobs[3] are scheduled.

Typically, client copy processes take several hours, need many gigabytes of storage space, and place a high load on both the source and the target system. For this reason, you should act with patience and care when planning, preparing, and performing client copy processes. This will save you many frustrating process aborts.

If you need to copy very large production clients to a test system, you should first reorganize the Oracle database in the target system (see Chapter 4). In

3 Refer to SAP Note 16083 for further information on this topic.

the case of remote copies, you must also reorganize the Oracle database in the source system. It is also useful to update the database statistics prior to the copy process. The runtime can be significantly affected by tables that are not reorganized as well as by statistics that haven't been updated. Moreover, you should update the statistics after each copy run. Because large datasets are moved in this process, you cannot use the previous statistics.

Because a copy run generates many redo log files, which decreases the system performance, you may want to deactivate the ArchiveLog mode of the Oracle system for the duration of the copy run. However, note that you should do that only if an up-to-date data backup exists and if you can be sure that the redo log files aren't needed for the duration of the client copy process. If, on the other hand, users continue to work on the system and enter critical data, you should not deactivate the ArchiveLog mode.

7.2.2 SAP Support Packages, Patches, and Corrections

We already mentioned that after installation, an SAP system is maintained and updated with support packages, patches, and note corrections and that the system is transferred to a new release after a specific period.

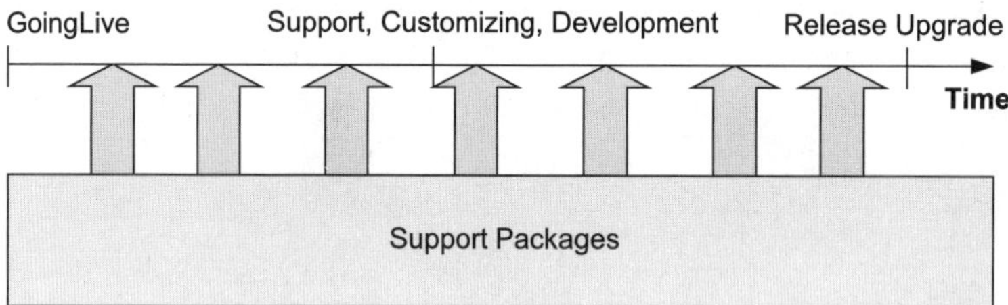

Figure 7.10 Life of an SAP System

Figure 7.10 illustrates the lifecycle of an SAP system. After the system has been installed and adapted in Customizing and Repository, the implementation project is completed with the *GoingLive*. From this time on, the underlying system landscape is used productively. Naturally, during this usage, changes are still made to the functionality and the processes of the SAP standard version via Customizing and development. Additionally, SAP provides code fixes, quality improvements, and new functionalities via support packages and SAP kernel patches that can be used for updating your system. Packages in the human resource area, for example, contain adaptations that comply with the latest statutory requirements. After a specific period, at the latest, when support is no longer provided for the installed release, the system can be upgraded to a new release.

SAP recommends that you always keep the system up-to-date to avoid known problems. It therefore makes sense to import support packages on a regular basis. Several tools exist for this purpose:

- The Support Package Manager (SPAM) in the ABAP environment
- The Java Support Package Manager (JSPM) in the Java environment

The Java Support Package Manager is introduced in Chapter 11, which explicitly deals with the Application Server Java. The JSPM is provided as of the SAP NetWeaver 7.0 release. Java Support Packages for SAP Web AS 6.20 and 6.40 are imported via an SAPinst installation using the Software Deployment Managers (SDM). More information on SDM can be found in SAP Note 544244. In this section, the main focus is on the ABAP support packages.

What are the characteristics of ABAP support packages? Every support package is valid for exactly one release version but can always be used for all underlying databases and operating systems. The objects delivered with a package are substituted in the system. Another important characteristic is that a support package always expects a specific number of predecessors. If these predecessors are not available, the package cannot be imported. Additionally, support packages must be imported in a specific order if various components are to be implemented in the system. This is ensured by the Support Package Manager. Some support packages depend on each other and should always be implemented together in the system. ABAP support packages are made available in a compressed SAR archive.

SAP categorizes the ABAP support packages in various types:

- SPAM/SAINT update
- Component Support Packages (CSP)
- Support packages for the SAP_HR component
- Conflict Resolution Transport (CRT)

Support packages for SPAM and SAINT contain corrections and innovations of the Support Package Manager and the add-on installation tool that will be discussed here later.

The *Component Support Packages* (CSP) are valid for one software component of the SAP system and provide updates for exactly that component. For example, there are packages for the SAP_BASIS, SAP_ABA, SAP_APPL components, and for add-ons. The packages for the SAP_HR component additionally contain adaptations for statutory changes.

A *Conflict Resolution Transport* (CRT) is used exclusively for add-ons. It is implemented when a support package needs to be adapted to an add-on. This is necessary in the Industry Solution (IS) area, for example. A CRT of a specific add-on release always includes all adaptations for previous releases of the same add-on and can contain quality improvements. De facto, a CRT can always be a specific component support package for an add-on component.

Java support packages are used to deliver fixes to Java software components. They communicate with the ABAP support packages and therefore must be implemented in the system in accordance with them. In contrast to an ABAP support package, a Java support package always provides the entire software component. Dependencies on predecessor packages of the same components do not exist; it is therefore not necessary to import those first. However, you should always check the corresponding SAP notes to ensure that the software component to be updated does not require a different procedure. Java support packages are delivered as *Software Component Archives* (SCA).

When importing support packages, a new or updated code is loaded into the system. Depending on the number and size of support packages, it requires additional space in the tablespaces of your Oracle database. Therefore, before starting the import process, take care that the tablespaces PSAP<SID><Basis Release> for ABAP code and PSAP<SID>DB for Java code have sufficient memory and that the disk systems provide a sufficient amount of physical memory in case you are using automatic memory management.

Support packages are provided on the SAP Service Marketplace under *http://service.sap.com/patches* or via DVD. The DVD can be ordered from the SAP Software Catalog at *http://service.sap.com/swcat*, for example.

Since April 2007, however, all support package components for SAP NetWeaver 7.0 and the SAP Business Suite 2005 are only available via the Maintenance Optimizer in the SAP Solution Manager. One exception is the patches for the SAP kernel and the Internet Graphics Service (IGS). SAP justifies this step because the flexibility of SAP applications results in a considerable increase of included software components that can be user-defined and installed both centrally on a server and in a distributed way on several servers, which is why professional support is necessary for efficiently managing the resulting combinations. The Maintenance Optimizer is part of the SAP Solution Manager and provides the customer with a complete and consistent process of software maintenance.

For receiving support packages, the following steps are performed:

1. The Maintenance Optimizer displays relevant maintenance updates.
2. Select the desired packages and accept the download.
3. As before, the packages are downloaded via the activated page on the Service Marketplace.
4. The import to the relevant systems is performed as usual via the SPAM, JSPM, or SAINT tools.
5. Afterwards, the maintenance process must be completed in the Maintenance Optimizer.

The Maintenance Optimizer is available in the Solution Manager 4.0 as of Support Package Stack 9 and with restricted functionality in the Solution Manager 3.2 as of Support Package Stack 15.

In addition to the support packages, it is important to regularly update the SAP kernel files and the files for the Internet Graphics Service (IGS) residing in the global */sapmnt/<SID>/exe* directory. Sometimes, dependencies between specific support packages of the SAP_BASIS and SAP_ABA components require you to implement a specific kernel version in the system. Patches can be selected in two ways:

1. For each kernel file, you select the current patch and thus compose your patch package.
2. You use the database-dependent and the database-independent packages defined by SAP. Both packages contain the latest patches of the relevant kernel files. The package with the dependent part of the database is called *SAPEXEDB_<patch level>-<platform identification>.SAR*, and the independent part is called *SAPEXE_<patch level>-<platform identification>.SAR*.

We recommend that you use the packages prepared by SAP. The patches for the kernel files are structured in the Service Marketplace as follows:

- Kernel release
- 32-bit or 64-bit architectures
- Unicode and non-Unicode
- Operating system and platform
- Database-independent part
- Database-dependent Oracle part

Therefore, when downloading the packages or the individual kernel files, you need to select the correct criteria for your installation. Be sure to download the `DBATOOLS` package for Oracle as well to be able to use the latest BR*Tools. The `DBATOOLS` are not included in the SAPEXEDB.SAR and SAPEXE.SAR packages. The IGS files can be found in a separate folder at the entry level to the patches of the kernel files. The folders underneath organize the IGS software according to operating system and platform.

Compared to previous releases, the update of the SAP kernel and IGS has been significantly improved since SAP NetWeaver Release 7.0 (Basis 7.00), particularly with regard to the Java part, because the kernel files are used by both ABAP and Java. We will not discuss the procedures for release 6.40 or earlier here.

As of release 7.00, the kernel and IGS files are stored in the *DIR_CT_RUN* directory. *DIR_CT_RUN* refers to the global kernel directory, which in homogeneous environments points to */usr/sap/<SID>/SYS/exe/run* and in heterogeneous environments points to */usr/sap/<SID>/SYS/exe/run/<codepage>/<OS>*. If the files are updated in this global kernel directory, the `SAPCPE` program distributes the files to the local instance directories under */usr/sap/<SID>/<instance_name>/exe* when the system is restarted. The automatic distribution of these files depends on the definition of the `DIR_CT_RUN` profile parameter for the global directory of executable files and of `DIR_EXECUTABLE` for the local directory of executable files. Check these parameters particularly when you perform an upgrade to release 7.0.

Let's look at the steps to be performed when you want to replace the kernel 7.00 for a standalone ABAP instance. In many cases, you can proceed as follows:

1. Log on as <sid>adm to the machine running the instance to be updated.
2. Unpack the SAR archives of the kernel files and the IGS to a temporary folder using the `SAPCAR` program.
3. Stop the SAP system.
4. Back up the current global kernel directory *DIR_CT_RUN* by storing it to tape or copying it to a backup directory.
5. Move the unpacked files from the temporary directory to the kernel directory.
6. Under UNIX, you must log on as the *root* user and change to the kernel directory. Then execute the `saproot.sh` script. This sets all necessary root permissions for the newly copied files.
7. You can then restart the system.

As described above, the system restart distributes the files to the *DIR_EXECUTBALE* local instance directories. Because the IGS is part of the Web Application Server as of version 7.00 and its files are now also stored in the *DIR_EXECUTABLE* directory, it is very simple to perform the update via the method described above.[4]

The kernel replacement for Java and double-stack systems, that is, ABAP systems with Java add-in, is a little different. This is where the Java Support Package Manager comes into play. In contrast to the SPAM on the ABAP side, it can exchange the kernel files. After updating the Java software components, the kernel can be exchanged in a single run. When several instances are run, they must be started manually by the JSPM on the other hosts after the kernel has been replaced. The Java Support Package Manager can only do so on the central instance. If you use a double-stack system where the ABAP server works with a non-Unicode kernel and the Java server works with a Unicode kernel, JSPM can update both parts. As described above, it makes sense to perform the replacement of the kernel files together with the Java support packages. For this purpose, SAP provides *Support Package Stacks* (SP Stacks) that will be discussed below on. The usage of JSPM is explained in Chapter 11.

The kernel replacement in JSPM requires the following steps:

1. JSPM automatically stops the central instance and asks you to manually stop the SAP Central Service Instance (SCS) and all other dialog instances.
2. After you confirm, the actual kernel replacement takes place.
3. Once the update has completed, you must restart the SCS instance.
4. Under UNIX, you now log on as the *root* user and change to the kernel directory. Then execute the `saproot.sh` script. This sets all necessary root permissions for the newly copied files.
5. As soon as the SCS instance is running, you can inform the JSPM. It will then deploy more patches (if any).
6. Meanwhile, you can start the dialog instances that then perform the kernel replacement via `SAPCPE`.

In 2003, the strategy of support packages for some products was extended to Support Package (SP) Stacks. This strategy is to improve customers' import behavior with regard to support packages as well as quality and service and is thus meant to reduce the ongoing operating costs. A Support Package Stack contains clear specifications for the packages and patches to be imported by

4 All changes to IGS versions after 6.40 can be found in SAP Note 917255.

providing permitted, tested, and best fitting combinations at a specific time. The SP Stacks are usually published quarterly via the methods described above. For downloading the stacks, SAP offers specific web pages that considerably simplify the downloading process for packages and patches. The import method of the individual support packages and patches does not change with the SP Stacks. An important condition is that the minimum requirements and dependencies between the individual components are considered. The support packages and patches delivered in the SP Stack must always be imported together. Import instructions are available that are specifically tailored to the combination to be imported, thus reducing the time and effort required for the import process.

Under *http://service.sap.com/sp-stacks*, you will find a table listing the product versions for which SP Stacks are provided or are about to be introduced. Every stack is determined by an application component or a support package component; thus, the corresponding support package is an essential part. Via the Support Packages Stack Schedule, you can find out when a new stack is available for a specific product version.

To be able to import a support package of the leading component, at least the status regarding the other components must be met. For most components, the import of a higher version is recommended only in the case of problems for which there is no local correction (such as a correction instruction) or a workaround.

The Support Package Manager is called via the SPAM transaction in client 000 by a user with the appropriate authorization (other than SAP*). The program name features the SPAM version and the current patch level. A basic prerequisite is that you always update the SPAM to the latest version before you import component support packages. This is achieved via **Support Package • Import SPAM/SAINT Update**. After you have imported the update, you need to restart SPAM. Figure 7.11 illustrates the initial screen.

There are two ways of providing packages obtained via download or DVD to the Support Package Manager:

1. Via your frontend (**Support Packages • Load Packages • From Frontend**) for archives to be imported that are smaller than 10 megabytes
2. Via the application server by copying the unpacked archives to the directory */usr/sap/trans/EPS/in* (`DIR_TRANS_EPS` parameter) and exposing them to the Support Package Manager via the function **Support Packages • Load Packages • From Application Server**

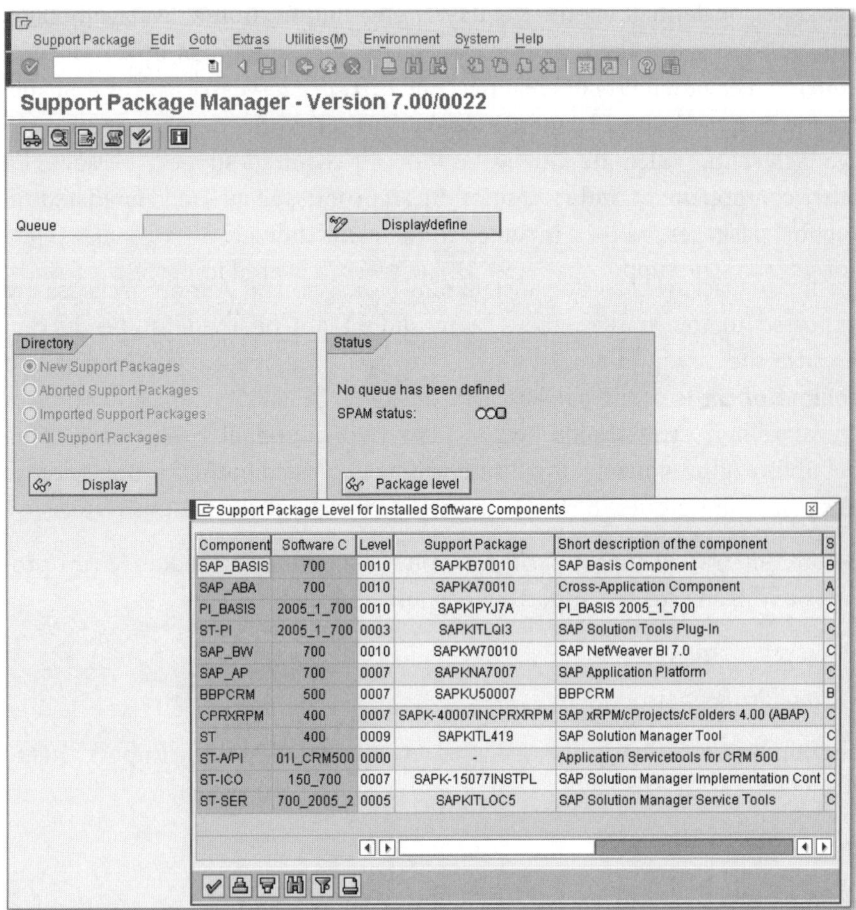

Figure 7.11 Support Package Manager (SPAM)

By defining a queue you determine, on the one hand, the support packages to be imported in the system and, on the other hand, the order in which this process is to be performed. A queue is specified via the support packages known to the SPAM. If such a queue is already specified, you can no longer change it. However, you can delete it if it has not yet been imported to the system beyond the step **Import 1**. If there are support packages in the system that do not fit the release or an installed add-on, SPAM does not include them in a queue. There are three ways of defining a queue:

1. From a software component
2. From several software components
3. From a target support package

The queue is defined via the **Display/Define** button. In the displayed dialog box, you can select the packages for exactly one component or for all components. The possibility of creating a queue from a target package is available via the **Display** button in the **Directory** area. From the desired target package, select the **Calculate Queue** button. All required support packages of other components, Conflict Resolution Transports, as well as related add-on support packages are then included in the calculation.

If support packages, add-on installation packages, and add-on packages are imported to the system, the system should not be used for production because the newly imported objects can cause interruptions. The size and volume of the current patches are considerable, and system downtime is therefore high. This should be considered when updating the system. One possibility of minimizing downtime will be described in this section because this restriction proves to be a disadvantage for many production systems.

Before importing support packages, you must define the queue. SPAM provides two scenarios for importing support packages:

- Test scenario
- Standard scenario

The import scenario can be specified via **Extras • Settings • Import Queue** (see Figure 7.12).

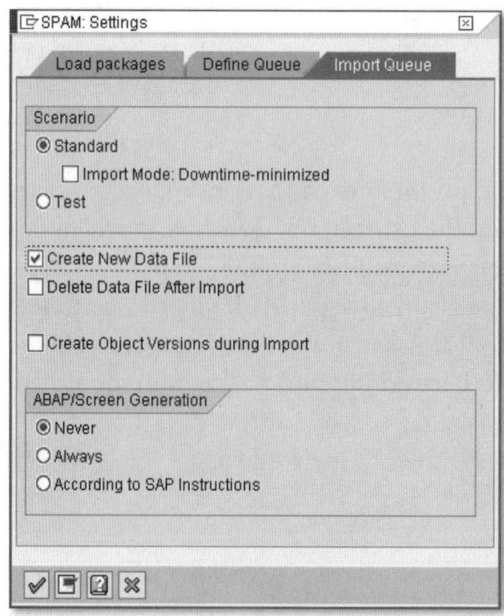

Figure 7.12 Settings for Importing the Queue

In the test scenario, you can determine even before the actual import process whether there will be conflicts or errors due to unreleased fixes or whether a modification adjustment is necessary, without importing data into the system. Additionally, you have the option of estimating the amount of time and effort for importing the packages. The test scenario must be selected via the queue import settings. Errors that occur in the test scenario can be ignored.

In the standard scenario, however, the queue is indeed completely imported into the system. If errors occur, they must be removed to successfully complete the import. In addition to the conventional mode, you can select the **Downtime-minimized** import mode to reduce the time of nonproductive system usage.

As a prerequisite to importing packages, you must define them in the queue and set up the standard scenario in the settings. To start the import process, select **Support Package • Import queue**. This command can also be used to set up an aborted process. The dialog box displayed presents several startup options for selection. For example, you can import the queue either in dialog mode or in the background and specify this decision for specific phases of the process. Processing is continued depending on the import mode (conventional or downtime-minimized):

- In conventional mode (without changing the standard options), the process is carried out in the dialog, and the status bar displays current information on the progress and the import phases. In this variant, the system should not be in productive operation. If you selected a start time or **continue manually**' in the start options for the Import 2 module, you can continue productive operation until Import 2 is started.
- The interruption of productive operation is prompted by the SPAM in downtime-minimized mode (provided you accepted the standard options without changing them). In the Import 1 step, the development environment is locked to prevent an inconsistency in the system caused by object changes. Before Import 2 is started, a dialog box indicates that productive operation should be suspended. The objects imported as inactive are enabled after productive operation has been suspended and the message has been confirmed.

If you have made changes to SAP objects, SPAM will prompt you to run a modification adjustment. Because the compiled code of the newly imported objects has been invalidated, a compiling message is displayed at first call. You can generate the newly imported objects later in one go via the SGEN transaction. Another option is to set **ABAP/Screen Generation** in the SPAM options for importing the queue.

Here, we would like to give you some more information on the downtime-minimized mode. As described above, the objects are imported as inactive into the system. Only during the Import 2 phase, new objects are enabled. This means the objects imported as inactive already reside in the Oracle database and consume more space. Thus, you exchange time for resources. You should ensure that sufficient storage space is available in the Oracle database and that imports of transport jobs don't take place simultaneously.

SAP provides add-ons as a supplement to the SAP system. These can be industry solutions, plug-ins, or customer-specific development projects. The installation and the update are performed via the Add-On Installation Tool. This tool is called in Client 000 via the transaction code SAINT by an authorized user. However, this user may not be SAP*. Updates of SAINT are delivered together with SPAM in the SPAM/SAINT support packages. You should always import the latest version before you perform the installation or the upgrade of an add-on. Figure 7.13 shows the initial screen of SAINT.

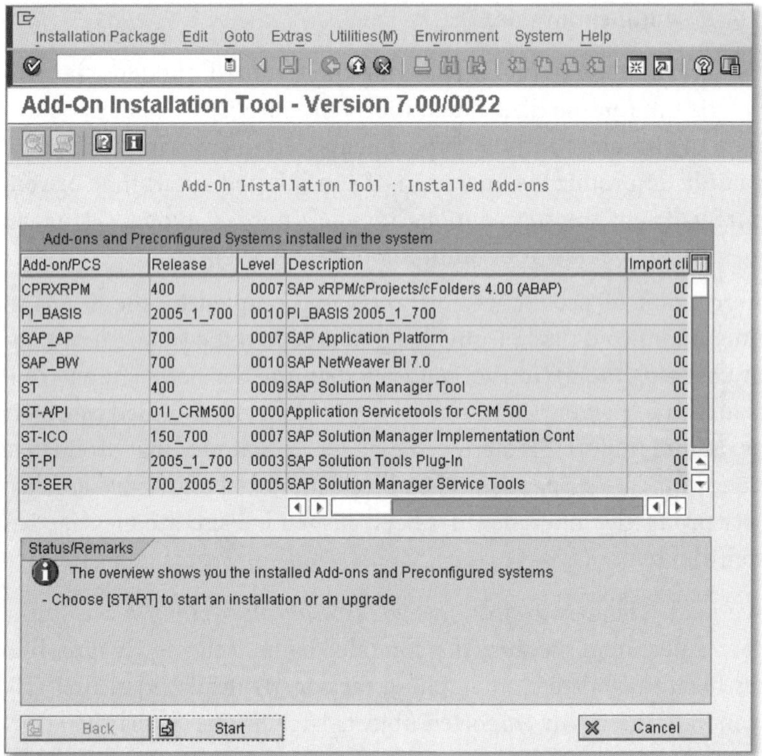

Figure 7.13 Add-On Installation Tool SAINT

It functions in a similar way to SPAM. Packages can be loaded via the application server or the frontend. The import conditions are checked before installation to ensure that only add-ons are installed that fit the existing SAP system and the imported support packages. If a specific support package is missing from the system to install the add-on and if it is known to the system, it is automatically added to the queue of objects to be imported.

For SAINT, you can also select the **Downtime-minimized** import mode to reduce system downtime. Via the start options, it is possible to change the import process. The functionality and scope of the SAINT transaction strongly resemble those of SPAM. If you understand the basic functions of one program, you can apply them in the other program.

Small ABAP program fixes or updates from SAP Notes can be implemented via the *Note Assistant*. The Note Assistant is called via the SNOTE transaction. It considerably simplifies the usage of correction instructions in the SAP Notes. The Note Assistant is available from release 4.5A with the corresponding support package version. For all other releases or with a lower support package version, the corrections indicated in the notes had to be implemented manually in the system. Apart from the high effort, this was a significant error source. Today, the notes can be loaded both from the SAP Service Marketplace and via the SAPNet to the SAP system and implemented automatically.

The SAP Notes describe how to correct known errors in SAP systems. They always contain a description of the symptoms, the error source, and the release and support package versions in which the error occurs. Depending on the type of error, you will find workarounds, correction instructions (corrections to repository objects), and references to other support packages. The Note Assistant can only process the correction instructions. It checks the validity of the instruction and implements it if the system state is within the specified validity area. It cannot perform workarounds, the implementation of support packages, and various pre- and postprocessing steps on the system. It is therefore very important that you read the notes thoroughly and carefully. In some cases, they may require specific prerequisites, interdependencies, and references to postprocessing steps that must be considered during implementation.

Working with the Note Assistant requires some basic settings. At first, you must control and maybe set the system change option via Transaction SE03. You must perform the following actions:

1. Set the software components in which notes are to be implemented to **Modifiable** or **Restrictedly Modifiability**.
2. Finally, you must set the general SAP namespace to **Modifiable**.

Depending on your preferred way of loading the SAP Notes into your system, you must set up an RFC connection[5]. You can download notes directly from the SAPNet, or you can provide notes you previously loaded from the SAP Service Marketplace in the Note Assistant. We recommend that you download notes from the SAPNet because you can directly load the notes to the system and update them in the application. Additionally, dependent notes are loaded automatically.

The notes are displayed in the Note Assistant as PDF documents. Therefore, you must install Adobe Reader Version 7.0.1 or higher on your local machine.

The Note Assistant is an extremely helpful tool that supports you with implementing the correction instructions. Although this implementation is performed automatically, it is important for the user to read the describing texts in the SAP Notes very carefully. Often, pre- and postprocessing needs to be done for the fix to function correctly.

Last, we will deal with the import of support packages into the system landscape (see Figure 7.14). As illustrated in Chapter 6, *SAP Change and Transport Management*, a development, a quality assurance, and a production system (DEV system, QAS system, PRD system) are operated in a three-system landscape.

Support packages and kernel patches are imported gradually in the system landscape, starting with the development system. At first, if necessary, the kernel replacement is carried out. Then, the SPAM imports the support packages into the system. The modification adjustment takes place during the SPAM session via SPDD and SPAU. This modification adjustment needs to be performed only once; you can then import modification adjustment transports into the other systems of the system landscape. For this purpose, you must record the modifications. More detailed information on this topic can be found in the SAP help under **Software Maintenance**.

5 To maintain the RFC connection, call Transaction OSS1. By default, a connection to the SAPNet is created here. The name of this connection is SAPOSS.

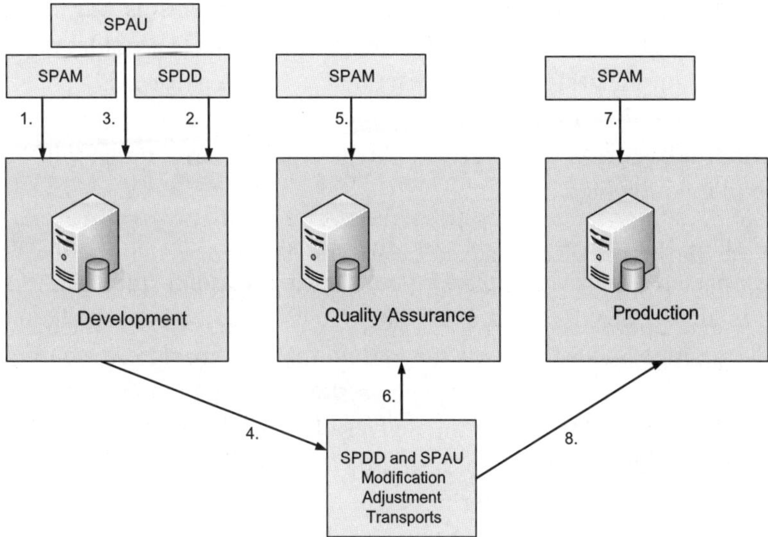

Figure 7.14 Support Packages in a Three-System Landscape

In the second step, the kernel patches and the support packages queue are imported in the quality assurance system. At the same time, you integrate the modification adjustment transports in the queue. In this way, you can avoid actions for manual adjustment. After the import has been completed, you can start with the test in the quality assurance system. If required, you might then be able to make first corrections to Customizing and Repository in the development system. These can then be imported into the QAS system and tested once more. If the support package version is released together with the changes, they can be imported along with the kernel patches into the production system.

When importing support packages via the SPAM, JSPM, and SAINT tools, you always receive SAP Notes that provide the latest information on known problems and conflicts. Read these carefully and follow the instructions and suggestions described in them before you continue importing the updates. Otherwise, your system may not be usable or data may be lost. Before updating the system, you should always check whether a usable data backup is available.

7.2.3 Maintaining the Oracle Database

In addition to maintaining the SAP systems, which was described in the previous section, another important task of the administrator is to maintain the Oracle database by installing patches.

Oracle provides corrections that eliminate specific problems as bug fixes, which are referred to as *interim patches* as of Oracle 9i. Oracle provides these interim patches on the basis of the patchset that's used. A *patchset* is a collection of corrections that are made available as self-contained bundles. If an interim patch is available for a current patchset, the interim patch will be contained in the next higher patchset.

When installing the Oracle database and the SAP system, you should install the highest patchset that's available for your Oracle release. In addition, it is advisable to always use the most up-to-date patchset. However, you should not install interim patches if you are not certain that it is absolutely required because you cannot always exclude negative side effects. The patchsets and interim patches offered by SAP on the delivery DVDs, sapservX[6], and in the SAP Service Marketplace have been tested by SAP. However, note that SAP offers only a subset of Oracle interim patches, namely, only those that are relevant for SAP installations. SAP checks all patches provided for download with regard to whether they affect other patches. If so, a *merge patch* is requested, which combines multiple patches. SAP does not check patches that are made available via Oracle Metalink. If you install this type of patch, it may deinstall other patches.

In general, not all interim patches are relevant for all SAP installations. This can differ from installation to installation. Consequently, you don't need to install all available patches in each database. We recommend the following procedure:

1. Install the currently valid patchset.
2. Check whether other interim patches are provided for download.
3. Analyze whether these are relevant for your system (SAP Notes).
4. If necessary, install these interim patches.

As of Patchset 8.1.7.3 for Oracle Release 8, SAP provides all patchsets and interim patches only in the SAP Service Marketplace. Older versions can only be downloaded from the sapservX servers. The URL, *http://service.sap.com/swcenter-3pmain*, provides access to the page that contains patches and support tools for the database systems of different vendors. There, you can navigate through a tree structure to the required releases, patchsets, and operating systems of your Oracle database and download the relevant files.

6 FTP servers provided by SAP from which you can download patches. The very latest versions are exclusively provided via the SAP Service Marketplace.

To install a patchset in the Oracle system, the main release must be installed. For an Oracle 10g database in Release 10.2.0, you can use all patchsets that are numbered as 10.2.0.x. Consequently, the current status of the patchset is always reflected by the fourth digit of the release number. If the release number is 10.2.0.2, it means Patchset 2 for Oracle 10.2.0 was installed. Patchsets are not based on each other. If Patchset 9.2.0.1 is installed in your Oracle 9i database and you want to update to 9.2.0.5, you don't need to install Patchsets 9.2.0.2, 9.2.0.3, and 9.2.0.4. A patchset always contains all patchsets whose numbers are lower. Furthermore, the software of the main release must be contained in the Oracle inventory (oraInventory), and the `ORACLE_HOME` variable,[7] in which the main release was originally installed, must be unchanged. The *installActions.log* file (located in */oracle/oraInventory/logs*) contains a list of all products of the Oracle inventory. Based on that list, you can check the prerequisites (main release) for the installation.

Patchsets are installed using the *Oracle Universal Installer*, which is also used to install the Oracle database itself (see Figure 7.15). The following SAP Notes contain information about which patchsets for the individual Oracle releases and operating systems have been released by SAP and what you need to know regarding their installation:

- SAP Note 362060: *current patchset for Oracle 8.1.7*
- SAP Note 539921: *current patchset for Oracle 9.2.0*
- SAP Note 871735: *current patchset for Oracle 10.2.0*

These SAP Notes are continuously updated. You should take the following tips into account when installing patchsets:

- When installing a patchset, you should always follow the instructions provided in the patchset documentation. This section of the book and SAP Notes about the installation process, which you may find, do not replace the documentation that comes with the patchset.
- Carefully read the SAP Notes for the latest patchset and required patches. Often it is not enough to just install the patchset, and you must also install various interim patches.

7 `ORACLE_HOME` is a defined variable that points to the */oracle/<DB-SID>/<Oracle release>* directory.

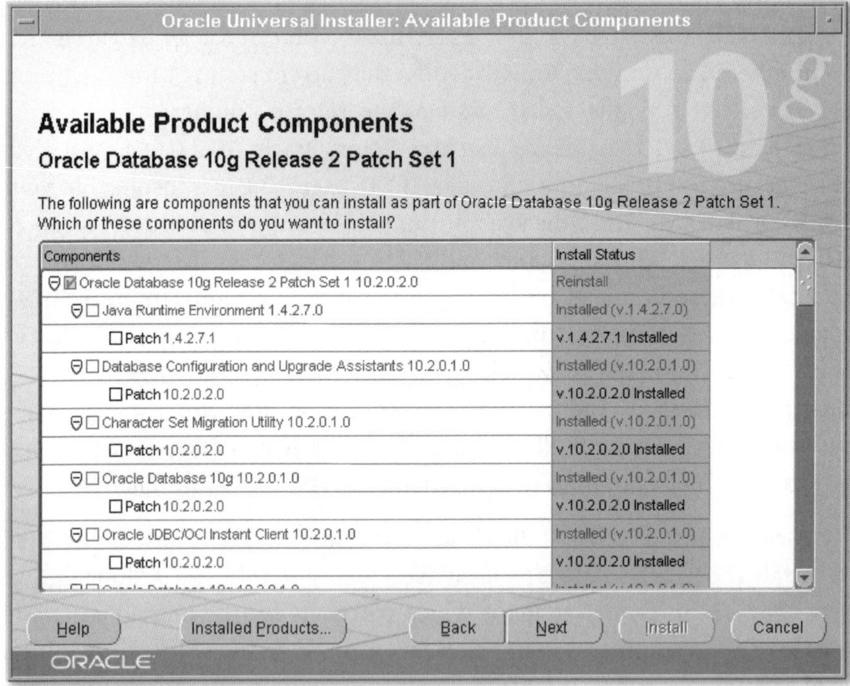

Figure 7.15 Oracle Universal Installer for Installing Patchsets

Let us now take a look at the main steps involved in installing a patchset in Oracle 10g:

1. **Preparing the installation**
   The preparatory steps are described in the documentation for the patchset. These include:
   - Identifying the Oracle database installation as the patchset to be installed is based on a database and does not represent a complete software distribution
   - Checking the notes regarding activities that must be carried out after the installation
   - Downloading and decompressing the software
   - Checking and setting the `ORACLE_HOME` and `ORACLE_SID` variables
   - Shutting down the database instance properly and stopping all relevant processes
   - Backing up the entire database

2. **Installing the patchset**
   You must install the patchset using the aforementioned programs as a ora<db-sid> *user*. For this purpose, you must set the display variable in a UNIX environment to display the graphical user interface and to be able to follow the instructions that display in the dialog that appears. Additional information can be found in the patchset documentation and the SAP Notes.

3. **Post installation**
   The instructions regarding the post installation are also contained in the patchset documentation. In this step, it is important that the SQL scripts, `catpatch.sql` (Release 10.1.0) or `catupgrd.sql` (Release 10.2.0), are executed. However, you may only execute these scripts if a database already exists for the `ORACLE_HOME` in which the patchset is installed. Only in this case is the installation of the patchset or an adaptation of the Oracle Dictionary to the new software version required. Be sure to use the scripts for the right Oracle release, as otherwise you may lose data. Do not run the scripts when reinstalling the database or during an upgrade. In that case, the scripts are called in the responsible process (check the relevant documentation for possible changes of this statement).

4. **Installing interim patches**
   Other interim patches must be installed using the OPatch program once you have completed the patchset installation and post installation processes. The following SAP Notes contain a list of interim patches to be installed at that point:

   - SAP Note 938986: *Oracle database 9.2: patches for 9.2.0*
   - SAP Note 871096: *Oracle database 10g: patchsets/patches for 10.2.0*

The interim patches must be installed and deinstalled using the OPatch tool, which has been available since Oracle Release 9i. In Release 9i, you must install it separately, whereas since Release 10g, it is part of the delivery. You can find OPatch for 10g in the following directory: */oracle/<DB-SID>/<Oracle release>/OPatch*. The OPatch versions for Oracle 9.2 and 10.1 were developed in Perl, whereas a completely new version was created in Java for Oracle Release 10.2. The reason for the decision to use Java was that the OPatch and runInstaller can be integrated more easily if both are based on Java.

In the following text, we will primarily refer to Oracle 10g. You can find information on installing OPatch for Oracle Release 9i and the use of interim patches in SAP Note 306408.

The newest OPatch versions are usually imported automatically into the system by means of a patchset. In general, it is not necessary to update OPatch using separate patches. However, should this become necessary, you can download an up-to-date version from the SAP Service Marketplace via the following URL: *http://service.sap.com/swcenter-3pmain*. Then, you must rename the directory of the previous OPatch version and extract the new version to `ORACLE_HOME`. After that, you can use the new version right away. You can find comprehensive documentation on OPatch on the Oracle web site. Additional information (FAQs and user manuals) is available in the following directory: */oracle/<DB-SID><Oracle release>/OPatch/docs*.

To be able to install patches, you must shut down the Oracle database and stop all processes of the instance. Follow the instructions in the documentation of the individual patches. The documentation is provided as a README.txt file along with the patches. This file contains information about whether you need to perform additional steps prior to or after the patch installation, and if so, which ones. You can install multiple interim patches one after the other without having to restart the database after each installation. The only exceptions to this rule are fixes that must be installed by means of a different procedure. The current status of the installed software is stored in the Oracle inventory (oraInventory). When you install patches, the status is updated and displayed by both OPatch and runInstaller. You can request the status of a patch using the `opatch lsinventory` command and archive it in a log file.

If you have installed multiple interim patches in the Oracle system and want to install a new patchset, you don't need to deinstall the patches. You can start installing the patchset right away, but make sure you follow the instructions in the associated documentation.

For installations on Windows, you should know that collective patches are available here for reasons related to the software technology. These collective patches contain several individual interim patches. Some of these collective patches are referred to as *critical patch updates*. With regard to performing the installation, there's no difference between a normal collective patch and a critical patch update.

Before you begin installing an interim patch, you must check for the following requirements:

- Create a backup copy of your database software. Check whether you have an up-to-date backup copy of your database files.

- Is the environment variable, `$ORACLE_HOME` (UNIX), or `%ORACLE_HOME%` (Windows), correct?
- Check the basic functions of OPatch using the following commands:
  - To display the Opatch version: `opatch version`
  - To display the installed patches: `opatch lsinventory`
  - To display all OPatch command options: `opatch -help`
- Finally, you must analyze the log files of OPatch. You can find these files in the following directory: *$ORACLE_HOME/cfgtoollogs/opatch*.

If the requirements are met, you can install the patches. To do that, you must log in to the operating system using the same user as the one you used to install the Oracle software.

- Create a separate base OPatch directory, <opatch_base_dir>, for each Oracle patchset. This enables you to easily find all patches that you install for a specific patchset. For Release 10.2.0.2, you could create such a directory using the

  ```
  mkdir /oracle/<DBSID>/opatch_base_dir_10202
  ```

  command.
- Then, copy and extract the patches to be installed to the base directory. During the extraction process, each patch is placed in a separate patch directory with a unique patch ID. This ID (5959612 in the example below) is usually identical to the patch number and hence to the number that's contained in the name of the patch file.

  ```
  cp p5959612_10202_HPUX-IA64.zip /oracle/<DBSID>/opatch_base_dir_10202
  cd /oracle/<DBSID>/opatch_base_dir_10202
  unzip p5959612_10202_HPUX-IA64.zip
  ```

- Next, you must install the patch. To do that, you must first shut down the database and stop all processes of this instance. Don't forget to stop the Listener. You now have two options regarding the call. The first option specifies the patch directory:

  ```
  $ORACLE_HOME/OPatch/opatch apply <patch_dir> [-verbose]
  ```

  The second option consists of a direct call from within the patch directory:

  ```
  cd <patch_dir>
  $ORACLE_HOME/OPatch/opatch apply [-verbose]
  ```

Here, the <patch_dir> directory stands for the path to the patch, that is, the OPatch base directory and the directory to the patch itself.

- Finally, you can view the installed patches using the `opatch lsinventory` command. Then restart the database and make a backup copy of it (both software and data).

If you need to install multiple patches, you can use the MOPatch tool. MOPatch stands for *Multiple Oracle Patch Tools* and is currently only available for Release 10.2 and UNIX platforms. This tool automates the process of extracting and installing the patches described above. You must install MOPatch as an addition to each database. If you want to use it, you should be aware of the following two limitations: You can use MOPatch only for the initial database installation in which no patches have been installed. In addition, you can use the tool to install patches but not to deinstall them. For further information, refer to SAP Note 1027012.

7.2.4 Maintaining the Operating System

In this section, we want to draw your attention to the maintenance of the operating system and give you some tips for operating system platforms. Maintaining the operating system is particularly important for security, performance, and stability of the SAP system and the Oracle database.

Regarding the maintenance of the operating system, you can differentiate between critical and general updates. Updates exchange, on the one hand, operating system-based software, such as kernels and libraries, and, on the other hand, applications that are supplied with the operating system. The manufacturer (or for Linux, the community) always provides patches for the operating system. For Linux, Novell and Red Hat, which are SAP-certified distributors, offer customized patch bundles that can be imported to a server. It is important that the operating system is always provided with the updates (such as error corrections, performance improvements, and functional extensions) of the critical area, particularly when patches involve security. They close known gaps and ensure that potential attackers cannot access the system. In addition to security gaps, such critical patches can also avoid data losses, for instance, if specific drivers are installed that are responsible for the communication based on the hardware but contain errors. However, now we refer to completely different software: the firmware in the individual hardware components. Its complexity has increased over the past years, and it is also provided with updates that must be included in the system maintenance.

SAP certifies operating systems for certain SAP solutions and then releases them for live operation. If you run your landscape on such a released operating system, you can be sure that SAP supports this system. When importing corrections to the operating system, you should always consider the compatibility of the new components. This is especially important for the operating system kernel and operating system-based libraries, especially for the Linux platform.

In Linux systems, in particular, you must determine which kernel and which glibc library are released by SAP. You can find this information in various notes in the SAP Service Marketplace with references to the individual patch levels. The most important notes are listed here:

- SAP Note 171356: *SAP Software on Linux: Essential Information*
- SAP Note 722273: *Red Hat Enterprise Linux 3 and 4: installation and upgrades*
- SAP Note 797084: *SUSE LINUX Enterprise Server 9: Installation Notes*
- SAP Note 816097: *Availability of SAP on Linux for x86_64 platforms*
- SAP Note 936887: *End of maintenance for Linux distributions*

SAP has not explicitly released single patches for other proprietary operating systems, such as AIX, HP-UX, SOLARIS, or Windows, but that does not mean that they can be imported arbitrarily. For this purpose, you should also search for certain remarks and documents for individual operating systems. Often, the manufacturers provide bundles that are not SAP-specific. Sometimes, patches are supplied that are specially tailored to SAP applications. Below, we list some notes on several operating systems that are continuously updated and provide information on minimum patch levels:

- SAP Note 30478: *Windows Service Packs*
- SAP Note 68440: *AS/400: AS/400: How do I upgrade to a higher OS/400 release?*
- SAP Note 360438: *SAP-relevant patches for Solaris 8 on SPARC*
- SAP Note 550585: *SAP-relevant patches for Solaris 9 on SPARC*
- SAP Note 816239: *General information about Solaris patches*
- SAP Note 832871: *SAP-relevant patches for Solaris 10 on SPARC*
- SAP Note 837670: *Minimum OS patch recommendations for HP-UX*
- SAP Note 908334: *SAP-relevant patches for Solaris 10 on x64*

Often, the reverse situation also occurs. Due to settings or certain patch levels, an error occurred in the SAP application or Oracle database. In this case, the SAP Service Marketplace also provides help and notes regarding which patch must be imported or exactly which setting must be configured to eliminate the error. If you can find no information, you must contact SAP Support.

In addition to the error that occurred, importing a new SAP kernel, support package, or Oracle patch set or interim patch can require that you update the operating system and adjust specific parameters. For these cases, various SAP Notes and documentations of the individual Oracle patches also provide help.

For example, a good point of entry is the Product Availability Matrix, which you can access via *http://service.sap.com/pam*. Each SAP solution contains a table with operating systems and databases that are certified and released by SAP for live operation. For each release of platform combinations, you can call information that is linked with a note and provides additional information on specific minimum requirements and maximum patch levels.

The update of the operating system for upgrades is particularly important. Here, the upgrade guides provide very detailed documentation with references to the most up-to-date notes.

7.3 Upgrades

All software products are subject to continuous development. This also applies to SAP products. In addition to continuous developments that are provided by support packages, significant version upgrades lead to new releases. Of course, the software cannot be reinstalled in a production environment. Instead, ways must be found for a transition that enables you to maintain all enterprise data. For this purpose, upgrade paths in an SAP environment allow for a change from a source release status to a current target release. The following sections provide an overview of the strategies in question, the tools used, and the processes during the upgrade.

7.3.1 SAP Upgrade

Upgrade means that your existing SAP system is upgraded to a new release. The SAP upgrade takes into account the existing customer data and dependencies to connected systems (particularly to integrated Java systems) or the add-ons and plug-ins used. Usually, an upgrade of the SAP system requires an update of the operating system and the Oracle release. An update may involve the import of specific patch levels or the upgrade of the Oracle software and the operating system. Section 7.3.2, *Oracle Upgrade*, describes the aspects of Oracle upgrades in greater detail. First, we want to explain the upgrade processes of SAP systems. For this purpose, the so-called *system switch upgrades* (see Section 7.3.1.3, *Phases and Processes*) are used. The following data is taken into account during the upgrade process:

- **Customer data**
  Customer data includes all enterprise data that is stored while working with the system. During the upgrade process, the data itself is not changed, but the structures of the tables that are used can be changed. For this purpose, the table structure is converted without changing the existing dataset; for instance, columns are added.
- **Control data and customizing**
  This data is a combination of SAP default data and customer data. During the upgrade process, the new SAP data is mixed with the existing customer data. In this way, customizing data for new functions can be included, for example.
- **Language data**
  As the name suggests, language data is all language-specific data of an SAP system. In the scope of the upgrade process, the language information is adjusted and updated to the new functions and developments. The standard languages, English and German, are always updated. All other languages must be additionally considered, which increases the upgrade runtime. Keep this in mind when planning your upgrade.
- **SAP repository and customer repository**
  The SAP repository contains all central objects of an SAP system. They are stored in several tables. For example, the objects are ABAP dictionary objects, ABAP source codes, GUI definitions, documentations, or table descriptions.

  Customer repository includes modifications and customer developments that are integrated in the SAP repository. During the upgrade process, the entire repository is exchanged. It is particularly important to maintain the customer developments and modifications of the existing system to allow a continuous functioning of customer applications. Therefore, all objects of the customer repository are copied to the new repository before they are exchanged. If conflicts arise, because modifications must be changed due to the upgrade, they are displayed during the process and can be solved by the developer. If possible, you should always try to reset modifications and return to the default settings.

- **SAP kernel**
  The kernel contains all kernel programs that are stored as files in the file system. As the customer cannot modify these files, they are simply exchanged in the file system.

As you can see from the objects that are affected by the upgrade process, nearly all parts of the system are subject to changes. Many of these changes can be made while the system is used in production, but for some modifications, the system must be shut down, which causes a nonavailability of the system. Among other things, the system needs to be shut down if you change transaction processes or data structures, which would cause data inconsistencies or data losses in live operation, or when you exchange the kernel.

To keep the necessary downtime as short as possible, SAP provides the upgrade strategy *downtime minimized*, that will be described in Section 7.3.1.1, *Upgrade Strategies*, in greater detail. Furthermore, careful planning of the upgrade prevents unnecessary offline times of the system. This includes, for example, adjusting the modifications during the live usage of the system, namely, in the PREPARE phase (see Section 7.3.1.3, *Phases and Processes*).

Complete and, above all, feasible planning before the actual upgrade process starts contributes to success. Take your time and plan to test the upgrade to be able to estimate the approximate runtime and the downtime period. It is particularly difficult to estimate the runtime of the technical upgrade, because this is influenced by numerous aspects. It starts with the hardware used (CPUs, RAM, speed of the disk subsystems) and continues in the SAP system with the numerous customer developments and modifications as well as the number of the necessary support packages in order to be consistent with the source release. Additionally, you must consider several direct and external dependencies when planning the general time frame of the upgrade. This planning does not directly affect the runtime of the actual upgrade process.

The release of the SAP system and thus the upgrade immediately affect the ITS server or SAP GUI. ITS servers must either be updated, too, or must even be replaced by the integrated ITS or Java component. Therefore, you should also consider the time for the installation of the new components or for the update process of the existing ITS server. Even simple things, such as a possibly necessary update of the SAP GUI of all users, should be considered in the upgrade process. Because all SAP GUI versions are downward compatible, you can and should run the update process at a very early stage.

You should also familiarize yourself with the external dependencies of the upgrade in advance. This includes analyzing the operating system required, the necessary Oracle version, and the compatibility of other connected systems, such as the archiving system or CAD interfaces. If the components mentioned must be updated or upgraded, consider whether you can perform these processes before the actual upgrade. This should be done as sequentially as possible to allow you to identify which action has caused an error. The number of error sources increases rapidly if problems occur when you update operating system, database, and SAP system in one step. Hence, a time-consuming analysis is usually needed to find the cause of the error.

During an upgrade of a multisystem landscape that consists of development, testing, and live system, the planning complexity increases considerably. In this case, comprehensive planning of the upgrade is inevitable for the *entire* landscape. Figure 7.16 illustrates a three-system landscape and a possible upgrade process based on the transport path. This process is also referred to as a *pipeline upgrade*.

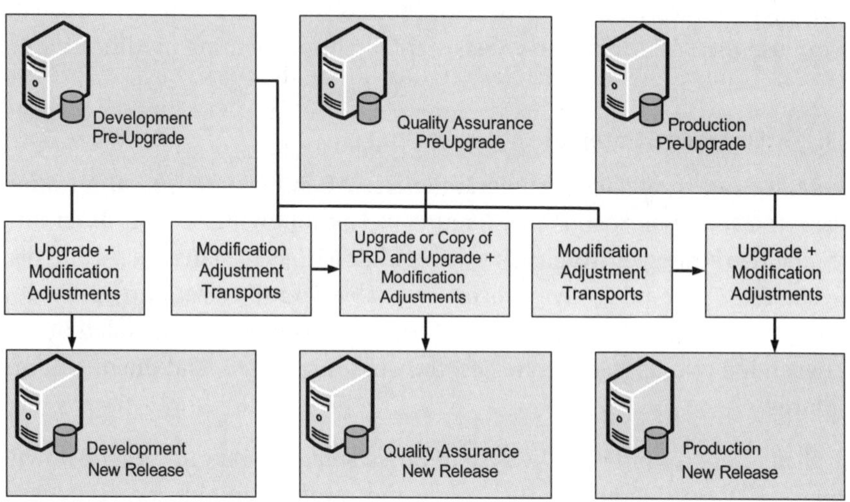

Figure 7.16 Upgrade of a Three-System Landscape

The upgrade of a landscape starts with upgrading the development system. During this upgrade, all modifications and developments are adjusted to the new release and stored in transports. These transports are imported during the upgrade of quality assurance and live system to reduce the time required for repeated adjustments.

Only developers, not system administrators or technical consultants, are supposed to adjust the modifications and customer developments. The users (at least some "test persons") should also be involved in the upgrade process to test the customized objects for their correct functionality. This example demonstrates that an upgrade cannot be implemented by one or two people. Instead, a team of people from various areas is needed to complete an upgrade project successfully.

Finally, here are some useful tips for simplifying the upgrade process:

- The upgrade runtime does not necessarily depend on the size of the database, but on the number of SAP objects that are supposed to be changed.
- If possible, use the downtime minimized upgrade strategy.
- To obtain a realistic estimation of the upgrade time and runtime, run a test upgrade with a similar configuration (for instance, a copy of the live system).
- Start as early as possible with updating the SAP GUI of all users.
- Try to set all modifications from source release to SAP standard. The more detailed the modifications of your system that are documented, the more easily upgrades will be performed. From SAP Release 4.5B onward, you can use the SAP Modification Assistant for implementing modifications.

7.3.1.1 Upgrade Strategies

There are two strategies for upgrading an SAP system: *the downtime minimized* and the *resource minimized* strategy. The following section differentiates the two strategies from each other and describes the advantages and disadvantages of the respective process to enable you to select one option for your upgrade process. Figure 7.17 shows a diagram of the relationship between the two upgrade strategies, the phases involved, and the downtime required.

All shaded phases indicate the system downtime. As you can see, the downtime begins considerably earlier when the resource minimized strategy is used. In comparison, when you use the downtime minimized strategy, *the system can still be used in the phases* SPDD, distribution, and activation, as well as delta import. However, with this strategy, the hardware resources, particularly RAM and CPU, are used considerably more for parallel operation of the shadow system, which is described in Section 7.3.1.3.

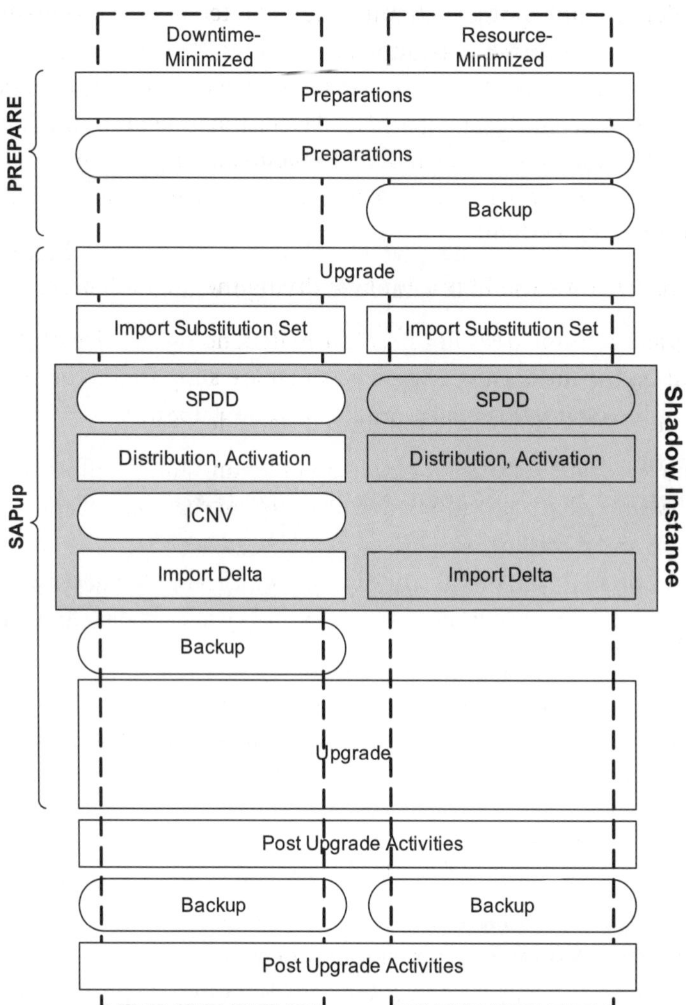

Figure 7.17 Upgrade Strategies and Phases

Whether the backup and import of substitution set phases can be performed online or offline depends on the archiving and backup strategy that you want to use during the upgrade. During the upgrade process, you can deactivate the archiving of the Oracle database to improve the upgrade performance and to limit the number of archive logs. As soon as the archiving is deactivated, you are not allowed to perform any live work in the system because data may be lost if an error occurs. Thus, the downtime increases. Moreover, after the archiver has been deactivated, you should run an offline backup to be able to restart the upgrade at the appropriate stage if an error occurs. For this purpose, additional memory space may be required.

The downtime minimized strategy tries to minimize the downtime required during the upgrade as much as possible. For this purpose, the shadow system is activated while the live system is still active. As already mentioned, this requires additional hardware capacities. This parallel operation of old and new releases enables you to perform some steps of the upgrade without affecting the live operation.

To do this, the following phases, which are partly very comprehensive and require much runtime (up to several hours), are executed while the live system is still running in the shadow system.

- **Import of substitution set**
  Import of the new release data into the shadow tables.
- **Modification adjustment**
  Adjustments of all modifications for the target release.
- **Activation and distribution**
  Activation of all ABAP dictionary objects, which are changed by support packages, and activation of modifications and customer developments.
- **ICNV – Incremental Table Conversion**
  Copying and converting tables from the source release to the target release. During this process, modifications and customer developments are maintained. With a conversion in advance, the downtime can be further reduced.

SAP recommends the *downtime minimized* strategy.

In contrast to the downtime minimized strategy, you don't need additional capacities for the shadow system if you use the resource minimized strategy. The shadow system is only started when the live system is stopped and then performs the conversions to the target release. This strategy is particularly appropriate if you have only few hardware capacities.

Table 7.2 summarizes the advantages and disadvantages of both strategies. Which of the mentioned strategies you use depends on two factors: permissible downtime and available hardware capacities. However, consider the restrictions and requirements of the strategy when planning the upgrade, for example, to be able to upgrade the server used in time or to provide sufficient memory capacities.

Strategy	Advantages	Disadvantages
Downtime minimized	▸ Reduced offline time ▸ Average memory consumption required to recover the database if errors occur (backup volume)	▸ Higher requirements for the system resources during parallel operation of live and shadow system ▸ Offline backup required if archiving was deactivated during the upgrade process
Resource-minimized	▸ No additional resources required during the upgrade process ▸ No additional memory space required to recover the database	▸ Long offline time ▸ Offline backup required after the upgrade has been completed

Table 7.2 Advantages and Disadvantages of the Upgrade Strategies

7.3.1.2 Upgrade Tools

SAP provides specific tools for upgrades. The following section provides a brief overview of these tools and their interactions. Depending on the characteristics of the source system, different tools are used. The programs PREPARE and SAPup are used for ABAP systems. For upgrades of Java instances, the counterparts JPREPARE and SAPJup are used. If you have installed a double-stack installation with both ABAP stack and Java stack the two tools are controlled centrally to enable a synchronous update of both system parts.

ABAP Tools

Several tools are used for upgrading an ABAP system. Figure 7.18 shows an overview of all used programs, whose importance and tasks are described in this section. However, `tp` and `R3load` are not mentioned, because they are used by SAPup in the background. Chapter 6 describes `tp` in detail.

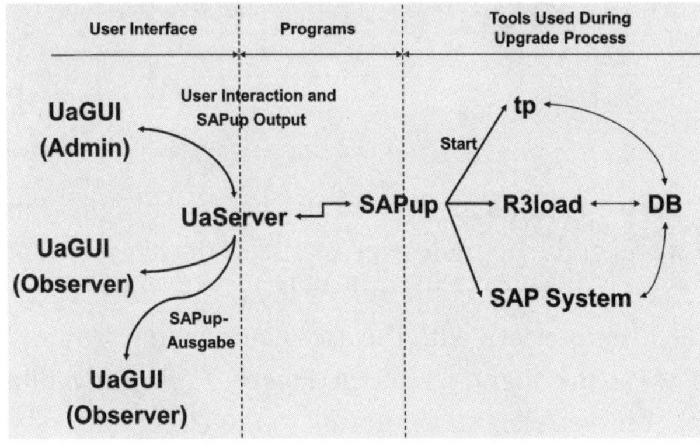

Figure 7.18 Relationship between the Upgrade Tools

The *Upgrade Assistant* is the user interface for the entire upgrade. For the command line, it is provided as a scroll variant, and as a Java-based version with a web user interface. Figure 7.19 illustrates the components of the graphical variant. This variant consists of the *Upgrade Assistant Server* (UaServer) that is started on the host of the central instance that should be upgraded. You can then start the *Upgrade Assistant GUI* (UaGUI) via the web browser and connect to the UaServer. For this purpose, call the following URL in the browser: *http://<Upgrade-Server-Name>:4239*. Figure 7.19 shows the HTML user interface that is displayed in the background and provides several options as a menu. Besides starting the UaGUI, you also have access to an overview of the upgrade phases and to upgrade guides.

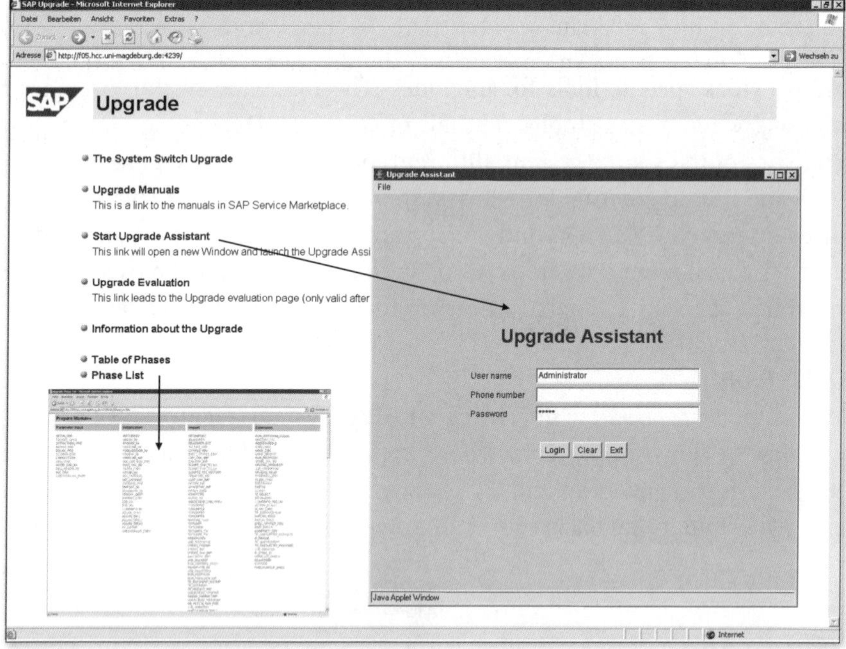

Figure 7.19 Upgrade Assistant

You can call the UaGUI in two operation modes: as the administrator that can perform activities in the scope of the upgrade process and as the *observer* that can observe the upgrade progress but has no influence on the process. For this purpose, log on to the user interface with the user name "administrator" or "observer." You can view the login screen in Figure 7.19. Only one administrator but several observers can be connected to the UaServer.

You can control the entire upgrade with the Upgrade Assistant. If you are logged on as the administrator, you can select from the menu illustrated in Figure 7.20. **Start PREPARE** and **Start Upgrade are** the two most important options. With these two menu options, you start the tools in the background. PREPARE runs checks and analyses that are described in Section 7.3.1.3. PREPARE can be executed while the SAP system is in production. Many upgrade requirements are checked, data is collected, and data and programs that are used throughout the upgrade process are copied to the upgrade directory. After PREPARE has been completed successfully, you can start with the actual upgrade using SAPup. To do so, select **Start Upgrade in the menu.**

SAPup is the central tool for the coordination of all upgrade processes. Internally, SAPup uses the transport tools, `tp`, `R3trans`, and `R3load`, to perform its tasks. *Before* starting an upgrade you should always check the SAPup version. If the SAP Service Marketplace provides a more up-to-date version, you should use it. During the upgrade, exchange SAPup only upon consultation with SAP.

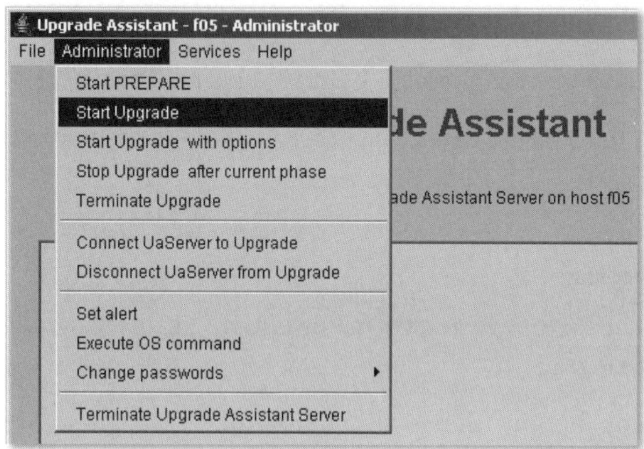

Figure 7.20 Upgrade Assistant Menu

Java Tools

For upgrading Java systems, SAP provides the SAPJup program. It upgrades a self-contained Java system. Section 11.3.3.3, *SAPJup*, describes SAPJup in detail.

Now, we want to point out the special aspects when upgrading an ABAP system with integrated Java stack. Because it is indispensable for a secure system operation that ABAP stack and Java stack have corresponding release and support package versions, you cannot update both systems independently. Therefore, SAP developed mechanisms that enable you to upgrade both components synchronously. The upgrade process of a double-stack system works as follows:

1. Start the upgrade of the ABAP system via the Upgrade Assistant. During the upgrade, SAPup determines that a Java installation is present for the system and prompts you to start SAPJup. SAPup waits until SAPJup is at the desired phase to keep both upgrade processes synchronous. If you start SAPJup first, it also determines that a corresponding ABAP instance is present and prompts you to start SAPup.
2. You start the SAPJup or SAPup requested and thus initiate the upgrade of the respective instance. Both upgrade processes communicate with each other and keep the upgrades synchronous. The upgrade progress, the user management, profile changes, and starting and stopping of the instances are important aspects for the synchronization of upgrade processes. Three synchronization stages are defined. They are at the beginning of the downtime, before the profiles are updated, and at the end of the downtime. If one of the upgrades reaches a stage prior to the other process, it waits until the second upgrade also reaches this stage.
3. After both upgrades have been completed, both systems are consistent.

If you must reset one of the two upgrades, the other upgrade must be reset, too.

7.3.1.3 Phases and Processes

The administrator can choose between two menu options in the Upgrade Assistant: **PREPARE** and **Upgrade**.

With the **PREPARE** menu option, the requirements for the upgrade are checked, information is collected, and data and programs are copied to the upgrade directory. This data is essential throughout the upgrade. You must run the individual phases in PREPARE before you can start with the upgrade. Many phases in PREPARE are automatically processed; some require specifications. The more carefully you work in PREPARE, the fewer errors occur in the actual upgrade phase.

You can start PREPARE while your system is in live operation. This is useful, as you can perform the preparation phase independently from the actual upgrade and thus can specify required system adjustments in advance. Therefore, you should start PREPARE well ahead of your planned upgrade date, so that all information can be collected, and the adjustments can be made in time.

After the basic preparatory work, such as creating the upgrade directory and checking the free memory space in the database, has been completed, you can start the installation of the Upgrade Assistant using the Upgrade Master DVD for your specific SAP solution. You can download the Upgrade Master DVD, the actual Upgrade Export DVDs, and the language DVDs as well as the detailed and helpful upgrade guides in the SAP Service Marketplace under *http://service.sap.com/installations* and *http://service.sap.com/instguides*. After the installation has been completed successfully, start the Upgrade Assistant and log on as the administrator user. Now, start the preparatory work via **Start PREPARE**. PREPARE responds with a screen that displays the target release to which you are supposed to change.

PREPARE processes specific modules. Some modules are mandatory; others are optional. Via a selection screen, you can select which modules PREPARE should process, but the actual upgrade can only be started if all mandatory modules are processed successfully.

In the individual modules, you must provide specific information. Often, default values are displayed that you can confirm or change. However, you should always refer to the upgrade guide and the mentioned notes before you close an entry. Depending on the entries made, PREPARE now processes the module you selected. These include:

- Initialization
- Import
- Extension
- Integration
- Installation
- General checks
- Activation checks
- Necessary checks for conversion
- Optional checks for conversion (optional)
- Modification support (optional)
- Preprocessing (optional)

Nearly all phases that are processed in the individual modules write log files. You can determine the names of these files using the list of the phases. After all modules selected have been completed, you receive a summarizing log file that describes which modules have been completed successfully and where you must interfere. The name of the file is *CHECKS.log*.

For example, the *initialization* module can prompt you to exchange the SAP kernel because it is too old. Also, the import of support packages and add-ons may be required. For this purpose, it is important that you close PREPARE, import the packages mentioned, and start running the individual modules using PREPARE.

Figure 7.21 shows the results log of a PREPARE run as an example. You can see, on the one hand, that Tablespace PSAPM85 is much too small and, on the other hand, that a new Tablespace PSAPM85640 must be created for the 640 dictionary objects. As soon as these activities have been executed, the modules that have not been completed successfully must be started again. The adjustments and checks must be repeated until all modules have been processed successfully.

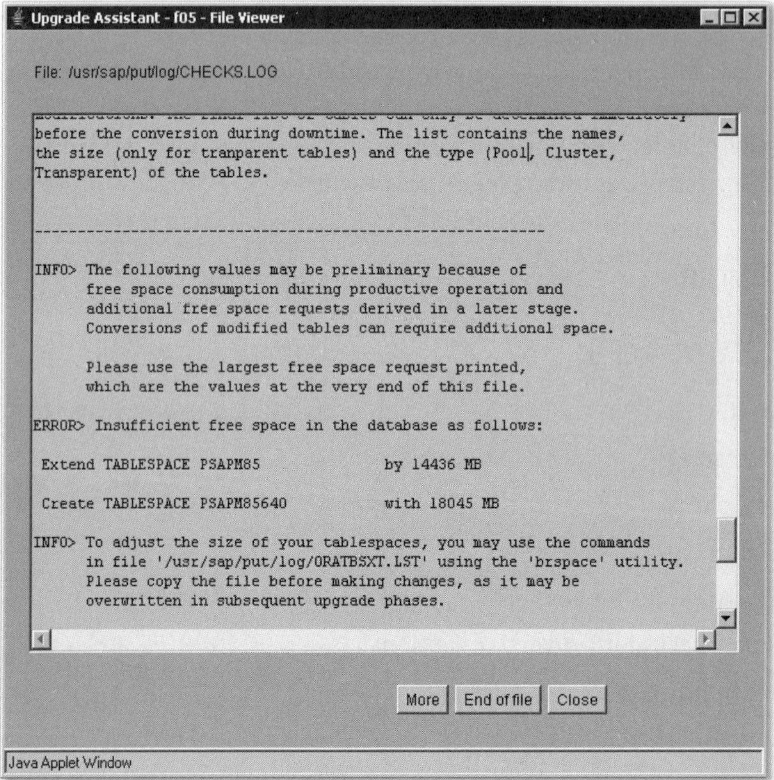

Figure 7.21 Results Log after a PREPARE Run

You can request the list of all phases via the already mentioned link of the PREPARE and upgrade phases in the modules when calling the Upgrade Assistant. This documentation is updated for every SAP solution that you want to upgrade to a new release.

After you have made all required entries in the modules, and all individual PREPARE phases have been processed successfully, you can start the actual upgrade.

The upgrade process is divided into different phases. The successful completion of a phase is required to successfully process the following upgrade phases. If errors occur in a phase, they must always be corrected, and the phase in which the error occurred must be repeated. If this phase is then completed successfully, you can continue the upgrade process. You start the upgrade via the Upgrade Assistant and the option **Start SAPup**. It is a basic requirement that all mandatory PREPARE modules were processed successfully and no data was deleted from the upgrade directory. If data is deleted from this directory, unpredictable inconsistencies may occur in your system.

The following groups of phases are processed during the upgrade:

- Import and modification transfer
- Shadow system installation
- Shadow system operations: SPDD and activation
- Shadow import
- Downtime phases I: switch tables and kernel
- Downtime phases II: conversion, main import, XPRAs
- Postprocessing

The documentation contains the description of the individual phases of these groups, the runtime of the phases as percentages of the total runtime, and the log files that are created. During the upgrade, you will be asked to store the data of the system, the Oracle database, and your upgrade directory. You should definitely store this data, because this enables you to reset your system to the status before the start of the upgrade if the upgrade fails, and you don't have to repeat PREPARE.

During the upgrade, a shadow instance is set up (see Figure 7.22). This shadow instance exists either as an SAP application server (in the form of the new kernel) or as shadow tables in your Oracle database. These tables are filled by the upgrade DVDs during the phases EU_IMPORT1 to EU_IMPORT7.

Thus, the target release and the source release are in the same database. The shadow system is also used to integrate the support packages, the add-ons, and the customer modifications into the target release. During this process, the tables of the new release are renamed so that they can be contained in the database. You can access these tables via the shadow instance and use Transaction SPDD to perform modification adjustments during live operation. If you use the downtime minimized strategy, you can also carry out activities for the upgrade before the system is shut down.

During the downtime, the new objects are renamed and activated, and missing objects are imported to the new repository during the EU_SWITCH phase. The objects of the source release are no longer required and thus are deleted. Then, the kernel is exchanged during the downtime in the KX_SWITCH_1 phase. The application tables are converted during PARCONV_UPG, and TABIM_UPG imports the data. Finally, XPRAS_UPG is executed. XPRA runs all programs required after the import.

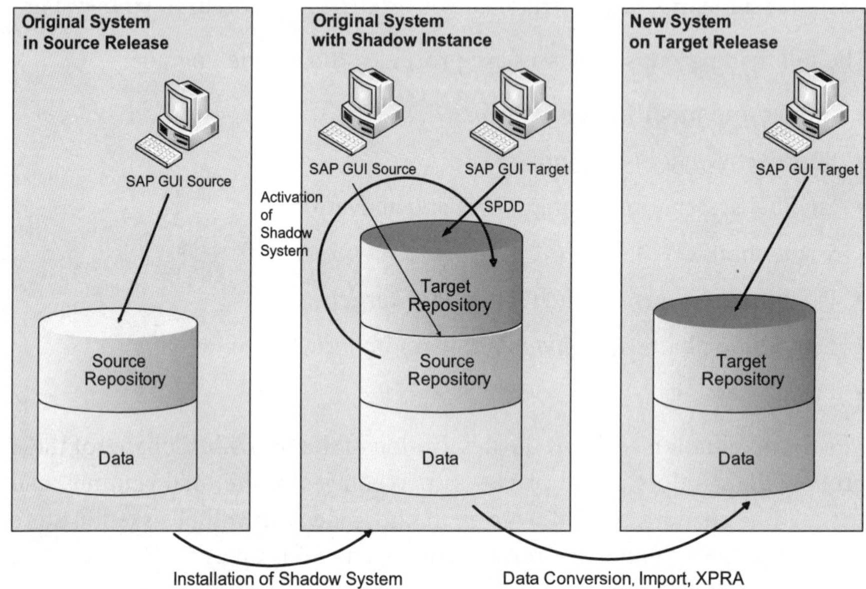

Figure 7.22 System Switch Upgrade

The downtime duration depends on the strategy selected (see Section 7.3.1.1, *Upgrade Strategies*). If you use the resource minimized strategy, the downtime of the system begins during the import of substitution sets to the system (which depends on the backup strategy), but at the latest during the REQSTOPPROD phase that shuts down the live system. The live instance and the shadow instance are not used simultaneously. In the downtime minimized strategy, the system is shut down during MODPROF_TRANS. This phase shuts down the system and changes the profiles of the system. The shadow instance and the live instance run in parallel, and the activities above mentioned are executed.

You must not forget to include the frontends in the upgrade process. You're on the safe side if you start to replace the old GUI installations with new ones during the upgrade phase. The new GUIs are usually downward compatible with older releases so that users can continue to work with the source system.

After the upgrade has been completed successfully, some important rework must be done. Depending on the importance of functioning, stability, and performance of the system, the rework can be done before the live operation is restarted, during limited live operation, or during live operation. The rework includes, among others processes:

- Running operating system scripts
- Importing additional programs
- Adjusting customer settings and developments
- Rescheduling background jobs
- Generating ABAP loads and BSP programs
- Adjusting roles in the authorization area
- Installing and upgrading dialog instances
- Importing support packages
- Configuring the transport management
- Cleaning up the Oracle database

You now know the basic principles of an SAP upgrade. Of course, the phases and processes are considerably more complex than this section could describe. The upgrade guides describe the individual steps, the parameters required during the phases, current SAP Notes, and dependencies in greater detail. The guides are available for any SAP solution. Always download the current guide for your upgrade and the respective SAP Notes that are referred to in the guides from the SAP Service Marketplace. An obsolete note may be missing important information that you need to run the upgrade without errors.

7.3.2 Oracle Upgrade

It can be necessary to upgrade the Oracle database to a new release when the SAP system is upgraded to a new SAP release. For example, this is always required when SAP no longer supports the old database release with the new release.

It is important to know the upgrade paths supported. For example, you can upgrade from R/3 4.6C to ECC 6.00, but SAP has not released the database upgrade from Oracle 8.1.7 to Oracle 10.2.0.2 yet. Oracle itself does support this process. That is, before upgrading an SAP system, you should upgrade the database to Version 9.2.0 and then to Version 10.2.0.2. In addition to this exception, you can also not change from Oracle Release 7.3.x to Release 8.1.7. This is only possible if an intermediate Release 8.0.6 or 8.1.6 is used.

Start Release	Target Release	Support	Intermediate Release
7.3.4	8.1.6	Yes	
7.3.4	8.1.7	No	8.0.6/8.1.6
7.3.4	9.2	No	8.0.6/8.1.6
8.0.x	8.1.6	Yes	
8.0.x	8.1.7	Yes	
8.0.x	9.2	No	8.1.7.4
8.1.6	9.2	No	8.1.7.4
8.1.7.x	9.2	Yes	8.1.7.4 recommended
8.1.7.4	10.2	No	9.2.0
9.0.1.x	10.2	Yes	At least Patch Set 9.0.1.4
9.2.0.x	10.2	Yes	At least Patch Set 9.2.0.4
10.1.0.2	10.2	Yes	

Table 7.2 Upgrade Paths of Oracle Releases

Table 7.3 lists the upgrade paths for the individual Oracle releases and indicates if you must use an intermediate release.

The tools that you use to change to a new Oracle release differ from release to release. Table 7.4 lists the tools that are used for upgrading various releases. In this table, ODMA stands for *Oracle Data Migration Assistant*, and DBUA stands for *Oracle Database Upgrade Assistant*.

Source Release	Target Release	Tool	Remarks
7.3.x	8.x	UNIX: orainst	Call with specific menu options
8.x	8.1.x	UNIX: ODMA	Call after software installation
8.1.x	8.1.7	UNIX: ODMA	Call after software installation
8.1.7	9.2	UNIX: scripts	Manual execution of scripts
9.2	10.2.0.2	UNIX: DBUA	Call after software installation
10.1	10.2.0.2	UNIX: DBUA	Call after software installation
7.3.x	8.0.5	Windows: mig80	Manual call
7.3.x	8.0.6	Windows: mig80	Call via the Universal Installer
8.x	8.1.x	Windows: ODMA	Call after software installation
8.1.x	8.1.7	Windows: ODMA	Call after software installation
8.1.7	9.2	Windows: DBUA	Call after software installation
9.2.	10.2.0.2	Windows: DBUA	Call after software installation
10.1.	10.2.0.2	Windows: DBUA	Call after software installation

Table 7.3 Tools for Changing Oracle Releases

In this respect, we also recommend downloading the respective guides for upgrading the Oracle releases from the SAP Service Marketplace. You can find the documents via the URL *http://service.sap.com/instguides* and then under **Other Documentation • Database Upgrades • Oracle**. Follow the steps and linked SAP Notes described in the guides exactly.

You must take the database offline for all upgrades. This means you must shut down your live system for upgrading the database. In addition to the actual upgrade, that is, exchanging the server software and migrating the data, you must store the entire database after the upgrade and also schedule the time for this process. To connect the SAP systems that run on an Oracle database, you must also import a newer version of the Oracle client software and change the paths to the client in the profile parameters of your instances accordingly.

7.4 Summary

In addition to the installation of the SAP system and the Oracle database, this chapter described the system maintenance of the two components and the operating system as well as a possible upgrade. Now you should have a rough idea of the work ahead of you during this process. For the installations, system maintenance via support packages and patches, and upgrades, it is important that you take you're the time to study the documentation provided and plan the processes carefully. Be aware of how a change in a system may affect other systems. With exact planning and careful execution, you can avoid numerous errors that cause problems, may have a negative effect on the system stability, or even lead to data losses.

The following chapters describe which tasks are supposed to be done during the normal operation of a system to ensure secure and consistent operation. You will learn how you can monitor and improve the system performance, analyze the general system status, and back up and restore all of your data.

Performance is not everything, but without performance everything is nothing, because most users find waiting almost impossible to bear.

8 Performance

In IT, performance describes a system's ability to carry out a task within a given timeframe. Therefore, performance is always measured in terms of tasks per time, such as FLOPS (*floating-point operations per Second*) or SAPS (*SAP Application Performance Standard*). One hundred SAPS are defined as 2,000 completely finished order items per hour, that is, 6,000 technical dialog steps and 2,000 update processes.

Usually, the transfer of a specific amount of data is the challenge, so that the unit can be described as quantity per time unit. Standardization of units is essential for comparing different systems and their performance. Such comparisons of defined and reproducible performance are referred to as *benchmarking*.

In the real world, it is the user who determines whether the performance of a system is good or poor. It's a matter of personal or subjective perception. A user does not necessarily recognize the scope of a task that has to be processed by a system. Consequently, on the one hand, good performance is an absolute characteristic when comparing systems, and, on the other hand, it has to be regarded in relation to the requirements. In addition, sociological factors play a role in this field: Five seconds of queue time for a data warehouse request is no problem for a user in an enterprise, whereas a customer of a web shop might be less patient.

Therefore, the overall goal of a system administrator must be to meet the different performance requirements to enable users to efficiently use a system.

Performance optimization is part of the lifecycle of every system and involves the steps of *implementation*, *operation*, and *revision*. Figure 8.1 shows a lifecycle including its different phases.

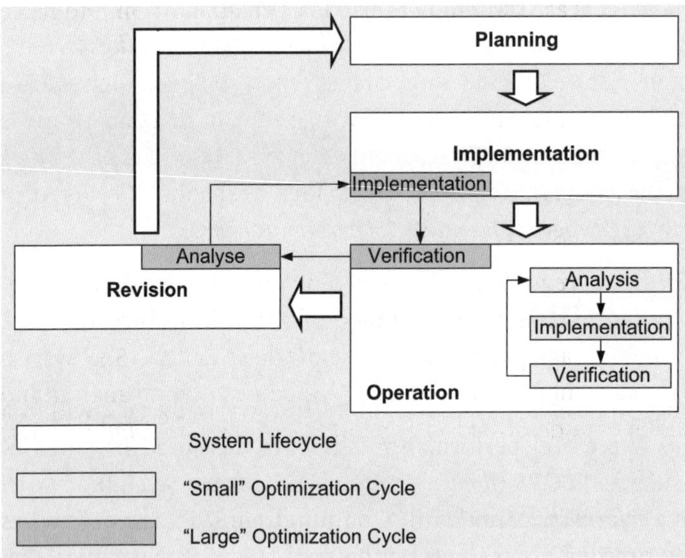

Figure 8.1 System Lifecycle and Optimization Cycles

The process of optimization is divided into the phases of *analyzing, implementing, and verifying*. There are two optimization cycles. The first, "small," cycle is carried out entirely in the lifecycle phase of *operation*. This is the phase of performance optimization, which has no or only short time effects on a system's availability. Examples of these processes include SAP kernel parameters for memory areas or work processes as well as the parameters of the Oracle database, some of which can be dynamically changed during runtime.

The "big" cycle covers the lifecycle phases of *implementation*, *operation*, and *revision*. Optimizations that require more time to be completed, as they involve tests and affect the system operation, must be performed within this wider context. Modifications on application code or extensive reorganizations of databases are also part of this cycle.

This chapter describes the *analysis*, *implementation*, and *verification phases:* Which analyses can be performed on a combination of SAP with an Oracle database and how can the results be implemented? To answer this question, we should first categorize the problems.

8.1 Administrative and Program-Based Problems

There are three sources of performance problems: program-based, administrative, and user-specific problems.

If performance problems are caused by the code of an application, the cause is *program-based*. Unfortunately, there are many examples of poorly coded software, as coding involves a wide range of bug types, such as memory leaks and inefficient algorithms, to name just a few. If, on top of that, a database is used, the probable bugs cover SQL statements that are required for the interaction. The issue of program-related performance problems is covered in Section 8.3, *Analyzing Program-Based Performance Problems*.

Administrative performance problems are caused by the configuration of hardware and software. This covers a wide range of areas, from incorrect disk layout to insufficient storage parameters of the database and the SAP system to the incorrect assignment of permissions. The methods used to analyze and solve these problems are described in Section 8.2, *Analyzing Administrative Performance Problems*.

The third source for possible problems is the behavior of users, in other words, *user-specific* causes. In this context, the problematic question is: Who caused the problem? The user who, for example, runs extensive queries and therefore causes the system performance to go down, or the programmer or administrator who does not prevent different kinds of "excessive use," by setting maximum values for input boxes or running plausibility checks? User-specific performance problems are not further discussed in this book. The solution to this type of problem is not the administration of SAP and Oracle databases but the development of applications or the administration of user permissions.

Besides the causes of the problems, the *locations of problems* represents the second part of a problem analysis, in this context, location means: Where does the performance problem occur? For a further specification of this issue, a system must be divided into its individual components. From a performance analysis point of view, an SAP system consists of the following components:

1. Hardware
2. Operating system
3. Database
4. SAP Basis (that is, SAP Kernel + SAP Basis = SAP NetWeaver Application Server)
5. SAP application

Table 8.1 shows an overview of the possible combinations of cause and location for the assignment of performance problems. Note that this chapter focuses only on the problematic points related to Oracle and SAP.

Cause\Location	Program-Based	Administrative
Hardware	Errors in firmware	Selection of inappropriate components, such as slow hard disks or storage
Operating system	▸ Inefficient storage management by operating system kernel ▸ Device drivers not optimized	▸ Incorrect parameterization of the operating system kernel ▸ Inappropriate layout for massive I/O operations
Database	▸ Use of "expensive" SQL statements ▸ Poor indexing	▸ Insufficient parameterization ▸ Inefficient table structures, for instance, because of too many extents
SAP Basis	Errors in the ABAP code for basic functions such as in communication components	▸ Inefficient buffer sizes ▸ Wrong parameters for the SAP kernel
Application	▸ Incorrect use of standard SAP functions in custom developments ▸ Bugs in the standard SAP system	None

Table 8.1 Overview with Examples of Performance Optimization Problems

We will now continue this chapter in two parts. The first part, Section 8.2 *Analyzing Administrative Performance Problems* deals with administrative performance problems in all fields including hardware, operating system, the Oracle database, and the SAP system, with a particular focus on Oracle and the SAP system, according to the intention of this book. Then, Section 8.3, *Analyzing Program-Based Performance Problems*, deals with the program-related issues, such as expensive SQL statements, indexing, and to a smaller extent, ABAP programming.

8.2 Analyzing Administrative Performance Problems

For an analysis of performance problems, two points of entry are quite useful: the *general analysis of the system status* or of the components and the *workload analysis*. The analysis of the components, which is also referred to as the system analysis, refers to the state, that is, the configuration and utilization of the system components, such as hardware, operating system, database, and the SAP Basis. The most important key figures for this type of analysis are filling levels, hit ratios, error statistics, and so on. Therefore, this section deals particularly with the examination of the components, gives information on how to solve problems, and provides configuration reference values.

The SAP workload analysis uses the times required for processing the individual dialog steps (roll-in and roll-out, database time, CPU time, and so on). These time values are collected in the system. This analysis used to monitor not only the components of the system, but also their interaction. Time is obviously the relevant key figure is in this context.

Experience has shown that starting with the workload analysis is useful when individual users complain about performance problems or when the problem occurs only at certain times. If the performance is generally poor or if a system analysis is carried out on a regular basis, starting with a general component analysis is preferable. For a complete analysis of the system performance, you should carry out both analyses.

The SAP workload analysis is not further covered here, as this would go beyond the scope of this chapter. Some excellent literature is already available on this topic, such as the following: *SAP Performance Optimization* by Thomas Schneider (SAP PRESS 2006).

A similar performance analysis method is available in the context of Oracle databases: the *wait event analysis*. As the name suggests, the flow of a transaction is analyzed on the basis of the different wait times of that transaction within a database. Section 8.2.2, *Analyzing the Database*, provides further information about the wait event analysis.

8.2.1 Analyzing the Hardware and Operating System

From the point of view of an SAP Basis administrator, no clear separation can be drawn when analyzing the hardware and the operating system, as the SAP Basis does not allow for that. However, such a separation is not necessary, as both the hardware and operating system form the basis of the SAP system and database and can therefore be viewed as one entity. If a performance problem is detected in the hardware or operating system, the system administrator or hardware partner often participates in the process of finding a solution, as the SAP partner normally does not have any access to the operating system level or lacks the required knowledge.

All data that is available for a hardware and operating system analysis in the SAP system is collected by the *SAP OS Collector* (SAPOSCOL), which is a component of the SAP Kernel that depends on the hardware and operating system. A background job (SAP_COLLECTOR_FOR_PERFORMANCE) reads the data and writes it to the performance database of the SAP system (Table MONI).

The analysis is started via the operating system monitor, which uses the data from the performance database or queries the SAPOSCOL directly. Transaction ST06 starts the OS monitor for the local instance of the system. For systems that have several instances on different servers, Transaction OS07 is used to navigate to the corresponding operating system monitor of an instance that is installed on a different server.

In general, the performance checks of hardware and operating system focus on four areas: CPU, memory requirement, I/O load, and network. All data for these components are collected by the SAP OS Collector and stored in the SAP database using a batch job. This allows access to current data as well as to a data history. Figure 8.2 shows the operating system monitor of an SAP instance.

Mon Jun 26 13:18:19 2006 interval 10 sec.

CPU

Utilization user %	1	Count	
system %	1	Load average 1 min	0,1
idle %	97	5 min	0,1
io wait %	1	15 min	0,1
System calls/s	2.371	Context switches/s	30
Interrupts/s	2.443		

Memory

Physical mem avail Kb	33.538.048	Physical mem free Kb	396.18
Pages in/s	0	Kb paged in/s	
Pages out/s	0	Kb paged out/s	

Swap

Configured swap Kb	54.525.952	Maximum swap-space Kb	88.064.00
Free in swap-space Kb	74.378.252	Actual swap-space Kb	88.064.00

Disk with highest response time

Name	c7t6d0	Response time ms	1
Utilization	1	Queue	
Avg wait time ms	0	Avg service time ms	1
Kb transfered/s	13	Operations/s	

Lan (sum)

Packets in/s	74	Errors in/s	
Packets out/s	75	Errors out/s	
Collisions	0		

Figure 8.2 Operating System Monitor (ST06 or OS07)

Table 8.2 provides information about the meaning of the most important key figures in the operating system monitor and states critical performance limits where possible or wherever it makes sense.

Field	Description	Critical Value
Utilization user	CPU load caused by user processes including SAP system and database	S > 80% (Ø per h)
Utilization system	CPU load caused by operating system kernel	
Utilization idle	CPU idle	<20% (Ø per h)
Utilization i/o wait	CPU load caused by waiting for I/O operations	>40% (Ø per h)
Count	Number of CPUs	–
Load average	Number of processes waiting for a CPU	>3.0 (specific OS, such as Solaris, also count the active processes, then >3 + number of CPUs)
Phy. mem avail	Complete main memory of the server	–
Phy. mem avail	Free memory of the server	<3% **Phy. mem avail** (except AIX, which uses the free RAM as file cache)
Pages in/out	Number of memory pages paged in and out between RAM and swap	Windows: Kb-in × 3600 > 20% RAM UNIX: Kb-out × 3600 > 5% RAM
Kb in/out	Size of memory pages paged in and out between RAM and swap	–
Swap-space (Free, Maximum, Actual)	Display depends on operating system (SAP Note 63906)	–
Disk	Hard disk with currently highest response time (menu path **Detail analyses menu • Disk**	**Utilization** > 50% (Ø per h)
Packets in/out	Number of sent and received network packets (total of all network interfaces)	–
Errors in/out	Error when sending and receiving network packets (total of all network interfaces)	Should no longer occur with the current state of technology; therefore should be checked in the case of >0
Collision	Collisions on the network	

Table 8.2 Overview of Operating System Monitor

The critical values are not absolute values; rather, they indicate problems. If one of these values is exceeded or fallen below, you should check further.[1]

8.2.1.1 Reference Values for Hardware Components

A CPU utilization of more than 80% per hour (also **idle + i/o wait** < 20%) is referred to as a CPU bottleneck. Many hardware partners, however, recommend a maximum utilization of 60% to 70% for production systems to ensure sufficient reserves for peak loads. However, you should keep in mind that the CPU values in Transaction ST06 are average values across all CPUs of the server; that is, a machine with two CPUs with a utilization of 70% has less reserve than a machine with eight CPUs with a utilization of 80% (at equal CPU performance).

Different values are available regarding the size of a swap memory. SAP recommends using three times more swap memory than physical memory, but at least 3.5 GB. This recommendation, however, is unrealistic for systems with a memory of more than 64 GB. In that case, it is difficult to reserve the appropriate amount of swap memory on the local disks. However, the operating systems often provide the corresponding solution, such as the use of a pseudo-swap for HP-UX.

Paging, that is, outsourcing memory pages from the memory and transferring them to the swap partition or the swap file on the hard disk, should generally be regarded as critical. The swap memory is merely a kind of emergency help for the operating system in order to be able to start more processes than the existing memory allows and to prevent processes from failing in situations of extreme memory load. With paging, you should always bear in mind that, theoretically, the factor that's responsible for the difference in access speed between the hard disk and RAM is approximately 500,000 (8 milliseconds for the positioning of the hard disk head — 15 nanoseconds of latency time for memory access). Although these values are only theoretical values that can be changed considerably by employing different hardware techniques, such as hard disk arrays or parallel memory access, a considerable difference still remains.

Generally, we advise that you not page out more than 5% of the memory within one hour. The best thing, however, is to entirely avoid paging and to size the memory according to your specific requirements. As a rule, when

1 Five percent can also be a poor result when the RAM is larger than 8 GB or the I/O for swap memory is too slow, for example due to a software RAID.

planning hardware resources, the memory should be of the highest importance.

The third component is the I/O load. When you double-click on the current **Disk with highest response time** in the operating system monitor, a list with all hard disks of the system displays including their current statuses. If a hard disk is indicated with **Utilization 100%**, this does not necessarily mean that there's a bottleneck. In fact, you should merely ensure that the average **Utilization** per hour does not exceed 50%. The history of the I/O load of each hard disk is displayed under **Detail Analysis Menu • Disk**.

The network can be checked from within the SAP system using a simple ping test. This LAN check of the presentation servers (SAP GUI) only works if the servers don't access the system via an SAP router. A second and much better way of checking the network is to use the `niping` program, which can be called from Transaction SM49 as an external operating system command. SAP Note 500235 contains detailed instructions on how you can use `niping`.

The operating system monitor displays the number of received network packets per second and provides a summary on an hourly basis. Critical points are the sent errors and collisions within a period of one hour. With today's modern network structures in a LAN, every value above 0 is suspicious and should be checked together with the network administrator (be insistent).

8.2.1.2 Identifying the Causes of Bottlenecks in Hardware Components

If a CPU, memory or I/O bottleneck is detected, you must search for the cause of the bottleneck in a second step.

The processes at the operating system level are responsible for the CPU utilization. In Transaction ST06, the current processes of the server are listed in the order of their CPU utilization under **Detail Analysis Menu • Top CPU**. The displayed CPU utilization percentage always refers to a CPU of the system; that is, in a system with multiple processors (*n* CPUs), the maximum utilization is *n* × 100%. If it is possible, you can also use the tools provided by the operating system, such as "top" that's available in the different UNIX derivatives.

The further procedure depends on the processes that are identified as CPU users. SAP work processes can be recognized by the <sid>adm user and the process names, dw.sap<instance> (UNIX) and Disp+Work (Windows). If these are the processes that produce the CPU load, these are further analyzed against the SAP process overview (Transaction SM50; see Section 8.2.3, *Analyzing the SAP System*). Individual processes are identified by a process ID (PID), which is displayed in the operating system monitor and in the SAP process overview.

Oracle processes are typically executed under the ora<sid> (UNIX) or SAPService<sid> (Windows) user, respectively, and have the identifier oracle<sid> (shadow processes) or ora_<process>_<sid> (Oracle system process). If one of the Oracle processes utilizes an unreasonably high CPU capacity, further analysis is performed using the database process monitor (Transaction ST04N; see Section 8.2.2, *Analyzing the Database*). Different reasons exist for an extensive CPU utilization by the Oracle processes; refer to SAP Note 712624 for further information.

Important Note

This book mainly refers to the application server of SAP Releases 6.40 and 7.00. Transaction ST04N, which will be mentioned frequently in the following sections, will no longer be available in the coming Release 7.10. In the new release, it will be called ST04 again. Moreover, from Release 7.00 onward, Transaction DBACOCKPIT for Oracle is available.

If an external process causes the high CPU load, this process has to be analyzed, and the bottleneck has to be eliminated in collaboration with the operating system administrator.

Analyzing the memory utilization by the processes is much more complicated than the analysis of the CPU utilization. On the one hand, that's because the memory is used in various different ways, for instance, as a local process memory or as a shared memory; on the other hand, the different operating systems use different methods of memory management.

There are considerable differences regarding the management of swap and memory — not only between the Windows and UNIX worlds but also between the different UNIX derivatives. In general, in-depth knowledge about the operating system is essential for a precise analysis.

First, you must use the options provided by the operating system to determine whether the memory utilization is caused by the SAP system or the Oracle database or by other processes. External and high memory utilization — which is not caused by SAP or Oracle — is often caused by the file system cache, which reserves a particular percentage of the memory as a buffer for data access. The maximum size that can be recommended depends on whether the server runs both the Oracle and SAP instances or only the SAP instance. Oracle generally recommends disabling all I/O buffers for the database access, as the access to database blocks then won't be buffered twice, namely, by the file system cache and the SGA memory. Instead, the memory should be completely allocated to the Oracle-optimized SGA buffer. If you use raw devices, you can't use the file system cache. The cache of a server with an SAP instance should not exceed 8% to 10% of memory, but no more than 1 GB. In AIX, you should also use the file system cache as little as possible. Refer to Section 8.2.2 for further information on the different types of I/O.

If the memory utilization occurs within the SAP system, that is, with the SAP work processes, a further analysis of the SAP memory areas is executed. Note that the SAP system is only capable of allocating the memory in accordance with the relevant instance parameters (see Section 8.2.3). The analysis of the memory usage of the Oracle database should be performed in the same way (see Section 8.2.2).

There are three possible causes for a high I/O load: massive paging in the swap area, a high load on the database, or an external program. If you recognize a high paging rate in the operating system monitor, you can use the disk analysis (**ST06 • Detail Analysis Menu • Disk**) to verify if the hard disk that contains the swap area has a high load. If that is the case, solving the paging problem also solves the problem with the I/O load. Because the swap area is never located on the same hard disk as the database, an I/O problem caused by paging usually never causes any I/O performance problems in the database.

If the high load occurs in the area where the database is installed, further analysis is required (see Section 8.2.2).

Problems with the communication hardware can theoretically occur for three connections:

- SAP instance: SAP GUI
- SAP instance: Oracle database server
- SAP instance: connected systems

The connection to the database server and possibly to the connected third-party system, for example, as a data source in SAP NetWeaver BI, has a particularly high bandwidth utilization. In this context, SAP requires the SAP instance and the database server to be located together in a 100-Mbit LAN. A network overload can only be recognized in the SAP system by means of indications such as collisions and long runtimes in the LAN. The SAP system administrator can perform further checks using the `niping` program. A precise analysis and identification of causes requires the use of external network tools and the profound knowledge of a system administrator.

8.2.2 Analyzing the Database

Because the database is the core of the SAP system, its performance is essential for the performance of the entire system.

The analysis includes the following performance-relevant components:

- **Buffers**
  The buffer areas of the Oracle database store frequently used information in the main memory of the server to provide a considerably faster access than is made possible by the hard disk storage.
- **Wait event**
  The analysis of wait events indicates when and which event the database has to wait for during the processing of a request. This is a relatively simple way to identify bottlenecks in the database.
- **General parameterization**
  In addition to the buffer parameters, there are many other performance-relevant Oracle parameters. These must also be included in the complete analysis.
- **Statistics**
  The Oracle Cost-Based Optimizer (CBO) calculates the costs of the potential access paths (for example, full scan, index range scan) to determine the fastest possible access path.
- **I/O**
  The task of a database is to read and write data blocks. Therefore, having the best possible I/O for the performance of an SAP system is essential.
- **SQL analysis**
  The quality of SQL queries affects the speed of the database significantly. Consequently, the identification and enhancement of bad SQL queries represent an important task in the context of performance optimization.

When is an analysis of the database useful? The amount of the total response time for the database in an SAP system is the best indicator. Usually, you can use a workload analysis to determine this amount, which should normally be less than 40%. A further indicator is the ratio between **Busy wait time** and **CPU time** (Transaction ST04N; see Figure 8.4), which should be approximately 60:40. If the **Busy wait time** is considerably higher, you can perform a wait event analysis (see Section 8.2.2.2, *Analyzing Wait Events*), whereas an increased **CPU time** indicates a CPU resource bottleneck. Another factor to be taken into account regarding the **Busy wait time** is the following: Possibly, Transaction ST04 also includes idle wait events in the **Busy wait time**. For this reason, you should check the correctness of the **Busy wait time** using the data from the V$SYSTEM_EVENT view.

As a prerequisite for the analysis of Oracle performance data, you must set the `TIMED_STATISTICS` parameter to `TRUE`. However, this is already the case after a standard SAP installation. Otherwise, you can set this parameter dynamically as a SYS database user (logon via sysdba):

```
f05:oram05 1>sqlplus "/as sysdba"
SQL> alter system set TIMED_STATISTICS = TRUE;
```

8.2.2.1 Analyzing the Database Buffers

Two factors determine the quality of a buffer: On the one hand, there is the logical access (*logical read*), which refers to every access to a block, and the physical access to a block on the hard disk (*physical read*). Figure 8.3 illustrates this concept.

The buffer quality can be calculated based on these factors by using the following formula:

Quality (hit ratio) = Number of hits/Number of queries × 100%

Basically, you must consider that all buffers are initialized after a system startup and therefore have no informational value. For a buffer analysis, the system has to be in an *established* state. In general, you can assume that this state is reached after one or two days of operation. The number of logical reads on the buffer cache of the database is another reference value for the established state. This value should be greater than 50,000,000.

The database buffers of the Oracle database are located in the system global area (SGA). You can find a detailed description of the individual buffer areas and their functions in Chapter 3, *Oracle Fundamentals*.

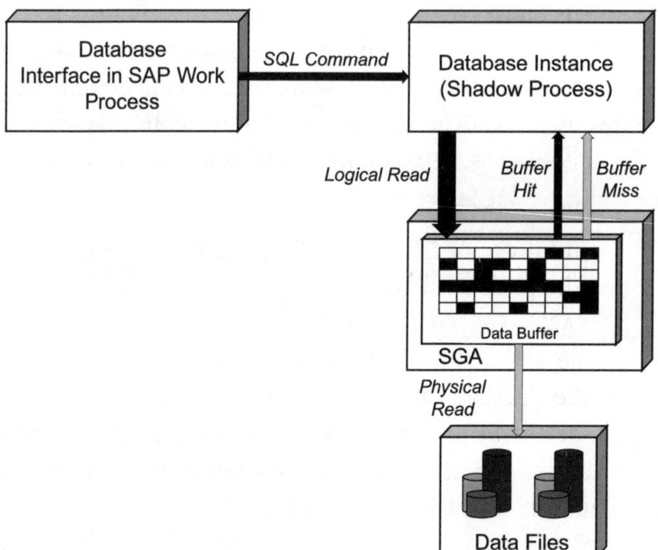

Figure 8.3 Access to Buffers and the Database

The overview in Table 8.3 includes the most important buffers in the SGA of the Oracle database.

SGA Buffer	Description
Data buffer	Contains the buffered data blocks from the data files on the hard disk. Parameter: DB_CACHE_SIZE
Shared pool	The two main subcaches: data dictionary cache and library cache. Parameter: SHARED_POOL_SIZE
Java pool	Used by the Oracle JVM, but not by the SAP system. Parameter: JAVA_POOL_SIZE
Large pool	Buffer for special data (for example, message buffer for processes running parallel queries). This buffer is very small and hardly used in SAP systems. Parameter: LARGE_POOL_SIZE
Streams pool	New buffer area in Oracle 10g for Oracle Stream, which manages data and events in distributed environments — not used in the SAP system. Parameter: STREAMS_POOL_SIZE
Redo buffer	Buffer for redo log data. Parameter: LOG_BUFFER

Table 8.3 Overview of SGA Buffers

As of Oracle Version 9i, the administrator can change the most important parameters (DB_CACHE_SIZE and SHARED_POOL_SIZE) of the SGA at runtime of the Oracle instance. This feature is referred to as dynamic SGA and should not be confused with the *Automatic Shared Memory Management* (ASMM). The old parameters from Oracle 8.1.x for the data buffer (DB_BLOCK_BUFFERS) can no longer be used. SAP has generally approved the use of the dynamic SGA, which is enabled by default during SAP installations based on SAP Basis 6.40.

As of Oracle 10g, you can fully automate the SGA management function. In that case, Oracle adjusts the individual areas, DB_CACHE_SIZE, SHARED_POOL_SIZE, JAVA_POOL_SIZE, LARGE_POOL_SIZE, and STREAMS_POOL_SIZE, to your current requirements. The SGA_TARGET parameter provides the total size of the SGA and enables the ASMM. Moreover, if the DB_CACHE_SIZE and SHARED_POOL_SIZE parameters are set, they provide the lower limits for each buffer area. Due to the lack of experience with ASMM, its use in an SAP system is not recommended. Nevertheless, it makes sense to use this parameter in a nonproduction environment to minimize the administrative effort, but only if you do not intend to use the system as an image of the production system for testing purposes.

Access to analysis data in the SAP system occurs via the Oracle database monitor (Transaction ST04N). This monitor provides you with all information about the Oracle database, which can be accessed from within the SAP system. The information about the database monitor originates from the Oracle database, specifically from the V$ views. Figure 8.4 shows the initial screen of the database monitor.

Table 8.4 explains the meanings of the most important key figures in the Oracle database monitor and provides recommendations for its optimal states after establishing the database.

In general, recommendations for particular buffers and characteristics are only reference values. The values may deviate significantly without affecting the performance of the SAP system. The user load on a training system, for example, barely reaches the user load of a production system, so the load that's generated by administrative tasks clearly prevails. Because these activities, such as the standard SAP background jobs and the creation of the database statistics, focus on different load aspects, the individual performance characteristics vary substantially. In this case, a ratio of User calls to Recursive calls or <0.5 would not be unusual.

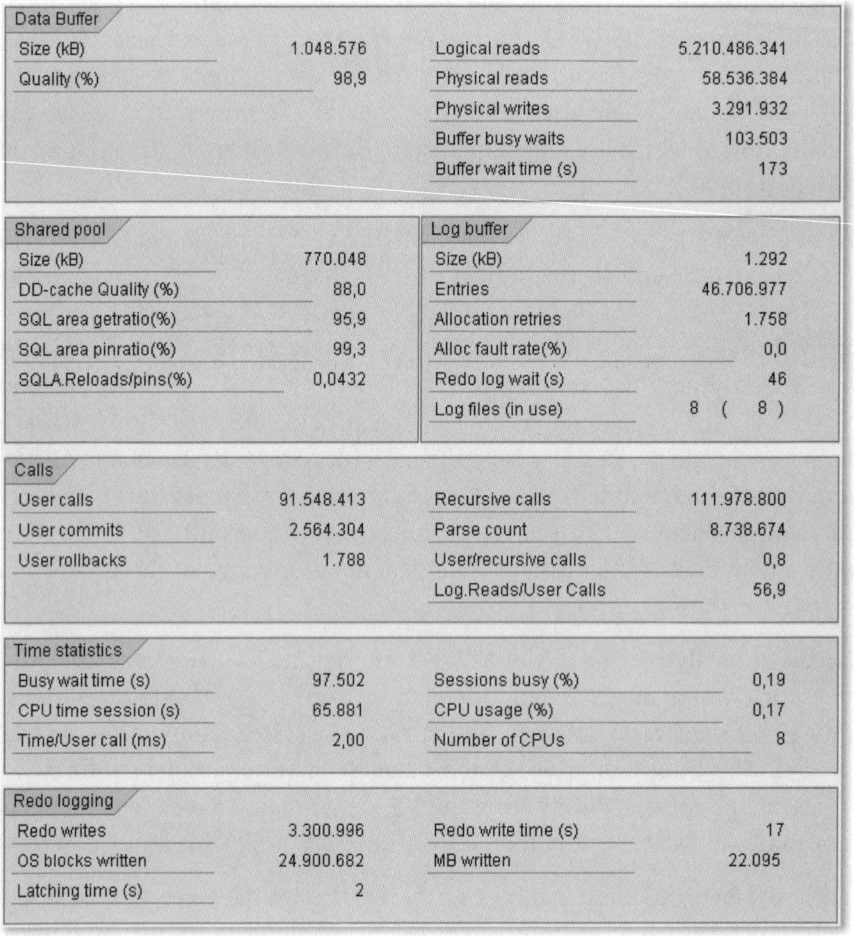

Data Buffer

Size (kB)	1.048.576	Logical reads	5.210.486.341
Quality (%)	98,9	Physical reads	58.536.384
		Physical writes	3.291.932
		Buffer busy waits	103.503
		Buffer wait time (s)	173

Shared pool / **Log buffer**

Size (kB)	770.048	Size (kB)	1.292
DD-cache Quality (%)	88,0	Entries	46.706.977
SQL area getratio(%)	95,9	Allocation retries	1.758
SQL area pinratio(%)	99,3	Alloc fault rate(%)	0,0
SQLA.Reloads/pins(%)	0,0432	Redo log wait (s)	46
		Log files (in use)	8 (8)

Calls

User calls	91.548.413	Recursive calls	111.978.800
User commits	2.564.304	Parse count	8.738.674
User rollbacks	1.788	User/recursive calls	0,8
		Log.Reads/User Calls	56,9

Time statistics

Busy wait time (s)	97.502	Sessions busy (%)	0,19
CPU time session (s)	65.881	CPU usage (%)	0,17
Time/User call (ms)	2,00	Number of CPUs	8

Redo logging

Redo writes	3.300.996	Redo write time (s)	17
OS blocks written	24.900.682	MB written	22.095
Latching time (s)	2		

Figure 8.4 Oracle Database Monitor – Main View

Buffer/ Characteristic	Descripton	Recom-mendation
Data buffer	Main database buffer for the data blocks (warning: This recommendation is very general, because there are extreme cases in both directions, which means there are systems running with 80% without problems and systems having serious problems at 98%.)	>94%
DD cache	Data Dictionary buffer contains metadata of the database (structures, users, authorizations)	>80%

Table 8.4 Essential Characteristics of the Oracle Database Monitor

Buffer/ Characteristic	Descripton	Recom-mendation
SQL area get ratio	SQL cache stores the parse tree and execution plan of previously run SQL statements Get ratio = S (hit)/S (request) × 100	>95%
SQL area pin ratio	Indicates the quantity of all requests (in percent) that still have required objects to be executed in the memory: Pin ratio = S (executions = pin hits)/S (requests for execution = pins) × 100	>99%
Reloads/Pin	Ratio between reloads of a SQL statement (for example, invalidated entry due to age) and execution requests	<0.04
User/Recursive calls	Ratio between user requests to the database and requests that the database executes in addition to the user requests (for example, due to a missing dictionary cache entry)	>2
Busy wait time	Total amount of all wait times of the database in terms of seconds, without idle events (see Section 8.2.2.2, *Analyzing Wait Events*)	Ratio approx. 60:40
CPU time	Total amount of CPU time consumed by all Oracle sessions	

Table 8.4 Essential Characteristics of the Oracle Database Monitor (Cont.)

In the following text, we will look more closely at the relevant Oracle buffers in the SAP environment with regard to performance.

Without a doubt, the *data buffer* for the actual data blocks of the database has the greatest impact on performance because it reduces the total number of physical disk accesses.

The logical reads include all reading requests to the database. During a *buffer get*, the system tries to read the corresponding data block from the data buffer for all requests that are not declared as *direct path*, which means they don't have an explicit direct access to the database. A successful read access is referred to as a *buffer hit*, whereas a failure leads to a physical read in which the block is read from the data files on the hard disk (see Figure 8.4).

The hit ratio for the data buffer can be calculated as follows:

Quality (hit ratio) = (Logical reads – Physical reads)/Logical read × 100%

To obtain a good database performance, the buffer should process at least 94% of all block accesses (except for direct path operations) to the database. You must check the following possible causes if the actual value falls below this reference value:

- The data buffer is too small
- Many direct path operations that circumvent the data buffer when accessing data blocks (Note: Direct path operations are deducted from the hit ratio when displayed in ST04N, but not in ST04. Therefore, there may be differences.)
- Expensive SQL statements (see Section 8.3)

The direct path operations include the following wait events:

- `direct path read` and `direct path write`
- `direct path read (lob)` and `direct path write (lob)` (Oracle 9i)
- `direct path read temp` and `direct path write temp` (Oracle 10g)

You can view the number of `direct path` operations in Transaction ST04N under **Additional Function • Display V$ • V$SYSTEM_EVENT** (see Figure 8.5). This number should be very small (<0.5%), primarily in comparison with the number of regular accesses to data blocks via the data buffer (`db file sequential read`). SAP NetWeaver BI systems are an exception in this case, because substantially higher values are acceptable here (see Chapter 12, *SAP NetWeaver BI and Oracle*). You can use direct path operations, for example, to access the PSAPTEMP tablespace. As an example, increasing the PGA memory of individual database work processes can help you reduce the number of these accesses to the temporary tablespace for `JOIN` or `SORT` operations. Figure 8.5 shows an excerpt of the V$SYSTEM_EVENT view. Another note regarding this view: This view contains only the wait events that occurred after the last database startup. You shouldn't be surprised if you don't see all of the wait events described above in this excerpt.

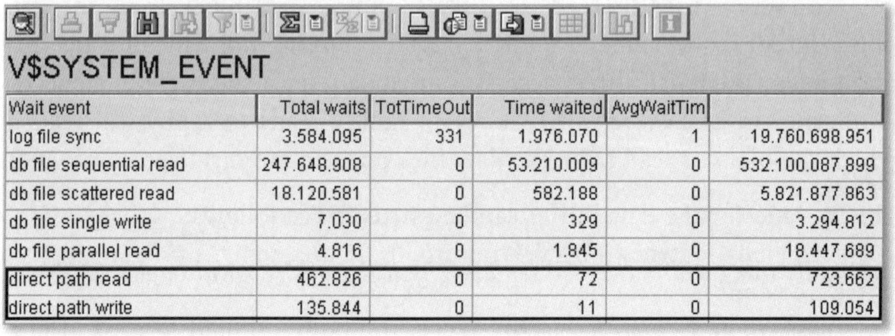

V$SYSTEM_EVENT

Wait event	Total waits	TotTimeOut	Time waited	AvgWaitTim	
log file sync	3.584.095	331	1.976.070	1	19.760.698.951
db file sequential read	247.648.908	0	53.210.009	0	532.100.087.899
db file scattered read	18.120.581	0	582.188	0	5.821.877.863
db file single write	7.030	0	329	0	3.294.812
db file parallel read	4.816	0	1.845	0	18.447.689
direct path read	462.826	0	72	0	723.662
direct path write	135.844	0	11	0	109.054

Figure 8.5 Direct Path Operations in V$SYSTEM_EVENT

If you can exclude expensive SQL statements and `direct path` operations as a reason for a poor hit ratio, you should, if possible, try to improve the performance by increasing the data buffer. If you can only implement this increase by extending the hardware, you should first exclude all possible causes for a performance degradation before making a corresponding investment.

The initial configuration of the data buffer depends completely on the intended use and the load on your system. In real life, many SAP production systems work with data buffers of more than 100 GB. Therefore, we cannot provide a general recommendation at this point. We would rather recommend that you have SAP experts perform sizing sessions.

Since the introduction of the dynamic SGA with Oracle 9i, the Oracle administrator can test changes to the data buffer in a simple and convenient way. The V$DB_CACHE_ADVICE view enables you to check how a change to the buffer size affects the number of physical reads. The factor representing the changes between the physical database accesses and the current status represents the possible reduction of the buffer in MB without a significant performance degradation or the efficient expansion of the buffer in MB to further minimize the physical reads. For this purpose, you must enable the dynamic SGA and set the Oracle parameter, `DB_CACHE_ADVICE`, to ON.

In addition to the actual data buffer, the *keep pool* and the *recycling pool* also buffer data blocks. If you use the dynamic SGA (Oracle 9i), you can see that these two pools are no longer part of the data buffer but are included separately in the SGA. The keep pool can be used for tables and blocks that should not be displaced from the data buffer. The recycling pool, on the other hand, can be used for tables that should not displace other blocks from the data buffer but whose own blocks can be displaced immediately. The standard settings in SAP do not use these pools; however, their usage is recommended under specific circumstances (see SAP Note 762808).

Apart from the data buffer, other important buffers of the Oracle database are located in the *shared pool*, namely, *SQL cache* and *dictionary cache*.

The SQL cache (formerly known as *shared cursor cache*) is located in the library cache and stores all Oracle-internal information for later reuse, if required. This information is related to an SQL statement call, such as the parse tree and the execution plan.

Another key figure for the SQL cache in the shared pool is the *pin ratio*. You can calculate the pin ratio as follows:

Pin ratio = (Pin hits/Pin) × 100%

Oracle processes an SQL statement by splitting it up into different components. A pin is the request for the reuse of one of the components resulting from the decomposition of the SQL statement, and, accordingly, a *pin hit* is the successful reuse. However, this is not always the case because cache entries may be invalidated by timeouts or displaced by other entries. If the described reuse fails, the system must reload the corresponding SQL command with its new components. The "Reloads per pin" key figure results from the relationship between requests (pins) and reloads (see Figure 8.4 and Table 8.4 above).

A buffer hit in the SQL cache simply means that the parsing of the queried SQL statement was already performed. However, the pin ratio indicates the number of successful reuses for a found cache entry. If the reuse fails, the system reloads the corresponding component.

In the Oracle library cache, you can find further subcaches for the PL/SQL (Procedural Language/Structured Query Language) packages as well as for the control structures, such as locks and library cache handles. These play only a minor role regarding the system performance.

The dictionary cache buffers rows from the dictionary of the Oracle database, that is, information about structures of tables, authorizations, and so on. This metadata of the database is needed regularly to process user requests.

According to SAP, the minimum size of the shared pool should be approximately 400 MB. If the hit ratio values are permanently under the values listed in Table 8.3, it may be useful to increase the value of the `SHARED_POOL_SIZE` parameter. However, you should take into account that, for instance, the structure of the database statistics may temporarily decrease the hit rate in the shared pool significantly.

Possibly, you can also minimize the shared pool again if the performance values (see Table 8.4) are acceptable and a larger subarea of the shared pools remains free (>50 MB). You can find the free area in the shared pool in Table **V$SGASTAT • free memory** or by using the following SQL command:

```
Select bytes from V$SGASTAT
where pool = 'shared pool' AND name = 'free memory';
```

In the V$SHARED_POOL_ADVICE view, you can also see how changes to the shared pool size affect the cache hits and then resize the pool accordingly.

As of Oracle 10g, you have the option to display the history of the load of the shared pool. Furthermore, the DBA_HIST_SGASTAT view displays the progress of the free space development.

The *Program Global Area* (PGA) component of the Oracle memory is locally assigned to a server process (shadow process or background process). The entire PGA memory of an Oracle instance can be calculated based on the amount of PGAs of all database processes. You can find the total amount of allocated PGA memory in Transaction ST04N or under **Additional Function • Display V$/GV$ Views and Values • V$PGASTAT • total PGA allocated** or by using the following SQL call:

```
SelectVALUE from V$PGASTAT
where name = 'total PGA allocated';
```

The PGA of a process contains only the data and information that is needed or to be processed. The size of the PGA plays a particularly important role for memory-intensive sort and hash operations. Consequently, the administrator should place special emphasis on the optimum configuration of this memory, in particular in the SAP NetWeaver BI environment (see Chapter 12).

However, the configuration of the PGA has been considerably simplified since Oracle Release 9i. Whereas the administrator of older Oracle versions had to specify the PGAs for individual operations (for example, SORT_AREA_SIZE and HASH_AREA_SIZE), you can now use the automatic PGA management function. Similar to the ASMM for the SGA, Oracle adjusts the PGAs for all server processes automatically. It is worth mentioning that, in contrast to earlier versions, PGA memory that is no longer needed is released using the automatic PGA management. You can limit the entire size of the PGA using the PGA_AGGREGATE_TARGET parameter. As of Oracle 9i, the automatic PGA management can be used (according to SAP Note 619876, it is even recommended) and is enabled by default in every SAP installation with SAP Basis 6.40 or higher.

To better understand the PGA tuning settings, we will now introduce some terms. To execute an operation, the Oracle process needs local memory, the *work area*. If the available PGA memory for the process is sufficient for the entire work area, we refer to this as an *optimal work area size*, and the corresponding operation is called *optimal execution*. If the PGA is not sufficient, the operation uses the temporary permanent storage (PSAPTEMP). The resulting I/O activities (direct path operations without buffering) have a significantly negative impact on the system's performance. If the first pass (first recursion level) of the PSAPTEMP is successful, we refer to it as a one-pass operation. If the PSAPTEMP is used for several passes, it is called multi-pass operation.

There are different indicators to determine if the configured PGA memory is too small. First, you should verify the following values in the V$PGASTAT view (this applies to the automatic PGA management; see Figure 8.6):

- **Over allocation count**
  Specifies how often the PGA memory was insufficient. This value should be around 0; otherwise, you must extend the PGA.
- **Cache hit percentage**
  Specifies the number of hits for the optimal work area size. Ideally, if the value is 100%, no one-pass or multipass operations exist. This value should be >70% for a normal ERP system and >90% for a BI system.

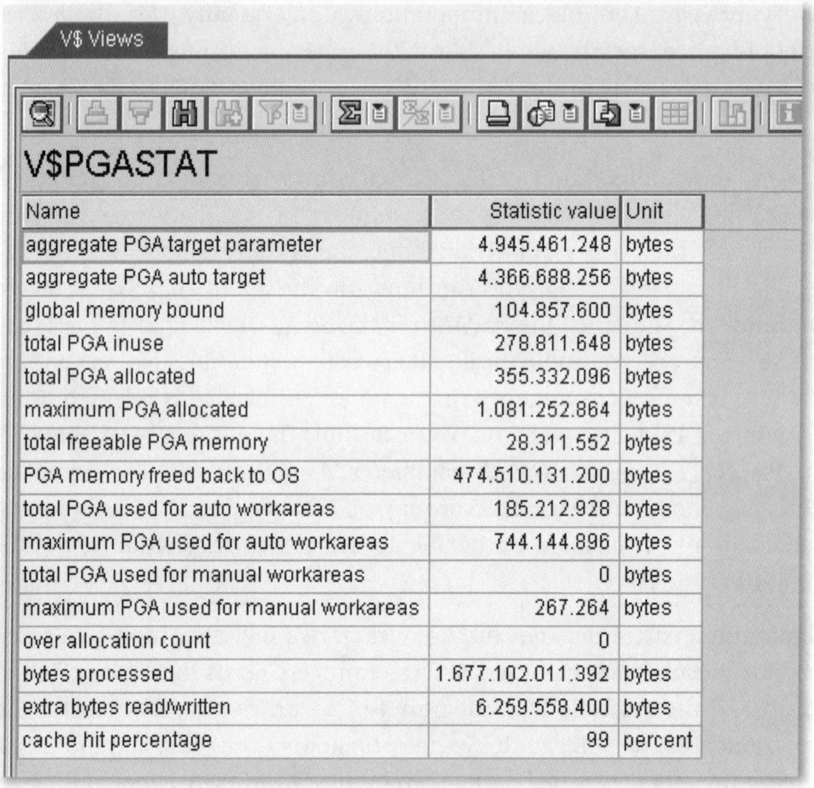

V$ Views

V$PGASTAT

Name	Statistic value	Unit
aggregate PGA target parameter	4.945.461.248	bytes
aggregate PGA auto target	4.366.688.256	bytes
global memory bound	104.857.600	bytes
total PGA inuse	278.811.648	bytes
total PGA allocated	355.332.096	bytes
maximum PGA allocated	1.081.252.864	bytes
total freeable PGA memory	28.311.552	bytes
PGA memory freed back to OS	474.510.131.200	bytes
total PGA used for auto workareas	185.212.928	bytes
maximum PGA used for auto workareas	744.144.896	bytes
total PGA used for manual workareas	0	bytes
maximum PGA used for manual workareas	267.264	bytes
over allocation count	0	
bytes processed	1.677.102.011.392	bytes
extra bytes read/written	6.259.558.400	bytes
cache hit percentage	99	percent

Figure 8.6 Characteristics of the PGA

The V$PGA_TARGET_ADVICE view displays how a change to the PGA_AGGREGATE_TARGET parameter affects the PGA quality (over allocation count and cache hit percentage).

The V$SQL_WORKAREA_HISTOGRAM view displays the frequency and quantity of the PGA memory used by a process and, accordingly, when an optimum, one-pass, or multipass operation was performed. The goal of sizing the PGA is to avoid multipass operations entirely. Depending on the type of system (ERP or BI), the percentage of optimum operations should be >70% or >90%, respectively.

8.2.2.2 Analyzing Wait Events

The quality of the individual buffer memories (data buffer, shared SQL, and so on) is not sufficient to make a reliable statement about the Oracle performance. If, for example, a query resulted in a hit, this does not tell you anything about the processing speed for the query and the output of results. That's where *Oracle wait events* come into play. The database response time consists of two elements:

- **CPU time:** the time during which the Oracle session uses the CPU
- **Wait event:** the times during which the Oracle session waits for an event, such as reading a data block from a hard disk

A wait event is a situation in which an Oracle session waits for an event. This event can come from different database areas. For example, the wait event, `log buffer space`, indicates that the session had to wait for free space in the redo log buffer. After starting the database, all wait events are collected in X$ tables and can be queried using different V$ views. The most important of these views are as follows:

- **V$SYSTEM_EVENT**
  Contains all wait events since the database was started including their frequency and average length.
- **V$SESSION_EVENT**
  Contains all waits since the database was started including their frequency and the average and maximum lengths for every Oracle session.
- **V$SESSION_WAIT**
  Contains the current waits for every Oracle session or the information that the CPU is currently being utilized.

With Oracle database Release 9i or lower, all monitoring data for the wait events are deleted after restarting the database. Oracle 10g, however, includes some history tables or views that store historical data. You can find the history of wait events in the DBA_HIST_SYSTEM_EVENT view.

The consideration of waits allows you to precisely determine which actions an Oracle session is currently performing or for which actions it is currently. This makes it easier for the administrator to identify potential problems. Moreover, the analysis of the system-wide collected waits provides details on the optimization potential within the database.

Wait events are always composed of an event name and up to three optional parameters to include more specific information on the event, as described in the following example:

- **Event:** `direct path read`: Waiting for a read operation on a data block from the hard disk while circumventing the data buffer
- **Parameter 1:** `file number`: File number of the file to be read
- **Parameter 2:** `first dba`: First block to be read in the file
- **Parameter 3:** `block count`: Quantity of blocks to be read

You can use the following SQL command to determine the file name for a file number and the corresponding tablespace:

```
Select tablespace_name, file_name
From dba_data_files
Where file_id = 'ID';
```

Oracle 10g contains more than 850 wait events (Oracle 9i has about 400), which are grouped in the classes shown in Table 8.5 to provide a better overview (as of Oracle 10g).

Wait Event Class	Number of Wait Events in Class
Administrative	46
Idle	62
Application	12
Network	26
Cluster	47
Scheduler	1

Table 8.5 Wait Event Classes (Number of Wait Events)

Wait Event Class	Number of Wait Events in Class
System I/O	24
Commit	1
User I/O	17
Concurrency	24
Other	591
Configuration	23

Table 8.5 Wait Event Classes (Number of Wait Events) (Cont.)

The following SQL statement can be used to determine to which class a wait event belongs:

```
Select WAIT_CLASS from dba_hist_event_name where EVENT_NAME='Name';
```

It is important to know that some wait events don't influence the database response time at all and can therefore be neglected in performance analyses. On the on hand, these are all events that belong to class `Idle`. These events are reported if an Oracle process is in idle state (that is, not performing any action). The most commonly known and used event of this class is `SQL*Net message from client`, which occurs if an Oracle shadow process is waiting for a new query. On the other hand, there are wait events that are irrelevant to the database, especially in the context of SAP. One reason for such a situation can be that the time of an event is already included in another event; for example, `log file parallel write` is already covered by `log file sync`. Furthermore, many (but not all) events that occur in Oracle shadow processes (`DBWR`, `PMON`, `SMON`, etc.) are only of secondary importance, because the corresponding operations are performed asynchronously to the Oracle work processes.

The following list shows the most frequent wait events that are usually irrelevant from the SAP perspective.

Oracle Wait Events not Relevant to SAP

- `db file parallel write`
- `log file sequential read`
- `smon timer`
- `SQL*Net message from client`
- `Log archive I/O`
- `ARCH wait on SENDREG`

Oracle Wait Events not Relevant to SAP

- `rdbms ipc message`
- `jobq slave wait`
- `log file parallel write`
- `pmon timer`
- `Streams AQ: <action>`

As already described in Table 8.4, the ratio between **Busy wait time** and **CPU time** (ideally 60:40) is generally a first indicator.

When starting a general wait event analysis, it is useful to create a list containing the top wait events, that is, a list with the totaled wait times in descending order. You can create this list in Transaction ST04N (see Figure 8.6) using the V$SYSTEM_EVENT view or by executing the following SQL command:

```
select EVENT, TIME_WAITED, AVERAGE_WAIT
from V$SYSTEM_EVENT
order by TIME_WAITED desc;
```

V$ Views

V$SYSTEM_EVENT

Wait event	Total waits	TotTimeOut	Time waited	AvgWaitTim	
SQL*Net message from client	127.281.305	0	5.677.404.718	45	56.774.047.184.223
rdbms ipc message	11.245.871	5.565.336	3.152.796.843	280	31.527.968.429.864
pmon timer	1.966.966	1.966.965	548.843.047	279	5.488.430.468.173
smon timer	19.338	17.315	529.726.249	27.393	5.297.262.486.895
db file sequential read	289.298.627	0	62.426.170	0	624.261.695.502
log file sync	4.239.257	341	2.344.644	1	23.446.443.696
log file parallel write	4.879.535	0	2.044.875	0	20.448.754.123
db file scattered read	21.427.723	0	772.395	0	7.723.951.864
control file parallel write	1.871.675	0	353.496	0	3.534.960.460
log file sequential read	50.781	0	71.087	1	710.873.862
control file sequential read	14.198.917	0	48.042	0	480.417.272
buffer busy waits	130.508	0	39.147	0	391.472.069
SQL*Net more data to client	1.029.243	0	32.746	0	327.458.767
enqueue	14.514	12	31.610	2	316.096.551
log buffer space	4.320	3	18.806	4	188.063.184
SQL*Net message to client	127.281.326	0	13.022	0	130.218.494
log file switch completion	2.979	0	10.717	4	107.170.463
rdbms ipc reply	15.908	0	8.082	1	80.822.031
library cache pin	1.499	5	6.696	4	66.962.562

Figure 8.7 Lists of Wait Events in the V$SYSTEM_EVENT View

The AVERAGE_WAIT column is formatted differently in Oracle 9i than in 10g. In Oracle 9i, the contained values are displayed as 1/100 seconds without decimal places, so they are not precise enough for a serious performance analysis. As an alternative, you can use the TIME_WAITED_MICRO column, which contains the total wait time in microseconds. The exact average wait time can then be calculated by dividing TIME_WAITED_MICRO by TOTAL_WAITS.

Table 8.6 provides an overview of the individual columns of the V$SYSTEM_EVENT view including their meaning.

Column	Description
TOTAL_WAITS	Number of occurrences of the wait event since the last start of the Oracle database
TOTAL_TIMEOUTS	Number of waits for which the corresponding event has not occurred
TIME_WAITED	Total wait time for the wait event in hundredths of a second
AVERAGE_WAIT	Average wait time for the event in hundredths of a second (AVERAGE_WAIT = TIME_WAITED / TOTAL_WAITS)
TIME_WAITED_MICRO (last column in Figure 8.7)	Total wait time for the wait event in microseconds

Table 8.6 Columns of the V$SYSTEM_EVENT View

Once the list has been created, it is searched from top to bottom to find critical wait events; during this step, idle wait events are ignored.

V$SESSION_WAIT

SID	SeqNo	Wait event	P1TEXT	Param. 1	Param. 1 raw	P2TEXT	P2	P2RAW	P3	P3	P3RAW	Wait Time	Sec. inWait	Session state
1	50.040	pmon timer	duration	300	...00000000012C		0	...00000		0	...00000	0	2.765.508	WAITING
2	63.456	rdbms ipc message	timeout	300	...00000000012C		0	...00000		0	...00000	0	1.732	WAITING
3	11.880	rdbms ipc message	timeout	300	...00000000012C		0	...00000		0	...00000	0	6	WAITING
6	2.355	rdbms ipc message	timeout	180.000	...00000002BF20		0	...00000		0	...00000	0	618	WAITING
8	41.164	rdbms ipc message	timeout	30.000	...000000007530		0	...00000		0	...00000	0	9.875	WAITING
7	21.897	rdbms ipc message	timeout	6.000	...000000001770		0	...00000		0	...00000	0	12	WAITING
4	34.471	rdbms ipc message	timeout	300	...00000000012C		0	...00000		0	...00000	0	0	WAITING
5	31.798	smon timer	sleep time	300	...00000000012C	failed	0	...00000		0	...00000	0	842	WAITING
9	42.101	SQL*Net message to client	driver id	1.413.697.536	...000054435000	#bytes	1	...00001		0	...00000	1-	0	WAITED KNOWN TIME
10	37.090	SQL*Net message from client	driver id	1.413.697.536	...000054435000	#bytes	1	...00001		0	...00000	0	9	WAITING
12	49.341	SQL*Net message from client	driver id	1.413.697.536	...000054435000	#bytes	1	...00001		0	...00000	0	114	WAITING
13	51.083	SQL*Net message from client	driver id	1.413.697.536	...000054435000	#bytes	1	...00001		0	...00000	0	54	WAITING
14	6.271	SQL*Net message from client	driver id	1.413.697.536	...000054435000	#bytes	1	...00001		0	...00000	0	5.694	WAITING
15	29.681	SQL*Net message from client	driver id	1.413.697.536	...000054435000	#bytes	1	...00001		0	...00000	0	291.092	WAITING
16	34.744	SQL*Net message from client	driver id	1.413.697.536	...000054435000	#bytes	1	...00001		0	...00000	0	27.532	WAITING
17	37.014	SQL*Net message from client	driver id	1.413.697.536	...000054435000	#bytes	1	...00001		0	...00000	0	291.066	WAITING
18	50.620	SQL*Net message from client	driver id	1.413.697.536	...000054435000	#bytes	1	...00001		0	...00000	0	291.087	WAITING
19	61.237	SQL*Net message from client	driver id	1.413.697.536	...000054435000	#bytes	1	...00001		0	...00000	0	291.066	WAITING
20	396	SQL*Net message from client	driver id	1.413.697.536	...000054435000	#bytes	1	...00001		0	...00000	0	26.988	WAITING
21	31.069	SQL*Net message from client	driver id	1.413.697.536	...000054435000	#bytes	1	...00001		0	...00000	0	29.537	WAITING
22	120	SQL*Net message from client	driver id	1.413.697.536	...000054435000	#bytes	1	...00001		0	...00000	0	2.765.474	WAITING
24	49.995	SQL*Net message from client	driver id	1.413.697.536	...000054435000	#bytes	1	...00001		0	...00000	0	54	WAITING
26	9.065	SQL*Net message from client	driver id	1.413.697.536	...000054435000	#bytes	1	...00001		0	...00000	0	354	WAITING
27	64.700	SQL*Net message from client	driver id	1.413.697.536	...000054435000	#bytes	1	...00001		0	...00000	0	27.500	WAITING
29	54.861	SQL*Net message from client	driver id	1.413.697.536	...000054435000	#bytes	1	...00001		0	...00000	0	173	WAITING
34	121	SQL*Net message from client	driver id	1.413.697.536	...000054435000	#bytes	1	...00001		0	...00000	3	414	WAITED KNOWN TIME
35	928	SQL*Net message from client	driver id	1.413.697.536	...000054435000	#bytes	1	...00001		0	...00000	1	293	WAITED KNOWN TIME
36	9.316	SQL*Net message from client	driver id	1.413.697.536	...000054435000	#bytes	1	...00001		0	...00000	0	54	WAITING
37	927	SQL*Net message from client	driver id	1.413.697.536	...000054435000	#bytes	1	...00001		0	...00000	2	54	WAITED KNOWN TIME

Figure 8.8 V$SESSION_WAIT View

You can obtain further important information in the V$SESSION_WAIT view (see Figure 8.8). This view displays the current or most recently active wait events of all Oracle processes.

Table 8.7 describes the meaning of the individual columns in the V$SESSION_WAIT view.

Column	Description
SID	Session ID of the Oracle process.
P1TEXT, P2TEXT, P3TEXT	Description and unit of the corresponding parameter.
P1, P2, P3	Parameter values of the wait event.
WAIT TIME	Time waited for the wait event (in hundredths of a second) once the wait event is no longer active. The value of an active wait event is 0. Moreover, there are two special values: Value = –1 if the duration of the event was below the measurement accuracy and value = –2 if TIMED_STATISTICS is not active.
STATE	Wait events can have the following statuses: ▸ WAITING: waiting/active (WAIT TIME = 0) ▸ WAITED KNOWN TIME: has expired and had a duration of more than 1/100 sec (WAIT TIME > 0) ▸ WAITED UNKNOWN TIME: has expired and had a duration of less than 1/100 sec (WAIT TIME = –1) ▸ TIME STATISTICS OFF: has expired, but statistics are not recorded (WAIT TIME = –2)

Table 8.7 Columns of the V$SESSION_WAIT View

Furthermore, it is often necessary or it simply makes sense to map the SAP work processes to an Oracle work process or vice versa. The easiest way to do this is to use the Oracle Session Monitor. In the **Clnt proc column,** this component includes the process ID of the linked SAP work process for every entry of an Oracle work process. This client PID corresponds to the **Pid** column of the SAP process monitor (Transaction SM50).

Warning

A CPU bottleneck can also cause a large number of different wait events. If the CPU load is very high, it is possible that Oracle processes that currently hold a lock are displaced. If other processes are waiting for this lock, several wait times can increase drastically. You should therefore first ensure that sufficient CPU resources are available.

Remark

As mentioned earlier, compared to the previous Release Oracle 9i, the number of wait events was increased considerably in Oracle 10g. This is reflected, for instance, in the splitting up of wait events for a more detailed root cause specification. We will mainly use the wait events from Oracle 10g and only point out the differences in comparison to Oracle 9i in a few situations.

The following sections describe the most important wait events and provide some background information on these. You'll find several tables with the most important details followed by a text section containing a description of the wait event.

Name	db file sequential read/db file parallel read
Parameter 1	File number(s)
Parameter 2	Block number(s)
Parameter 3	One or a number of parallel reads
Meaning	These events represent the process of waiting for one or more parallel read operations to be performed on blocks on the hard disk. In this case, parallel does not refer to reading several blocks successively, but to simultaneous reads of different, nonsuccessive blocks.
Rating	Average wait time should be less than 2, i.e., 2/100 s = 20 ms.

Table 8.8 db file sequential read/db file parallel read

If there are problem values for the average wait time, this primarily indicates an I/O performance bottleneck. For information on the analysis of I/O problems, refer to Section 8.2.2.3, *Analyzing the Database I/O*. Another important factor apart from wait time is the occurrence frequency of `db file sequential read`. If this value is very high, the wait event usually occurs in conjunction with a bad hit ratio of the data buffer. In this case, there are two solution scenarios: You either tune potentially existing bad SQL statements (see Section 8.3) or you increase the data buffer size.

Name	db file scattered read
Parameter 1	File number
Parameter 2	Block number
Parameter 3	Number of blocks

Table 8.9 db file scattered read

Name	db file scattered read
Meaning	If this event occurs, an Oracle session is waiting for a successive read operation on several blocks from the hard disk.
Rating	A maximum of 10% of the WAIT_TIME of `db file sequential read` (exception: in case of SAP NetWeaver BI, a higher value can be accepted).

Table 8.9 db file scattered read (Cont.)

A successive read operation on several blocks usually occurs only with `Full table scan` or `Index fast full scan`. These access types reduce performance significantly and should thus be avoided if possible. Once again, SAP NetWeaver BI represents an exception to this rule (see Chapter 12). If the occurrence of `db file scattered read` exceeds the values listed in Table 8.9, you should determine the SQL commands that cause this situation. Information on these commands can be found using the function **SQL Request** in Transaction ST04N or following menu path **Resource Consumption • SQL Request**. Pay attention to SQL statements with high disk reads. Better yet, focus only on commands that include a full scan in their process.

SAP Note 619188 describes an SQL command that can be used as of Oracle 9i. Using this command, you can determine the 20 SQL statements that generate the largest number of disk reads because of full scans. You should then determine if these commands can be tuned. **Attention**: If you make extensive use of the Oracle transactions in the SAP system (for example, Transaction ST04N) during performance analysis, this may be reflected in the results. In this case, some of the top 20 SQL statements contain queries on Oracle specifications or Oracle monitoring data that are not associated with the normal business-related SQL queries. These SQL statements should be ignored in your analysis.

Name	direct path read/direct path read temp direct path write/direct path write temp
Parameter 1	File number
Parameter 2	Block number
Parameter 3	Number of blocks

Table 8.10 direct path [read|write|temp]

Name	direct path read/direct path read temp direct path write/direct path write temp
Meaning	This wait event is registered if the data buffer is circumvented when data blocks are accessed. As of Oracle 10g, waits are categorized by either access to "normal" blocks or access to temporary blocks from the PSAPTEMP tablespace (temp).
Rating	None of these events should be among the first 10 in the wait event list (in descending order according to the totaled wait time; see Figure 8.7). Furthermore, similar to `db file sequential read`, a maximum value of 2 applies to the average wait time, i.e., 2/100 s = 20 ms.

Table 8.10 direct path [read|write|temp] (Cont.)

If the problem is caused by a too long average wait time, this is probably also caused by an I/O bottleneck. In this case, you should perform the steps described in Section 8.2.1.2, *Identifying the Causes of Bottlenecks in Hardware Components*.

If the `direct path` operations are performed too often and are therefore displayed among the first entries in the list, you must distinguish between the reasons for these operations in subsequent actions.

For the Oracle database, there are three reasons why `direct path` operations are performed:

1. PSAPTEMP accesses
2. Parallel queries
3. Access to LOB data (large object)

For many operations on the PSAPTEMP tablespace (these can be recognized by the wait event, `direct path read/write temp`), increasing the PGA storage (see Section 8.2.2.1, *Analyzing the Database Buffers*) is a possible solution to the problem. Operations that are performed for the second or third reason cannot be distinguished in Oracle 10g. In contrast, when accessing unbuffered LOB data in Oracle 9i, a separate wait event is generated: `direct path read/write (lob)`. LOB data, that is, large unstructured data in table columns, is primarily used by the SAP system in tables with ABAP code. Because of their size (up to four gigabytes), these LOBs are no longer buffered in the data buffer. This again results in `direct path` operations. If problems occur, buffering special LOB data might be advisable (see SAP Note 563359).

Parallel queries, that is, performing special actions such as a full table scan in parallel, are generally not used by SAP. They are only used for SAP NetWeaver BI systems. The reason for this is that these queries have several disadvantages regarding the CBO and the resulting resource allocation (see SAP Note 651060).

Name	log file sync/log buffer space/log file parallel write
Parameter 1	Number of buffers/ - / file number
Parameter 2	- / - / Number of blocks
Parameter 3	- / - / Number of I/O requests
Meaning	▸ `log file sync` Represents the process of waiting for the full synchronization of the log files with the redo buffer by the LGWR (e.g., after a `COMMIT`). ▸ `log buffer space` Represents the process of waiting for a free block in the redo buffer. ▸ `log file parallel write` Occurs if there is a wait time for the writing of blocks in the redo log files.
Rating	For all three wait events, a maximum average wait time of 4 applies, i.e., 4/100 s = 40 ms. However, for current hardware, significantly lower values should be obtained that allow for about 15 ms.

Table 8.11 log file [sync|parallel] and log buffer space

All three wait events described above usually depend directly on I/O performance during write operations for redo log files. You should therefore first analyze and examine if there are I/O problems and whether these areas can be optimized (see Section 8.2.1.2, *Identifying the Causes of Bottlenecks in Hardware Components*, and Section 8.2.2.3, *Analyzing the Database I/O*). The redo log files are the most I/O-intensive area of an Oracle database and therefore have special requirements regarding their storage location and parameterization. Section 5.2.3, *Storage and SAN Infrastructure*, provides further information on this topic.

Under certain circumstances, it makes sense to completely deactivate logging when importing or modifying large data volumes. This takes place, for instance, during the initial loading of the SAP system in the database. However, after deactivating logging, you can only restore and recover data up to the time when this action was performed. This means you need to create a new full backup of the system once you reactivate the logging function.

Another aspect is the size of the redo buffer. If this buffer is configured with less than one megabyte – contrary to the SAP recommendation – this may also result in log buffer space wait events. If this situation occurs, you need to change the `LOG_BUFFER` parameter to the size of one megabyte (offline). There are a few other cause of the `log file sync` wait event, such as enqueue wait situations (see SAP Note 745639, Section 12).

Name	log file switch completion/(archiving needed)/(checkpoint incomplete)/(private strand flush incomplete)
Parameters	–
Meaning	These wait events are reported if the system needs to wait for a log file switch for different reasons (see below).
Rating	▸ `archiving needed` Should never occur ▸ `checkpoint incomplete` Should never occur (special SAP Note 79341) ▸ `completion` Should not be among the top 10 of the wait event list, at most one log switch per minute ▸ `private strand flush incomplete` Should never occur

Table 8.12 log file switch completion

The term *log file switch* is a generic term for several wait events that occur when switching to the next redo log file:

- **log file switch (archiving needed)**
  Occurs if the log switch cannot be performed, because the next redo log file has not been archived yet
- **log file switch (checkpoint incomplete)**
  Represents the process of waiting for completion of the checkpoint of the subsequent redo logs before the log switch
- **log file switch completion**
  Represents the process of waiting for completion of the log switch
- **log file switch (private strand flush incomplete)**
  Occurs if the LGWR waits for the DBWR to completely write the in-memory UNDO buffer (IMU) into the log buffer

An "archiving needed" event always has an average wait time of 98–100 (time in one-hundredth of one per second), because the writing Oracle processes (LGWR, DBWR, etc.) always wait for exactly one second in case of an archiver stuck before a new write attempt is carried out. An archiver stuck must not occur in an SAP production system, as this would cause a system standstill. Only in a nonproduction system is a short archiver stuck acceptable under certain circumstances, if the system reaches a very high load, for instance, during client copies or data loading at night-time. To avoid this standstill of the Oracle database, your backup strategy must ensure that the disk volume on which the offline redo logs are saved (usually the directory *oraarch*) is always backed up and purged so that there is sufficient space for new offline redo logs after a redo switch. If you define other archiver destinations using the `LOG_ARCHIVE_DEST` parameter, you need to ensure that these are backed up as well.

In the case of a `log file switch (checkpoint incomplete)` wait event, the "checkpoint not complete" error has occurred and was recorded in the Oracle alert log. Checkpoints are performed during every log switch. Several checkpoints can be active at the same time. The "checkpoint not complete" error is recorded if a log switch is to be performed to a redo log with a checkpoint that has not yet been completed.

The following four situations can cause a repeated occurrence of the wait event or the "checkpoint not complete" situation:

1. Numerous redo logs are being written.
2. DBWR performance bottleneck.
3. Not enough redo logs.
4. Redo logs are too small.

If the Oracle database writes many redo logs, you should first examine whether you are dealing with an operational load, that is, whether the number of redo logs is caused by the normal system usage. If there is no indication that your applications are responsible for the high redo log frequency, there are several other possible reasons, such as misconfigurations and Oracle bugs. Read SAP Note 584548 for a description of the possible causes.

Usually, the reason for a high amount of redo logs can, of course, be found in the system operation. As a first step, you should ensure that no more than one redo log switch is performed per minute. If this is not the case, you should increase the size of your redo log files. To do that, proceed as follows:

1. Log on to the database as sysdba:

   ```
   sqlplus "/ as sysdba"
   ```

2. Delete a log file group:

   ```
   ALTER DATABASE DROP LOGFILE GROUP 11;
   ```

   If the error ORA-01623 is reported, use the following command to switch to a new redo log file and wait for a few seconds before you repeat the `DROP` command:

   ```
   ALTER SYSTEM SWITCH LOGFILE;
   ```

   If the error ORA-01624 is reported, the current checkpoint has not yet been completed. Wait for a few seconds and repeat the `DROP` command.

3. Delete the corresponding operating system files in the redo log directory.
4. Set up the log file group 11 with a new larger size (<new_size> in MB):

   ```
   ALTER DATABASE ADD LOGFILE GROUP 11
   ('/oracle/<sid>/origlogA/log_g11_m1.dbf',
   '/oracle/<sid>/mirrlogA/log_g11_m2.dbf')
   SIZE <new_size>M;
   ```

5. Repeat steps 2 through 4 for all existing redo log groups.

In the standard SAP installation, the redo log files of the four groups have a size of 50 MB each. Increase the files incrementally and verify whether this solves the problem. The scope of the increase depends on the number of redo logs that are written per minute. If five log switches are performed per minute with a size of 50 MB, there is no point in increasing the log size to 100 MB, but, change the size to, for instance, 300 MB right away.

If the `log file switch (private strand flush incomplete)` wait event occurs or there are other indications of a bottleneck in the DBWR process, for example, from the `free buffer waits` wait events (see below), you can increase the number of DBWR processes to enhance write performance. To do this, set the `DB_WRITER_PROCESSES` parameter using the following command (prerequisite: parameter management with SPFILE):

```
alter system set db_writer_processes=X scope=spfile;
```

Attention: The number of DBWR processes should not exceed the number of available CPUs.

Another way to enhance write performance is, of course, to tune the Oracle environment, that is, all I/O relevant components. Refer to Section 8.2.2.3 for further information on this topic.

The `log file switch completion` wait event occurs if an Oracle shadow process must wait for the completion of a log switch. As described above, if too many redo log switches exist during operation (more than once per minute), this results in a critical condition regarding the database performance. However, if this happens, proceed as described earlier.

Name	read by other session/buffer busy wait
Parameter 1	File number
Parameter 2	Block number
Parameter 3	ID
Meaning	These wait events describe the process of waiting for a block in the data buffer, because this block is currently being read (`read by other session`) or modified (`buffer busy wait`).
Rating	The average wait time value should be below 2, i.e., 2/100 s = 20 ms.

Table 8.13 read by other session/buffer busy wait

In Oracle 9i, both events were named `buffer busy wait`, and parameter value 3 indicated the reason: The IDs started with 1 or 2 and contained further places depending on the exact reason. If the ID starts with 1 (ID = 1xx), the event deals with the reading of a block. If it starts with 2 (ID = 2xx), the wait event is caused by a write or change operation for a block. As of Oracle 10g, the name of the wait event already distinguishes whether the event was caused by a read or write operation. Detailed information on the event cause can be obtained from the parameters.

As all data that are read from or saved in the database "pass through" the data buffer (an exception is the already mentioned direct path access), high I/O loads always result in `buffer busy waits`. You always have the option to reduce I/O load to decrease the amount of waits on the data buffer. This can either be done by redistributing data loads or by tuning SQL statements so that fewer data blocks must be read (see Section 8.3).

The second criteria besides I/O load is the management of the data blocks themselves. In this area, in particular, Oracle 9i provided significant enhancements with the introduction of *Automatic Segment Space Management* (ASSM). Previously, the individual blocks of a tablespace or a segment were managed using the PCTUSED, PCTFREE, FREELISTS, and FREELISTGROUPS parameters. These parameters were used, for example, to define the fill level of a block (PCTUSED): As long as this value was not reached, the block would accept new data. From this group of parameters, only one was also implemented in ASSM so that you can still use its function: PCTFREE.

Without ASSM, the database administrator had to or could decide for each table how the individual blocks of the segments were used. This made it possible to choose between performance and efficient space usage depending on the change frequency. This task is now performed by ASSM. SAP made the use of ASSM possible as of Version 9.2.0.5, and on installations with SAP Basis 6.40 and higher all data tablespaces are set to ASSM by default. If problems occur that are related to buffer busy waits, you can now switch to ASSM to resolve issues relating to segment management. In Oracle 9i, this switching procedure involves downtime, whereas Oracle 10g allows you to make the transition online. SAP Note 620803 provides step-by-step instructions for this transition.

Name	write complete waits/free buffer waits
Parameter 1	File number
Parameter 2	Block number
Parameter 3	ID
Meaning	These wait events occur if an Oracle process must wait for the DBWR process to write a block into the relevant data file.
Rating	Both wait events must not be among the first 10 entries in the wait event list.

Table 8.14 write complete waits/free buffer waits

If these wait events occur too often, the data buffer may be too small or the performance of the DBWR process is poor. If possible, resolve this problem by increasing the value for the DB_CACHE_SIZE parameter or optimizing the I/O performance (Section 8.2.2.3). Furthermore, you can raise the number of DBWR processes as described in the previous section.

Name	rdbms ipc reply
Parameter 1	PID of the background process
Parameter 2	Timeout in seconds
Parameter 3	–

Table 8.15 rdbms ipc reply

Name	rdbms ipc reply
Meaning	This wait event occurs if an Oracle shadow process must wait for a background process.
Rating	This event must not be among the top 10 entries in the wait event list.

Table 8.15 rdbms ipc reply (Cont.)

In general, the occurrence of the `rdbms ipc reply` wait event is not a problem, as there are various reasons why a process must wait for a background process. The crucial factor is the duration of the wait time for the background process. The main reason for this event is wait situations in the `BEGIN BACKUP`, `TRUNCATE`, and `DROP` operations, because the CKPT process must perform a checkpoint in these operations. In Oracle 9i and lower, there is the additional drawback of a design weakness that results in the entire data buffer being searched for affected blocks in a `DROP` or `TRUNCATE` operation; this process can take quite some time with larger buffer sizes. This problem does longer exists in Oracle 10g.

In general, the duration of `rdbms ipc reply` wait events is very short. For this reason, the average wait time should not exceed 10 ms, as this would indicate several wait periods that are much too long and increase the average value. In this case, it is advisable to examine the enqueue wait events, because some of them are closely related to the `rdbms ipc reply` wait event. Refer to SAP Note 745639 for further information on this topic.

If you suspect a problem with this wait event, you can use the Oracle Session Monitor (Transaction ST04N; **Resource Consumption • Oracle Session**) and V$SESSION_WAIT to determine which Oracle work process is waiting for which background process. In V$SESSION_WAIT you'll find the SID of the process that is waiting for the `rdbms ipc reply` wait event, while parameter 1 (column P1) displays the PID of the background process for which the work process is waiting. Subsequently, you can use the Session Monitor to find out which actions the background process is currently performing. For a more detailed analysis of the actions performed by Oracle processes, you should use the functions of the ORADEBUG trace. The procedure is described in SAP Note 613872.

Name	latch free/latch: <latch_name>/wait list latch free
Parameter 1	Latch address
Parameter 2	Latch number

Table 8.16 Latch Wait Events

Name	latch free/latch: <latch_name>/wait list latch free
Parameter 3	Number of sleeps
Meaning	This wait event occurs if a process must wait for the release of a latch.
Rating	The rating heavily depends on the specific latch wait event. In general, latch wait events should not appear among the top 10 entries in the wait event list.

Table 8.16 Latch Wait Events (Cont.)

A *latch* is a very low-level lock mechanism for the SGA memory structures. In contrast to a lock, a latch is applied only for a very short time. For this reason, latch requests are not placed in a queue, but the requesting processes permanently try to apply the latch. This so-called spinning process is performed as many times as set in the `_SPIN_COUNT` parameter. If a process applies a latch and another process tries to access the respective memory area, but does not succeed in doing so during the spin phase, a latch `<latch_name>` wait event is activated. Oracle 10g contains 27 latch wait events, and their names specify the location or the memory structure in which the latch is applied. All "irrelevant" latches are referred to as "latch free."

In older Oracle releases (before 10g), all waits are summarized under the term *latch free*. As an analysis of the different latch wait events would go far beyond the scope of this chapter, we refer you to SAP Note 767414 for more detailed information on this topic.

Name	enqueue (9i)/enq: <type> - <description> (10g)
Parameter 1	Type
Parameter 2	ID1 (9i)/Detailed information in plain text (10g)
Parameter 3	ID2 (9i)/Detailed information in plain text (10g)
Meaning	An event of this type occurs if a process is waiting for the release of an Oracle lock.
Rating	The average wait time value (of all enqueue events) should be below 10, i.e., 10/100 s = 100 ms. As all possible lock situations are collected under one event in 9i, it is generally not a problem if these events are listed among the lower top 10 entries in the wait event list. With Oracle 10g, however, the different enqueue waits should not appear among the top 10 (an exception is TX "row lock contention").

Table 8.17 Enqueue Wait Events

Finally, we want to introduce another important Oracle wait event related to Oracle database locks (enqueues and locks). The meaning of this event can be seen from the development between 9i and 10g. In Oracle 9i, all enqueue waits were still accumulated as one event so that it was rather difficult to perform an analysis. With 10g, however, 184 enqueue wait events were introduced, which, are grouped in different classes (see Section 8.2.2.4, *Other Performance-Relevant Aspects of the Oracle Database*; this section describes database locks in greater detail).

8.2.2.3 Analyzing the Database I/O

If you have found a hint on problems in the I/O area in one of the preceding analyses, for example, due to an anomaly of a corresponding wait event, you inevitably get to the I/O analysis. Unfortunately, from the SAP administrator's point of view, the analysis of an I/O system is restricted. In addition, an I/O bottleneck can generally not be solved during the operation if it is caused by hardware or the distribution of data.

Term Clarification

- Before getting started with the analysis, we should clarify the term *hard disk*. (Also refer to Figure 8.11.) Regarding server systems for business-critical applications, namely, the world of SAP and Oracle, the term *hard disk* has two meanings:
- Physical: magnetic memory; the hardware part
- Virtual: operating system resource (device); the software part

In the following text, the term *hard disk* is always used with the second meaning, because the SAP system or the database considers only the operating system with the resources available as the underlying level. Regardless of whether the hard disk is visible as a hard disk with file system or as a raw device, the virtual hard disk in a modern IT infrastructure is far more than a physical hard disk. In fact, there is a complex storage architecture with many different components behind the operating system as the abstraction layer. All of these parts of a storage system, for instance, interface cards to a SAN, storage switches, or array controllers, can be relevant for I/O problems. Unfortunately, you as an SAP or Oracle administrator have no chance to identify and solve problems but need assistance from specialists of the respective hardware partner. You should keep this definition in mind and remember the "veiled" complexity of the term in the relevant parts of the following sections.

Critical points in the structure of an Oracle database are as follows: The most I/O intensive areas are without any doubt the redo log files followed by the data files. Out of those, the undo (or rollback) and PSAPTEMP tablespaces can be pointed out, which always (undo) or, especially in the OLAP environment (PSAPTEMP), show increased access rates. Offline redo logs and Oracle executables are less important. Read Section 5.2.3, *Storage and SAN Infrastructure,* to find out more about the optimal distribution of Oracle files.

We already briefly touched upon analyses in Section 8.2. In the operating system monitor (ST06) you can view the current utilization of all hard disks of the operating system (see Figure 8.9) under **Detail Analysis Menu** using the **Disk** button.

Local (f42) / Local disks snapshot

Refresh display

Thu Sep 7 09:44:44 2006 interval 10 sec.

Disk	Resp. [ms]	Util. [%]	Queue Len.	Wait [ms]	Serv [ms]	Kbyte [/s]	Oper. [/s]
c0t6d0	17	2	0	1	16	29	4
c0t5d0	16	6	0	0	16	38	10
c7t6d0	16	2	0	0	16	30	4
c4t6d0	13	4	0	0	13	31	8
c35t4d4	1	0	0	0	1	11	1
c41t2d6	1	1	0	0	1	214	18
c34t10d2	0	0	0	0	0	0	0
c34t12d7	0	0	0	0	0	0	0
c35t2d0	0	0	0	0	0	0	0

SAPMSSY0 | f42 | INS

Figure 8.9 Overview of the Hard Disks in the Operating System Monitor

By double-clicking on one of the displayed disks, you can view the utilization of the selected disk during the last 24 hours. The most important key figure, **Utilization**, shows a mean value over a period of one hour (see Figure 8.10).

Local (f42) / Disk c41t2d6 last 24 hours

Disk-- | Disk ++ | Graphics by column

Thu Sep 7 09:44:44 2006

Hour	Utiliz. [%]	Queue length	Wait Time [ms]	Srv. Time [ms]	[Mbyte/h]	Oper. [/h]	[Kbyte/s]	Oper. [/s]
22	9	0	0	0	1.417	153494	403	43
21	9	0	0	0	1.573	164182	447	46
20	13	0	0	0	1.804	176518	513	49
19	13	0	0	0	1.513	165669	430	46
18	13	0	0	0	1.496	156706	426	44
17	11	0	0	0	1.446	155576	411	43
16	10	0	0	0	1.656	166661	471	46
15	8	0	0	0	1.515	157714	431	44
14	13	0	0	1	1.482	157530	422	44
13	13	0	0	1	1.930	186984	549	52
12	10	0	0	0	1.469	155935	418	43

SAPMSSY0 | f42 | INS

Figure 8.10 History of a Single Hard Disk

If you discover a problem with a hard disk via the I/O utilization, you must identify which parts of the Oracle and SAP installation are on the disk. Unfortunately, the SAP system does not enable you to retrace the direct assignment of files and raw devices to hard disks. The reason is the already mentioned resource of the virtual hard disk that is displayed in the operating system monitor. Between the virtual hard disk and the actual files, server systems have another virtualization layer, such as the typical Logical Volume Manager (LVM) for UNIX operating systems. Figure 8.11 illustrates the relationship between the individual components.

For example, if you want to create a connection between the hard disk and the Oracle data files or raw devices, you must use tools of the operating system.

You have two options to increase the I/O performance: You can increase the performance of the hard disk(s) or try to reduce the I/O load.

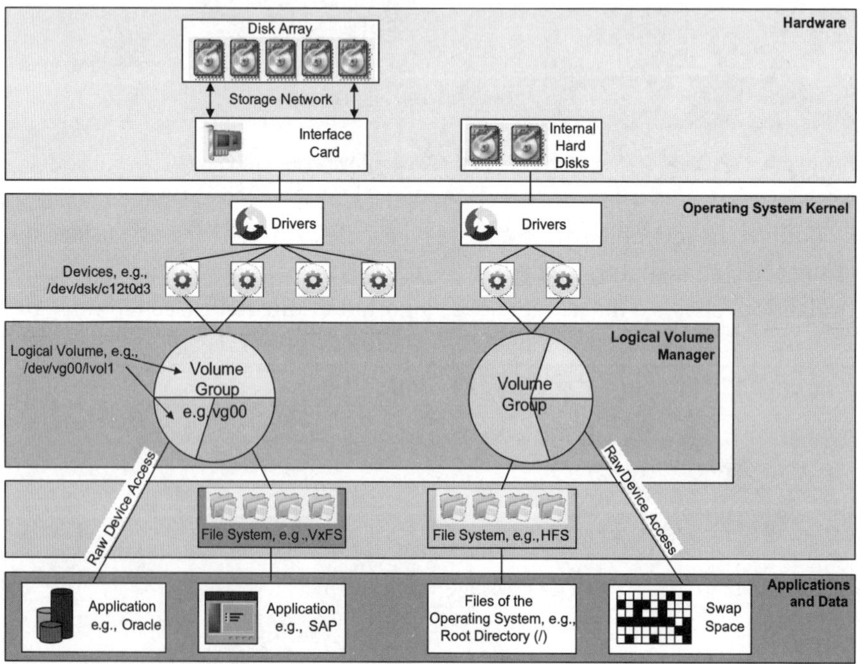

Figure 8.11 Overview of a UNIX System with Logical Volume Manager

Let us first take a look at the options to increase the hard disk performance. First, you should check if you have used all options of the operating system for optimal performance:

1. Does the layout of the structure of your Oracle files correspond to the recommendations, especially regarding the separation of load-intensive files (see Chapter 5, *Planning the System Landscape*)?
2. Have you used all possible options of I/O processing?
3. Are all current drivers for I/O subsystems installed?

You should pay particular attention to the options of I/O processing. In general, all operating systems provide two functions for I/O operations: the *file system caching* and *file lock mechanisms*. File system caching works in a similar way to the Oracle data buffer (but is easier) as a temporary storage for the access of applications to I/O systems. File locks serve as write locks so that data or files cannot be changed simultaneously by two different processes. For the options of I/O processing, the handling of the mentioned operating system functions is decisive. Table 8.18 lists all options in descending order of their performance.

Name	Description
Raw I/O	When raw I/O (or raw devices) is used, the operating system functions are bypassed completely, and logical volumes and hard disks are directly accessed. Furthermore, there is no file system and correspondingly no data in the traditional sense.
Concurrent I/O	As is the case for raw I/O, file system caching and file locks are bypassed completely, but there is a file system and thus normal files. Of course, the used file system must support concurrent I/O (e.g., Veritas VxFS). This I/O type can be used for Oracle databases, as the Oracle-internal locking functions already provide a collision-free access and hence ensure the integrity of data. Caution: Only volumes that contain only Oracle data or redo log files may be operated in this mode (Oracle executables are also excluded).
Direct I/O	Direct I/O disables only the file system caching of the operating system but uses the locking mechanism for the data access.
Cached I/O	Uses all operating system functions for I/O and is generally the default setting for I/O processing.

Table 8.18 Options of I/O Processing

In addition to the I/O modes already mentioned, there are two more independent options: *synchronous I/O* and *asynchronous I/O*. When a process performs a synchronous input or output, the process must wait until the operation is completed and only then can continue to work or perform the next input or output. This is not the case for asynchronous I/O. Thus, the process can continue working simultaneously with the I/O operation. Generally, you should use asynchronous I/O.

SAP Note 834343 provides a table with the currently supported combinations of operating system, file system, and I/O options.

Another remark on raw I/O: Basically, with raw I/O, you can assume that you can reach an I/O performance that is about 20% higher than the performance with other I/O options. Why is raw I/O not always used? The main disadvantage of raw I/O is that it always involves significantly increased administration efforts for setting up and managing the Oracle database. However, a psychological aspect also assumes an important role regarding the usage of raw I/O: The administrator "misses" his files. The Oracle recommendation for the usage of raw devices is as follows:

"Oracle recommends that raw devices should only be considered when the Oracle database is I/O bound."[2]

Raw I/O is fully supported and integrated by SAP, Oracle, and all relevant monitoring and backup solutions so that it can be especially used for performance-critical installations, such as SAP Business Information Warehouse. In this case it is also possible to operate only parts of the Oracle database, for instance, redo log files or the temporary tablespace, on raw devices.

For the usage of the described I/O options, the administrator also has to keep two relevant Oracle parameters in mind:

- **DISK_ASYNCH_IO** (Default: `TRUE`)
  This option ensures that asynchronous I/O is always used when it is offered by the operating system.
- **FILESYSTEMIO_OPTIONS** (Default: none on the part of Oracle, however, depending on the version SAP uses `ASYNC` (9i) or `SETALL` (10g))
  This parameter overrides `DISK_ASYNCH_IO` when file systems are used and includes the following options:
  - **NONE**
    No direct I/O and no asynchronous I/O.
  - **DIRECTIO**
    Enables direct I/O.
  - **DIRECTIO**
    Enables asynchronous I/O.
  - **SETALL**
    Enables concurrent I/O (if available), direct I/O, and asynchronous I/O.

2 Oracle recommends that raw devices should only be considered when the Oracle database is I/O bound. See *www.oracle-training.cc/oracle_tips_raw_devices.htm*.

For example, this can be used for installations with the combination of raw devices and file system to use asynchronous I/O on the raw device (DISK_ASYNC_IO=TRUE) on the one hand, but also to use cached I/O for file system data (FILESYSTEMIO_OPTIONS=NONE).

In addition to the options for I/O processing, SAP supports further parameters for the different systems that can affect the I/O performance. SAP Note 793113 is a good starting point that refers to the individual operating system-specific notes. To increase the hard disk performance, you can also exchange hardware. Especially regarding the already described complex storage systems that are now used in important areas, many components can be significantly enhanced when they are replaced by a new generation. Together with your hardware partner, you should decide whether such an exchange makes sense or not. Let us now take a look at the second option for increasing the I/O performance: the attempt to reduce the I/O load. Here, you must bear in mind which I/O type occurs where. Table 8.19 provides notes on the I/O reduction.

Data type/ I/O type	Read I/O	Write I/O
Redo log files	/	▸ Keep data files no longer than necessary in backup mode (parameter backup_dev_type) ▸ If possible, use NOLOGGING ▸ Avoid long transactions with timeouts and rollbacks (because changes are unnecessarily logged) ▸ Avoid unnecessary INSERT-, UPDATE, and DELETE operations ▸ Avoid unnecessary indexes
Data files	▸ Tuning of expensive SQL statements (Section 8.3) ▸ Caching of LOB accesses (SAP Note 563359) ▸ Extension of the Oracle buffer pool ▸ Extension of the PGA	▸ Time between log switches more than one minute ▸ Distribution of data files across different volumes or hard disks ▸ Extension of the PGA ▸ Extension of the buffer pool (at free buffer waits)
Temporary data files (PSAPTEMP)	▸ Tuning of expensive sorting with sort, hash, or bitmap functions ▸ Extension of the PGA	▸ Tuning of expensive sorting with sort, hash, or bitmap functions ▸ Extension of the PGA

Table 8.19 Notes on the I/O Load Reduction

Regarding the reduction of I/O load, we will concentrate on one aspect in more detail: the distribution of data files to reduce the accesses to individual volumes and hard disks. "File system requests" in the Oracle monitor (Transaction ST04N; **Overall Activity**) are suited to get an impression of the number of accesses to the individual data files. Figure 8.12 shows the corresponding view, sorted by the number of read accesses.

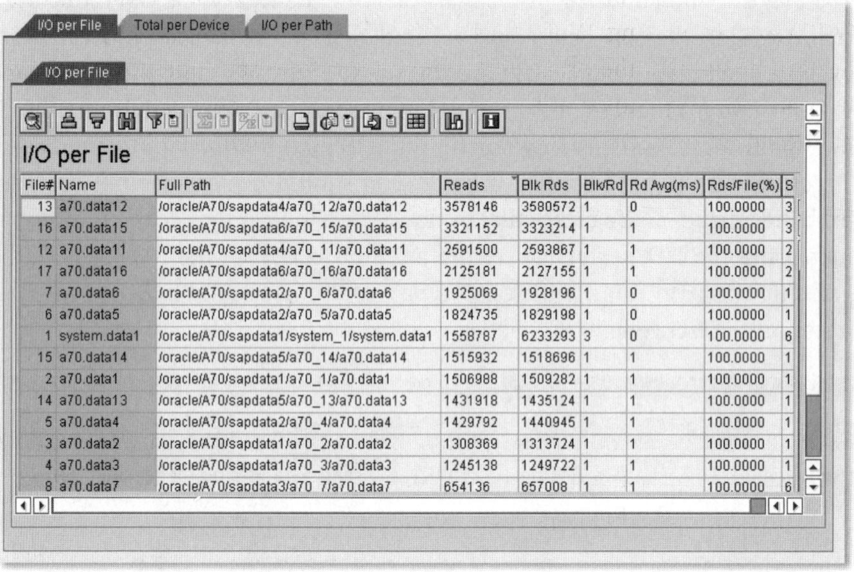

File#	Name	Full Path	Reads	Blk Rds	Blk/Rd	Rd Avg(ms)	Rds/File(%)	S
13	a70.data12	/oracle/A70/sapdata4/a70_12/a70.data12	3578146	3580572	1	0	100.0000	3
16	a70.data15	/oracle/A70/sapdata6/a70_15/a70.data15	3321152	3323214	1	1	100.0000	3
12	a70.data11	/oracle/A70/sapdata4/a70_11/a70.data11	2591500	2593867	1	1	100.0000	2
17	a70.data16	/oracle/A70/sapdata6/a70_16/a70.data16	2125181	2127155	1	1	100.0000	2
7	a70.data6	/oracle/A70/sapdata2/a70_6/a70.data6	1925069	1928196	1	0	100.0000	1
6	a70.data5	/oracle/A70/sapdata2/a70_5/a70.data5	1824735	1829198	1	0	100.0000	1
1	system.data1	/oracle/A70/sapdata1/system_1/system.data1	1558787	6233293	3	0	100.0000	6
15	a70.data14	/oracle/A70/sapdata5/a70_14/a70.data14	1515932	1518696	1	1	100.0000	1
2	a70.data1	/oracle/A70/sapdata1/a70_1/a70.data1	1506988	1509282	1	1	100.0000	1
14	a70.data13	/oracle/A70/sapdata5/a70_13/a70.data13	1431918	1435124	1	1	100.0000	1
5	a70.data4	/oracle/A70/sapdata2/a70_4/a70.data4	1429792	1440945	1	1	100.0000	1
3	a70.data2	/oracle/A70/sapdata1/a70_2/a70.data2	1308369	1313724	1	1	100.0000	1
4	a70.data3	/oracle/A70/sapdata1/a70_3/a70.data3	1245138	1249722	1	1	100.0000	1
8	a70.data7	/oracle/A70/sapdata3/a70_7/a70.data7	654136	657008	1	1	100.0000	6

Figure 8.12 Access Statistics for Oracle Data Files

With the access statistics, the administrator can, for example, distribute the top 10 data files to different media or data subsystems. You find an example for moving data files below:

1. Log in as sysdba user. The corresponding tablespace must be set to offline for moving the data files:

```
alter tablespace PSAP<SID> offline;
```

2. Move the file at the operating system level (to simplify matters from the Oracle shell with a preceding "!"):

```
! mv /path with old volume/<sid>.dataX /path with new volume/
<sid>.dataX
```

3. Change the path of the file in the Oracle database:

```
alter tablespace PSAP<SID> rename file
```

```
'/path with old volume/<sid>.dataX' to '/path with new volume/<s
id>.dataX';
```

4. Set the tablespace to online again:

```
alter tablespace PSAP<SID> online;
```

Because the data files are generally rather big and the corresponding tablespace needs to be offline, it is not possible to move the files while the SAP system is running. When files of the SYSTEM or of the UNDO tablespace need to be moved, the procedure mentioned above does not work. Instead, the database needs to be offline to move the files. The new path to the file is published in the MOUNT status with the following command:

```
alter database rename file ...
```

8.2.2.4 Other Performance-Relevant Aspects of the Oracle Database

At the end of this section we will discuss two additional very important and performance-relevant aspects:

- Oracle enqueues and Oracle optimizer statisticsare locks at database level that ensure permanent access to Oracle resources, such as objects or data records in tables. For example, if an Oracle process wants to change a data record, an enqueue is created to protect this modification as an atomic operation. If a second process wants to change this data record, it also creates an enqueue that is placed in a queue. The processing of the queue follows the FIFO principle (*first in, first out*). Oracle enqueues are often referred to as *exclusive lockwaits* or *Oracle locks*. If an enqueue or a lock situation occurs, the corresponding enqueue wait event is generated. Generally, Oracle distinguishes between two types of enqueues that are again differentiated by type: User enqueues are the enqueue types that occur with "normal" data changes, for instance, inserting or deleting data records or restructuring an index. There are three types:
  - TX (transaction enqueue): Evolves from every change made to a data record when the system needs to wait for this change. This is the most frequent enqueue type.
  - TM (DML enqueue):
  - Occurs when a complete object, for example, an index, is locked.
  - UL (user enqueue): Is generated when a user sets a lock with DBMS_LOCK.REQUEST. This function is not used in the SAP standard.

- System enqueues are the enqueue types that occur in many Oracle-internal management mechanisms. There are more than 40 different types. However, most of them are only partially or not at all relevant. The most important type in the SAP environment should be mentioned, though: ST (space transaction enqueue). This enqueue is generated during extent management in DMTS (dictionary-managed tablespace).

A data lock mostly affects a row of a table if it is changed via `update`, `delete`, `insert`, or `select for update`. Such locks, as described above, are called TX enqueues. Other enqueues, for example, also lock entire segments (e.g., TM enqueues) or critical paths (ST enqueues). The set lock is always kept up to the data base command `COMMIT` and is then released again. Because a `commit` or `rollback` is carried out after every SAP transaction step (caution: not transaction), the database locks should generally be kept no longer than a few seconds.

Of course, *database locks* are generally important for data consistency in the database. Therefore, their occurrence is normal and presents no problem for the performance. However, this only applies when the locks are only held as long as necessary and no serialization effects occur. This would mean that increasingly more processes wait for the release of a database lock. You should therefore observe the Oracle lock monitor in Transaction ST04N or by following menu path **Exceptional Conditions • Lock Monitor** (or Transaction DB01). **Caution**: You will *not* see the current locks that are kept in the Oracle database but only the lockwaits and thus the requested locks that have not been immediately assigned (that are being waited on). Information about the current database locks can be found in the views V$LOCK and V$LOCKED_OBJECT. Figure 8.13 shows these two views — also called via Transaction ST04N or by going to **Additional Function • Display V$/GV$ Views and Values**.

The figure demonstrates how the Oracle Process **31** (**Session ID**) locks the object with ID **18.992**. **V$LOCKED_OBJECT** illustrates that it is a **TM** enqueue in Mode **3**. Furthermore, **V$LOCK** demonstrates that Process **31** also keeps another **TX** enqueue in Mode **6**.

The mode shows how restrictively the object is locked. Table 8.20 illustrates the possible modes of locks.

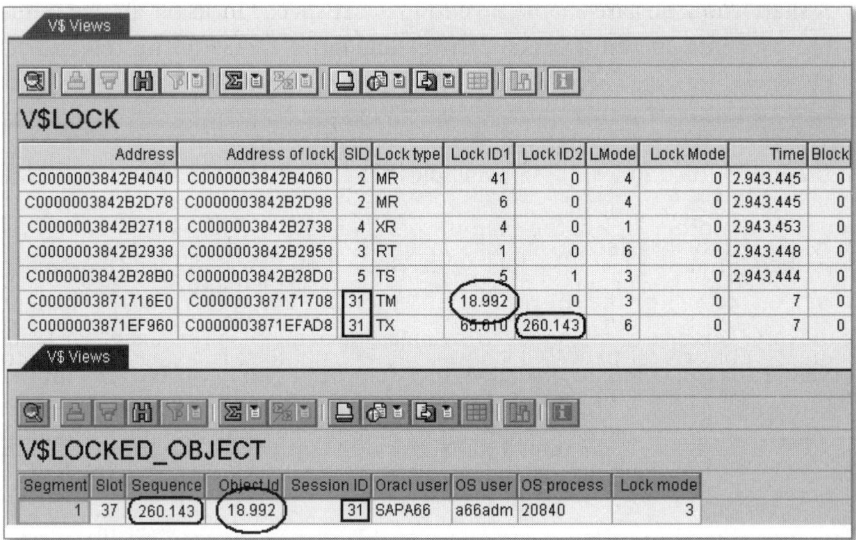

V$ Views

V$LOCK

Address	Address of lock	SID	Lock type	Lock ID1	Lock ID2	LMode	Lock Mode	Time	Block
C0000003842B4040	C0000003842B4060	2	MR	41	0	4	0	2.943.445	0
C0000003842B2D78	C0000003842B2D98	2	MR	6	0	4	0	2.943.445	0
C0000003842B2718	C0000003842B2738	4	XR	4	0	1	0	2.943.453	0
C0000003842B2938	C0000003842B2958	3	RT	1	0	6	0	2.943.448	0
C0000003842B28B0	C0000003842B28D0	5	TS	5	1	3	0	2.943.444	0
C0000003871716E0	C000000387171708	31	TM	18.992	0	3	0	7	0
C0000003871EF960	C0000003871EFAD8	31	TX	65.610	260.143	6	0	7	0

V$ Views

V$LOCKED_OBJECT

Segment	Slot	Sequence	Object Id	Session ID	Oracl user	OS user	OS process	Lock mode
1	37	260.143	18.992	31	SAPA66	a66adm	20840	3

Figure 8.13 Locks of the Oracle Database

Mode	Name
0	Not hold or not requested
1	Null mode
2	Row shared table locks (RS)
3	Row exclusive table locks (RX)
4	Shared table locks (S)
5	Shared row exclusive table locks (SRX)
6	Exclusive table locks (X)

Table 8.20 Modes of Oracle Locks

The description of the individual modes and their corresponding effects would fill several pages. You should therefore refer to the Oracle documentation at *www.oracle.com/pls/db102/homepage* under **Concepts • Data Concurrency and Consistency**. We will only give a brief description of the basic difference between *shared* and *exclusive* locks:

- An exclusive lock protects a resource against a shared or another exclusive lock. It is set when the resource is supposed to be changed. The first process that requests and receives an exclusive lock for a resource is the only process that can change the resource until it releases the lock.

- A shared lock on a resource also allows other shared locks on that resource but prevents exclusive locks. That means write access to the resource is not possible with a shared lock. Therefore, the resource can be read consistently.

In the individual modes, these principles are linked at table and row level.

Let us take another look at the example of Figure 8.13. What is happening? As described, Process 31 holds a lock with Mode 3 on Table 18992. That means it has a shared lock on the entire table (TM enqueue) and wants to make changes to the row. This also corresponds to the meaning of mode — row exclusive table locks. Of course, changing the rows also determines an exclusive lock on the corresponding row, which can be seen in V$LOCK. The last entry demonstrates that Process 31 holds an exclusive lock (Mode 6) on a row (TX enqueue). That is, Process 31 only makes entries or changes in Table 18992.

The Oracle session monitor (Transaction ST04N; **Resource Consumption • Oracle Session**; see also Chapter 4, *SAP and Oracle*) shows which SAP work process is linked with Oracle Process 31. Using the following SQL command, you can determine which object is specified by the object ID:

```
SQL> select object_name, object_type from dba_objects where object_
id=41733;
```

Finally, we will take another look at the V$LOCK view and, in particular, at the lock mode column in Figure 8.13. (Caution: Don't confuse this with the column with the same name in V$LOCKED_OBJECT.) This column contains the mode of a requested lock. That is, in case of a value >0, the process waits for a lock from the lock mode that it requested. At this point, you can recognize a lockwait. As mentioned before, such a requested but not assigned lock would also be displayed by the Oracle lock monitor (Transaction DB01) in the SAP system. Furthermore, you can also determine the Oracle process that holds the lock on the "demanded" object (lock mode = 0) via the columns Lock ID1 and Lock ID2 (objects).

If you discover Oracle locks that are held longer or that are being waited on, you should identify the SAP work process that causes the lock via the client host and the client ID. Afterwards, you can determine which program sets the lock for which user and does not release it. A further analysis can then be made with the help of the user or the developer.

If you cannot identify an SAP process with the respective lock, there are two possibilities: First, the SAP work process was cancelled and the "attached" database shadow process was not closed properly. In this case, you can delete the lock manually by cancelling the corresponding database shadow process using tools of the operating system. (Caution: Ensure that you don't cancel the wrong database shadow process or even an Oracle system process.) To prevent such a situation, you can set the parameter SQLNET.EXPIRE_TIME in the file sqlnet.ora, which enables an automatic cleanup of cancelled sessions. See SAP Note 20071 for further information. Second, the lock could also be kept by an external process or its attached database shadow process.

See the corresponding Oracle documentation and SAP Note 745639 for further information on Oracle enqueues.

The *table statistics* of the Oracle database provide another essential performance aspect. The Oracle Database Optimizer is supposed to determine the optimum access path for accessing the data. Generally, there are two types of optimizers: the *Rule-Based Optimizer* (RBO) and the *Cost-Based Optimizer* (CBO). The RBO calculates the access paths according to rules that derive from the "where" clause of the SQL statement to be optimized. However, because all databases running on SAP systems use the CBO, the exact process of the RBO is not relevant for us. The R/3 systems version 3.x or older on Oracle older than 7.3.3 were the only exceptions, because the SAP applications for the RBO were developed on these systems due to technical problems with the newly introduced CBO.

The cost-based optimizer calculates the access path to the data on the basis of the costs required for the access. In Oracle systems, you recognize the usage of the CBO with the parameter OPTIMIZER_MODE. In SAP systems on Oracle 9i, the parameter has the CHOOSE value, which determines that the CBO is always used when statistics are available for a table and that otherwise the RBO is used. From Oracle 10g onward, the RBO is no longer supported, so different levels of the CBO are provided for selection. As of Version 10g, the SAP default value for the parameter is therefore ALL_ROWS.

The exact definition of the access costs depends on the database. For Oracle releases older than 9i, the costs are exclusively determined via the blocks to be read, whereas versions higher than Oracle 10g allow several key values (single-block reads, multiblock reads, and CPU) for cost determination. The exact working method of the CBO is kept secret by Oracle. A description and summary of the known facts regarding the CBO can be found in SAP Note 750631, *Rules of Thumb for Cost Calculation of the CBO*. The most important thing to keep is mind is that the costs are mainly calculated on the basis of table statistics. Therefore, the generation of these statistics is an important task of administrators. Optimizer statistics are generated in two steps:

1. Analyzing the table
2. Creating the statistics

In the first step, all tables of the database are analyzed to determine for which table statistics have to be renewed. Because the actual creation of statistics is very resource-intensive, this two-phase process prevents unnecessary new statistics from being created when the content of a table is insignificantly changed. SAP urgently recommends that you use only the SAP tools to create optimizer statistics, as these tools are especially customized to meet the requirements of the SAP software for the Oracle database. The BR*Tools introduced in Chapter 4 can be called for the creation of statistics by means of the command line (as <sid>adm user)

```
brconnect -u / -c -f stats -t [<TABLESPACE_NAME>|ALL]
```

or can be scheduled via the DBA planning calendar (Transaction DB13) (see Figure 8.14).

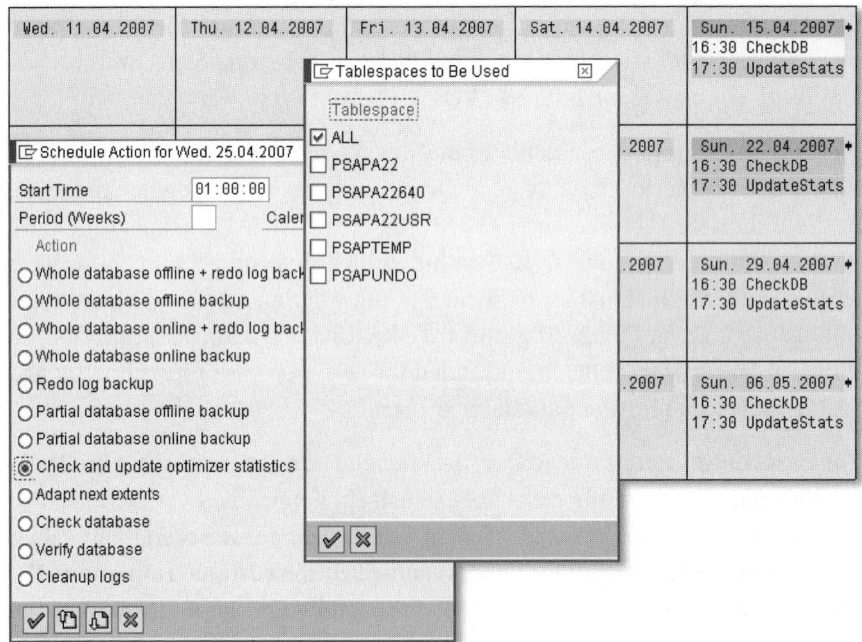

Figure 8.14 DBA Planning Calendar

Chapter 9, *System Operation and Monitoring*, provides further information on the DBA planning calendar.

For every execution of the BR*Tools, and thus for every table analysis run and statistics creation, you find the corresponding log file in the log display for DBA operations (Transaction DB14). There, by clicking on the **BRCONNECT** button, you can view all `brconnect` logs. You can identify the logs for the update of the optimizer statistics by means of the description or abbreviation "sta" in the FID column. By double-clicking, you can view the log file and find an entry for every table, whose statistics are recalculated (`method = C`) or estimated (`method = E`), such as:

```
BR0881I Collecting statistics for table SAPA22.CCMSBIDATA with
method/sample C ...
BR0881I Collecting statistics for table  SAPA22.CPRTYPET with
method/sample E/P30 ...
```

Which table of the Oracle database is analyzed and how it is analyzed is controlled by two aspects:

- Most important are the rules that are programmed in the `BRCONNECT` program. Those are:
  - First, it is determined whether new statistics are required or not (on the basis of the number of changed rows), followed by the actual creation of the statistics (two-phase concept).
  - No statistics on pool and cluster tables for Oracle 9i or earlier.
  - Accuracy of the statistics based on the number of entries in the table and so on.
- The second aspect is the content of the DBSTATC table. Using this table, the system administrator can influence the statistics creation for individual tables. Therefore, the table is also referred to as exception table. In every row of DBSTATC, the parameters for running the statistics creation are set for a specific table. The maintenance of table DBSTATC is performed via Transaction DB21 (see Figure 8.15).

Table 8.21 lists the most important columns of the DBSTATC table.

You can also implement new tables in the DBSTATC table that were, for example, created through developments. See SAP Note 106047 for further information on the maintenance of the DBSTATC table.

Configuration of Statistics Creation

Database Object	Database	Use	Active	ToDo	Method	Sample	Hist.	Cus
AFPO	ORACLE	A	A		C		X	
AFRU	ORACLE	A	A		E	R6	X	
AFVC	ORACLE	A	I		E	P30	X	
AFVU	ORACLE	A	A		E	P30	X	
AFVV	ORACLE	A	A		E	P30	X	
AGR_1016	ORACLE	O	A		C			
AGR_1250	ORACLE	O	A		E	P10		
AGR_1251	ORACLE	O	A		E	P3		

Figure 8.15 Excerpt from the DBSTATC Table

Column	Description
Database object	Name of the table
Usage	A = Application Monitor (ST09) and Optimizer O = Only for the optimizer
Active	Controls if the statistics for the table are renewed. Possible values are, for example: ▸ A: Active (is checked and updated, if required) ▸ I: Ignore ▸ U: Unconditional (statistics are always updated) ▸ N: No statistics ▸ R: Only temporary statistics
ToDo	Forces the statistic to be generated once.
Method	How the statistic is generated — either by the exact analysis of the entire table (C) or by the estimation according to procedure <sample> (E).
Sample	You have two options: ▸ P <*n*> – *n* = Percent of the table rows are analyzed ▸ R <*n*> – *n* × 1,000 table rows are analyzed

Table 8.21 Columns in the DBSTATC Table

8.2.3 Analyzing the SAP System

Having discussed the analysis of the hardware and operating system as well as of the Oracle database, we now turn to the analysis of the SAP system, or more precisely, the individual instances of the SAP system.

The criteria that are relevant for the performance of an SAP instance can be divided into two main categories:

1. Configuration of the characteristics of an instance, for example, the number of work processes and their types or, even more importantly, the memory configuration of the instance.
2. Configuration of the SAP buffers, that is, the analysis and administration of table buffering, of number range buffering, and of program buffering in other internal SAP buffers.

The following sections briefly describe these categories and give an overview of the most important options and settings.

8.2.3.1 Configuring the Memory of an SAP Instance

In general, the importance of the SAP memory configuration (not of the SAP buffer) has decreased due to the technological progress in recent years. Above all, the enhancement of the main memory capacities, which also involves changing to the 64-bit technology, means the main memory is usually no longer the limiting factor of an SAP instance. However, the configuration must still be performed so that the instance can work with high performance. In the following text, we will briefly introduce the SAP memories and their configuration and provide information that is relevant to performance. However, we won't go into too much detail, as the SAP memory configuration depends on the operating system and would thus fill an entire book if it was described thoroughly.

The memory configuration of an SAP instance must be defined in the instance profile. The parameters of the individual memory areas are also in these sections.

> **Note**
>
> The following text refers only to the SAP memory management for typical UNIX operating systems (HP-UX, Solaris, and AIX). The concepts for configuring the memory of other platforms supported by SAP, such as Linux, Windows, or IBM iSeries, sometimes deviate considerably. For example, Windows and Linux provide an option for Zero Administration Memory Management, where only one parameter defines the total memory that is available for the instance and where the individual memory areas are automatically configured.

The SAP memory areas are:

- **Roll memory**
  Every work process contains a roll memory area that is located in the local process memory. It stores the initial user context that is swapped to the

roll buffer when the process is changed (SAP process multiplexing). The roll buffer itself (don't confuse it with the roll memory) is also referred to as the roll area and, like the extended memory, is a shared memory area. From SAP R/3 3.0 onward, the roll memory plays only a minor role, because the main part of the user context is directly stored in the extended memory and the access change is performed through the pointer. This method is significantly faster than copying the data in the memory.

- **Extended memory**
  This shared memory is used by all work processes and is the most important memory area of an SAP instance. It contains all user contexts of the users that are logged in to the instance, with the exception of the small initial context that is being copied between roll memory and roll buffer.
- **Heap memory**
  This memory area is a local memory that belongs to one work process. The work process type determines when the heap memory is used. It is used for dialog processes when the extended memory or at least the part of the extended memory that may be used by a single work process is entirely utilized. For nondialog processes, the local heap memory is used immediately after the roll memory, because here no process multiplexing is performed, and the extended memory is therefore reserved for the dialog processes.
- **Paging memory**
  Previously, this memory area served to reduce the load of the roll memory for operations with large amounts of data via a paging procedure similar to the paging process of an operating system. Today, the memory is only used when the ABAP commands, `EXTRACT` and `EXPORT ... TO MEMORY...`, are used.

Table 8.22 provides an overview of the most important parameters of the SAP memory areas. The SAP Help provides a complete overview of all parameters.

SAP Memory Area	Parameter	Description
Roll memory and roll buffer (area)	`ztta/roll_first`	Defines the size of the initial local roll memory of a work process. The default value is only 1 byte.
Roll memory and roll buffer (area)	`ztta/roll_area`	Defines the size of the entire local roll memory of a work process.

Table 8.22 Parameters for the SAP Memory Areas

SAP Memory Area	Parameter	Description
Roll memory and roll buffer (area)	rdisp/ROLL_SHM	Defines the size of the roll buffer in the shared memory.
	rdisp/ROLL_MAXFS	If the roll buffer is not sufficient, an overflow file exists whose size is specified with this parameter.
Extended memory	em/initial_size_MB	Defines the total size of the extended memory of an SAP instance.
	ztta/roll_extension	Defines the maximum amount of extended memory that can be used by a single work process. Two other parameters can also be used to specify the maximum memory for dialog and nondialog processes.
	abap/ heap_area_total	Defines the total size of the local heap memory as the total of all work processes in one SAP instance.
	abap/heaplimit	If one work process uses more heap memory than this parameter specifies, the process is started again at the end of the transaction to release the memory.
Paging memory	rdisp/PG_SHM	Specifies the size of the paging memory of an SAP instance.
	rdisp/PG_MAXFS	If the paging memory is not sufficient, an overflow file exists whose size is defined with this parameter.

Table 8.22 Parameters for the SAP Memory Areas (Cont.)

Transaction ST02 (memory monitor) gives you an overview of the configuration and the current status of the SAP memory areas. Figure 8.16 shows the section that is relevant for the memory areas.

SAP memory	Current use [%]	[kB]	Max. use [kB]	In memory [kB]	On disk [kB]
Roll area	0,66	1.725	15.744	131.072	131.072
Paging area	0,01	16	35.888	65.536	196.608
Extended Memory	4,70	196.608	692.224	4.186.112	
Heap Memory		0	110.778		

Figure 8.16 SAP Memory Areas in Transaction ST02

The **Current use** column provides information on the current use of the instance. **Max. use** lists the maximum use since the last start of the instance. The **In memory** column contains the maximum values of the individual areas in kilobytes. The areas are defined according to the parameters from Table 8.22. Note that the parameters of the extended and heap memories are defined in megabytes or bytes, whereas the roll buffer **(roll area)** and paging memory **(paging area)** sizes are specified by the number of blocks with a size of 8k. The last column, On disk, shows the maximum sizes of the overflow files of the roll buffer and of the paging memory.

The **Detail analysis menu** button in Transaction ST02 enables you to obtain a selection with further analysis options. Using the **SAP memory** function, you can display a detailed analysis of the SAP memory areas. Here, the administrator can view which user is using how much of which SAP memory at a given time. You can also obtain a historical overview.

Before the extended memory was implemented, the roll-in and roll-out processes were critical for performance during process multiplexing, that is, copying the user context. Thanks to the usage of pointers, this problem has become obsolete. What needs to be done now is to configure the SAP memory areas with enough memory of each area and without wasting memory space that could be of more use somewhere else (for instance, for SAP buffers or the Oracle database). However, if not enough memory is available for one of the areas, the performance of the SAP instance may automatically decrease considerably, or program aborts may occur. The following list summarizes the most important rules for the configuration of SAP memory areas:

- Choose the roll buffer and the paging memory so that the overflow files are never used, that is, the value in Max. use is always smaller than the value in In memory, as shown in Figure 8.16. The SAP default values for these areas are usually sufficient. An exception is SAP NetWeaver BI, which sometimes places considerably more load on the paging memory.
- The extended memory is the most important SAP memory area. Therefore, you should calculate it more generously. Earlier recommendations of 6 to 10 MB per user are too small for today's requirements. Consequently, you should consider 20 to 30 MB per user.
- As a contingency reserve, 20% of the extended memory should remain free, that is, the Current use should never exceed 80% of the In memory value. If the Max. use value indicates that this rule has not been adhered to, you should check if the history if this contingency reserve was often used and increase the extended memory, if required.

If Max. use or the history clearly shows that the extended memory is never used up to 80%, you can reduce it accordingly and use the memory somewhere else.

- Regarding the maximum amount of the extended memory of a single work process, SAP recommends 10% to 20% of the entire extended memory.
- You can use heap memory (Current use) without a problem as long as you use it only for nondialog processes. However, if dialog processes use local heap memory, they change to the so-called PRIV mode, that is, they can no longer perform a user change and are bound to the running transaction. You can identify this status in the SAP process overview (Transaction SM50). You should avoid this status by all means. If required and possible, you should specify more extended memory.

Of course, you should keep an eye on the hardware resources when configuring the memory for an SAP instance. It is important that there is enough space in your operating system for all SAP memory areas plus the SAP buffers plus a contingency reserve. If there isn't enough space, the SAP instance won't start. The best option for the performance is that everything (including the maximum heap memory) can be mapped onto the physical memory of the server.

Note on SAP Memory Management

The extended memory is not created completely at the start of the instance but, depending on the usage, grows to its maximum size. During this process, the extended memory, which has been allocated once, is not released for the operating system even if it is no longer used by the SAP instance and is thus actually available. This is a problem if a memory bottleneck occurs on the server, because "available" memory is not recognized as being really available by the operating system and therefore can be removed during swapping, for example. Some new instance parameters that are provided as of Kernel 4.6D (with the relevant patch) can solve this problem. For more details, see SAP Note 724140.

8.2.3.2 SAP Buffers

The SAP system also uses the buffers concept to access data quickly that is often reused. This concept is equivalent to that of buffers in the database. Figure 8.17 illustrates the two-level buffer architecture and the relationships between the buffers. Note that, of course, each instance of an SAP system has its own buffers.

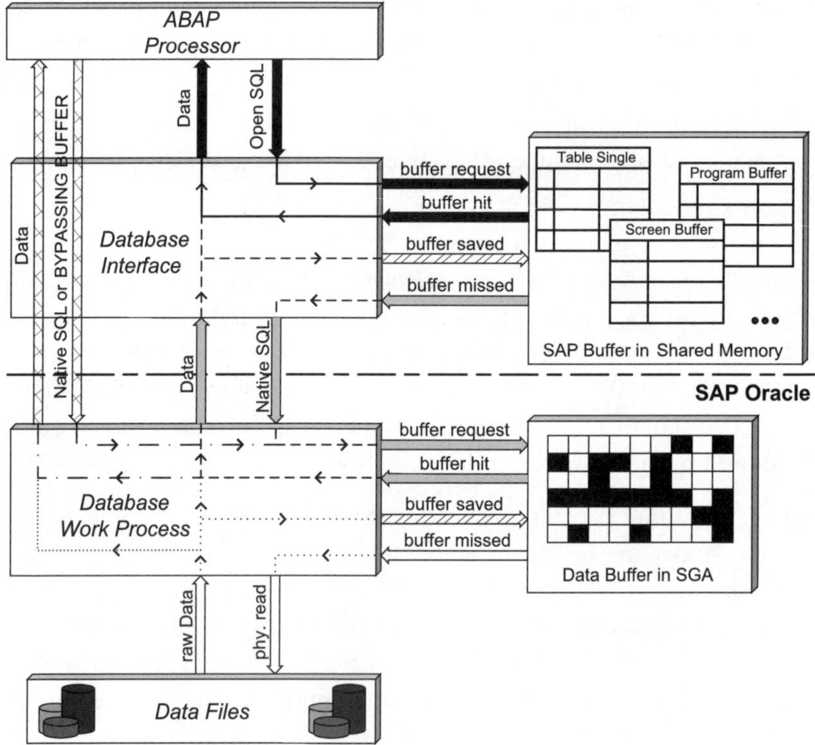

Figure 8.17 Two-Level Buffer Architecture of SAP-Oracle

The combination of database and SAP buffers involves a performance-relevant feature. Let's take a data record for currency conversion as an example. This data record is loaded from the Oracle database if a relevant transaction is performed by the user. First, the Oracle database loads the data record from the data files (or from the raw device) and stores it or the data blocks in the data buffer. The SAP system or the work process receives the data record for the current transaction and stores it also in the SAP buffer for table entries (table single buffer or table generic buffer) if the table that originally contained the data record is provided for buffering.

If the currency conversion is performed again, the data record is provided by the SAP table buffer if it has not become invalid, due to changes, for example. As a result, the data record or the respective blocks are swapped from the Oracle data buffer after a short period of time (depending on the buffer size). If they are also swapped from the SAP table buffer, for example, because other objects have been loaded in the meantime and the buffer size is not large enough, another query of the currency conversion leads inevitably to a physical read of the database. That is, the objects and data that are buffered in the SAP application server are generally swapped from the database buffer, which causes a physical data access when they are queried again from the database.

Therefore, SAP buffers primarily contain other data than the database buffer. Table 8.23 shows which individual buffers are available.

SAP Buffer	Description
Table definition (TTAB)	Buffers the entries of the DDNTT table. Explanation: The name table (NTAB) contains all information on the table and field definitions in the ABAP repository. It consists of the DDNTT (table definitions) and DDNTF (field descriptions) tables.
Field descriptions (FTAB)	Buffers the entries of the DDNTF table.
Short NTAB	Stores a combination of TTAB and FTAB buffers.
Initial record	Stores the layout of the data records.
Program	Here, the compiled executable versions of the ABAP codes are buffered. The swaps are performed on the basis of the LRU concept (least recently used).
CUA	Buffers objects from the SAP GUI, such as menus or button definitions based on the LRU concept.
Screen	Stores the dynpro screens that have been generated previously.
Calendar	Here, all defined factory and holiday calendars from the TFACS and THOCS tables are buffered (also on the basis of the LRU concept).
OTR	This is the Online Text Repository buffer that stores texts that are, for example, used in BSPs.
Table generic/ Table single	These are the entries for table buffering in an SAP instance (as described below).
Export/Import Exp/Imp SHM	This buffer is used for all work processes and stores data clusters using specific ABAP commands (see SAP Note 702728).

Table 8.23 SAP Buffers

To carry out a qualitative evaluation of the buffers, it is required that they be in an established state, as is the case with database buffers.

Transaction ST02 enables you to access the memory monitor of the instance to which you are currently logged in. Figure 8.18 shows the part of the monitor that lists and evaluates the individual SAP buffers. The individual fields and their meanings are described in Table 8.24.

Buffer	Hitratio [%]	Allocated [kB]	Free space [kB]	Free space [%]	Dir. size Entries	Free directory Entries	Free directory [%]	Swaps	Database accesses
Nametab (NTAB)									
Table definition	99,80	11.917	4.560	49,68	50.000	24.837	49,67	0	36.598
Field description	99,79	103.906	31.600	31,60	50.000	26.307	52,61	0	25.079
Short NTAB	99,85	5.563	2.918	72,95	12.500	7.763	62,10	0	4.738
Initial records	99,55	11.563	7.394	73,94	12.500	2.919	23,35	18.311	27.895
Program	99,67	500.000	1.217	0,25	125.000	111.847	89,48	141.283	471.732
CUA	99,88	8.000	35	0,51	4.000	2.389	59,73	27.745	3.450
Screen	99,75	24.415	14.066	59,03	10.000	9.199	91,99	4.792	5.652
Calendar	99,67	488	287	60,04	200	109	54,50	0	91
OTR	100,00	4.096	3.531	100,00	2.000	2.000	100,00	0	0
Tables									
Generic key	99,85	48.829	3.052	6,55	10.000	1.267	12,67	222	217.250
Single record	99,07	30.000	15.730	52,69	500	281	56,20	0	101.131
Export/import	89,88	40.000	1.581	5,01	30.000	15.760	52,53	0	0
Exp./Imp. SHM	85,09	4.096	3.529	99,94	2.000	1.999	99,95	0	0

Figure 8.18 SAP Memory Monitor (Excerpt Containing the SAP Buffers)

Field	Description
Hit ratio	The hit ratios of a buffer are indicated as a percentage. They are calculated in the same way as the hit ratio of the database buffers: *Buffer quality (hit ratio) = (Buffer requests – Database requests)/ Buffer requests × 100%*
Allocated	Memory space (in RAM) occupied by the SAP buffer.
Free space	Memory space that is available for the buffer.
Dir. size	Maximum number of possible buffer entries.
Free directory	Number of buffer entries that are available.
Swaps	Number of swaps from the buffer since the last start of the instance.

Table 8.24 Fields in the Memory Monitor

Hit ratio and swaps are the essential criteria for SAP buffers. SAP recommends that the hit ratio of the buffers should be >98%. The two export and import buffers are an exception with an optimum hit ratio that is supposed to be >80%. If possible, swaps from buffers should be avoided. However, depending on the utilization and usage of the SAP instance, it is not always possible to avoid them. For example, if an instance runs in another operating mode to execute more batch jobs at night, other ABAP programs and tables are required that are loaded into the program or nametable buffer. This usually leads to swaps. You can therefore tolerate a small number of swaps (a few hundred swaps per day). SAP recommends that up to 10,000 swaps per day can be accepted for the program buffer.

If the number of swaps increases considerably, you must check if the *free space* or the number of *free directory entries* of the buffer is insufficient. The respective instance parameter must then be increased step by step to eliminate the swaps. You can find the parameters for the SAP buffers using the **Current parameter** button in the memory monitor.

In addition to the hit ratio and swaps, you should also keep an eye on the free space for SAP buffers. You can possibly find unused memory resources if large parts of a buffer are not used in the established state. For example, in Figure 8.18, this is the case for the field description buffer because 30 MB are unused. It makes more sense to use this memory somewhere else.

There are three types of table buffering in an SAP system:

1. **Single buffering**
   In this process, each record (row of a table) is stored individually in the TABLP buffer if it has been read once on the database. To use single buffering, it is important that all key fields are qualified in the `where` condition for a query
2. **Full buffering**
   If a record is read from the database, the entire table is stored in the TABL buffer.
3. **Generic buffering**
   This buffering type is specified by the number of key fields used for selection. If a record is read from a table buffered as generic 1 from the database, all other data records are buffered that are identical to the record initially read in key field 1. Corresponding buffering with *n* key fields is also possible. The generic buffered data records are in the TABL buffer.

Note

When full buffering is activated, a client-dependent table, that is, a table that always has the MAN key first, is automatically buffered as generic 1.

The entire buffer management is mapped onto the database interface of the individual SAP work processes, that is, here it is decided when which buffer is accessed. For the access of the buffer, it is decided whether all required keys of a table are specified in the `where` condition. Let us assume that the TAB table with the key fields KEY1, KEY2, and KEY3 is buffered as generic 2, that is, via KEY1 and KEY2. The following call would benefit from a buffering process:

```
SELECT * FROM TAB WHERE KEY1=X and KEY2=Y;
```

In contrast, the following calls could not be buffered and would thus cause an access to the database:

```
SELECT * FROM TAB WHERE KEY1=X;
SELECT * FROM TAB WHERE KEY1=X and KEY3=Z;
```

Additionally, there are numerous exceptions where the table buffer is not used either:

- When the SQL commands `SELECT FOR UPDATE` or `SELECT DISTINCT` are used
- When the aggregate functions `SUM`, `MIN`, `MAX`, and `AVG` are used
- When the Native SQL statements or the Open SQL condition `BYPASSING BUFFER` is used

Because all SAP buffers are kept separately for each instance, the table buffer is forced to synchronize the instances. If the content of a table buffer is changed, the running work process writes a corresponding entry to the DDLOG database table. The instances read this table regularly to invalidate data records in their own table buffers that are affected by the changes. That is, if a table is individually buffered, only the affected data record is declared as invalid; however, if tables are generic or fully buffered, the complete generic part of the table or the entire table in the buffer is invalidated.

This synchronization process is controlled via the profile parameters `rdisp/bufrefmode` (controls reading and writing of the DDLOG table) and `rdisp/bufreftime` (specifies the frequency at which the DDLOG table is read — default: 60s). Furthermore, you can monitor the buffer synchronization in the SAP memory monitor: **SAP_memory monitor (ST02) • Detail analysis menu • Buffer syncron**.

The synchronization of the table buffers between the instances may have a negative effect on the system performance. Therefore, some criteria must be met by tables and views (they can also be buffered) for useful buffering:

- The table must be small and read very often.
- The change rate must be very low, for example, less than 1% changes per day for tables with a size of one megabyte.
- A short-term inconsistency must be acceptable because delays during synchronization between the instances (`rdisp/bufreftime`) may occur.

On the basis of the characteristics mentioned, the individual data classes in an SAP system can be assigned relatively rigidly to one buffering procedure. SAP distinguishes between three data classes that are contained in a database in the system (apart from the actual ABAP code and "technical" data):

1. **Transaction data**
   All data that is generated and changed in large quantities during operation, such as invoices, delivery notes, sales orders, material movements, and so on. The tables grow rapidly during operation and can thus reach a size of several gigabytes. Therefore, they are generally not suited for buffering in the SAP system.
2. **Master data**
   Master data is changed rarely or never during live operation and contains information on material, customers, vendors, and so on. The respective tables change less than the transaction data but still reach a size of several hundred megabytes. Therefore, master data tables are also not included in the SAP table buffer.
3. **Customizing data**
   Data that is generated when mapping the enterprise processes onto the SAP system (customizing). The most common examples are company codes, factories, sales organizations, conditioning, and so on. The respective table records are changed or supplemented rarely during operation and are therefore usually buffered in the SAP system.

On the basis of SAP's own experience, table buffering functions are already configured in the supplied versions of the different SAP software solutions.

To decide when and how a table is buffered reasonably or not, you have to monitor the SAP table buffering processes. This can be done in the SAP memory monitor (ST02) via **Detail analysis menu • Call statistic** or using Transaction ST10. A selection screen is displayed where you must select the Table type, Period, and SAP instance factors. Because every instance has its own buffers, you must theoretically analyze each instance. However, this is only virtually relevant if different tasks are performed on these instances, such as batch against dialog instances, or if organizational enterprise parts (for example, international branch offices) are distributed across different instances and thus other data must be buffered.

Figure 8.19 shows an excerpt from the table access statistics, and Table 8.25 lists the most important columns and their meanings. (Note: You can expand the individual detail columns via buttons.)

Table	Buffer State	Buf key opt	Invali-dations	Buffer size [bytes]	Size maximum [bytes]	ABAP/IV Processor requests				DB activity	
						Total	Direct reads	Seq. reads	Changes	Calls	Rows affected
Total			20.271	48.462.095	162.951.206	402.251.527	143.788.848	247.375.811	11.086.868	60.760.932	548.532.003
ATAB RFCDOC	pending	sng	1.548	0	273.920	39.937	2.915	35.166	1.856	462.844	52.157.699
REPOSRC			0	0	0	30	0	30	0	31.966	49.370.925
WBCROSSGT			0	0	0	32	0	32	0	102.513	37.602.420
GLFUNCA			0	0	0	24.500.366	0	24.500.132	234	161.849	24.690.245
AGR_HIERT	pending	gen	0	0	17.690	21.147.134	0	21.147.134	0	46.038	21.466.945
PTDW_PWS_DB			0	0	0	12.794.570	0	12.794.570	0	18.995	13.119.475
PPOIX			0	0	0	11.655.573	0	11.655.573	0	34.938	11.889.189
DD02L			0	0	0	349.514	1.940	347.391	183	360.956	11.064.837
CROSS			0	0	0	96	0	35	61	20.347	10.713.541
TTREE_EXTT	absent	gen	0	0	0	4.002	0	4.002	0	16.238	10.385.190
GLIDXA			0	0	0	5.842.514	0	5.842.279	235	12.928	6.015.078
MC13VD0HDRSETUP			0	0	0	5.851.192	0	5.613.320	237.872	555.827	5.882.627
MC13VD0ITMSETUP			0	0	0	5.850.926	0	5.613.054	237.872	555.565	5.882.365
TBTCO			0	0	0	3.723.172	2.182.411	264.091	1.276.670	5.945.800	5.794.643
BDCPS			0	0	0	5.395.811	0	5.395.340	471	5.577	5.722.114
TBTCP			0	0	0	1.267.692	0	811.929	455.763	1.275.488	5.672.479
TST01			0	0	0	3.744.841	2.654.251	480	1.090.110	6.410.476	5.497.628
TPRI_PAR			0	0	0	4.880.317	0	465.901	4.414.416	4.882.155	5.083.642
D010INC			0	0	0	75.479	0	75.479	0	75.708	4.176.566
ALTSTLOD			0	0	0	69.256	0	34.628	34.628	69.696	3.912.964
T5C2H	absent	gen	0	0	0	3.530.270	0	3.530.270	0	4.155	3.756.500
D010SINF			0	0	0	4.256.916	4.767	4.252.149	0	4.262.268	3.634.093
TADIR	valid	sng	2	23.808	7.127.616	11.344.509	601.267	10.743.087	155	10.745.569	3.167.033
USR13	absent	gen	0	0	0	2.927.742	0	2.927.742	0	5.400	3.149.796
FILCA			0	0	0	2.654.231	0	2.654.230	1	22.890	2.825.347

Figure 8.19 Excerpt from the Table Access Statistics

Column	Description
Table	Name of the table
Buffer state	The most important possible states are: ▸ Valid: Table is in the buffer and valid. ▸ Invalid: Table buffer has become invalid and cannot be loaded yet because the change has not been completed. ▸ Pending: Table buffer has become invalid and cannot be loaded yet because the grace period is still running. ▸ Loadable: Table buffer was invalid and can be loaded again. ▸ Absent: Table has never been loaded. ▸ Displaced: Table was swapped from the buffer. ▸ Error: Very important state, particularly regarding the performance, because it indicates that table buffering was cancelled (see SAP Note 618868, Section 9, Table Buffering)
Buffer key opt	Buffering type: ful = full, gen = generic, sng = single.
Buffer size	Space in the buffer currently occupied by the table.
Size maximum	Maximum space in the buffer occupied by the table.
Invalidations	Indicates how often the table buffer was invalid.
ABAP/IV processor requests	Number of ABAP requests for the table, which can be broken down as follows: direct reads, sequential reads, and changes (update, inserts, deletes)
DB calls	Combination of direct and sequential fetches (transferring the results of an SQL request to the calling SAP work process).
DB rows affected	Number of data records that are transferred from the database to the SAP system. Exception: initial load of the buffer.

Table 8.25 Columns of the Table Access Statistics

The following list describes how to check the buffered tables and how to decide if it makes sense to buffer them:

- **Estimation of the database accesses (DB rows affected)**
  The database accesses of buffered tables should be considerably smaller than those of unbuffered tables at a similar number of requests. If there are buffered tables at the beginning of the table access statistics after the table was sorted by "DB rows affected," you should further examine them.
- **Change rates of the tables**
  They are calculated on the basis of the following formula:

  (Values from the table access statistics from the ABAP request area): Change rate = Changes/(direct reads + seq. reads) × 100%

  Reference values for acceptable change rates are:
  - Table size < 1 MB ↔ Change rate < 1%
  - Table size > 1 MB and < 5 MB Change rate < 0.1%
  - Table size > 5 MB are rarely buffered; if buffered, change rate < 0.01%
- **Size of the table in the buffer**
  Sort the table access statistics by the buffer size column and ensure that all larger buffered tables (>100,000 bytes) are set to valid, if possible. If this is not the case, the table buffer should be extended, if possible. Note: The **Analyze table** button enables you to perform a complete table analysis in the background. This analysis indicates, for instance, the size of the table in the database or the distribution of the generic areas.
- **Select quality**
  When you double-click on a row of the table access statistics, a detail screen for the respective table opens. There, you will find the select quality as the ratio between ABAP requests and database calls (**Fetches/Exec**: fetching/changing data records). The quality should be approximately >95%.

Vice versa, the administrator searches for tables that are not buffered but should or could be buffered. For this purpose, here is a brief overview of the most important criteria:

- **Number of ABAP requests**
  Sort the table access statistics by total ABAP requests (for a better overview, you can view only the unbuffered tables). The ABAP Dictionary tables, DDNTF and DDNTT, are usually listed at the top. However, these tables are already stored in the nametab buffer. Look for Customizing or customer-specific tables in the top request entries (see the Remark box on the next page).

- **Change rates of the tables**
  Once you have found the relevant tables, determine the change rates as described above and compare them with the recommendations.

Remark

How do you recognize customizing tables? There are numerous customizing tables, such as the condition tables Axxx (xxx = 000 – 999). If you search for a table in the standard SAP system, you can find further information as follows:

1. Look at the short text of the table in the Data Dictionary (Transaction SE11) and check the specifications under **Goto • Technical Settings** in the Logical storage parameters field (see Figure 8.20).
2. Search for the table for your application (for example, ERP or SCM) in the SAP documentation under *http://help.sap.com*. Because Customizing is documented very well, this documentation mentions or describes nearly all Customizing tables.
3. Look for SAP Notes on the table in the SAP Support Portal. There are some explicit notes on buffering for some tables.

The buffering settings for a table can be made in the Data Dictionary (Transaction SE11). There, you must enter the respective table and view and change it via **Goto • Technical Settings** (see Figure 8.20).

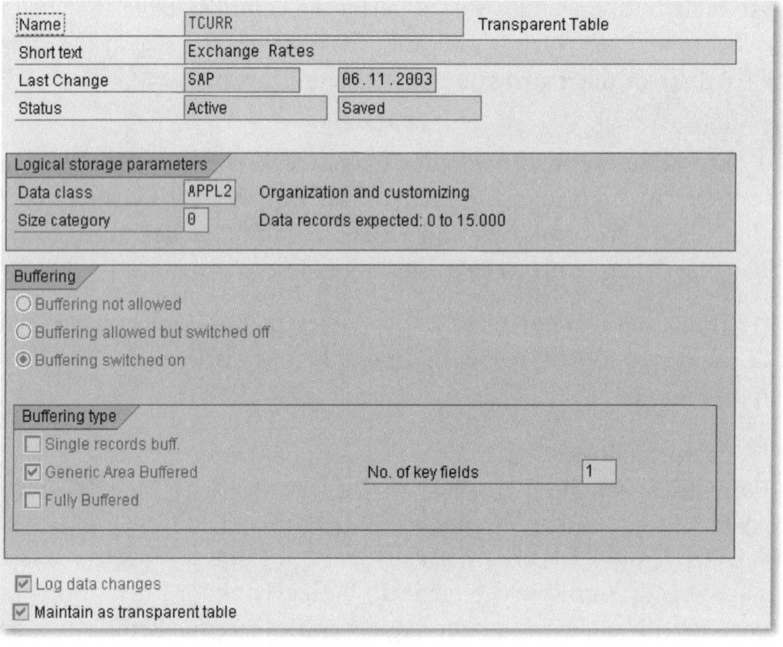

Name TCURR Transparent Table
Short text Exchange Rates
Last Change SAP 06.11.2003
Status Active Saved

Logical storage parameters
Data class APPL2 Organization and customizing
Size category 0 Data records expected: 0 to 15.000

Buffering
Buffering not allowed
Buffering allowed but switched off
Buffering switched on

Buffering type
Single records buff.
Generic Area Buffered No. of key fields 1
Fully Buffered

Log data changes
Maintain as transparent table

Figure 8.20 Table Buffering Settings

Some final remarks on table buffering: Always check whether it is a table from the standard SAP system or a customer-specific table. As already mentioned, SAP provides your standard tables with the relevant buffering settings. You should only change them if SAP explicitly recommends or authorizes this (for example, in an SAP Note). Regarding customer-specific tables, you should discuss with the developer of the table or application that uses the table if buffering is possible or makes sense.

In general, activating the buffering function is more dangerous than deactivating it. If you deactivate a buffering function, performance problems of applications that use the table are the worst that can happen. In contrast to that, if the table buffering is switched on — caused by a delay in the synchronization between instances of the SAP system — logical inconsistencies may occur.

Having viewed the individual components and areas of an SAP system with an Oracle database regarding the performance under administrative aspects, the last section deals with aspects related to the program.

8.3 Analyzing Program-Based Performance Problems: SQL Optimization

In Chapter 3, *Oracle Fundamentals*, the possibility of optimizing the query language SQL via DBMS is described as one of the strengths of relational databases. The SQL query describes the desired result and leaves it up to the database system to calculate the result set. In general, the DBMS provides much better ways to create the best execution plan . Theoretically, expert software developers should design a better plan only in exceptional cases. However, in practice, the Optimizer is not able to locate the best plan in all cases. A developer with knowledge of the interdependencies between the attributes and of the value distribution often must support the Optimizer by providing hints.

As an SAP-Oracle administrator, you are responsible for detecting and avoiding program-based bottlenecks. Thomas Schneider reports that quite frequently, situations occur in which a few expensive SQL statements cause more than 50% of the database load (*SAP Performance Optimization,* SAP PRESS, 2005). These issues can often only be handled with the support of the development team, even if you as an administrator can immediately alleviate the problems by creating an additional index or using other technical measures.

Our examples show you how to develop high-performance programs, demonstrate a few typical errors, and describe their impact on the interaction between SAP and Oracle. In this context, we will introduce essential SAP tools for analyzing SQL statements in the following sections. In addition, we'll also demonstrate how you can use and create indexes.

On the one hand, this will provide you with material for advising the developer team regarding a high-performance use of SQL in a qualified manner. On the other hand, you will learn how to use these tools to identify problems in that area, and you will get to know basic solution approaches.

8.3.1 Two Goals: Functionality and Performance

ABAP programs are often developed by application experts whose IT knowledge is rather limited. You have to ensure not only that the programs provide functionally correct results, but also that the tools be implemented in such a way that they provide high performance.

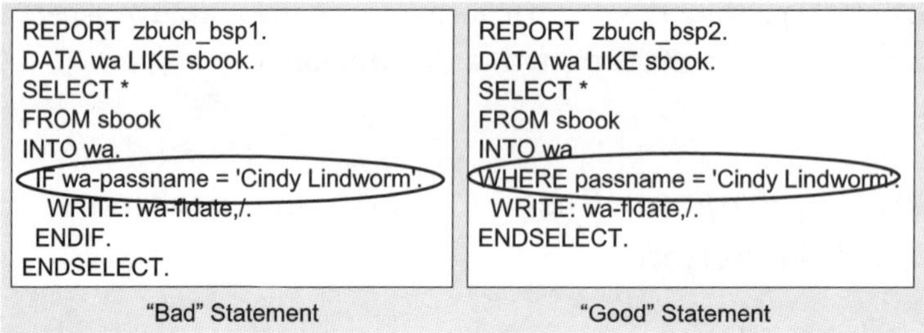

Figure 8.21 Inefficient and Efficient Use of SQL

The example shown in Figure 8.21 shows two functionally identical variants of a report that — based on the flight data table, SBOOK — lists all days on which Cindy Lindworm booked flights. For this purpose, in the variant on the left, all data records of the SBOOK table are read from the database. After that, the data records determined for further processing (here: output) are selected. In the other variant, the selection is performed by the `where` clause, which is triggered by the Oracle DBMS. The second variant has two advantages:

1. The Oracle server process transfers only the data that is really needed for the work process.
2. Oracle can select the correct data records very quickly by using existing help data structures.

An old IT saying goes that you make mistakes whenever they are possible. Functional errors can either be avoided by using proper specifications or identified by means of testing. A performance-critical programming style may remain undetected for a long time. That's because hardware performs at different speeds or the SAP systems in use have different loads. Consequently, the statement that the execution of the SAPBC_DATA_GENERATOR report takes about 138 seconds for creating the flight data model is of no real relevance.[3]

Note

Not every "bad" SQL statement causes performance problems. SAP and Oracle proactively provide mechanisms to process such statements quickly (see Chapters 2, 3, and 4). On the other hand, not every optimized SQL statement is fast. Some processes simply need a lot of time.

8.3.2 Effects

A poorly formulated SQL statement has both indirect and direct effects on performance. Figure 8.22 illustrates the direct effects. In the example shown in this figure, the transferred data packages between Oracle and the SAP application server consists of exactly one SQL query that is submitted and requests the entire SBOOK table. Therefore, the Oracle database needs to deliver the entire table, which can involve many physical reads (❶). In addition, the transfer of the entire table with delivery of an unnecessary number of data packages is involved (❷). The Oracle system itself cannot perform any optimization action because it does not know that numerous data records in the application are discarded. In the application server itself, all data records are (sequentially) verified with regard to whether they correspond to the `IF` condition (❸). This is quite time-consuming for the generated flight database that contains 90,000 data record in the SBOOK table.

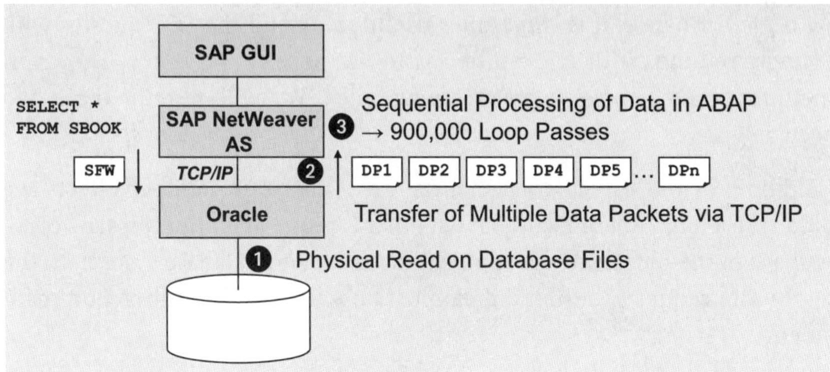

Figure 8.22 Effect of a "Bad" SQL Statement

3 We have chosen the monster data record variant and created the database in a background job (Transaction SM36).

Figure 8.23 shows the processing of a good SQL statement. The statement is improved because not all attributes of the desired data records that are marked with * are requested — only the FLDATE attribute is. Based on an exact description of the desired result quantity, the Oracle system can deliver the minimum result set. Consequently, only a small number of loop passes is necessary for the work process (❸), and only some data is transferred, which fits into a single package in our example (❷). Moreover, Oracle can create an optimized execution plan. For example, by using indexes, the physical read operations can be limited to some index data blocks as well as to those data blocks containing the requested data records.

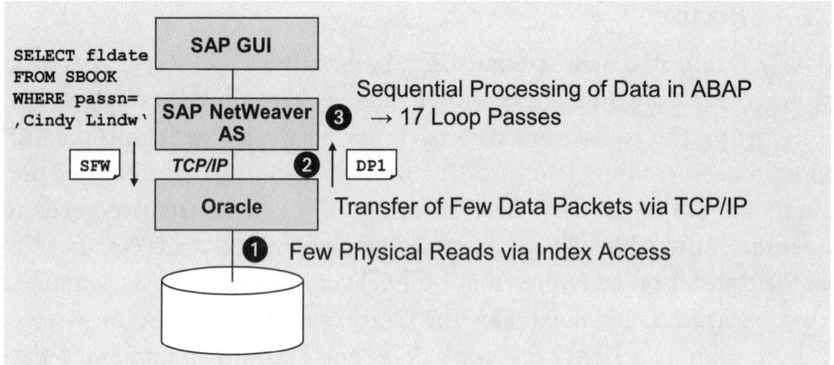

Figure 8.23 Effect of a "Good" SQL Statement

However, not every SQL statement that requests only the necessary data, like the one in Figure 8.23, is optimized. You also need to consider the processing by the Oracle system, particularly the use of indexes. From the point of view of performance, it is sometimes useful to extend the SQL queries with seemingly redundant where conditions to use an existing index. However, sometimes you may have to create a new index. We will describe these two aspects in greater detail in Section 8.3.6, *Indexes for Faster Access*.

In addition to the direct effects, there are also some indirect effects we should take a look at. For example, data that is requested unnecessarily occupies space in the buffers of the application server and database system. In the case of write requests, buffered data must be processed by transaction management.

For experiments and optimizing operational processes, SAP tables allow you to define whether and to what extent they are buffered in the table buffer of the application server. To do that, you must select a table in Transaction

SE11 (ABAP Dictionary), go to **Display** or **Change** and then select **Technical Settings**. Figure 8.24 shows the buffering settings. You can define whether you want a table to be buffered, whether buffering is allowed but switched off, or whether buffering is not allowed at all. If you allow buffering, you can also specify if individual data records, table sections, or entire tables should be buffered. Because the SCARR table used in the example is part of the standard SAP system, the settings can only be changed using an object key, which must be requested from SAP. If a table is buffered, it is very likely that the Oracle database is not accessed in experimental runs, which you should take into account when discussing the results.

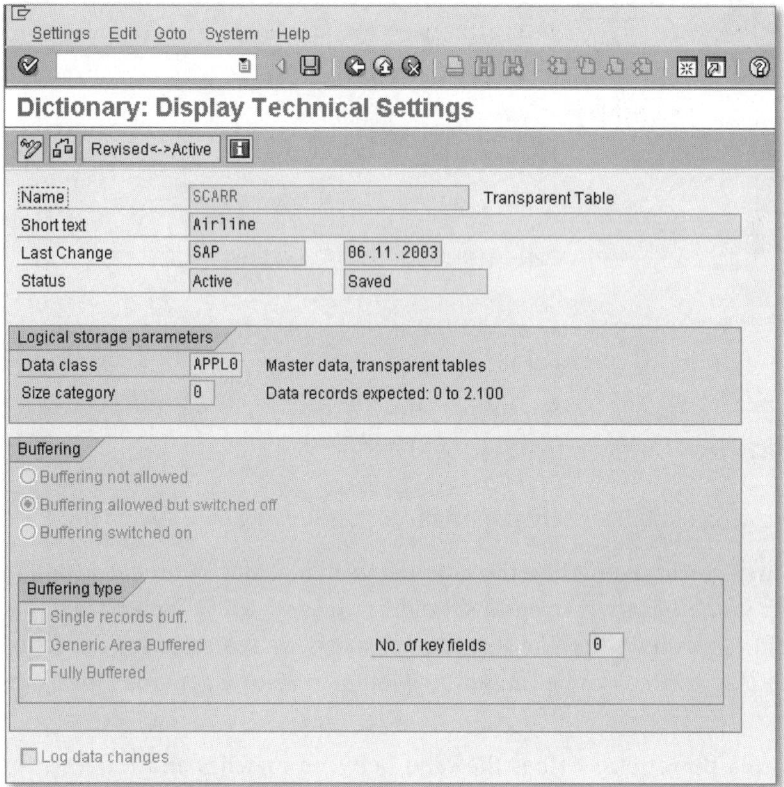

Figure 8.24 SCARR Is Not Buffered

8.3.3 Problem Analysis Tools

SAP provides a range of tools to detect and analyze performance problems that are related to SQL queries. There are tools that support the examination of the entire system and others that enable a detailed analysis of an SQL statement or program.

In this context, the analysis of the transaction profiles (Transaction ST03) and Oracle performance (Transaction ST04 or ST04N) again plays a major role (see Figure 8.25). You can use these tools to identify and isolate problems from the point of view of the entire system first.

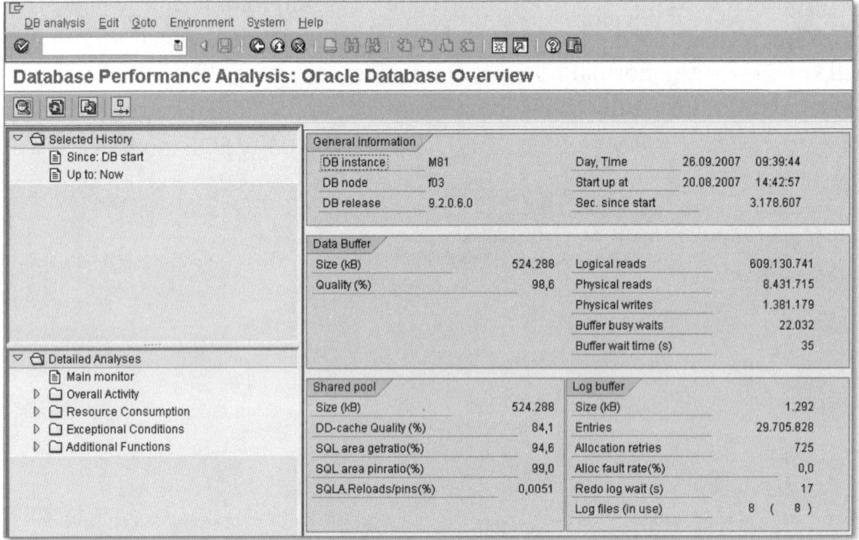

Figure 8.25 Oracle Performance Analysis with ST04N

The following parameters are important for optimizing SQL statements:

- **SQL area getratio** describes the ratio between matches and requests for an object in the library cache and should be close to 100% for a production system. This shows that the shared pool size is well selected for the actual query load, which can be caused by good queries or a generous measurement.
- **SQL area pinratio** describes the ratio between matches and requests for reading and executing objects and should also be close to 100%. Here again, expensive queries can have a negative impact due to displacements.
- Vice versa, **SQLA.Reloads/Pin** describes the ratio between the necessary reloads (SQL query parsing) and the accesses. Consequently, a value close to 0 should be reached here.

The quality of the dictionary cache should also be close to 100 because it is required for the plan creation and query processing. In addition, the size of the data dictionary is known because of the fixed structure[4]. Therefore, the system can size the memory area in an optimal manner. This is not the case with the system used in Figure 8.25 because it has been in use only for a short period.

You should know the typical values for your own system. Deviations may occur when maintenance work is carried out on the system. Usually, you as an administrator will carry out this work or at least will be involved. In this respect, you will develop a feeling for the behavior of your system.

Deviations in the normal operation, however, must be checked thoroughly. The goal is to locate the cause of the problem, which might be related to the use of an inefficient SQL statement. The analysis of the SQL requests may be an option to identify this type of statement. In Transaction ST04, you can access a sorted list of all SQL statements that are stored in the Oracle system by selecting **Detail Analysis • SQL Request**. If you want to select the requests of a specific user in the selection screen, note that only the UNIX users of the SAP system are referred to here, but not the SAP users that are unknown to the Oracle system. As of SAP Basis 8.1, the CLIENT_ID will be available, which corresponds to the SAP end user.

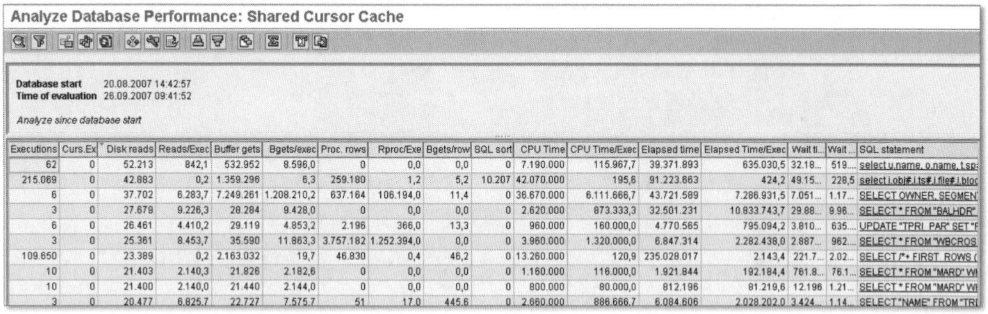

Analyze Database Performance: Shared Cursor Cache

Database start 20.08.2007 14:42:57
Time of evaluation 26.09.2007 09:41:52

Analyze since database start

Executions	Curs.Ex	Disk reads	Reads/Exec	Buffer gets	Bgets/exec	Proc. rows	Rproc/Exe	Bgets/row	SQL sort	CPU Time	CPU Time/Exec	Elapsed time	Elapsed Time/Exec	Wait ti...	Wait ...	SQL statement
62	0	52.213	842,1	532.952	8.596,0	0	0,0	0,0	0	7.190.000	115.967,7	39.371.893	635.030,5	32.18...	519....	select u.name, o.name, t.sp
215.069	0	42.883	0,2	1.359.296	6,3	259.180	1,2	5,2	10.207	42.070.000	195,6	91.223.663	424,2	49.15...	228,5	select i.obj#,i.ts#,i.file#,i.bloc
6	0	37.702	6.283,7	7.249.261	1.208.210,2	637.164	106.194,0	11,4	0	36.670.000	6.111.666,7	43.721.589	7.286.931,5	7.051...	1.17...	SELECT OWNER, SEGMEN
3	0	27.679	9.226,3	28.284	9.428,0	0	0,0	0,0	0	2.620.000	873.333,3	32.501.231	10.833.743,7	29.88...	9.96...	SELECT * FROM "BALHDR"
6	0	26.461	4.410,2	29.119	4.853,2	2.196	366,0	13,3	0	960.000	160.000,0	4.770.565	795.094,2	3.810...	635....	UPDATE "TPRI_PAR" SET "F
3	0	25.361	8.453,7	35.590	11.863,3	3.757.182	1.252.394,0	0,0	0	3.960.000	1.320.000,0	6.847.314	2.282.438,0	2.887...	962....	SELECT * FROM "WBCROS
109.650	0	23.389	0,2	2.163.032	19,7	46.830	0,4	46,2	0	13.260.000	120,9	235.028.017	2.143,4	221.7...	2.02...	SELECT /*+ FIRST_ROWS (
10	0	21.403	2.140,3	21.826	2.182,6	0	0,0	0,0	0	1.160.000	116.000,0	1.921.844	192.184,4	761.8...	76.1...	SELECT * FROM "MARD" WI
10	0	21.400	2.140,0	21.440	2.144,0	0	0,0	0,0	0	800.000	80.000,0	812.196	81.219,6	12.196	1.21...	SELECT * FROM "MARD" WI
3	0	20.477	6.825,7	22.727	7.575,7	51	17,0	445,6	0	2.660.000	886.666,7	6.084.606	2.028.202,0	3.424...	1.14...	SELECT "NAME" FROM "TR

Figure 8.26 Analysis of the Shared Cursor Cache

The top SQL statements should be primarily analyzed in terms of disk reads, buffer gets, and elapsed time. The read access per execution (**bgets/exec**) and the read access per record (**bgets/row**) provide important information. They are important when performing a thorough and individual analysis of an SQL statement. **bgets/exec** can be critical if a request carries out many buffer accesses that may be redundant, as shown earlier in the example in Figure

4 Apart from custom developments, patches, and upgrades, the database structures generally remain stable.

8.21. If the value for **gbets/row** is high, many blocks must be read from the database to deliver a small number of data sets to the application server. In this context, the database access is possibly performed without using appropriate indexes. However, complex joins and several inlists can entail high values for **bgets/exec** without having the technical potential for optimization.

8.3.4 Detailed Analysis of SQL Statements

Furthermore, you can view the execution plan for individual SQL queries (Ctrl-Shift-F6). The query plan for the query

```
SELECT * FROM SBOOK
INTO WA
WHERE PASSNAME = 'Cindy Lindworm'
```

provides the execution plan shown in Figure 8.27. Because no appropriate index is available, the entire table is accessed using the primary index.

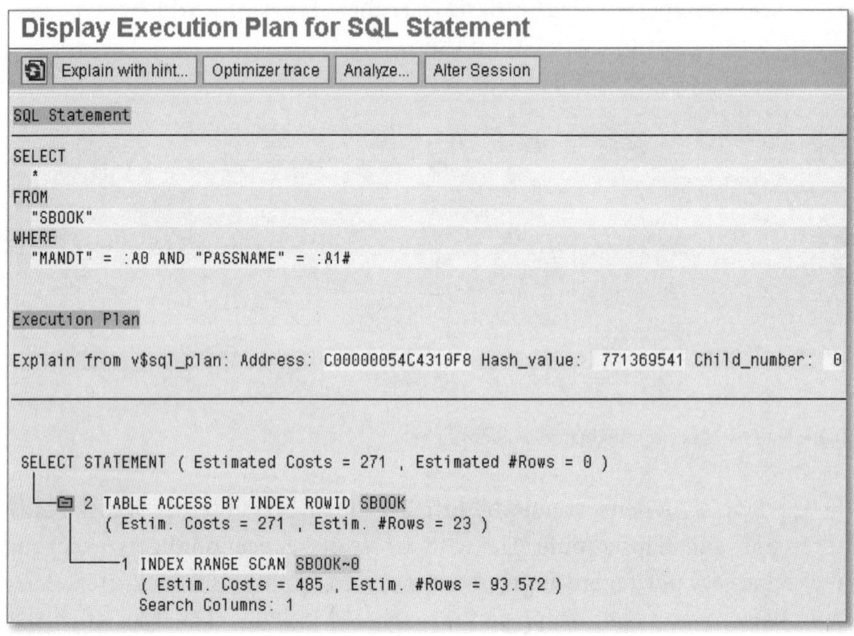

Figure 8.27 Execution Plan for an SQL Query

The ABAP Dictionary (Transaction SE11; see Figure 8.28) provides more information about the available indexes. No index is defined for the SBOOK table via the `PASSNAME` attribute queried by the `where` clause.

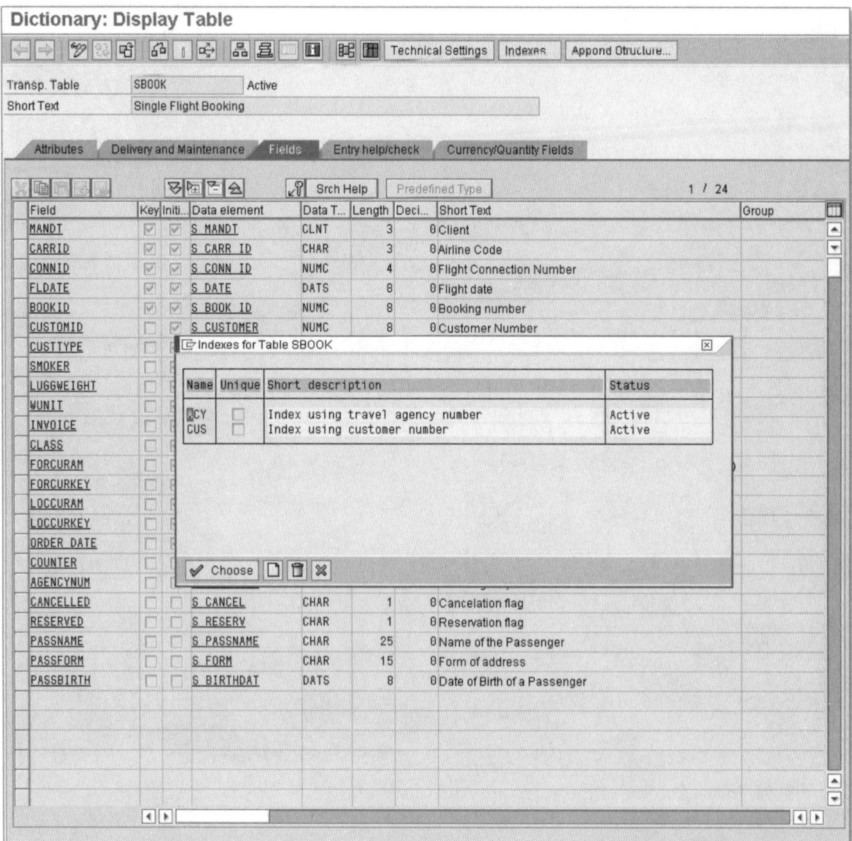

Figure 8.28 Transaction SE11 for Displaying Available Secondary Indexes

8.3.4.1 Analyzing Programs

An alternative approach is to examine the programs that produce high loads or send SQL statements causing these loads. The ABAP Dictionary provides the **Where used** function to enable the identification of programs that use the table. The list of found programs can be very long. In that case, the use of the shared SQL analysis table is more appropriate (see Figure 8.26), which also contains the name of the program that submitted the listed SQL statement first.

Starting from here, a runtime analysis of the program can be carried out (use Transaction SE30 or follow menu path **Tools • ABAP Workbench • Test • Runtime Analysis**). In the first step, the program to be examined must be executed. In the second step, you can view the evaluation (see Figure 8.29).

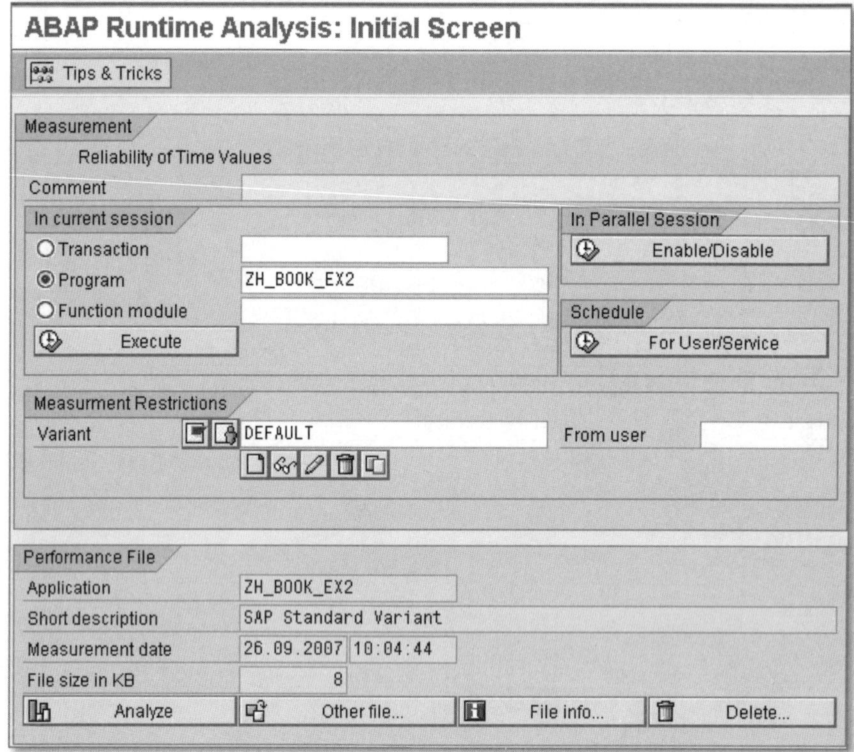

Figure 8.29 Initial Screen of the Runtime Analysis

Figure 8.30 shows the results of the "bad" SQL statement used at the beginning including the use of the `IF` condition. With a total execution time of three seconds, the program has already slowed down noticeably. Most of the time is assigned to the database system that has to transfer about 900,000 records of the SBOOK table to the application server. From the point of view of the architecture, this is absolutely necessary because the buffering of the SBOOK table is not permitted.

In contrast, the program, which has been optimized by shifting the name verification into the `where` condition, shows a runtime behavior that has been improved by a factor of >10 (see Figure 8.31). Whereas the processing with `IF` requires approximately 3 seconds, the variant using `WHERE` only takes 0.2 seconds. On the one hand, the load in the database system is lower, because only a few records needed to be delivered. On the other hand, the application server is also less stressed, because it has to perform the `SELECT` loop only a few times.

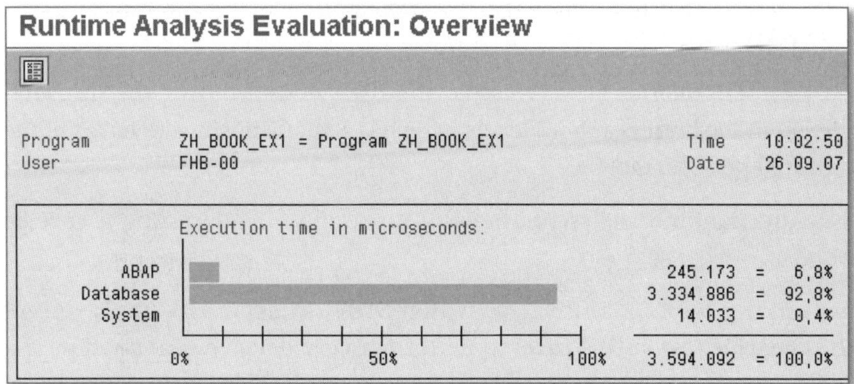

Figure 8.30 Runtime of a Bad Statement

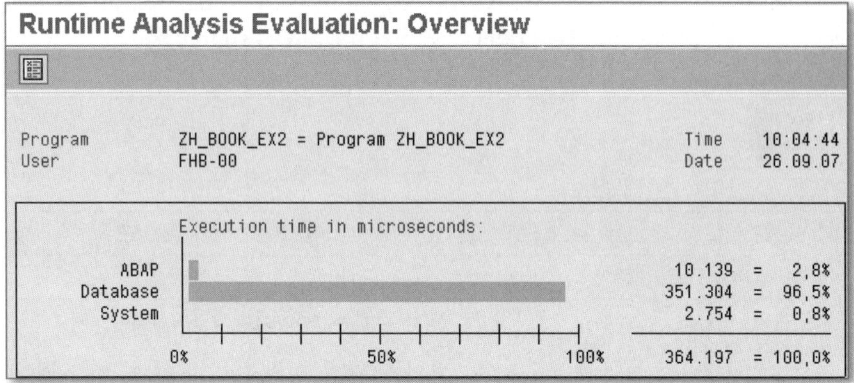

Figure 8.31 Runtime of a Better Statement

Note that the runtime measurements do not always provide the same results. For buffered tables, the initial execution can involve a high database load, whereas the second execution can leverage the data from the buffer of the application server, and the query does not access the Oracle database. The Oracle buffers behave in a similar manner. Consequently, the Oracle data buffer also buffers tables for which no buffering (in the application server) is allowed from the point of view of the SAP system. In this respect, it is not always easy to construct clear examples. The actual system behavior also has an impact on the measurements:

- Other transactions generate loads and require CPU time and data transfer volume.

- Other SQL queries displace data from the buffers to the application server and Oracle levels.
- Other SQL queries already stored the data viewed during the measurement in the buffers at both levels (which is actually positive in terms of the overall performance).

Thus, the runtime analysis is helpful, especially for addressing a specific problem.

You can use the SQL Trace (Transaction ST05 or menu path **Tools • ABAP Workbench • Test • SQL Trace**) to perform a very detailed examination of a single program. Here, the database interface on the side of the SAP system logs the processing steps for SQL queries in detail. This includes the operations provided by the record-oriented interface of the five-layer architecture (see Chapter 3). Figure 8.32 shows the large number of fetch operations that occur with an unspecific SQL query against the SBOOK table.

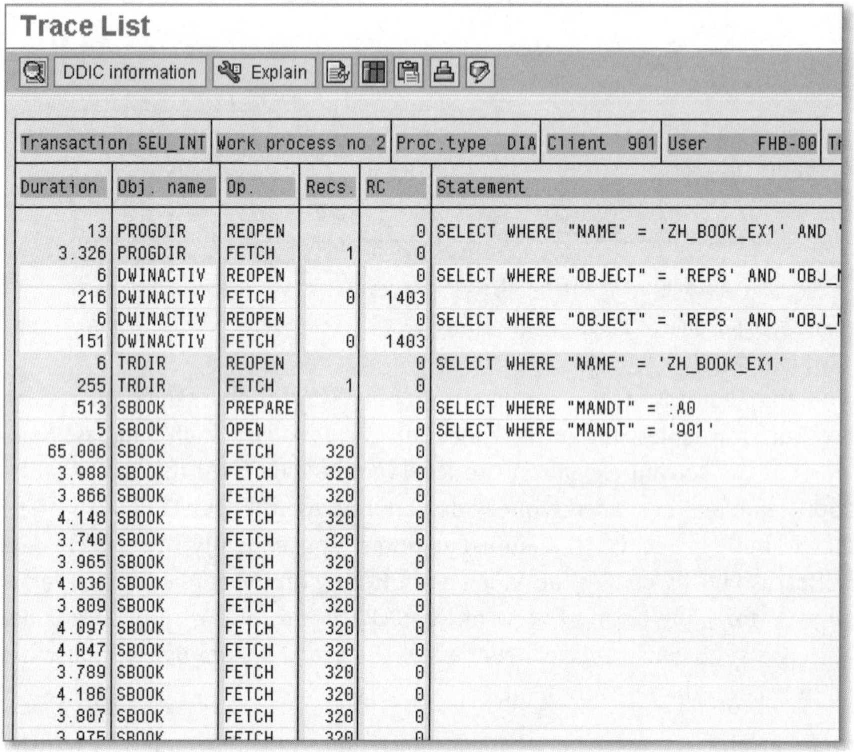

Trace List

DDIC information | Explain

Transaction SEU_INT | Work process no 2 | Proc.type DIA | Client 901 | User FHB-00 | Tr

Duration	Obj. name	Op.	Recs.	RC	Statement
13	PROGDIR	REOPEN		0	SELECT WHERE "NAME" = 'ZH_BOOK_EX1' AND '
3.326	PROGDIR	FETCH	1	0	
6	DWINACTIV	REOPEN		0	SELECT WHERE "OBJECT" = 'REPS' AND "OBJ_N
216	DWINACTIV	FETCH	0	1403	
6	DWINACTIV	REOPEN		0	SELECT WHERE "OBJECT" = 'REPS' AND "OBJ_N
151	DWINACTIV	FETCH	0	1403	
6	TRDIR	REOPEN		0	SELECT WHERE "NAME" = 'ZH_BOOK_EX1'
255	TRDIR	FETCH	1	0	
513	SBOOK	PREPARE		0	SELECT WHERE "MANDT" = :A0
5	SBOOK	OPEN		0	SELECT WHERE "MANDT" = '901'
65.006	SBOOK	FETCH	320	0	
3.988	SBOOK	FETCH	320	0	
3.866	SBOOK	FETCH	320	0	
4.148	SBOOK	FETCH	320	0	
3.740	SBOOK	FETCH	320	0	
3.965	SBOOK	FETCH	320	0	
4.036	SBOOK	FETCH	320	0	
3.809	SBOOK	FETCH	320	0	
4.097	SBOOK	FETCH	320	0	
4.047	SBOOK	FETCH	320	0	
3.789	SBOOK	FETCH	320	0	
4.186	SBOOK	FETCH	320	0	
3.807	SBOOK	FETCH	320	0	
3.975	SBOOK	FETCH	320	0	

Figure 8.32 SQL Trace: High Number of Fetch Operations

An optimized statement that performs the selection using the `where` clause needs only one fetch for the few Cindy Lindworm records. However, this fetch runs relatively long (see Figure 8.33).

Note that when you use an SQL trace, all SQL queries are logged if no filters are used for specific tables, users, or work process numbers. The result can thus be falsified by the side effects of other transactions. Therefore, you should use the filtering options. Tracing processes are time-consuming and may falsify the result.

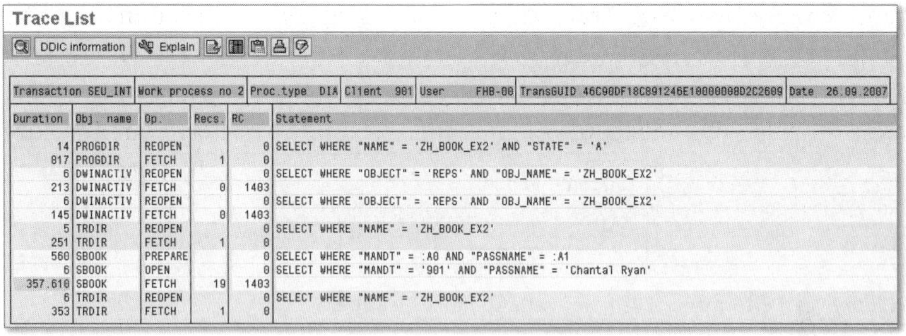

Trace List

DDIC information | Explain

Transaction SEU_INT	Work process no 2	Proc.type DIA	Client 901	User FHB-00	TransGUID 46C90DF18C891246E10000008D2C2609	Date 26.09.2007

Duration	Obj. name	Op.	Recs.	RC	Statement
14	PROGDIR	REOPEN		0	SELECT WHERE "NAME" = 'ZH_BOOK_EX2' AND "STATE" = 'A'
817	PROGDIR	FETCH	1	0	
6	DWINACTIV	REOPEN		0	SELECT WHERE "OBJECT" = 'REPS' AND "OBJ_NAME" = 'ZH_BOOK_EX2'
213	DWINACTIV	FETCH	0	1403	
6	DWINACTIV	REOPEN		0	SELECT WHERE "OBJECT" = 'REPS' AND "OBJ_NAME" = 'ZH_BOOK_EX2'
145	DWINACTIV	FETCH	0	1403	
5	TRDIR	REOPEN		0	SELECT WHERE "NAME" = 'ZH_BOOK_EX2'
251	TRDIR	FETCH	1	0	
560	SBOOK	PREPARE		0	SELECT WHERE "MANDT" = :A0 AND "PASSNAME" = :A1
6	SBOOK	OPEN		0	SELECT WHERE "MANDT" = '901' AND "PASSNAME" = 'Chantal Ryan'
357.610	SBOOK	FETCH	19	1403	
6	TRDIR	REOPEN		0	SELECT WHERE "NAME" = 'ZH_BOOK_EX2'
353	TRDIR	FETCH	1	0	

Figure 8.33 SQL Access with the Where Clause

The large number of logged operations can be reduced to a more manageable amount by defining suitable restrictions during the preselection. It is useful to specify the SAP user (FHB-00 in the example), because the SAP application server logs the operations of the database layer.

You can also view the execution plan for individual SQL statements from within the SQL trace (Explain – F9). In addition, you can change and test SQL statements on a trial basis (Ctrl-F6).

We have now briefly discussed some of the main approaches for detecting and analyzing problematic SQL queries. Let's take a closer look at the solution to these problems.

8.3.5 Prevention: The Silver Bullet

The best way to avoid problematic SQL requests is prevention. The SAP system itself offers numerous good and bad examples via the **Tips and Tricks** function of the runtime analysis (Transaction SE30) or through the ABAP Workbench (Transaction SE80 or **Environment • Examples • Performance Examples**). Based on small code examples, you can become familiar with the alternative programming methods and can start measuring the runtime right away. The examples illustrate typical programming errors including their effects and troubleshooting options (see Figure 8.34). As a prerequisite, you need the flight data model in each case.

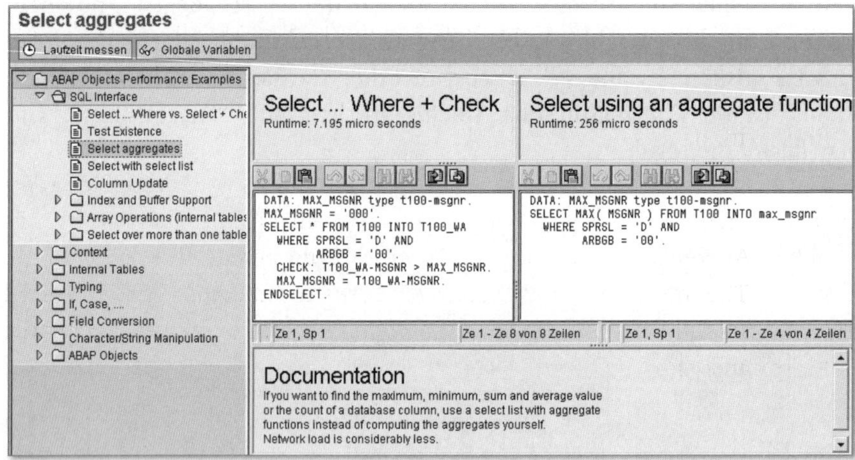

Figure 8.34 Performance Examples with Runtime Measurement

The examples also illustrate the *five golden rules of high-performing SQL programming* (see Schneider, Thomas: *SAP Performance Optimization*, SAP PRESS, 2005), which we will describe briefly here:

1. The number of data records to be transferred between the DBMS and SAP application server must be kept as small as possible. The impact of nonspecific SQL requests that transport large amounts of data has been discussed several times in this section. In addition, multiple reads of identical data by a program can cause large data volumes. You can detect such behavior in the SQL Trace using the **Display Identical Selects** function (Ctrl-Shift-F8).
2. The transported data volume must be kept as small as possible. In addition to Rule 1, you must ensure that no complete data records are transferred, that is, you should avoid using `select *`. Furthermore, for typical calculations, such as calculating averages or totals, you should use the aggregate functions of the Oracle system (see the example in Figure 8.34).
3. The number of transfers between the Oracle database and the application server should also be kept small. Consequently, it is better to use a few SQL requests with large[5] return quantities than many SQL requests with

5 Of course, taking into account Rules 1 and 2.

very small return quantities. On one hand, this is because processing SQL requests involves a certain overhead. On the other hand, data packages that contain small amounts of data and have a constant size on the network unnecessarily consume resources. With many small selects, the transferred gross quantity of data can be a multiple of the net quantity of data. If you succeed in determining all necessary data with a single SQL request, waste occurs only in the last package, which is probably not completely filled with data.

For this reason, you should avoid using SQL requests with nested loops. In current SAP versions, join operators are available for this purpose. In older SAP versions (older than 4.0), joins could be emulated by defining views. The alternative and intuitive way of formulating joins as nested loops can still be found in older developments and offers some potential for optimization.

4. You can keep the overhead for processing the request small by using a `where` clause that corresponds to the existing indexes. For this purpose, the `where` condition should be simple, that is, it should consist of `AND` links as far as possible. `AND` constrains the search area, whereas `OR` extends it. When formulating a request, it is often possible to transfer `OR` conditions into `AND` conditions.[6] We'll describe the use of the correct index in this context in greater detail later in this chapter.
5. It can be useful to shift the load more toward the application server. The architecture of the SAP system can best be scaled at the level of the application server. It is possible to use a larger number of instances to increase the computing performance at that level. However, most SAP installations use only a single integrating database server (see Chapter 2, *SAP Fundamentals*). For operations such as sorting or grouping, which can be performed equally at the database server and application server levels, a shift toward the application server is advisable. Here, you can also use particularly efficient algorithms internally, such as a sorting algorithm. Of course, you need to take Rules 1 to 3 into account in this context, that is, this procedure only makes sense if the entire data quantity considered is used in the application.

Whereas Rules 1 through 4 are universally valid to a large extent, Rule 5 sometimes doesn't make sense or may even be counter-productive in your

6 Procedures for the conversion into disjunctive normal form and conjunctive normal form (by negation) are described in the algorithm literature, for example the application of De Morgan or the Quine-McCluskey procedure.

specific installation. If the application level and database level are located on the same server computer, this would cause a load on the same CPUs, irrespective of the execution level. If the database server computer is comparably overdimensioned, an execution in the database layer would certainly have some advantages. In this context, it is essential to understand the underlying mechanisms to obtain a working solution.

8.3.6 Indexes for Faster Access

Indexes support the quick access to specific data in tables. Take this book as an example: Without a doubt, you can find the key word *Runtime analysis* by reading all pages of the book in their entirety. However, this kind of search is pretty time-consuming. Instead, you may want to use the index at the end of the book where — thanks to the alphabetic sorting — you will only need to search one or two pages more closely to find the reference to the correct page. Ultimately, you will only have to read 3 to 5 pages instead of approximately 800 pages (in the worst case).

For tables, you can create several indexes, which connect single attributes or combinations of attributes. First, there is always the primary index that contains the key attributes. It can be mapped by means of a sorted storage of the data records. Other indexes are referred to as secondary indexes. These secondary indexes store the combinations of attribute values with references to the associated data records in additional memory pages. The organization can occur, for example, as a B-tree, via hash procedures, or as a bitmap index.

An important aspect in this context is that an index has a highly efficient selection function, which means it can help you significantly reduce the number of accesses to the data record blocks. Furthermore, the index should be necessary, that is, the attribute combination should be frequently used by application programs in the `where` clause. Moreover, it is useful if an index consumes significantly fewer memory pages than the data, that is, it is composed of only a few attributes.

In addition to the memory consumption, the maintenance of indexes costs time as well. Insert, change, and delete operations require the adjustment of associated indexes. If many indexes exist, this can considerably slow down the system operation. For this reason, you should act with special care when creating indexes. The creation of unnecessary indexes should be avoided.

8.3.6.1 Using Indexes

In the following text, we will demonstrate the effectiveness of indexes and optimization options on the basis of some examples. Figure 8.27 showed the execution plan for a selection by passenger names. In this context, the primary index is used, it doesn't provide any advantage. Actually, 277 seems to be a pretty high value for the costs.[7] However, the passenger name can be replaced with the customer ID, because the sample data contains a customer ID for every passenger name and vice versa. If you modify the request by performing an additional selection via the `CUSTOMID` attribute, the Oracle Optimizer leverages the secondary index via the `CUSTOMID` attribute (see Figure 8.28). This is shown in the plan in Figure 8.35, which now displays an estimated cost of 3.

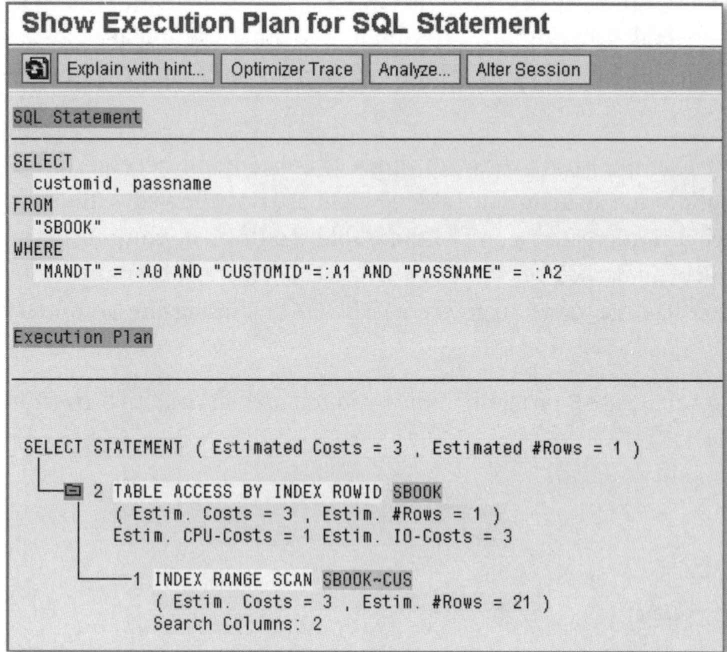

Figure 8.35 Plan with Additional CUSTOMID

Note that by taking into account existing indexes, you can often accelerate the program execution considerably. In this context, you should particularly consider attributes that do not change from the perspective of a specific

7 The costs (Estim. Costs, Estim. Rows) are relative values, which support the comparison of alternative plans. See also SAP Note 766349.

application and are therefore often ignored when a request is formulated. Important examples in this context include the MANDT and BUKRS attributes. Sometimes these attributes must be added to the where clause to make the optimizer use a specific index.[8]

8.3.6.2 Creating Indexes

It may become necessary to create an additional index. However, note that this is a substantial intervention in the system. You should only create indexes for tables of the standard SAP system after consulting the SAP Notes and by taking into account the above considerations. Also, note that creating an index takes some time, and the affected table may be locked for that time. For this reason, you should create the index at times of low usage. Because indexes consume additional resources, you should check the effectiveness of the index. In general, however, the creation or deletion of secondary indexes does not affect the functionality of the system, if they are not unique indexes.

The following example shows how an index is created and becomes effective. As changes to the structure of Table SBOOK are not allowed without an access key, we'll first create a copy of that table. To do that, you must start Transaction SE11 and click on the **Copy** icon. This creates an empty table, ZBOOK, which has the same structure as SBOOK including the secondary indexes.

The following small ABAP program allows you to copy all data records from SBOOK to ZBOOK:

```
REPORT  zh_sbook_copy.
DATA booking LIKE sbook.
SELECT * FROM sbook INTO booking.
  insert into zsbook values booking.
ENDSELECT.
```

For Table ZBOOK, the runtime analysis shows the values measured in Figure 8.36 for a selection by "Cindy Lindworm." No index is used here, because no suitable index exists for that passenger name. Compared to a selection using Table SBOOK, the values shown here are slightly different. One possible reason might be the different physical characteristics of the two tables.

8 See Schneider, T.: SAP Performance Optimization. SAP PRESS 2005.

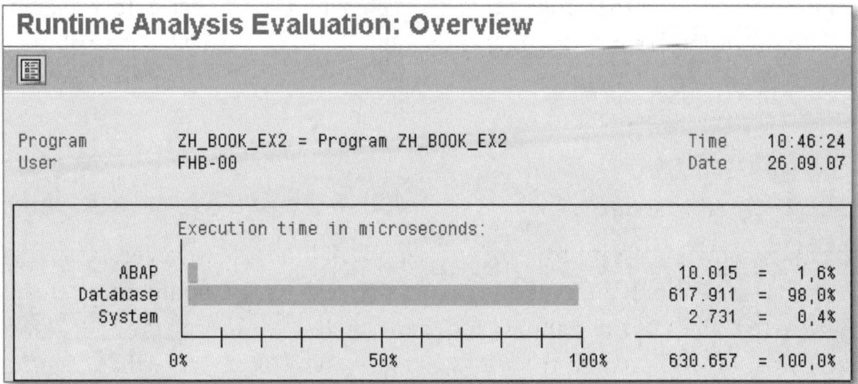

Figure 8.36 Runtime Analysis Without Index

As shown in Figure 8.37, you can use Transaction SE11 to create an index, PNI, for the PASSNAME attribute.

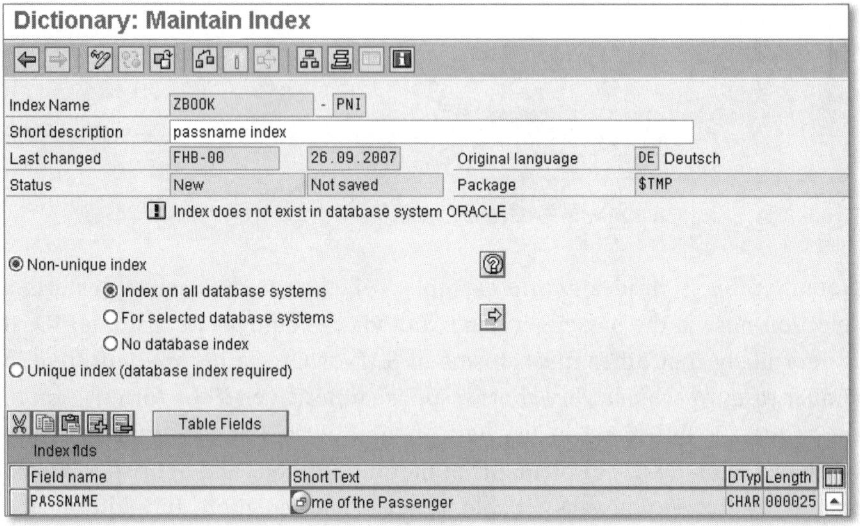

Figure 8.37 Creating the PNI Index for PASSNAME

When measuring the unchanged program, the new results are significantly better, as shown in Figure 8.38. The processing in the application server requires a similar amount of time. The number of packages transported between the database and application server is the same. However, in the example, processing in Oracle is 250 times faster due to the use of the index.

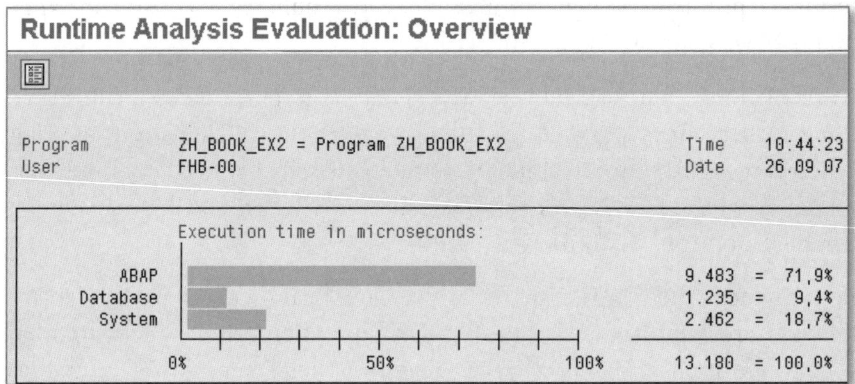

Figure 8.38 Runtime Analysis with Index

The display of the selected plan (see Figure 8.39) shows the use of index PZBOOK-PNI via the PASSNAME attribute, as expected.

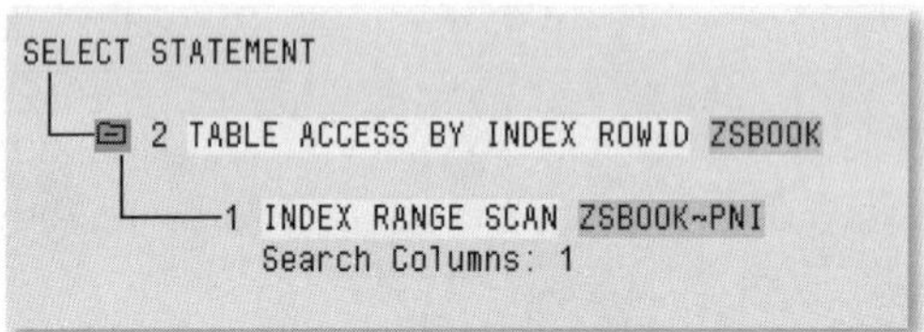

Figure 8.39 Execution Plan with PASSNAME Index

Note that this is an ideal-world example. It makes more sense to perform a selection not via the passenger name, but via the equivalent customer ID. It is very likely that other mechanisms of SAP or Oracle become effective in similar cases to achieve very short response times, even if the formulation of the request is not made in the best possible way. The powerful statistical optimizer from Oracle implements numerous methods and heuristics, which frequently (but not always) enable an ideal plan creation. In addition, the optimizer is enhanced continuously.

8.4 Summary

Performance is a far-ranging and complex topic. Hardware – operating system – Oracle – SAP system: Nobody knows everything. The intention of this chapter was to provide an overall picture to enable you to handle performance problems. Whenever possible, you should try to consult an expert on the topic you need help with.

Avoid making snap decisions. Performance is important, but isn't everything. Data security is always the top priority. If the system halts, immediate action is required, but this situation should generally happen very rarely. Try to adhere to the small or big optimization cycle: Problem analysis – troubleshooting – verification.

Performance-critical SQL statements may significantly affect the overall system and are often caused by the primarily function-oriented programming style of the application developers. Prevention helps here as well as training the developers with regard to a high-performance programming style. You can often improve problematic SQL statements in collaboration with the development team. In this chapter, we demonstrated ways to recognize and precisely analyze this type of statement. Another option, which, however, should be the responsibility of an experienced Oracle administrator, is to create additional secondary indexes. If you identify a problem with an original SAP program, you're probably not the first to encounter that problem. In this case, the SAP Service Marketplace or the SAP Notes often contain essential information for problem handling, either by means of a correction or a workaround.

The administrator of a system landscape must be able to get an overview of the status of the components at any time. If problems are recognized too late or if the system fails, substantial financial damage may result.

9 System Operation and Monitoring

The increasing complexity of distributed network and system structures requires consistent information on the components' conditions, resource utilization, and quality of service. Therefore, *monitoring* is an important process of modern electronic data processing and has the task to monitor hardware, software, and communication networks.

The following sections provide an overview of the general meaning of monitoring and which components should be included in the process. We will then describe how you can monitor an SAP system that runs on an Oracle database.

9.1 Monitoring in the SAP Environment: Motivation and Scope

Today, monitoring is a basic function of each data center and is used to monitor all vital operational functions. It continuously penetrates an increasing number of areas of the IT system landscape and therefore provides more and more detailed information on the performance and status of hardware and software components.

In the context of electronic data processing (EDP), monitoring is responsible for detecting and avoiding undesired system statuses. In networked IT infrastructures, individual components cooperate with each other, so an error in one component can immediately affect the entire infrastructure. If the IT systems of the individual departments in an enterprise, such as purchasing, marketing, sales, and production, are networked to automate business processes, a failure in one of the systems immediately affects the other systems and thus the business process. Therefore, modern interacting IT infrastructures need processes that detect and correct errors as quickly as possible. Consequently, monitoring is "mission critical" for IT service providers.

The monitoring data is used for error detection and prevention as well as for documenting rendered services. However, it is even more important to detect potential sources of error or error situations as early as possible than to recognize known errors. You thus have the possibility to interfere and find adequate solutions at an early stage.

The forecast of future developments of the infrastructure has a similar aim. Using this forecast, you can plan the resources and control the further expansion of your infrastructure. The data used for forecasting purposes is mainly based on dimension and utilization data from the monitoring process.

The following sections describe the characteristics of monitoring when using Oracle and the areas of monitoring that are of interest when using an SAP system.

9.1.1 Monitoring Areas

For monitoring within the SAP environment, usually three main areas are important:

1. The hardware on which the landscape is based
2. The software, that is, the SAP systems, connected systems, and other software required for operating the landscape
3. The network that provides the infrastructure for all of the communication between the systems and users

The network and hardware are only briefly described because a detailed explanation would go beyond the scope of this book. Especially when hardware is monitored, the specifications of the individual manufacturers must be observed. The basic requirements, such as disk space as well as CPU and memory requirements, are, of course, general aspects that are described in Section 9.2.3, *Monitoring the Hardware and Operating System.*

9.1.1.1 Hardware

The hardware of the landscape constitutes the basis for all other components. If there are already problems with the hardware, the software will probably be affected in the short or medium term. For example, an increase in the ambient temperature due to a defective fan or failure of the air-conditioning can lead to a shutdown or failure of the server. Thus, the software that runs on the server is also affected. Due to this obviously close connection between hardware and software, both need to be monitored. The following sections deal with some aspects that you should consider when setting up the monitoring process for the hardware.

The hardware of a computer can be categorized as follows:

- **Central processing unit (CPU)**
  In addition to the availability that can only be monitored for multiprocessor systems, the temperature of the CPU is a critical issue. If the temperature gets critical for the CPU, the load needs to be reduced, and the heat problem must be solved quickly. The utilization of the CPU is also important for the analysis of system bottlenecks and for the historical evaluation of monitoring processes.
- **Memory (volatile and nonvolatile)**
  In this context, the utilization is essential to avoid bottlenecks, and it is important to monitor whether the stored data is correct. In the random access memory (RAM), the information is checked for bit errors to determine faulty memory cells. For permanent storage and disk and tape drives, read and write errors on the medium are registered.
- **Internal communications links (buses)**
  The I/O queues of the buses are monitored to detect overflows. Additionally, the transferred information is checked for communication errors (wrong check amounts).
- **I/O devices (for example, network card, keyboard, and so on)**
  I/O devices are also mainly monitored regarding their availability and utilization.
- **Peripherals (for example, power supplies, fans)**
  Here, the most important objects that need to be monitored are the environment parameters and the power supply. Temperature and humidity are the essential parameters for computer operation that are supposed to be monitored, as well as the functionality of the existing fans. The power supply is essential for the system stability, too, and must therefore be monitored for quality and quantity. For example, failed power supplies must be immediately indicated and replaced.

To enable a holistic monitoring process, all the previously mentioned components must be included in the monitoring solution. If one of the first three components is affected, this leads to a system failure or, at least, performance problems. Therefore, immediate monitoring is indispensable. Responsible administrators can benefit from even short reaction times before a failure occurs to take measures against resulting damage. A failure of I/O devices or peripherals doesn't affect the system immediately. In this case, you have a certain period of time to react to errors. Due to redundancy within one server, these errors can be partly corrected without interruptions.

The redundancy capability and, above all, the actually used redundancy of components can considerably decrease the likelihood of a breakdown. Nearly all current server and operating systems can monitor the hardware status independently and inform the administrator when errors occur. At this stage, the availability is, due to the integrated redundancy, not endangered, and you can initiate measures to correct the error. The measures can often be taken during operation, for example, when fans, power supplies, or redundant hard disks (use of RAID) are replaced.

9.1.1.2 Network

The network plays a special role, because it consists of hardware and software. For example, cables, switches, and routers are hardware. Furthermore, software (e.g., IOS on Cisco switches) that is responsible for the actual functionality, such as routing or firewall functions, is used on many network components. Due to their specific properties regarding their role as an essential linking element, networks are considered separately in the monitoring process. For the SAP system landscape to function correctly, a continuous availability of the network is important, because the user cannot work with the SAP GUI or web browsers on the systems without a network connection.

9.1.1.3 Software

Software can be divided into several categories regarding the monitoring process. These include:

- **Availability**
  When is the service available? This aspect is the main criteria for software monitoring.
- **CPU utilization**
  When and how long does a software process use the CPU? In this way, "dead" or stuck processes can be determined. This is very important for

system availability and performance, because they are directly affected by a high CPU load.

- **Memory consumption**
  When does a software process use memory, and how much does it use? The problem of memory leaks should be given special attention. These leaks can lead to considerable performance problems or to a system shutdown when a process occupies memory but doesn't make it available again to be used by other processes.
- **Users**
  When do users work with the software, and how many of them use it? In this way, the current system utilization, the user behavior, and the load optimization is evaluated. This information can also be used for accounting.
- **Storage consumption**
  How much permanent storage does the software use? To plan the future properly, it is important for an administrator to know how much the consumption increases per time unit is.
- **I/O utilization**
  How often does the software access I/O devices? Knowing this allows performance problems to be identified and solved. The throughput of memory and hard disk accesses plays an important role in this context.
- **Security**
  Security and its monitoring is a very important issue that applies to all types of software. It determines the integrity and confidentiality of the data directly and the system availability indirectly. The system administrators are responsible for monitoring and maintaining the software security within their range of capabilities. For this purpose, the integrity of files is checked by means of previous system copies. In addition, the current state of the software must be monitored for security updates.

In the context of SAP monitoring, we will concentrate in particular on the first issues and omit security, because the security in SAP systems is a complex construction of roles, profiles, and authorizations that goes beyond the scope of this book. Chapter 5, *Planning the System Landscape*, includes some security notes related to the entire infrastructure.

9.1.2 Monitoring Problems

Monitoring includes some problems that should be considered when setting up and configuring monitoring processes.

The timeliness of data is often very important Of course, you, as an administrator, want to see the current state of a parameter and not states that are outdated. However, it is problematic to request data from a system too often, because these requests create loads in the system. This may lead to a part of the system capacity being only used for responding to monitoring requests. Therefore, it is important to find a balance between parameter timeliness and load generated by monitoring processes. Important parameters, such as availability or archiver stucks, should be monitored more often than values that change only slowly, for example, the database size or its filling level.

To avoid or solve such problems, you should adjust the monitoring configuration consistently. Monitoring "out of the box" is usually impossible because each landscape has its own specific properties. Without adjusting the process to the landscape properties, error messages may occur too quickly, too late, or not all. If too many error messages are provided by monitoring processes, messages may be ignored, and thus critical situations may escalate.

The filling level of the tablespace is a good example. If the threshold value for an alert is set to 95%, you have free space of 100 megabytes for a small tablespace of two gigabytes. In comparison, an 80-gigabyte tablespace still has 4 gigabytes available at the same threshold value. Therefore, it might not be necessary to interfere at this point. In this case, you should adjust the threshold value to activate an alert at a later stage. The same applies to the update interval for parameters that don't change much. The less often they are read, the less load is imposed by monitoring.

Another issue regarding the monitoring setup is the adjustment to specific products and customer developments. If no predefined solutions exist, you must generate your own monitoring process. When using a monitoring tool, there are often possibilities provided to develop your own monitors and add the desired functions. These custom developments and the future maintenance are associated with costs that should be kept in mind.

A system that monitors other systems must be active for as long a time as possible. Therefore, when setting up the monitoring process, you should ensure that monitoring tools are set up with high availability and that installations are distributed across the system (for example, by using agents), which to an extent monitors itself and initiates alerts at component failures.

9.1.3 Solutions for SAP Monitoring

Most of the components described in Section 9.1.1 can be monitored via the regularly repeated execution of commands or transactions in the operating and SAP systems. Because it is not efficient to waste your time as an administrator by calling the same commands for half of the day, *monitoring tools* were developed to automate this task. These tools can be custom scripts to regularly collect and analyze data or they can be complex software packages to monitor entire landscapes. Irrespective of which tools you use, you as an administrator are automatically alerted via several channels (SMS, email, pager, and so on).

For monitoring SAP systems, there is a range of solutions that support the automatic monitoring of threshold values. Because the SAP system or the entire SAP landscape is usually the basis for nearly all business processes, monitoring assumes a special role to ensure continuous system operation. There are several possibilities for how to set up an automatic monitoring infrastructure:

1. **Using internal SAP monitoring**
   The *Computing Center Management System* (CCMS) is a collection of monitoring functions within the SAP system that covers nearly all parameters related to an SAP infrastructure.
2. **Using SAP Solution Manager**
   The SAP Solution Manager is a self-contained SAP system that collects and analyzes data from other systems. Furthermore, this information can be processed in reports and linked to monitor business processes.
3. **Using an external monitoring tool**
   In external tools, the type and scope of the monitoring process differ considerably, but in comparison with the first two options, the degree of flexibility is much higher.

The advantages and disadvantages of all possibilities are summarized in Table 9.1.

Monitoring solution	Advantages	Disadvantages
Using internal SAP monitoring	▸ Part of the SAP system, so very close to the system. ▸ To a certain extent, the system monitors itself and partially takes countermeasures independently.	▸ Complex configuration. ▸ Difficult to enhance, for example, to monitor other, non-SAP products. ▸ If the system fails, the monitoring process stops, too; no alert may be initiated unless an additional SAP system is installed.

Table 9.1 Advantages and Disadvantages of Monitoring Options

Monitoring solution	Advantages	Disadvantages
Using SAP Solution Manager	▸ SAP product that is available free of charge for licensees. ▸ Based on internal monitoring processes of SAP systems. ▸ Allows for reporting based on data from the monitoring process. ▸ Monitoring of business processes via several systems.	▸ Additional SAP instance, so there are additional costs for hardware and software. ▸ High availability for SAP Solution Manager should be provided.
Using an external monitoring tool	▸ Very flexible. ▸ Other components can be integrated. ▸ Can serve as the central basis for the entire monitoring process. ▸ External monitoring, so an alert is initiated if the SAP system is not available.	▸ Often very expensive. ▸ Effort and costs for installation and configuration. ▸ Costs for maintenance, upgrades, and enhancements.

Table 9.1 Advantages and Disadvantages of Monitoring Options (Cont.)

For the following sections, it doesn't matter which option you choose to monitor your systems. We will describe how you can manually, that is, via the operating system or SAP system, check the status of your system and how you can determine errors and solve potential problems. The most important monitoring approaches are also introduced. A monitoring solution to be used in the SAP environment (with an Oracle database) should at least include the basic monitoring parameters described below.

9.2 Parameters for Monitoring an SAP System Based on Oracle

In this chapter, components of an SAP system are all components that can be monitored and possibly managed directly or indirectly from within the SAP system:

1. Oracle database
2. Backup
3. Instances of the SAP system
4. Underlying operating system

The following sections discuss the possibilities for monitoring the system and advise you how to solve related problems.

9.2.1 Monitoring the Oracle Database

The general availability and accessibility, the remaining space for storing data, and the performance are important for monitoring a database. Additionally, you have to monitor whether the data files and archive logs are regularly saved.

The availability of the database is based on the proper functioning of all required processes. Chapter 3 has already introduced these processes. You can check the status of the processes by using the UNIX command `ps` or the process overview in Windows. If all required processes are active, you can usually assume that your database works properly at least at process level.

In addition to the functionality of the Oracle database, the availability of the Oracle Listener is also relevant for using Oracle in an SAP system. The database can be made available by testing the connection and reading the data by means of SQL Plus. For example, this data can also contain other monitoring information. Besides database availability, SAP work processes also depend on the availability of the Oracle Listener. The accessibility of the Oracle Listener can be checked using the `tnsping` command. The following listings show the outputs of a functioning and not functioning Listener:

```
f01:oras01 10> tnsping S11
TNS Ping Utility for HPUX: Version 10.2.0.2.0 - Production on 23-AUG-2006 20:40:10
Copyright (c) 1997, 2005, Oracle.  All rights reserved.
Used parameter files:
/oracle/S01/102_64/network/admin/sqlnet.ora
Used TNSNAMES adapter to resolve the alias
Attempting to contact (DESCRIPTION = (ADDRESS_LIST = (ADDRESS =
(COMMUNITY = SAP.WORLD) (PROTOCOL = TCP) (HOST = f03) (PORT = 3010)))
(CONNECT_DATA = (SID = S11) (GLOBAL_NAME = S11.WORLD)))
OK (10 msec)
```

A ping signal is sent to the Oracle Listener of Database S11. When the name is resolved by means of the file */oracle/<SID>/102_64/network/admin/tnsnames.ora*, you obtain host f03 and port 3010. If the Listener is contacted successfully, you receive an OK message and information on the output of the response time (in the example above, 10 milliseconds). If no Listener can be contacted, the message

```
TNS-12541: TNS:no listener
```

is displayed. This message can be analyzed, for example, by using a monitoring tool.

There must always be sufficient memory space to store all data in the database when an SAP system is used. The memory space is stored on the file system in the form of tablespaces and managed via extensions and segments (see Chapter 3).

You can use the SAP tool, `brspace`, to check the space that is currently occupied in the files. For this purpose, call the `brspace -f tsextend` statement as the ora<sid> user. Figure 9.1 shows the call and the subsequent menu.

```
f03:/root#su - oras10
f03:oras10 1> brspace -f tsextend
BR1001I BRSPACE 7.00 (14)
BR1002I Start of BRSPACE processing: sdtjiegq.tse 2006-08-28 09.22.20

BR0280I BRSPACE time stamp: 2006-08-28 09.22.22
BR1009I Name of database instance: S10
BR1010I BRSPACE action ID: sdtjiegq
BR1011I BRSPACE function ID: tse
BR1012I BRSPACE function: tsextend

BR0280I BRSPACE time stamp: 2006-08-28 09.22.22
BR0656I Choice menu 301 - please make a selection
-------------------------------------------------------------------------------
Tablespace extension main menu

 1 = Extend tablespace
 2 - Show tablespaces
 3 - Show data files
 4 - Show disk volumes
 5 * Exit program
 6 - Reset program status

Standard keys: c - cont, b - back, s - stop, r - refr, h - help
-------------------------------------------------------------------------------
BR0662I Enter your choice:
```

Figure 9.1 brspace –f tsextend Command

In addition to requesting information on the tablespaces, its data files, and the distribution across the connected hard disks (disk volumes), the tablespaces can be extended. Figure 9.2 shows a list of tablespace data as an example.

```
-------------------------------------------------------------------------------
List of database tablespaces

Pos.  Tablespace      Type  Status    ExtMan.  SegMan.  Backup  Files/AuExt.
      Total[KB]     Used[%]    Free[KB]  ExtSize[KB]  FreeExt.    Largest[KB]

  1 - PSAPSR3          DATA  ONLINE    LOCAL     AUTO       NO          9/9
      18432000      97.87       391744     11755520          2      8192000+:3563520+:361408:30336:0
  2 - PSAPSR3700       DATA  ONLINE    LOCAL     AUTO       NO          6/6
      27013120      84.19      4270720     11755520          5      5959680+:5795840+:3805184:462784:960
  3 - PSAPSR3DB        DATA  ONLINE    LOCAL     AUTO       NO          2/2
       2334720      55.56      1037440     11755520          3      9216000+:2539520+:1023936:13248:256
  4 - PSAPSR3USR       DATA  ONLINE    LOCAL     AUTO       NO          1/1
         20480       2.19        20032     10219520          1     10219520+:20032:0:0:0
  5 - PSAPTEMP         TEMP  ONLINE    LOCAL     MANUAL     NO          1/1
       1239040       0.00      1239040      9000960          0      9000960+:0:0:0:0
  6 - PSAPUNDO         UNDO  ONLINE    LOCAL     MANUAL     NO          1/1
       6594560       1.02      6527168      3645440         21      3645440+:3274304:2531264:375040:208128
  7 - SYSAUX           DATA  ONLINE    LOCAL     AUTO       NO          1/1
        204800      77.66        45760     10035200         15     10035200+:38848:2048:2048:832
  8 - SYSTEM           DATA  ONLINE    LOCAL     MANUAL     NO          2/1
        716800      63.56       261184      9779200          3      9779200+:255936:5056:192:0

Standard keys: c - cont, b - back, s - stop, r - refr, h - help
-------------------------------------------------------------------------------
BR0662I Enter your selection:
```

Figure 9.2 Tablespace Output

You can obtain the same information within an SAP system if you have no access to the operating system level. To do so, go to **Tools • Administration • Monitor • Performance • Database • Tables/Indexes** (Transaction DB02) in the SAP system. Figure 9.3 shows the output.

Database performance: tables and indices

Tab/Ind | History of tablesp. | Storage management | Freespace analysis | Data files / Temp files | Critical tables/ind.

28.08.2006 09:50:57 S10 f03
Storage check on 25.08.2006 07:00:50

Tablespace	Freespace		Fragments	Max next	Critical objects		
Maximum/kb	Maximum/kb	Total/kb		extent/kb	now	after reorg	a. autoext
SYSTEM	255936	261184	3	1024	0	0	0
PSAPUNDO	4801408	6517952	24	1024	0	0	0
SYSAUX	38848	45888	6	1024	0	0	0
PSAPTEMP	0	0	not calc.	not calc.	not calc.	not calc.	not calc.
PSAPSR3	361408	391872	2	65536	0	0	0
PSAPSR3700	4267968	4270720	4	65536	0	0	0
PSAPSR3USR	20032	20032	1	64	0	0	0
PSAPSR3DB	1023936	1037440	3	8192	0	0	0

Figure 9.3 Free Space in the Tablespace in the SAP System

We recommend that you use `brspace`, because tablespaces can also be extended when problems related to the permanent storage are detected.

The memory space is allocated by means of *extents*. An extent is a coherent area of a database that is assigned to a segment. Unlike a segment, an extent cannot span over several data files.

Chapter 3 already described how managing extents has been simplified by implementing *locally managed tablespaces* (LMTS). Either only four permanent extent sizes is used that depend on the segment size (*LMTS autoallocate*), or a standardized size is used that is defined when creating the tablespace (*LMTS uniform*). Table 9.2 lists the segment sizes and the assigned extent sizes for LMTS autoallocate.

Segment size	Size of the next extent
SEG < 1 MB	64 KB
1 MB ≤ SEG ≤ 64 MB	1 MB
64 MB ≤ SEG ≤ 1 GB	8 MB
1 GB ≤ SEG	64 MB

Table 9.2 Extent Sizes for LMTS

The usage of the defined sizes can also be found in Figure 9.3 in the **Max next extent/kb** column. If the tablespace is an LMTS uniform type, the extent size can be determined using the following SQL statement:

```
SELECT NEXT_EXTENT FROM DBA_TABLESPACES
WHERE TABLESPACE_NAME = '<Tablespace>';
```

With LMTS, you only have to ensure that sufficient free space — in percent or absolute values — is available in the tablespace for increasing segments. LMTS does not use the segment as the monitoring unit or the `NEXT` parameter as the control parameter. The monitoring unit for LMTS is the entire tablespace, and the value to be monitored is the free space in the tablespace.

By exactly defining the extents, free memory can be reused more efficiently. This reduces the fragmentation within the data files. Furthermore, the new algorithm allocates, if necessary, the free memory using the next smaller extents. In this way, smaller areas are also reused. If an initial extent size is defined during the creation of a new object, the new extent sizes are used for allocation. The following examples clarify this procedure:

- **Case 1: very small initial values**
  If you select, for example, 16 KB or 80 KB as the initial extent sizes, the first extents are automatically allocated with 64 KB. If you select higher values, Oracle skips the smaller categories. Especially for SAP NetWeaver BI systems with many small objects (previously 16 KB), this may lead con-

siderably more memory space being required in the database when changing to LMTS.

- **Case 2: very high initial values**
  From an initial extent size of 1,025 MB, only 8-MB extents and 64-MB extents will be assigned. SAP systems no longer use 64-KB blocks.
- **Case 3: intermediate sizes**
  If you create an object with sizes in between the above-listed segment limitations, the extents are divided into the sizes defined. Thus, a segment with an initial size of 65 MB is divided as follows: Extent 0 with a size of 8 MB, extents 1 through 49 with 1 MB each, extent 50 with 8 MB. The following extents are then created according to the above schema.

When implementing LMTS, the background job of adjusting the extent sizes becomes redundant. If the job is still scheduled, you can check in the job's log file whether it can be deallocated. If the message

```
BR0906I All selected tables/indexes are in locally managed table spaces
```

is displayed in the log, you can deactivate the job.

If the job is still scheduled and all data files are set to `autoextend=OFF`, the free space in the tablespace is checked. If at least one data file is set to `autoextend=ON`, the free space in the file system is checked, too, to ensure that not only the tablespace provides sufficient space, but also that the data file can be extended to the maximum size in the file system.

In systems with *dictionary-managed tablespaces* (DMTS), the job for the next-extent-calculation is supposed to be scheduled via **Tools • CCMS • DB Administration • Planning Calendar • Local** (Transaction DB13) (recommendation: once a week). You can also call the calculation via `brconnect -f next -t all`. This avoids having a quickly increasing segment occupying — due to a too small extent size — many extents and eventually reaching the MAX_EXTENTS limit. This limit is only set for DMTS.

You can use the following command to check the maximum extent (`segment` corresponds to a table or an index):

```
SELECT MAX_EXTENTS FROM DBA_SEGMENTS
WHERE SEGMENT_NAME = '&lt;segment&gt;';
```

You can use the commands given below to adjust the number of the maximum extents and the extent increase:

```
ALTER &lt;segment&gt; STORAGE (NEXT &lt;new_next&gt;);
ALTER &lt;segment&gt; STORAGE (MAXEXTENTS &lt;new_maxextents&gt;);
ALTER &lt;segment&gt; STORAGE (PCTINCREASE &lt;new_pctincrease&gt;);
ALTER TABLE &lt;segment&gt; STORAGE (NEXT &lt;new_next&gt;);
ALTER INDEX &lt;segment&gt; STORAGE (NEXT &lt;new_next&gt;);
```

If no more coherent free space is available for an extent that must be newly allocated, and if the automatic data file extension via AUTOALLOCATE is not activated, the running transaction is cancelled with an error message. If the transaction is an SAP update transaction, the update of the SAP system will be deactivated.

Besides the memory space for the data files, the Oracle database also requires memory for writing the redo logs. It is particularly important to save the offline redo logs. If the available memory space does not suffice to save the logs, this leads to a database shutdown, which is referred to as an *archiver stuck.*

An archiver stuck occurs if no disk space is available for the archiver process to save the online redo logs as offline redo logs. The database is stuck until you can save the online redo files again. You must monitor the target directory of the offline redo logs, */oracle/<SID>/oraarch* by default, to avoid an archiver stuck. The log files contained in this directory are usually saved on tape by means of a periodic or filling level-controlled backup. If data is not saved, for example, due to a backup error, an archiver stuck may result. You can avoid an archiver stuck by permanently monitoring the filling level. For I/O-intensive operations, such as loading and storing mass data or generating authorization profiles, the filling level of the archive log directory changes very fast. Therefore, its monitoring is time-critical.

You have several options to check the filling level. You can regularly check the relevant file system using operating system commands, such as `df` or `bdf` in UNIX, or you can call **Tools • CCMS • DB Administration • Backup Logs** (Transaction DB12) in the SAP system. There, you can determine the current filling level via **Archiving Directory Status**, as shown in Figure 9.4. Moreover, you get an overview of all redo log backups and their return codes, for example, to identify failed backups as causes of an error.

You can delete and remove log files, define a temporary directory as an archiving target, or create a dummy file in the log directory to eliminate the archiver stuck. However, you shouldn't delete logs, because, in a worst case scenario, this may prevent the backups from being restored because consistent recovery information is no longer available. For testing and development systems, which you don't want to recover, you may delete the logs, but in other cases you should avoid this. By moving the logs or writing them temporarily to another directory, the backup of the logs may be made more difficult because it can no longer run completely automatically. The log files won't be lost, though. Simply save all logs and restore them in a recovery process. Working with a dummy file enables a quick release of memory space in the archiving directory without any interruption of the usual work. Section 10.2.3, *Online Data Backup*, describes the exact procedure and handling in detail.

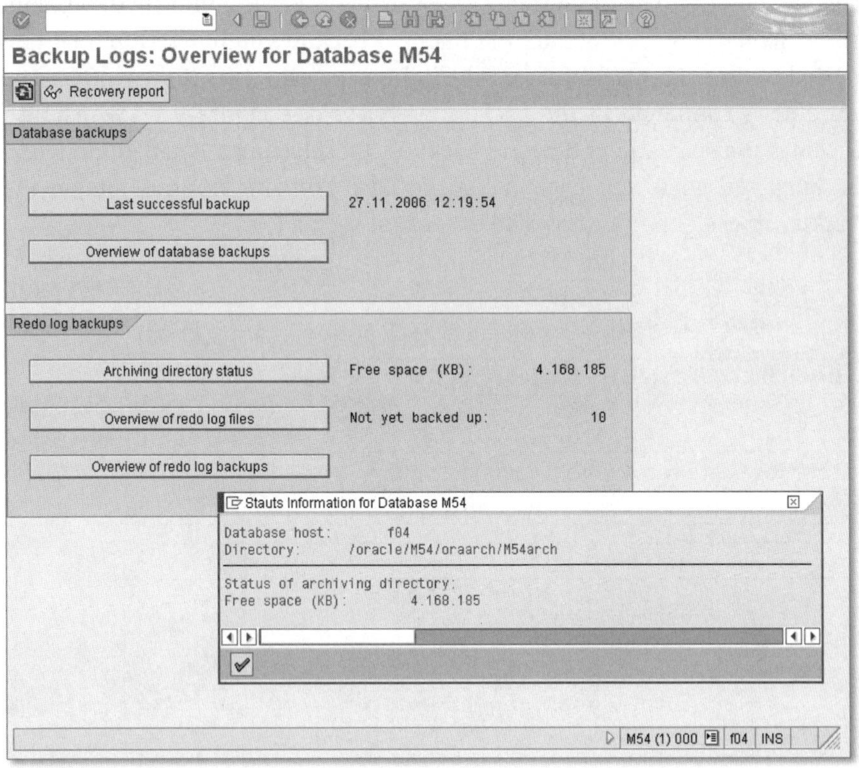

Figure 9.4 Filling Level of the Archiving Directory

In addition to the backup of the archive logs, you must also run a periodic online backup of the systems. SAP recommends that you run the backup of the systems daily. It is important that the respective redo logs are saved after an online backup of the database. This is the only way you can ensure that consistent restore and recovery processes are executed. If possible, you should check at regular intervals if you can restore the system with the saved data. If such an error is only detected in an emergency, it can lead to severe problems when restoring the system or even cause a comprehensive data loss. Regular backups of the offline redo logs are mandatory to enable a recovery of all changes between two online backups. Information on the last successful backup as well as all previous backups can be found under **Tools • CCMS • DB Administration • Backup Logs** (Transaction DB12). Chapter 10, *Backup, Restore, and Recovery*, contains more information on the backup aspects.

By means of the backup logs, you can also obtain information on the backup time and the backup size. If the runtime deviates much from previous values based on experience, problems may have occurred during the writing process of the backup (for example, tape or disk errors). Monitoring the backup sizes enables you to schedule the planned backup volume within a certain period of time. This is useful for scheduling tape capacities, for example. The runtime is contained in the backup overview (see Figure 9.5), which also includes the start and end of the backups. By selecting a detailed view of a backup, you go to the backup log that also contains information on the backup size. Figure 9.6 shows an excerpt of such a log.

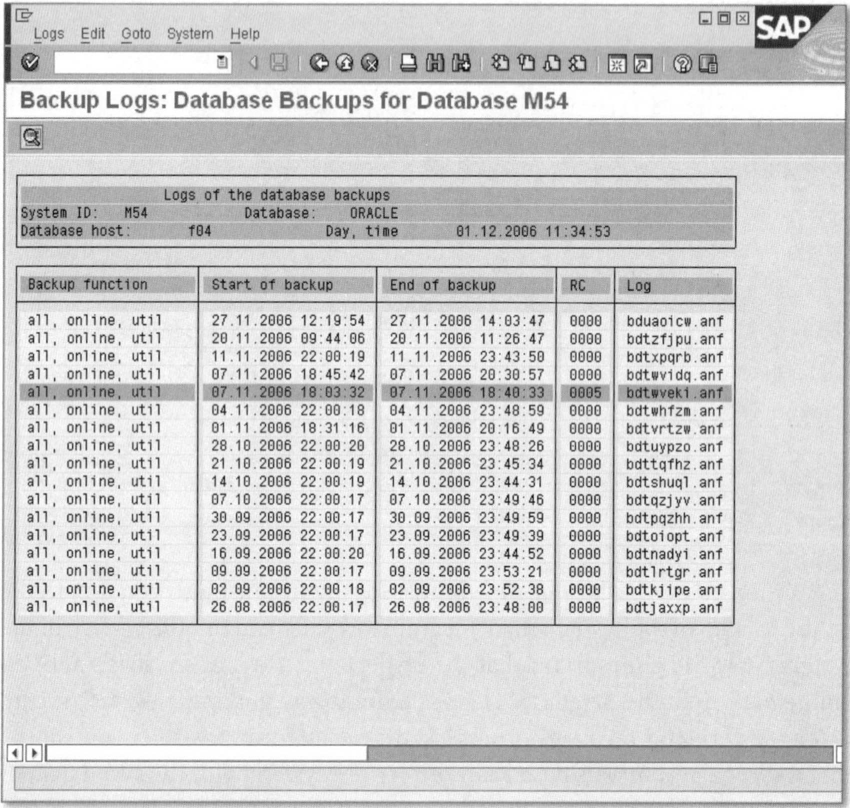

Backup function	Start of backup	End of backup	RC	Log
all, online, util	27.11.2006 12:19:54	27.11.2006 14:03:47	0000	bduaoicw.anf
all, online, util	20.11.2006 09:44:06	20.11.2006 11:26:47	0000	bdtzfjpu.anf
all, online, util	11.11.2006 22:00:19	11.11.2006 23:43:50	0000	bdtxpqrb.anf
all, online, util	07.11.2006 18:45:42	07.11.2006 20:30:57	0000	bdtwvidq.anf
all, online, util	07.11.2006 18:03:32	07.11.2006 18:40:33	0005	bdtwveki.anf
all, online, util	04.11.2006 22:00:18	04.11.2006 23:48:59	0000	bdtwhfzm.anf
all, online, util	01.11.2006 18:31:16	01.11.2006 20:16:49	0000	bdtvrtzw.anf
all, online, util	28.10.2006 22:00:20	28.10.2006 23:48:26	0000	bdtuypzo.anf
all, online, util	21.10.2006 22:00:19	21.10.2006 23:45:34	0000	bdttqfhz.anf
all, online, util	14.10.2006 22:00:19	14.10.2006 23:44:31	0000	bdtshuql.anf
all, online, util	07.10.2006 22:00:17	07.10.2006 23:49:46	0000	bdtqzjyv.anf
all, online, util	30.09.2006 22:00:17	30.09.2006 23:49:59	0000	bdtpqzhh.anf
all, online, util	23.09.2006 22:00:17	23.09.2006 23:49:39	0000	bdtoiopt.anf
all, online, util	16.09.2006 22:00:20	16.09.2006 23:44:52	0000	bdtnadyi.anf
all, online, util	09.09.2006 22:00:17	09.09.2006 23:53:21	0000	bdtlrtgr.anf
all, online, util	02.09.2006 22:00:18	02.09.2006 23:52:38	0000	bdtkjipe.anf
all, online, util	26.08.2006 22:00:17	26.08.2006 23:48:00	0000	bdtjaxxp.anf

Figure 9.5 Overview of the Database Backups

```
BR0280I BRBACKUP time stamp: 2006-11-27 12.19.59
BR0057I Backup of database: M54
BR0058I BRBACKUP action ID: bduaoicw
BR0059I BRBACKUP function ID: anf
BR0110I Backup mode: ALL
BR0077I Database file for backup: /oracle/M54/sapbackup/cntrlM54.dbf
BR0061I 64 files found for backup, total size 120740.438 MB
BR0143I Backup type: online_cons
BR0130I Backup device type: util_file_online
BR0109I Files will be saved by backup utility
BR0142I Files will be switched to backup status during the backup
```

Figure 9.6 Backup Size in the Backup Log

When operating system, hardware, software, and firmware errors occur, corrupt Oracle blocks can be generated in your database. These blocks are only detected in the next read access to a database object that is stored in them. Because they might not be accessed very often and corrupt blocks are not detected when running a database backup, they can remain undetected for a long time. Additionally, such blocks may cause your backups to become unusable. Therefore, you have to check the database regularly for consistency, if possible, once a week. The consistency of the log files should also be monitored. Depending on the procedure used and on the type of corruption, the inconsistencies are logged in the alert log, */oracle/<SID>/saptrace/background/alert_<SID>.log*, in the trace files in the directory */oracle/<SID>/saptrace/usertrace,* or only in the consistency check log. The analysis is time-consuming and should therefore be performed during a downtime or a period of low system load, for example, on the weekend. The three procedures for consistency analyses are explained in the following sections.

9.2.1.1 Complete Analysis

The complete analysis usually requires the definition of an SQL script. Not only the database tables will be analyzed, but also the respective indexes and the cross references between tables and indexes. This causes a long runtime. Another problem is the temporary lock of the analyzed tables against changes. Therefore, these methods should only be carried out during periods of low load or — better — when the SAP system is stopped. Additionally, reading the blocks to be analyzed into SGA causes a temporary decrease of the buffer quality in the database block buffer. From Oracle 9 on, the analysis can be performed via `analyze table validate structure cascade ONLINE;` without locking the tables.

Call the following command for a complete analysis via `brconnect`:

```
brconnect [ -u / ] -c -f stats -v cascade -t all -e null
-p <number>
```

`<number>` refers to the number of Oracle tables that are analyzed at the same time. Do not set this value higher than your CPU number. The `-e null` option ensures that tables that were excluded from the statistics calculation are analyzed nevertheless.

Check at least the objects of the SYS user with this procedure, because when a corruption of an object of SYS remains undetected, an considerably time-consuming full database export and import is required in the worst case. You can use `brconnect -u / -c -f stats -t oradict_tab -v` for a dedicated analysis of the objects of the SYS user.

9.2.1.2 DBVerify

The second procedure for a consistency analysis is to use DBVerify. By using DBVerify, tables, indexes, and empty database blocks are analyzed. Cross-references between tables and indexes are not analyzed. DBVerify reads the blocks without importing them into SGA. Therefore, the buffer quality of the database block buffer is not affected.

This is the only procedure that can also be used for data files that were restored by a backup but does not require that these files are included in a database. The analysis can run during normal operation and has a short runtime.

DBVerify can be started via the DBA planning calendar, as shown in Figure 9.7, directly from the SAP system. For this purpose, go to **Tools • CCMS • DB Administration • Planning Calendar • Central** (Transaction DB13). You can also use the BR*Tools. Here, the call is `brbackup [-u] -c -w only_dbv -t online`. The name of the log file is *b*.dbv*, and it can be found in the directory *$ORACLE_HOME/sapbackup/*. The `–t online` option means that the database remains open. If you set the parameter to `offline`, the database is closed during the process. Instead of setting the option, you can set the `backup_type` parameter in the standard profile, `$ORACLE_HOME/dbs/init<SID>.sap`. This is particularly useful for scheduling with the planning calendar in the SAP system.

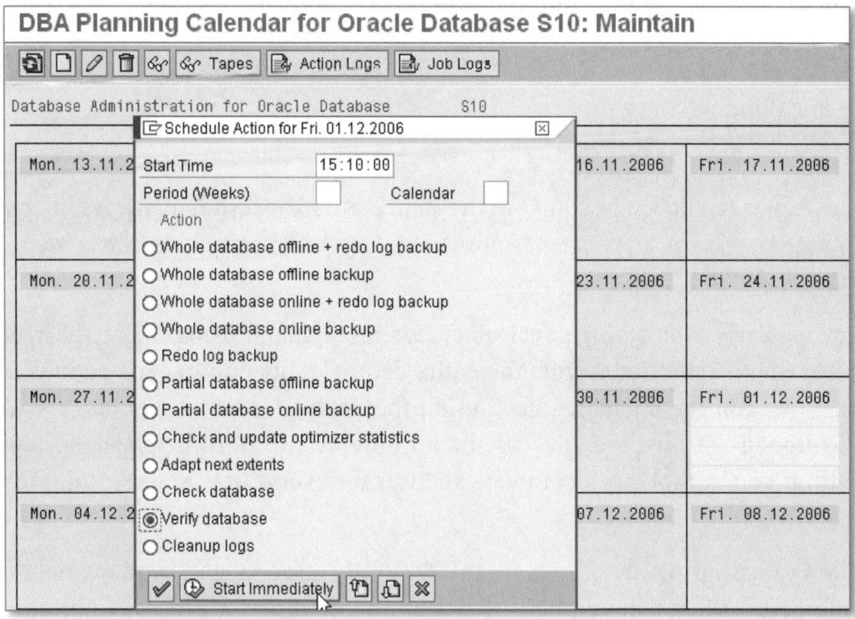

Figure 9.7 DBVerify in the DBA Planning Calendar

9.2.1.3 Export

The idea of the export method is that a table cannot be corrupt when it can be exported. This is not quite correct, because some errors are exported without an error message. In this case, the corrupt blocks can only be detected when you try to import them at a later stage. Therefore, we only recommend the export as a check procedure in addition to the procedures mentioned previously.

You can export the database on the running system, but the export processes will decrease performance. Because only tables are checked, the runtime is reduced compared to a complete analysis. If you access comprehensive tables in write mode during the export, the error message ORA-1555 ("Snapshot too old") may be displayed. This can be avoided with sufficiently dimensioned rollback segments. Furthermore, all blocks to be checked are imported into SGA, which temporarily decreases the buffer quality of the database block buffer.

Depending on the operating system, you use one of the following commands for the export at the operating system level:

- For UNIX systems:

```
exp system/****** full=y file=/dev/null volsize=0 buffer=3000000 log=<logfile>
```

- For Windows systems:

```
exp system/****** full=y file=NUL: buffer=3000000 log=<logfile>
```

The export result can be found in the *log file*. An export should always be terminated with the message "Export terminated successfully without warnings."

For regularly monitoring consistency, we recommend using DBVerify with `brbackup` (parallelized) across the entire database. In addition, you should, if possible, run the database check using the analysis method. For the above mentioned reasons, the analysis should only be run during periods of low load. If you cannot run a complete analysis for everything, at least run it for the SYSTEM tablespace.

The evaluation of the results of the DBVerify process and perhaps of the automatic analysis should be included in the monitoring process to be able to interfere properly when consistency errors occur. In addition, the alert log should be checked regularly for messages that relate to corruptions. For this purpose, you can use the database check.

Options for scheduling and performing a database check (*DB check*) can also be found in the DBA planning calendar. Figure 9.7 shows the **Check database** option. In the scope of the database check, the configuration and log files as well as the database environment and structure are checked for faulty or critical entries. The relevant information is displayed as the result of the database check. Call the command `brconnect [-u] -c -f check` to start the database check with `brconnect`.

You can go to **Tools • CCMS • DB Administration • Operations Monitor** (Transaction DB14) for a log overview of nearly all operations mentioned previously. In the overview, you can access the logs of the individual database operations, as shown in Figure 9.8.

The methods for the check of the data files cannot be used for checking the consistency of the archive logs. It is not reliable to simply dump the archive log. If a dump signals an error, you can assume that corruption is present. However, although no error is signaled, a corruption can be present in the archive logs. You can only reliably check archive logs by importing a standby database. The standby database for analyzing the archive logs requires the same disk space but almost no CPU and memory resources at all. An SAP system is not required.

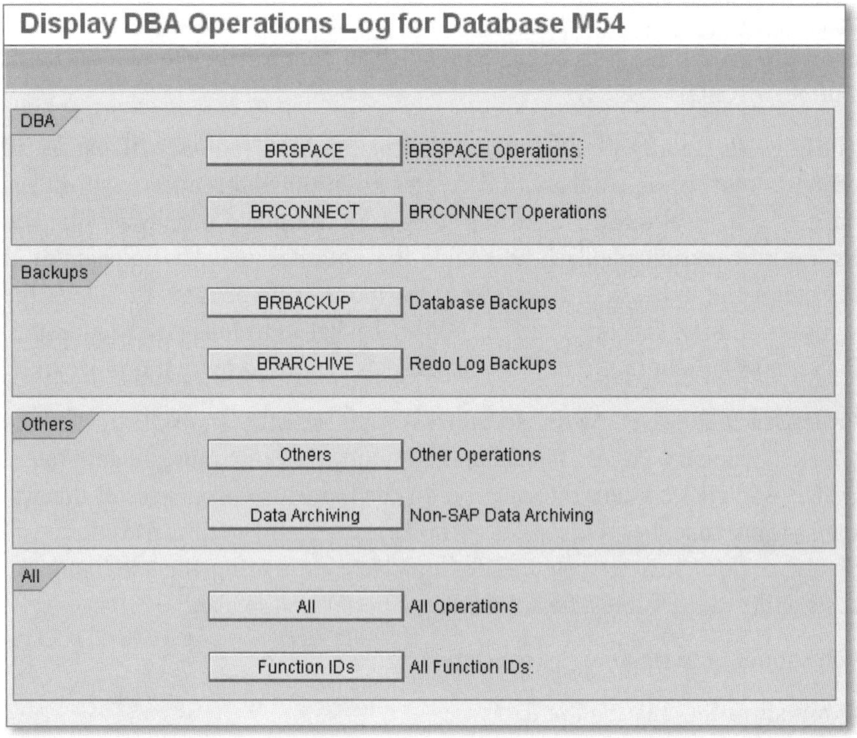

Display DBA Operations Log for Database M54

DBA
BRSPACE | BRSPACE Operations
BRCONNECT | BRCONNECT Operations

Backups
BRBACKUP | Database Backups
BRARCHIVE | Redo Log Backups

Others
Others | Other Operations
Data Archiving | Non-SAP Data Archiving

All
All | All Operations
Function IDs | All Function IDs:

Figure 9.8 Log Display of DBA Operations

Another situation that can considerably hinder work with the database is lock conflicts, so-called *deadlocks*. A deadlock can occur if two or more users wait for the same data and have blocked each other. Real deadlocks are soon detected by Oracle and eliminated by cancelling a blocking transaction with the ORA-00060 error within seconds. Database accesses that are stuck for longer can have different reasons (enqueues, archiver stuck, and so on), but are not Oracle deadlocks. You can call **Tools • Administration • Monitor • Performance • Database • Exclusive Locks** (Transaction DB01) in the SAP system to check whether objects are locked exclusively.

If you receive hints at existing deadlocks during checks using `brconnect -f check`, analyze them with the trace files in */oracle/<SID>/saptrace/usertrace* and */oracle/<SID>/saptrace/background* to determine the cause.

All previously mentioned areas serve to monitor the database availability and consistency. Additionally, the database performance is also important for high performance. Chapter 8 already described the determination and optimization of performance data in detail. Therefore, this section only concentrates on the creation of current statistical data for the *Oracle Cost-Based Optimizer* (CBO).

The CBO is an important tool for optimizing SQL requests. It parses all requests sent to the database and creates an optimized request plan on the basis of statistical information. It is necessary to update the underlying statistical information regularly to enable the optimizer to react to changes in the tables and indexes. In the scope of the monitoring process, the age of the statistics and the success of the scheduled background jobs (see Section 9.3, *Background Jobs in the Scope of Monitoring*) is supposed to be monitored.[1]

From Oracle Release 10g on, so-called system statistics and statistics for the Oracle Dictionary (access to schemas SYS and SYSTEM) must be generated. System statistics contain information on the hardware properties of the system, for instance, I/O performance or process speed. The CBO uses these statistical performance key figures for precisely estimating the CPU and I/O costs and is therefore useful for finding a better access plan.

You should prepare new system statistics:

- Initially after creating the database
- After creating new tablespaces
- After a database upgrade in Oracle 10g
- When changing the hardware of the database server (other or more CPUs, more disks, faster network)
- Simply once every quarter

Call `brconnect -u / -c -f stats -t system_stats` to create system statistics.

You should create dictionary statistics when larger changes have been made in the Oracle Dictionary, for example:

- After installing a database patch set
- After an SAP upgrade
- After another SAP system has been installed or uninstalled (Multiple Components in One Database [MCOD]).

1 Note that the age of statistics cannot automatically be used as an index of quality. With systems that are used exclusively in read-only mode, even old statistics can be of good quality.

In other cases, the dictionary statistics should also be updated once per quarter using `brconnect -u / -c -f stats -t oradict_stats`.

The automatic creation of the two statistics with Oracle 10g is not yet supported by SAP and has to be deactivated. In new installations on the basis of Kernel 7.00, SAPINST deactivates them automatically. You can manually deactivate the statistics using the following command:

```
sqlplus / as sysdba
SQL>EXECUTE DBMS_SCHEDULER.DISABLE('GATHER_STATS_JOB');
```

To update the optimizer statistics, schedule the job **Check and Update Optimizer Statistics** in **Tools • CCMS • DB Administration • Planning Calendar • Central** (Transaction DB13) once a week. For live systems on Release Oracle 10g, SAP recommends changing to daily checks.

For updating with `brconnect`, call the command `brconnect -u / -c -f stats -p [n] -t all`. By means of the `-p` option, you can use `[n]` parallel processes for creating the statistics. As an option, you can set the `stats_parallel_degree` parameter in the file `/oracle/<SID>/102_64/dbs/init<SID>.sap`. By changing the `-t` option to `missing`, you can define that only missing statistics will be created. If you set the parameter to `dbstatc_tab`, the entries in the DBSTATC table are used for creating the statistics.

9.2.2 Monitoring the SAP System

The monitoring of the SAP systems is the second important aspect of basic monitoring of the system landscape. This section first introduces the options for analyzing the general availability of the system. Then you will learn where you can detect errors in the system that, for example, affect the performance in a negative way or lead to problems in the system operation in the medium term. Chapter 8 describes performance monitoring.

9.2.2.1 Problems in SAP Work Processes

The availability of an SAP system depends on several work processes that were explained in Chapter 2. Single points of failure (SPOF) are the message server, the enqueue server, and the dispatcher of each instance. If one of the servers fails, parts of the SAP system (failure of the dispatcher leads to a failure of the instance) or even the entire system (failure of the central message or enqueue server) are no longer available or are affected in some way. Therefore, at least the availability of these work processes needs to be monitored. Additionally, work processes (batch, dialog, update (-2), spool, gateway) are specified for each instance of an SAP system. If one of these processes fails or no longer works properly because of another error, the system is still available, but the function of the instance is limited. You should therefore also monitor the work processes of the instance.

Two programs, `msprot` and `msmon`, are provided for monitoring the message server. Moreover, you can query information via the message server in the SAP system or via a web browser. In the following text, we will look at the individual options.

`msprot` stands for *SAP Message Server Protocol Program* and can be used for a simplified availability check. For this purpose, call `msprot` as the user <sid>adm. The program connects to the message server and logs all logons, logoffs, and status changes of the logged-in instances. The return codes shown in Table 9.3 are returned for the use of `msprot` in monitoring scripts.

Return value	Meaning
0	Process completed without errors.
1	Missing or invalid parameters used in the call.
2	The machine name the message server runs on (`rdisp/mshost`) could not be determined from the profile, or the profile is invalid (wrong path?).
3	The service name (`sapms<SID>`) could not be determined from the profile, or the profile is invalid.
4	The logon to the message server failed. Either wrong parameters were specified or the message server does not run, or a network problem occurred.
5	Request to make changes in the server list failed. The message server does not run, or a network problem occurred.
6	Retrieval of the server list failed. The message server does not run, or a network problem occurred.
7	The connection to the message server was cancelled. The message server does not run, or a network problem occurred.

Table 9.3 Return Codes of msprot

Additional information on potential errors can be found in the *dev_msprot* file that is created in the current directory during the call. From the SAP Web Application Server 6.20 on, the `msprot` program is part of the supplied kernel. You can download an actual downward-compatible version for older releases from the SAP Service Marketplace.

Figure 9.9 illustrates an exemplary `msprot` output where you can see that Instance dis01_S01_03 was stopped and started. By using the `-1` option for the call, you only receive an output of the current status, and the program is shut down afterward.

`In comparison to msprot, msmon` provides not only display functions, but also the option to manage the message server. As the user <sid>adm, call the command `msmon pf=/sapmnt/<SID>/profile/ <SID>_<Inst>_host` or `msmon name=<SID>` to get an overview of the active application servers. You can change various settings for the message server by using the menu (key (M)). An overview of the options provided is shown in Figure 9.10.

```
f00:s01adm 15> msprot name=S01 -d J2EE/ABAP -s
SAP Message Server Protocol Program, Version 1.3 (built: May 13 2006 06:03:17)


INFO CLIENT-NAME          HOST                SERVICE (NET)  STAT      SERVICES (SAP)
-------------------------------------------------------------------------------------
LIST dis01_S01_03         dis01               sapdp03        ACTIVE    DIA BTC ICM J2EE
LIST cis01_S01_01         cis01               sapdp01        ACTIVE    DIA UPD BTC SPO UP2 ICM J2EE
MOD  dis01_S01_03         dis01               sapdp03        ACTIVE    DIA BTC ICM
MOD  dis01_S01_03         dis01               sapdp03        SHUTDOWN  DIA BTC ICM
SUB  dis01_S01_03         dis01               sapdp03        STOP      DIA BTC ICM
ADD  dis01_S01_03         f01                 sapdp03        STARTING  DIA BTC ICM
MOD  dis01_S01_03         dis01               sapdp03        STARTING  DIA BTC ICM
MOD  dis01_S01_03         dis01               sapdp03        STARTING  DIA BTC ICM
MOD  dis01_S01_03         dis01               sapdp03        ACTIVE    DIA BTC ICM
MOD  dis01_S01_03         dis01               sapdp03        ACTIVE    DIA BTC ICM J2EE
```

Figure 9.9 Sample Output of msprot

```
Message Server monitor, connected to cis01 / sapmsS01 (Wed Dec 13 14:47:39 2006)
--------------------------------------------------------------------------------
Main menue
--------------------------------------------------------------------------------
  1  : display client list
  2  : display hardware id
  3  : security menu
  4  : statistics menu
  5  : server parameter
  6  : server release informations
  7  : expert menue
  8  : connect to server
  9  : disconnect from server
  11 : display logon group list
  12 : display logon group list with snc
  13 : group logon data
  14 : group logon data with SNC
  15 : group logon data with LB
  16 : group logon data with LB and SNC
  17 : free memory of logon data
  18 : force reread of logon data
  19 : counter menu
  +  : increase trace
  -  : decrease trace
  q - quit
->
```

Figure 9.10 msmon Menu

The same functions can be found under **Tools • Administration • Monitor • System Monitoring • Message Server Monitor** (Transaction SMMS) and in the respective menus in the SAP system. Figure 9.11 shows part of the menu available in the message server monitor.

If you have access to neither an SAP system nor to the operating system, you can use a web browser to obtain information on the message server. For this purpose, call the URL *http://host:MS-HTTP-Port/msgserver* (for example, *http://cis01:8100/msgserver*). You can determine the HTTP port of the message server in the profile of the message server (profile parameter, `ms/server_port_0`) or in the trace file, *dev_ms*.

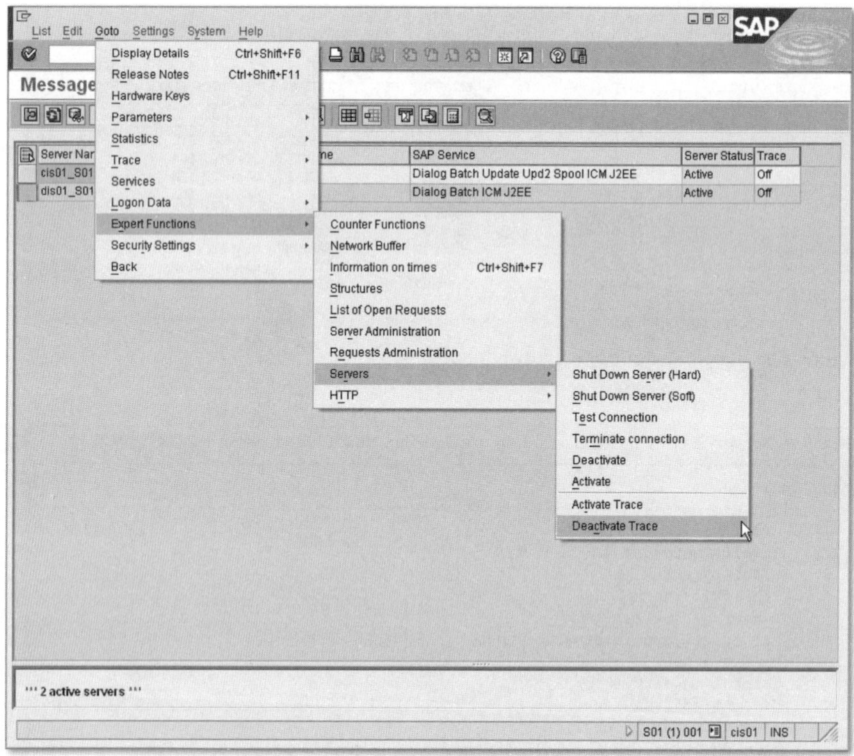

Figure 9.11 Message Server Monitor

There, at the beginning, you find an output similar to the following output that also contains the HTTP port:

```
[Thr  1] HTTP logging is switch off
[Thr  1] set HTTP state to LISTEN
```

```
[Thr  1] ms/icf_info_server : deleted
[Thr  1] *** I listen to port sapmsS01 (3600) ***
[Thr  1] *** I listen to internal port 3900 (3900) ***
[Thr  1] *** HTTP port 8100 state LISTEN ***
```

The web display (an example is shown in Figure 9.12) provides a general overview of the work processes available, namely, the J2EE engine and logon groups.

Logon groups combine application servers and distribute the logged-in users across these servers (load balancing). Furthermore, they can specify groups, which work on certain servers, for different departments or tasks.

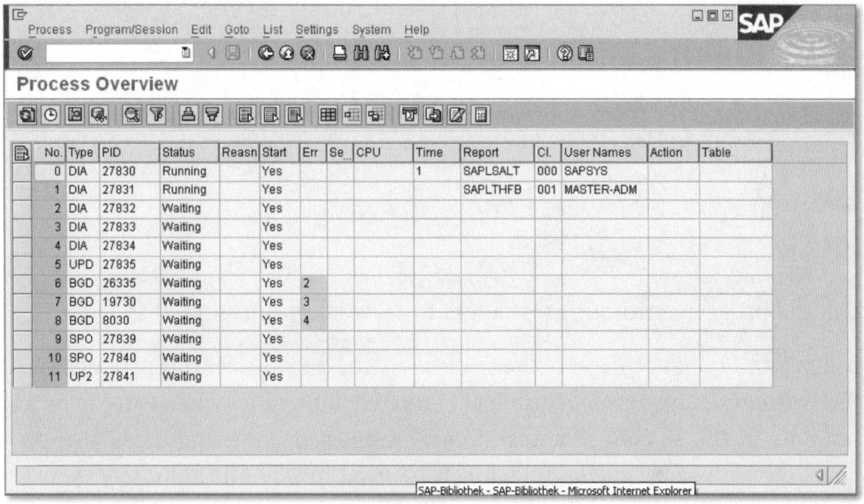

Process Overview

No.	Type	PID	Status	Reasn	Start	Err	Se	CPU	Time	Report	Cl.	User Names	Action	Table
0	DIA	27830	Running		Yes				1	SAPLSALT	000	SAPSYS		
1	DIA	27831	Running		Yes					SAPLTHFB	001	MASTER-ADM		
2	DIA	27832	Waiting		Yes									
3	DIA	27833	Waiting		Yes									
4	DIA	27834	Waiting		Yes									
5	UPD	27835	Waiting		Yes									
6	BGD	26335	Waiting		Yes	2								
7	BGD	19730	Waiting		Yes	3								
8	BGD	8030	Waiting		Yes	4								
9	SPO	27839	Waiting		Yes									
10	SPO	27840	Waiting		Yes									
11	UP2	27841	Waiting		Yes									

Figure 9.12 Web Frontend of the Message Server

If the information on the logon groups is not available, the user can only log on to the server immediately. For this purpose, the data in the SAP Logon must be changed, which the end user usually can't do. Therefore, the administrator must monitor the logon groups and the servers included. As we already know how to monitor the server, the following section only describes the determination of the logon groups and the assigned servers.

In an SAP system, the administration of the logon groups can be found under **Tools • CCMS • Configuration • Logon Groups** (Transaction SMLG). There, you can define new groups and assign servers. SAP provides the message server and logon group test tool `lgtst` to analyze the existing groups and the respective active servers in the operating system. The basic syntax of `lgtst` is `lgtst -H <Hostname Messageserver> -S sapms<SID>` and provides a list divided into two segments that contains the active server and its services as well as the existing logon groups. The call is logged in the dev_lg file in the current directory. The following listing demonstrates the sample call and its result:

```
f00:s01adm 1> lgtst -H cis01 -S sapmsS01
using trcfile: dev_lg

list of reachable application servers
-------------------------------------
[dis01_S01_
03] [dis01] [10.10.1.3] [sapdp03] [3203] [DIA BTC ICM J2EE ]
[cis01_S01_01] [cis01] [10.10.1.1] [sapdp01] [3201]
[DIA UPD BTC SPO UP2 ICM J2EE ]

list of selectable logon groups with favorites
----------------------------------------------
[HCCMD] [10.10.1.3] [3203] [700]
[SPACE] [10.10.1.3] [3203] [700]
```

Call the program without parameters to view all options of `lgtst`.

Besides the message server, the *enqueue* is the second central process of an SAP system. If the enqueue process is not available, lock management is not possible in the system. For testing and monitoring the enqueue, SAP provides the program `ensmon`, which can be used locally and remotely. Specify the host name and server instance or the port of the enqueue service to start `ensmon`. The following listing shows the call via the instance name and the subsequent menu:

```
f00:s01adm 29> ensmon -H cis01 -I ASCS00
Try to connect to host cis01 service sapdp00
Enqueue Server monitor main menu
================================
   1: Dummy request
   2: Get replication information
   3: Get a file from the enqueue server
   4: Set/get trace status information on/from the enque server
   q: quit
   h: help
 ==>
```

You can test the connection to the enqueue, read the trace files (Option 3), and change the trace level (Option 4) by means of the options shown. Option 2 returns information on whether the lock table of the enqueue service is mirrored with a replication server to be able to continue work during a failure without any interruption.

In addition to the interactive mode, ensmon also supports an automatic mode where you can transfer the command code in the command line. The following listing shows the call for building up a test connection and the respective return:

```
f00:s01adm 29> ensmon -H cis01 -I ASCS00 1
Try to connect to host cis01 service sapdp00
Dummy request executed successfully with rc=0
```

The command codes correspond to the number in the interactive mode (for instance, 1 = dummy request).

For managing the locks and the locked objects, enqueue uses an internal table. This table contains all user locks for specified objects of the SAP system. Usually, these locks are removed when the work is stored or terminated, which enables other users to obtain write access to the objects again. If these locks are not removed, for example, due to a machine failure, further work is not affected. The age of the lock entries must be monitored to detect such error situations. If the age is higher than the defined threshold value, appropriate measures (clearing the situation with the user, removing the lock) must be taken. You can check the currently existing lock entries in **Tools • Administration • Monitor • Lock Entries** (Transaction SM12).

For further monitoring of the instances and all other kinds of work processes of a system, you can use Transaction SM51 (**Tools • Administration • Monitor • System Monitoring • Servers**) and Transaction SM50 (**Tools • Administration • Monitor • System Monitoring • Process Overview**).

By double-clicking, you can directly go from the server overview (Transaction SM51) to the process overview (Transaction SM50) of a server to obtain detailed information on the individual processes (see Figure 9.13). Information on the dispatcher of the instance can be found by selecting **Process • Trace • Dispatcher** in the process overview. There, in the submenu, you can control the trace file and change the trace level of the dispatcher.

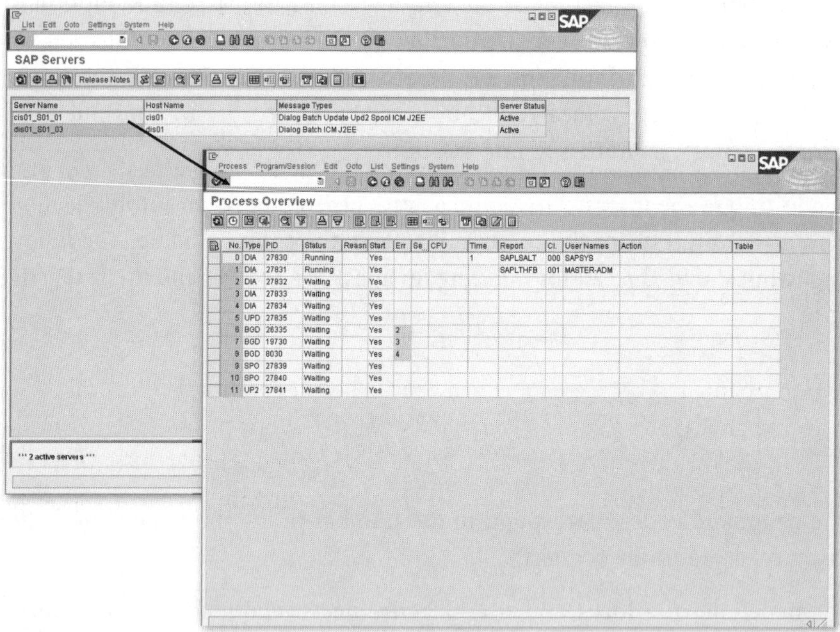

Figure 9.13 Relationship between Server and Process Overview

From the overview of the work processes, you can obtain more information on the status of the instance. The column Status refers to the activity of the processes. If the Start column contains Yes, the process is restarted after an error occurs. If problems already exist during the start, the restart is automatically set to No to prevent the process from being restarted endlessly if the reasons for the problem are external factors (for example, the database system is not available). After correcting the error, you can reactive the automatic restart via **Process • Restart After Errors • Yes.** To find information on the error causes, you can view the trace file of a work process via **Process • Trace • Display File.**

The Reason column shows you why a work process has the Waiting status. Typical reasons are debugging, CPIC activities, locks, updates, and GUI (system waits for a response from the SAP GUI frontend program, for example, when an RFC is called). The **PRIV** reason assumes a special role. It refers to a "private" process usage.

PRIV means the work process requires so much memory for a certain user that it exceeds the extended memory. Heap memory is used to be able to still occupy memory, but this means the user context can no longer be rolled in and out, which assigns the process exclusively to the user. The work process is in the PRIV mode and cannot be used by other users. The more PRIV work processes exist, the higher is the risk that the response times increase or even that no connection to work processes is available at all.

To avoid this problem, you can limit the maximum number of work processes that are allowed to remain in the PRIV mode longer than a defined period of time. For this purpose, the following two SAP profile parameters exist:

- `rdisp/max_priv_time # standard value: 600`
- `rdisp/wppriv_max_no # standard value: MAX(1, number Dialog WPs - 5)`

If more than `rdisp/wppriv_max_no` work processes are in the PRIV mode for longer than `rdisp/max_priv_time` seconds, the work process that is in the PRIV mode for the longest period of time is cancelled. This is continued until maximal `rdisp/wppriv_max_no` work processes are in the PRIV mode for longer than `rdisp/max_priv_time`.

For certain system configurations you may want processes change to the PRIV mode, for instance, during the debugging process. However, if you see that the PRIV mode is caused by a memory bottleneck, adjust the size of the extended memory (parameter `em/initial_size_MB`) to your system or eliminate the reason for the high memory consumption.

Table 9.4 lists the other columns of the process overview and their meaning.

Column	Meaning
CPU	Specifies the accumulated CPU time since a work process has been started. The time is shown in seconds and hundredths of seconds. It is very time-consuming to determine the CPU time. Therefore, you must explicitly query this information via **List • CPU** or by clicking on the CPU icon in the menu. If you see that some work processes are not used, you can reduce the number of these work process types.
Time	Indicates how much time the work process has already required for the dialog step that is processed at the moment.
Err	Indicates the number of failures since the work process has been started.
Sem	Specifies the number of the semaphore for which the work process is waiting. This field is supposed to be empty. If a semaphore number appears unusually often, check the performance of your system with the performance monitor.
Report	Indicates the ABAP reports or programs that run at the moment.

Table 9.4 Columns of the Process Overview

Column	Meaning
Cl./User Names	Specifies the client and user whose data is processed.
Action	Indicates the action that is executed by the current program. The actions displayed are logged by the SAP performance monitor. The performance monitor must be active (SAP profile parameter `stat/level=1`, standard value) so that the actions or accesses to the database tables can be displayed.
Table	When accessing the database, this column contains the names of the tables that are accessed.

Table 9.4 Columns of the Process Overview (Cont.)

The dispatcher manages the individual work processes of an instance. It distributes the requests to the appropriate work processes. For this process, the dispatcher uses queues that record and store requests if no free process is available at that moment. If your system generates several syslog entries that indicate that the dispatcher queues have an overflow in individual work process types, you should check the queues, for example, by means of the SAP program `dpmon`. The profile of the instance is used to start `dpmon`. The following listing shows a sample call for UNIX:

```
cd /usr/sap/C11/DVEBMGS00/work
ls -l dw.sap* ;: indicates the EXE directory
head stderrl ;: indicates the profile
/usr/sap/C11/SYS/exe/run/dpmon \
pf=/usr/sap/C11/SYS/profile/C11_DVEBMGS00
```

After `dpmon` is called, an output similar to the output shown in Figure 9.14 is displayed.

You can identify the individual work process types of the instance (here, DIA, UPD, ENQ, BTC, SPO, and UP2) as well as their current and maximum utilization. For example, if you determine that all work processes are permanently utilized and thus wait times are caused, you must analyze why the processes are permanently utilized and perhaps increase the number of work processes.

The same queue overview can be found with Transaction SM51 (**Tools • Administration • Monitor • System Monitoring • Server**) and from there going to **Goto • Server Information • Queue Information in the SAP system.**

```
Dispatcher Queue Statistics                              Fri Sep  8 07:42:17 2006
===========================


+------+--------+--------+--------+--------+--------+
|  Typ |    now |   high |    max | writes |  reads |
+------+--------+--------+--------+--------+--------+
| NOWP |      0 |      4 |   2000 |  79284 |  79284 |
+------+--------+--------+--------+--------+--------+
|  DIA |      0 |      4 |   2000 |  35167 |  35167 |
+------+--------+--------+--------+--------+--------+
|  UPD |      0 |      5 |   2000 |    133 |    133 |
+------+--------+--------+--------+--------+--------+
|  ENQ |      0 |      0 |   2000 |      0 |      0 |
+------+--------+--------+--------+--------+--------+
|  BTC |      0 |      1 |   2000 |    513 |    513 |
+------+--------+--------+--------+--------+--------+
|  SPO |      0 |      2 |   2000 |   5410 |   5410 |
+------+--------+--------+--------+--------+--------+
|  UP2 |      0 |      1 |   2000 |     45 |     45 |
+------+--------+--------+--------+--------+--------+


max_rq_id                 59461
wake_evt_udp_now          0

wake events               total107228,  udp 95794 ( 89%),  shm 11434 ( 10%)
since last update         total      0,  udp     0 (  0%),  shm     0 (  0%)



    q - quit
    m - menue

--> 
```

Figure 9.14 dpmon Display

The work processes Update (V1) and Update2 (V2) are responsible for writing all data to the database. Update writes all data records that are supposed to be updated time-critically, and Update2 processes all statistical data that can be updated any time. If Update2 is not available, the data records are also periodically processed by the V1 process. If the update processes is cancelled due to a system error or a manual shutdown, an entry is logged in the system log, and all other data records are listed in the update queue. You can view the queue via transaction SM13 or menu path **Tools • Administration • Monitor • Update** in the SAP system. You can also reactivate the update processes or update the accumulated data records later.

Update problems must be divided into two categories and can have the following reasons:

- The "simple" errors are isolated and occur sporadically and only affect some transactions or updates. These are usually errors in the update function module or respective programs, such as customer developments. They are found in the CCMS alert monitor, or the user affected can query the reason. These errors are usually not serious, unless business-critical transactions are affected. You can limit the reason and correct the error partly or let it be corrected by the system log and the update management.
- The second, considerably more critical, error type is update problems that affect the entire system and thus all updates. All larger database and system problems (for example, table overflow in the Oracle database) can cause update problems. In this case, the update problem is only a symptom of a larger problem. After eliminating the main problem, you should check the system in the update management for cancelled updates and, if necessary, update them later.

```
f03:s10adm 6> gwmon pf=S10_DVEBMGS01_f03
Gateway monitor, connected to f03 / sapgw01
Connection table (Used: 0, Connected: 0)

---------------------------------------------------------------------------------
NO  CLIENT(LU/TP)      USER        STATE       SDEST     CONVID   PROT WP REQTIME
---------------------------------------------------------------------------------

  q - quit
  m - menue
-->m
Gateway monitor, connected to f03 / sapgw01
Main menue
---------------------------------------------------------------------------------
  1 : display connection table
  2 : display work process table
  3 : display client table
  4 : display remote gw table
  5 : connection attributes
  6 : statistics
  7 : gateway parameters and attributes
  8 : gateway release info
  9 : security information
 10 : expert functions
  + : increase gateway trace
  - : decrease gateway trace
  q - quit
-->
```

Figure 9.15 gwmon Menu

In the context of work processes, the last task to be mentioned is the monitoring of the gateway process. This process can be run at the operating system level and from the SAP system. SAP provides the gateway monitor, `gwmon`, for monitoring the command line. To start, select the profile of the preferred application server as a parameter, for example, `gwmon pf=/sapmnt/S01/profile/S01_DVEBMGS01_cis01`. The name of the trace file is dev_gwmon. Figure 9.15 illustrates the menu options. The same monitoring and administration options are provided under **Tools • Administration • Monitor • System Monitoring • Gateway Monitor** (Transaction SMGW) in the SAP system.

The gateway monitor at the operating system level also provides the option of a script-controlled usage. By using `cmdfile [file name]`, you can run all commands of the defined file consecutively. You get an overview of the commands when you run `gwmon pf=<profile> -cmdfile -` and then enter `HELP` as a command.

Now that you know the options for monitoring the different kinds of work processes to ensure a general availability of the SAP system, the following sections deal with errors within the system. They do not necessarily affect the availability directly, but are usually caused by problems that occur when you work in the system.

9.2.2.2 Problems in the SAP System

Errors in the SAP system are mainly logged in the system log and in the overview of short dumps. You go to the system log via **Tools • Administration • Monitor • System Log** (Transaction SM21). All application servers of an instance record events and problems in system logs. If your SAP system runs in a UNIX environment, you have two logging options: *local* and the *central* logging. Each SAP application server has a local log that contains the messages issued by this server. To provide central logging, each application server copies its local logs into a central log. To select a specific log, call the menu **System log • Choose** and choose the desired log (see Figure 9.16).

For Windows and AS/400 hosts, only local logs (one per application server) are generated. They are not combined in a central log.

Numerous messages in the sys log explain themselves or contain hints at the reason or at approaches for troubleshooting. By means of these hints or error codes, you can often find appropriate SAP Notes in the SAP Service Marketplace (quick link *Notes*) to help you with solving the problem.

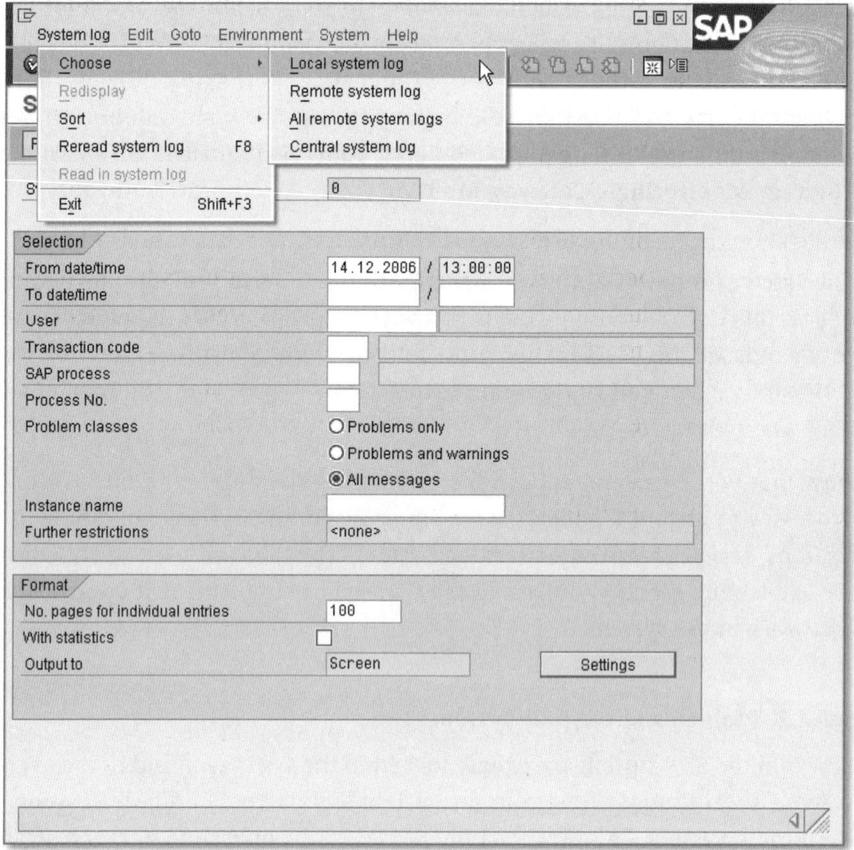

Figure 9.16 Log Selection in the System Log

ABAP dumps, also called short dumps, are logged in the system log as well. They indicate errors in ABAP programs. Usually, program errors are caught and an error message is displayed. If this is impossible or if no exception management was implemented, the information on the system environment is stored in a dump at the time the error occurs. Go to **Tools • Administration • Monitor • Dump Analysis** (Transaction ST22) to analyze failures in the system.

In addition to the error messages and short dumps, you also obtain the information on which user has caused the error in which client. If you also require information on currently logged-on users and their operations for other tasks, you can go to **Tools • CCMS • Configuration • Logon Groups** (Transaction SMLG). Select **Goto • User List** in the menu to get a list of all users logged on to the system. You can also determine the distribution of the users across the existing instances via **Goto • Load Distribution**. Select **Tools • Administration • Monitor • System Monitoring • User Overview** (Transaction SM04) to determine the users of the instance that you are logged on to at the moment. When performance problems occur, you can then draw conclusions if they are caused by a high number of users or by poor performance data of other components.

Besides the determining users and user numbers, the data can also be relevant for license aspects. If, for example, the number of users has increased considerably and the number of users specified in a license agreement will be reached soon, measures can be taken at an early stage. Therefore, the maximum number of users logged on simultaneously and the number of users created in the system (named users) should also be included in the monitoring process.

For determining operating-system-specific data, such as CPU utilization, memory consumption, and so on, and their provision in the SAP system, the SAPOS Collector is started when the system is started. This is a background job that has root authorization and can therefore access comprehensive information on the operating system. From SAPOSCOL Version 20.85 on, SAPOSCOL can run on some operating systems without root authorization. The platforms HP-UX, SUN, AIX, and OS390 support this function. On these operating systems, the <sid>adm user can install and start `saposcol`. As the user <sid>adm, you can determine the SAPOSCOL version with the call `saposcol -v`.

For installations with root authorization, set the SAPOSCOL group to sapsys using the `chgrp sapsys saposcol` command. Then, set the setuid authorization for SAPOSCOL. For this purpose, run `chmod 4750 saposcol` so that you, as the <sid>adm user, can start the OS Collector, but the process is run as the root user.

For an installation without root authorization, also set the group `sapsys` to limit the access to `saposcol`. With `chmod 750 saposcol`, you set the changed authorizations that are supposed to be carried out. This procedure ensures that all <sid>adm users can access SAPOSCOL during the installation of several systems on one machine. Therefore, SAPOSCOL must be installed as <sid>adm, and the sapsys group must be able to run it.

If more than one SAP system runs on one server, only one SAPOSCOL is started that provides information for all systems. Regarding the SAP release, SAPOSCOL is downward compatible. This means the SAPOSCOL release can be higher than the SAP Basis release, so no problems occur on the server during data collection even though releases are "mixed." In contrast, SAPOSCOL depends on the release of the operating system. Keep this in mind when downloading a new SAPOSCOL version. Usually, the collector is also updated when a new kernel patch is imported.

Go to **Tools • Administration • Monitor • Performance • Operating System • Remote • Activity** (Transaction OS07) and **Tools • Administration • Monitor • Performance • Operating System • Local • Activity** (Transaction OS06/ST06) in the SAP system to analyze and manage (start, stop) SAPOSCOL.

Figure 9.17 shows Transaction ST06, which contains the operating system data of the local server. Click on the **OS collector** button or go to **Goto • Operating System collector** to view information on the OS Collector. Using the options in the **OS Collector** menu, you can start and stop SAPOSCOL as well as view the details.

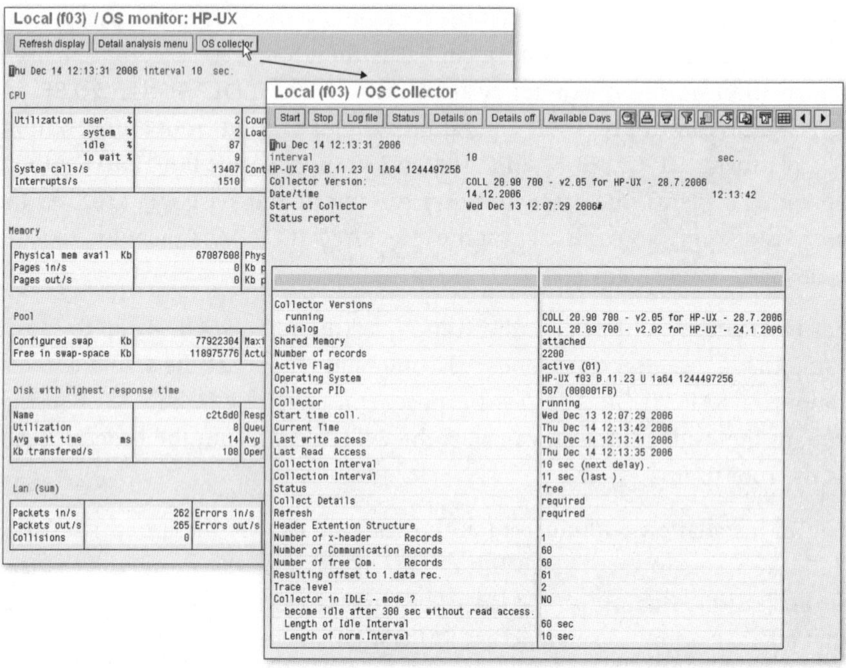

Figure 9.17 SAPOSCOL in Transaction ST06

In contrast, Transaction OS07 first provides a popup window that lists all SAPOSCOL destinations that are known by the central system. Here, a distinction is made between:

- The local server
- Other application servers of the same system in the form of <host name>_<SID>_<instance>
- CCMS agent destinations in the form SAPCCMSR.<host name>.99 or SAPCCM4X.<host name>.< NR>

The functions **Start**, **Stop**, **Status**, and **Log File** are only implemented for the local call and for calls via CCMS agents. If you choose another application server of the same system in the popup window, some functions may not be displayed.

As the <sid>adm user, you can manage SAPOSCOL at the operating system level. For this purpose, the options listed in Table 9.5 are available. Simply enter the desired option when starting SAPOSCOL, for example, `saposcol -k` to stop the collector.

Option	Meaning
-l	Starts the collector.
-k	Stops the collector.
-s	Status retrieval.
-d	Calls the dialog mode. In the dialog mode, you can process the SAPOSCOL shared memory segments and retrieve the information collected.

Table 9.5 Command Line Parameter of SAPOSCOL

If the SAPOS Collector is not active, the SAP system cannot collect the relevant information and thus signals no alerts when CCMS is used. Therefore, you should include the availability check for SAPOSCOL in the monitoring process. Section 9.2.3, *Monitoring the Hardware and Operating System*, describes the usage of the SAPOS Collector data for monitoring the operating system.

Performance monitoring of an SAP system is mentioned here for the sake of completeness. In addition to potential sources of errors, the performance must also be monitored to observe the efficiency of a system. A system that runs well but very slowly is not satisfying for the user. Chapter 8 explains the individual parameters that affect the system performance in greater detail.

9.2.3 Monitoring the Hardware and Operating System

The underlying operating system and the hardware used are the third important component in the monitoring process. This aspect may sound simple but is divided into relatively small areas that must be considered. Depending on the operating system used, some aspects may assume a special role, such as different approaches for hard disk management in UNIX and Windows environments. However, generally speaking, the issues mentioned always have a similar structure.

Let's start with the physical landscape components, namely, servers, disk systems, and communication infrastructure. Most modern servers have their own internal monitoring systems (for instance, the *Event Monitoring System* (EMS) in HP UX systems) that can initiate an alert automatically (usually via email) in cases of failures or redundancy losses of components. In general, this also includes the accessibility of hard disk systems. The status of the hard disk systems is mainly monitored by an internal controller that can also inform the administrator. Other infrastructure components can be monitored by the SNMP log. For this purpose, a central server is used that can evaluate the so-called SNMP traps and, based on this data, determine information on the hardware condition.

First, you should ensure in the scope of the monitoring process that all operating system processes run properly and are configured for the use of an SAP system. An operating system that runs but is incorrectly configured for SAP operation has the same value as a faulty system: nearly none. The kernel is the essential component of any system. If the kernel cannot run properly due to problems with general conditions (for example, memory error or lack of memory), it usually results in a failure, shutdown, or serious damage to the entire system. If the general availability of the system is ensured and monitored, you can now focus on the individual system areas. You can find an overview of some important kernel parameters under **Tools • Administration • Monitor • Performance • Operating System • Local • System Configuration** (Transaction OS04).

The files of the SAP system and the database can be stored in the following directories mentioned in Chapters 2 to 4:

- */usr/sap/<SID>*
- */sapmnt/<SID>*
- */oracle/client*
- */oracle/<SID>/.....*

If you can no longer access these directories or if no free memory is available, a stable system operation is no longer possible. Therefore, the free space and availability must be monitored.

In addition to access to directories, the performance data is also important to detect bottlenecks. For example, if a certain hard disk is frequently accessed, you can analyze whether this problem can be solved when faster systems are used. However, perhaps the individual directories are not properly distributed and thus they are simultaneously accessed during operation. The data of response time, throughput (reading and writing), and access frequency can be used as the basis for such evaluations.

You can query information on the free space of your file systems by following the path **Tools • Administration • Monitor • Performance • Operating System • Remote • Activity** (Transaction OS07). There, you can call detailed information on the hardware via the **Detail analysis Menu** button. Figure 9.18 shows this task. With the other options provided, you can determine nearly all necessary data about your hardware and operating systems.

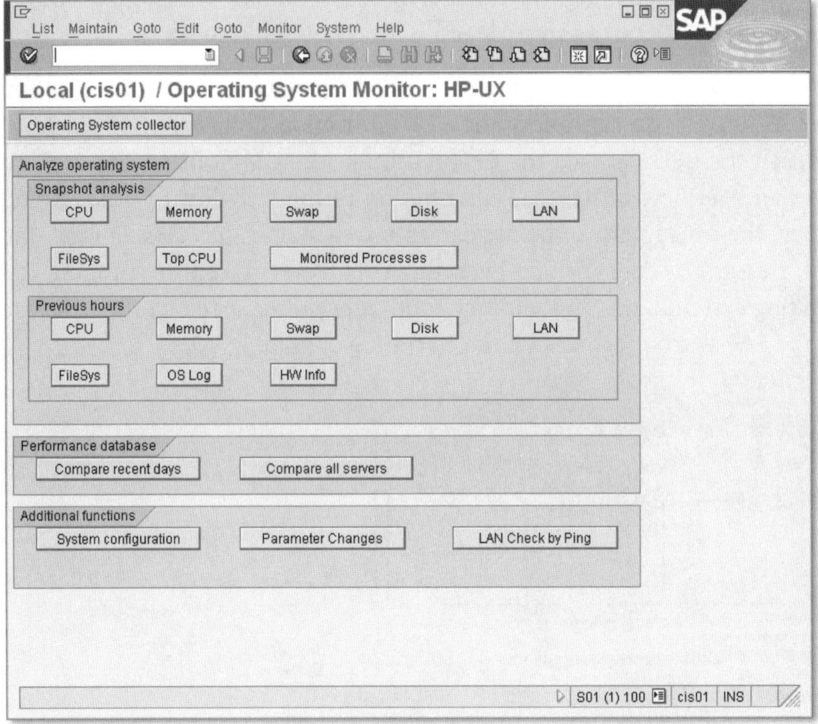

Figure 9.18 File System Information in Transaction OS07

In addition to the hard disk consumption, the SAP system also requires resources, such as CPU performance and main memory. The main memory is supposed to be divided into a physical memory and a swap memory.

The physical memory is provided as RAM modules in the server and can therefore only be extended by adding or replacing RAM modules, whereas the swap memory can be created on internal hard disks or disk arrays and can be easily extended compared with the physical memory. Here, the restrictions of the operating system must also be considered, and the swap memory cannot be understood as a "universal remedy" for insufficient main memory.

For monitoring the memory consumption, you can also use the buffers (nametab, CUA, tables, export/import, and so on) and memory areas (roll area, heap/extended memory, and so on) discussed in Chapter 8. For determining the utilization, you can go to **Tools • Administration • Monitor • Performance • Setup/Buffers • Buffers** (Transaction ST02). You can find a detailed description of the individual values and their effects in Chapter 8.

For querying information on the swap memory, you can also use Transaction OS07, which has been mentioned already several times. There, go to the **OS monitor** via the **Detail analysis Menu** button and select **Swap**.

CPU performance is required for processing the data, as is the case for any other software. You can query the CPU utilization in Transaction OS07 as well. Call the CPU data via the **CPU** button in the **OS monitor**. Figure 9.19 shows an overview of the load distribution of the individual CPUs. As you can see, the consumer can be divided into two main categories. On the one hand, *system processes* include everything that is required for running the operating system, and, on the other hand, *user processes* reflect the database and the SAP work processes on the operating system.

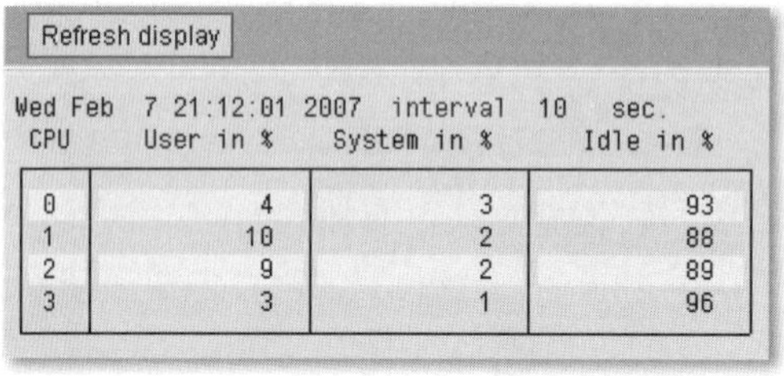

Refresh display

Wed Feb 7 21:12:01 2007 interval 10 sec.

CPU	User in %	System in %	Idle in %
0	4	3	93
1	10	2	88
2	9	2	89
3	3	1	96

Figure 9.19 CPU Overview in Transaction OS07

In Transaction OS07, you can follow the path **Goto • Current Data • Snapshot • Top CPU Processes** to determine which processes are using how much CPU load at a given time. You get a detailed overview of the processes that currently generate the greatest load. This overview contains, among other things, the process ID, the user name of the operating system, the executed command, the used CPU load, and the allocated memory. The same information can be found using top in UNIX operating systems and in the **Task manager** on the **System capacity** tab in Windows environments.

All processes that are required for the provision of the different operating system services (swap, hard disk management, cron, memory allocation, and so on) and therefore use CPU time are combined under *system processes*. However, compared to the database and the SAP system, this time is quite short. Usually, a misconfiguration is the cause of a permanent utilization of the CPU by the operating system. Here, the use of software RAID systems assumes a special role. The more often an application accesses disk systems in the software RAID group, the more CPU performance is used for implementing the RAID. In this case, we recommend changing to hardware RAID with the appropriate controllers.

Nearly all processes that are not included in the first category are *user processes*. In the context of SAP systems, Oracle and SAP work processes are user processes. Processing the user data in the work processes uses CPU performance. If sufficient CPU capacity is not available, wait times result, and system performance decreases. This results in longer response times for the user when working with the system. You can check the response times by going to **Tools • Administration • Monitor • Performance • Workload • Aggregated Statistical Records – Local** (Transaction ST03N) in the system. There, the individual parts of the total response time are broken down. Figure 9.20 shows this kind of display as an example. With this display, you can determine the work process and task type (**ABAP**, **BACKGROUND**, **DIALOG**, and so on). For each type, detailed information is given on the steps performed, their total processing time, as well as the breakdown into CPU, database, wait, and roll times. With this breakdown, you can draw conclusions about the cause or causes of performance problems.

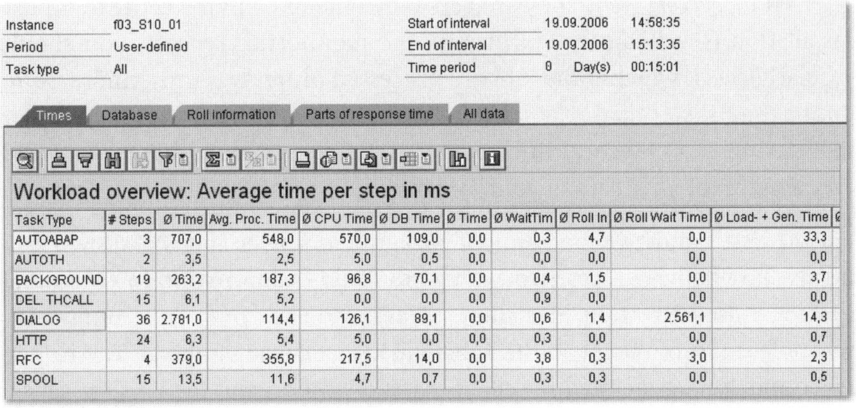

Instance	f03_S10_01	Start of interval	19.09.2006	14:58:35
Period	User-defined	End of interval	19.09.2006	15:13:35
Task type	All	Time period	0 Day(s)	00:15:01

Times | Database | Roll information | Parts of response time | All data

Workload overview: Average time per step in ms

Task Type	# Steps	Ø Time	Avg. Proc. Time	Ø CPU Time	Ø DB Time	Ø Time	Ø WaitTim	Ø Roll In	Ø Roll Wait Time	Ø Load- + Gen. Time
AUTOABAP	3	707,0	548,0	570,0	109,0	0,0	0,3	4,7	0,0	33,3
AUTOTH	2	3,5	2,5	5,0	0,5	0,0	0,0	0,0	0,0	0,0
BACKGROUND	19	263,2	187,3	96,8	70,1	0,0	0,4	1,5	0,0	3,7
DEL. THCALL	15	6,1	5,2	0,0	0,0	0,0	0,9	0,0	0,0	0,0
DIALOG	36	2.781,0	114,4	126,1	89,1	0,0	0,6	1,4	2.561,1	14,3
HTTP	24	6,3	5,4	5,0	0,0	0,0	0,3	0,0	0,0	0,7
RFC	4	379,0	355,8	217,5	14,0	0,0	3,8	0,3	3,0	2,3
SPOOL	15	13,5	11,6	4,7	0,7	0,0	0,3	0,3	0,0	0,5

Figure 9.20 Response Times in Transaction ST03N

We will now complete the general overview of the monitoring process of the operating system. You cannot determine data about the status of other hardware components, such as fans, power supplies, or similar, in an SAP system. Use the hardware-specific tools and commands for monitoring these components.

9.3 Background Jobs in the Scope of Monitoring

Numerous background jobs are responsible for the proper operation of an SAP system and for collecting data for the monitoring process. In addition, we recommend that you schedule some optional standard jobs that, for example, aggregate statistical data and are provided in the system. In the context of this chapter, we will deal with SAP jobs for system cleansing and data collection.

Because logs for certain actions are also written to the Oracle database and to Oracle directories, the next sections describe how you can delete obsolete data.

Furthermore, a range of background jobs exist in a live SAP system that are responsible for business-critical tasks, for example, forwarding jobs to a supply system. In such a scenario, it is, of course, relevant to monitor these jobs, too.

9.3.1 SAP Standard Jobs

Standard jobs are background jobs that should run regularly in a live SAP system. Usually, these jobs perform specific reorganization work in the system, such as deleting obsolete spool orders or dumps. Therefore, they are also referred to as *reorg jobs*. They are generally scheduled in the context of post-installation (see Chapter 7). Through the monitoring process, you should regularly check whether the jobs are processed properly. Furthermore, some optional jobs, so-called *collector jobs*, collect and aggregate data for detailed monitoring and statistical information. You can schedule these jobs when you require the that data in your system.

For the first standard scheduling of background jobs in the SAP system during the installation process, you can go to **Tools • Administration • Monitor • System Administration Assistant** (Transaction SSAA). This transaction schedules most of the jobs from Table 9.6 in any chosen interval. The respective options are generated for client-dependent jobs, and the jobs are scheduled by clients. You can plan all other reorg jobs via **Tools • CCMS • Background Processing • Define Job** (Transaction SM36). For monitoring or scheduling missing jobs, you get an overview of the jobs already scheduled and the status of the last jobs via **Goto • Standard Jobs**. Figure 9.21 shows a sample overview of jobs. You can request to schedule all jobs by clicking on the **Default scheduling** button, as shown in Figure 9.21.

If you cannot find a job, you can search for a specific job and check the job logs via **Tools • CCMS • Background Processing • Jobs - Overview and Administration** (Transaction SM37). You can get a graphical overview of all jobs scheduled in the system under **Tools • CCMS • Background Processing • Job Scheduling Monitor** (Transaction RZ01). As illustrated in Figure 9.22, all jobs are combined in a Gantt diagram. You can call detailed information and logs by selecting a certain job.

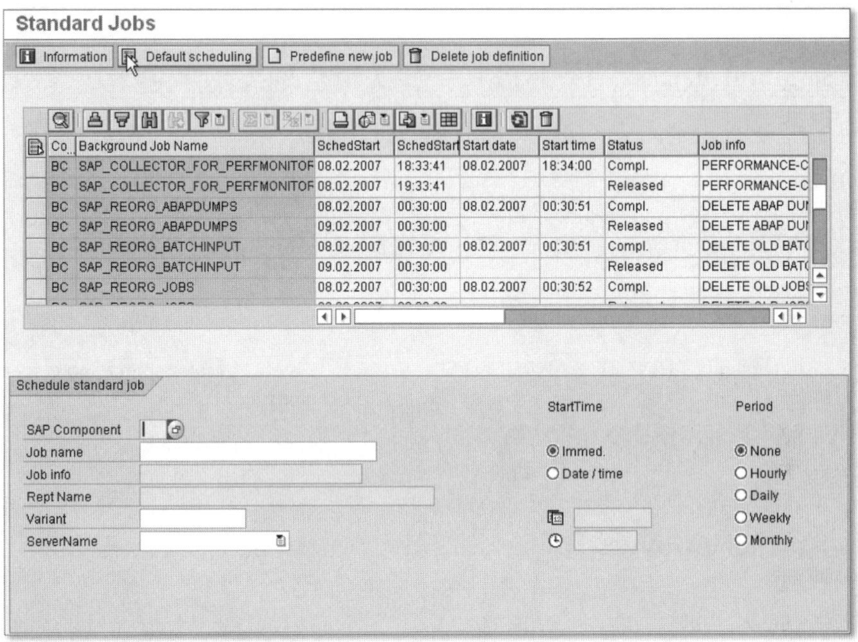

Figure 9.21 Standard Jobs in Transaction SM36

The left side of Figure 9.22 shows the four background processes available for job processing. The right side displays which job is used at what time and how long the job occupies the process.

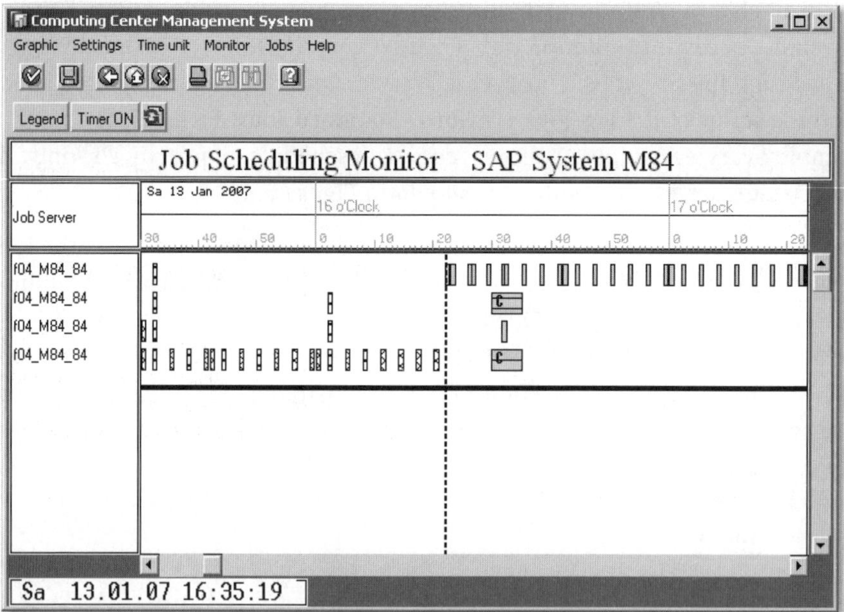

Figure 9.22 Job Scheduling Monitor

Job Name/Period/ Client-Dependent	Report	Function
SAP_REORG_JOBS/ Daily/No	RSBTCDEL(2)	Reorganizes jobs, deletes obsolete background jobs.
SAP_REORG_BATCHINPUT/ Daily/Yes	RSBDCREO	Deletes obsolete batch input sessions.
SAP_REORG_SPOOL/ Daily/Yes	RSPO0041 (old) RSPO1041 (new version)	Deletes obsolete spool data.
SAP_REORG_ABAPDUMPS Daily/No	RSSNAPDL	Deletes obsolete dumps caused by ABAP program failures.
SAP_REORG_JOBSTATISTIC/ Monthly/No	RSBPSTDE	Deletes job statistics for jobs that have not run since the defined date (statistics are no longer required, because the job now runs only once or not at all).
SAP_SPOOL_CONSISTENCE/ Daily/Yes	RSPO01043	Deletes spool inconsistencies.

Table 9.6 Background Jobs in the System Administration Wizard

Job Name/Period/ Client-Dependent	Report	Function
SAPREORG_PRI_PARAMS/ Monthly/No	RSBTCPRIDEL	Reorganizes the print parameters of batch jobs.
SAP_REORG_ORPHANED_ JOBLOGS/ Weekly/No	RSTS0024	Deletes job logs without existing jobs.
SAP_REORG_ XMI_LOGS/ Weekly/No	RSXMILOGREORG	Reorganizes the TXMILOGRAW table.
SAP_CCMS_MONI_BATCH_DP/ Hourly/No	RSAL_BATCH_TOOL_ DISPATCHING	This job is not a "real" reorg job but is required to start tools and methods needed for monitoring the system in the background.

Table 9.6 Background Jobs in the System Administration Wizard (Cont.)

Some jobs listed in Table 9.6 have release-specific features or are only required in certain environments. These jobs are described in the following list in greater detail:

- **SAP_REORG_SPOOL/SAP_SPOOL_CONSISTENCE**
  In addition to the two reorg jobs, you should also perform a regular consistency check of the TemSe database[2] and spooler. Inconsistencies can occur, for example, if you manually delete table entries from the spool and TemSe tables, if you delete spool and TemSe objects from the file system, or if you don't perform the consistency check properly. Report and transaction failures also lead to inconsistencies.

  To check the consistency of spooler and TemSe, you can follow the path **Tools • CCMS • Print • Spool administration** (SPAD) **• Administration • Check Consistency and Tools • CCMS • Print • TemSe Administration** (Transaction SP12) **• TemSe Data Storage • Check Consistency**. For a full consistency check, both checks must be run. If you want to automate the consistency check of spooler and TemSe, you can schedule the RSTS0020 report along with the SAP_REORG_SPOOL_CONSISTENCE job.

  From Release 4.0A on, the RSPO1043 report is used to check the spooler in batch mode via SAP_REORG_SPOOL_CONSISTENCE. If required, you can schedule it daily. The report can delete inconsistencies in the batch if

2 TemSe is a storage area for temporary sequential data, that is, TemSe stores objects that are usually not stored in the system permanently. The spool system uses TemSe to store output data temporarily.

it has detected them repeatedly. This ensures that no temporary inconsistencies are deleted. Temporary inconsistencies occur if no data is written to the TemSe or in the spooler at runtime, or the job itself cause these inconsistencies. Therefore, RSPO1043 may list its own spool job as an inconsistently, but you can ignore this entry.

You can use the RSTS0020 report to check TemSe inconsistencies in the batch. The result is a list of the found inconsistencies that cannot be deleted. You must run the report for a second time and select the objects to be deleted. Optionally, you can use the TemSe administration as described above. When using this method, consider that long-lasting jobs of the current day can also be listed in the logs as inconsistencies.

- **SAP_REORG_ABAPDUMPS**
  If this job is not scheduled, you can also run the ABAP report, RSNAPJOB, from the ABAP Editor to manage jobs. This report schedules RSSNAPDL using the following information:
  - Job name: RSSNAPDL
  - Variant: DEFAULT (You must create this variant.)
  - Start time: 1 a.m.
  - Period: Daily
- **SAP_REORG_PRIPARAMS**
  From Release SAP R/3 4.6A on, the print parameters are managed separately from the job steps. Thus, the RSBTCDEL(2) report deletes no longer print parameters. Therefore, the RSBTCPRIDEL report, which reorganizes the print parameters client-independently, must be scheduled additionally. Because the number of print parameters increases — compared with the batch steps — more slowly, you can run this report at larger time intervals (≥1 month).
- **SAP_REORG_XMILOG**
  SAP_REORG_XMILOG reorganizes the TXMILOGRAW table. This table contains log information of the XMI interface that is required for the use of external job scheduling tools. In this process, XMI log entries are written to the table. The RSXMILOGREORG program is available since Release 4.6C. Use the `ZRSXMILOGREORG` program for earlier releases.
- **SAP_CCMS_MONI_BATCH_DP**
  SAP_CCMS_MONI_BATCH_DP is not a reorganization job but is required to start tools and methods needed for monitoring the system in the background (Transactions RZ20 and RZ21). The RSAL_BATCH_TOOL_DISPATCHING is provided since Release 4.6A.

Besides the reorg jobs already mentioned, SAP recommends that you also schedule other collector jobs. These implement the data collection for the performance monitor. Table 9.7 gives an overview of the jobs. You can schedule the jobs using Transaction SM36.

Job Name/Period/ Client-Dependent	Report	Function
SAP_COLLECTOR_FOR_ JOBSTATISTIC/ Daily/ No	RSBPCOLL	Generates runtime statistics for background jobs.
SAP_COLLECTOR_FOR_ PERFMONITOR/ Hourly/ No	RSCOLL00	Creates statistics for system performance. This job was referred to as COLLECTOR_FOR_ PERFORMANCE_MONITOR in the past. Ensure that you schedule the job under its new name. RSCOLL00 schedules all reports that are required for the performance monitor. It obtains the names of the reports to be executed from the TCOLL table.
SAP_COLLECTOR_FOR_ NONE_R3_STAT/ Hourly/ No	R2N3_STAT_ COLLECTOR	Available from Web Application Server 6.20. Collects data from SAPCCMSR agents. These agents can monitor external components of an SAP system (components without SAP instance).

Table 9.7 Performance Collector Jobs

With the information provided in this section you can schedule the basic clean up and reorganization jobs for an SAP system. Depending on the solution used, application-specific jobs do sometimes exist. These jobs can be found in the installation documentation. With the tools described, you can schedule these jobs and check their results.

9.3.2 Oracle Jobs

In addition to the already mentioned standard jobs to clean up the SAP system, some jobs reorganize the logs in the Oracle database and check the Oracle database itself. These jobs, for instance, move log files and table entries to old backups and checks. Earlier releases provided the `sapdba` tool for these jobs. This has been replaced by the BR*Tools. Currently, both products are maintained, particularly for older releases. Generally, you should use the BR*Tools, because they are the future SAP development. You can find further information on the BR*Tools and their development in Section 4.5. No special versions of the BR*Tools or SAPDBA are available for Unicode systems, because both programs are also suitable for Unicode. The `brconnect` program of the BR*Tools is used for running the mentioned jobs.

Table 9.8 shows an overview of the sapdba calls and the respective call of `brconnect` as well as a short description of the corresponding functions. Section 4.5 describes further `brconnect` functions and details of other BR*Tools.

SAPDBA "sapdba"	BR*Tools "brconnect -f"	Function
-check	check	Runs a database check
-next	next	Recalculates the values for the next extent
-checkopt | -analyze	stats	Recalculates the database statistics
-statistics	stats -p [n]	Recalculates the database statistics with *n* parallel threads (default = 1)
-delete	stats -d	Deletes statistics
-cleanup	cleanup	Cleans the DBA logs

Table 9.8 SAPDBA and BR*Tools Options

You should schedule the creation of statistics and the cleanup of log files as regular background jobs. They can be planned, as is the case with planning DBVerify (see Section 9.2.1, *Monitoring the Oracle Database*), by following the path **Tools • CCMS • DB Administration • Planning Calendar • Local** (Transaction DB13). We recommend a weekly schedule.

9.4 Summary

Based on the information in this chapter, you should be able to perform basic monitoring tasks in your system. Depending on the requirements and properties of your system, additional monitoring objects can be included in the continuous monitoring process.

Data is money! One fact is absolutely clear: data security is essential for the financially valuable data resources of a company.

10 Backup, Restore, and Recovery

In no event and under no circumstances should data be lost. If a huge problem in the area of storage[1] causes a system to crash, *system downtime* occurs in addition to the data loss. Every hour, or indeed every minute in some applications such as the area of e-commerce, for example, that a system is not available for production due to database downtime can and will cost a lot of money. Legal requirements that stipulate that data is stored securely also apply.

Before you set up your SAP system, you should ensure that everything possible is done both technically and structurally to prevent any system downtime. In Chapter 5, we provided you with planning criteria and introduced techniques and concepts in the sections about availability and security to help you reduce the possibility of system downtime.

Nevertheless, you can (or should) never assume that all redundancies and all security precautions will prevent downtime. The following is therefore essential:

- You must back up your Oracle database and your SAP system, including the required software components, properly and at strictly defined intervals, and the backups must be controlled.
- You must be able to restore your Oracle database and your SAP system if errors occur.

In addition to the theoretical knowledge that we offer you in this chapter, to restore the SAP system, you, as the administrator, also require completely practical preparation in the form of regular restore and recovery exercises based on different error scenarios.

1 Primary and secondary storage from individual local hard disks, disk arrays, DAS, or SAN.

Many of the errors that can occur and damage the database are grouped into four different error classes:

- **Software errors**
  All errors that occur in the Oracle software, the operating system, and the SAP software can be categorized in this class. For example, importing a current software update can result in errors, for which data is overwritten or deleted.
- **Hardware errors**
  All errors that cause data losses due to hard disk or controller downtimes or through downtimes with the actual technical equipment are grouped in this class. Through a redundant setup of the technology and the data store, the effects of the downtime can at least be partly reduced to the extent that they do not affect the functions of the system. A service and support contract with the hardware manufacturer that is tailored to the company's requirements can also further minimize the system downtime if a major hardware failure occurs.
- **Operating errors**
  These errors occur frequently and must not be ignored. Incorrect administration, wrongly assigned authorization within the SAP system, or defective customer developments cause data to be deleted to a lesser or greater extent. Although SAP concepts such as the SAP system landscape and the transport system associated with it (see Chapter 6) cannot exclude the sources of these errors, they can significantly reduce them.
- **External factors**
  These can include catastrophes such as fire, water leaks, earthquakes that occur in other parts of the world, or rats that enjoy gnawing on buried cables. In addition to taking out good insurance, you should remember that the data is backed up on hardware that is physically and (more beneficially) locally operated separately from the actual productive technical equipment (see Chapter 5 for more information).

All errors can occur in the lifecycle of an SAP system. It is all the more important, therefore, to have a well-conceived backup concept. Only such a concept can prevent loss of your data treasure. By also being experienced in restoring the system and in dealing expertly with any situation by using precise actions, you can significantly reduce the system downtime if a failure occurs.

10.1 What Must Be Backed Up?

In this section, we will show you at a glance what you must store in a data backup and the circumstances you should watch closely when planning a backup concept.

We will first look at the Oracle database objects, SAP objects, and other possible data for your installation that you must back up.

Figure 10.1 shows the data backup objects of an SAP system with an Oracle database. The physical database objects of an Oracle database are:

- The data files where the actual tables with the data are contained in tablespaces
- The online and offline redo log files
- The control files
- The parameterization files of the Oracle database
- The log files

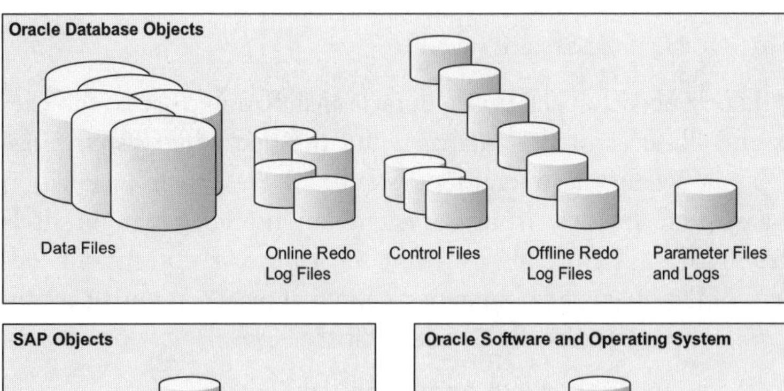

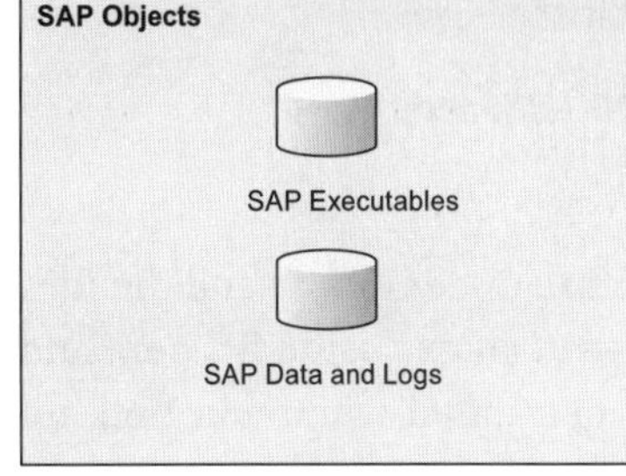

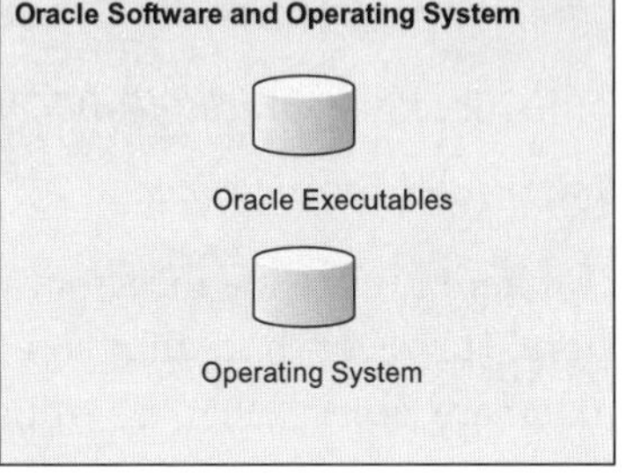

Figure 10.1 Data Backup Objects of an SAP System with Oracle

You *must* back up some of these objects, but there are others that you *can* back up. Why do we make this distinction? The crucial factor in terms of what you must and can back up is based on the data backup method used in each case. We will introduce the methods in Section 10.2, *Data Backup*

Methods. We will look at the different backup objects again separately in Section 10.1.1, *Interaction of Oracle Processes and Database Objects*, in particular, to help you understand the online backup of an Oracle database.

In addition to Oracle database objects, you must also back up SAP objects. These include:

- Executable SAP system files located in the */usr/sap/<SID>/SYS/exe/run* global kernel directory and in the local kernel directory under */usr/sap/<SID>/<instance name>/exe*
- SAP data files such as the */usr/sap/trans* transport directory, the */usr/sap/<SID>/<IN STANZ_NAME>/data* statistics files created by the SAP system, and the SAP profiles under */sapmnt/<SID>/profile*

Rather than backing up individual selected subdirectories, the sensible thing to do is to back up the complete directory structure with the files located in the */usr/sap/trans*, */usr/sap/<SID>*, and */sapmnt/<SID>* paths. Do not forget to back up the home directories of the <sid>adm and ora<sid> (UNIX) operating system user or <SID>ADM and SAPService<SID> (Windows). These contain the configuration files where the environment variables for the SAP system and the Oracle database are saved.

You will ultimately need to back up the Oracle installation, that is, the executable files and libraries of the database, and the operating system files. Although you can set up the operating system and the Oracle installation again after a system crashes, from a system downtime viewpoint, it is quicker to restore the system. This also applies for the SAP objects and configuration files of the operating system users listed above. You must back up the following, in particular, for the Oracle database:

- Oracle home directory */oracle/<DBSID>/<DB release>*[2]
- Oracle client under */oracle/client*

It is also useful here to save the directory structure under */oracle* and the files contained there. However, note that you maintain an exclusion list here and exclude all database objects that we initially mentioned when you back up the Oracle installation.

---

2 The system ID of the database instance is referred to as <DBSID>. The system ID of the SAP system is represented as <SID>. On individual instances, the system ID of the database instance is the same as the system ID of the SAP system (DBSID = SID).

It is also important to back up the complete operating system. Bear in mind here that if the bootable hard disk crashes, it does not make much sense to purely back up the files, because you will subsequently begin to reinstall the operating system in the event of the particular situation. At this point, you should use products that back up a mapping of the operating system that you can later use to restore the system using bootable options.

If you do not want to back up the SAP and Oracle directories regularly (although this is what we recommend), you should on all accounts back them up after you install your SAP and Oracle systems and after an SAP or Oracle upgrade, and then ensure that you can access these back ups. The loss of temporary files of an SAP system as found in the instance directories is not critical – it does not result in any loss of data. You can reset any links of these files to the database using SAP tools.

In the following section, we will look in more detail at the individual Oracle database objects and how they interact with processes and memory areas. In addition, we will discuss the operating modes of the Oracle database and archiver stuck.

10.1.1 Interaction of Oracle Processes and Database Objects

The basis for understanding the different backup methods is the process of how the Oracle database writes data into the individual physical database objects. Figure 10.2 shows a simplified view of how and under what circumstances the data is written into the database objects. Chapter 3 provides a detailed description of the individual Oracle processes that are outlined in Figure 10.2.

Shown in a very simplified way, a user process (for example, this can be an SAP dialog work process) communicates with an Oracle server process. The server process reads the data (provided that this does not already exist in the data buffer) from the data files into the buffer and changes it.

These changes are asynchronously saved in the data files by the DBWR process (Database Writer). There are different events and situations in which the DBWR becomes active:

- The fill level of the database buffer reaches a certain threshold value.
- The server process does not find a free data block.
- The checkpoint process (CKPT) triggers the writing of data.
- A timeout occurs.

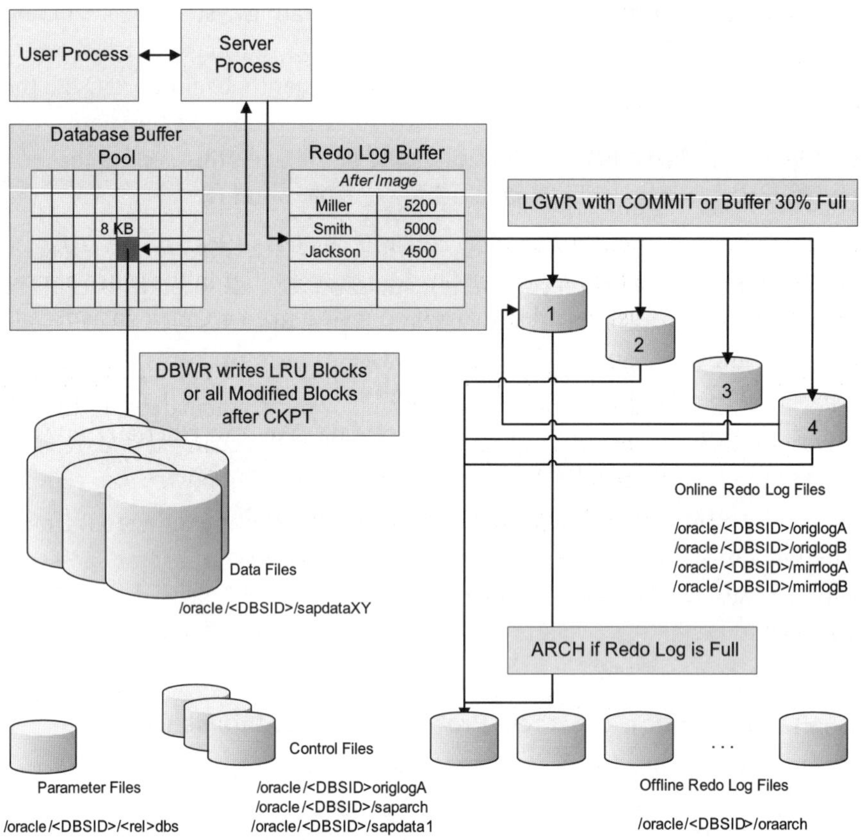

Figure 10.2 Writing Data into Data and Redo Log Files

Except in the case of a checkpoint, the DBWR process writes the least recently used blocks into the data files of the Oracle database. *Least recently used* is a page replacement strategy for cache memories. It stores the particular page, the last referencing of which dates back to the least recently used. A checkpoint prompts the DBWR to write all of the buffer blocks into the data files. In both cases, only the database buffer changes committed using `COMMIT` are written into the Oracle data files.

In addition to the database buffer cache, a server process also retains all change operations such as inserting, changing, and deleting data in the redo log buffer. After-images of the changed data record are saved sequentially and circularly here. If the redo log buffer is full, it is written again from the beginning. The LGWR process (Log writer) writes redo log entries into online redo log files. The LGWR then becomes active when one of the following conditions is met:

- You perform a COMMIT.
- The DBWR writes blocks from the database buffer into the data files.
- The buffer is filled to 30%.
- A period of 3 seconds has passed.

This sequential writing into the redo log files is significantly faster than writing into the dispersed blocks of very large database files. This is a major advantage. The redo log files are binary files, not log files in the sense of protocol files. There must be at least two redo log files in an Oracle instance.

What are the other advantages of the redo log buffer and writing into online redo log files? A COMMIT commits the changes and immediately writes the corresponding entries, that is, the after-images of the changed data record, in the redo log buffer into the current redo log file. If a power outage now occurs, for example, although the changes have not yet been stored in the data files, they are contained in the redo log file. You can now restore the database buffer from this file and consequently return the database to its status from before the power outage occurred. Only the changes committed by COMMIT are reloaded into the database buffer in this case. The recovery process of redo logs is called *instance recovery* (see Section 10.3, *Recovery Methods*).

We will first look at the control files before returning to the redo logs. The control files contain data such as the structure and status information of the database. This includes the *System Change Number* (SCN), storage locations of files, and database name, for example. Due to the key significance of the control file for the database instance, this file is mirrored in different locations of the file system. Three copies of the file are stored in the standard SAP installation. However, note that this mirroring is not a substitute for backing up the control files on an external medium. We will discuss the backing up of these files throughout the chapter.

The SCN is very important. It is an internal transaction counter. Each time you perform a COMMIT, a unique SCN is incremented internally in the Oracle database and written together with the change into the redo log file and data file where the data record was inserted or changed. The assignment of the data file to the last SCN is also saved in the control file. This will tell you up to which transaction you must restore this data file if a restore is required.

The *checkpoint process* is responsible for updating this information in the control and data files. This process only saves control information, so it triggers the DBWR once again before writing the data in order to write all data from the buffer into the data files. It is automatically started if:

- A redo log file is full and the redo log group needs to be changed
- The Oracle database is stopped
- A specified number of data changes were made
- A defined period of time has expired

If a power outage occurs, all changes would then first be saved in the data files if all blocks with the `COMMIT` status were written out of the buffer using a checkpoint.

Now let's return to the redo log files. An Oracle database does not just consist of an individual online redo log file; it also has a defined number and size of files. The LGWR process writes the files cyclically. If a file is full, the next online redo log file is used. This change to another online redo log file is called a *redo log switch*. A redo log switch involves the new online redo log file receiving a unique number known as the *Log Sequence Number* (LSN). When the system switches to an online redo log file that is already full, the data saved there is overwritten. Online redo logs are always reused. The control file also saves the initial SCN and the SCN that was current at the time of the log switch, in combination with the LSN of the redo log file.

You can organize redo log files in groups. Because they are written alternately, you need at least two groups. The groups enable a mirroring of the online redo log files, because all files of a group are identical and can be easily distributed on different physical media. The redo log groups are also written cyclically. Figure 10.3 shows an example of four redo log groups[3] that each contain two files. The two files are in different directories, hence the reason you can place these directories on different physical media. If the hard disk crashes, this reduces the possibility of data being lost due to the loss of the redo log file.

A redo log file can adopt different statuses. These include:

- **UNUSED**
  The online redo log files were never written before. A file obtains this status if you added it or opened the database using the `resetlogs` option.

3 This is the configuration you will find after you install an SAP system on Oracle.

- **CURRENT**
  This is the current file. The status implies that the file is also active. You can open and close the file.
- **ACTIVE**
  Although the log file is active, it is not current. You need it for the instance recovery process and can also use it for the media recovery.
- **CLEARING**
  This log is created using the `ALTER DATABASE CLEAR LOGFILE` command. After you have completed this process, the status changes to unused.
- **INACTIVE**
  You no longer need the redo log file for an instance recovery, but you can use it for a media recovery.

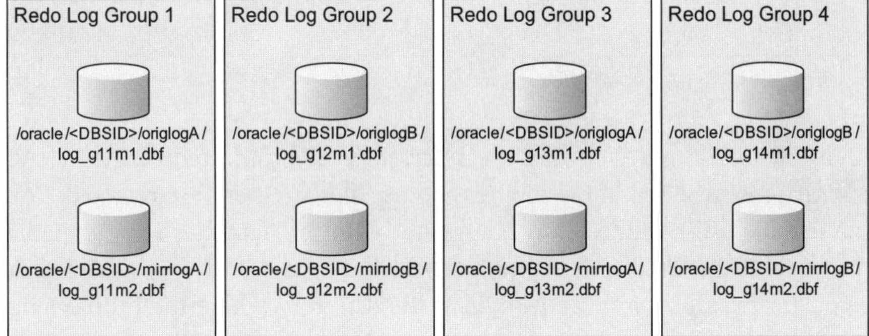

Figure 10.3 Redo Log Groups

10.1.2 Operating Modes of the Oracle Database

In addition to the database objects and processes already described, there are also (as shown in Figure 10.2) *offline redo log files* and the *archiver process* (ARCH). The archiver process becomes active when the database is in *ArchiveLog mode*. The situation where this process remains inactive is the *NoArchiveLog mode* (see Figure 10.4).

In ArchiveLog mode after a redo log switch, the archiver process backs up the online redo log file that is no longer current but is still used before the switch and copies this file into a special directory that is */oracle/<DBSID>/oraarch* by default as of SAP Basis Release 6.20. Earlier versions used the */oracle/<DBSID>/saparch* directory.

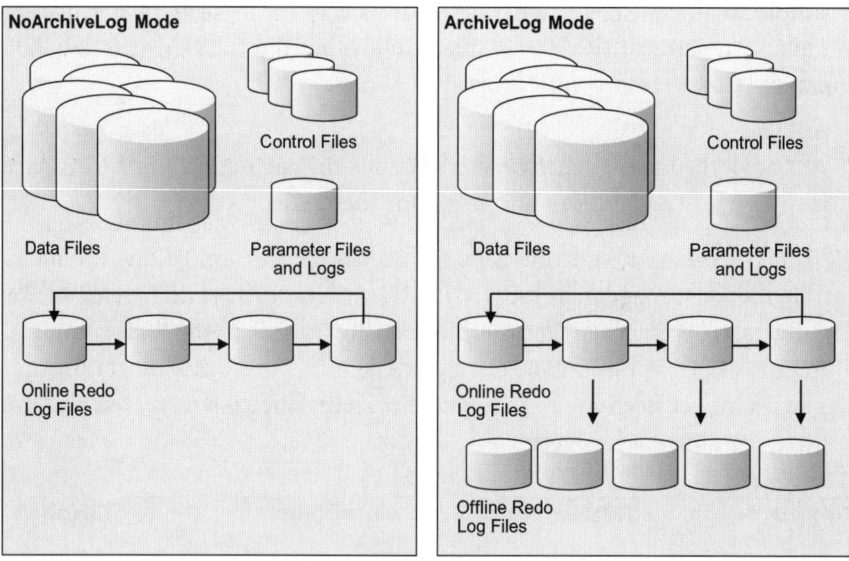

Figure 10.4 Operating Modes of an Oracle Database

Archived online redo log files are referred to as offline redo log files. All transactions specified in the online redo log files are therefore retained. You can use the offline redo log files together with the data files for the media recovery. If the database crashes, for which data is lost due to a hard disk error, for example, you can (provided the directory where the offline redo log files are saved is not affected by the disk error) restore the Oracle database up to the last completed transaction.

The number of offline redo log files written into the archiver directory depends, in addition to the activities running on the SAP system, on the PC and storage hardware equipment. For example, if you perform client copies or process batch runs, some offline redo log files can already be created per minute and over several hours. In test or development systems, however, only a few offline redo log files may be created per day.

If you operate the database in NoArchiveLog mode, the changes entered in the online redo log are then lost if the online redo log file written first is overwritten with new changes by the implemented cycle. This means you cannot subsequently restore the data. You can therefore only use the online redo logs for the instance recovery already mentioned. You must select the operating mode depending on the backup method in question. We recommend that you operate the database in ArchiveLog mode, because this significantly increases the possibility of restoring the database.

A simple way to discover whether your Oracle database is in ArchiveLog mode and whether the archiver process was started is to execute the SQL command:

```
ARCHIVE LOG LIST;
```

If the ArchiveLog mode is deactivated, you can easily activate it using the BR*Tools. To do this, start the `BRTOOLS` or `BRGUI` program. Follow the menu path **Instance Management • Alter Database Instance • Set archivelog mode**. Another option is to activate the mode using the following SQL command lines. It is important that you start up the database in the *Mount* status.

```
CONNECT / AS SYSDBA
STARTUP MOUNT
ALTER DATABASE ARCHIVELOG;
ALTER DATABASE OPEN;
```

To start the archiver process (if this is deactivated), enter the commands:

```
CONNECT / AS SYSDBA
ALTER SYSTEM ARCHIVE LOG START;
```

The archiver process (if it was not already activated) will subsequently remain active until you shut down the database. You must repeat the process after you next open the database.

The parameter files of the Oracle database provide a default activation of the archiver process. The *init<DBSID>.ora* parameters

- `log_archive_start = true`
- `log_archive_dest = <directory>/<file_prefix>`
- `log_archive_format = <Oracle default>`

can enable the archiver process to be activated by default when you boot up the Oracle database. The `log_archive_start` parameter in this case specifies whether the archiver process is to be activated automatically or not. You use the `log_archive_dest = <directory>/<file prefix>` profile parameter to specify the directory path and the prefix of the offline redo logs. The prefix is set to <ORACLE_SID>arch by default after an SAP installation with Oracle. The `log_archive_format` parameter defines how you want the archived redo log files to be named. The Oracle standard is used after the installation.[4]

4 This is a combination of the thread number that the file has written and the LSN.

An offline redo log file for an SAP installation is contained in the */oracle/ <DBSID>oraarch* path and is called arch<DBSID><Thread_Number>_<LSN>.

Alternatively, as of Oracle 9i, you can use the `log_archive_dest_n` parameter to specify the archiver directory. However, this can only be defined if `log_archive_dest` is not set. You can specify up to 10 directories where Oracle can archive redo log files. You can use `log_archive_dest_state_n` to activate or deactivate such a directory. The syntax of the profile parameter is `log_archive_dest_n = 'LOCATION=<directory>/<file prefix>'`. When specifying several archiver directories, you can switch between the directories (see next section) or archive in several directories.

After you install the SAP system, the Oracle database operates in ArchiveLog mode by default.

10.1.3 Archiver Stuck

As described earlier, it would be fatal if the offline redo log files were to be lost due to a hard disk crash. The */oracle/<DBSID>/oraarch* directory and its files should therefore be on a physically separate medium that must be protected by a RAID (see Chapter 5).

The capacity of the archiver directory is not unlimited. Your SAP users work in the SAP system and your Oracle database processes one transaction after the other and fills one online redo log after the other. The archiver process continually archives these online redo log files into the archive directory. The capacity of the directory will sooner or later reach its limits, regardless of how large it is. If no more space is available in the */oracle/<DBSID>/oraarch* directory, the archiver process cannot write any more online redo logs into the directory as offline redo logs. Oracle cannot perform any more redo log switches. The database now waits with the processing of other database transactions until the archiver can write log files into the directory again. This defined problem is known by the name *archiver stuck*. Users who are logged on to the SAP system and execute a transaction will recognize the archiver stuck by the fact that the system comes to a complete standstill and an hourglass appears: the system hangs.

The archiver directory must therefore either be emptied depending on the fill level or emptied continually. Because you need the redo log files to restore the system, you do not simply delete these files; you usually save them instead on a backup tape. How often you back up the offline redo logs depends entirely on the number of activities in the SAP system. If many redo log entries are written and the online redo log files are therefore changed very frequently, a higher number of redo logs are created. You must monitor this directory and, if necessary, back up and then delete the files. Another option is to continually write the redo log files on a backup medium using program options (see Section 10.4.2, *Backing Up Redo Log Files Using BRARCHIVE*).

The bigger the archive directory, the later an archiver stuck occurs if there is a high load. The number of existing redo log files depends on the specific SAP system load (normal operation, client copy, batch runs) and the performance of the hardware. The current SAP installation guidelines specify a value of at least 400 MB for the size of the archiver directory and a data quantity from 300 MB to 1 GB to be archived daily for live systems. In our experience, these specifications are too small. Irrespective of your hardware and the load on the systems, you should initially create the directory with 5 GB. If you operate a lot of SAP systems, you will not connect a tape drive for each system exclusively for backing up redo log files. In this case, you should select an even bigger size for the archiver directory to avoid an archiver stuck. Another option is to store the files of all SAP systems temporarily in a very large hard disk directory and save them from there to tape. The actual final size of your directory is a rule of thumb that you determine over time for your specific hardware and software environment.

This backup of redo log files should not only be performed based on the fill level of the directory, but should be performed once a day because, as already mentioned several times, the redo log files are very important for restoring the database. In addition to the RAID protection for the directory, we recommend that you back up each log file twice onto backup tapes or onto other backup media. When errors occur, a second copy of the redo log files will therefore always be available. You should always perform the second backup on a different backup medium than the first backup (see Figure 10.5).

Each offline redo log file receives a status that is recorded in a log file located by default in the */oracle/<DBSID>/saparch* directory and called arch<DBSID> .log. If the archiver writes an online redo log file into the archive directory, this file gets the ARCHIVED status. If the backup method is the one defined in Figure 10.5, the next step involves saving a redo log to tape, which changes the status of this file to SAVED. You will only be able to delete the file once you have backed it up again and its status has changed to COPIED. The deletion process is immediately activated after the status changes to COPIED. In addition to the status, the current backup run is recorded to help you establish, when you are carrying out a recovery process, from which backup the required log file was written.

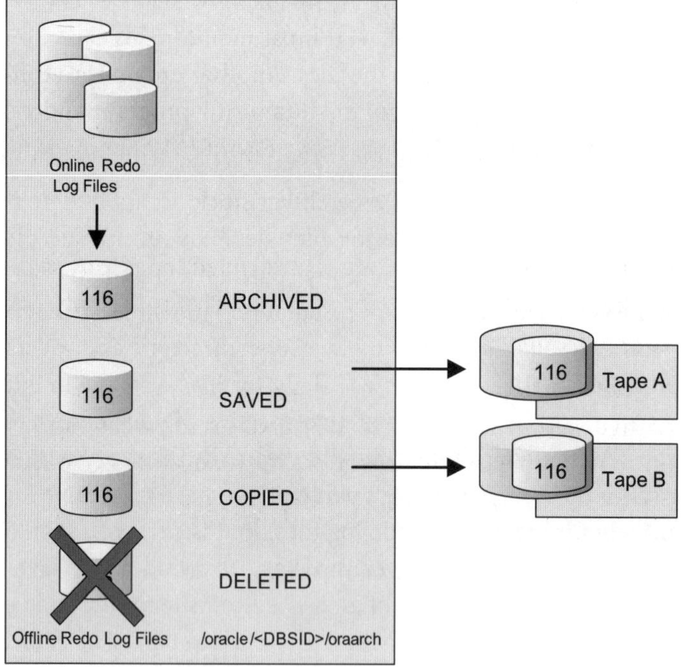

Figure 10.5 Duplicate Backup of Offline Redo Log Files

Redo log files, without exception, must be available for a recovery. A defective current backup of data files can always be replaced by an older backup if the redo log files between these backups are available and can therefore be used for a recovery.

Back to the problem of the archiver stuck: What should you do if an archiver stuck occurs despite all of the described measures? You have the following options:

- **Dummy file**
  The quickest and smartest option is to place a sufficiently large dummy file into the archiver directory that you can delete when an archiver stuck occurs. Users can then continue working in the system, and you gain time to back up and delete the redo log files from the directory. You must make the dummy file so large that at least enough space is created by deleting this file so that enough time remains for you to empty the directory without another archiver stuck occurring. Although this solution means that additional memory is used, its attraction is that all redo logs are consistently saved to tape, and you can perform a recovery without any prob-

lems. Section 10.8, *Tips and Tricks*, describes a command that you can use to create a dummy file on UNIX operating systems.

- **Move offline redo logs**
  Another method involves using operating system commands (`mv`, `move`) to move the files from an archiver directory to an area that contains sufficient space. This can be done very quickly, and your users can continue working in the system. However, you must then ensure that these moved files are subsequently saved to tape and are also retained for as long as the automatically backed up redo log files, for example. This is the only way you can guarantee consistent recovery.
- **Change the archiver directory**
  The third alternative is to change the directory path for the archiving process temporarily to gain time to back up the offline redo log files. You can choose this alternative if you have sufficient hard disk space available in another directory. You must execute the following SQL commands for this using `sqlplus`:

  ```
  alter system archive log stop;
  alter system archive set log_archive_dest=<temp_path and prefix>;
  alter system archive log start;
  ```

  The first command stops the archiver process so that it no longer copies the online redo log files into the archiver directory. The second command changes the directory into which you want the copy process to save the files temporarily. Here, you specify the same prefix as the one defined in init<DBSID>.ora. Finally, you can use the last command to activate the archiver again. If you have emptied the original archiver directory, you can use the same command sequence to set this again by default for the database. Afterward, you must not forget to copy the offline redo log files saved in the temporary directory back into the original archiver directory and to back them up. If you choose this alternative, you do not have to worry that, by deactivating the archiving process, the online redo log files will be cyclically overwritten and that this will cause important changes of completed transactions (customer master data, purchase orders, sent invoices) to be lost. The online redo log files will be written in ArchiveLog operating mode until there are no more redo log groups with the ARCHIVED status free. Oracle then waits until the archiver process updates the online redo log files that still have to be archived. Once this has been completed, the processing of transactions is resumed. A gap in the chain of redo log files does not occur in this case. Alternatively, you can use the `log_archive_dest_n` and `log_archive_dest_state_n` parameters and arrange the switching of the archiver directories more easily.

- **Delete the offline redo logs — not a solution**
  The fourth alternative involves deleting the redo logs. Although this solves your archiver stuck problem very quickly, the major disadvantage of this option is that you permanently delete the files, and if the database fails due to hardware errors, you will only be able to recover the Oracle database up to the point up to which you backed up the last redo log onto a tape. You also subsequently need to back up your system completely, from which time onward, the redo logs will be consistently backed up again. However, what do you do if this backup is faulty for the recovery?

You can, incidentally, back up offline redo log files for a database that has been shut down. The tools provided by SAP support this function (see Section 10.4.1, *Data Backup Using BRBACKUP*).

We already mentioned the LSN as a unique numbering for redo log files. Each redo log file receives a unique, sequential number that is very important for the recovery (see Figure 10.6).

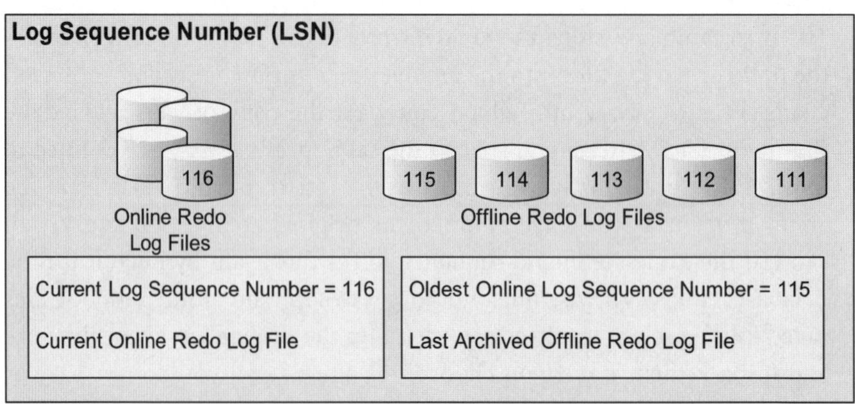

Figure 10.6 Log Sequence Number (LSN)

The current LSN belongs to the online redo log file with the CURRENT status. The number is assigned to the online redo log file during the redo log switch to this. The last offline redo log file archived is logged during an online backup (see Section 10.2.3, *Online Data Backup*) and defines the start of the archived redo log files for the backup. All older redo log files archived are not necessary for a recovery based on this backup. The LSN is particularly important for recovering an Oracle database.

10.2 Data Backup Methods

We now come to the individual data backup methods in this section. We differentiate between *logical* and *physical* methods (see Figure 10.7).

The logical method involves exporting data from the Oracle database, whereas the physical method entails backing up data onto any backup medium. When backing up data, we distinguish the status of the Oracle database. An offline data backup is performed from a database that is shut down but available to users, and an online data backup takes place from an open database, also available to users. We will discuss the individual methods in more detail in the following sections.

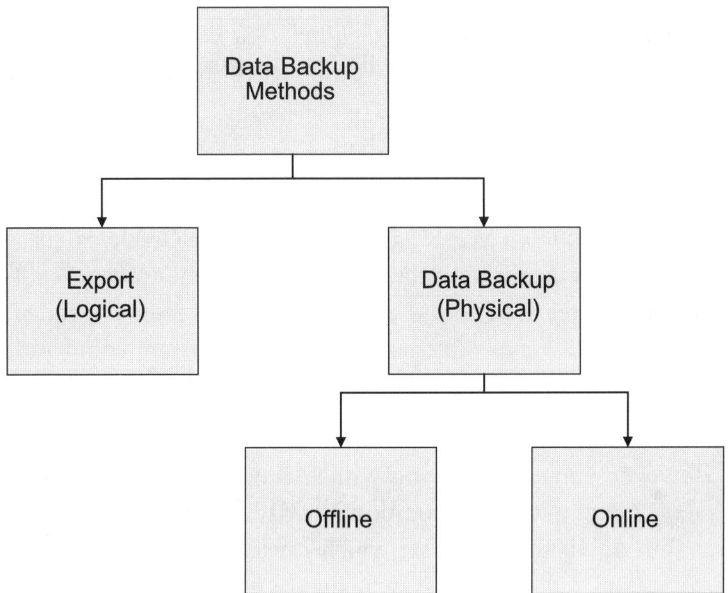

Figure 10.7 Data Backup Methods

10.2.1 Data Export

When you export data, you use Oracle functions to export database structures, indexes, and content from the database into files and later import them into the same or different databases.

Under no circumstances does a data export replace the physical methods of data backup discussed later in this section. A major drawback compared to a physical backup is that an import as the recovery method for a database means that only the status that was backed up when the export was saved can be restored. All changes that were performed after an export in the SAP system and therefore in the Oracle database are lost.

However, the logical exports and imports are used for reorganizing the database. Structural information, indexes, and the data are exported from selected tablespaces or data files, and these are reorganized, and the data is finally imported into the reorganized objects.

Exports are also used for the data transport. You can copy individual tables or the entire database in this way. For example, you can export an installation-enabled copy from the Oracle database from your SAP system this way. You can use this export to set up training or test systems, for instance.

When you migrate the Oracle database to a new release, it can also be useful to export the data. We will not deal with the export and import options and their use any further in this chapter. We will now discuss offline data backups in the next section.

10.2.2 Offline Data Backup

Offline data backup, also known as *cold backup*, backs up the Oracle database when this is stopped. This means the database instance is shut down, the different memory areas are released, and the background processes are ended. The data is backed up at file level. You can use operating system commands (such as `dd` or `cpio`) to write the data files to a backup medium.

The main disadvantage of this backup method is that you have to shut down the database. However, you cannot do this with SAP systems that must operate 24 hours a day, 7 days a week. In addition, the database buffers are emptied when you shut down the database, which causes the performance to suffer. This also applies for the SAP system that you would have to stop. Nevertheless, you can use the reconnect mechanism here.[5]

If you set this in the SAP start profiles, you can take the Oracle database offline and have the advantage of all buffers of the SAP system remaining filled. After you start the database, the performance is considerably better than when you shut down the complete system (SAP and Oracle). Users who are still logged on to the SAP system cannot do any work in it, however.

5 Each SAP dialog, batch, update, and spool work process establishes its own connection to the database when it is started. If this database connection is broken, the work process tries to establish a new connection. For more information, see SAP Note 98051.

Where offline data backups are concerned, we differentiate between two other options related to operating modes:

- Offline data backup of an Oracle database in NoArchiveLog mode
- Offline data backup of an Oracle database in ArchiveLog mode

The process of backups does not change in the different operating modes (see Figure 10.8). You must first shut down the database to ensure that the database objects can no longer be accessed. You then begin to back up the individual database objects (including online redo log files, control files and, optionally, parameter and log files) to a backup medium.

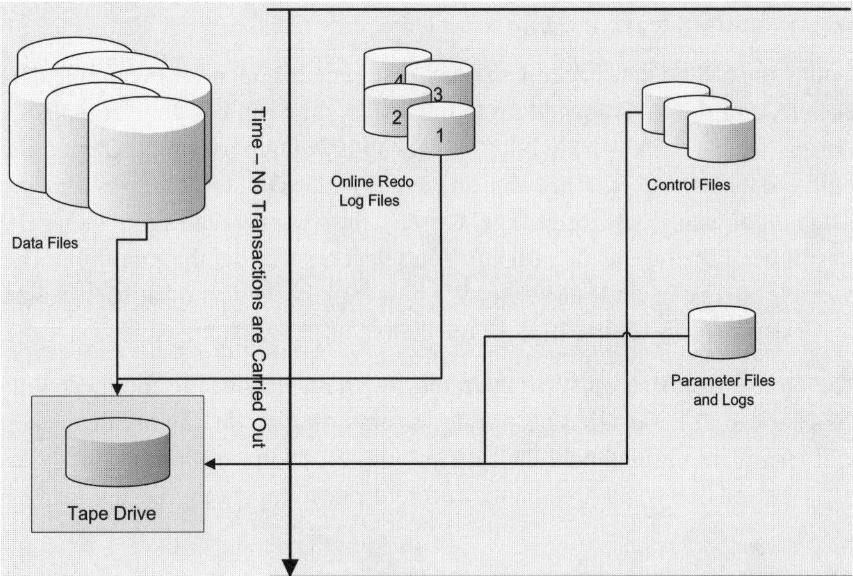

Figure 10.8 Process of an Offline Data Backup

After you perform the backup, you can restart the database. The SAP processes connect with the database, provided you set the reconnect mechanism.

After an offline data backup, you receive a completely consistent backup. When you continue working with the SAP system, the backup is no longer current. The two backup types differ at this point. If you operate the database in NoArchiveLog mode, the online redo log files (as already described in Section 10.1.2) that are no longer current after a redo log switch are not archived, and the transactions they contain are lost. If a media recovery is necessary, you can only access the last full data backup, and all changes between this backup and the system failure are lost. The situation worsens if you discover that your last offline backup is defective.

The situation looks different if you operate the database in ArchiveLog mode and perform an offline data backup. In this case, you can restore the database up to the last transaction before the crash. From the perspective of a loss of data, even a defective backup will not cause problems because you can access an older backup and apply the offline redo log files completely.

The downside in both cases is the nonavailability of your SAP system when you are performing a backup. This is unacceptable for most users.

10.2.3 Online Data Backup

Unlike the offline data backup, the database remains open for the online data backup, and the users logged on to the SAP system can continue completely normally with their work while the backup is being performed. During the online data backup, the interaction between the Oracle processes and the database objects does not change. Nevertheless, you should ensure that the start time of the online data backup you select is such that the minimum load possible is created on the system. We will explain the technical background that exists for this information in the course of this section.

The Oracle database must be operated in ArchiveLog mode for the online data backup. If the database is not in this operating mode, the online backup will terminate immediately. During an online backup, offline redo log files must be and are written — many different ones, depending on the load on the SAP system.

A major difference compared to the offline data backup is that the backup is performed based on the *tablespace*. However, the backup of a tablespace backed up from an open database is inconsistent.

Let's assume that a tablespace consists of several dozen data files, and changes are continually being made to the data files due to user activities, whereby a change is saved to several data files of the tablespace. We now begin to back up the tablespace as of the first data file. The parts of the changes that are written into this first data file during the overall runtime of the backup are not also included in the backup and are consequently ignored. To be more specific, even when the first data file is backed up, the changes written into this file are already no longer considered if the copy process has exceeded the point when the change was inserted. However, the last backed-up data file contains almost all parts of the changes. If we recreate the tablespace from the backup, the changes that were written into the individual data files during the backup are not complete, and the data in the tablespace is inconsistent. A backup of the tablespaces alone is a fruitless exercise.

To restore an Oracle database consistently, you must consider the redo log files created during the online data backup. You create an online backup using operating system commands such as `cpio` or `dd` under the control of SAP or Oracle tools. Because these operating system commands are not part of the Oracle database, you must set a kind of starting point that is used to inform Oracle that an online backup has been started. All changes made to data after the starting point and their recording in the redo log files are required for a consistent backup of the data.

The process of an online data backup, which is often described as a hot backup, is shown in Figure 10.9. The SQL command

```
alter tablespace <tablespace name> begin backup;
```

is used to prepare every tablespace for the backup and therefore sets the starting point of the backup. You can now copy the files of the corresponding tablespace using the operating system commands mentioned above. During the copy process, users can work completely normally in the system and create redo log files that are archived in the archiver directory as offline redo log files. After the data files of the tablespace are copied, you can reset this tablespace back to normal mode. You do this using the command

```
alter tablespace <tablespace name> end backup;
```

You then back up a control file and copy it to the backup medium using operating system commands. You copy the file using the command

```
alter database backup controlfile;
```

You then perform a redo log switch, whereby you switch and archive the current online redo log file. This is necessary because this current redo log file still contains changes that were recorded during the online backup. You can perform the log switch and the archiving using the command

```
alter system archive log current;
```

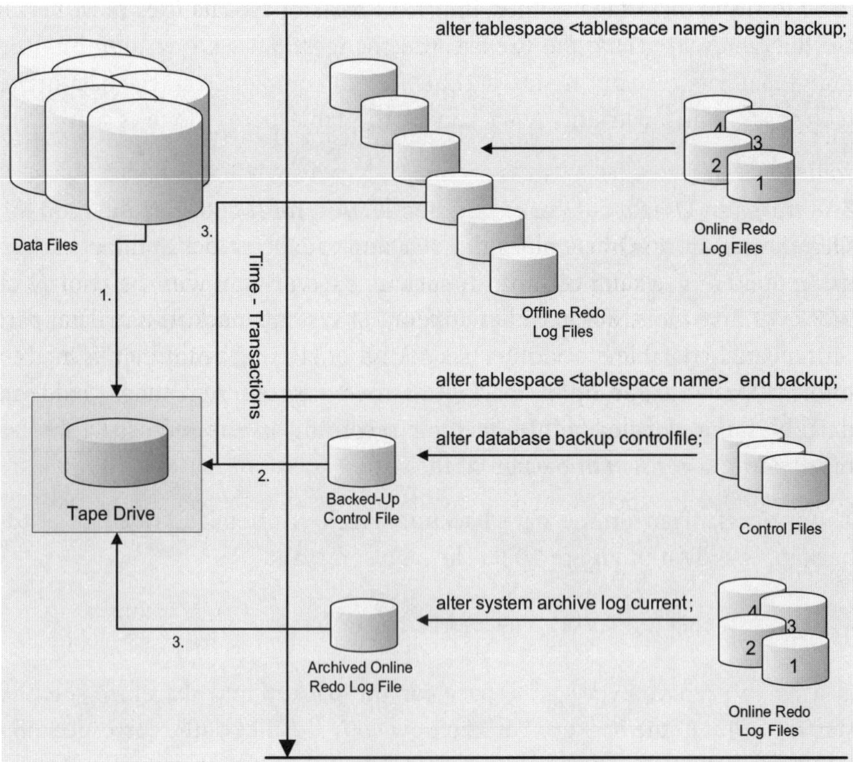

Figure 10.9 Process of an Online Data Backup

You must now save all generated offline redo log files to the backup medium.

Let's take a look at what changes the `alter tablespace begin backup;` SQL command makes to the internal behavior of the Oracle database. The first important change is in the redo log files. Not only is one after-image of the changed data record logged in the redo log files for each changed data record, but a before-image of the entire Oracle block that contains the changed data record is also recorded. The second change applies to the SCN. This is frozen by executing the SQL command. All backed up data files therefore have the SCN that they had when the backup began.

The SCN needs to be frozen, because the Oracle database is not notified of when the operating system backs up the header of the data file where the SCN is saved. If you were not to retain the SCN, this could be bigger in the data files of the backup than it was at the beginning of the `alter tablespace begin backup;` command. To be able to apply redo log files correctly if you have to restore a database, the SCN of the backed up data files must match the SCN at the beginning of the backup.

Why are the before-images of the blocks in question saved in the redo log files? The size of an Oracle block is defined using the `db_block_size` initialization parameter. These values are typically between 2 KB and 8 KB in size. SAP does not support block sizes of less than 8 KB (see SAP Note 105047). Therefore, such an Oracle block can be a multiple of a block at the operating system level. For example, if the operating system works with a size of 2 kb, blocks of 2 kb are always read and copied when you back up the data files. This means an Oracle block of 8 kb is not backed up as one unit but is instead backed up across the operating system blocks at different times. This can quickly lead to Oracle block inconsistencies in the backup, especially if parts of an Oracle block were backed up across operating system blocks, the complete Oracle block is then changed, and, finally, the remaining parts of the Oracle block that have not yet been backed up are copied. The restored Oracle block would then have a part with data where there are no changes and a part with data where the changes are contained. This phenomenon is called *block split*. This is where the before-images of the Oracle blocks that were recorded in the redo log files come into effect: When you restore a backup with the split blocks mentioned above, these inconsistent blocks can be overwritten and changed from the recording of the original blocks and the changes made to them in the redo log files. The Oracle blocks are subsequently consistent.

The `alter tablespace <tablespace name> end backup;` SQL command resets the relevant tablespace back to the normal status. The SCN is written into the data files of the tablespace again, and the redo log files only record the after-images of the changes.

We now come to the reason why you should run the online backup at times when there is minimal work load. When you set the tablespace in backup mode, the number of redo log files increases because, as described, the before-images of the Oracle block are also recorded. In times of minimal work load, you therefore reduce the "production" of these particular redo log files.

You should also note that you only set each tablespace to backup mode when you are really beginning to back up the data files. When you set all tablespaces of the database to backup mode, redo log files with before-images are written for all changes made in the database, although the operating system, if possible, only backs up the data files of one tablespace. This means that you minimize the time that a tablespace is in backup mode.

In SAP releases that use the new tablespace layout[6] with very few tablespaces, a tablespace backup almost corresponds to a complete database backup. The so finely grained distribution of individual tablespaces on online data backups is no longer possible. For the reasons described above, you should therefore check a backup strategy based on several tablespace backups, in particular, on large database systems that are run using the new tablespace layout (for more information, see also Section 10.7, *Backup Strategies*).

An online data backup is one option you can use to back up the Oracle database if you cannot shut this database down. However, an online backup can only be consistent if the offline redo log files generated in the meantime are also backed up. Online and offline data backups therefore differ in terms of recovery. You must always apply the redo log files for the database backed up online, to transfer the Oracle database in a consistent state.

10.3 Recovery Methods

Because we have described the different backup types, we will now discuss the recovery methods in detail.

Before you recover the SAP system, you should be clear about what exactly is causing the problem, what the condition of the database is, and which method is suitable for getting the system running again in the quickest way. If you are unclear about this, you should seek help. The costs that are additionally suffered due to the system failing because the database recovery has been incorrectly performed or delayed are usually higher than the consultancy costs incurred in such a situation. The recovery is a complicated procedure that is supported by different SAP tools (see Sections 10.4.3, *Restoring Using BRRESTORE*, and 10.4.4, *Recovering the Database Using BRRECOVER*). When you perform a recovery, you need to know about the different problem cases. It is always helpful to perform recovery exercises regularly on a test system. This test system should be identical to the live system. If you port your system to another hardware system, change your system land-

6 This is standard as of SAP Web Application Server Release 6.10 and higher. As of this SAP release, you can no longer choose the classic layout for new installations or system copies. See also SAP Note 355771.

scape, or perform a migration to a new release, you should associate such an exercise with this work in any case.

Let's use Figure 10.10 and first distinguish the terms *restore* and *recovery* from each other. The term *restore* refers to restoring one or more faulty data files of the Oracle database. The restore is divided *logically* and *physically*. The logical restore, the import, involves importing the data, which was previously stored during an export, into the Oracle database again. The physical restore means restoring data files that were previously backed up onto a different backup medium. This is known as a *media restore* and can be divided into a *full* and *partial* restore. These two terms refer to the way in which the data is copied back from the backup medium. *Full* specifies that all data files of a data backup run are written back. A partial restore only restores some selected data files of a run.

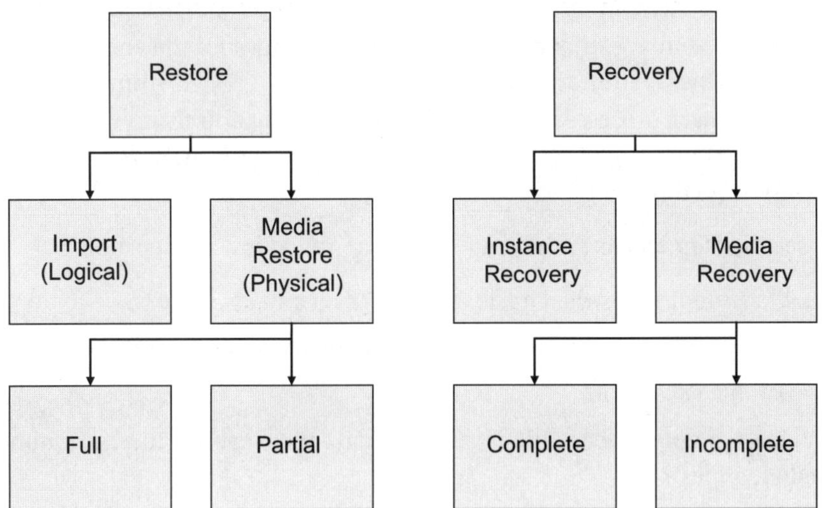

Figure 10.10 Restore and Recovery Methods

A recovery is always required if either a restore is not possible or data is lost due to obsolete data in a restore already performed, which is nevertheless unacceptable and can only be adjusted by a full or partial recovery run. We differentiate between two types of recovery here. If all data files physically exist and are not faulty, an instance recovery is performed. This is necessary after a power outage or if errors occur in the software. An instance recovery is performed automatically when you start the database. However, if a data file is damaged or has been lost and you restore this using the restore function, you must perform a media recovery on this data file. Again, there are also two types here: *complete recovery* and *incomplete recovery*. Complete recovery means that all redo log files up to the time of the Oracle database crashing are applied, so no data is lost except for the transactions not completed. All redo logs up to this point must be available without exception in this case. Incomplete recovery means that not all redo log files up to the time of the crash are available for recovery or they are available but, up to the time of the crash, are not to be used for a recovery. Data is lost with an incomplete recovery.

We will now look at the steps you must perform if a database is damaged and you must deal with a recovery using the restore and recovery options.

The first step involves analyzing the problem. To do this, you can check the Oracle ALERT log and the trace files belonging to the background and user processes of the database. The Oracle ALERT log is available in the[7] *<SAPDATA_HOME>/saptrace/background/alert_<DBSID>.log* directory. Important system events and significant error messages for the entire system are continually saved in this log. The trace files are created from the background and user processes and contain more information than exists in the database's ALERT log. These are available in the *<SAPDATA_HOME>/saptrace/usertrace* directory.

The second step entails asking and answering the following questions:

1. In what condition is the Oracle database? Is it still available?
2. What type of error has occurred? Is this a media or user error?
3. Which file is corrupt?
4. Which type of database file is affected (data files, control files, or online redo log files)?
5. If a media error has occurred, is software or hardware RAID set up and available? What is the status of the RAID array?
6. Do you have a standby database or another high-availability solution such as split mirror databases?

If a user error has occurred, the database is still available and generally operational. In the next step, you should perform a complete offline data backup before you start the database recovery.

If a media error has occurred, you must first exchange the defective hardware affected and create the file systems as they were before the error

7 <SAPDATA_HOME> is an environment variable and defines the */oracle/ <DBSID>* directory.

occurred. Before you exchange the hardware, back up the database objects that you can still access, if possible. You can always delete these again when the database is subsequently recovered and running. However, if a recovery run is incorrect, you therefore have a backup of the defective database that you can restore again to perform a new recovery on the defective database.

You can now start the database recovery. We have grouped the most important scenarios in Table 10.1. You can select an appropriate scenario based on the source of the error and purpose of the recovery.[8]

Error	Purpose	Scenario
Media error, for example, a disk crash	Recovery up to the time of the crash	Complete database recovery
User or software error	Recovery up to a certain time before the error occurred	Database point-in-time recovery
User or software error in an MCOD database component	Recovery of the affected component at a certain time before the error occurred	Tablespace point-in-time recovery
Media, user, or software error but: ▸ All copies of the redo logs are permanently lost, although a backup of the data files exists or ▸ Backup was performed immediately before the database crashed	Resetting of database to a status that it had the last time the data was backed up	Database reset
Entire database lost with all logs	Recovery of the database to a status, as far as possible, before the error occurred	Disaster recovery

Table 10.1 Recovery Scenarios

The recovery scenarios listed in the table are explained in more detail in Section 10.3.3, *Error Scenario: Loss of a Normal Tablespace*, where the loss of a normal tablespace is used as an example. We discuss in detail disaster recovery as a special form in Section 10.4.7, *Disaster Recovery Using BR*Tools*. However, we will first look at the recovery methods based on different data back ups.

8 You can install and use other SAP systems in an existing database of an SAP system. For more information, see SAP Note 388866 and go to *http://service.sap.com/mcod*.

10.3.1 Recovery from an Offline Data Backup

When you recover data from an offline data backup, you must first note the operating mode of the Oracle database. We will discuss the NoArchiveLog mode first.

Recall that in NoArchiveLog mode, the online redo log files where the changes are logged are not archived. Because the online redo log files are written cyclically, the changes are lost when the redo log file that is active when you start the database is overwritten.

When there is damage to individual or several data files, or the entire database, you can only recover the complete database from the offline data backup. All changes that take place in the normal operation of the system after this backup are lost forever.

We have already explained that the online redo log files are written cyclically. If such a cycle has not yet been processed, all changes that were performed on the database after the last offline data backup are still contained in the online redo log files. You can then recover the faulty data files from the offline backup and use a recovery run to apply the changes still contained in the online redo log files to these data files. This applies to both active and all inactive redo log files. Admittedly, it is very unlikely that you will find yourself in such a situation.

Nevertheless, you will recognize the serious disadvantage of backing up data in NoArchiveLog mode: Under no circumstances will you be able to recover all data. The database can only be recovered up to the time of the last backup – the changes cannot be recovered (with the exception of the improbable case mentioned above).

If the database is in ArchiveLog operating mode, online redo log files are copied into the archive directory when a log switch occurs. If these offline redo log files and the online redo log files (where the last changes were held before the database crashed) are fully available, you can restore all data.

You must first restore the incorrect data files from the offline data backup. If you restore individual files, this is called a partial restore; if you restore all files, this is a full restore. After a full restore from an offline backup, you will have a consistent database with which you can work. However, the changes that were made between the last backup and the crash will be missing in this case. You must therefore restore the offline redo log files (provided they are not still in the archive directory) and use them to recover the database. When you implement all changes into the database, including the changes that are still in the online redo log files, this is known as a complete recovery. If users, whether intentionally or not, have removed data records from tables, for example, you certainly do not also want to include these logged changes in the recovered database. You will finish your recovery run before the deletion change is imported and then perform an incomplete recovery.

You can see that all data can be restored for an offline data backup in ArchiveLog mode. The disadvantage is that you must shut down the database during the time of the backup, which means the SAP system will not be available to users.

10.3.2 Recovery from an Online Data Backup

To perform an online data backup, you must operate the database in ArchiveLog mode. The online data backup enables the database to continue operating during the backup. Users of the SAP system can therefore continue with their work. In addition, you can recover all data. Like the recovery of data from an offline data backup in ArchiveLog mode, all offline redo log files and online redo log files must be available for this without exception.

You must first restore the incorrect data files from the backup medium. Again, we differentiate between a partial and a full restore. Unlike the database restored from the offline data backup using a full restore, the database from the online data backup, which was restored using a full restore, is not consistent. You cannot open the database at this point and therefore cannot work with it because it is inconsistent (this relates to block splitting; see Section 10.2.3) This requires performing a recovery run to import all those redo log files that accrued during the database backup. If you do this, the database would be consistent, although the data that was added between the online backup and the crash would still always be missing. To retrieve this data, restore the remaining offline redo log files and import these together with the online redo log files using the recovery run mentioned above. This method also enables you to cancel the recovery run early; in other words, to perform an incomplete recovery.

Restoring data from an online data backup is more time-consuming. During the backup, significantly more redo log files are generated because, due to the before-images recorded for backups, the dataset is bigger than it would be for the normal recording of changes. The increased number of redo log files and their application in the recovery run prolongs the recovery of the Oracle database.

10.3.3 Error Scenario: Loss of a Normal Tablespace

In the text that follows, we will use an error scenario to introduce individual restore and recovery scenarios. These are scenarios that are normally used to recover a damaged database.

Let's look at Figure 10.11. The horizontal arrow indicates the time. Below this are the database objects, that is, the control files, offline and online redo log files, and data files. The numbers in the offline and online redo log files represent the LSN. As you already know, the changes from the redo log buffer together with the current SCN are stored in the redo log files when you execute a `COMMIT`. In the redo log, we therefore find a set of changes with SCNs that are all defined using a unique LSN. The other database objects are labelled using the SCN. For the sake of simplicity, these are identical for the represented data files. This is correct for a full online data backup. This must not be the case for an offline data backup. When the represented database crash occurs, it is also a simplification that all data files have the same SCN.

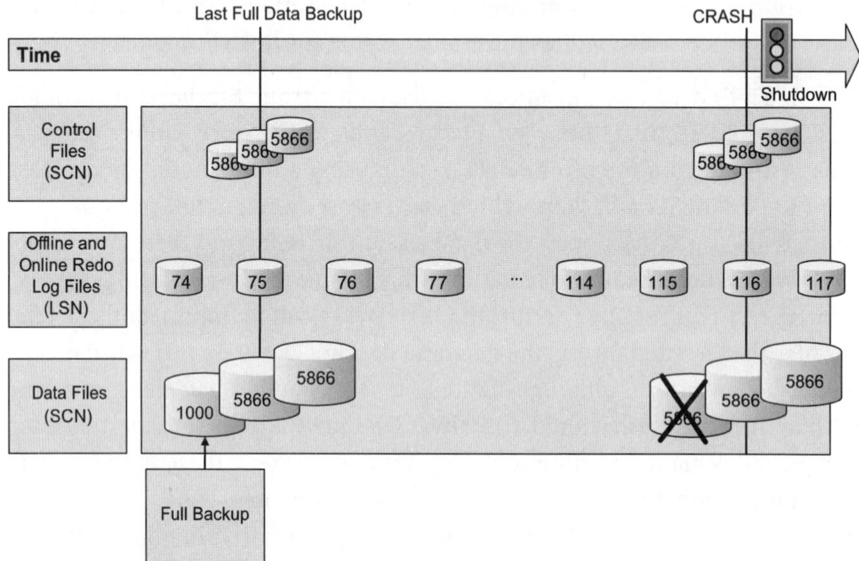

Figure 10.11 Data File of a Normal Tablespace Is Faulty

At the time of the last full data backup, the SCN of all database objects is 1,000. The redo log file that still belongs to the backup has an LSN of 75. When the database crashes, the SCN of the objects is 5,866. If we assume that each mapped data file represents exactly one tablespace, this crash means that we lose a complete tablespace with the data file. A hard-drive error, for example, is the reason we lose the data file. The database is shut down, and you cannot open it again because of the missing data file.

10.3.4 Partial Restore and Complete Recovery

Based on this situation, we will now look at individual scenarios. The first scenario is *partial restore and complete recovery*. Partial restore means that (as shown in Figure 10.12), only the faulty data file is restored from tape. After the restore, the SCN of the data file is 1,000 again. In this situation, you can run the database in the Mount status, and a recovery run is possible. A complete recovery is performed, which means that all redo log information, up to the last transaction before the crash, which was written into the redo log files by a COMMIT, is restored. All redo log files up to LSN 116 are applied. You can subsequently open the database again, and SAP users can continue working with the system as normal.

You can use this scenario if individual data files that were located on a separate hard disk, for example, have been lost and you want to recover the data up to the point when the crash occurred. No data is lost, because all transactions completed with COMMIT are recovered. This procedure does not enable a recovery at an earlier time (for example, LSN 100) because all other nonfaulty data files already contain changes that were saved in redo log 116.

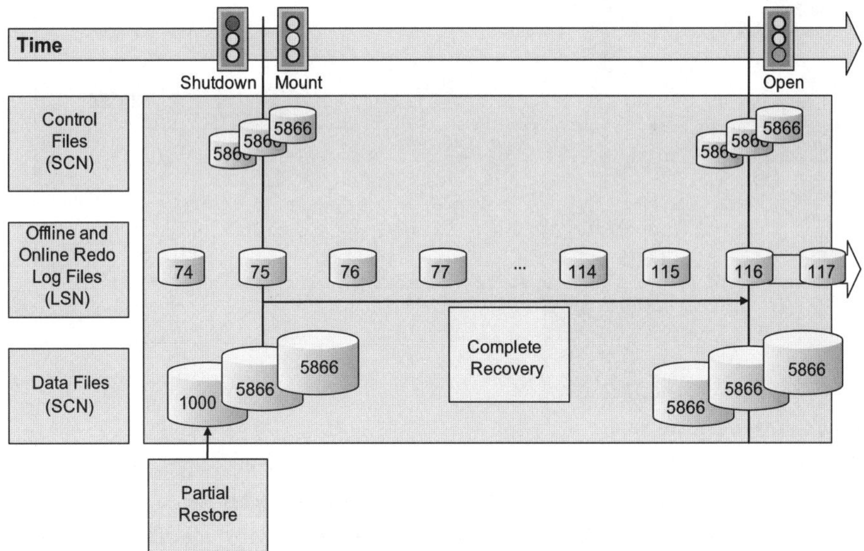

Figure 10.12 Partial Restore and Complete Recovery

10.3.5 Database Reset

You can use the *database reset* function to reset your database to the status it had after the last available offline or consistent online data backup.

You perform this reset in two circumstances:

- If all copies of the redo log files have been permanently lost but the backup of the data files (fortunately) still exists and works.
- If you performed a backup immediately before the database crashed. This can be the case during a migration, for example. This means you will not have to restore the database from a much older backup and apply numerous redo log files.

Figure 10.13 shows how the database reset works. An offline data backup is fully restored; in other words, a full restore takes place. After this full restore has been processed successfully, the database (which is already consistent) is opened easily. SAP users can work with the system again or the migration mentioned above can be continued.

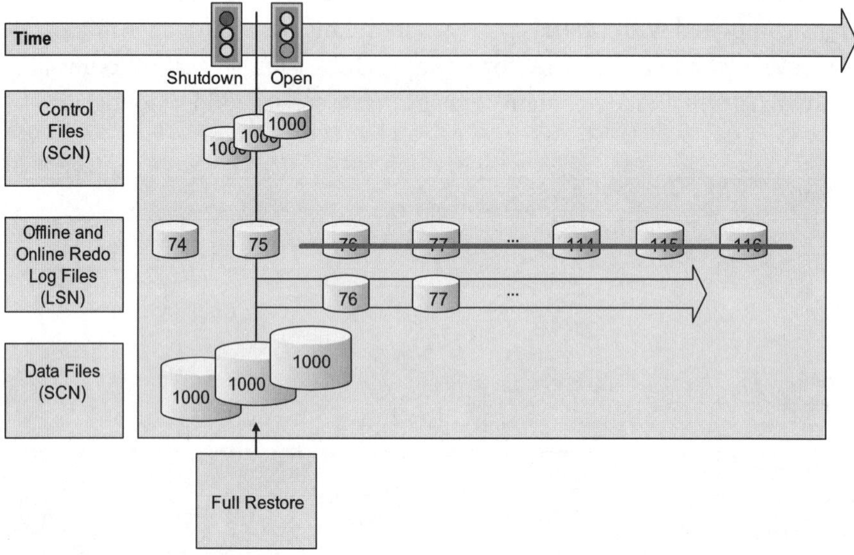

Figure 10.13 Database Reset

If the full restore is based on an online backup, the database is still not consistent after the restore. It is run in the Mount status, and all offline redo log files that are added during the online backup must be applied to the data files. This achieves the required consistency, and you can open the database.

The Oracle database then writes the redo log files again as normal, beginning with LSN 76. If there are still old redo log files with the same LSN in the archive directory, these are overwritten. Very high levels of data are lost in this recovery scenario.

10.3.6 Point-in-Time Recovery

The *point-in-time recovery* described here is performed for errors that were caused by users or by the software itself. For example, this could be an error where the contents of a database table have been deleted. Point-in-time means the database is restored up to a specific time or up to a particular redo log file. For a recovery due to a media error, it is, of course, possible that there is a certain "gap" in time up to the point when the hardware crashed.

Figure 10.14 shows a database point-in-time recovery. This scenario can also be referred to as a full restore and incomplete recovery. All database data files are first written back from the tape. It is important that the control files are not touched so that any structural changes in the database that have occurred since the last backup and the crash can be integrated once again. These changes are not held in the redo log files. After the restore has been completed, the database is run in the Mount status, and the offline redo log files are applied to the data files up to the specified LSN or up to the particular time. If this process is completed, you can restart the database using an Open Resetlog. The SQL command

```
alter database open resetlogs;
```

resets the online redo log files of the Oracle database, because these can no longer be used for an incomplete recovery. The LSN in this case is reset to 1. You can restore the data up to the point where the user or software error occurred. We can therefore say that a small amount of data is lost. We have to qualify this statement if data continued to be entered in other SAP applications not affected by the error.

In addition to the database point-in-time recovery, there is a *tablespace point-in-time recovery*. This type of recovery is mainly used for the Multiple Components in One Database systems (MCOD) already mentioned. You can use it to recover the tablespace of a single component, which cannot be used because of a user error or an upgrade, without affecting the other components contained in the same MCOD database. You first use a restore to recover all data files of the component tablespace. You then apply all offline redo log files up to the time you require, and you can greatly minimize the loss of data, similar to the database point-in-time recovery. In this case, you must open the database again using the `open resetlogs` option.

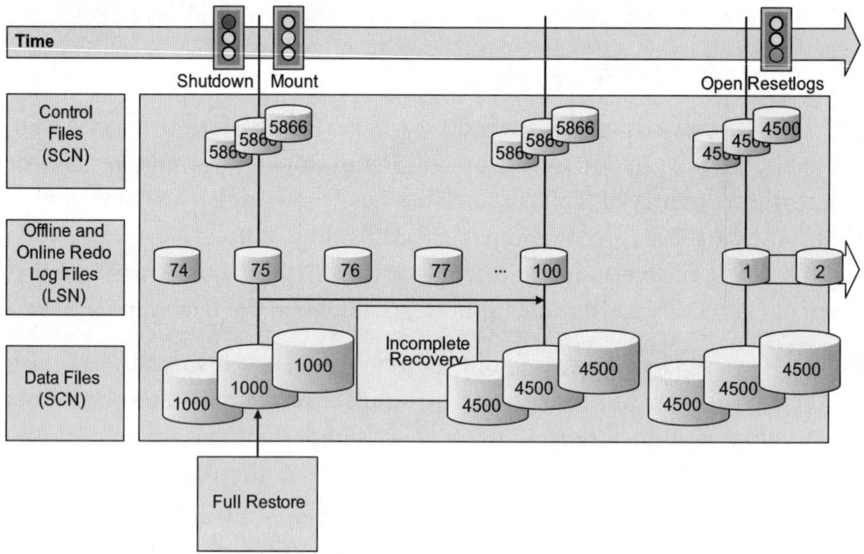

Figure 10.14 Database Point-in-Time Recovery

When recovering a component tablespace, note that you must take the complete database offline, and the (undamaged) MCOD systems are therefore also not available.

10.3.7 Full Restore and Complete Recovery

This scenario is very similar to the recovery we discussed in Section 10.3.4, *Partial Restore and Complete Recovery*. Figure 10.15 displays the process.

You use the full restore and complete recovery scenario if all data files were deleted or are faulty and you want to restore the database up to shortly before the crash.

You first restore all data files of the Oracle database from the backup again using a full restore. You should retain the control file again in case there are structural changes. After you have run the restore, you can mount the database and begin applying the redo log files. When you finish this, you can open the database, and the SAP users can work with it again. Like the partial restore and complete recovery, you can restore all data here that was written into the redo log files by `COMMIT` before the crash.

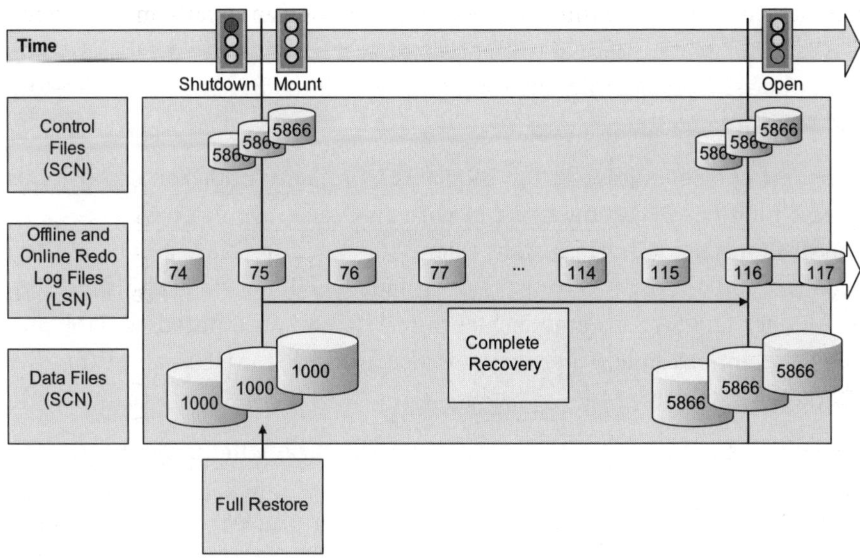

Figure 10.15 Full Restore and Complete Recovery

The difference in the partial restore is the runtime of the recovery, because you must restore all data files here. However, you can still always choose to perform a point-in-time recovery in this case.

10.4 BR*Tools for Backup, Restore, and Recovery

SAP provides tools that you can use to administer and protect the Oracle database. These are combined in a program package called BR*Tools. The topic of this section is the tools that you use to back up and restore data and that therefore help protect the Oracle database.

In Chapter 4, we discussed the program components that you use for database administration and the tools that provide the text menus or a graphical interface to call the BR*Tools. Chapter 8 deals with the BR*Tools in relation to monitoring SAP systems.

In addition to the BR*Tools, SAP also provides the SAPDBA tool for SAP Basis Release 6.20 or lower. The administration, backup, recovery, and reorganization functions mapped there for the Oracle database are also followed step-by-step in the BR*Tools. SAP therefore recommends that you use the BR*Tools. The last release developed is SAPDBA 6.20. You can use this release for SAP systems that are running with the Oracle database in Releases

8.1 and 9.2. You can also use this version for SAP systems with Basis Release 6.40 and for administering tablespaces or reorganizing the database easily. Nevertheless, compatibility problems occur with the BR*Tools in the restore and recovery areas.

The most current release of the BR*Tools is Version 7.00. You can use this release for all SAP systems that run with an Oracle 10g database or — after you have installed Oracle Instant Client 10g — an Oracle 9.2 database.[9] In addition, you can use BR*Tools 7.00 without functional restrictions for non-ABAP stack and SAP systems such as pure J2EE systems, portals, MDM, and Requisite, for example. This version is also available for UNIX and Windows operating systems.

The name itself is a little confusing: BR*Tools means the program package that contains programs such as BRBACKUP, BRARCHIVE, BRRESTORE, BRRECOVER, BRSPACE, BRCONNECT, and BRTOOLS. BRTOOLS is a program where the other parts of the BR*Tools are integrated. It provides menu options in a text-based interface that can be used to call the other BR programs. The BR*Tools are automatically installed in the */usr/sap/<SID>/SYS/exe/run* directory when the SAP system is installed.

The BR programs are classified into different categories. As you will see, some programs can be assigned to several classes, because they can be used in different ways:

- **Functional**
  These are the programs that work directly on the Oracle database files and objects such as BRBACKUP, BRARCHIVE, BRRESTORE, BRRECOVER, BRSPACE, and BRCONNECT, for example.
- **Help**
  This includes the BRTOOLS and BRCONNECT programs again. As mentioned above, BRTOOLS provides a menu and calls all other programs. However, the BRTOOLS and BRCONNECT programs can also be started internally by other BR*Tools, for example, BRBACKUP can start the BRCONNECT tool.
- **Batch**
  This category groups BR programs that can run without a menu display and on their own in a batch, such as BRBACKUP, BRARCHIVE, BRRESTORE, and BRCONNECT. They can also be called using BRTOOLS.

9 For more information about current versions of BR*Tools, see SAP Note 12741.

- **Interactive**
  All BR programs that offer a menu for interaction with the user are assigned to this category. These include BRTOOLS, BRRECOVER, and BRSPACE. In addition, BRRECOVER and BRSPACE are batch-enabled.

Figure 10.16 displays the BR*Tools that are provided for backing up and restoring data. These are BRBACKUP, BRARCHIVE, BRRECOVER, and BRRESTORE. BRBACKUP is used to back up the data, control, and online redo log files of the Oracle database. To back up the offline redo log files, the BRARCHIVE program is used. BRRESTORE is used to ensure that the database files are restored. BRRECOVER applies redo log files to the data files and recovers profile and log files. The BRARCHIVE and BRBACKUP tools create detailed and summary log files when you back up database objects. These are stored by default in the */oracle/<DBSID>/saparch* directory and saved to the selected backup medium at the end of the backup. The log information is used by the BRRESTORE and BRRECOVER recovery tools. We will look at the tools in more detail in the following sections.

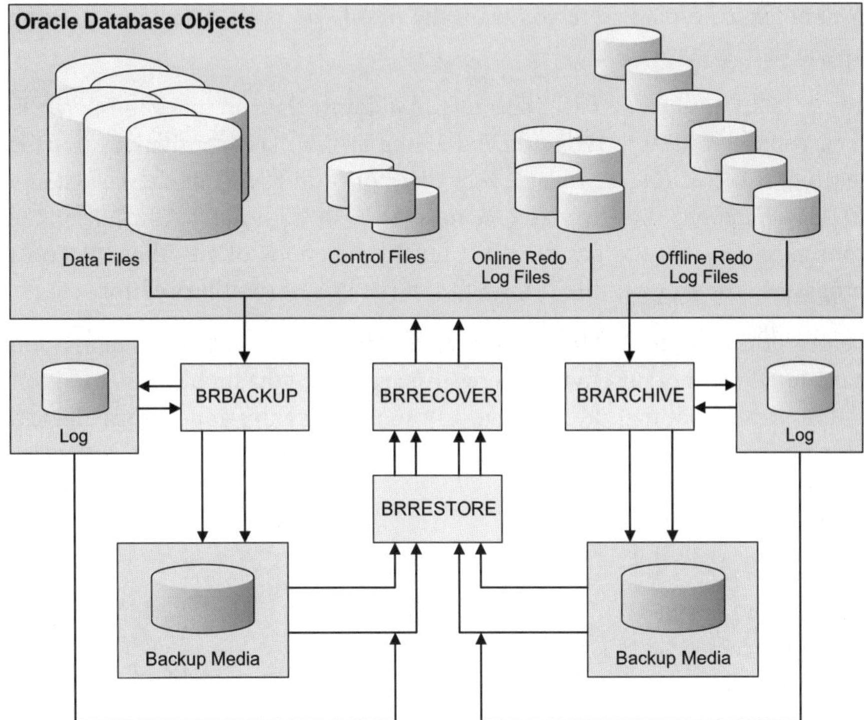

Figure 10.16 BR*Tools for Backup, Restore, and Recovery

10.4.1 Data Backup Using BRBACKUP

In addition to backing up the Oracle database objects already mentioned, you can use BRBACKUP to back up files and directories that do not belong to the Oracle database. You can also use this program to create a database copy.

BRBACKUP itself does not have a graphical interface and can be started directly at command level using the required options. Another option is to use the BRTOOLS program that can call the data backup with BRBACKUP using menu options. In addition to these textual alternatives, you can call the functions using BRGUI (see Chapter 4). You can also use the Computing Center Management System for Oracle directly from the SAP system under **Tools • CCMS • DB Administration • Planning Calendar • Local** (Transaction DB13).

BRBACKUP operating system commands are used to back up the relevant files. If you operate your Oracle database based on files, the cpio or dd programs are used to back up data to a backup tape, or cp or dd are used to back up to hard disks. If you operate the database on raw devices, the dd program is used to back up to tape or hard disk. You can use the backup_root_dir parameter to define where you want the files to be written to when backing up the data to hard disk.

To be able to use BRBACKUP, you must first adjust the configuration parameters. You can do this in the *init<DBSID>.sap* profile. This configuration file is located in the *<ORACLE_HOME>/dbs* directory (on UNIX) or the *<ORACLE_HOME>\database* directory (on Windows).[10] In addition to the BRBACKUP configuration, this file has an effect on the functions of all other BR*Tools programs. You can edit the configuration file in a normal text editor.

Before you use the BR*Tools, you should find out which parameters you have to adjust in your environment. In particular, you should pay attention to the parameters that do not have any standard values and require device-specific information or special platform-based commands.

The parameters and their values are stored in the *init<DBSID>.sap* file in the form:

```
<Parameter> = <Wert>
<Parameter> = (<Wert_1>,<Wert_2>)
```

10 <ORACLE_HOME> is an environment variable. It defines the */oracle/<DB SID>/<DB release>* directory.

Figure 10.17 shows a small extract of this configuration file. Individual values in a list of values are separated by a comma and enclosed in parentheses. If the parameter values need to be continued on the next line, you can simply continue on the next line. The line break is then treated as a blank space. If a parameter contains special characters such as a blank space or a $, you must place the values in quotation marks:

```
rewind = "mt -f $ rewind"
```

If you are unsure about the syntax or formatting, you can check and compare the initSID.sap sample file. You will find this file in the */usr/sap/ <SAP-SID>/SYS/exe/run/initSID.sap* directory of executable files of the SAP system.

```
# @(#) $Id: //bas/700_REL/src/ccm/rsbr/initHP.sap#5 $ SAP
########################################################################
#                                                                      #
# SAP backup sample profile.                                           #
# The parameter syntax is the same as for init.ora parameters.         #
# Enclose parameter values which consist of more than one symbol in    #
# double quotes.                                                       #
# After any symbol, parameter definition can be continued on the next  #
# line.                                                                #
# A parameter value list should be enclosed in parentheses, the list   #
# items should be delimited by commas.                                 #
# There can be any number of white spaces (blanks, tabs and new lines) #
# between symbols in parameter definition.                             #
#                                                                      #
########################################################################
# backup mode [all | all_data | full | incr | sap_dir | ora_dir
# | all_dir | <tablespace_name> | <file_id> | <file_id1>-<file_id2>
# | <generic_path> | (<object_list>)]
# default: all
backup_mode = all
# restore mode [all | all_data | full | incr | incr_only | incr_full
# | incr_all | <tablespace_name> | <file_id> | <file_id1>-<file_id2>
# | <generic_path> | (<object_list>) | partial | non_db
# redirection with '=' is not supported here - use option '-m' instead
# default: all
restore_mode = all
# backup type [offline | offline_force | offline_standby | offline_split
# | offline_mirror | offline_stop | online | online_cons | online_split
# | online_mirror
# default: offline
backup_type = online
# backup device type
```

Figure 10.17 Small Extract from init<DBSID>.sap

If you do not make any changes to the configuration file, the default values are used. The values stored by default in the configuration file perform a complete offline database backup with BRBACKUP, which includes data files, control files, and online redo log files, to a tape drive without compression.

Many parameters that exist in the init<DBSID>.sap configuration file can be overwritten using BRBACKUP command options (and the other BR*Tools). The values from the configuration file are used by default. Values in the BRBACKUP command options overwrite the values from the configuration. Note that the changes to the parameter values only become active when you call the required BR tool.

The default configuration for BR*Tools often requires the user to enter data. This does not make sense for backups that run overnight and for which administrators are not to be present. Functions that enable an unsupervised data backup to be executed are therefore implemented. You must ensure that enough backup devices and backup media are available for this purpose. BRBACKUP enables these devices to be backed up in parallel without intervention by the administrator. Another alternative is to use devices that automatically change the tape when it becomes full.

In addition to the database objects already mentioned, BRBACKUP (like BRARCHIVE also) backs up the following files to the backup medium:

- A copy of the init<DBSID>.ora and init<DBSID>.dba profile files
- A copy of the init<DBSID>.sap profile file
- The detailed log file for the current BRBACKUP run (or BRARCHIVE run)
- The summary log file for the BRBACKUP runs, back<DBSID>.log, or BRARCHIVE runs, arch<DBSID>.log
- The summary log file for BRSPACE runs, the log file that adds the changes to the database structure (struc<DBSID>.log), and the log file that logs the changes to the parameters (param<DBSID>.log)

The profile and log files are written to the backup medium each time BRBACKUP (or BRARCHIVE) runs a backup. If the database objects and log files of the BRBACKUP and BRARCHIVE runs are lost due to a hard-drive error, you can determine the content of the backup medium by recovering the backed-up log files.

Irrespective of which of the above-mentioned alternatives you use to start the data backup, the menu options in the BRTOOLS program are in all cases identical to the possible command options and the parameters in the configuration file. If you create regular backups from database objects that are always the same, you should adapt the configuration in the init<DBSID>.sap file, instead of using the command options. BRBACKUP uses functions for this that Oracle recommends for creating online and offline data backups.

You can use the `backup_mode` configuration parameter (command option `-m`) to control which objects you want to back up using `BRBACKUP`. The following list shows possible values. You can only specify a single value for a BRBACKUP run that is used to back up the corresponding objects. If you also want to include other objects in a backup, you always need to run another BRBACKUP with the required value:

- **all**
  Backs up the complete database.
- **all_data**
  Backs up all tablespaces that are not pure index tablespaces or empty.
- **full**
  Performs a full database backup (level 0) for incremental backups using RMAN.
- **incr**
  Starts an incremental backup (level -1) using RMAN.
- **<tablespace>**
  Backs up the data files of the specified tablespace.
- **<file_ID>**
  Backs up the file with the specified file ID. This is the Oracle file ID for data files. Control files are specified using the ID 0. Online redo log files are addressed using the ID 0<n>, where <n> is the redo log group. ID 00 backs up all existing online redo log files. Temporary files are identified by negative numbers.
- **<file_ID1>-<file_ID2>**
  Backs up the files in the interval.
- **<generic_path>**
  When you specify a full path name, you can back up all database objects, nondatabase files, or the specified directory. If you specify a generic path, all data files of the database, the names of which begin with the path name, are backed up. If you specify a directory, this is backed up with the content and name of the subdirectories. However, the directory structure and the content of the subdirectories are not copied.
- **sap_dir**
  Backs up all files of the SAP environment that are in the */sapmnt/<SID>*, */usr/sap/<SID>* and */usr/sap/trans* directories. You can only use this option if you back up to tape and do not perform a backup check.

- **ora_dir**
  Backs up all files of the Oracle environment, excluding database objects in the *<ORACLE_HOME>* directory. You can also only use this option if you back up to tape and do not perform a backup check.
- **all_dir**
  Combination of `sap_dir` and `ora_dir`.
- **<object list>**
  You can specify an object list. This list can contain the keyword "all." However, you should back up the database objects and nondatabase objects separately.

If you want to back up the SAP or Oracle environment on Unix, you should start `BRBACKUP` as the root user. Otherwise, you may not have the necessary authorizations to back up the directories. An advantage of performing the back up as the *root* user is that all settings for users and file authorizations are retained when you carry out a restore. However, the *root* user must have the environment of the ora<sid> user to be able to start `BRBACKUP`. Under no circumstances should backing up the SAP and Oracle environment using the `sap_dir`, `ora_dir`, or `all_dir` options replace the regular backup of the file system using operating system tools. As described, these options only back up parts of the SAP and Oracle installation, but not the remaining operating system files, user directories, and other files on your server.

The `all` and `full` options back up all database objects and, automatically, a control file. It is therefore not absolutely necessary to update the control file, especially using a single backup. One member of each redo log group is also saved when data is backed up offline. The file ID 00 can be used to back up online redo log files outside of offline data backups. However, this type of backup only makes sense if you perform partial offline backups.

In addition to the `backup_mode` parameter described above, other parameters and options are used to control the backups. We would like to introduce some of the important ones now. As already mentioned earlier, you should find out about the parameters before you use `BACKUP` for the first time:

- **backup_type/-t|-type**
  You use this parameter to define whether you want an online or offline data backup to be performed. Valid values are `online | online_cons | offline | offline_force | offline_standby | offline_stop | online_split | offline_split | online_mirror | offline_mirror`. The default value is `offline`. The vertical bar in the list indicates that, for a `BRBACKUP`

run, you can only use a single value from those specified. We also use this notation for the other lists.

An online data backup is performed using the online_cons option, and BRBACKUP is used to also include the redo log files added during the backup into the same backup. The backup of the redo log files in this case is not based on BRARCHIVE runs. The online option, in contrast, only backs up the data files and the control file. Both options correspond to the online data backup described in Section 10.2.3.

The offline option shuts down the database. However, this only happens when no more users are logged on to the SAP system. In contrast, offline_force shuts down the database for backing up, even if users are working in the system. These options correspond to the offline data backup described in Section 10.2.2. All other options are used for split mirror and standby databases (see Sections 10.7.3 and 10.7.4).

- **backup_dev_type/-d|-device**
  You use this parameter to specify which backup medium you want to use. The media available for selection are disk | tape | pipe | tape_auto | pipe_auto | tape_box | pipe_box | disk_copy | disk_standby | util_file | util_file_online | stage | stage_copy | stage_standby | rman_prep | rman_util | rman_disk | rman_stage. The default value here is tape.

  The disk option backs up the database objects to a hard disk. The directory is defined using the backup_root_dir parameter. You use the tape option to back up data to a tape. You can use the pipe value to trigger a backup to a remote system. All functions available for a local backup to a tape drive can also be used (on UNIX) with pipe.

  For a backup, the utile_file and utile_file_online values use a backup program that is integrated using the BACKINT interface. The second option always sets the tablespace in backup mode when it is being backed up, whereas the first option sets all tablespaces in backup mode. If you want to use utile_file_online, ask the manufacturer of your external backup program whether they support BACKINT. You can also set this value for offline data backups. The database is only shut down when you want the first file to be backed up using BACKINT and is restarted when the last file is written. Both options allow you to use other memory media (such as optical disks) that can be written using the provider's backup program and use BACKINT. The rman and stage options are used for backups with the Oracle Recovery Manager.

- **tape_copy_cmd**
  This parameter specifies which command you want to use to copy database files and nondatabase files from hard disk to tape drive. Possible values are cpio | dd | rman | rman_dd | cpio_gnu | dd_gnu | rman_gnu, and rman_dd_gnu. The default value is cpio.

  You use rman and rman_dd to perform the backup with the Oracle Recovery Manager. The data is copied from the SAP backup library, which is installed in the Recovery Manager, directly to tape. In the case of rman_dd, the data is transferred by the dd command.

- **compress/-k| compress**
  You use this parameter to specify whether and how you want the files to be compressed. The values no | yes | hardware | only are available, and no is the default value.

  The yes option uses software compression during the backup. If you use backup devices that support a hardware compression, set the hardware option. However, setting this option does not activate the hardware compression; rather, it is information for BRBACKUP. You must activate the compression directly on the device. Furthermore, the value supports backups to hard disks with file systems on Windows NT and AIX that are compressed using hardware.

  The only option calculates the compression rate for the software compression. However, a backup of the files is not started. You use the compress_dir = <dir>|(<dir_list>) parameter to specify the directories where file compression is performed. If you do not define this parameter, the directory that was defined using backup_root_dir is used by default.

- **exec_parallel/-e|-execute**
  You can use this option to process your backup in parallel. You set the maximum number of copy processes that can be run in parallel as value n. The default value is 0 and is automatically linked with the number of available backup devices. The n value should be smaller than or the same as the number of available tape drives. If you define an n value that is smaller than the number of connected tape drives, you actually use the number of drives specified by n. If the tape in one of the drives used in parallel needs to be changed, the system automatically changes to the next free tape drive, and the backup is continued there.

  If you back up to hard disks, the n value can be greater than the number of connected hard disks (but not greater than 255). The hard disks are then written simultaneously with several processes. If the n value is smaller than the defined hard disks, only n disks are used. If one of these hard disks used in parallel is full, the system automatically changes to the next one, and the backup continues.

- **volume_backup/-v|-volume**
  BRBACKUP uses this parameter to identify the volumes that must be used for backing up the database and nondatabase objects. A default value is not used. As values, you use names of volumes, with a maximum length of 10 characters. If you use more than one volume, you separate these with a comma and enclose all in parentheses. If you use the name SCRATCH, the automatic volume management is deactivated.

  When BRBACKUP is started, the automatic volume management checks all volumes in the sequence in which they were defined in the parameter. Volumes are written cyclically. However, only those volumes whose validity date has expired are used for a backup. These are the volumes that are consequently free. You configure the validity period using the expir_period parameter. Because volume management only uses free volumes, you must ensure that you provide a sufficient number of volumes. You must be able to perform all of the backups that accumulate up until the validity period of the volumes from the first backup expires. The greater the validity period you set, the more volumes you require.

  If you perform a data backup every day, require four tapes for this, and set the retention time to 14 days for each tape, you must reserve 56 tapes. A possible database growth is not taken into consideration in this case. If you allow for a buffer of 25%, you must reserve 70 tapes.

  However, if you use the SCRATCH value, any volumes whose validity period has expired are used. The name of the volume is retained during the backup.

- **util_par_file/mount_par_file/-r|-parfile**
  This option defines a BACKINT or Mount parameter file. There is no default value. If you use backup devices such as a jukebox or autoloader with BRBACKUP, you can use this option and an additional parameter file to also specify the configuration settings for the mount and dismount commands for BRBACKUP.

  When you use external backup programs through the BACKINT interface using the -d util_file | util_file_online options, you can use the parameter file to store additional information. This information is required to be able to complete the backups using the external backup programs. The content of the parameter file in this case depends exclusively on the external backup program. To store the correct parameter with the correct syntax in the parameter file, you should refer to the manual or contact the support group of the manufacturer of the external backup program.

There is a distinction between two parameters in the BR*Tools configuration file. `mount_par_file` is the parameter for BRBACKUP backups, and `util_par_file` is the parameter for backups using external backup programs.

When you specify the parameter file, you must enter the full path and the file name. If you do not specify the path, the system searches in the *<ORACLE_HOME>/dbs* directory (on UNIX) or the *<ORACLE_HOME>\database* directory (on Windows NT).

- **-c | -confirm**
  You use this command to perform backups in unattended mode. The default value is that confirmation messages appear during the backup process and the user must react to these messages. When you use this option, most messages that you have to confirm are suppressed. However, the following messages continue to appear:
  - Interactive password entry
  - Request for another volume (if several are simultaneously required)
  - Request for another tape (if cpio continuation tape is used)

  You can use the `–c force` option to avoid interruptions caused for the reasons mentioned above. Except for the password entry, all messages that you would have to confirm are suppressed.
- **-u | -user**
  You can use this command for the backup run to specify the user name and relevant password for accessing `BRBACKUP` on the Oracle database. The syntax is `-u | -user [<user> [/<password>]]`. The default value is `system/<default password>`.

  If you only specify the `–u` option, `BRBACKUP` will request the user and password. When you specify `–u <user>`, `BRBACKUP` only requests the password. This password is not displayed when you enter it.

  If you are working with an OPS$ user (such as the r ora<sid> Oracle operating system user on UNIX), for example, you use `brbackup -u /` as the call. In this case, `BRBACKUP` tries to log on to the database as the OPS$ user. The OPS$ user must be defined for this in the database. It must at least have SYSOPER rights and be assigned to the SAPDBA role. If you use RMAN, this user must also have SYSDBA rights. This method means you do not have to enter or store the password for the BRBACKUP call. For more information, see Chapter 4.

- **-w | -verify**
  After the backup of database objects has been performed, you can use this option to start a verify. The following additional values are allowed: use_dbv | only_dbv | only_conf. The default setting is that no verification is performed.

  You should start a verify to ensure that a performed backup can be read and is complete. If the backup has been performed, all saved objects are recovered from the volumes, decompressed, read by a check program, and compared to the original objects. The file contents are compared at binary level during an offline data backup, and the size of the saved files is determined and checked during an online data backup.

  The use_dbv value restores the backup in a temporary directory and executes a check of the Oracle block structures using the DBVERIFY tool.

  You can perform an internal check of the block structure of the database objects using the only_dbv value with the DBVERIFY tool and without a backup.

  BRBACKUP uses only_conf to call the external backup program to confirm that the performed backup is known. No data is verified.

  Note that a verification can almost double the time required for the backup, in particular, for verifying an offline data backup. For security reasons, you perform a verification at least once in the validity period of your complete backups, although once a week is better. This verify helps you find potential hardware problems and enables you to implement measures in time. If all error-free backups have been overwritten with the error, you only have a few options to restore an error-free database after you have eliminated the hardware problems.

- **-bd | -backup_delete**
  This command backs up the data backup that was saved to hard disk and then deletes this. Possible options include <log_name> and last, the latter being the standard value.

  The name of the log file of the hard-drive backup that is to be copied and deleted is specified using <log_name>. The last option automatically selects the last successful hard-drive backup, copies it to tape, and then deletes it. The backups are deleted automatically.

You have now learned about some of the most important parameters for BRBACKUP and their values in a very condensed way. You have seen that some parameters depend on, or even require, other parameters. If you have to learn more about the subject, we recommend that you refer to the SAP help. The BRBACKUP options and parameters and all other BR*Tools programs are described in great detail here. When using an external backup program, you should always consult the relevant manual provided by the manufacturer.

10.4.2 Backing Up Redo Log Files Using BRARCHIVE

The BRARCHIVE program enables you to back up and delete the offline redo log files that are written into the archive directory when you operate the Oracle database in ArchiveLog mode (see Section 10.1.2). This helps you prevent an archiver stuck (see Section 10.1.3). The backup of redo log files is very important because a media recovery of the database up to the last transaction made can only be performed when all accumulated redo log files are available without exception. Usually, BRARCHIVE backs up the offline redo log files to a tape. However, for certain purposes, the redo logs may also be backed up to local or remote hard disks.

BRBACKUP and BRARCHIVE have some characteristics in common. For example, before you use BRARCHIVE for the first time, you must adapt the init<DBSID>.sap configuration file from the *<ORACLE_HOME>/dbs* directory, which is also the case for BRBACKUP. In the previous section, we described an example of using this configuration file. By default, BRARCHIVE starts a backup of the archived offline redo log files to a tape with a storage capacity of 1.200 MB. The file compression is deactivated.

In addition to the offline redo log files, BRARCHIVE backs up (exactly like BRBACKUP) the files described below to the backup medium:

- A copy of the init<DBSID>.ora and init<DBSID>.dba profile files
- A copy of the init<DBSID>.sap profile file
- The detailed log file for the current BRARCHIVE run
- The summary log file for the BRARCHIVE runs
- The summary log file for BRSPACE runs, the log file that adds the changes to the database structure (struc<DBSID>.log), and the log file that logs the changes to the parameters (param<DBSID>.log)

Like BRBACKUP, the listed log files are saved to the backup medium for each backup run to ensure that you can restore the backed up log files and therefore determine the content of the backup medium if data is lost.

You can start a BRARCHIVE run regardless of the database status. You can easily back up offline redo log files from an Oracle database that has been shut down. In contrast to BRBACKUP, BRARCHIVE cannot continue writing the running backup to another backup medium when this becomes full. The backup terminates, and you must start another BRARCHIVE run on a different medium. Due to the current tape capacities, however, this is not an actual restriction.

In Section 10.1.3, *Archiver Stuck*, we described that you should back up the offline redo log files twice for security reasons. BRARCHIVE fulfils this requirement with different options or parameters that you can specify for a BRARCHIVE run. In the init<DBSID>.sap configuration file, you can set the behavior of BRARCHIVE using the archive_function parameter. The values save | second_copy | delete_saved | deleted_copied | save_delete | second_copy_delete | double_save | double_save_delete | copy_save | copy_delete_save are available for selection in this case. A leading minus sign is simply specified before these values for the command options, or their short form –s | -sc | -ds | -dc | -sd | -scd | -ss | -ssd | -cs | -cds is used. The default value is save.

Table 10.2 shows the individual options in detail.

Parameter values for archive_function	Description
save, -s	Backs up offline redo log files.
second_copy, -sc	Creates a second copy of the offline redo log files that were already backed up a first time.
delete_saved, -ds	Deletes the offline redo log files that were backed up once.
delete_copied, -dc	Deletes the offline redo log files that were already backed up a second time.
save_delete, -sd	Backs up offline redo log files and then deletes them.
second_copy_delete, -scd	Creates a second copy of the offline redo log files that were already backed up once and then deletes them.
double_save, -ss	Backs up the offline redo log files to two backup media in parallel, that is, the second copy is created immediately.

Table 10.2 Values Available for the archive_function Parameter and Their Descriptions

Parameter values for archive_function	Description
`double_save_delete, -ssd`	Similar function to `double_save`, but the files are subsequently deleted.
`copy_save, -cs`	Creates a second copy of the offline redo log files that were already backed up and then backs up the offline redo log files that were generated in the meantime.
`copy_delete_save, -cds`	Works like `copy_save`, but the offline redo log files that were backed up a second time are subsequently deleted.

Table 10.2 Values Available for the archive_function Parameter and Their Descriptions (Cont.)

Depending on the number of connected tape drives, the specification of the duplicate backup of offline redo log files can be fulfilled using the combination of parameters and the number of `BRARCHIVE` runs.

If you have only connected a single tape drive, you can use the `copy_save` or `copy_delete_save` option. You therefore ensure that `BRARCHIVE` creates a second copy of the offline redo log files, deletes these if necessary, and subsequently backs up the files that were meanwhile regenerated by the Oracle database. A disadvantage of this variant is that you may write the first and second backup of the redo logs to the same tape. If this tape is faulty, all files are lost. Calling `BRARCHIVE` twice could be the solution in this case. Initially, you back up the redo logs to a tape for the first time using the `save` option. In the second run, you use the `second_copy` or `second_copy_delete` option and use a different tape for the backup. The second variant requires changing the tape in the drive. If a high number of redo log files arises and tapes need to be changed manually, this variant is no longer feasible. Instead of manually changing the tapes, it then makes sense to use an autoloader.

We recommend the parallel backing up of the offline redo log files, which, in contrast to the serial backup described above, requires two tape drives. You can use the `double_save` and `double_save_delete` options for this purpose. The advantage of this approach is that the redo log files are archived on two different tapes in one `BRARCHIVE` run.

For all variants that can be set using the `archive_function` parameter, `BRARCHIVE` only backs up exactly as many files as those backed up using the `-n` parameter. The default value is set at 10,000. Practically all files contained in the archive directory are backed up.

Another important parameter is the -f option with the optional values <number> | stop | suspend | resume. BRARCHIVE writes a backup medium continually by waiting for the next offline redo log file to be backed up. BRARCHIVE writes all redo logs contained in the archive directory to tape by default. After it has done this, the program ends. If you want to back up the next files from the directory, another run is required. You can use this option to ensure that the archive directory does not become full. As soon as Oracle writes an offline redo log file, BRARCHIVE uses the -f option to back this up to the backup medium. This process lasts until the medium is full or a previously specified number of files have been backed up.

The individual parameter values are each described as follows:

- **<number>**
  You use this value to arrange BRARCHIVE, rather than back up each redo log file individually to tape, to wait until a specific number <number> of redo log files has been accumulated. These files are then backed up as a group. If you use external backup programs through the BACKINT interface, you should group the redo log files. Each Oracle archiving process activates this interface, repositions the tape in the drive, and writes a complete backup record. If the number of backup records is reduced by grouping offline redo log files, the overall backup can be speeded up.

  If the <number> number of files was generated, BRARCHIVE writes this to tape. This process is repeated until the process is stopped by the stop option or until the previously defined maximum number of files to be backed up has been reached.

- **stop**
  You can use this option to stop a BRARCHIVE run that was started with the -f option.

- **suspend**
  This value suspends a BRARCHIVE run that was started with the -f option. This can be useful, for example, if an offline data backup is created from the database.

- **resume**
  You can use this value to resume a BRARCHIVE run that was stopped with the suspend option, for example, if you start the database again after the offline data backup.

The status of the offline redo log files is recorded in the arch<DBSID>.log log contained by default in the *<ORACLE_HOME>/saparch* directory. To ensure that the redo logs are archived effortlessly, this log must exist in a legible format for BRARCHIVE. Therefore, under no circumstances should you delete or manually change this file.

Each offline redo log file in this log contains an entry that has a different syntax based on the backup medium used and on the use of an external backup program. Figure 10.18 and Figure 10.19 show a small extract from the archM54.log summary log file. The following list provides an overview of the possible entries in this log file:

- **#ARCHIVE**
  Details about the offline redo log file saved on a tape drive. The details consist of the LSN, the path and file name, time of creation, file size, start SCN, and thread number.
- **#SAVED**
  Details about the first backup of this log file that is based on the backup medium and is composed of:
  - Backup to tape drive: the action ID with encoded time stamp, function ID (extension of log name), name of tape and position of file on the tape, time stamp when the backup process was ended, compression rate, and size of compressed file (if the compression was activated)
  - Backup using an external backup program: the action ID, function ID, backup ID that was returned by the external program, and time stamp when the backup process was ended
- **#COPIED**
  Information about the second backup of this redo log file, where the details are the same as those in the #SAVED section.
- **#DELETED**
  Data about deleting this redo log file from the archive directory that consists of the action ID, the function ID, and a deletion time stamp.
- **#***
  Details about the status of the BRARCHIVE run that consist of the Oracle SID, the device type, action ID, function ID, time stamps that specify the start and end of the backup, a return code, the compression rate, an internal indicator for the BRARCHIVE command options and, finally, the BRARCHIVE version.
- **#DISK/#STAGE**
  Details about the offline redo log file saved on a local or remote disk (identical to those under #ARCHIVE).

- **#DISKSAV/#STAGESAV**
  Information about backing up this redo log file, which includes the action ID, function ID, path and file name, time stamp, compression rate, and size of the compressed file (if active).
- **#DISKDEL / #STAGEDEL**
  Information about deleting this log file from the archive directory, such as the action ID, function ID, and time stamp of the deletion.
- **#DELDISK**
  Details such as the action ID, function ID, and time stamp of this redo log file if it was deleted from the backup disk.
- **#APPLIED**
  Information about this offline redo log file if this was applied on a standby database.

The action ID and function ID combined form the name of the detailed log files that can be found in the same directory as the arch<DBSID>.log summary file.

We now return to Figures 10.18 and 10.19, already mentioned.

```
#ARCHIVE.. 12712  /oracle/M54/oraarch/M54archl_12712.dbf  2006-11-26 02.05.39  52422656        43650571  1
#SAVED.... aduahmpx sve  *20061126.0002.00 2006-11-26 03.07.01 ........... ............
#COPIED... aduahnod cpd  *20061126.0015.00 2006-11-26 03.15.56 ........... ............
#DELETED.. aduahnod cpd  2006-11-26 03.15.56
#
#* M54  util_file  aduahmpx sve  2006-11-26 03.00.05  2006-11-26 03.07.26  0 ...........     12666    12712         0
      0  ------- 6.40 (36)
#
#* M54  util_file  aduahnod cpd  2006-11-26 03.10.35  2006-11-26 03.16.35  0 ...........         0        0     12666
  12712  ------- 6.40 (36)
#
#ARCHIVE.. 12713  /oracle/M54/oraarch/M54archl_12713.dbf  2006-11-26 05.00.28  52427776        43650997  1
#SAVED.... aduajnje sve  *20061126.0037.00 2006-11-26 12.57.18 ........... ............
#COPIED... ........ ...  ................. .......... ........ ........... ............
#DELETED.. ........ ...  .......... ........
#
#ARCHIVE.. 12714  /oracle/M54/oraarch/M54archl_12714.dbf  2006-11-26 10.30.28  52427776        43665480  1
#SAVED.... aduajnje sve  *20061126.0037.00 2006-11-26 12.57.15 ........... ............
#COPIED... ........ ...  ................. .......... ........ ........... ............
#DELETED.. ........ ...  .......... ........
#
#ARCHIVE.. 12715  /oracle/M54/oraarch/M54archl_12715.dbf  2006-11-26 12.36.05  15121408        43691205  1
#SAVED.... aduajnje sve  *20061126.0037.00 2006-11-26 12.57.18 ........... ............
#COPIED... ........ ...  ................. .......... ........ ........... ............
#DELETED.. ........ ...  .......... ........
#
#* M54  util_file  aduajnje sve  2006-11-26 12.54.18  2006-11-26 12.57.24  0 ...........     12713    12715         0
      0  ------- 6.40 (36)
#
```

Figure 10.18 Extract 1 from the arch<DBSID>.log Log

The offline redo log files were backed up to a tape drive using an external backup program. Figure 10.18 shows that the redo log file with LSN 12712 generated on 16.11.2006 at 02:05 hours was initially backed up with the -`save` option for the first time on 26.11.2006 at 03:07 hours. The second backup and the deletion from the archive directory occurred with the

-second_copy_delete option in a run at 03:16 hours. Entries about both BRARCHIVE runs then follow. For example, you can see that the backups required approximately 7 minutes, and all redo log files were backed up with LSN 12666 up to 12712. Below this, in the section, you can see that a backup run has written exactly three redo log files (12713, 12714, and 12715) within three minutes in one of the first backups to tape.

Figure 10.19 shows the status of the log file after the second backup of the three redo log files and their deletion from the archiver directory. You can see that all backup and deletion processes are meticulously recorded in this file. This figure displays which redo log files can be found in which backup run and on which backup medium these files were backed up.

```
#ARCHIVE.. 12712  /oracle/M54/oraarch/M54archl_12712.dbf  2006-11-26 02.05.39  52422656          43650571  1
#SAVED.... aduahmpx sve  *20061126.0002.00 2006-11-26 03.07.01 .......... ...........
#COPIED... aduahnod cpd  *20061126.0015.00 2006-11-26 03.15.56 .......... ...........
#DELETED.. aduahnod cpd  2006-11-26 03.15.56
#
#* M54  util_file  aduahmpx sve  2006-11-26 03.00.05  2006-11-26 03.07.26  0  ..........    12666    12712        0
       0  ------- 6.40 (36)
#
#* M54  util_file  aduahnod cpd  2006-11-26 03.10.35  2006-11-26 03.16.35  0  ..........        0        0    12666
   12712  ------- 6.40 (36)
#
#ARCHIVE.. 12713  /oracle/M54/oraarch/M54archl_12713.dbf  2006-11-26 05.00.28  52427776          43650997  1
#SAVED.... aduajnje sve  *20061126.0037.00 2006-11-26 12.57.18 .......... ...........
#COPIED... aduajnyw cpd  *20061126.0038.00 2006-11-26 13.04.12 .......... ...........
#DELETED.. aduajnyw cpd  2006-11-26 13.04.12
#
#ARCHIVE.. 12714  /oracle/M54/oraarch/M54archl_12714.dbf  2006-11-26 10.30.28  52427776          43665480  1
#SAVED.... aduajnje sve  *20061126.0037.00 2006-11-26 12.57.15 .......... ...........
#COPIED... aduajnyw cpd  *20061126.0038.00 2006-11-26 13.04.08 .......... ...........
#DELETED.. aduajnyw cpd  2006-11-26 13.04.08
#
#ARCHIVE.. 12715  /oracle/M54/oraarch/M54archl_12715.dbf  2006-11-26 12.36.05  15121408          43691205  1
#SAVED.... aduajnje sve  *20061126.0037.00 2006-11-26 12.57.18 .......... ...........
#COPIED... aduajnyw cpd  *20061126.0038.00 2006-11-26 13.04.13 .......... ...........
#DELETED.. aduajnyw cpd  2006-11-26 13.04.13
#
#* M54  util_file  aduajnje sve  2006-11-26 12.54.18  2006-11-26 12.57.24  0  ..........    12713    12715        0
       0  ------- 6.40 (36)
#
#* M54  util_file  aduajnyw cpd  2006-11-26 13.01.06  2006-11-26 13.04.18  0  ..........        0        0    12713
   12715  ------- 6.40 (36)
```

Figure 10.19 Extract 2 from the arch<DBSID>.log Log

The detailed log files mentioned above, which follow the a<encoded time stamp>.<ext> naming convention, contain information about actions that were performed during the backup process. The relevant parameters from the init<DBSID>.sap file that were used during the BRARCHIVE run are logged. In addition, the whole process of writing the offline redo log file and the log files that are part of the run are recorded. If a backup has failed, you can find valuable information here when searching for the errors. The <ext> ending indicates the different options that were used to start BRARCHIVE.

You can also set the hardware compression for the BRARCHIVE backups using the -k / -compress option. The no | yes | hardware | only values presented in the previous section are available. However, the only option is not of practical importance, because the calculated compression rates are not saved in the database. You can use the data to check the compression rates of the offline redo log files. Consequently, the compression rates of a previous run are not used for the backup of the redo log files currently pending. A default value of 1 is assumed as the rate. With a tape that is 200 GB in size, up to 4,096 redo log files can be saved for a size of 50 MB each. However, if a larger number of files was written to tape due to the compression set, you can adjust the `tape_size` parameter to meet your requirements. Experience shows that hardware compression can reduce the size of the offline redo log files by up to a third. You could therefore increase the `tape_size` value by 50%, thus to 300 GB in our example. This value then forms the compression rate. You will consequently be able to save more files to tape. In the example here, this is 2,048 logs. If you successively adjust this value, you can optimize the use of your tapes for the backups of the offline redo logs.

A number of other options and parameters are available in addition to the ones described in somewhat more detail above. These are often identical to those of `BRBACKUP` and only differ minimally in terms of individual values. You do not have to maintain parameters that are identical and that you have already maintained for `BRBACKUP` or other BR*Tools again. These are jointly used by all BR*Tools. The following list names the most important options:

- **-a | -archive**
  Copies offline redo log files to a tape that were copied earlier to disk during a backup.
- **-b | -backup [<brb_options>]**
  Starts `BRBACKUP` after the `BRARCHIVE` run with the options that can be specified in `<brb_options>`. The `BRARCHIVE` program assumes the control and volume management. The main advantage is that you only have to start or schedule one program, and you can use the tapes to their optimum capacity (not automatically like when the BACKINT interface is used). If you want `BRARCHIVE` to be started under the control of `BRBACKUP`, you must specify the `-a | -archive` option for the `BRBACKUP` run. SAP recommends this variant.
- -c **| -confirm**
  Performs the backup in unattended mode (see Section 10.4.1, *Data Backup Using BRBACKUP*).
- **-d | -device**
  Specifies on which backup medium you want the backup to be run (see Section 10.4.1). The `util_file_online` value is not supported for `BRARCHIVE`. If you specify this value, `util_file` is automatically used.

- **-m | -modify**
  This option is used for BRARCHIVE to apply offline redo log files to a standby database (see Section 10.7.3, *Standby Databases*). A <delay> value in this case can be specified in minutes, which means the recovery on the standby database can be delayed after the redo log file is generated on the live database. A delay is not set by default.

- **-r | -parfile**
  You use this value to define a BACKINT or Mount parameter file (see Section 10.4.1).

- **-u | -user**
  Specifies the user name and password for accessing the Oracle database (see Section 10.4.1).

- **volume_archive / -v | -volume**
  Specifies all volumes that must use BRARCHIVE to back up the offline redo log files. The functionality and syntax for this parameter or option are identical to BRBACKUP. If you use the –b option for a BRARCHIVE run, the data of the subsequent BRBACKUP run is written to tapes that were defined in volume_archive.

- **-w | -verify**
  Verifies the backed-up redo log files. The only_conf value is also available. No checks are performed by default. You can use this option to ensure that a backup was written legibly and completely. After the backup has been completed, the offline redo log files are restored, decompressed (provided the compression is activated), read by a check program, and compared with the originals.

  If you use the -s, -sc, -ss, or -cs options, the comparison is performed at binary level. When you use -sd, -scd, -ssd, or -cds, the size of the backed-up files are determined and checked.

  You use the only_conf value to call the external backup program, like BRBACKUP, to confirm that the backup is known. Data is not verified.

We conclude this section with a note about a potential problem with BRARCHIVE that can lead to an archiver stuck in some circumstances.

Up to SAP Basis Release 6.10, the logs that BRARCHIVE generates and the offline redo log files were saved in the same directory, namely */oracle/<DBSID>/saparch*. If an archiver stuck occurs, the BRARCHIVE program may not start, even though it should remain executable in such a situation.

As a precautionary measure, two changes to the configurations are proposed:

- The solution recommended by SAP and implemented by default as of Basis Release 6.20 is to change the archiver directory of Oracle by changing the `log_archive_dest von /oracle/<DBSID>/saparch` parameter in the init<DBSID>.ora file to a different directory (such as */oracle/<DBSID>/oraarch*, for example). You should refer to the measures described for this in Section 10.1.3, such as a separate physical medium and RAID protection when creating the directory.
- The second solution is to change the log directory for `BRARCHIVE`. You can do this by setting the `SAPARCH` environment variables. The offline redo log files continue to be written into the directory that is defined using the `log_archive_dest` parameter, whereas the log files are written into a different directory (for example, */oracle/<DBSID>/sapbackup*). However, to ensure that the logs saved in this way can be viewed in the SAP system, you must set the `SAPARCH` variable both in the environment for the Oracle operating system user and for the SAP operating system user. In the Oracle system, these are ora<sid> for UNIX and <SID>ADM for Windows and in the SAP system, they are <sid>adm for UNIX and SAPService<SID> for Windows. This solution is only useful if the archive directory is on a different physical medium or mount point than the set log directory. Otherwise, there would be just as little chance of `BRRACHIVE` starting if an archiver stuck occurs as there would be in the outbound case.

In Section 10.1.3, we mentioned temporarily changing the directory as the third variant of the solution for the archiver stuck error. After you empty the original directory, it is important to copy the offline redo log files from the temporary directory into the original directory to ensure that all redo log files are backed up properly. This is easier with `BRARCHIVE` as of Version 7.00 Patch Level 17. On the basis of the V$ARCHIVED_LOG view, `BRARCHIVE` is then able to find the offline redo log files in different directories, in particular, those that were defined using the `log_archive_dest_n` and `log_archive_dest_state_n` parameters. All older versions of `BRARCHIVE` only ever back up the redo log files from the archiver directory currently specified, which is why gaps can occur, which you can only eliminate using a manual copy process. Even when using `BRARCHIVE` 7.00 (17), ensure that the redo log files are backed up correctly in the temporary archiver directory before this directory is deleted again.

10.4.3 Restoring Using BRRESTORE

You can use the BRRESTORE SAP tool to restore the database objects backed up using BRBACKUP and BRARCHIVE. In addition to restoring the complete database, you can select the individual files or tablespaces and the nondatabase files and directories for a BRRESTORE run.

In this case, you should know that BRRESTORE only ever restores the objects of a specific backup run selected by you. The database is not recovered. You must start recovery runs after a restore run. You can do this either using the BRRECOVER tool, which we will deal with in the next section, or manually using the Oracle sqlplus tool.

As is already the case with the other two BR*Tools tools that we introduced here, you must maintain some parameters for BRRESTORE in the *init<DBSID>.sap* configuration file. These are:

- backup_dev_type | -d
- compress | -c
- util_par_file / mount_par_file / -r|-parfile
- restore_mode | -m

Except for the last parameter, we have already described all of these parameters and their mandatory or optional values in detail in Section 10.4.1, where we discussed the BRBACKUP tool. You only maintain the parameters once in the file for all BR*Tools that use these parameters. In reverse, this means that, if you have already maintained these parameters for BRBACKUP or BRARCHIVE, you do not need to do this again for BRRESTORE.

The restore_mode parameter is functionally identical to backup_mode for BRBACKUP and BRARCHIVE. It indicates which restore activity must be performed. The possible characteristics are similar to those of BRBACKUP, but there are some differences that we will highlight. We already explained the all | all_data | full | incr | <file_ID> | <file_ID1>-<file_ID2> | <object_list> options in relation to backup_mode. These options restore the specified objects when you use BRRESTORE.

The incr | incr_only | incr_full | incr_all | <tablespace> | partial, and nondb options are also available. The first four are used in conjunction with RMAN and incremental backups. incr_only therefore restores all changes to the files that were available in the last successful and full data backup. In contrast, incr_full restores the files that were added since the last full backup. In addition to an incremental backup (restore with incr),

incr_all restores all redo log files, the control file, and the nondatabase files and directories if those exist in the backup.

If you specify the name of a <tablespace> tablespace, its data files are restored again by BRRESTORE. This option can be useful if you need to restore a complete tablespace or for components of an MCOD database. The partial parameter restores all files, without having to specify them, that were saved in a partial backup. Last, you can use non_db to write back all nondatabase files from the backup medium without explicitly specifying the objects.

Other options are available for BRRESTORE that you can specify when you call the command. We will describe these briefly, as follows:

- **-a | -archive | -a1 | -archive1**
  BRRESTORE uses this option to restore offline redo log files of the first copy. The default value setting is such that no redo logs are restored. When you specify this option, BRRESTORE searches the BRARCHIVE summary logs to find out which medium contains the required redo log files as the first copy. The <DBSID>, <log_no>, <log_no1>-<log_no2>, <rest_dest>, and <log_no_list> values are optionally available. Here, <DBSID> specifies the database instance, which is only used, however, if you use the Oracle Parallel Server. <log_no> is used to specify an LSN for an offline redo log file. You use <log_n01>-<log_n02> to specify an interval of redo log files. You can also use <log_list> to indicate different LSNs. You must separate the individual numbers with a comma in this case. You use <rest_dest> to identify the directory where you want the redo logs to be restored. If you do not specify this option, all files end up in the default archive directory.
- **-a2 | -archive2**
  Restores the offline redo log files from the second copy. The default value, function, and option available are identical to -a.
- **-b | -backup | -b1 | -backup1**
  You use this to restore all data files that were backed up using BRBACKUP. The last successfully run backup is set as the default value. With this option, you must either specify the name of a detailed b<encoded time stamp>.<ext> log file of a BRBACKUP backup or last is used, which, as described above for the default value, restores the data backup.
- **-b2 | -backup2**
  Data files are restored using the BACKINT interface and the connected external backup program. You must either specify <util_backup_id>,

which indicates the backup ID of a backup of the external backup program, or #NULL, which restores from the last successful backup run using BACKINT.

- **-c | -confirm**
  This option performs an unattended restore by suppressing all messages that appear if a backup medium has to be changed (for example, a tape). The additional force option suppresses all other messages that might appear. For example, this is useful if database copies are regularly created by a live system to have an adequate test system available.
- **-e | -execute**
  You can use this option to perform a parallel restore. BRRESTORE uses a maximum of just as many copy processes to restore the data as were used for the backup. The n value to be specified can only reduce the number of processes, not increase them.
- **-k | -compress**
  If the value for decompressing the data to be restored does not match that of the backup when you start BRRESTORE, a warning message is issued. The data that was saved with software compression is decompressed with BRRESTORE in each case. If you did not store the software compression in the configuration file with compress -= yes, start BRRESTORE with -kyes. The restore handles the hardware option exactly like the no option.
- **-n | -number**
  This option enables you to restore a file directly from a tape drive, without having to specify a backup log. <file_pos> | init_ora | spfile | init_sap | space_log | det_log | sum_log | init_all | all_log | control_file are available as mandatory values.
- **-n2 | -number2**
  A data backup on hard disk under <back_file> is restored into the directory specified using <rest_dest>.
- **-q | -query**
  You can use this option to determine which volumes have to be inserted and which additional resources BRRESTORE requires. A restore is not started. With –q check, you can check that an already mounted tape in the tape drive is correct for the pending run.
- **-u | -user**
  You can specify the user name and password for accessing the Oracle database (see also Section 10.4.1).

- **-w | -verify**
  Without another option being indicated, BRRESTORE tests the legibility of the data from the backup medium and saves this, although not to the hard disk. If you use the use_dbv option, the files in the directory that was specified using the compress_dir parameter are restored, checked by DBVERIFY, and then deleted. A normal restore is not performed in any of the two cases. You can also specify the only_conf option. The external backup program is called again here to confirm that the backup is known. No data is verified.

You can only set one option from the -a, -a2, -b, -b2 or -n, -n2 options presented above. If you do not specify any of these options, the -b last default applies, that is, the data files from the last successful backup are restored. However, you can start BRRESTORE with the -a option parallel to a BRRESTORE -b or -n. Offline redo log files and data files or log files will then be restored in parallel in two runs.

Exactly like BRBACKUP and BRARCHIVE, BRRESTORE supports restoring database objects in parallel. If you want to restore offline redo log files in parallel, these must be on several volumes. Several backup devices must be available, and the number of parallel processes that are specified when you start BRRESTORE must match these.

When you start a run to restore data, and the SAPDATA directories under */oracle/<DBSID>* have not yet been created, this is done automatically by the BRRESTORE run. You specify the restore of a complete database using the –m full or restore_mode=full option. If you use –m all, all tablespaces, but not the control file and online redo log files, are restored. However, you can combine this option with an object list for nondatabase files or directories, for example. Nevertheless, as already described, you should not back up database objects and nondatabase files in a BRBACKUP run. In this respect, these are then restored separately from each other. If online redo log files are restored, the mirroring of the files is set automatically.

BRRESTORE writes log files about all of the activities performed. As already applied with BRARCHIVE and BRBACKUP, the log files here are divided up into a detailed file and a summary file.

The detailed logs are known by the syntax r<encoded time stamp>.<ext>. The <ext> ending can adopt the values *rsb* (for a restore from a BRBACKUP run), *rsa* (restore from a BRARCHIVE run), *rsf* (for a restore of files) and *qur* (if the –q option was used). The parameters of the init<DBSID>.sap configuration file and the restore process are recorded in the detailed log files in this case. Depending on the database object or nondatabase file restored, you will find an entry that begins with a #FILE, #NDBF, #DIR, #ARCHIVE, and #RESTORED field and is followed by additional information about the path, file name, tape name, and backup ID (if the objects were restored using an external backup program).

Also provided is the summary log file called rest <DBSID>.log, which, like the detailed files, you will find in the */oracle/<DBSID>/saparch* directory. The summary log file contains information about each BRRESTORE run including the following:

- Action ID (encoded time stamp of the name of the detailed log file of the run)
- Function ID (file extension of the detailed log file)
- Time stamp of the start of the restore
- Time stamp of the end of the restore
- Return code
- Absolute number of file restored
- Number of database objects restored
- Number of nondatabase objects restored
- Type of restore and device used

We have now handled all of the important points for restoring data using BRRESTORE. Remember that after you restore the Oracle database with BRRESTORE, this database is only consistent and can only be used from a full offline data backup. All other BRRESTORE runs require a recovery run that you can perform using the BRRECOVER tool, for example. We deal with this in the next section.

10.4.4 Recovering the Database Using BRRECOVER

In categorizing the individual tools at the beginning of this section, we established that BRRECOVER provides a menu for interaction with the user but is not batch-enabled. However, all previously presented tools from BR*Tools are batch-enabled and do not directly provide a menu for interaction.

You can use the BRRECOVER tool to perform a recovery of an Oracle database that was restored in a BRRESTORE run, for example. BRRECOVER here supports the following recovery scenarios that you already know from Section 10.3:

- Complete database recovery (through a partial or full restore)
- Point-in-time recovery (database or tablespace)
- Database reset
- Recovery of individual files from a data backup
- Recovery and application of offline redo log files
- Disaster recovery

You may justifiably wonder what "recovery of individual files from a data backup" and "recovery of offline redo log files" have in common with a recovery scenario. BRRECOVER provides these options in its interactive user menu and calls BRRESTORE with the required command options to be able to restore the required files. These two points are more like options to help you than actual recovery scenarios. They allow the user to restore database objects from the BRRECOVER menu. In this context, it is worth mentioning that you can use BRRESTORE through the menu options to restore database objects in all other recovery scenarios mentioned above. This shows that BRRECOVER and BRRESTORE work very closely together.

One scenario that we did not discuss in Section 10.3 is *disaster recovery*. You use this recovery in the following situations:

- The entire database, profiles, and even the BRBACKUP and BRARCHIVE logs have been lost.
- Only the profiles and the BRBACKUP and BRARCHIVE logs have been lost.

To recover the logs and profiles, BRRECOVER does not call BRRESTORE, as you would perhaps expect, but instead performs this process itself. BRRESTORE would already require the log files for a recovery run.

When you perform a disaster recovery, neither the data files nor the redo log files are restored. Only the missing logs and profiles from copies of previous data backups are restored. The scenario prepares the database for a subsequent restore and a recovery through a database point-in-time recovery or database reset by making the necessary files available.

A complete database recovery and a tablespace point-in-time recovery are not possible because the current control file required for this is missing. You should only perform the disaster recovery if you have already tested all other recovery options provided by BR*Tools. If you use the disaster recovery incorrectly, you can cause data loss and additional downtime. Section 10.4.7, *Disaster Recovery Using BR*Tools*, contains additional information about disaster recovery.

Like all other BR*Tools, BRRECOVER is called by the ora<sid> user on UNIX operating systems and by the <sid>adm user on Windows operating systems. BRRECOVER connects to the Oracle database through the SYSDBA authorization. This authorization is derived from the dba group, to which these users belong. You therefore do not normally need to specify the database user and password using the -u option when you call BRRECOVER.

To achieve a successful BRRECOVER run, you must set the required and optional parameters in the init<DBSID>.sap configuration file. You can also specify different command options for the BRRECOVER call. This means you override the parameters that were defined in the configuration file and restrict the menu structure in some cases:

- backup_dev_type | -d
- util_par_file / mount_par_file / -r|-parfile
- recov_degree | -e
- recov_interval | -i
- scroll_lines | -s
- recov_type | -t

No doubt, you are familiar with the first two parameters, which we explained in the previous sections. The other four parameters are used as special BRRECOVER settings:

- **recov_degree | -e**
  BRRECOVER uses this parameter or command to initiate SQLPLUS to apply redo log files to the data files in parallel. The parameter is followed by a <number> number that defines the number of parallel Oracle recovery processes or threads. The standard Oracle value is used by default here. A parallel process reduces the time required to recover the database. If you set the 0 value, the Oracle default value is used. Value 1 sets the serial application of redo log files.
- **recov_interval | -i**
  You can use this option to specify the interval when BRRECOVER searches for data backups. By default, 30 days are preset. The 0 value searches for all available data backups, whereas the 1 value looks for all backups for the current day.
- **scroll_lines | -s**
  You use this option to specify how many lines are output for scrolling lists in the menus. The default value is set at 20 lines. If you use the value 0

here, a list to be output is displayed in one step, whereas all values above 0 display the defined number of lines.

- **recov_type | -t**
  This parameter specifies the recovery scenario to be used from those specified for selection. You are obliged to specify one of the following values:
  - **complete:** complete database recovery
  - **dbpit:** database point-in-time recovery
  - **tspit:** tablespace point-in-time recovery
  - **reset:** database reset
  - **restore:** individual files are restored using BRRESTORE
  - **apply:** offline redo log files are restored and applied
  - **disaster:** disaster recovery

  A full database recovery is performed by default.

In addition to the parameters, individual commands can also be executed. The most important ones are listed below:

- **-a | -tsp | -tablespace <tsp_name> | <tsp_name_list>**
  This optional parameter enables you to define an individual tablespace or a list of tablespaces that you want to be recovered by a tablespace point-in-time recovery.
- **-b | -backup [<log_name> | last]**
  You can specify exactly one BRBACKUP run, from which the database files are recovered. You use `<log_name>` to specify the log file of the required run. The `last` value automatically pulls the last successfully performed backup. This value is used by default.
- **-c | -confirm [force]**
  As is the case with the other tools, you can use this option to perform an unattended recovery. The `force` value suppresses all queries and automatically selects default entries and values in the menus. This is useful if you perform regular database copies for your test system to keep up it up-to-date or if you are absolutely sure about which result this automatism returns. Under no circumstances should you use this option to recover live systems. Instead, you should go through the menus step-by-step and check the default entries and values. From a general point of view, this option is more of an exception.

- **-g | -scn | -change <scn>**
  You can use this parameter to specify the last Oracle System Change Number that you want to be used for a point-in-time recovery. No value is specified by default.
- **-m | -pit | -time <yyy-mm-dd hh-mi-ss>**
  You can use this parameter to indicate the time for a point-in-time recovery up until which the database or a tablespace must be restored.
- **-n|-seq|-sequence <seq_nr>]**
  This specifies the LSN of the last redo log file that you want to be used for a point-in-time recovery.
- **-n1|-seq1|-sequence1 <seq_nr>]**
  With this parameter, you specify the LSN of the first redo log file that you want to be applied using the `-t apply` option.
- **-u | -user [<user>[/<password>]] |**
  You can use this option to specify the user name and password for accessing the Oracle database (see Section 10.4.1).
- **-w|-own|-owner <own_name>|<own_name_list>**
  The owner for a tablespace point-in-time recovery is determined using this option.

At the beginning of 2005, there was a very big leap between the patch levels of BR*Tools 6.20. Patch level 100 was delivered at that time, with which a completely revised BRRECOVER has been available since then. The functions provided with this version replaced the previously implemented logic in the recovery area in SAPDBA. In particular, functional enhancements were made for supporting MCOD configurations and disaster recovery scenarios. As of this patch level, BRRECOVER enables a seamless connection to the current BR*Tools such as BRARCHIVE, BRBACKUP, and BRRESTORE already available at the time. The leap in the patch number illustrates the main functional enhancements of BRRECOVER.

BRRECOVER, which has been delivered in Release 6.20 since patch level 100, can execute the recovery procedure beyond structural changes to the database. If data files are added to a tablespace, BRRECOVER determines the structural change. When it is running, BRRECOVER can then create any of these files that may be missing. You therefore no longer need to execute a full data backup of the Oracle database directly after these types of changes. The backups that take place regularly are completely sufficient.

Like all other tools presented earlier, BRRECOVER writes the two known types of log files, namely, a detailed and a summary log.

All information that occurs during a recovery run is entered in the detailed log file. The log collects data about the following:

- Relevant parameters that were used from the init<DBSID>.sap configuration file during the recovery run
- Recovery scenario used
- Menus that were displayed and the options that were selected by the user
- Commands that were used in each phase of the restore and recovery and the results of executing these commands
- Remounting of the Oracle database
- Status of the individual tablespaces, data files, control files, and redo log files
- Names of database objects that were restored or underwent a recovery

The structure of the detailed log file is similar to that of the other tools of BR*Tools. The syntax is v<encoded time stamp>.<ext>. The ending can have the values *crv* (for a complete database recovery), *dpt* (for a database point-in-time recovery), *tpt* (for a tablespace point-in-time recovery), *drs* (for a database reset), *rif* (for restoring individual files), *alf* (for restoring and applying offline redo log files), and *drv* (for a disaster recovery).

The summary log file is called recov<DBSID>.log. This log contains information about all BRRECOVER runs. The entries cover the following:

- Action ID (encoded time stamp of the name of the detailed log file of the run)
- Function ID (file extension of the detailed log file)
- Time stamp of the start of the recovery
- Time stamp of the end of the recovery
- Return code
- Recovery scenario chosen

We have now discussed all of the basic points that are important in relation to using BRRECOVER to recover the Oracle database.

10.4.5 Post-Processing for an Incomplete Recovery

In certain cases, incomplete recovery runs require opening the database with the `open resetlogs` option. This initializes the online redo log files of the Oracle database again. The information still remaining in these files cannot be used for the current operation or another recovery of the database. The `open resetlogs` option resets the LSN of the redo log files to a value that is lower than the current value.

Let's look at the following two cases in detail:

1. Recovering a complete offline data backup and opening the database, without performing a full recovery
2. Recovering a complete offline or online data backup and performing a point-in-time recovery and then opening the database using the `resetlogs` option

In both cases, problem situations can occur relating to the additional backup of the data files using `BRBACKUP` and the redo log files using `BRARCHIVE` after a restore and recovery:

1. The information about the last backups and the volumes used are lost by restoring the database and therefore the SDBAH and SDBAD tables that contain this information. As a result, the volumes are queried in the next backup, which, although they are free from a logical perspective, are physically locked because they were already written.
2. As already mentioned, the recovery changed the LSN of the redo log files. In case 1, this is a value that is smaller than the current value before the recovery; in case 2, this value equals 1. Problem: `BRARCHIVE` would not be able to find the files written after the recovery, because offline redo log files were already written earlier with the LSN. The summary arch<DBSID>.log log file contains entries of successfully performed backup runs of earlier redo log files with the same LSN, and `BRARCHIVE` would therefore not be able to determine the new redo log files as files that would have to be backed up.

What do you do in such situations? For the first problem, you initially refer to the detailed log file of `BRBACKUP` for the last backup performed to establish which volume was last used there. You can use the `backup_volumes` parameter in the init<DBSID>.sap configuration file to determine the volume that you want to use for the next backup. Then start the `BRBACKUP` backup using the `-v` option and the name of this volume. The next volume according to the one specified using the -v option will then be used automatically for the next scheduled backup.

The second problem described was eliminated very early, specifically as of SAP Release 2.2E, by BRARCHIVE identifying the resetting of the LSN for the open database. You therefore do not have to do anything else.

For the sake of completeness, you should note the following: When you use release versions lower than 2.2E, you must change the summary log file for BRARCHIVE in one of the following ways:

- In case 1, the LSN that was active before the start of the backup, which was used to restore the data, is entered in the last line of the log.
- In case 2, the "zero" LSN is entered in the last line of the log.

We will use an example to make this procedure for releases lower than 2.2E clearer. In case 1, the database was restored with a backup that had 1,000 as the current LSN. The last entry in arch<DBSID>.log after the restore looks as follows:

```
#ARCHIVE.. 1313  /oracle/A24/oraarch/A24arch1_1313.dbf  2007 - 01 - 20 13.50.41
```

The LSN must now be entered before the start of the backup to ensure that BRARCHIVE backs up the redo log files once again as of the LSN:

```
#ARCHIVE..  999  /oracle/A24/oraarch/A24arch1_1313.dbf  2007 - 01 - 20 13.50.41
```

After the first backup has been performed with BRARCHIVE, reset the changed line again.

In case 2, the value of the last entry in arch<DBSID>.log is set to zero:

```
#ARCHIVE..    0  /oracle/A24/oraarch/A24arch1_1313.dbf  2007 - 01 - 20 13.50.41
```

Here too, you should reset the line again after the first archiving process. As already described, you no longer have to perform this process for all releases as of Release 2.2E.

However, note for all releases that all redo log files that were restored for a recovery from the tape in the archiver directory are deleted after the successful recovery. If you use the BR*Tools, the system will issue a prompt after the recovery, asking you if you want to delete the files. In this case, you should choose the relevant option to confirm that you do.

10.4.6 BR*Tools and Temporary Tablespaces

The backup of locally managed temporary tablespaceswith temporary content (LMTS/T) was adapted with BRBACKUP 6.20 as of Patch Level 100 in such a way that this is no longer performed in online or partial data backups. Tablespaces with permanent content (DMTS/P) that are managed temporarily by a dictionary continue to be included in the backup. Chapter 3 provides additional information about the functions and use of temporary tablespaces.

From an Oracle point of view, the locally managed temporary tablespaces can be recreated again after the database is restored. This is why a backup is no longer necessary. However, the offline data backup with BRBACKUP remains unaffected by this. The locally managed temporary tablespaces continue to be included in the backup here.

A backup of these tablespaces using RMAN did not occur before BRBACKUP was adapted. The functions mapped by Oracle relating to the temporary tablespaces in the BR*Tools were therefore consistently transferred.

If you are recovering an online data backup, the files of the locally managed temporary tablespaces are no longer available (if you use BR*Tools as of 6.20 Patch Level 100). If you recover the database using BRRECOVER, if necessary, the files of the temporary tablespace are automatically created again. You therefore do not have to be surprised if these are missing in the backup. On no account should you access the recovery manually and create the tablespaces ahead of time.

If you do not use BRRECOVER and you restore the database using BRRESTORE and perform a recovery using the SQLPLUS tool, you must manually create the new files for temporary tablespaces. You can do this using the SQL command

```
alter tablespace <temp_tsp> add tempfile '<temp_file>';
```

where `<temp_tsp>` specifies the tablespace, such as PSAPTEMP, for example, and `'<temp_file>'` indicates the data file.

10.4.7 Disaster Recovery Using BR*Tools

In Section 10.4.4, we briefly touched on disaster recovery using the BRRECOVER tool. This type of recovery scenario is necessary if the entire database with all profiles and log files of the BR tools, or only the profiles and logs from the BRBACKUP or BRARCHIVE runs, have been lost but a restore and recovery of the database must be performed. The disaster recovery supported by BRRECOVER does not recover the data files. The profiles of the database and the logs are in fact recovered. BRRECOVER therefore prepares the database to the extent that a database point-in-time recovery or a database reset subsequently sets the database to an operational status again. However, data is lost in both cases. You cannot perform a complete recovery or tablespace recovery because of the missing control files.

You should only use disaster recovery if you are an expert in Oracle database administration, have full knowledge of all activities in the phases to be performed and have already tested the other recovery scenarios that are supported by the BR*Tools, or these cannot be applied. If you perform the disaster recovery incorrectly, you may cause data loss and additional downtime.

The prerequisites for disaster recovery are:

- The SAP software and Oracle software are installed correctly
- The file systems are configured exactly as they were before they failed.

To prepare the database with the disaster recovery for a database point-in-time recovery or a database reset, the following steps must be performed:

1. Select the BRBACKUP and BRARCHIVE data backup that contains the required profiles and logs.
2. Choose the device that you want to use to start the recovery.
3. Specify the relevant parameters based on the device you just chose.
4. Select the profiles and logs to be recovered. These can be the:
   - Data backup profile
   - Oracle profile
   - BACKINT/Mount profile
   - Detailed log file of BRARCHIVE or BRBACKUP
   - Summary log file of BRARCHIVE, BRBACKUP, or BRSPACE
   - BRSPACE log files of structural changes and parameter changes
5. Recover the selected profile and log files. BRRECOVER carries this out without calling BRRESTORE (because the logs that exist for this are missing).
6. Choose the detailed log that you want to recover. You can only choose logs that exist on the recovery device you chose earlier. The detailed logs are recognized on a tape drive by the inserted tape.
7. In the last phase, you recover the detailed log files selected. Again, BRRECOVER does this without calling BRRESTORE.

When performing the disaster recovery, bear in mind that the usual security precautions that were implemented for the other recovery scenarios in BRRECOVER are not available. A status check of the database does not take place, and the user is not guided step-by-step through the recovery as is otherwise usual. All pending actions can be processed independently of each other; in other words, the user must know exactly when each phase must be performed and in which order. This procedure requires some expert knowledge.

The backup medium with the required files needs to be available in all phases. The administrator must know exactly which files have to be recovered. He or she must also know exactly where these files are located. During the recovery, a copy of the files from the backup medium is created at the operating system level. BRRECOVER stores these copies in the standard directory.

If you use an external data backup program, the BACKINT repository with the last available backup must be accessible because the tapes are managed through this repository in the external data backup program. To access the data, the parameter file for BACKINT must be available and set in such a way that it meets the requirements for the specific implementation. If these settings are lost, they must be set up again before the disaster recovery starts. If everything is installed and configured correctly, BRRECOVER calls BACKINT to perform the recovery. BACKINT then restores the profiles and logs of the last successful backup.

You can view the result of the recovery of the objects in the logging of the BRRECOVER run. The detailed log is located in the */oracle/<DBSID>/saparch* directory and has the syntax v<encoded time stamp>.drv. If the recovery has been successfully completed, you can then start one of the two recovery scenarios — database point-in-time recovery or database reset. How you choose between the two scenarios depends on the number of redo log files since the last backup and how far the last successful backup dates to since the database failed. In this context, we refer you to Section 10.3 and Table 10.1.

10.4.8 BR*Tools in Windows Environments

The NTBACKUP program is available in Windows environments in addition to the BR*Tools. You can use this program to perform offline data backups of your Oracle database. The following database objects are backed up:

- SAP data files
- System and rollback data files
- Control files

- Online redo log files
- Offline redo log files

NTBACKUP cannot, however, perform an online data backup. You use the same program to restore your backup that you previously created with NTBACKUP. You cannot use BRRESTORE and BRRECOVER for the restore and recovery.

SAP recommends that you only use NTBACKUP for small installations or for test systems that you can regularly take offline for a data backup.

The BRBACKUP and BRARCHIVE BR*Tools, in contrast, are suitable for backing up large databases and live systems. You can use them to back up the complete Oracle database or individual tablespaces online. You must operate the database in ARCHIVELOG mode for this. Section 10.2, *Data Backup Methods*, contains detailed descriptions of the offline and online data backup of an Oracle database. The operating modes are presented in Section 10.1.2.

Some parameters that you set in the init<DBSID>.sap configuration file for using the BR*Tools are specific to operating systems and must be adapted accordingly. It is important that the BR*Tools can be called from anywhere and are therefore entered in the system's PATH path variable.

10.4.9 Backup Media and Volume Management

In the previous sections, we briefly discussed the different backup media and the volume management associated with the parameter settings and command options of BRBACKUP and BRARCHIVE. We will now take another look at some of the interesting points.

You can perform the backup and recovery of database objects on locally connected devices such as tape drives, hard disks, or an SAN, on remotely connected devices in LAN or WAN, or using the BACKINT interface to external backup programs with the underlying locally or remotely connected backup hardware.

The variant most frequently encountered is the local connection of the backup media to the database server. When you use remotely connected devices, you should pay particular attention to the stability of the network connection. Performing a backup of test systems using this type of connection is not as critical as the backup of live systems. You should only use remotely connected backup media to perform the data backup of live systems if the database is not very big or the network connection is stable. In all other cases, you should perform a backup using locally connected backup media. A test run with the test system to the remotely connected backup media can provide some clarity here because you can use the results to check whether serious problems occur with this type of connection. One secure solution is a database backup of the test system to back up media that are locally connected to the database server of the live system.

You will require a pool of tapes to back up the Oracle database and the offline redo log files using a tape drive. Enough tapes must be available to cover a complete backup cycle. You must also allow for the possible growth of the database and, furthermore, for unscheduled backups. You should provide 20% more tapes in the pool than are actually used at that moment. You can reuse tapes when the backup cycle finishes. A backup cycle usually takes 28 days to complete (see Section 10.7, *Backup Strategies*). You should regularly check the utilization of the tapes: if the tapes run low, you must reorder a sufficient number and integrate them into the pool.

In addition to backing up to tape, you can also back up your Oracle database to hard disk. Sufficient memory must be available for this, and you should subsequently copy the backup from this hard disk to tape. The SAP `BRBACKUP` tool provides suitable command options to help you do this, which we presented in Section 10.4.1, *Data Backup Using BRBACKUP*. A backup of the database to hard disk and then to tape is used for the two-phase database backup (see Section 10.7.2 for the relevant advantages and disadvantages).

When you calculated the pool size, you must consider the following factors:

- Size of the Oracle databases
- Number of backup devices used in parallel
- Duration of the backup cycle
- Frequency of the data backup
- Number and size of the redo log files in a backup cycle
- Database growth and unscheduled backups (+ 20%)

You can compress the data to save memory on the tapes. We differentiate here between software and hardware compression. *Software compression* is set by the configuration parameters or command options of `BRARCHIVE` and `BRBACKUP`. *Hardware compression* occurs directly through the backup devices. You must also implement a setting in the BR*Tools, indicating that hardware compression is used (see Section 10.4, *BR*Tools for Backup, Restore, and Recovery*).

If the backups occur through the BACKINT interface of the BR*Tools, you can use the volume management of the external backup software. To help you with its setup and functions, you should refer to the manual or consult the support group of the manufacturer of the external backup program. Nevertheless, you can also use the volume management of the BR*Tools with external backup tools.

If you use locally or remotely connected backup devices, however, by default, you first use the volume management implemented in the BR*Tools.

Before you can use a volume of `BRBACKUP` and `BRARCHIVE`, it must be initialized correctly. Initialized means the tapes are assigned an SAP-specific tape name. A file called .tape.hdr0 is written during the initialization. This file is read each time the volume is checked. If the label does not exist, the check is incorrect and the tape is not used. If you use tools other than `BRBACKUP` and `BRARCHIVE` on a tape that was initialized using these, the name can be overwritten, and all of the data that was contained on the tape will be lost. You always need to initialize tapes when:

- You use new tapes
- You want to use tapes that have never been used with `BRBACKUP` or `BRARCHIVE`

You only ever need to initialize a tape once. You do not have to do this before each data backup. To change the name of a volume, you need to carry out a reinitialization. You cannot perform this name change during a data backup. The name change deletes all information on the tape.

If you want to use the automatic tape management, you must store all volume names of the pool in the init<DBSID>.sap configuration file under the `volume_backup` or `volume_archive` parameters. Labeling the tapes with the volume names is extremely useful for being able to quickly retrieve the tapes required by the BR*Tools. The following options are available for the initialization:

- **-i | -initialize**
  You can only use this option for tapes that were already initialized with the BR*Tools. You mainly use it to rename volumes. However, you can only do this if the expiration period of the volume has been reached.
- **-i | -initialize force**
  You use this option if you want to initialize new or non-SAP tapes. You can also reinitialize tapes that have already been initialized, because this

option does not check the expiration period. We recommend that you only use this option if really necessary.

- **-v | -volume**
  This option specifies the name of the volume (for more information, see also Sections 10.4.1 and 10.4.2).
- **-n | -number**
  This option indicates the number of volumes to be initialized.

The following command initializes 10 new tapes, whose volume names are defined in the `volume_backup` parameter in the init<DBSID>.sap configuration file:

```
brbackup -i force -n 10
```

You use the following command to initialize three new tapes for the `BRARCHIVE` backups, whose volume names are not defined in the init<DBSID>.sap configuration file:

```
brarchive -i force -v archive_1,archive_2,archive_3
```

You must mount all tapes in the correct sequence in the tape drive.

As soon as you initialize the tapes, you can use them in `BRBACKUP` and `BRARCHIVE` runs. Before this type of run writes to a tape, the name of the volume is checked. If the volume name is correct, the expiration period of the volume has elapsed, and the tape use count is not exceeded, the data can be written. You use the `tape_use_count` parameter to define the counts of the use of the tape and to specify the maximum number of times a volume can be written to tape. The default value is 100 possible repetitions. This count is to ensure that a tape is replaced with a new one after a specific number of runs. Otherwise, incorrect data could be written or read. The default setting is only a benchmark. You should consult the manufacturer for the exact value for your tapes.

Each `BRBACKUP` or `BRARCHIVE` run overwrites the volumes if the conditions mentioned above are met. The BR*Tools never utilize any free memory remaining on the tapes that was not used by a previously performed backup. This means you must insert new tapes, or tapes whose expiration period has elapsed, for each backup. The expiration period incidentally ensures that a volume and therefore the backup contained on it are not deleted by being unnecessarily overwritten prematurely, and, consequently, all required backups are made available for a restore at any time of the set backup cycle.

We have already discussed the different uses of volumes. Volumes can be selected as follows:

- Manually
- Automatically
- Using external tools

You set the first option by deactivating the automatic volume management. You do this by using the reserved volume name SCRATCH. However, the BR*Tools check the expiration period of the volume in each case. You have two options to start a backup with a manual volume selection:

1. You can assign the SCRATCH value to the `volume_backup` and `volume_archive` parameters in the init<DBSID>.sap configuration file. You can then start `BRBACKUP` and `BRARCHIVE`.
2. You do not touch the parameters in the configuration file (you can define a pool here). You start the backup using the `-v SCRATCH` option when you call `BRBACKUP` and `BRARCHIVE`.

In both cases, the two BR*Tools will require the necessary number of volumes, whose periods have expired, with any names. The names are not changed by the backup.

Automatic volume management automatically selects the volumes that are intended for the next backup. The name of the volume entered is compared to the name found in the defined pool. There is also a check to ensure that the current backups are not overwritten. The following steps are required to set up automatic volume management:

1. Define a pool of volumes. You do this using the `volume_backup` and `volume_archive` parameters by entering all names that physically exist and that you want to use.
2. Check whether the expiration period of the volumes is set in the `expir_period` parameter. Change this parameter if necessary.
3. Start the backups without the `–v` option. In this case, only volumes that are not locked are used.
4. Mount the required volumes. During the next backups, `BRBACKUP` and `BRARCHIVE` will write all available volumes of the pool in sequence.

5. Display the names of the volumes used for the next backup by calling the `brbackup -q` or `brarchive -q` commands.
6. Check the inserted volumes using the `brbackup -q check` or `brarchive -q check` commands.

For the name for the volumes for automatic volume management, SAP suggests a syntax that uses the database instance and a serial number, for example, <DBSID>A<nn> for tapes that are to contain the archive backups and <DBSID>B<nn> for tapes that are to contain the database backups.

External volume management systems or specifically written shell scripts can manage the volume names externally. For a pending backup, you use the `-v` option to transfer the names of the required volumes to `BRBACKUP` or `BRARCHIVE`. You can use this option to deactivate automatic volume management that may be set in the configuration files. As always, the BR tools check the expiration period of the specified volumes. You should therefore ensure that the external tools only propose those volumes for a backup that are free and can be used. If this is not the case, `BRBACKUP` and `BRARCHIVE` may terminate.

10.5 Oracle Recovery Manager (RMAN)

So far, we have described in detail SAP's BR*Tools for backing up and restoring the Oracle database. Oracle provides the proprietary tool, Oracle Recovery Manager (RMAN), for performing backups and restores.

The Oracle RMAN tool has the following options:

- You can use RMAN to create incremental backups. Only the changes that have occurred since the last full backup performed are backed up in this case. This reduces the time required for a backup and the number of tapes required, but it increases the time required to restore the database, because several incremental backups must be integrated.
- Another feature is the consistency check that RMAN performs during a backup to each logical database block that is backed up. This ensures that each backup is consistent and free of errors. You can therefore omit the recommended weekly database check (see Chapter 9, *System Operation and Monitoring*) using `DBVERIFY`.

- Because only the logical database blocks that are actually in use are backed up, the amount of data to be backed up is reduced. This results in a reduction in the number of tapes required for a full data backup.
- You can use RMAN to verify backups. This ensures that the data is written to tape without any errors.
- RMAN considerably reduces the amount of redo log information that accumulates during an online backup of the database. The reason for this is that tablespaces of the Oracle database must not be set in a backup mode.

You can call RMAN from the command line and use it from a graphical interface in the *Oracle Enterprise Manager* (OEM). You should consider three important points when using RMAN:

1. RMAN uses a *recovery catalog* to save the information about a backup. For security reasons, you should keep this catalog on a separate server in a separate database. This requires additional administration work.
2. Particularly in disaster situations where the database of the live SAP system and the recovery catalog have been lost, a restore and recovery are very complicated. You cannot restore the database without the information that was written in the recovery catalog, because the backups are not available. In this case, you have to fall back on Oracle Support.
3. The user of the database who is responsible for the backups requires SAPDBA authorizations. Simple SYSOPER authorizations are not enough.

SAP supports RMAN with the `BRBACKUP` and `BRARCHIVE` BR*Tools. They can be used to integrate the RMAN features mentioned above into the existing backup strategies and tools:

- The described recovery catalog is not used. The information about your backups is stored in the control file. Because the control file is subsequently also included in the backup after a backup has been performed, after you restore the control file, you immediately have all of the information for restoring the database. Because the control file is held in three copies in different directories of the database, there is little likelihood of a failure.
- Integrating RMAN with `BRBACKUP` and `BRARCHIVE` means you can display all of the necessary information about the data backup in the SAP *Computing Center Management System* (CCMS).

- As described in Section 10.4.9, *Backup Media and Volume Management*, you can back up data with the volume management functions through the SAP backup library.
- You can also use the BACKINT interface provided by SAP in the BR*Tools for external backup tools.
- All backup strategies known with the BR*Tools are supported with RMAN. As of BR*Tools 7.00 Patch Level 15, you can use RMAN for backups of standby and split mirror databases. Older BR*Tools do not support this.

To be able to use the enhanced functions, such as incremental backups, for example, made available with the BR*Tools, you must install a backup library that uses the *System Backup to Tape* (SBT) interface of the Oracle Recovery Manager. You can choose from the following backup libraries:

- SAP backup library of the BR*Tools (*libsbt*)
- LSM backup library of the Legato Storage Manager (*liblsm*)
- Backup library of a third party's backup tool (external backup library)

Using such a library is optional. If you do not specify a library, RMAN performs the backup on the local hard disk. For more information about installing a backup library, refer to SAP Note 142635.

When you use the Oracle Recovery Manager and which backup library you want to use for this depends entirely on the strategy you want to use to back up the data. The strategy is affected by the following factors:

- Size of the database to be backed up
- Amount of data that is actually changed and added to the database
- Backup medium that is used
- Basic security requirements

Table 10.3 lists backup media available for backups with and without RMAN, differentiated according to backup method.

The complete database backup (`backup_mode = all` parameter) backs up all database files but does not catalog these as reference for an incremental backup. The complete backup (`backup_mode = full` parameter), the level 0 backup in the RMAN context, also updates the database files but catalogs these as reference for incremental backups. You can only execute the incremental backups (level 1 backup in the context of RMAN) with RMAN. They also always require a level 0 backup as reference.

If you perform a level 0 backup without RMAN, you must activate RMAN to catalog this backup. This occurs automatically when you use BRBACKUP if you use the corresponding parameter to call the backup. If you perform a level 0 backup with RMAN, all database blocks that were ever written or changed are updated and immediately cataloged in this backup.

Backup	Complete database	Full backup (level 0)	Incremental backup (level 1)
Without RMAN	▸ Tape drive (local/remote) ▸ Hard disk (local/remote) ▸ BACKINT (external tool)	▸ Tape drive (local/remote) ▸ Hard disk (local/remote) ▸ BACKINT (external tool) ▸ You must start RMAN to catalog the backup	Not possible
With RMAN	▸ Tape drive (SAP backup library) ▸ Hard disk (locally without backup library) ▸ Supported device (external backup library)	▸ Tape drive (SAP backup library) ▸ Hard disk (locally without backup library) ▸ Supported device (external backup library)	▸ Tape drive (SAP backup library) ▸ Hard disk (locally without backup library) ▸ Supported device (external backup library)

Table 10.3 Backup Devices with and without RMAN

RMAN provides different types of incremental backups. These are the differential incremental backup and the cumulative incremental backup.

The *differential incremental backup* updates all blocks that have changed since the last backup at level 0 or level 1. If RMAN establishes that the last backup is a level 1 backup, all changes to blocks since this backup are backed up. If a level 1 backup is not available, all changed blocks since the last level 0 backup are written. During a restore, all differential incremental backups that are run after the level 0 backup are restored again. Figure 10.20 illustrates this concept. On Sundays, level 0 backups are always performed and all blocks that were ever used are backed up. The differential incremental backups are run on the subsequent days, that is, Monday to Saturday. The backup on Monday is based on the level 0 backup from Sunday and updates the changed blocks between Sunday and Monday. The level 1 backup on Tuesday is based on the level 1 backup from Monday and saves all changed blocks since this backup.

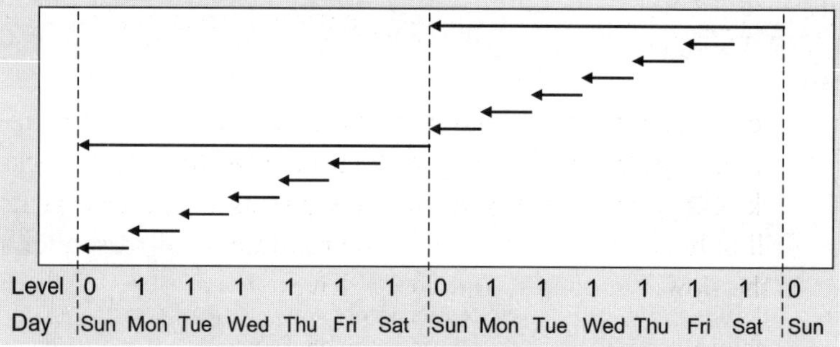

Figure 10.20 Differential Incremental Backup

The *cumulative incremental backup*, however, updates all blocks that were changed since the last level 0 backup. Changed blocks are written several times in incremental backups. In terms of data volume, the cumulative incremental backups always become bigger with the ever increasing time intervals from the last level 0 backup and always last longer. This type of backup reduces the work involved in restoring data, because only the last level 1 backup must be imported. Figure 10.21 shows an example of this type of backup. The level 0 backups are always scheduled on Sundays. The subsequent backups from Monday to Saturday are based on the level 0 backup from Sunday and back up all changed blocks since Sunday.

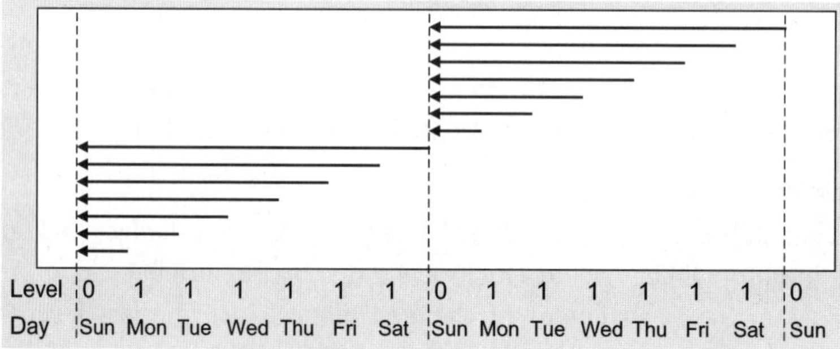

Figure 10.21 Cumulative Incremental Backup

The cumulative level 1 backups must then take preference over the differential level 1 backups if the time for restoring data is more important than the space used for a backup. The differential incremental backup is set by default.

Only the cumulative incremental backup is implemented in the BR*Tools. This means that, when restoring data, you must always restore the last successful incremental backup. Because only the changed blocks are updated for the incremental backup, we recommend this type of backup as a backup strategy for very large databases. You can only perform incremental backups using RMAN.

You may not see any significant reduction in the backup runtime for incremental backups. One reason for this may be that the algorithm that checks whether a block was used or changed occupies just as much time as its backup. You will only achieve a reduction in the runtime if the reason for a long backup is the slow throughput to the tape drives.

One possible backup scenario with incremental backups is that a full database backup (level 0) is performed every Sunday and an incremental backup (level 1) is performed on all other days. The pending redo log files must also always be backed up because otherwise you will not be able to perform a recovery up to the last completed transaction.

In addition to backing up the database, you can use RMAN to back up offline redo log files with BRARCHIVE. You do this using either the SAP backup library or an external backup library. It is possible to back up offline redo log files using RMAN as of Basis Release 6.10. The advantage of backing up the offline redo log files using RMAN is that a consistency check is performed during the backup. If you believe this type of check is important, this is a good alternative to the missing functions with DBVERIFY (for more information, see Chapter 9). In the next sections, we will discuss the individual RMAN backups again with the different backup libraries using BR*Tools.

10.5.1 Backups Without Backup Library

If you do not use a backup library, RMAN backs up on the local hard disk. To map an incremental backup and ultimately copy the data to a tape drive, you must first create a level 0 backup and then the level 1 backup. You have two options for the level 0 backup:

1. You create a backup on the local hard disk using RMAN. As soon as this is completed, you use BRBACKUP to copy the backup to tape.
2. You create a backup to tape drive or hard disk using BRBACKUP or an external tool. You must then start RMAN to catalog this backup.

In the second step, you can then run the incremental level 1 backups. In this case, you create a backup on the local hard disk and then use BRBACKUP to copy this backup to a tape.

The advantage of the backup using RMAN with the subsequent BRBACKUP run is that the RMAN functions such as the automatic block check are used and less redo log information is written during the backup because the backup mode for the tablespaces is missing. A significant disadvantage is that you must subsequently back up the data to a tape. This generates additional work.

The benefit of using BRBACKUP or another external tool and then cataloging the backup using RMAN is that you can also restore and recover data without RMAN. You then recover the database using the redo log files backed up during the BRBACKUP run, and this replaces restoring the incremental backups. The backup may also run faster, because the data is run directly using tools such as dd and cpio and not using RMAN. Obvious disadvantages include the missing check for blocks and using the backup mode for tablespaces with its associated features such as a higher occurrence of redo logs and a possible archiver stuck.

10.5.2 Backups with the SAP Backup Library

The SAP backup library is an SAP implementation of the Oracle System Backup to Tape interface in the form of a library. The Oracle server process calls this library to write data to tape. BRBACKUP and BRARCHIVE must be configured in such a way that they call RMAN for the backup. We discussed the configuration parameters in the init<DBSID>.sap file in Sections 10.4.1 and 10.4.2. For local tape drives, you must adapt the backup_dev_type parameters with the tape | tape_auto | tape_box values and the tape_copy_cmd parameter with the rman | rman_dd values. For remote tape drives, the pipe | pipe_auto | pipe_box values are available for the backup_dev_type parameter.

You can also back up data to remote hard disks. However, you can only run incremental backups. For this purpose, you must set the backup_mode = incr, backup_dev_type = stage and remote_user parameters with the user and password and remote_host with the host name of the remote server as a prerequisite for SAPFTP (SAP-Specific File Transfer Protocol). This variant is suitable for standby databases to copy the offline redo log files to the standby server using BRARCHIVE and, in doing so, get the benefits of the RMAN consistency check.

10.5.3 Backups with an External Backup Library

Finally, you can also install backup libraries from third parties. The backup media that are subsequently available depend on the external backup program and the corresponding backup library. You can obtain the relevant information from the manufacturer of the external library.

The database backup with the BR*Tools using an external library occurs in three phases:

1. BRBACKUP or BRARCHIVE call RMAN. This starts the Oracle server process, which reads the data of the Oracle database to be backed up and writes the data to the external backup library. The backup library works as a backup client and forwards the data to a backup server, which ultimately writes this data to the backup medium.
2. After the backup has been completed, the information about it is written in the control file that is then backed up together with the profiles and log files. In this case, the BR*Tools can do one of two things:
   - Use the BACKINT interface and forward the data mentioned above directly to the backup server
   - Write the data mentioned above to a local or remote hard disk (without using BACKINT)
3. If the BR*Tools have written the data to a local and remote hard disk, another backup program must back up this data to tape in a third step. This process does not occur under the control of the BR*Tools.

Up until Basis Release 6.10, backups had to be performed using the BACKINT interface if RMAN was used with an external backup library. This procedure was activated using the `backup_dev_type = rman_util` parameter. As of Release 6.20, you no longer have to use BACKINT. You use `backup_dev_type = rman_disk` or `backup_dev_type = rman_stage` to back up the database files to the external backup medium using the option described in step 1 and to write the control file, the profiles, and the logs to a local (rman_disk) or remote (rman_stage) hard disk.

10.6 Other Error Scenarios

In Section 10.3.3 and subsequent sections, we presented the *loss of a normal tablespace* error scenario and used it to explain the different recovery methods. Naturally, other objects can be lost from an Oracle database. In the following, we want to describe other error scenarios and explain how you can eliminate errors because it is often difficult to decide which files you must restore to get the Oracle database up and running again.

10.6.1 Loss of a Control File

The loss of a single control file should not cause you too much concern because at least two other copies of the control file are mirrored in the directories of the Oracle database. You can only apply the solution described below if the control file copies still exist.

You notice that the file is missing or that Oracle cannot write on the control file because it is corrupt when you want to shut down or start up the database. You then receive the following error messages:

```
ORA-00210: cannot open the specified controlfile
ORA-27041: unable to open file
ORA-00205: error in identifying controlfile, check alert log for more info.
```

You do not have to perform a recovery in this case; replacing the corrupt or missing control file is sufficient.

However, you should first find out why the control file is missing. For example, you may no longer be able to access the hard disk where the file is located. You should search the ALERT log file and trace files of the database for errors. In the error messages, you establish which file is missing. You may also discover why the file is missing.

If you have eliminated the cause of the error, you can copy the control file as follows:

1. Copy a remaining control file at the operating system level to the location from which the control file is missing. Pay attention to the user, group, and access authorizations of the copied file.
2. Stop and start the database.
3. Check the ALERT log file and trace files for error messages again.

If you cannot copy the control file to the location from which it is missing, you can change the destination of the control file in init<DBSID>.ora and copy the file to this new location.

Another alternative is to reduce the copies of control files by the one incorrect file. Nevertheless, at least two copies should still always be available.

However, you should refrain from using this variant or at least only use it in the short term and recover the situation with three copies as quickly as possible.

10.6.2 Loss of All Control Files and the System Tablespace and Rollback Tablespace

A more precarious situation is when all control files and possibly the system tablespace and rollback tablespace are lost. Figure 10.22 illustrates this scenario.

Oracle notices that control files are missing when, for example, a checkpoint is written or a data file is added to the database. The system then automatically ceases all work.

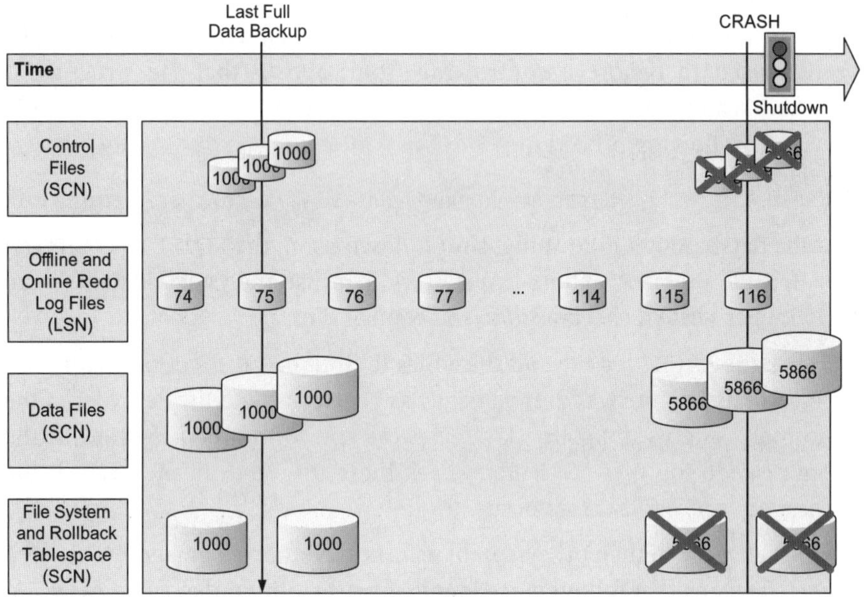

Figure 10.22 Loss of All Control Files, the System Tablespace, and Rollback Tablespace

In this case, you can recover the database if one of the following three points applies:

1. Oracle has not yet "noticed" that the control files are missing, and the structure of the database can be exported.
2. An old copy of the control file exists in which the current structure of the database is mapped.

3. A log of all database data files exists and you can use this to create a control file.

These points or conditions indicate how you can recover your control files. The first option is the easiest, whereas the last option, a manual one, is the most difficult. We now want to use these points to describe the different ways you can recover the control files.

We start with the first situation: You notice before Oracle that all control files are missing, and you can still continue to use the database. You can then use the SQL command

```
alter database backup controlfile to trace;
```

to generate a script that contains the structure of the database and can build the control file again. However, this file is built in the NoMount status, which means you must shut down the database. The process differs from the process used to restore a control file from tape in that the structure is exported while the database is running and the file is not restored. We advise the following procedure:

1. Execute the `alter database backup controlfile to trace;` command.
2. If the database is still running, shut it down using the SQLPLUS command `shutdown abort`. An abort is necessary, because the Oracle database can no longer write a checkpoint in the control files.
3. Check the ALERT log file and trace files to find the causes of the error. You can also determine whether damage has been caused to the data files of the normal, system, and rollback tablespaces and to the redo log files. If the online redo log files are legible, back these up. You can then repeat the recovery process if errors occur.
4. Then check whether other database files have been damaged. This step and the steps that follow it are identical to the option described for point 2 (where there is an old copy of a control file). We ignore an additional description at this point and refer to step 4 in the subsequently described procedure.

If you can no longer access the database and create an export, you must restore an old copy of a control file. When you perform a backup with the BR*Tools, a copy of the control file is always backed up after the data files are written. In this respect, the requirement for point 2 must always be met, and you must have the option to restore a control file from the last successful backup. We will now look at what this type of restore and recovery can look like:

1. If the database is still running, shut it down using the SQLPLUS command `shutdown abort`.
2. Check the ALERT log file and trace files to find the causes of the error and establish whether data files or redo logs were damaged. If the online redo log files are legible, back these up. You can then repeat the recovery process if errors occur.
3. Restore the control file from the last backup. You can use the BR*Tools to do this and select **Restore of individual backup files • Restore files from BRBACKUP backup** to trigger the process. Then copy the file to the areas provided for this (see `control_files` parameter in init<DBSID>.ora). You only use these control files to enable you to set the status of the database to Mount.
4. If other files are damaged, restore these again. If some tablespace data files are damaged, you must restore all data files of the backup for a point-in-time recovery but only the damaged data files for a complete recovery. Because a recovery is then required, you must restore the offline redo log files that have accumulated since the last backup.
5. You can use the SQLPLUS command `sqlplus "/ as sysdba"` and then `startup mount` to set the status of the database to Mount.
6. Now export the structure of the database using

   ```
   alter database backup controlfile to trace;
   ```

   (if you were not already able to perform this for a running database like in point 1). A trace file is created in the *$ORACLE_HOME/saptrace/usertrace* directory. Copy this file as another file and change the name and ending of the file to .sql (for example, create_controlfile.sql). Look at the file: If the online redo log files exist and are not damaged and you can therefore perform a complete recovery, delete the first lines and the "Set #2" section from the file. If the online redo log files are damaged, only leave the "Set #2" commands in the file. The first command of the script must be `startup nomount` in both cases.
7. Check your ALERT log file to see whether data files were created during the time between the backup of the control file and the current status of the database. If this is the case, you must include these files in the relevant section in the script in the same sequence in which they were created.

8. When you shut down the database using ABORT, the status of the data files changes to OFFLINE. You must set the status to ONLINE again for a recovery. You can use

   ```
   select * from v$datafile
   ```

   to display all data files that are set to OFFLINE.

   ```
   alter database datafile '<file name>' online;
   ```

   resets the status of the affected data files to ONLINE.
9. Now start the script created earlier with

   ```
   @ORACLE_HOME/saptrace/usertrace/create_controlfile.sql
   ```

   to create the control file again and recover the database. The database then opens.
10. Finally, back up the recovered database.
11. If you performed an incomplete recovery such as a point-in-time recovery, you may have to carry out post-processing (see Section 10.4.5, *Post-Processing for an Incomplete Recovery*).

For example, if you want to perform the recovery irrespective of the control files being created, you must deactivate the commands in the SQL script. You can then carry out the restore and the recovery in the BR*Tools. You must select the relevant recovery variant there based on the status of the online redo log files. However, ensure that you select **yes** for the **Use backup control file** option in the recovery options when performing an incomplete recovery. The reason for this is that the control files in this case were created again without being based on the redo log files.

The fact that the control file mirrors the current structure of the database is enormously helpful. This should therefore contain the exact number of files and, indirectly, those of the database's tablespaces. Information such as the path name for the data files and redo log files and status of the LSN is not as important, because you can change these details using SQL commands, or you may not need them.

However, if you do not recover a control file from a backup and cannot export a structure, you can create a new control file manually (point 3). To do this, you need a current log that contains all database files. This can be a BRBACKUP log, for example. Note that this option is much more complicated and must be performed very conscientiously. You should also have basic knowledge of the syntax of the SQL commands to be executed. The structural contents of the control file could consequently be incomplete, and a restore would fail. Proceed as follows:

1. If the database is still running, shut it down using the SQL command `shutdown abort`.
2. Check the ALERT log file and trace files to find the causes of the error and establish whether data files or redo logs were damaged. If the online redo log files are legible, back these up. You can then repeat the recovery process if errors occur.
3. If other files are damaged, restore these again. If some tablespace data files are damaged, you must restore all data files of the backup for a point-in-time recovery but only the damaged data files for a complete recovery. Because a recovery is then required, you must restore the offline redo log files that have accumulated since the last backup.
4. Start up the database in the NoMount status using `startup nomount`.
5. Use the following SQL commands to build the control file. Refer to the Oracle documentation for additional information.

   ```
   create controlfile
   database <name>
   logfile '<online redo log groups>'
   noresetlogs|resetlogs
   maxlogfiles 10
   maxlogmembers <your value>
   datafile '<names of all data files>'
   maxdatafiles 1022
   archivelog;
   ```

   You must specify full path and file names for the online redo log files and data files. You can obtain these from the log file mentioned above. If the database is very large, you have to proceed very carefully at this point. Only use the `resetlogs` command if an online redo log group has been lost in addition to the control files. In all other cases, always use `noresetlogs`.
6. Then mount the database using `startup mount`.
7. You now start the recovery with the command

   ```
   recover database until cancel [using backup controlfile];
   ```

   The `using backup controlfile` option is only used here if you created the control file using the `resetlogs` option, that is, without being based on the redo log files.

8. Finally, you can open the database. Use

   ```
   alter database open noresetlogs;
   ```

   if you reconstructed the control file with the `noresetlogs` option and performed a full recovery. Use

   ```
   alter database open resetlogs;
   ```

   to open the database if you created the control file using `resetlogs` or you performed an incomplete recovery.
9. Then back up the recovered database. Refer again to the details about post-processing (see Section 10.4.5) if you used an incomplete recovery (for example, a point-in-time recovery).

You can also access the BR*Tools here but only if you have recovered the control file manually using SQLPLUS. Ensure that you specify the above-listed options correctly for the recovery run.

10.6.3 Loss of the System Tablespace and Rollback Tablespace

If the system tablespace and rollback tablespace are lost because of a crash, and the control files and online redo log files are not damaged (as shown in Figure 10.23), two types of recoveries are useful.

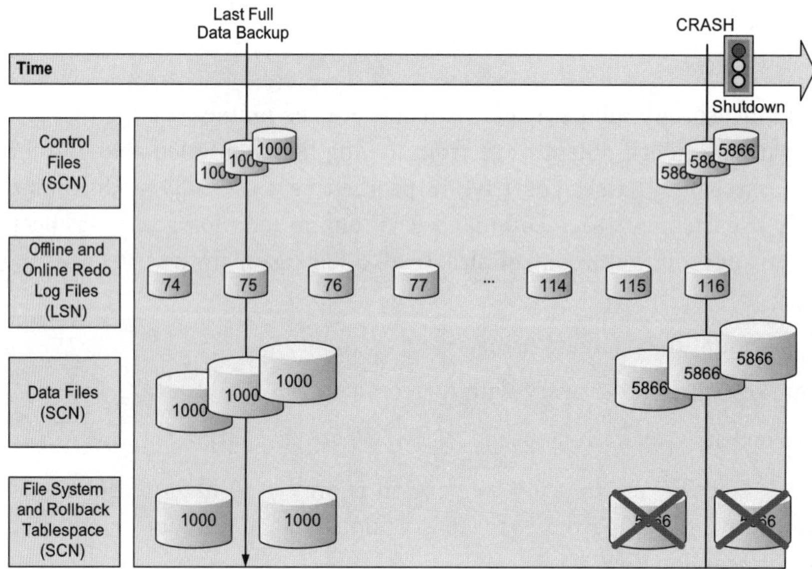

Figure 10.23 Loss of the System Tablespace and Rollback Tablespace

These are the *complete recovery* and the *point-in-time recovery*. We have already described both variants. In each case, you must take the Oracle database offline for the recovery.

If all redo log information up until the crash is available, you can perform a complete recovery. You only have to reload the damaged files of the affected tablespace from a backup and all of the required offline redo log files and recover these data files. For the point-in-time recovery, you recover all of the data files of the Oracle database and the offline redo log files from a backup. The recovery then takes place on all data files. In both cases, you must not recover the control file.

You can carry out the restore and recovery easily using the BR*Tools. You can, of course, also do this using SQLPLUS. To perform the complete recovery with this, use the SQL command

```
recover database;
```

to initiate the recovery and

```
alter database open;
```

to open the database. For the point-in-time recovery, you can use the command

```
recover database until cancel;
```

to cancel the process using a `CANCEL` command or

```
recover database until time 'YYYY-MM-DD:HH24:MI:SS';
```

to let the process run up until a certain time. You can then open the database using

```
alter database open resetlogs;
```

Again, consider the work that you must perform after an incomplete recovery (see Section 10.4.5).

10.6.4 Loss of a Data File of a Temporary Tablespace

In Section 10.4.6, *BR*Tools and Temporary Tablespaces*, we explained that, with the BR*Tools as of Release 6.20 Patch Level 100, you cannot back up locally managed temporary tablespaces with temporary content (LMTS/T) anymore and that these are therefore no longer available for a recovery. If you recover the complete database, BRRECOVER ensures that the LMTS/T temporary tablespace is recreated.

If a data file of the temporary tablespace is lost, you will find information in the ALERT log file and trace files as soon as an attempt is made to write to this file. If you execute the SQL command

```
select file#, substr(A.name,1,50) "data file", status from v$datafile A;
```

you obtain the status of each data file. The file that is no longer available gets the RECOVER status (see Figure 10.24). First, place the data file offline. To do this, use the SQL command

```
alter database datafile '<path/file name>' offline;
```

Then check whether the data files are temporary data files. To help with this, you can use the SQL command

```
select contents from dba_tablespaces where tablespace_name='PSAPTEMP';
```

If TEMPORARY is output as the result of this query, you can correct the error by deleting the missing file and creating it again. You can do this because temporary data files are optional files. You can open the Oracle database without these files. Delete the temporary data file with

```
alter database tempfile '<path/file name>' drop;
```

and use

```
alter tablespace PSAPTEMP add tempfile '<path/file name>' size <size>;
```

to add the temporary data file to the tablespace again.

If the result of the above query is PERMANENT, check which database users access the temporary tablespace:

```
select username, temporary_tablespace from dba_users;
```

You can now alter this for each database user for the time of the recovery of the temporary tablespace. You can create a new tablespace for this or use an already existing one with sufficient free memory. In both cases, note that the tablespace you want to use uses the same extent management (DMTS/P versus LMTS/T). You can alter the database users with the `alter user <username> temporary tablespace <tablespacename>;` command.

```
SQL> select file#, substr(a.name,1,50) "Data files", status from v$datafile A;

     FILE# Data files                                         STATUS
---------- -------------------------------------------------- -------
         1 /oracle/M54/sapdata1/system_1/system.data1         SYSTEM
         2 /oracle/M54/sapdata1/m54_1/m54.data1               ONLINE
         3 /oracle/M54/sapdata4/m54_2/m54.data2               ONLINE
         4 /oracle/M54/sapdata5/m54_3/m54.data3               ONLINE
         5 /oracle/M54/sapdata5/m54_4/m54.data4               ONLINE
         6 /oracle/M54/sapdata6/m54_5/m54.data5               ONLINE
         7 /oracle/M54/sapdata6/m54_6/m54.data6               ONLINE
         8 /oracle/M54/sapdata1/m5446c_1/m5446c.data1         ONLINE
         9 /oracle/M54/sapdata2/m5446c_2/m5446c.data2         ONLINE
        10 /oracle/M54/sapdata2/m5446c_3/m5446c.data3         ONLINE
        11 /oracle/M54/sapdata3/m5446c_4/m5446c.data4         ONLINE

     FILE# Data files                                         STATUS
---------- -------------------------------------------------- -------
        12 /oracle/M54/sapdata3/m5446c_5/m5446c.data5         ONLINE
        13 /oracle/M54/sapdata6/m5446c_6/m5446c.data6         ONLINE
        14 /oracle/M54/sapdata1/m54usr_1/m54usr.data1         ONLINE
        15 /oracle/M54/sapdata1/roll_1/roll.data1             ONLINE
        16 /oracle/M54/sapdata1/temp_1/temp.data1             ONLINE
        17 /oracle/M54/sapdata6/m54_7/m54.data7               ONLINE
        18 /oracle/M54/sapdata1/temp_2/temp.data2             RECOVER

18 rows selected.

SQL>
```

Figure 10.24 Status of Data Files of System M54

Instead of now recovering the missing data file from a backup, you can, provided no permanent objects have been stored, delete the tablespace and create it again with the identical file size and same extent management and storage parameters. This process is considerably faster to implement. If you have created the new PSAPTEMP tablespace, you can move the database users back to the original tablespace again using the SQL statement described above. You can subsequently delete a newly created temporary tablespace created for this action.

10.6.5 Loss of an Online Redo Log File

The loss of an online redo log file can be quickly remedied once you heed the recommendations from Oracle and mirror your online redo log files.

Again, you should first find out why the log file has been lost and which errors have occurred. You can check the ALERT log and trace file for this. Even if an error lets you continue working with the database, you should solve the problem as quickly as possible. For example, if a redo log file is lost from a redo log group, Oracle continues operating the database because it can store the information in the other redo log file that still exists.

If the online redo log files are not mirrored, the risk of losing data and the consequences associated with this are significantly greater. As we have already explained, you can only perform a complete recovery of the Oracle database up to the last completed transaction if all of the last redo log information about the online redo files is still available. You can only protect yourself against this type of loss by mirroring the redo log file in a group. If the mirroring has not been arranged, you may only be able to perform an incomplete recovery if you lose the online redo log files and the database. All information that was contained in the online redo log file is missing.

Let's assume there is a second copy of a lost active online redo log file in the redo log group (SAP default value) and no other database files are damaged. If this is not the case, you must recover these and the missing active online redo log file and then perform a recovery according to the type of recovered files.

You can use the `select * from v$logfile` SQL command to discover the missing online redo log file with the `INVALID` value in the **Status** column. When you have shut down the database, simply carry out the following steps:

1. Investigate the error that caused the redo log file to be deleted. Use the log files to help you.
2. Create a copy of the active redo log file that still exists in place of the missing file.
3. Pay attention to the users and groups to which the file belongs as well as to the access rights. Rename the copied file. The redo log files are unique. The first part of the file name is the same for each group; they only differ at the end of the file name. A number is incremented.
4. Start the database. The system will automatically perform an instance recovery. When this has been completed, you can use the system again.

If the database is still open, proceed as follows:

1. Investigate the error that caused the redo log file to be deleted. Use the log files to help you.
2. Use

   ```
   select * from v$logfile;
   ```

   to determine the missing online redo log file.
3. Delete this file using

   ```
   alter database drop logfile member '<path/filename>';
   ```

4. Create the file again. Use the SQL command

   ```
   alter database add logfile member '<path/filename>' to group
   <group number>;
   ```

If the hard disk where the redo log file was contained no longer exists, you can use the path for the file with the add command provided above.

In both cases, you will use

```
select * from v$logfile
```

to determine the INVALID status for the new redo log file created. This status will only change when the group to which the file belongs is written. By executing the SQL command

```
alter system switch logfile;
```

multiple times, you can speed up the switching and writing of the group, and the INVALID status should then disappear.

10.6.6 Loss of an Online Redo Log Group

If an entire online redo log group is lost, that is, both members of the group, the actions that must be performed to bring the database back to an operational status again totally depend on the status of the redo log group. We discussed the different statuses of the redo log files in Section 10.1.1, *Interaction of Oracle Processes and Database Objects*. You can use the SQL command

```
select * from v$log;
```

to display the status of each online redo log group. Figure 10.25 shows the output of the command. You can see that everything was fine in this system. The archiving status of the redo log group is provided under the **ARC** column. A distinction is made between the values **YES** and **NO**. All groups, apart from those that are being written at that moment, are archived.

We will now discuss the individual error scenarios when an online redo log group is lost. In the first case, let's assume the group that has been lost has the INACTIVE status and was archived. You must then carry out the following steps:

1. Check the log files to find out why the group was lost or to see if the redo log files have been damaged.
2. If you shut down the database, open it in the Mount status using

   ```
   startup mount
   ```

3. Delete the damaged redo log group using the SQL statement

   ```
   alter database drop logfile group <groupid>;
   ```

4. Then create the redo log group again using

   ```
   alter database add logfile group <groupid> ('<path/filename
   member1>', '<path/filename member2') size <size>;
   ```

Because the group is inactive and archived, the loss of the group is less dramatic.

```
SQL> select * from v$log;

    GROUP#    THREAD#  SEQUENCE#      BYTES    MEMBERS ARC STATUS           FIRST_CHANGE# FIRST_TIM
---------- ---------- ---------- ---------- ---------- --- ---------------- ------------- ---------
         1          1      13201   52428800          2 NO  CURRENT          51073368      21-JAN-07

         2          1      13199   52428800          2 YES INACTIVE         51047183      21-JAN-07

         3          1      13198   52428800          2 YES INACTIVE         51035478      20-JAN-07

    GROUP#    THREAD#  SEQUENCE#      BYTES    MEMBERS ARC STATUS           FIRST_CHANGE# FIRST_TIM
---------- ---------- ---------- ---------- ---------- --- ---------------- ------------- ---------
         4          1      13200   52428800          2 YES ACTIVE           51053550      21-JAN-07

SQL>
```

Figure 10.25 Status of the Online Redo Log Group

In the second case that we will consider, the group, which has the ACTIVE status but has already been archived, has been lost. If the database is shut down and you open it again, the redo log files of this group are required for the instance recovery. Proceed as follows:

1. Set the status of the database to Mount. Oracle now requires the files of the missing group for the instance recovery.

2. Use the following command to determine the LSN that was assigned to the redo log files of the incorrect group:

   ```
   select * from v$log;
   ```

3. Then execute the following SQL command to determine the path and file name of the current online redo log file:

   ```
   SELECT v$logfile.member FROM v$logfile, v$log
   WHERE v$log.status='CURRENT'
   AND v$logfile.group#=v$log.group#;
   ```

4. Use the SQL command

   ```
   recover database until cancel using backup controlfile;
   ```

   to start the recovery. An archive for applying the file is proposed. If the proposed LSN matches the LSN from step 2, confirm this log file. After you have applied this redo log file, you are prompted for the current online redo log file. Specify the path and file name that you determined in the last step. After you have applied both redo log files, enter `CANCEL`.

5. Open the database using

   ```
   alter database open resetlogs;
   ```

   Then perform a complete backup of the database.

If the database is still open in this second case, wait until the next checkpoint has been written or initiate this manually using the SQL command

```
alter system switch logfile;
```

The group subsequently becomes INACTIVE. You can then eliminate the error as described in the first case. In the third case, the status of the lost group is INACTIVE and the files are not yet archived. As soon as the Oracle database attempts to perform a redo log switch to this group, it will inevitably hang because this switch cannot be executed. The still inactive group, to which the switch is to be made, cannot be read or written. If this problem is of a more temporary nature, for example, if the user and group affiliation and the access rights are incorrectly set but the files themselves are not destroyed, you can continue using the redo log group after a correction. The database then continues working from the spot where it had earlier stopped.

However, if the redo log files of this inactive group are destroyed, you can no longer use this group. You must delete it and create a new one. You carry out this procedure as follows:

1. If the database is running, shut it down using the SQL command `shutdown abort`.
2. Use the ALERT log file and trace files to discover the reason for the loss of or damage to the redo log files.
3. Use `startup mount` to put the database in the Mount status.
4. If you operated the database in ArchiveLog mode, temporarily switch to NoArchiveLog mode:

   ```
   alter database noarchivelog;
   ```

   You need to do this because, otherwise, the system will be prevented from subsequently deleting the faulty files of the redo log group.
5. You can now delete the damaged online redo log group. You can do this with the

   ```
   alter database drop logfile group <group number>;
   ```

   SQL command.
6. You must use the following command now to create the group again:

   ```
   alter database
   add logfile group <groupid>
   ('<path/file name member 1>' ,
    '<path/file name member 2>')
   size <size>;
   ```

7. Then open the database with

   ```
   alter database open;
   ```

8. If you have set the status of the database to NoArchiveLog mode, shut down the database using `shutdown;` and start it up using `startup mount`. Now change the operating mode back to ArchiveLog mode using `alter database archivelog;`. You can now open the database again using `alter database open;`.
9. You must then ultimately follow up a backup if the database is operated in ArchiveLog mode by default and the archiving had to be stopped. This is exactly when a gap occurs in the sequence of offline redo log files. If another media error occurs, you can only recover the database using an incomplete recovery. There is a risk that data may be lost.

In the fourth case, the damaged redo log group has the ACTIVE status and is not archived. If the database is still open, wait for the next redo log switch. The group is then assigned the INACTIVE status, and you can take action as described previously in the third case. If the database is offline, the files of this redo log group are required at the start for an instance recovery. There is no way you can open the database without this redo log file. Because it was not archived, you must recover all data files of the last backup and perform an incomplete recovery with all available offline redo log files (see Section 10.6.7, *Loss of All Online Redo Log Files*).

The last case we will look at in this section is the loss of the current redo log group, the group with the CURRENT status. The files for this group cannot be archived because they are still being written. If you shut down the database smoothly (all changes are consistent in the data files), you may find yourself in the fortunate position that the redo log files of this group are not required for an instance recovery. You can check the ALERT log file to see whether the database was actually shut down with a `shutdown immediate` or `shutdown`. If that is the case, you can test the following steps:

1. Start up the database in the Mount status.
2. Start a recovery using the SQL command

   ```
   recover database until cancel using backup controlfile;
   ```

   If you are prompted for a redo log file, do not specify a file and immediately cancel the recovery using CANCEL. Background: this SQL command sets the database to Backup mode. If you did not execute the command, you would not be able to open the database with the `resetlogs` option to reinitialize the online redo log file.
3. You do this using the `alter database open resetlogs;` SQL command.
4. If errors do not occur, create a full backup of the database.

However, if the database was not shut down smoothly or if errors occur when you open the database in the procedure described above, you must perform a full restore and an incomplete recovery. We describe this procedure in the next section.

10.6.7 Loss of All Online Redo Log Files

The loss of all online redo log files requires recovering all data files and an incomplete recovery. Only the offline redo log files that are available can be applied in the recovery. A loss of data is unavoidable here. You must not reload the control file for the recovery.

1. Shut down the database using the `shutdown abort` command.
2. Check the ALERT log file and trace files to find the causes of the error. You can also determine whether damage has been caused to the data files of the normal, system, and rollback tablespaces and to the redo log files.
3. Recover all data files. Leave the control file unchanged.
4. Use the `startup mount` SQLPLUS command to start up the database in the Mount status.
5. If you cannot restore certain files to the original location or if the file name has changed, you must update the control file in this step. You can use

   ```
   alter database rename file '<file name'> to '<file name'>;
   ```

   to change the location or the name.
6. You start the recovery using the SQLPLUS command

   ```
   recover database until cancel;
   ```

   or

   ```
   recover database until time 'YYYY-MM-DD:HH24:MI:SS';
   ```

   Specify the path for the required offline and online redo log files when you are prompted to do so. If you apply all redo log files with the first command, cancel the process using the `CANCEL` command. The process terminates automatically for the second command as soon as the required time has been reached.
7. After you have cancelled the recovery with `CANCEL`, you can open the database. To do this, you must execute the `alter database open resetlogs;` command. The online redo log files are then reinitialized.
8. Finally, back up the recovered database and bear in mind the post-processing that you must perform here (see Section 10.4.5).

The entire recovery process is supported by the BR*Tools.

10.6.8 Loss of Offline Redo Log Files

The loss of offline redo log files, for example, from the archiver directory or a backed up tape, creates a gap in the chain of the redo logs required to recover the database. In each case, it is better to discover a loss of individual offline redo logs during the normal operation of the database than to only notice this in an exceptional situation. It might already be too late then. You should therefore always follow up errors in the logs of the `BRARCHIVE` runs.

When offline redo log files have been lost, we must differentiate between two different cases:

1. The offline redo log file is older and may have already been backed up to a tape.
2. The offline redo log file was recently archived.

In the first case, ensure that you have a valid backup that is more recent than the time stamp of the lost redo log file. Also, start a database check as quickly as possible (see Chapter 9) to ensure that there are no corrupt blocks and that you may have to access an even older backup. If the time stamp of the missing redo log file is more recent than the last backup, start a complete backup of your database.

In the second case, initially check whether the online redo log file from which the archive was created still exists. You can use the `select * from v$log;` SQL command to display the LSN and status of the individual log groups. If you find the LSN of the missing offline redo log file in the list again, you can use the SQL command

```
alter system archive log logfile '<path/file name online redo log>
to '<path/file name offline redo log>';
```

to create the archive manually again. If the online redo log files have been overwritten, perform a complete backup of the database.

10.6.9 Database Crash During an Online Backup

As we described in Section 10.2.3, you begin an online backup of the database with `begin backup` by setting individual tablespaces or all tablespaces to Backup mode. After you back up the tablespace's data files or all of the database's tablespaces, you must reset their status to normal with `end backup`. This mechanism is not used for backups using RMAN.

If the Oracle database crashes during this type of online backup or if you shut down the database using the `shutdown abort` SQL command, not only does the backup cancel, but the tablespaces remain in the Backup mode. As soon as you try to restart the database, Oracle issues a message that the data files require a media recovery, it terminates opening the database, and remains in the Mount status. Figure 10.26 illustrates such a situation. The database of SAP system M54 was backed up online — all tablespaces were in Backup mode. A `shutdown abort` was performed in this state. After the first data file of the */oracle/M54/sapdata1/system_1/system.data1* tablespace has been checked, the opening of the Oracle database terminates with the message that a media recovery is required.

In this case, you must manually bring about the `end backup` status. If a database crash caused the backup to terminate, first check the ALERT log file and trace files to find the cause of the error. When you check the ALERT log file after you have tried to open the database, you will find error number ORA-01113 there. The exact message that you received as output when you opened the database was thus documented. Do not be confused; you do not have to perform a restore and recovery at this point. Begin by resetting the data files to the normal status.

```
SQL> startup
ORACLE instance started.

Total System Global Area 1147105848 bytes
Fixed Size                   737848 bytes
Variable Size             620756992 bytes
Database Buffers          524288000 bytes
Redo Buffers                1323008 bytes
Database mounted.
ORA-01113: file 1 needs media recovery
ORA-01110: data file 1: '/oracle/M54/sapdata1/system_1/system.data1'


SQL> █
```

Figure 10.26 Start of Database that Crashed During the Backup

For this purpose, you need to get an overview of the data files, whose statuses are still in Backup mode. You can output these files using the following `SELECT` command:

```
select substr(A.NAME,1,50) "datafile",
A.FILE# "file#", B.STATUS "Status"
from V$DATAFILE A, V$BACKUP B
where A.FILE# = B.FILE#
order by A.FILE#;
```

Figure 10.27 shows the output of the `SELECT` command on SAP system M54. The ACTIVE status shows that the data files of tablespace PSAPM54 were set to Backup mode.

```
/oracle/M54/sapdata1/m54_31/m54.data31                  47 ACTIVE
/oracle/M54/sapdata1/m54_32/m54.data32                  48 ACTIVE
/oracle/M54/sapdata1/m54_33/m54.data33                  49 ACTIVE
/oracle/M54/sapdata1/m54_34/m54.data34                  50 ACTIVE
/oracle/M54/sapdata1/m54_35/m54.data35                  51 ACTIVE
/oracle/M54/sapdata1/m54_36/m54.data36                  52 ACTIVE
/oracle/M54/sapdata1/m54_37/m54.data37                  53 ACTIVE
/oracle/M54/sapdata1/m54_38/m54.data38                  54 ACTIVE
/oracle/M54/sapdata1/m54_39/m54.data39                  55 ACTIVE

Data file                                     File number Status
--------------------------------------------- ----------- ------------------
/oracle/M54/sapdata1/m54_40/m54.data40                  56 ACTIVE
/oracle/M54/sapdata1/m54_41/m54.data41                  57 ACTIVE
/oracle/M54/sapdata1/m54_42/m54.data42                  58 ACTIVE
/oracle/M54/sapdata1/m54_43/m54.data43                  59 ACTIVE
/oracle/M54/sapdata1/m54_44/m54.data44                  60 ACTIVE
/oracle/M54/sapdata1/m54_45/m54.data45                  61 ACTIVE
/oracle/M54/sapdata1/m54_46/m54.data46                  62 ACTIVE
/oracle/M54/sapdata1/m54_47/m54.data47                  63 ACTIVE

63 rows selected.

SQL>
```

Figure 10.27 Output of the Data Files with SELECT Command

You can now use the SQL command

```
alter database datafile ''<file name>' [,'<file name>']' end backup;
```

to reset the affected data files to the normal status manually. Specify the complete path name for each data file. If the complete tablespace is in Backup mode, as an alternative, you can use the command

```
alter tablespace <tablespace> end backup;
```

to set all of the tablespace's data files to the normal status.

When you subsequently open the database, Oracle performs an instance recovery. You can check this using the ALERT log file. Finally, do not forget to repeat the aborted backup.

10.7 Backup Strategies

This section mainly covers the backup of large and highly available SAP systems and associated Oracle databases. However, before we discuss the alternatives provided for backing up these comprehensive systems, we will look at some of the basic details, concepts, and strategies.

In this chapter, we have frequently talked about the complete backup of the Oracle database, be it an online or offline backup. You are now probably wondering how often you have to perform such a backup.

The frequency of a complete backup depends on the level of activity in your database. When lots of data records are entered and many changes are made, a very high number of redo log files are written. As a result, if an error occurs and you must perform the associated restore and recovery of the database, you will need a great deal of time to recover the redo log files and apply them to the data files. However, if you perform many complete backups, the number of redo log files required for a recovery is reduced. At the same time, this decreases the downtime. The frequent backing up of the database also reduces the loss of data that could occur due to the redo log files being missing.

However, the bigger the database to be backed up, the more difficult it is to place the complete backups in a timeframe (*backup window*) that was defined for performing the backup.

If you now lose a redo log file and cannot find this file in the recommended second backup, you cannot recover the database completely, even if you have several complete backups. To avoid this threat of data loss, you must back up the redo logs twice (see Section 10.1.2).

In this context, we refer you once again to the archiver stuck that we dealt with in Section 10.1.3. The continuous monitoring and backing up of the archiver directory and the exclusiveness of a tape drive for backing up redo log files is elementary. What use are all of the precautions to prevent an archiver stuck if the tape drive that backs up the redo log files is occupied for several hours by a backup of the data files?

You should also keep several complete backups and the relevant redo log backups. This ensures that you can also restore and recover the database if, for example, the last complete backup has been lost. You can then still restore the data files from the penultimate backup and apply all redo log files:

- Of the penultimate backup
- From the period between the penultimate backup and the lost backup

- Of the lost backup itself
- From the period since the lost backup

SAP has summarized all of these details and advocates a backup cycle of at least 14 days — the 28-day backup cycle (4 weeks) is recommended. This backup cycle defines the time for which a backup that was written to a tape is kept. After this time has elapsed, the tape with the backup is released and is available for the next backup.

You should carry out the following in this cycle:

- Perform a daily online backup of your Oracle database.
- Run an offline backup once a week (though at least once in the cycle), preferably when the system is not being used (such as the weekend, for example).
- Back up the offline redo log files daily, depending on the redo logs that occur, and always after the online and offline data backup. Make sure that you carry out the backup on two separate tapes.
- At least once in the cycle, you should check a verify of an offline backup for physical errors and a verify of the database for logical errors. You should take the tapes with the verified offline backup from the pool for the backup cycle and keep them separately for long-term storage. You must replace the tapes you have taken out with reinitialized tapes.
- Although no longer necessary, you can perform additional backups if the database structure has changed. When you perform these types of backups, you should set aside the tapes for long-term storage.

Remarks

Legislation may stipulate the duration for storing backups in this type of long-term pool. This must be taken into consideration in project planning and when buying technical equipment for storing the backups (see Chapter 5).

Although the backup cycle presented (see Figure 10.28) contains all of the important requirements you must fulfill to protect your data, it can not effectively be used for SAP systems whose Oracle database is very large and therefore cannot be backed up within a backup window and must be used 24 hours a day, 7 days a week.

We consider databases to be large if they have between 500 gigabytes and 10 terabytes or more. In this case, it is almost impossible to back up the database as frequently as recommended above. When you back up these types of databases, basic problems occur. These include:

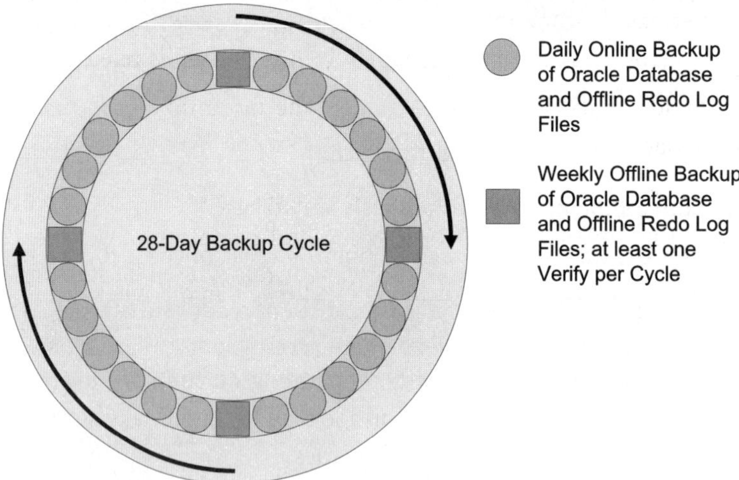

Figure 10.28 28-Day Backup Cycle

- **Performance**
  A backup burdens the resources of the database server. These are mainly the CPU, the system and I/O buses, and the hard disk and tape controller. While a database is being backed up, only limited actions can be executed in the SAP system.
- **Time**
  The backups are usually performed if there is no load on the systems, so this is frequently done at night. However, the larger the database, the more time is required for its full backup. The backup may run into the normal daily rhythm again and noticeably slow down the system.
- **Size of data volume**
  As described in the previous point, the size of the database influences the backup time. If the database is too large, it cannot be backed up in the specified time.

Different factors determine how you can now back up very large databases with BRBACKUP. For example, the capacity and throughput of tape drives play a crucial role. If these have a high throughput rate, you can back up more data by using several drives in parallel. However, this also depends on the access time on the hard disks where the database is saved, the maximum throughput of the system and I/O buses, and the performance of the `dd` and `cpio` operating system tools used, which ultimately update the data. The `BRBACKUP` backup tool, however, has negligible hardware requirements. Bear in mind that the scalability of the data backup is limited. The performance during the data backup does not increase in proportion to the number of tape drives you add. The more drives you use, the more time each device requires for the backup.

The hardware configuration for very large database systems and their backup must be planned in advance in a very detailed and complete way. Several tape changes must be made to connected drives for this type of backup and, most importantly, several hundred tapes must be kept ready and managed in the backup pool. Consider purchasing tape jukeboxes, robots, or autoloaders in this case.

Several alternatives are available to cause the backups to be performed at different times or to considerably reduce the amount of data during the backup.

One variant that we have already introduced involves performing incremental backups. You can only perform these backups using the Oracle Recovery Manager (RMAN). Only the database blocks that are actually changed are backed up in incremental backups. For more information, refer to Section 10.5, *Oracle Recovery Manager (RMAN)*.

Another option is to use snapshot technology. This technology is provided by the hardware partners in different instances in conjunction with memory systems. We will introduce the principle and advantages and disadvantages briefly here.

A snapshot freezes all data of a point-in-time at the level of the I/O system. Creating a snapshot normally only takes a few seconds in which the database cannot be used. After you create the snapshot, regular access to the database is enabled again. The changed data is then also stored as a new version. The snapshot mechanism is displayed in Figure 10.29. The XY data file consists of three disk blocks: A, B, and C. A snapshot was created for this file. It also references blocks A, B, and C (left side of display). If you now change block C, the system writes a new disk block C' (right side of display). The data file now consists of the disk blocks A, B, and C', whereas the snapshot of the file still references blocks A, B, and C.

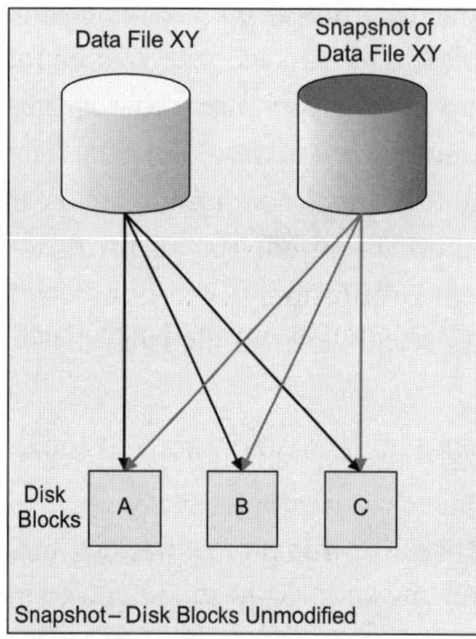

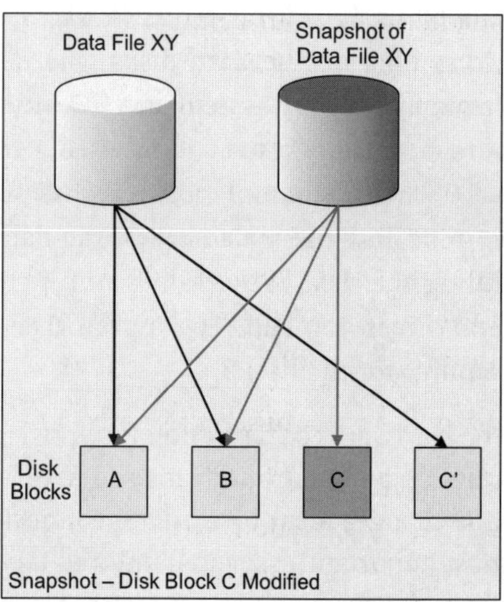

Figure 10.29 Snapshot Mechanism

The snapshot itself initially remains on the central memory system and is immediately available for the possible restore of the database. Several snapshots are usually stored and kept on the memory system. Data is always backed up to tapes from the snapshot. The major advantage of this is that the database server is not affected by the backup load. The most recent and therefore most frequently required versions of the data backups remain on the memory system as snapshots. Older versions of the snapshots are backed up, as usual, to tape drives or other media and then deleted from this memory system. You can access the database without any restriction during the backup process. The advantages are:

- You can create a hard disk backup very quickly.
- Several snapshots of different points-in-time are possible.
- Less additional space is required than for a split mirror backup (see Section 10.7.4, *Split Mirror Databases*), because only the changed blocks must be stored in duplicate.
- You can restore the database more quickly if the snapshot is kept longer.

The disadvantages are:

- The backup runs in the same memory system as the live database, so a conflict of resources is possible.
- If block corruptions occur due to problems with the hardware, these will probably also be corrupt in the snapshot.

In addition to your complete backup, another alternative is to back up individual tablespaces that are changed frequently. This can reduce the time for restoring the database. If a more recent backup of a tablespace that is used very intensively is available, you have to apply fewer redo log files to restore a database than you would from a complete backup. It only makes sense to back up individual tablespaces if you do not place the backup of the entire database within your backup window. You can also use this method to back up very large databases (also refer to the information about the partial backups in Section 10.7.1).

We will discuss other alternatives for backing up large and highly available databases in the next sections.

So far in this section, we have dealt with backups of live systems. You may not have to back up the data of test and development systems as often. The backup cycle here mainly depends on how frequently these systems are used. Restoring the last successfully performed offline backup is often sufficient for test systems. In this case, you can operate the database in NoArchiveLog operating mode and ignore the online backups and backup of the redo log files. The strategy can, in turn, be completely different for development systems, because you place great emphasis on backing up all development and customizing work here. In this case, you operate the database in ArchiveLog mode and continuously update the redo log files for the offline backup on two tapes. In both cases, you can, of course, use the very secure strategy that you use with your live system.

10.7.1 Partial Backups

One option to back up a large database that must be available 7 days a week and 24 hours a day is to use *partial backups*. With partial backups, the backup of the Oracle database is distributed over several days (or, preferably, nights). By night, each of the defined pools of data files (or tablespaces) is updated using an online backup. The weekend should then be used to back up the database completely online.

This mechanism is very prone to error. The administrator is responsible for dividing the data on the different partial backups. He must ensure that all data files are incorporated into the total partial backups so that all tablespaces are ultimately backed up. The risk of a loss of data is higher than with other procedures. An online data backup is only consistent in this situation if all partial backups are correct and all redo log information was backed up. If changes are made to the database structure, you must also keep an eye out that these changes are taken into account for the partial backup. If a data file that is not contained in any of the partial backups is missing, you cannot restore the database. The administrator decides what is updated with this type of backup. BRBACKUP supports the administrator in the backup process but does not help him decide which of the tablespaces must still be backed up.

You can use the BRBACKUP parameter or command options to set up partial backups. You can achieve a split for a partial backup of the database by specifying the tablespace using the backup_mode parameter. You can use this for backing up MCOD databases. You can therefore back up the different components on different days of the week. For a database that only contains an SAP system and still uses the new tablespace concept (see Chapter 4), the backup using tablespaces makes little sense. There are a few tablespaces with the new concept, and the PSAP<SID> tablespace also contains most of the data in the Oracle database. You can use the specification of the file ID of the data files in the backup_mode parameter here.

On no account should this type of backup fully replace a regular complete backup of the database. If you only perform partial backups over a very long period, you increase your dependency on your redo log files. This is because with individual backups of tablespaces, you do not perform a consistent backup of the database. You therefore require all redo log files since the last consistent and complete backup of the database to be able to restore this if an error occurs. The risk of data being lost due to a missing redo log file therefore increases considerably.

We will now summarize the advantages and disadvantages. The advantages are:

- Partial backups require less time so that you can perform these daily.
- You can restore the database at any time. You must have all of the required redo log files.
- You can restore your database very quickly, because you only have to restore the affected files.

The disadvantages are:

- It takes a very long time to restore the complete database because you have to restore all partial backups.
- You must ensure that all data files in the cycle of the partial backups are backed up. This situation intensifies if a complete backup is not possible within a time when the database load is low.

- Dependency on the redo log files is very high. If redo log files are lost, the risk of a loss of data increases considerably.

10.7.2 Two-Phase Data Backup

Another alternative for backing up large databases is the *two-phase data backup*. In the first phase, the data is backed up on a hard disk. You can do this more quickly than with a tape drive. In the second phase, the backup on the hard disk is then updated onto tapes. Both phases are supported by BRBACKUP. You can perform the second phase using external backup tools, because the files cannot be accessed by the database and are open.

A restore occurs directly and quickly from the hard disks used in phase 1 to the original directories of the database. If the backup is already on tape and has been deleted from the hard disk, it can also be restored from the tape. The prerequisite is that this backup was performed using BRBACKUP.

The benefits are obvious:

- The backup to hard disk in phase 1 is significantly shorter.
- If you have to restore a backup, this is much faster if the data is still available on the hard disk.
- If you have to restore a backup from a tape, you can do this directly in the database directories (if BRBACKUP was used).
- You first use the volume management of BRBACKUP in the second phase.

There are also the following disadvantages:

- Greater hardware requirements for hard disk space must be met. For the one-off temporary storage in phase 1, a maximum amount of memory equal to the size of the database is required.
- You perform two backups and therefore need to call BRBACKUP twice (if you do not use an external tool for phase 2).

In addition to backing up the data files of the database, you can back up the redo log files the same way. You should also back up the redo log files in phase 2 twice to different tapes. There is hardly any difference in the advantages and disadvantages that we listed for backing up with BRBACKUP. However, one important advantage in relation to BRARCHIVE is that the archiver directory in phase 1 can be emptied much more quickly and an archiver stuck is better avoided.

10.7.3 Standby Databases

Another way to back up large and highly available Oracle databases is to use a *standby database*. This is officially supported by Oracle as of Release 8.

Figure 10.30 illustrates the concept of the standby database. Two identical servers are set up. An Oracle database is running on each of the two servers. In our example, the primary and live database is running on server A. The database is open; the SAP instance accesses it and changes are written. However, the standby database on server B is running in the Mounted Standby status and is only used as a recovery system. When you create an offline redo log file in the live database, this is copied to the archiver directory of the standby database and applied to the data files immediately or after a certain delay, depending on the setting. All changes in the live database are replicated in the standby database. You therefore get an identical copy.

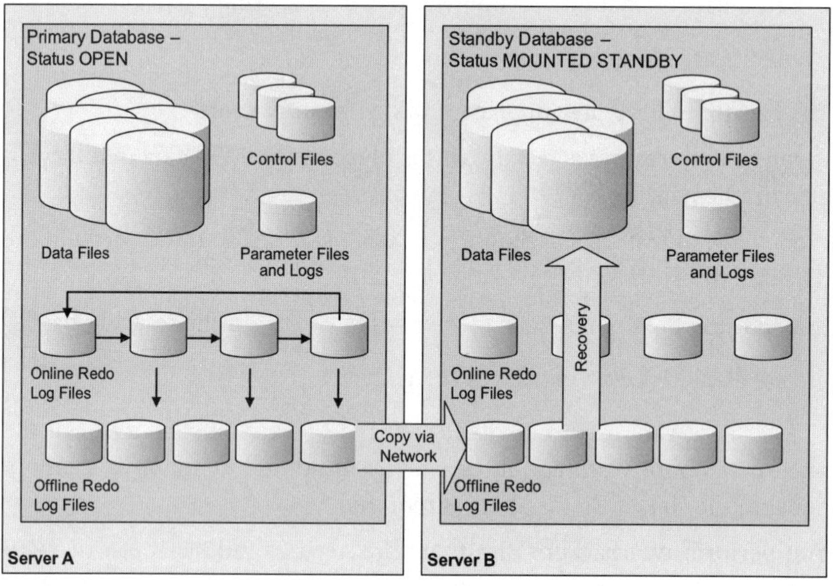

Figure 10.30 Standby Database

If you cannot use the primary database now because of an error, you can switch to the standby database through a *takeover*. The SAP application works from there on the database of server B. The standby database abandons the recovery status, and its status changes to Open. You subsequently have sufficient time to repair the hardware for server A.

You can switch to the standby database much more quickly than you can restore and recover a database. Before you can use the standby database, you still have to apply the remaining redo log files of the primary database. You can also try to archive the current online redo log file (using SQL command `alter system archive log current;`) and import this into the standby database.

After a takeover, you must set up the standby database again. This is usually done on the server where the primary database was previously running (server A in our case).

You back up the database to tape from the standby database. The advantage of this is that the live system is not burdened with the backup process at any time, and all resources are exclusively available for live operations. Because activities do not take place on the server that contains the standby database, the full resources of the server that contains the standby database can be used for the backup. This can also be started at any time and last any length of time depending on the size of the database.

The BR*Tools comprehensively support the standby solution. `BRARCHIVE` is therefore used on the primary database to constantly copy the offline redo log files to the archiver directory of the standby database. `BRARCHIVE` is used on this to apply the redo log files and then back them up twice and delete them, if necessary. `BRARCHIVE` starts the recovery process of the database in this case.

You can only back up the standby database offline (`backup_type = offline_standby`). `BRBACKUP` connects to the primary database at the start and obtains from there all information about the database structure, which is then written into the log files of the backup. `BRBACKUP` notes the status of the database at the beginning of the backup to reset this after the backup has been completed. No redo log files can be applied during the backup. `BRARCHIVE` will only execute this function again once the database has the Mounted Standby status again.

Let's take a look at the advantages of this solution:

- **Low error rate**
  The fact that all system components are available twice, in other words, they are redundantly available, reduces the error rate considerably. Primary and standby databases run on two completely separate servers, and there is very little likelihood of both crashing at the same time. For security reasons, both can also be locally separated from each other. They do not have to be in the same data center.
- **Short downtime**
  If the primary database crashes, the downtime of the SAP system is very low. After you have applied the last redo log files of the primary database

on the standby database, you can open this through the takeover and use it. The time gained is significant compared to the time-consuming restore and recovery.

- **Reduced load on the live database**
  The load on the primary database is reduced. The data backup that mainly burdens the CPU, the system and I/O buses, and the controller is totally omitted, and the resources are fully available for the live operation. There will not have to be any restrictions on or interruptions to the live operation.

There are also the following disadvantages:

- **High costs**
  To illustrate the scenario, duplicates of all components must exist and be operated. In addition to the purchase costs for the servers, you must also calculate costs for a possible additional data center infrastructure and its operation.
- **More time and effort for the system administration**
  You must first set up the standby database together with the server. During the operation, a check must be carried out to see whether structural changes that were made on the primary database are also included in the standby database. This is usually done automatically. If this is not the case, the recovery process stops until the administrators intervene. If the standby database eventually becomes the primary database because of an error, you must subsequently (after you have eliminated the error) set up a new standby database.
- **High requirement of switchover software**
  In addition to the database takeover, you must also switch over to the SAP central instance. Hardware and software manufacturers provide solutions for this purpose that must be evaluated, selected, purchased, installed, and managed.

You have now learned about all of the advantages and disadvantages of this solution. Weigh these carefully against each other before you decide in favor of or against this solution.

10.7.4 Split Mirror Databases

The last variant we will present is *split mirror databases*. This means that a mirror is created between hard disks at the level of the disk system. The changes made to the database files by the database server are mirrored between these hard disks.

You should always implement this mirroring with hardware, because a software solution would increase the load on the database server enormously. If you choose this type of solution, you should, on all accounts, consult with your hardware partner. The mirror is split and the hard disks are synchronized using scripts and programs that are not provided by SAP. You must contact the manufacturer of the operating system or backup software about this.

As the name suggests, a mirror is split for a backup, that is, the array of hard disks to be synchronized is split. Online and offline backups of the database can be performed. The advantage is that the time when the database is either offline or in Backup mode is very short. The BR*Tools support the split mirror technology.

You can implement the principle using a server and an additional backup server. We will first look in more detail at the split mirror backup with a server (see Figure 10.31).

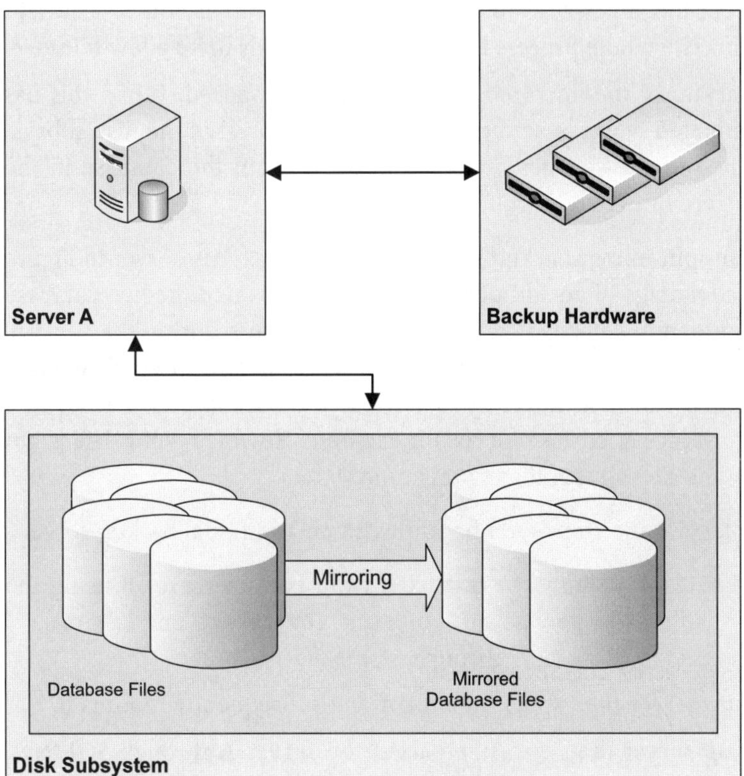

Figure 10.31 Split Mirror Backup with a Server

The disk subsystem is responsible for mirroring the hard disks, which contain the database objects, onto other hard disks on a one-to-one basis. In normal operations, the server A database server accesses the database files and modifies them. The disk subsystem immediately synchronizes these changes to the blocks on the mirrored hard disks. The synchronization of the changes has nothing in common with the redo log files that log the changes.

If you now perform a backup, the following steps are required:

1. You start the backup with `BRBACKUP`. You must execute the `brbackup -t offline_split` command for an offline backup and `brbackup -t online_split` for an online backup. In the first case, you shut down the database; in the second case, you set the status of the tablespaces to Backup mode.
2. The database server (server A) then splits the mirror and subsequently mounts the mirrored file system.
3. You can now use `BRBACKUP` to start up the database on server A again or set the status of the tablespaces to Normal mode. You can use the SAP system fully again. The whole process lasts for a few seconds up to a few minutes.
4. A data backup of the mirrored hard disks is then started. When this has been completed, you can set up the mirror at the level of the disk subsystem again, and the changes that have been made in the database in the meantime are integrated through synchronization.

We show the split mirror backup with an additional backup server in Figure 10.32. The advantage of an additional backup server is that the live database server is completely detached from the load that occurs during the backup. Consequently, the performance on the live server is not affected. If the identical Oracle software is installed, you can use the backup server itself as a standalone instance to create reports, for example. However, your data is not mirrored by the live system during this time.

Let's take a look at the steps for a backup with an additional backup server:

1. First, the backup on server A is started from backup server B using the `BRBACKUP` command `brbackup -t offline_split` or `brbackup -t online_split`. This occurs through SQL*Net.
2. The backup server then splits the mirror and subsequently mounts it.
3. The backup server then ends the backup on server A through SQL*Net. You can use the SAP system fully again, and there is no system load from

the copy process that now follows, because this takes place on the backup server. The process itself lasts for a few seconds up to a few minutes.

4. The data backup of the mirrored hard disks is then started on the backup server. When this has been completed, the backup server restores the mirror at the level of the disk subsystem, and the changes that have been made in the database in the meantime are integrated through synchronization.

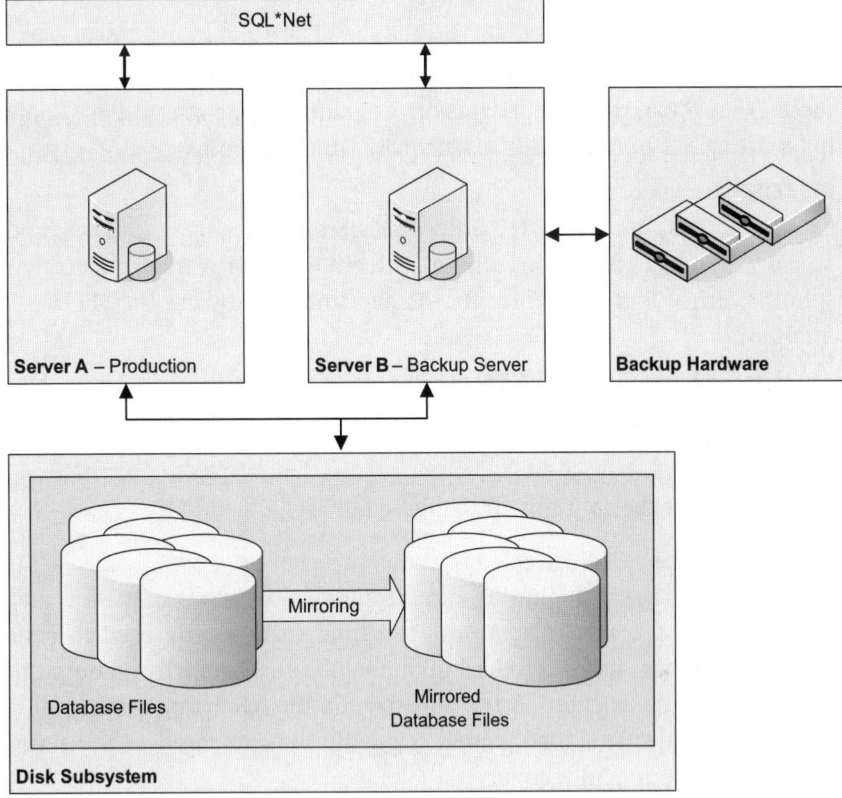

Figure 10.32 Split Mirror Backup with Two Servers

In both cases presented, it is important that the data that you back up to tape is consistent; otherwise, you cannot restore the database.

You can use the BACKINT interface to perform mirror backups without any restrictions.

However, split mirror technology is only supported by `BRBACKUP`. The backup of offline redo log files using `BRARCHIVE` continues to be performed from the live server to connected or remote backup media or using the

BACKINT interface. In any case, the load that occurs when the redo log files are being backed up is very low. To keep the BRBACKUP runs synchronous with the BRARCHIVE runs, you can start BRARCHIVE directly after the mirror is split, not only at the end of the BRBACKUP run. The Oracle database itself already regards the backup of the database with the split as ended.

BRBACKUP can assume control of the splitting and the subsequent synchronization of the hard disks. Two scenarios are supported for this:

- **Split command scenario**
  The split_cmd and resync_cmd parameters are used for this purpose. For these BRBACKUP parameters, scripts or programs are run that call BRBACKUP for splitting the mirror or for resynchronization purposes.
- **SPLITINT scenario**
  BRBACKUP uses the SPLITINT interface here. The split_options and split_resync parameters are used to integrate the software products that split the mirror and resynchronize the data and thereby use the SPLITINT interface.

  The database handling in the SPLITINT scenario is considerably faster than in the split command scenario, and SAP therefore recommends this scenario.

The advantages of the split mirror database are:

- **Short downtime**
  The time between the beginning and the end of a backup is very short and can take from seconds to minutes. The time span is only used to shut down the database or set it to Backup mode, to split the mirror, mount the file system on the backup server, and start up the database again or set it to Normal mode. The time gained is significant compared to the time-consuming restore and recovery.
- **Reduced load on the live database**
  As already mentioned, the load on the primary database is reduced when you use an additional backup server. The data backup that particularly burdens the CPU, the system and I/O buses, and the controller does not take place on the live database, and the resources are fully available for the live operation. There do not have to be any restrictions on or interruptions to the live operation.
- **Hard disk backup created quickly**
  Due to the mirroring, a backup to hard disk can be created very quickly from the live system. You may be able to use this as a system copy for the quality backup system.

When making your decision, you have to carefully weigh the following disadvantages with the advantages:

- **Higher costs**
  To illustrate the scenario, at least an equal amount of hard disk space to that of the live database must be available. If you want to use an additional backup server, you will have to factor in other purchase costs and costs for the cost center infrastructure and its operation.
- **Greater time and effort for system administration**
  If you want to use an additional backup server, you must build and set this up. You must also install and set up the hardware and software for creating the mirror. During the operation, you must monitor whether the mirroring is working correctly and whether the mirror is split and resynchronized again if a backup is performed.
- **Additional time and effort for split software and hardware for the mirroring**
  You may have to purchase software to structure, split, and resynchronize the mirror. You will also have to schedule the hardware that you want to handle the mirroring. You must evaluate, select, purchase, install, and manage the solutions provided by software and hardware manufacturers.

For more information about split mirror technology in live environments, refer to SAP Notes 170607, 378818, and 968507.

10.8 Tips and Tricks

In this section, you will find important instructions and information that you may be able to use in your system environment for backing up and restoring data.

- **Change the archiver directory in the live system**
  If there is not enough hard disk space for the offline redo log files on the hard disk, or if an archiver stuck has occurred and there is no more time left to copy the existing offline redo log files, you can change the directory into which the archiver process writes the redo log files during the live operation. The automatic archiving by the ARCH process can be stopped and started again with `STOP` / `START`:

  ```
  alter system archive log stop;
  alter system archive log set log_archive_dest = <temp_path/suffix>;
  alter system archive log start;
  ```

- **Manually archive online redo log files**
  You can use the following SQL command to manually archive all online redo log files that are not currently archived

  ```
  alter system archive log all;
  ```

- **Redo log switch on the next redo log group**
  You can implement a redo log switch on the next redo log group using the command

  ```
  alter system switch logfile;
  ```

- **Query status of redo log file**
  You can query the status of the redo log files using the command

  ```
  archive log list;
  ```

  and use

  ```
  select * from v$log;
  ```

  to obtain information about the redo log groups.

- **Execute a manual checkpoint**
  Executing a manual checkpoint results in all database buffers being written into the data files. You can initiate this type of checkpoint using the command

  ```
  alter system checkpoint;
  ```

- **Create a dummy file**
  To prevent an archiver stuck, we mentioned using a dummy file as an alternative. You use the following UNIX operating system command to create such a file of 1 GB in size:

  ```
  dd if=/dev/zero of=dummy bs=1024 count=1024k
  ```

- **Useful SAP Notes**
  SAP Notes 424102, 786921, 914174, and 968507 are useful if you have already installed a standby database.

10.9 Summary

Two of the most important tasks for an administrator are backing up the Oracle database, SAP system, and operating system and professionally restoring them. In addition to the aspect of data loss, that of system downtime must also be considered. Every minute that the live SAP system is not available can cost a lot of money.

In this chapter, you first learned about the backup objects and, particularly, the interaction of Oracle processes with the Oracle database objects. We then discussed the two Oracle operating modes and presented the archiver stuck caused by the archive mode as well as possible prevention strategies and various solutions if this error occurs.

The data backup methods differentiate between offline and online data backups. When performing an online backup, bear in mind the special features for the tablespace backup, namely, the freezing of the SCN and the phenomenon of the block split.

The most common recovery scenarios are:

- Partial restore and complete recovery
- Database reset
- Point-in-time recovery
- Full restore and complete recovery
- Disaster recovery

You cannot use the 28-day backup cycle as a backup strategy for large Oracle systems, because an online backup of the system may not fit into the defined backup timeframe. You can use the following options to reduce the time and the data volume of a backup:

- Incremental backups using RMAN
- Snapshot technology
- Partial backups
- Two-phase data backups
- Standby databases
- Split mirror databases

The Java programming language has become more and more widespread since its introduction. Particularly since Java 2 Enterprise Edition has been available, it is an inevitable part of every large application system.

11 Administrating the Java Stack

SAP first offered a Java application server with SAP Web Application Server 6.10. In the meantime, in the release SAP NetWeaver 7.0 (2004s), version 7.0 of the J2EE server is available (SAP NetWeaver Application Server Java). Based on that, SAP has developed a number of products in the past few years. The best-known examples are SAP NetWeaver Portal and SAP NetWeaver Exchange Infrastructure (XI). Due to its distributed and component-oriented architecture, SAP NetWeaver Application Server Java is built for scalability and fail-safety. Many familiar concepts from the ABAP world were taken into the Java application server and integrated into the architecture.

Just as in the ABAP environment, SAP offers a complete development environment for Java. This includes a separate implementation for software logistics, the *SAP NetWeaver Development Infrastructure* (NWDI). It allows the versioning and distributed development of Java applications. Together with the *SAP NetWeaver Developer Studio* (NWDS), based on Eclipse, you have all of the tools you need to develop your own applications.

The following section will first provide a basic look at the architecture and internal structure of an SAP NetWeaver AS Java, with particular attention paid to its interplay with the Oracle RDBMS.

Moreover, we'll also take a look at the most important parameters of an ABAP system of interest when connecting to an SAP NetWeaver AS Java, as well as a look at the particular features of Java software logistics.

11.1 Using Java in SAP Systems

Besides the traditional use of an SAP ABAP system, there are also a number of applications that rely at least partly on the use of Java applications or that are entirely Java based. The best-known examples, as mentioned previously, are the SAP NetWeaver Portal, which is fully Java-based, and the SAP NetWeaver Exchange Infrastructure, which consists of both ABAP and Java components. To manage the requirements of these solutions, SAP has developed an application server to use according to the J2EE specification. This part of the application server is often called the *Java stack*.

There are two basic usage scenarios for using the Java stack:

- **SAP NetWeaver Application Server with ABAP and Java**
  A schematic diagram of this variant is shown in Figure 11.1. The system consists of an ABAP stack that also has an iterated Java instance. In the database of the ABAP stack, an additional schema is created for the data of the Java stack. Alternatively, a separate database instance can also be installed. Communications between the two instances are carried out through the Java Connector (JCo). Access to the systems is possible using either the SAP GUI or a web browser. Depending on the form of application called up in the web browser, the Internet Communication Manager (ICM) is capable of distributing the requests to the corresponding instance. Thus, calls from Business Server Pages (BSPs) are passed to the ABAP stack, whereas web dynpros, for instance, are processed by the Java stack.
- **SAP NetWeaver Application Server with Java (stand-alone)**
  The system consists of a stand-alone Java server with its own database. This installation variant is used in SAP NetWeaver Portal, for instance, or in the SAP NWDI. The corresponding applications are created in the Java Engine in either case. Figure 11.2 shows an example structure for a Java cluster. This consists of three instances and one instance for the central services, the message server, and the enqueue service. Within the instances, server processes are defined that handle the processing of requests.

A more detailed explanation of the architecture follows in Section 11.2, *Architecture of the J2EE Engine*.

The two scenarios mentioned allow a variety of options for the extension and reorientation of existing landscapes, as well as high flexibility when designing new infrastructures.

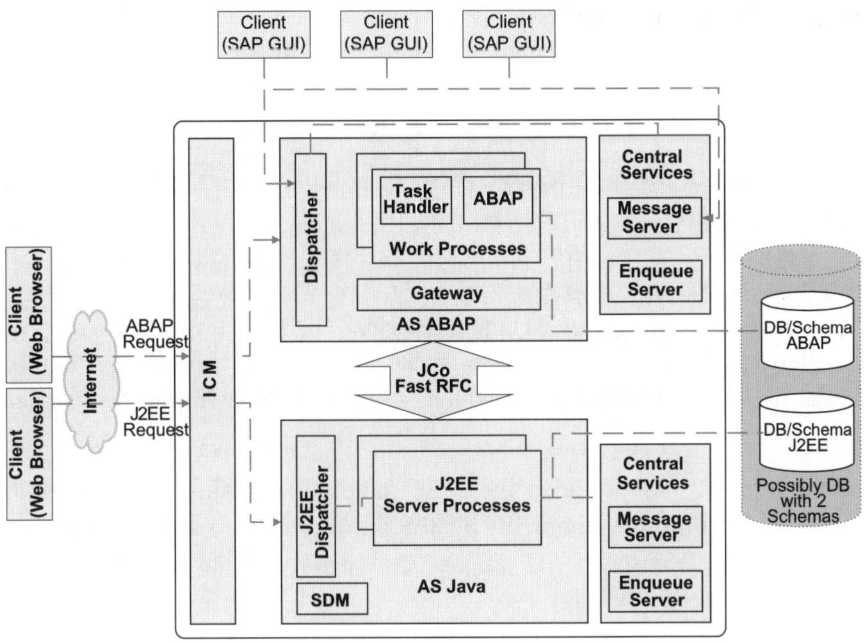

Figure 11.1 Architecture of SAP NetWeaver Application Server ABAP and Java

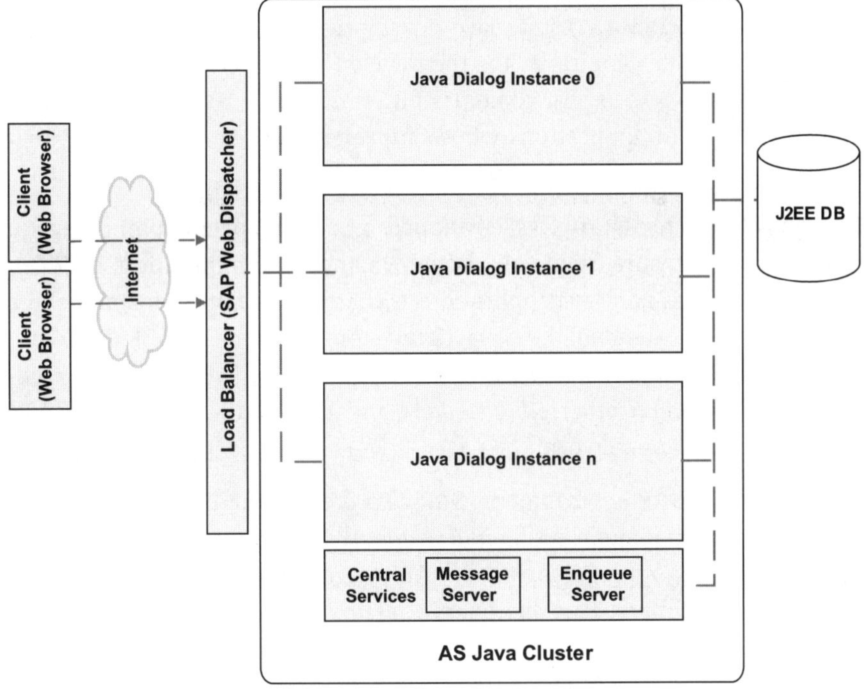

Figure 11.2 Architecture of an SAP NetWeaver Application Server Java

The basis for construction of a Java application server is the *J2EE specification*. The reference implementation is predefined by Sun Microsystems, but it can be extended or easily changed. Version 5 of the Java Platform Enterprise Edition was approved on May 5, 2006.

In the context of the specification, there is a complete description of all APIs, services, and properties to be implemented by a J2EE server. Some important APIs are *Enterprise Beans* (sometimes also called Enterprise Java Beans), *Enterprise Servlet API*, *Java Persistence API*, *Java Naming and Directory Interface* (JNDI), and *Java Database Connectivity API* (JDBC). Currently a variety of certified application servers are available, for instance Apache Geronimo, Jboss, IBM WebSphere, and, of course, SAP NetWeaver Application Server Java.

Moreover, SAP has extended the J2EE standard with their own developments. The central developments by SAP are *Web Dynpro* and the *SAP Java Connector*. The Persistence API was also extended by SAP to enable database-independent programming.

Web Dynpro is, in principle, an extension of servlets, implementing a programming model for the creation of graphical user interfaces. The MVC pattern (*Model-View-Controller*) is implemented, allowing the strict separation of the data model (*Model*), interface development (*View*), and business log (*Controller*). At the same time, for the development of Web Dynpro a uniform metamodel is in use for all kinds of user interfaces, which simplifies the implementation of applications whose appearance should be uniform, that is, when using a corporate design.

The *Java Connector* (JCo) was developed as an independent middleware component to ensure stable, high-performance communication between ABAP applications and Java applications (J2EE, web dynpros, or stand-alone Java). SAP also extended the Java Connector Architecture API (JCA) and developed it into the SAP *Java Resource Adapter* (JRA), which permits communication between other J2EE servers and the ABAP stack. The JRA is based on the JCo framework.

Just as in the ABAP environment, SAP also created the option in the Java stack of developing applications independently of the underlying database. To do this, an SAP-specific persistence API was developed that implements a central Java dictionary. This dictionary contains the descriptions of uniform, database-independent data types, which can be used to define tables. These table descriptions are also stored in the dictionary. *Open SQL for Java* is used to access the data, which allows database-independent definition of SQL statements in a way similar to Open SQL in ABAP systems. Finally, the concept of logical locks from the ABAP world was adapted to the Java persistence layer, so that the programmer can set logical object locks without needing to worry about locking objects at the database level.

SAP has also extended the Eclipse open-source development environment with a series of its own plug-ins, and this environment is available under the name of SAP NetWeaver Developer Studio (NWDS) as a tool for Java development. The NWDS allows developers in the SAP environment to use all of the possibilities inherent in the SAP J2EE engine. To handle software logistics during programming, SAP developed the NetWeaver Development Infrastructure (NWDI). Among other things, it supports the software logistics of Java development, which differs from that in the ABAP world. We will take a closer look at these changes and their effects in Section 11.3.1, *SAP NetWeaver Development Infrastructure*.

11.2 Architecture of the J2EE Engine

You can see a rough overview of the architecture in Figure 11.2. We will flesh that out in the following sections, to give you an understanding of the structure of an SAP NetWeaver Application Server Java. The entire architecture of the J2EE engine is designed for scalability and high availability to handle the requirements of large applications.

For this reason, it is possible to use multiple instances in one J2EE installation, which are all responsible for receiving and processing requests. Additional dialog instances can be installed, all of which work on the same database and share central services. To distribute requests over the different instances, for instance, the SAP Web Dispatcher can be used. Such a structure is shown in Figure 11.5.

For instance-internal scaling, you can define additional server processes for each instance. As you can see in Figure 11.3, this can be done by simply adding them in the Config Tool of the instance. To start the Config Tool from */usr/sap/<SID>/<instance>/j2ee/configtool*, depending on the operating system, start either the configtool.sh (UNIX) or configtool.bat (Windows) file. The framework of the SAP J2EE engine ensures that the new process is built and added. No further action is needed to use the process.

In Figure 11.3, you can also see that for each process, a two-digit number is appended to the instance ID. This makes unique identification of all server processes within an instance possible.

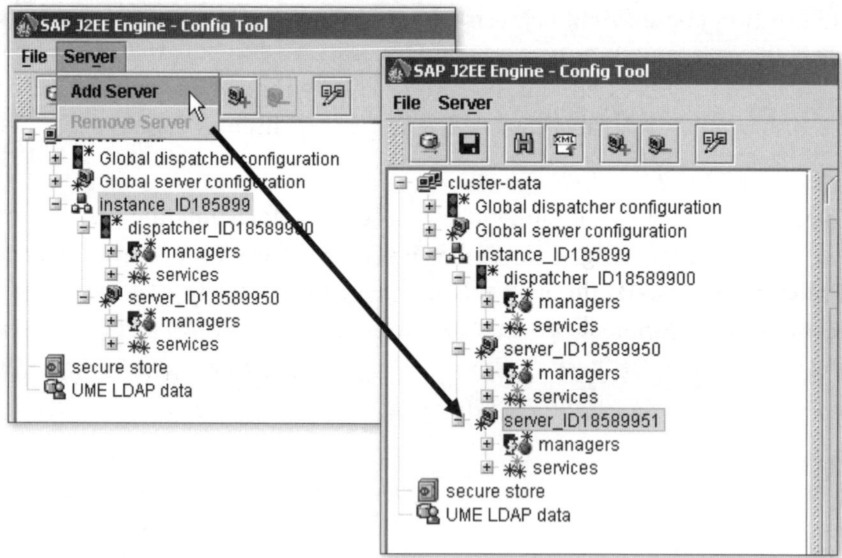

Figure 11.3 Adding a Server in the Config Tool

The instance ID in Figure 11.3 is 185899 and can be found as the first part of each server process as well. There, 00 is appended for a dispatcher process and 50 and up for server processes, so that the structure shown results. In the file system, the processes are reflected in the subdirectories */usr/sap/<SID>/<instance>/j2ee/cluster*, as shown in the example in Figure 11.4. There, besides the directory *dispatcher* are also the directories server0 through server<n>, as well as the file instance.properties, which contains the configuration of the cluster and basic bootstrap information. In this file, you can also find the assignment of each instance ID to a directory.

```
f01:/usr/sap/S01/DVEBMGS01/j2ee/cluster#11
total 42
-rwxr-xr-x   1 s01adm    sapsys       2008 Oct 27 11:23 .hotspot_compiler
drwxr-xr-x   2 s01adm    sapsys       1024 Aug 23 11:48 bootstrap
drwxr-xr-x   7 s01adm    sapsys       1024 Oct 27 11:18 dispatcher
-rw-r--r--   1 s01adm    sapsys       3631 Oct 27 11:23 instance.properties
-rw-r--r--   1 s01adm    sapsys       4977 Aug 23 11:49 instance.properties.vmprop
drwxr-xr-x  10 s01adm    sapsys       2048 Oct 27 11:18 server0
-rw-r--r--   1 s01adm    sapsys       3503 Oct 27 09:56 system.log
-rw-r--r--   1 s01adm    sapsys       1065 Oct 27 11:17 version.bin
```

Figure 11.4 J2EE Engine in the File System

The distribution of load over many individual instances and processes also increases failure safety. By using Java serialization, the data for a user session can be stored persistently in the database after every HTTP round trip. As a result, when a server process or even an entire instance fails, the session can be forwarded to a different process or server, which can read its data back out of the database. If the dispatcher for an instance fails, all existing sessions continue to be processed, but the instance won't receive new requests until the dispatcher is available again. The dispatcher itself is stateless, so that there is no data loss.

Single points of failure of an installation are therefore only the central service instance, consisting of the message server and enqueue service and the database. If necessary, these must be implemented in a fail-safe manner with additional high-availability solutions.

Now that we've addressed a few components of the SAP NetWeaver AS Java, let's look at their interplay and how they work. An SAP NetWeaver AS Java can be broken down into four elements: the load balancer (for instance, SAP Web Dispatcher), the central service instance (message server and enqueue service), the database, and the Java dialog instances. A dialog instance is internally composed of a dispatcher and an arbitrary number (at most 16) of server processes.

The dispatcher handles the function of internal load distribution over the server processes, which process the requests. A schematic diagram is shown in Figure 11.5. The process for the *Software Deployment Manager* (SDM) is also shown there. It is responsible for the loading of new applications into a Java engine, so-called *deployment*. During deployment, all of the components of an application are transferred to the server and stored in the database.

The database is used to store all configuration data and for the storage of binary data (archives of applications). Central administration of the cluster is therefore possible, because there is always central processing and storage of data, for example, a deployment in the database and not to the file system for the instance. In addition, it is possible to integrate external databases as data sources and access their data. The details of how this works and how the communication with the Oracle database is implemented from a technical standpoint are explained in Section 11.2.2, *Interplay of the Java Stack and the Database*.

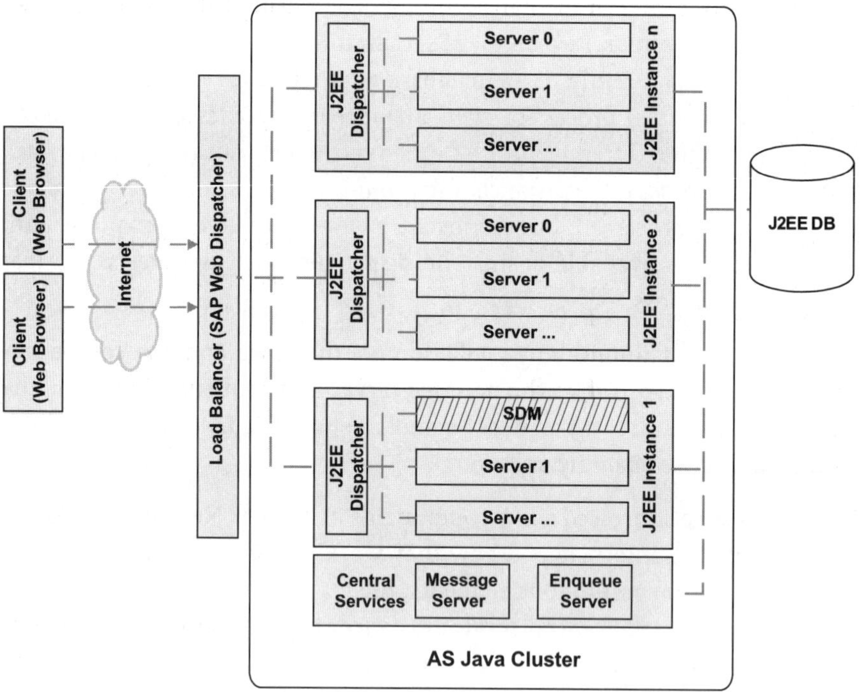

Figure 11.5 Architecture of a Java Cluster

The SDM is a central component of a J2EE installation and consists of a client and a server. In the server mode, it exists only once for the entire cluster and allows only exclusive accesses from the clients. The server is responsible for the consistency of the whole of the deployed content of an installation. The unique ID of a component is based on the version, the component name, and the manufacturer of the component. The client is used to download individual patches or other Java archives. All activities during upgrade or loading of a support package stack are also handled through the SDM.

The enqueue service, just as in the ABAP world, handles the central lock administration for all processes within a Java installation. To do this, when a central object is used, a lock is first requested and then released after the processing is complete. This lock is held by enqueue in that time, and the object will not be released for other processes. In addition to the central objects, a Java Virtual Machine (JVM) also provides resources for general access. These are not administered through enqueue, but by Java mechanisms. The goal of this separation is to keep the number of scenarios needing locking in enqueue as low as possible. Normally, enqueue locks are needed when starting and stopping server and dispatcher processes, when working on configuration files in the database, and when using EJB (Enterprise Java Bean)-CMP[1] containers.

Besides the Enqueue service, the *message server* (MS) is one of the central components of any SAP installation. The message server is the central point of message exchange within a cluster environment. These are primarily messages concerning the current status of the cluster and the participating components. The entire communication between server nodes is also performed by the message server. The nodes are each connected with the message server by a persistent TCP connection. This means it is not necessary for every node to communicate with every other node, which would result in a significantly higher load on the network and the nodes themselves.

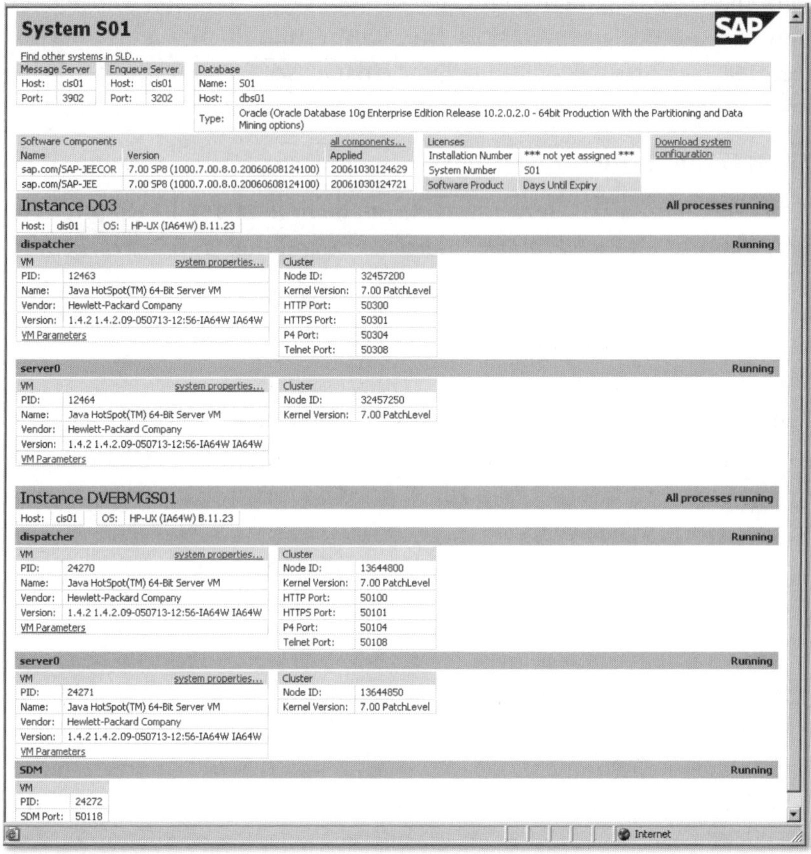

Figure 11.6 System Info for a J2EE Installation

1 Container managed persistence (CMP) is a form of transparent persistence. The developer needn't worry about synchronizing data in main memory with the database. This is done for both data retrieval and for writing by an automatic mechanism in the EJB container.

All information about the structure of a J2EE clusters can be shown by calling the system information page. This is located at the URL *http://<host>:<Port>/sap/monitoring/SystemInfo*. The port of a J2EE engine can be determined as follows: *5<system number>00* or *50,000 + <system number> × 100*.

Figure 11.6 shows an example of the system data. The system S01 shown there consists of the two instances DVEBMGS01 and D03, each of which provide a dispatcher and a server process. The instance DVEBMGS01 is also assigned to the SDM process.

Now that you are familiar with the general structure of the J2EE engine, let's take a closer look at a few areas below. We will first look at the internal structure of a J2EE engine to understand the processes during starting and stopping. Of particular interest is the administration of the connection between the Java processes and the Oracle database.

11.2.1 Internal Structure

The "innards" of each Java server process can be broken down into three layers. This division into *applications*, *components*, and the *Java Enterprise Runtime* is shown in Figure 11.7.

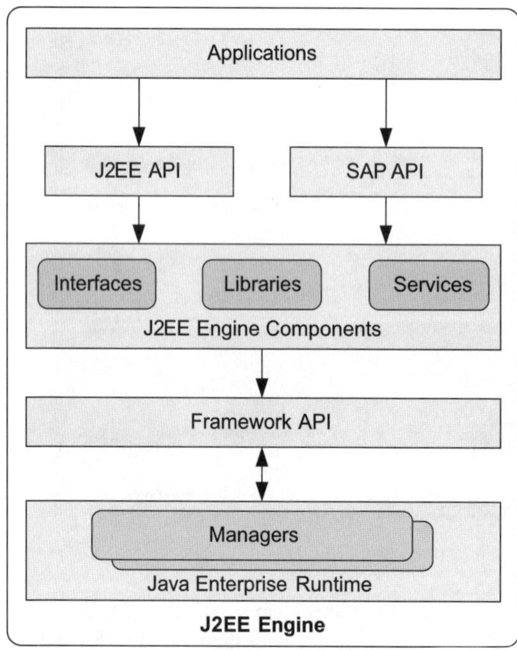

Figure 11.7 Architecture of a J2EE Engine

In general, for all layers, the basic rule is that components from a higher level can use the components of a lower level, whereas the components from the lower level know nothing of the existence of the higher levels and can therefore not use the functions on that level. The effects of this rule can be see in the start sequence of the individual layers. First, the runtime is started, which then starts the services (loads the libraries, resolves the interface definitions) that the applications need.

The components of the higher levels thus each use a series of APIs that access the functions of the lower levels. That means the J2EE engine components use the framework API to access the functions of the Java Runtime, and the applications use the APIs of the J2EE specification and the APIs by SAP to access the J2EE engine components.

The Java Enterprise Runtime represents the basic system that provides all of the central functionality for the runtime environment. These functions are divided into *managers*. Table 11.1 shows the most important managers and their functions. In Figure 11.8, you can see how the managers are listed under the managers entry in the Config Tool. There, you can administrate their settings as needed.

Manager	Function
Log Manager	Logs system events
Ports Manager	Opens communication ports for the engine
Pool Manager	Pooling of Java objects
Application Thread Manager	Administration of the threads in which the code of the applications is executed
Thread Manager	Administration of the threads in which J2EE system operations are executed
Connections Manipulator Manager	Administration of the connections of clients to the J2EE engine on the TCP/IP socket level
Locking Manager	Creation of the connection to enqueue
Configuration Manager	Administration of reading and writing of configuration data (properties, deployment information, etc.) from and to the database
Classloading Manager	Administration of Java classes and references to one another
Licensing Manager	Administration of the SAP license

Table 11.1 Managers in an SAP J2EE Engine

Manager	Function
Cluster Manager	Administration of the internal cluster communications between nodes (status and modules in the nodes)
Service Manager	Container for all components of the J2EE engine, loads and starts all components

Table 11.1 Managers in an SAP J2EE Engine (Cont.)

The *Service Manager*, also called the Service Container, is the central element of the J2EE engine, because it contains all of the components. Without the other managers and their functions, however, it could not run. The Server Manager is responsible for starting the applications when the J2EE engine is started up, so it is the last subsystem to be started. When the system is stopped, the Service Manager also coordinates the shutdown of the components.

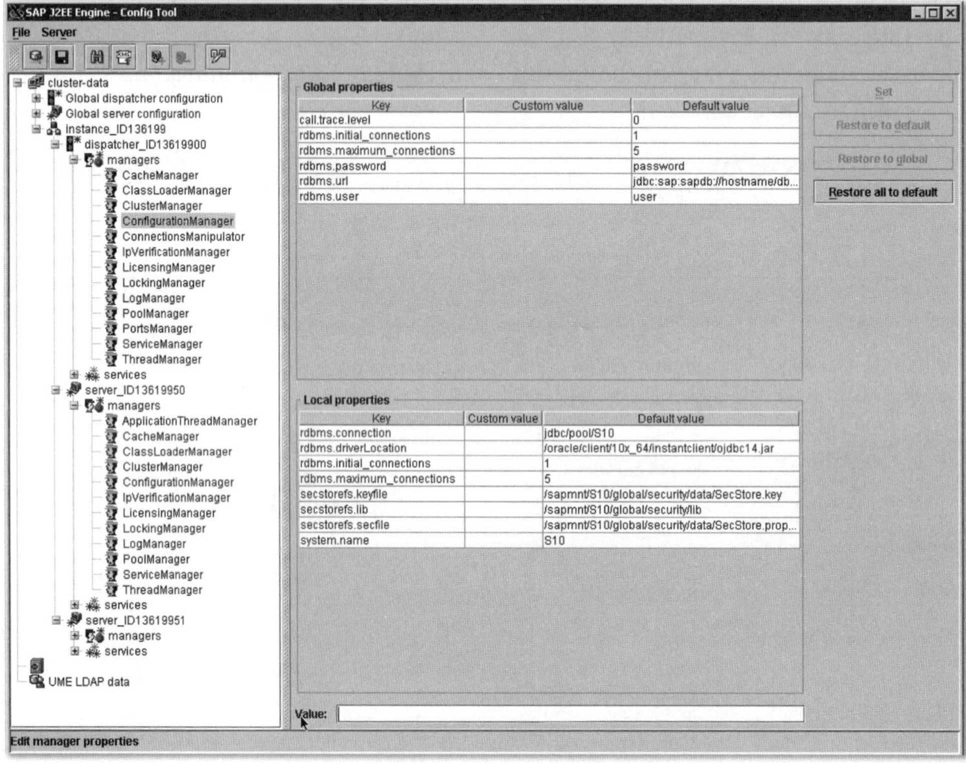

Figure 11.8 Managers in the Config Tool

Three types of J2EE components can be distinguished: *interfaces*, *libraries*, and *services*:

- **Interfaces**
  Interfaces define which components of the system work together and how. They provide a name and a list of methods and are used through a service that implements this interface.
- **Libraries**
  Libraries are generally useful auxiliary classes that provide a name, a set of classes, and methods. They are not capable of assigning resources on their own and have no configuration data in the system. A component that uses a library must instantiate it and generate the objects desired. Functions are generally accessed via static methods.
- **Services**
  Services provide a name, classes, and runtime objects. These objects are registered in the system once the class has been loaded. Service components can use the framework API to use functions in the runtime. They are also called active components. Moreover, they can assign resources when started and release them again when finished.

Applications represent the top layer of Java components. They are capable of using all functions provided by the J2EE API and SAP's own APIs. They consist of a series of subcomponents, each of which is responsible for specific areas. Figure 11.9 shows a schematic diagram of the structure. The servlets and JSPs in the web container provide the frontend functionality, the Enterprise Java Beans in the EJB container encapsulate the business logic, and the JDBC drivers on the persistence level provide functions for the reading and writing of data. The containers each provide the specific functions for the components and handle the administration of the life cycles of the components. Applications can reference other applications and thus use their functions.

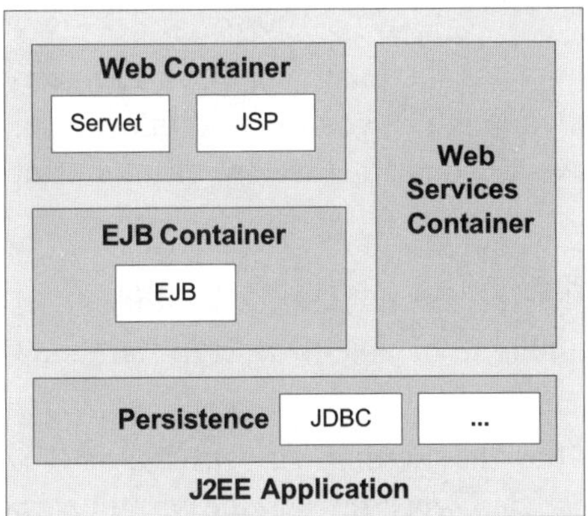

Figure 11.9 Components of a J2EE Application

With the knowledge we now have about the structure and dependencies of the individual server components, we can turn our attention to the start process of an SAP Java instance.

The two binaries `jcontrol` and `jlaunch` are responsible for the start process of a J2EE engine. The two together are called the *Java Startup and Control Framework*. `jcontrol` controls the entire lifecycle of the `jlaunch` process. Both files are located in the global executable directory */usr/sap/<SID>/SYS/exe/run*. Moreover, for each instance there is a copy of the exe directory under */usr/sap/<SID>/<instance>/exe*. `jcontrol` starts, stops, and monitors the processes of a Java instance (both the dispatcher and the server processes), which are represented by `jlaunch`. To process commands to start and stop, `jcontrol` is capable of reacting to SAP signal handling.

`jlaunch` itself starts at the beginning of a JVM in its own reserved memory range and then represents one element of the Java cluster. The process receives named pipes signals from `jcontrol` to stop or restart the process as needed. If the connection to `jcontrol` is lost, the `jlaunch` process stops as well.

Both processes have a *bootstrap process* in common. This synchronizes the information from the database with the configuration files on the file system level, before the actual processes start. To do this, the information is read from the database and the corresponding updated property files, which are then used to start the Java process. For this reason, it doesn't make sense to change the configuration files of the J2EE engine at the operating system level, because these entries are simply overwritten on every restart. The Java archives used for the applications are also synchronized with data from the database.

In all, the start process of a J2EE engine has the following form. For every individual step, the log files are specified in which you can find information about each process. Figure 11.10 shows a schematic diagram of the startup process.

1. `jcontrol` is started by the SAP start service or the `startsap` script.
2. `jcontrol` initializes SAP signal handling to be able to react to start, stop, and restart requests.
3. `jcontrol` starts `jlaunch` (❶) with the settings in */usr/sap/<SID>/<instance>/j2ee/cluster/bootstrap/bootstrap.properties* and the current parameters from the file instance.properties.

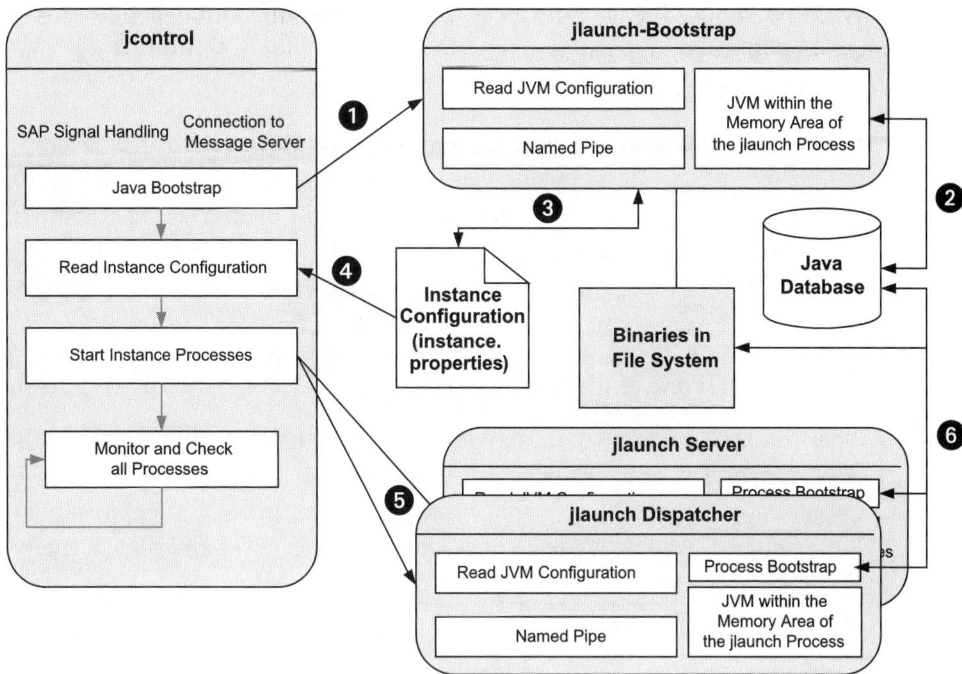

Figure 11.10 Schematic Diagram of the J2EE Startup Process

4. A JVM is generated, which starts the bootstrap process and synchronizes (❷) the data from the database with the file system. The bootstrap process reads the configuration of the Java instance from the database and updates it, if necessary, in the file instance.properties. This file then contains all of the information about the cluster elements to be started (❸). The bootstrap process ends:

```
/usr/sap/<SID>/<instance>/work/dev_bootstrap | jvm_
bootstrap | std_bootstrap.out
```

5. `jcontrol` uses instance.properties to generate a list of all cluster elements (❹), starting a `jlaunch` process (❺) for each one:

```
/usr/sap/<SID>/<instance>/work/dev_jcontrol
```

6. A JVM is generated for each node, which starts a new bootstrap process to synchronize the data about managers and services from the database with the file system (❻). These are also stored in property files:

```
/usr/sap/<SID>/<instance>/work/log_bootstrap_<node
ID>.[*].log | jvm_bootstrap_<node ID>.out | dev_bootstrap_<node
ID> | std_bootstrap_<node ID>.out
```

7. The bootstrap is stopped, and the Java Enterprise Runtime is started with the properties stored. The properties can be found in this directory:

   `/usr/sap/<SID>/<instance>/j2ee/cluster/<node>/cfg/kernel`

8. The Service Framework (Service Manager) and the services are started:

   ```
   /usr/sap/<SID>/<instance>/work/
   dev_server[*] | std_server[*].out | jvm_server[*].out
   dev_dispatcher | std_dispatcher.out | jvm_dispatcher.out
   dev_sdm | std_sdm.out | jvm_sdm.out
   ```

9. After starting, the status of the server process is monitored continually by `jcontrol`. If one of the processes fails, `jcontrol` automatically restarts it.

After the J2EE engine is started, you can find the individual processes in the process overview of your operating system. Figure 11.11 shows a call to `ps -ef|grep -e jcontrol -e jlaunch` and its results in a Unix environment. For a better overview, we have highlighted the processes and their form.

```
f01:/root#ps -ef|grep -e jlaunch -e jcontrol
  s01adm 13702 13677  0  Jan 14  ?         1:16 jcontrol pf=/usr/sap/S01/SYS/profile/S01_DVEBMGS01_cis01 -DSAPS
TART=1 -DCONNECT_PORT=51165 -DSAPSYSTEM=01 -DSAPSYSTEMNAME=S01 -
    root 23365 20715  2 21:51:26 pts/1     0:00 grep -e jlaunch -e jcontrol
  s01adm  3105 13702  0  Jan 15  ?        46:31 /usr/sap/S01/DVEBMGS01/exe/jlaunch pf=/usr/sap/S01/SYS/profile/
S01_DVEBMGS01_cis01 -DSAPINFO=S01_01_dispatcher -nodeId=0 -file=
  s01adm 14570 13702  0  Jan 14  ?       1304:12 /usr/sap/S01/DVEBMGS01/exe/jlaunch pf=/usr/sap/S01/SYS/profil
e/S01_DVEBMGS01_cis01 -DSAPINFO=S01_01_server -nodeId=1 -file=/usr
  s01adm 14571 13702  0  Jan 14  ?         8:49 /usr/sap/S01/DVEBMGS01/exe/jlaunch pf=/usr/sap/S01/SYS/profile/
S01_DVEBMGS01_cis01 -DSAPINFO=S01_01_sdm -nodeId=2 -file=/usr/sa
```

Figure 11.11 Process Overview of a J2EE Server

The writing of all of the log files described here is activated by default. Due to errors, it may be necessary to increase the trace level to get more detailed information about the internals of the processes. The standard trace level is 1, and it can be increased to 3. If the trace level is set to 0, no trace information will be written. The additional information is written to developer traces (*dev_* files*). Depending on the operating system in use, the process of changing the trace level is different:

- **Microsoft Windows**
  Under Microsoft Windows, the SAP Microsoft Management Console (MMC) is used. There, as shown in Figure 11.12, you can increase the trace level in the context menu under **All Tasks (Increase trace level)**, or you can reduce it (**Decrease trace level**). After the processes are restarted, the trace level is set back to the default level.

- **UNIX**
  Under UNIX, you need the tool JControl Monitor Program (JCMon) for activation. Start JCMon, and use the process overview to search for the

PID of the desired process. Then use the command `kill -USR1 <PID>` to increase the trace level. To lower the trace level, use `kill -USR2 <PID>`. You can find more detailed instructions on calling and working with JCMon and in Section 11.2.3, *Monitoring*.

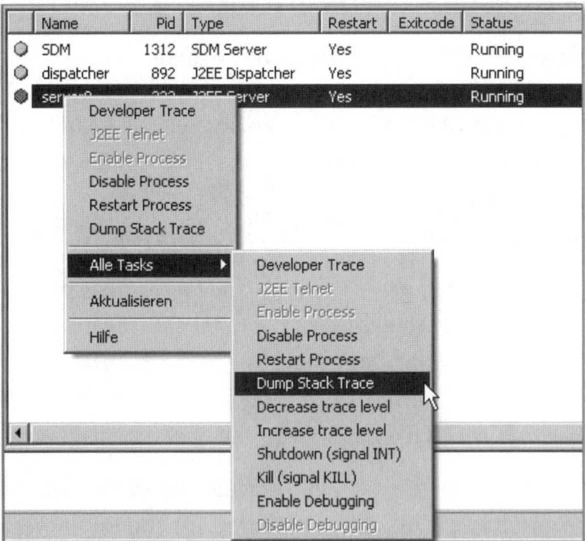

Figure 11.12 Adaptation of the Trace Level under Windows

It is also possible to write a complete dump to the log file. To do this, select the option Dump Stack Trace.

After this overview of the start process of a Java engine, we will take a quick look at the processes involved in stopping the system. They are much simpler.

During stopping of the instance, `jcontrol` receives a `SIGINT` from the SAP start service or the `stopsap` script, which causes `jcontrol` to send a stop signal to all of the server processes through their named pipes. The `jlaunch` process stops all servers and then terminates the JVM. The `jcontrol` process then ends.

When starting or stopping an entire cluster, the communication of the `jcontrol` processes through the message server is used. During the start process, `jcontrol` registers the instance with the message server, and it is added to the internal instance list. `jcontrol` is thus capable of receiving commands from the message server.

When stopping a J2EE cluster, the message server receives the message to shut down and forwards it to the individual `jcontrol` processes. Finally, `jcontrol` sends a response about the shutdown to the message server.

The restart of a cluster works similarly. After the shutdown of the instances, a start command is sent by the message server to the instances that perform the restart.

11.2.2 Interplay of the Java Stack and the Database

In the Java environment, as shown in the previous section, a great deal of information and programs is stored in the database, just as in the ABAP world. Any product that has been approved for SAP NetWeaver can be used for a database. It is also possible to establish connections to other databases if a JDBC driver is available for them. In the following text, however, we'll concentrate on Oracle as the schema database and connecting to Oracle through JDBC/ODBC.

When a Java instance accesses the database, two basic scenarios can be distinguished. The first is access by the executables to the database, for instance, when the bootstrap processes read the configuration and executables or deployment is performed via SDM. The second is access of Java applications within the J2EE runtime, which is carried out by the Java persistence layer.

What the two have in common is the use of JDBC drivers to implement the physical connection to the database. JDBC is the standard for the implementation of a database access in Java applications. Whereas the processes perform access to the JDBC driver independently, the applications in the SAP J2EE environment use preconfigured resources provided by the managers and services (*JDBC Connector Service*). This allows other external databases to be integrated as data sources and the data stored there to be used. By using *Open SQL for Java*, moreover, database-independent development of applications can be accomplished.

11.2.2.1 Connections from the Server Processes

Before covering the configuration of database access, we will first take a quick look at the general setup of Java schemas. There are two options here, depending on the installation variant:

1. The schema is added to an existing ABAP database and therefore needs no separate Oracle database installation. All existing file systems and backup mechanisms of the ABAP installation can be used. You only need to provide a little extra storage space in the database and the file system.
2. If the Java instance is installed as an instance of its own, you can choose whether the schema should be added to an existing (ABAP) Oracle database, or if a new installation of a database instance will be performed. This

installation variant offers the possibility of creating a separate SAN connection for the database (on the logical unit level). This allows access to the ABAP and Java database to be distributed better under high-load conditions to increase performance. It also makes a separate backup of the database possible. Which of the installation variants fits your requirements depends on their use in the context of your landscape. If there is a high load requirement, we recommend the use of a separate database.

The name of the Java schema is built the same in either case; it is PSAP<schema ID>DB. This tablespace is used for all SAP objects in the Java stack as a default tablespace. SAP currently uses SR3 as the template for the schema ID. However, this can be changed using the BR*Tool.

As mentioned earlier, a suitable JDBC driver is needed for access to an Oracle database. Currently, only the Oracle JDBC thin driver[2] is supported. The JDBC OCI driver, like drivers by other providers, have not been approved for use in SAP Java applications. The version of the JDBC driver must agree with the main version number of the version of the database software, for example, Oracle 10. The driver version must not be less than the database version. All three levels are supported by SQL (Open, Vendor, and Native; for more information on this, see Section 11.2.2.2, *Persistence for Java Applications*).

If the Oracle database is used as an external database, the same restrictions apply. In addition, it must also be taken into consideration that only connections to SAP J2EE schemas are supported within the external database, and the database version used must be supported by the J2EE version used. Information about which Oracle versions are released for which J2EE releases can be found in the Product Availability Matrix and at *http://service.sap.com/pam*.

The primary JDBC driver archives for Oracle databases are the files *classes12.jar* and *ojdbc14.jar*. Which of the two files you use depends on the JDK version you are using. The archive *classes12.jar* is for use with JDK versions 1.2 and 1.3, whereas *ojdbc14.jar* is designed for use with JDK 1.4 and 5.0. In the SAP environment, the `ojdbc14.jar` driver is almost always used. The driver class to be used and contained there is `oracle.jdbc.driver.OracleDriver`.

Copies of the driver class can be found in three places in the file system. These are, first, the copies within the Oracle database software and the

2 The thin driver has the advantage over the OCI driver of being developed entirely in Java and is therefore platform-independent.

Instant Client and, second, stand-alone isolated storages that are independent of the Oracle installation.

Within the Oracle installation, the driver archives are stored in the directories *$ORACLE_HOME/jdbc/lib* and */oracle/client/10x_64/instantclient*. If an update or upgrade of the database or the client is performed, these archives are automatically updated. The Oracle software is generally only found in the central instance, which is why you should prefer a link to the driver within the client software.

Because an Oracle client is not necessarily installed, an alternative possibility is to store a copy of the JDBC driver in the */usr/sap/<SID>/JC<XX>|DVEBMGS<XX>/j2ee/* directory. When updating the database software, you must then perform a manual update of the driver file.

To determine which driver file is used by a J2EE instance, use a text editor to open the config.properties file in the */usr/sap/<SID>/<instance>/j2ee/configtool* directory. You will find a parameter `rdbms.driverLocation` there that specifies the path for this instance. In the example in Figure 11.13, the directory of the Oracle client is set up as storage, and the file ojdbc14.jar is used.

```
/usr/sap/S10/DVEBMGS01/j2ee/configtool
f03:s10adm 13> more config.properties
#Generated by Config Tool
#Mon Jun 19 19:38:05 CEST 2006
rdbms.maximum_connections=5
system.name=S10
secstorefs.keyfile=/sapmnt/S10/global/security/data/SecStore.key
secstorefs.secfile=/sapmnt/S10/global/security/data/SecStore.properties
secstorefs.lib=/sapmnt/S10/global/security/lib
rdbms.driverLocation=/oracle/client/10x_64/instantclient/ojdbc14.jar
rdbms.connection=jdbc/pool/S10
rdbms.initial_connections=1
config.properties: END
```

Figure 11.13 JDBC Drivers in the File config.properties

The configuration for access to the schema database is done in the *Secure Store*[3]. The information contained there can be edited using the Config Tool. You can specify the class names of the JDBC driver archive and the connection data for the database. The user specified is a user of the J2EE engine, not

3 The Secure Store stores in encrypted form all data that is needed to build the primary database connection as well as connection data for the J2EE engine. These are used by SDM, for instance.

a database user. This results in the definition of DataSources explained in Section 11.2.2.2. Figure 11.14 shows an example configuration of a Secure Store for the use of an Oracle database. The information contained in the Secure Store is not synchronized with the database content, but rather stored in encrypted form in the file */usr/sap/<SID>/SYS/global/security/data/SecStore.properties*. Never change the settings there directly, as this will destroy the file's data consistency. Always use the Config Tool.

The database URL for the Oracle JDBC thin driver is stored in the parameter jdbc/pool/<SID>/URL and has the following syntax: jdbc:oracle:thin:@<host>:<port>:<sid>. The port specified is the port for the Oracle listener. In the example in Figure 11.14, the listener can be reached at port 3010. If there are changes to the host or port, it is enough to adapt those settings in the database URL. Adaptation of the JDBC driver is a little more involved if the class name of the driver changes, for instance.

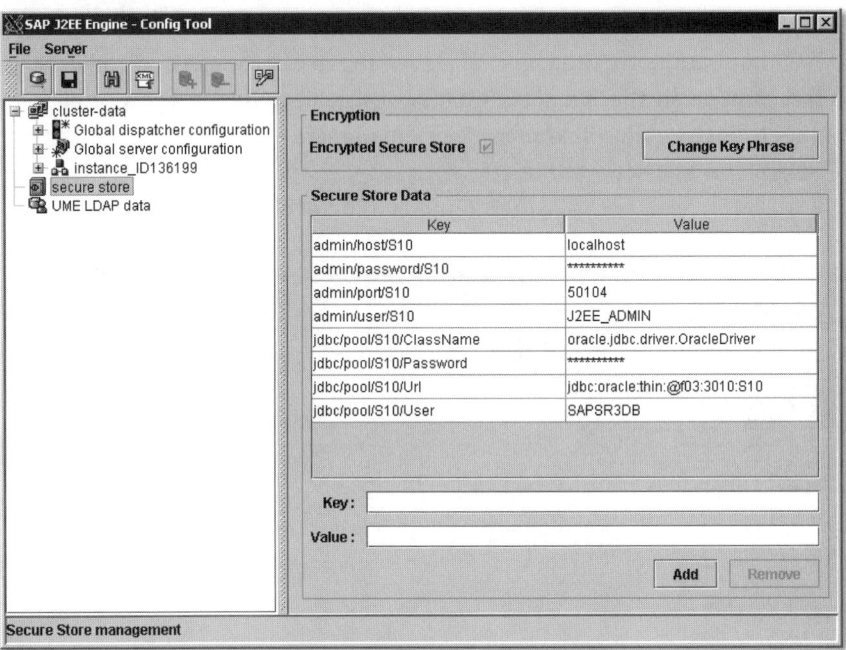

Figure 11.14 JDBC Configurations in the Secure Store

Start the Config Tool and open **Cluster Data • Secure Store**. Adjust the parameter jdbc/pool/<SID>/URL correspondingly (port, database system, and host). If the name of the driver or the class used changes, the parameter jdbc/pool/<SID>/ClassName must also be changed. To store the changed values, use **Add**. You must then go to **File • Apply** to save the changes to the Secure Store.

To change the file name, you must perform a series of adjustments in different places, because many processes need direct access to the JDBC drivers. These particularly include the bootstrap processes and the SDM. These adjustments are described in the following list:

- **Bootstrap settings**
  Use a text editor to change the pathname of the parameter `rdbms.driverLocation` in the file */usr/sap/<SID>/<instance>/j2ee/cluster/bootstrap/bootstrap.properties* to the new name.
- **Config Tool**
  Use a text editor to change the pathname of the parameter `rdbms.driverLocation` in the file */usr/sap/<SID>/<instance>/j2ee/cluster/configtool/config.properties* to the new name.
- **Configuration Manager**
  The Configuration Manager contains the path for each dispatcher or server node in the instance. Change it for all nodes in the Config Tool under **cluster-data • Instance_IDxx • managers • Configuration Manager**, where you will see a parameter `rdbms.driverLocation` for each (see Figure 11.15). Save your settings with **Set** and **Save**.

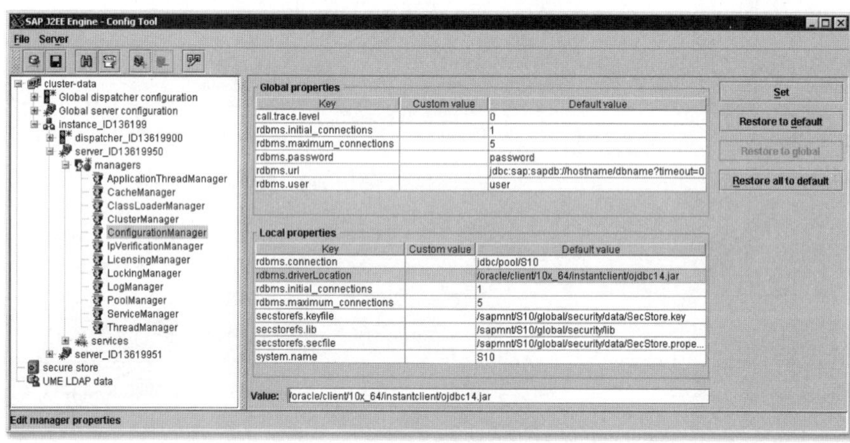

Figure 11.15 JDBC Drivers in the Configuration Manager

- **Software Deployment Manager**
  Use a text editor to search the file */usr/sap/<SID>/ <instance>/SDM/program/config/sdmrepository.sdc* for the entry "CONFIG_DB." Under that ID

is an XML tag `<FixedSizeParamContainer>`. Change the path specification there appropriately and save your changes:

```
<ID> CONFIG_DB </ID>
      ...
        <FixedSizeParamContainer>
...            <![CDATA[/oracle/client/10x_64/instantcli-
ent/ojdbc14.jar]]>
          </Param>
        </FixedSizeParamContainer>
```

- **Deploy Tool**
  Use a text editor to change the parameter `rdbms.driverLocation` in the file */usr/sap/<SID>/<instance>/j2ee/deploying/rdb.properties.*
- **Template Configuration Tool**
  Use a text editor in the file */usr/sap/<SID>/<instance>/j2ee/templateconfigurator.properties* to change the `${RDBMS_DRIVER_LOCATION}` parameter:

```
##################################
#     System dependencies       #
##################################
...
${OS_UNICODE}=true
${OS_BIT_LENGHT}=64
${RDBMS_DRIVER_LOCATION}=/oracle/client/10x_64/instantcli-
ent/ojdbc14.jar
${R3_ENV_YES_NO}=no
...
```

- **Java parameters for the instance nodes**
  Use the Config Tool to add the Java startup parameter `Drdbms.driverLocation` to every instance node with the new value or path of the driver.
- **Profile of the instance**
  In the instance profile, change the value of the parameter `j2ee/dbdriver` to match your requirements. This change is only necessary as of SAP NetWeaver 7.0.

All changes only take effect after restarting the cluster.

If inconsistencies, typos, or incorrect paths lead to errors, there are normally two major error classes to distinguish:

1. `java.lang.ClassNotFoundException:<jdbc_class>` exceptions indicate that the path of the class was specified incorrectly. Check it against the locations given above.

2. `java.sql.SQLException: No suitable drive` exceptions indicate that the class was found, but the driver found there cannot be used or the class specified was incorrect. Check the entries in the Secure Store and correct them.

Logging of problems with database access is done for each individual process. A log file database.*.log is written to the system subdirectory of the log directory for each node. The path of the log directory is */usr/sap/<SID>/<instance>/j2ee/cluster/<node>/log/*.

11.2.2.2 Persistence for Java Applications

The persistence layer of the J2EE runtime is primarily of interest to application developers. It is also important for administrators to know how the interplay of the individual J2EE components with the JDBC drivers and the database works, in order to react properly in case of startup problems with the components or even with the entire J2EE engine. Furthermore, a developer usually has no access to the SAP NetWeaver Visual Administrator and can therefore not create DataSources for access to external databases.

To give Java developers the ability to develop applications independent of a particular database, the Open SQL standard also exists in the Java world. The developer can also write applications based on Native SQL or Vendor SQL. The relationships between these three SQL levels are shown in Figure 11.16.

In the figure, you can see that Vendor SQL includes the manufacturer-dependent version of SQL. This corresponds to the JDBC implementation of the database manufacturer, which only encapsulates the connections. By using these JDBC drivers, in principle, all databases can be connected to the J2EE server. Moreover, the use of database-dependent SQL tools is also possible. However, note that the portability of applications using these drivers is lost. A check of SQL syntax or buffering is not done by the Open SQL API.

Things are similar when using Native SQL, but in contrast with Vendor SQL, the access layer of the Open SQL API is used. However, here the statements are simply passed through to the database, but at least there can be traces of the access and buffering of statements.

EJB Container Managed Persistence (EJB CMP) and *Java Data Objects* (JDO) provide object-relational access to data objects. Instead of using SQL statements, the developer can implement data access using Java classes and objects. Data retrieval and storage is performed by mechanisms in the EJB container and is transparent for further use. You can find more information about JDO at *http://java.sun.com/products/jdo/*.

In general, the use of Open SQL or the other specializations, JDO or EJB CMP, should be preferred during development. Among other things, it simplifies the transport of development to different application servers.

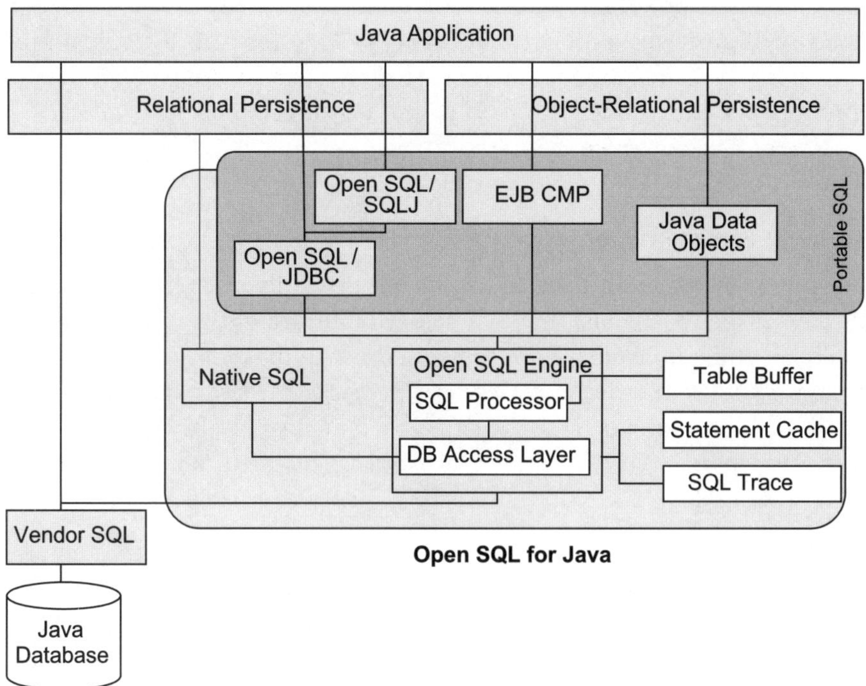

Figure 11.16 SQL Access Options using Open SQL

All JDBC connections are set up and administrated through the Visual Administrator. This administration of connections can be found in the nodes of a server under **Services • JDBC Connector**. A connection consists of the driver for access and the DataSource as connection target. Figure 11.17 shows the standard connection and standard driver after installation of a system. A series of aliases for these drivers (ADS, SAP/BC_ADM, etc.) are used by the individual services within the J2EE engine.

To integrate a new database, a driver for that database must first be added. For Oracle 10g, for instance, this is the library odbc14.jar. If the system database is already based on Oracle, as in our example, this driver can be used. The creation of a new DataSource is next. The name and the aliases of the DataSource are later placed in the JNDI for developers and are available for connections. The actual connection information is specified using the database URL and the user information.

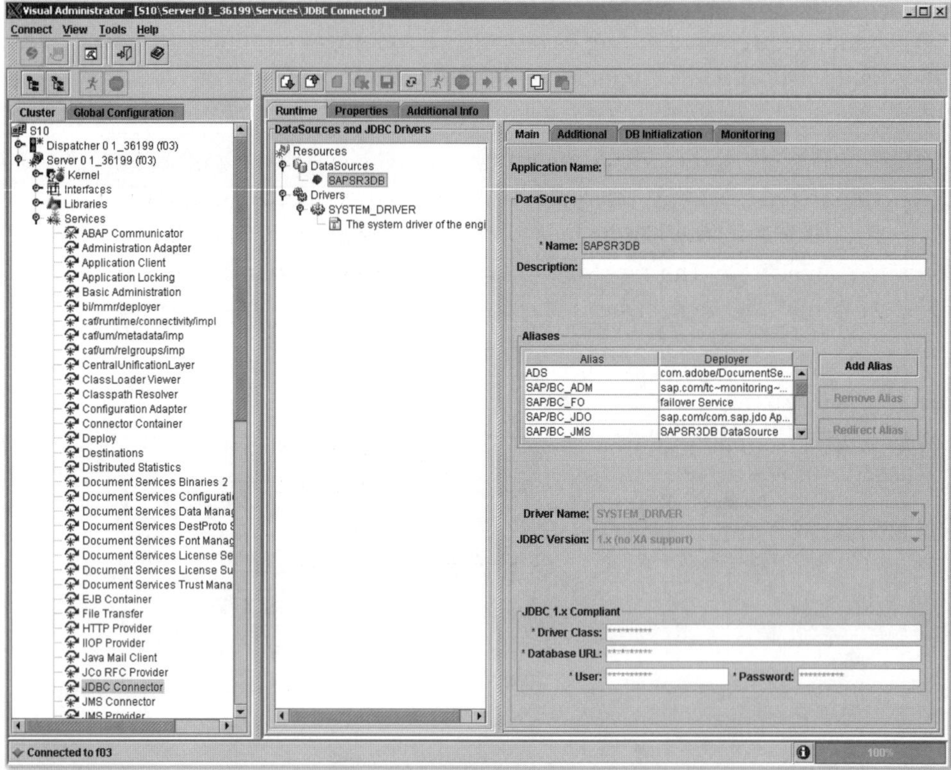

Figure 11.17 Administration of JDBC connections

On the Additional tab, you also have the option of specifying whether Open, Native, or Vendor SQL should be used for access. Due to the restriction that the Java Dictionary can only be used for the system database, the setting **Open SQL** is only possible for the default database.

The integration of a DataSource CAR_RENTAL_POOL in the Java source code might thus look something like this:

1. For access, there is first a lookup in the JNDI:

   ```
   DataSource ds = (DataSource) context.lookup("java:comp/env/jdbc/
   CAR_RENTAL_POOL")
   ```

2. Then, we open a connection to this DataSource:

   ```
   Connection conn = ds.getConnection();
   ```

3. Using this connection object, we then receive access to the methods to generate and process statements (`createStatement`, `createPrepared-Statement`, `executeUpdate`, etc.):

```
java.sql.Statement stmt = conn.createStatment();
stmt.executeUpdate ("insert into VEHICLE " + "(NAME, PRICE,
CURRENCY)" + "values ('Audi_A3', 25000, 'EUR')");
ResultSet rs = stmt.executeQuery ("select NAME, PRICE, CURRENCY from VEHICLE");
```

The code fragments shown don't represent a complete implementation, but are only intended as an example. After setting up connections, the administrator also needs to know how to monitor the servers of an instance and the database connections. The monitoring of our J2EE installation needed for this is the subject of the next section.

11.2.3 Monitoring

Of course, for the administrator, the monitoring of system status of an SAP NetWeaver AS Java is of interest. A detailed treatment of the individual possibilities is far beyond the scope of this book, so we will only present an overview and mention some pointers about which tools you can use to perform monitoring. For more information, consult more detailed documentation, such as SAP Help (*http://help.sap.com*).

In principle, as when monitoring an ABAP instance, the two areas of server problems and application problems must be differentiated and are monitored with different tools. Table 11.2 shows an overview of the areas and the appropriate tools. There are also a number of external monitoring tools that allow central monitoring. However, we will leave those out here, because our object is to examine the use of the tools SAP includes as standard.

Monitoring area	Type	Tool
General server problems	Availability	CCMS/ICM external tools
	Distributed Statistics Records (DSR)	CCMS/ Visual Administrator
	Status monitoring	CCMS/ICM/ Visual Administrator
	Log monitoring	CCMS/Log Viewer
Application problems	Performance trace	CCMS
	Application trace	Visual Administrator
	Single activity trace	Visual Administrator
	Java Application Response Time Measurement (JARM)	Visual Administrator

Table 11.2 J2EE Monitoring

Monitoring area	Type	Tool
	SQL trace	Visual Administrator
	Developer trace (Logging API)	Visual Administrator

Table 11.2 J2EE Monitoring (Cont.)

The availability of the J2EE engine can be measured in different ways, as follows. For a simple installation, besides the database, the following processes must be running: The central instance includes a message server and an enqueue server, which appear at the operating system level as the processes `ms.sap<SID>_<instance>` and `en.sap<SID>_<instance>`. Moreover, at least a dispatcher and a server process are needed, as well as (optionally) an active SDM process. These three processes are represented by `jlaunch`. The type of process can be seen from the `–DSAPINFO` parameter.

Under Unix, you can use the command `ps -ef | grep jlaunch` to observe the processes. Figure 11.18 shows an example for a system S10. Under Windows, you can use the SAP Management Console to monitor processes.

```
f03:/root#ps -ef|grep jlaunch|grep S10
  s10adm  6212  6116  0  Oct 25  ?        54:36 /usr/sap/S10/DVEBMGS01/exe/jlaunch pf=/usr/sa
p/S10/SYS/profile/S10_DVEBMGS01_f03 -DSAPINFO=S10_01_server -nodeId=1 -file=/usr/s
  s10adm  7032  6116  0  Oct 25  ?        78:23 /usr/sap/S10/DVEBMGS01/exe/jlaunch pf=/usr/sa
p/S10/SYS/profile/S10_DVEBMGS01_f03 -DSAPINFO=S10_01_sdm -nodeId=2 -file=/usr/sap/
  s10adm  6211  6116  0  Oct 25  ?        56:59 /usr/sap/S10/DVEBMGS01/exe/jlaunch pf=/usr/sa
p/S10/SYS/profile/S10_DVEBMGS01_f03 -DSAPINFO=S10_01_dispatcher -nodeId=0 -file=/u
f03:/root#
```

Figure 11.18 Output of ps –ef|grep jlaunch

Besides this simple monitoring, there is also the possibility of integrating monitoring into the *Computing Center Management System* (CCMS) of an existing ABAP system, thereby getting much more precise information about the status of a J2EE cluster. This can be done using the *Generic Request and Message Generator* (GRMG). Using the GRMG, the CCMS is capable of sending regular requests to the J2EE engine to determine its availability and the status of its dispatcher and server processes. Moreover, a so-called CCMS agent is used, which can forward the log files and the statistical information from the *Distributed Statistic Records* (DSR) service to the ABAP server. Figure 11.19 shows the schematic structure for the implementation of such a monitoring scenario. This kind of implementation can transmit a large portion of the monitoring data to an ABAP system and integrate it into an existing central monitoring system.

A lot of transmitted data can also be called up in the Visual Administrator through the Monitoring Service (**Services • Monitoring**). If you don't have an

ABAP system for a monitoring system and you have no external monitoring tool, you still have one way of getting to information about the J2EE engine. As shown in Figure 11.20, you can query for information from the areas of applications, kernel, performance, services, and system.

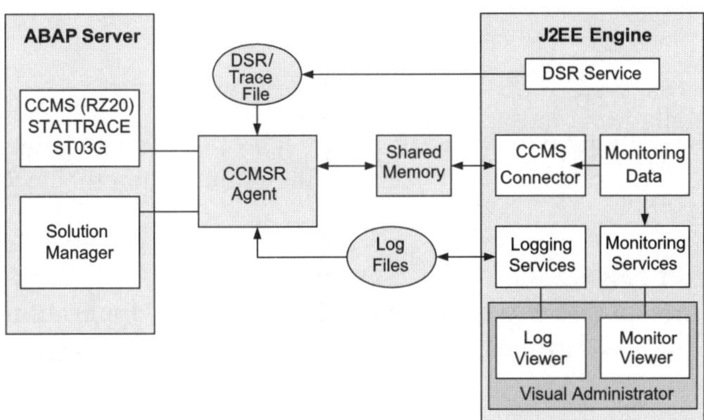

Figure 11.19 Monitoring of a J2EE Engine

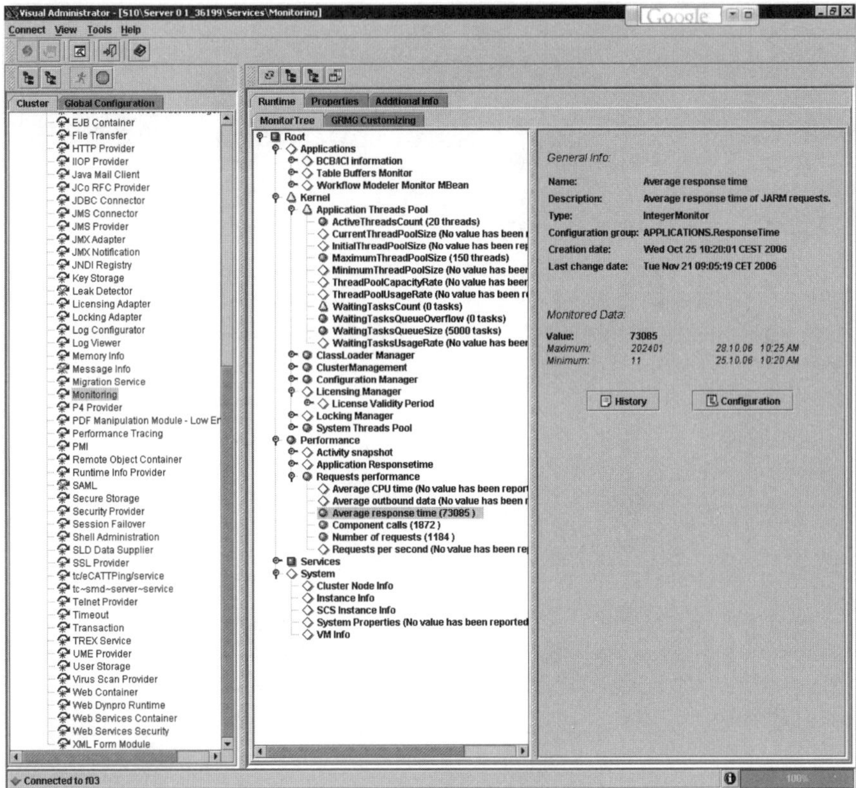

Figure 11.20 Monitoring Service of the Visual Administrator

If an error is registered in the context of server monitoring, whether it's the crash of a process or only of one application, additional tools are required to search for the cause of the error. The options listed in the "Application problems" part of Table 11.2 are available for that purpose, and we will briefly examine them in the following list:

- **Performance trace**
  A performance trace can be activated if you find irregularities in the running times of J2EE components. The performance trace provides information for all of the individual modules. It is more fine-grained than the DSR statistics.

- **Application trace**
  The application trace provides the option of debugging an application without placing the server in debug mode or deploying the application again (see Figure 11.21).

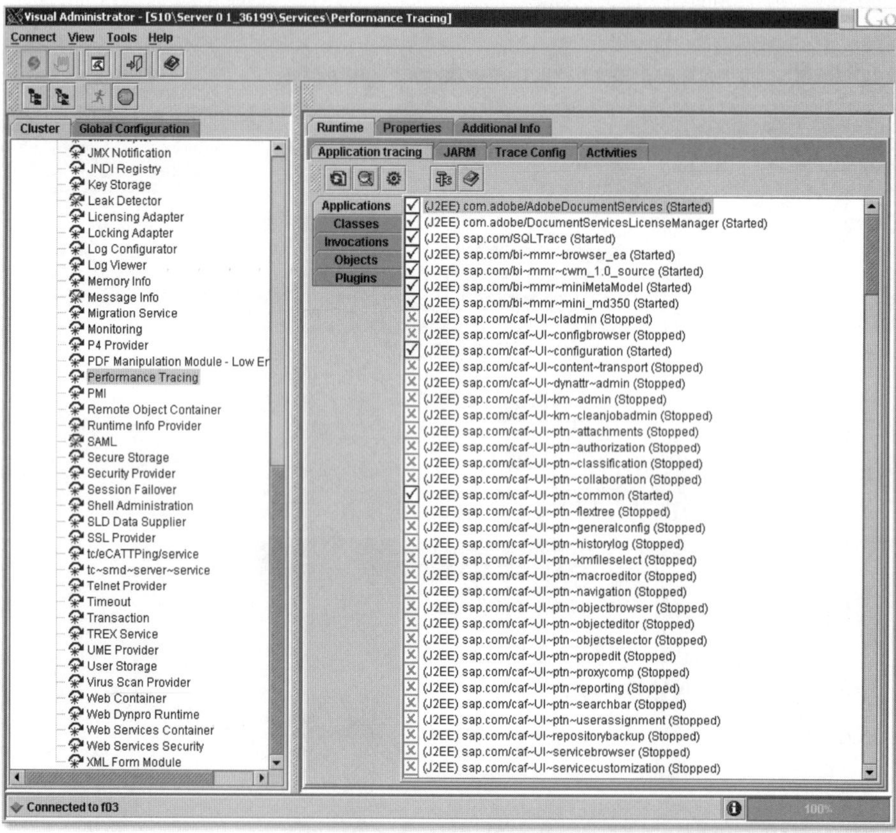

Figure 11.21 Application Trace in the Visual Administrator

- **Single activity trace**
  The single activity trace and Java Application Response Time Measurement (JARM) work together very closely. A single activity trace makes it possible to track a particular request in detail, gaining insight into performance problems, or following its execution to discover any logical errors. JARM, besides collecting response times, also measures the quantity of data sent and discovers the user who initiated the request (see Figure 11.22).

- **Developer trace (Logging API)**
  The developer trace allows the developer to print error messages from the program using the SAP Logging API.

  All specified traces can be activated and evaluated from the Visual Administrator. To do so, call up the path **Services • Performance Tracing** under the desired server node in the Visual Administrator.

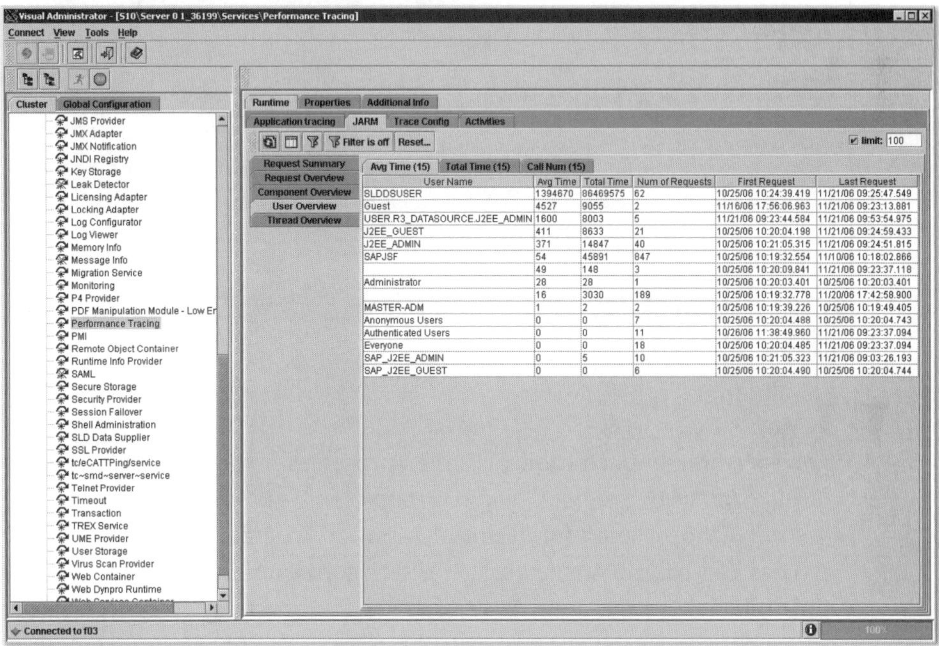

User Name	Avg Time	Total Time	Num of Requests	First Request	Last Request
SLDDSUSER	1394670	86469575	62	10/25/06 10:24:39.419	11/21/06 09:25:47.549
Guest	4527	9055	2	11/16/06 17:56:06.963	11/21/06 09:23:13.881
USER.R3_DATASOURCE.J2EE_ADMIN	1600	8003	5	11/21/06 09:23:44.584	11/21/06 09:53:54.975
J2EE_GUEST	411	8633	21	10/25/06 10:20:04.198	11/21/06 09:24:59.433
J2EE_ADMIN	371	14847	40	10/25/06 10:21:05.315	11/21/06 09:24:51.815
SAPJSF	54	45891	847	10/25/06 10:19:32.554	11/10/06 10:18:02.866
	49	148	3	10/25/06 10:20:09.841	11/21/06 09:23:37.118
Administrator	28	28	1	10/25/06 10:20:03.401	10/25/06 10:20:03.401
	16	3030	189	10/25/06 10:19:32.778	11/20/06 17:42:58.900
MASTER-ADM	1	2	2	10/25/06 10:19:39.226	10/25/06 10:19:49.405
Anonymous Users	0	0	7	10/25/06 10:20:04.488	10/25/06 10:20:04.743
Authenticated Users	0	0	11	10/26/06 11:38:49.960	11/21/06 09:23:37.094
Everyone	0	0	18	10/25/06 10:20:04.485	11/21/06 09:23:37.094
SAP_J2EE_ADMIN	0	5	10	10/25/06 10:21:05.323	11/21/06 09:03:26.193
SAP_J2EE_GUEST	0	0	6	10/25/06 10:20:04.490	10/25/06 10:20:04.744

Figure 11.22 JARM in the Visual Administrator

- **SQL monitor**
  To monitor database connections and SQL traces, besides the Visual Administrator (**Services • Performance Tracing • Trace Config**), you can also use a web frontend.

The overview **Open SQL Monitors** shown in Figure 11.23 can be called up at *http://host:Port/OpenSQLMonitors*. Besides the SQL trace, this also shows monitors on the buffer and JDBC connections. The SQL trace can also be called directly through the URL *http://Host:Port/SQLTrace*.

The JDBC connections themselves can also be monitored in Visual Administrator using the JDBC Connector. By selecting the Monitoring tab of a DataSource, you can get an overview of the currently active connections and the maximum number permitted.

A general overview of the key data of the J2EE engine can be found in the Monitoring service in the Visual Administrator.

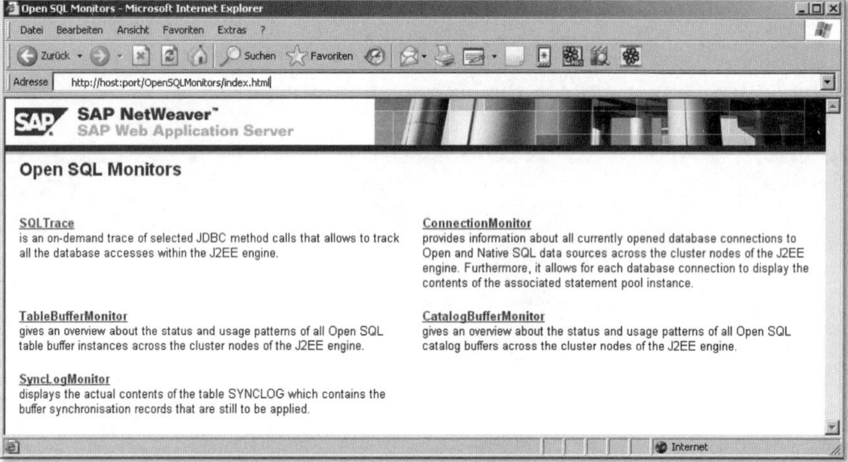

Figure 11.23 Open SQL Monitor

- **JCMon**

  For specific administration of server processes at the operation system level, SAP also provides the program /usr/sap/<SID>/SYS/exe/run/jcmon. JCMon stands for JControl Monitor Program and is part of the startup and control framework. It offers correspondingly varied options for influencing processes. At the start of the program, you use the user <sid>adm. You must then specify the path to the profile of the desired instance as a parameter:

  ```
  jcmon -pf /usr/sap/<SID>/SYS/profile/<instance profile>
  ```

  Within JCMon, you have the option of administrating the entire cluster or individual processes. After startup, the menu shown in Figure 11.24 is provided.

The two subsequent menus **Cluster Administration Menu** and **Local Administration Menu** can be seen in Figure 11.25 and Figure 11.26. These give you an introduction to the administration options.

```
f03:s10adm 5> jcmon pf=S10_DVEBMGS01_f03
[Thr  1] MtxInit: -2 0 0

============================================================
JControl Monitor Program - Main Menu
============================================================
0  : exit
------------------------------------------------------------
10 : Cluster Administration Menu
------------------------------------------------------------
20 : Local Administration Menu
------------------------------------------------------------
30 : Shared Memory Menu (Solid Rock, experimental)
------------------------------------------------------------
command =>
```

Figure 11.24 Start Menu of JCMon

```
|Idx|Name               |PID     |State               |Error|Restart|
|---|-------------------|--------|--------------------|-----|-------|
|  0|dispatcher         |    6211|Running             |    0|yes    |
|  1|server0            |    6212|Running             |    0|yes    |
|  2|SDM                |    7032|Running             |    0|yes    |
------------------------------------------------------------


============================================================
JControl Monitor Program - Administration Menu  (Local)
Instance : JC_f03_S10_01
============================================================
0  : exit
1  : Refresh list
2  : Shutdown instance
3  : Enable process
4  : Disable process
5  : Restart process
6  : Enable bootstrapping on restart
7  : Disable bootstrapping on restart
8  : Enable debugging
9  : Disable debugging
10 : Dump stacktrace
11 : Process list
12 : Port list
13 : Activate debug session
14 : Deactivate debug session
15 : Increment trace level
16 : Decrement trace level
17 : Enable process restart
18 : Disable process restart
19 : Restart instance
------------------------------------------------------------
40 : Enable bootstrapping for all processes with specified process type
41 : Enable bootstrapping for all processes excluding specified process type
------------------------------------------------------------
99 : Extended process list on/off
------------------------------------------------------------
command =>
```

Figure 11.25 Cluster Administration Menu of JCMon

Most of the options visible in the menus are self-explanatory, so we won't look at them further.

```
==============================================================
JControl Monitor Program - Cluster Admin Menu
==============================================================
0  : exit
1  : Display Instance List
2  : Shutdown Cluster
3  : Shutdown Cluster (Async)
4  : Shutdown Cluster and wait for Restart
5  : Shutdown Cluster and wait for Restart (Async)
6  : Start waiting Cluster
7  : Free Cluster wait lock without Restart
8  : Shutdown Cluster and wait for Restart without SDM
9  : Shutdown Cluster and wait for Restart without SDM (Async)
--------------------------------------------------------------
10 : Shutdown Instance
11 : Shutdown Instance (Async)
12 : Shutdown Instance with Restart
13 : Shutdown Instance with Restart (Async)
14 : Restart Instance
15 : Enable processes with specified process type
16 : Disable processes with specified process type
17 : Enable processes excluding specified process type
18 : Disable processes excluding specified process type
19 : Shutdown and Restart Instance (Async)
--------------------------------------------------------------
21 : Process Administration Menu (remote)
--------------------------------------------------------------
30 : Enable all processes with specified process type
31 : Disable all processes with specified process type
32 : Enable all processes excluding specified process type
33 : Disable all processes excluding specified process type
--------------------------------------------------------------
40 : Enable bootstrapping for all processes with specified process type
41 : Enable bootstrapping for all processes excluding specified process type
--------------------------------------------------------------
50 : Shutdown and Restart Cluster (Async)
--------------------------------------------------------------
98 : Display monitor clients
99 : Display process types
--------------------------------------------------------------
command =>
```

Figure 11.26 Local Administration Menu of JCMon

- **ICM Monitor**

  If there is no possibility of using JCMon or the operating system level, you can still perform administration of the J2EE engine from a connected ABAP system. To do this, go to **Transaction Tools • Administration • Monitor • System monitoring • ICM Monitor** (Transaction SMICM). There, you can use **Go To • HTTP Server • Data** to display a status overview of the J2EE engine and the communication port. The application server shown in Figure 11.27 has an active J2EE engine (J2EE Server operational and configured = TRUE) and is reachable by HTTP on port 50100. All URLs that don't start with the prefixes in the URL prefix table are passed to the J2EE engine (**Default root access handler = J2EE**). The prefix table shown is active (**URL Prefix Table loaded = true**). If this is not the case, an orderly forwarding of URLs to the ICM or J2EE engine can be done. In the ICM Monitor transaction, you can then follow the path **Go To • HTTP Server • Load URL prefixes** to force loading of the prefix table.

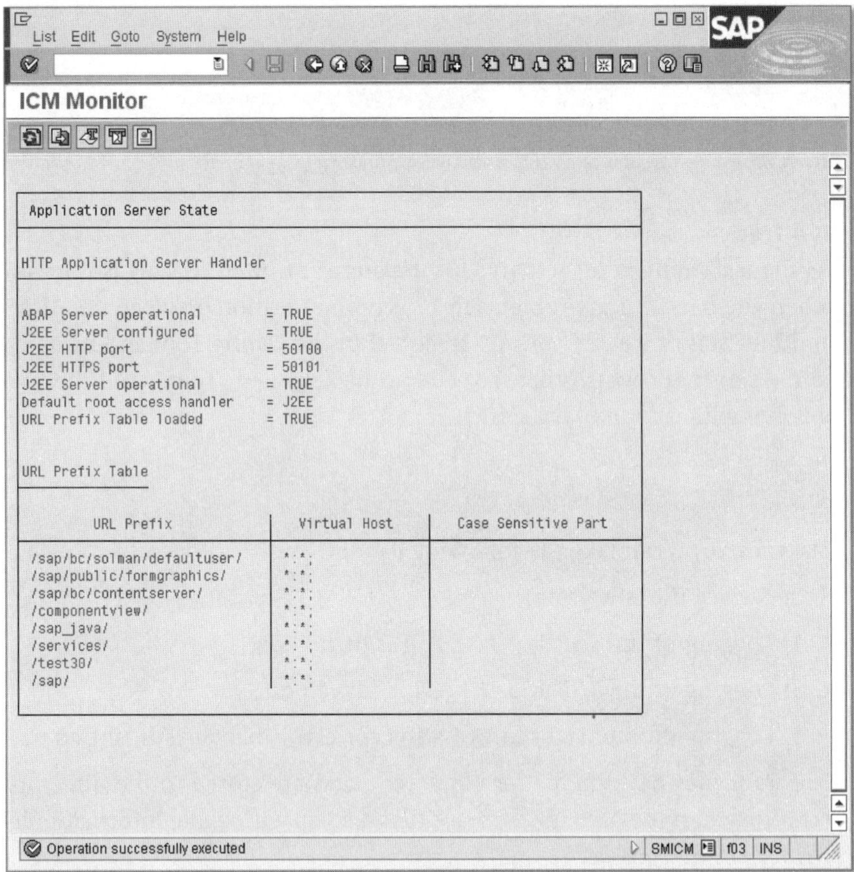

Figure 11.27 ICM Monitor

Moreover, within the ICM Monitor, you also have the option of starting or stopping an individual J2EE instance or the entire cluster. To do this, you can use either a soft mode, which waits until the processes have ended, or a hard mode, which performs a strict termination of the processes. To do this, call up the menu entry Administration in the ICM Monitor. Figure 11.28 shows an overview of the options. The same options exist for the entire J2EE cluster.

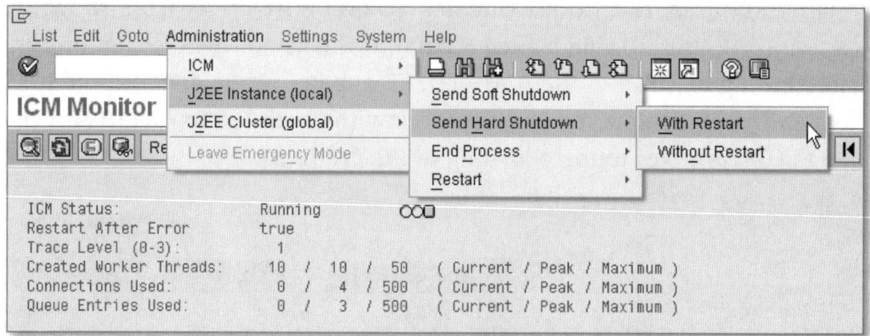

Figure 11.28 Administration of a J2EE in the ICM Monitor

- **JCo Trace**

  As the last monitoring activity, JCo tracing is of interest. This is relevant when you have found problems in JCo communication between the ABAP and Java stacks. To activate JCo traces, start the Config Tool and navigate to the server for which the trace should be activated. There, add the two following lines to the Java start parameters.

  ```
  -Djco.trace_level=<trace_level>
  -Djco.trace_path=<trace_path>
  ```

  The trace level can take the following vales:

  - 0: A trace file is written.
  - 1: Logging of the SAP JCo Java API is turned on.
  - 3: Logging of the SAP JCo JNI API is turned on.
  - 5: Logging of important information for error diagnosis is turned on.

  The trace files have the pattern `JCO*.trc` and are stored to the directory `trace_path`. If the path for the trace files isn't specified, the information is written to the console.

- **JRA Trace**

  If you are using the SAP Java Resource Adapter, which is based on the JCo, you can trace it using similar options. Use the following two lines to activate logging in that case:

  ```
  -Djra.trace_level=<trace_level>
  -Djra.trace_path=<trace_path>
  ```

  After entering or changing the parameters, restart the J2EE engine.

Now that you know something about the architecture of the J2EE engine, in the following sections we can point out a few features of the J2EE engine.

We'll cover the different software logistics, which also influences the patching and upgrading of a Java engine. The tools used are also covered in the following chapter.

11.3 Java Software Logistics

The software logistics of the J2EE engine differ from those in the ABAP engine. SAP has developed a concept that provides a similar development landscape, but there is no transport of delta changes of programs, for instance. Instead, components are replaced in the Java environment. Due to this difference, in the following sections, we will first address the structure and functionality of a Java development landscape, the *SAP NetWeaver Development Infrastructure*, and then we'll take a look at how to patch Java instances and applications. Particularly relevant for both topics is the changed structure of Java applications in comparison with ABAP programs. This structure, the *component model*, is explained in more detail in Section 11.3.2, *SAP Component Model.*

11.3.1 SAP NetWeaver Development Infrastructure

The SAP NWDI provides a complete infrastructure for the development of Java-based applications. It regulates the versioning, compilation (build), and further administration of an application during its entire lifetime. When working with the NWDI, a development environment — the SAP NetWeaver Developer Studio (NWDS) — and a series of web-based tools are available. These make it possible to manage compilation and distribute components.

11.3.1.1 SAP NetWeaver Developer Studio

The SAP NWDS provides the option of local development of components. In conjunction with the local installation of a J2EE engine, these can also be tested at a given workplace. If this studio is also connected to the NWDI, development in teams is possible. Here, individual components are checked out for changing, freezing them at a certain version for the global development process until they are released again. After completion of programming work, the completed components can then be transferred back to the central infrastructure and combined with other components. The components of the NWDI handle the following tasks:

- The Design Time Repository (DTR) provides central storage for all source files in the database. These can be exported from there for further use. The DTR is also used to synchronize source code in a distributed development environment.
- The Component Build Service (CBS) gives the developer access to the current Java archive of components, as well as starting a central build process to check the behavior of locally developed components in the overall context. To reduce the running time of the build process, there is an incremental build procedure, so that only changed components and dependencies will be recompiled.
- The Change Management Service (CMS) is presented as a web frontend, providing a central point for the administration of the entire development landscape. This includes the definition of the development landscape in so-called development tasks and the transport of components within those tasks.

Figure 11.29 shows how the development process works with NWDI and the interplay of the individual NWDI components.

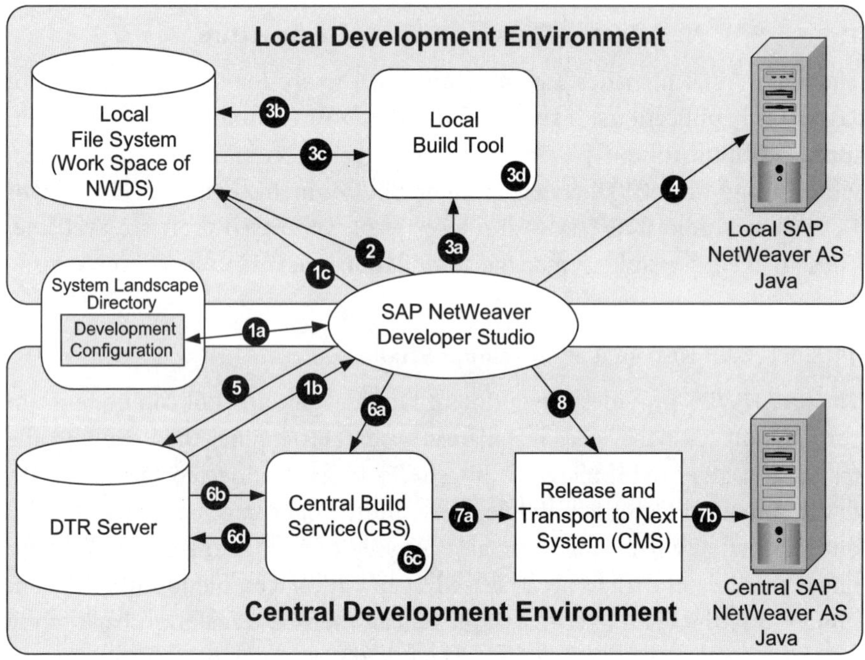

Figure 11.29 Process of Development Using the NWDI

This process works as follows:

- 1a – The developer logs into the NWDI with his NWDS, and imports a development configuration from the System Landscape Directory (SLD). This development configuration defines the developer's view of the NWDI. This includes a complete description of all components, sources, libraries, and services that the developer needs for further work.
- 1b/1c – Once the development configuration is loaded, all referenced objects from the DTR and CBS are synchronized with the local files.
- 2 – The developer now works with the local source and can create new objects, which are initially stored locally.
- 3a / 3b / 3c / 3d – For local compilation of the developed objects, the build tool in the NWDS is used. The result of this process is stored in the local workspace.
- 4 – Ideally, the developer has a local SAP NetWeaver AS Java available on which the developed objects can be tested. There, the developer can perform a deployment from the NWDS and test the functionality of the application.
- 5 – After development is complete, the local source is transmitted or updated back to the DTR.
- 6a / 6b / 6c / 6d – From the NWDS, the source is downloaded from the DTR for a central build, and that archive is stored back into the DTR if the build is successful.
- 7a / 7b / 8 – All parts stored by the different developers in the DTR, after compilation, are then combined into a complete application, centrally tested, and transported as a product through the CMS into the system landscape.

11.3.2 SAP Component Model

In the previous section, we spoke of the development process for components and their combination into a product. The *SAP component model* plays a very important role in this regard, because it is used to structure the organization of a development project. The component model represents an extension of the familiar Java package concept and the public/private concept. SAP has extended these concepts with metadata, particularly to avoid coordination and synchronization problems in large projects developed by teams.

For instance, these problems include the lengthy analysis of dependencies between classes or packages that is impossible without either extensive source code analysis or a view of packages as complete units, which makes distributed development difficult. In addition, the component model also allows the use of packages or components in different versions to ensure maintenance for applications.

The components are available to the developer as simple, maintainable, reusable objects. Components can use other components, contain subcomponents, or provide functions through defined interfaces (public parts).

The component model consists of the four elements *product, software component* (SC), *development component* (DC), and *development object* (DO), which allow an ever finer analysis of a project. The elements are defined as follows:

- **Products**
  Products consist of a set of SCs that can have identical parts (DCs). An SC can belong to multiple products.
- **Software components**
  SCs are available after development as deliverable or installation and are the smallest installable unit of a package. They are composed of multiple nonoverlapping DCs.
- **Development components**
  DCs are a part of the developed software (assigned to an SC) and can be composed of multiple development objects. They are compiled in the context of the build process. DCs can be nested in one another and access functions from other DCs.

  The DC contains meta-information about the module itself. This includes, for instance, the relationships to other DCs and the parts used in common. Examples of a few existing DC types are web dynpro applications, data dictionary objects, and Web Services.

  In the context of development projects, the developer is normally assigned a DC that represents a bounded part of the project (for instance, a posting module). Within the DC, the developer can then create DOs (classes, views, table definitions) that represent complete components.
- **Development objects**
  DOs are the smallest unit of development and are created and changed during development. Within a DC, they provide a certain functionality whose source code is stored in the DTR as a versioned file. A development object can be a Java class or a package, a web dynpro view, a table definition, a Java Server Page, or something similar. DCs cannot be executed alone — only in the context of the DC.

The relationship between these four elements of the component models is represented graphically in Figure 11.30. The figure shows that a product can consist of multiple SCs, which in turn can belong to different products. An SC consists of multiple DCs, which in turn are made up of multiple DOs.

For delivery, deployment, or maintenance purposes, it is possible to mark the current status of an SC as *Release*. The decision to do this can be made by those responsible for the SCs. In the NWDI and the NWDS, no information is stored about this status. An SC can therefore be part of a release, but it need not be. A release of an SC can be found when patching a J2EE engine, for instance. There, the support packages of the individual SAP Java components each correspond to a release level. The support package contains a number of special characters, which provide a current version of the J2EE components.

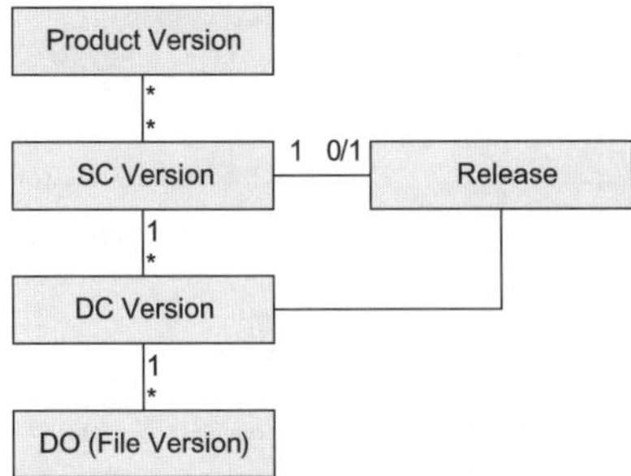

Figure 11.30 Interplay of Elements in the Component Model.

Development in the context of these components is fully supported by the NWDI and particularly by SAP NWDS.

11.3.3 Patching Java Instances and Applications

After the installation or development of an SAP NetWeaver AS Java and Java applications, the later lifecycle is also of interest to the administrator. SAP has developed new tools in the Java environment for this purpose, which are intended to simplify the patching, downloading, and upgrading of Java components. As the central tool, all of these tools use the *Software Deployment Manager*. It is used by the *Java Support Package Manager* (JSPM) and the *SAP Java Upgrade program* (SAPJup).

11.3.3.1 Software Deployment Manager

The SDM is already familiar to you from the description of the architecture and the NWDI. All activities that require deployment use the SDM of a J2EE instance. *Deployment* is the downloading or updating of a software archive in a J2EE engine. The deployment of developed objects through the SDM is entirely integrated into the NWDS. At the same time, however, you also have the option of loading archives through the *SDM Remote GUI*. To do this, call the program /usr/sap/<SID>/ <instance>/SDM/program/RemoteGui.sh. After logging into the SDM, you will see a screen similar to that shown in Figure 11.31, showing an overview of all components deployed and their versions. You can use the SDM to delete or update them, or even load entirely new components.

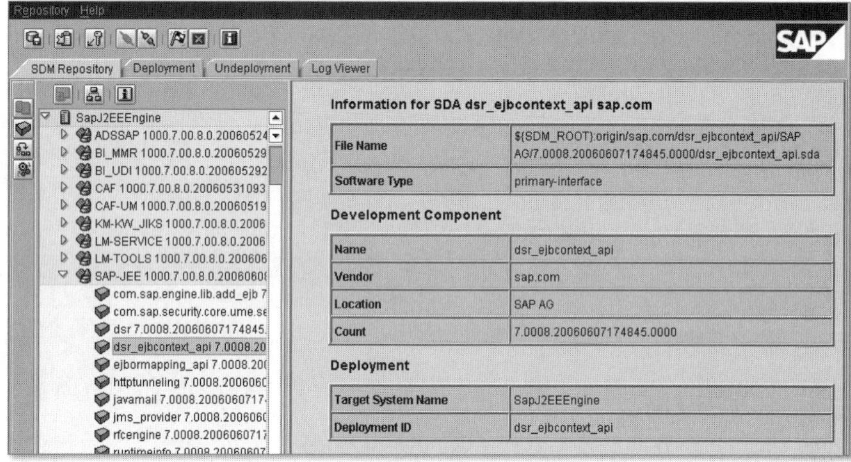

Figure 11.31 SDM Repository in the Remote GUI

The SDM allows only one exclusive connection. Note this when you are working with the Remote GUI, for instance. During that time, nobody else can connect to the SDM, for instance, to deploy archives.

As a client, an independent program, the Remote GUI, or a development environment like the NWDS, can be used. Similarly, the CMS can act as a client to deploy the archives to the server of an NWDI.

A password is needed to log into the SDM, which is set during installation. You can change the password in the Remote GUI through **Repository • Change SDM Password**. For security reasons, the SDM is automatically shut down after three incorrect password specifications.

To start the SDM, there are multiple operating modes. First, the SDM can be operated in integrated mode. This means it is automatically started during the startup of the J2EE engine by jcontrol. Second, it can be started in standalone mode. That means the SDM must be started manually when needed, and only then is it ready for deployment or other tasks. After conclusion of the work, the SDM is stopped again.

To start the SDM in stand-alone mode, perform the following commands as <sid>adm:

```
cd /usr/sap/<SID>/< instance>/SDM/program
./sdm.sh jstartup mode=standalone  (UNIX)
sdm.bat jstartup "mode=standalone" (Windows)
```

To set it back to integrated mode, perform the following:

```
./sdm.sh jstartup mode=integrated  (UNIX)
sdm.bat jstartup "mode=integrated" (Windows)
```

If the host on which your J2EE engine is running with the SDM process has multiple network cards or IP addresses, we recommend editing the *bindHost* property for the P4 port of the dispatcher. There, enter all of the IP addresses (if possible, no host names, to avoid domain name service problems) at which the J2EE engine should be reachable. As shown in Figure 11.32, navigate in the Config Tool to **Global dispatcher configuration • services • p4** and select the parameter bindHost. Enter the desired IP addresses and confirm with Set. Save your settings using **File • Apply**. Then, restart the J2EE engine.

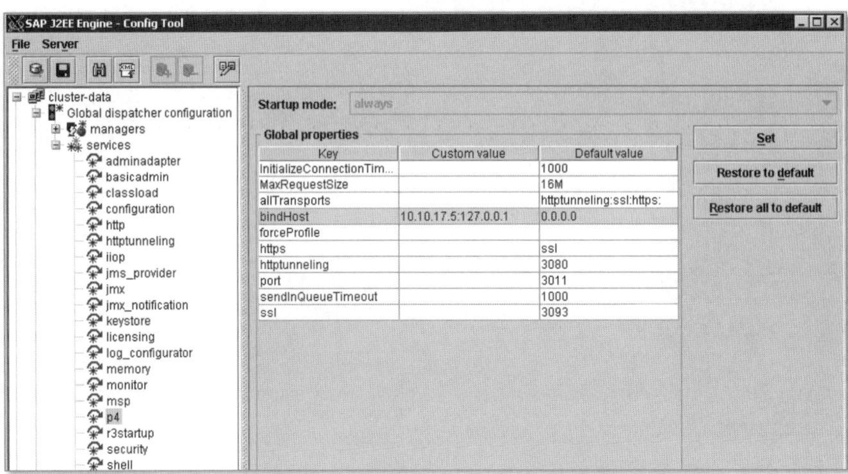

Figure 11.32 Adjustment of the bindHost Parameter of the P4 Port

We recommend making this adjustment, particularly when using virtual IP addresses.

11.3.3.2 JSPM

As of SAP NetWeaver 7.0, the JSPM is available for use of support packages on the SCs used. Moreover, you can perform deployments for new SCs that aren't part of the SAP standard. These can also be updated using support packages. JSPM recognizes and automatically offers only those components that can upgrade the components used. It also checks deployment dependencies between components.

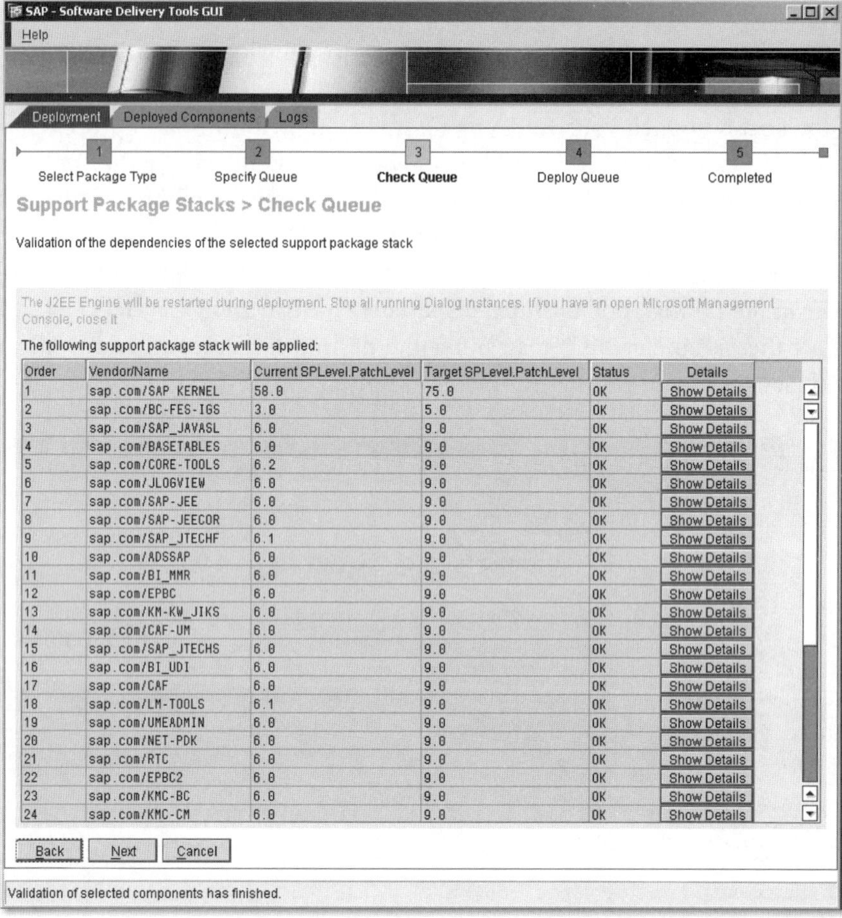

Figure 11.33 Importing an SPS in JSPM

Furthermore, JSPM supports the updating of kernel binaries, the SDM, and even the JSPM itself. Support packages can be loaded individually or as a complete stack. Support Package Stacks (SPSs) represent a complete set of support packages that have been tested by SAP. Such a definition is shown in Figure 11.33. In the context of this stack, the kernel and all of the other J2EE components are updated at once. The definition of a support package stack can be saved as an XML file when downloading. JSPM is capable of evaluating these XML files and performing corresponding patching of all J2EE components.

If it should be necessary to restart the J2EE engine during patching, JSPM informs you of this in advance and then performs the restart automatically later.

JSPM logs the entire deployment processes and provides the log files in an integrated log viewer. Alternatively, you can find the log files in the */usr/sap/<SID>/<instance>/j2ee/JSPM/log* folder.

If the loading of packages is interrupted, JSPM supports the resumption of deployment.

To load support packages, first you download the desired packages and store them in the directory */usr/sap/trans/EPS/in*. If this is an SPS, you also store the file SPSTab.xml there, which you can also download when you retrieve the SPS. When JSPM is called, this file is automatically read, and you have the option of loading the entire SPS. To start the JSPM, go to */usr/sap/<SID>/<instance>/j2ee/JSPM* as <sid>adm and call `go` or `go.bat`.

Then first patch the JSPM itself by selecting the Single Support Package option and only loading the support package for the JSPM. Then restart the JSPM and load the support package stack. During patching, all packages are unpacked into the */usr/sap/<SID>/<instance>/SDM/prog/temp* directory. Be sure to keep sufficient free storage available there (about one and a half to two times the size of the support packages).

In larger landscapes with a lot of systems, to avoid the files from different support package stacks being mixed together or even overwritten, you can adapt the Inbox of the JSPM. For instance, you have the option of creating a separate directory for each SPS. To change the Inbox directory of the JSPM, there are two techniques:

- **Temporary change to the Inbox**
  To do this, start the JSPM with the option `config=jspm/inbox=<path of inbox>`. The changed path is only valid for this call and overrides the setting in the configuration file.

- **Permanent change to the Inbox**
  To change the Inbox permanently, add a new parameter, `/jspm/inbox`, in `/usr/sap/<SID>/<SYS>/j2ee/JSPM/param/jspm_config.txt` and set the desired (full) path there. It will take effect on the next start of the JSPM.

11.3.3.3 SAPJup

The *SAP Java Upgrade Program* (SAPJup) controls the upgrade of SAP NetWeaver Application Server Java and the software based on it. It is available as of Release SAP NetWeaver 7.0.

SAPJup can be used to perform upgrades of SAP NetWeaver AS Java standalone installations and of integrated systems consisting of SAP NetWeaver AS ABAP and Java (add-in installations). If you installed SAP NetWeaver Application Server Java as an add-in, you must update SAP NetWeaver AS ABAP and AS Java in parallel. SAPJup is synchronized with the ABAP upgrade program SAPup to achieve the shortest downtime possible. Like SAPup, SAPJup provides the option of integrating support packages for the target release into the upgrade so that your system is immediately at the latest level after the upgrade. To manage this feat, SAPJup can detect and determine the software installed on the starting release, which components must be updated, and which must be installed, to reach a valid target release configuration. The installation of additional components is then performed by SAPJup. The basic data and table structures are converted as needed into *migration containers*.

All of the custom development performed to date is retained, meaning it is all still contained in the target release. If you made changes to SAP software in the starting release, you will have to make them again to the newly delivered software before the upgrade. You can then have SAPJup perform the deployment of the corresponding archive during the upgrade.

11.4 Tips and Tricks

This section is intended to give you a few important tips and tricks for the profile parameters of Java instances and offer help in particular error situations.

11.4.1 Profile Parameters for the J2EE Engine

To couple a J2EE engine to an ABAP system, different profile parameters must be edited. This is particularly relevant in add-in installations. If you encounter problems when starting or stopping, or with ICM communication, check the corresponding profile parameters as well. The following overviews present the most important parameters. Note that for executables under Windows you need to append the extension *.exe*.

For the J2EE Engine 6.30/6.40, the parameters shown in the following listing must be entered into the instance profile:

```
exe/j2ee = $(DIR_INSTANCE)/j2ee/os_libs/jcontrol
rdisp/j2ee_start_control = 1
// control start J2EE engine
rdisp/j2ee_start = 1
// Enable start of J2EE engine
rdisp/j2ee_timeout = 600
// Reconnect timeout for J2EE Engine, default=60
rdisp/frfc_fallback = on
jstartup/trimming_properties = off
jstartup/protocol = on
exe/jlaunch = $(DIR_INSTANCE)/j2ee/os_libs/jlaunch
jstartup/instance_properties = $(INSTANCE_PROPERTIES);$(SDM_PROPERTIES)
ms/server_port_0 = PROT=HTTP, PORT=81<InstNo>
INSTANCE_PROPERTIES = $(DIR_INSTANCE)/j2ee/cluster/instance.properties SDM_
PROPERTIES = $(DIR_INSTANCE)/SDM/program/config/sdm_jstartup.properties
icm/HTTP/j2ee_0 = PREFIX=/,HOST=<j2ee_host>,CONN=0 - 500,PORT=<j2ee_http_port>
```

For SAP NetWeaver 7.0, the following parameters must be entered into the instance profile:

```
jstartup/trimming_properties = off
jstartup/vm/home = <path to the JDK directory>
jstartup/max_caches = 500
jstartup/release = 700
jstartup/instance_properties = $(jstartup/j2ee_properties);$(jstar-
tup/sdm_properties) #Path separator is system-dependent
j2ee/dbdriver = <path to JDBC driver jar files> #Path separator is
system-dependent
j2ee/instance_id = <instance id>
jstartup/protocol = on
rdisp/j2ee_start_control = 1
rdisp/j2ee_start = 1
rdisp/j2ee_libpath = $(DIR_EXECUTABLE)
exe/j2ee = $(DIR_EXECUTABLE)/jcontrol$(FT_EXE)
rdisp/j2ee_timeout = 600
```

```
rdisp/frfc_fallback = on
icm/HTTP/j2ee_0 = PREFIX=/,HOST=localhost,CONN=0 - 500,PORT=5 $$00
icm/server_port_0 = PROT=HTTP,PORT=80 $$
```

In case of an error, the ABAP system automatically tries to restart the J2EE engine. The number of attempts can be configured using the `rdisp/j2ee_error` parameter. The default value is 10.

There may also be conflicts due to longer startup times in the ABAP or J2EE server. To avoid this, you can use the `rdisp/j2ee_start_lazy` parameter to start the startup of the J2EE engine only after conclusion of the ABAP startup phase. Set the value of the parameter to 1 to do this.

All the parameters that start with `jstartup` are passed to the Java Startup and Control Framework and affect the settings there. For further information on these options, see Section 11.4.2, *Parameters of the Property File*.

Using the parameter `icm/HTTP/j2ee_<xx>`, you can define how the ICM can communicate with the J2EE engine. Due to their importance, we will look at the individual options in more detail. How to monitor the connection between ICM and the J2EE engine was covered in Section 11.2.3, *Monitoring*.

The parameter has the following syntax:

```
icm/HTTP/j2ee_<xx>=PREFIX=<uri prefix>,[HOST=<host>,] CONN=<number
of connections >, PORT=<port> [, SSLENC=<n>, TYPE=<t>, CRED=
<file>, SPORT=<HTTPS-port> ]
```

In Table 11.3, you can see a description of the individual options.

Option	Description
PREFIX	All the HTTP URLs starting with this string will be checked as to whether they should be forwarded to the J2EE engine. `PREFIX=/` means that by default, all URLs will be passed to the J2EE engine. The only exceptions are the entries from the URL prefix table in the ABAP system.
HOST	Host on which the J2EE engine is running. If the parameter is not specified, `localhost` is assumed. If the secure socket layer (SSL) is forwarded to the J2EE engine, the subject canonical name that appears in the SSL server certificate of the J2EE engine (name of the computer on which the certificate was created, for instance, "help.sap.com") must match this value.

Table 11.3 Profile Parameters for the J2EE Engine

Option	Description
CONN	This parameter can be used to define the number of network connections to the J2EE engine. You can either configure a fixed number of connections or a range (`min-max`). If a range is specified, the ICM opens `min` connections to the server during startup. New connections are opened on an as-needed basis until the maximum value of `max` is reached. If a fixed number is specified (or if the minimum value is equal to the maximum), these connections are already opened during startup.
PORT	Port number or name of the HTTP listener ports of the J2EE engine with which the ICM should connect.
SPORT	Port number or name of the HTTPS listener ports of the J2EE engine with which the ICM should connect.
SSLENC	Specifies whether the data stream should be SSL-encrypted again; the following values are possible: ▸ **0**: Data is not SSL-encrypted again. ▸ **1**: Data is SSL-encrypted again, if it came to the ICM with encryption (HTTPS). ▸ **2**: Data is SSL-encrypted in any case. If nothing is specified, the data is not encrypted again (value 0).
TYPE	Specifies whether client authentication should be used and which X.509 certificate the ICM should use to do it. The following values are possible: ▸ **0**: No certificate ▸ **1**: Default certificate ▸ **2**: Use certificate specified by the parameter `CRED`
CRED	Name of the personal security environment file used for authentication on the server; this option is only relevant for `TYPE=2`!

Table 11.3 Profile Parameters for the J2EE Engine (Cont.)

11.4.2 Parameters of the Property File

The parameters in the property file are passed to `jlaunch` during startup to start the process with the settings specified. For add-in installations, some of the parameters can also be passed to the start routine by the SAP system. If this is possible, the name of the SAP profile parameter must still always be specified. Table 11.4 shows the parameters of the property file.

Description	jlaunch parameter	SAP profile parameter
Path to SAP instance profile; profile containing all parameters for the J2EE instance	pf=<filename>	-
Path to instance.properties file	-file=<filename>	jstartup/ instance_properties= <filename>
Node name for jlaunch; the process is started under this name, and the matching parameters are filtered out of the *instance.properties* file (for instance SDM, bootstrap, dispatcher, server(n)	-nodename=<nodename>	-
Name of the trace file for jcontrol and jlaunch	-tracefile=<filename> Default=<home-directory> /dev_<Nodename>	-
Activate and deactivate bootstrap	-bootstrap=[yes/no] Default=yes	jstartup/bootstrap
Detailed information in the trace files	-protocol=[on/off] Default=off	jstartup/protocol
Process mode for jlaunch; depending on mode, different internal default values are used	-mode=[STANDALONE/J2EE] Default=STANDALONE	-
Output for messages from the JVM	-jvmOutFile=<filename> Default=<home-directory> /jvm_<Node name>.out	-
Output mode for the JVM messages; either a new file is generated or the messages are appended to the existing file	-jvmOutMode=[new/append] Default=new	-
Log files for the output of the jlaunch processes	-locOutFile=<filename> Default=<home-directory> /dev_<Nodename>	-
Activation of debug mode for a node	-debugMode=[yes/no] Default=no	jstartup/debug_mode

Table 11.4 Parameters of the Property File

Description	jlaunch parameter	SAP profile parameter
Security level of the J2EE instance, which determines how jcontrol reacts to signals from the message server. A value between 0 and 3. 3 means there will be no reaction; 0 allows all signals.	-securityLevel=[0...3] Default=0	jstartup/security_level
Additional environment variables These must be passed as a list in the form Variable1=Value1; Variable2=Value2.	environment= <list of environment variables>	jstartup/environment

Table 11.4 Parameters of the Property File (Cont.)

11.4.3 Minimum Configuration of the instance.properties File

All the parameters in the file are stored in the database. If this file is defective for some reason and access is no longer possible, you can restore access with a minimal set of parameters. This minimal instance.properties file has the following content:

```
bootstrap.ClassPath=./bootstrap/launcher.jar
bootstrap.JavaParameters=-Djco.jarm=1
bootstrap.JavaPath=/opt/java/j2sdk1.4.2_09 #your path
bootstrap.MainClass=com.sap.engine.offline.OfflineToolStart
bootstrap.MaxHeapSize=128
bootstrap.Name=bootstrap
bootstrap.Parameters=com.sap.engine.bootstrap.Bootstrap  ./bootstra
p ID0098278 # all on one line!!!
bootstrap.RootPath=/usr/sap/<SID>/<instance>/j2ee/cluster
bootstrap.Type=bootstrap
```

This minimal configuration will make it possible to restore the original instance.properties file from the database. In addition, you'll need the bootstrap.properties file, which contains the connection information for the database.

Table 11.5 gives a brief description of the options specified.

Property name	Description
ClassPath	Path to the file launcher.jar
JavaParameters	Additional Java parameters passed to the JVM during startup
JavaPath	Path to the Java directory, corresponding to the JAVA_HOME variable
MainClass	Main class of the Java program
MaxHeapSize	Heap storage size in megabytes
Name	Name of the process; in this case, bootstrap
Parameters	Parameter with which the process should be started
RootPath	Root path of the Java program
Type	Type of Java process; possible values are unknown, bootstrap, dispatcher, server, sdm

Table 11.5 Bootstrap Parameters of the Property File

An example bootstrap.properties file looks like this:

```
install.dir=/usr/sap/S10/DVEBMGS01/j2ee
secstorefs.lib=/sapmnt/S10/global/security/lib
rdbms.driverLocation=
/oracle/client/10x_64/instantclient/ojdbc14.jar
rdbms.connection=jdbc/pool/S10
instance.prefix=ID136199
rdbms.initial_connections=1
secstorefs.keyfile=
/sapmnt/S10/global/security/data/SecStore.key
secstorefs.secfile=
/sapmnt/S10/global/security/data/SecStore.properties
rdbms.maximum_connections=5
system.name=S10
```

11.5 Summary

With the SAP NetWeaver AS Java, SAP provides a complete infrastructure for the construction of Java-based applications. We hope this chapter has given you an overview of how this technology works and where you, as an administrator, may be involved. For additional information, we recommend the Java-specific works of SAP PRESS, which will give you not only more technical information, but also the basics of programming in this environment (for instance, *Java Programming with the SAP Web Application Server* by Kessler et al., 2005).

If you are interested in "playing" with SAP NetWeaver AS Java a little, you can download a test version from the SAP Developer Network (SDN; *http://sdn.sap.com*). There, you will also find extensive information and tutorials on all aspects of the architecture and programming with the entire SAP NetWeaver stack.

The goal is to provide large amounts of data in such a way that it can be understood and analyzed.

12 SAP NetWeaver BI and Oracle

SAP NetWeaver Business Intelligence (SAP NetWeaver BI) is one of SAP's most popular developments of ERP software (Enterprise Resource Planning). In the NetWeaver architecture, SAP's Data Warehouse supports the enterprise in the strategic structuring of its business based on well-founded analyses and forecasts. In this chapter, we'll be looking at the technical side of SAP NetWeaver BI. First, however, we'll look at the particular features and methods of data warehouse databases from a general perspective and cover data warehousing with Oracle. Then we'll turn our attention to SAP NetWeaver BI. We'll cover the application first, and then examine the concrete technical questions of BI administration, particularly in connection with Oracle.

12.1 Basics and Concepts of Data Warehousing

Data warehousing is a special kind of database use. The concepts, structures, and procedures associated with it are the subject of this section.

12.1.1 OLAP and OLTP

Traditionally, database systems had two major sets of tasks. On the one hand, they supported a set of business processes as interactive as possible, handling compact, short transactions very quickly. This mode of operation is called *online transaction processing* (OLTP). On the other hand, they were designed to provide collected or aggregated data in the form of reports. The first task was usually carried out in dialog operation, and the second usually at night in background jobs. Log running reports require analysis and calculations, and can disturb business operations during the day.

Today, every manager has his own notebook computer and needs to be able to access a variety of reports and analyses online, which should include data right up to the minute, if possible. The *online analytical processing* (OLAP) needed for this capability requires special support from a dedicated database — the *data warehouse*.

The requirements of OLTP and OLAP for database management system (DBMS) configuration differ from one another. OLAP queries can be executed on a system configured for OLTP applications, but the probable result will be a hindrance of daily OLTP business. In addition, such OLAP queries are significantly slower than in a specially configured OLAP database.

Table 12.1 shows some differences between OLTP and OLAP. The significant property of the OLAP system is that it works on the basis of historical data. That means that from the point of view of the database system, the basis data is only written once (when loaded) and is then never changed. The database of the data warehouse can therefore dispense entirely with costly transaction mechanisms. The fragmentation of the OLAP database can be lower, because blocks can be filled optimally once and need not reserve free space for updates.

On the other hand, sifting through a large historical data inventory can lead to high load and the multiple replacement of the system global area (SGA) contents.

Aspect	OLTP system	OLAP system
Usage profile	Transaction-oriented	Analysis-oriented
Application area	Daily operations	Planning, strategic support
Users	Staff	Manager
Typical operations	Reading, writing, modification, deletion	Reading, periodic insertion
Complexity of queries	Frequent, simple queries	Less frequent, but more complex queries
Data volume	Small data volume per query	Large data volume per query
Time reference	Operates primarily on the basis of current data	Operates primarily on current and historical data
Optimization goal	Fast updates important	Fast calculation important

Table 12.1 Comparison between OLTP and OLAP

12.1.2 Data Warehouse Architecture

William H. Inmon defines a "data warehouse as a department-oriented, integrated, stable, historical collection of data for the support of management decisions" (see *The Data Warehouse and Data Mining*, 1996).

Integration of data is an important task of the data warehouse, because in an enterprise or its environment, numerous information systems generate and collect data (see Figure 12.1). With SAP, you already have an integrated system that can provide all significant operational data, but the fact that the ideal and the real seldom match in practice is something you surely already know from your own experience. For this integration, however, the NetWeaver architecture includes some powerful integration tools.

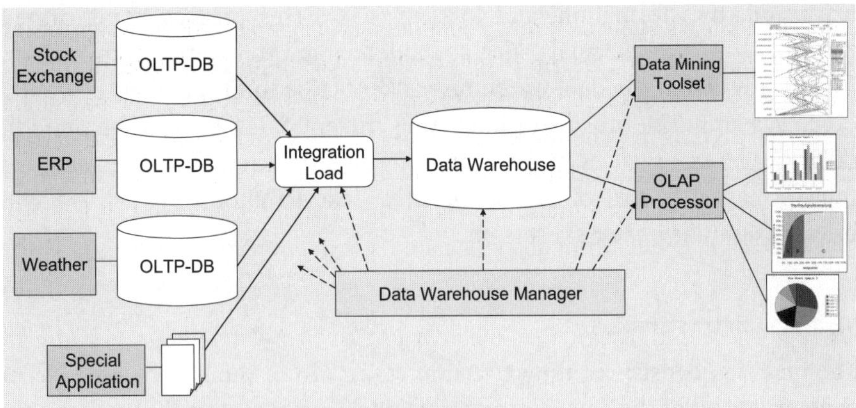

Figure 12.1 Simplified Data Warehouse Architecture

Figure 12.1 sketches the architecture of the entire system and the data flow in a data warehouse landscape. Production information systems store their transaction data in databases or files. It can be very important to be able to access external data, such as the weather or the stock market. The Integration Engine acts as a data pump to copy the data, collecting it in the data warehouse. In the data warehouse, special data structures are used, which we will briefly introduce in this chapter. Based on the homogenized and integrated data, an OLAP processor can generate reports according to defined specifications. Another possibility is the use of data mining tools to find hidden relationships in the data, which help optimize production, business operations, and the strategy of the enterprise. For example, do the sales of diapers depend on the weather?[1] The process of administration of the entire system

1 A classic example of the motivation for data warehousing is the significantly frequent purchase together of diapers and beer on Friday evening (see Potts, W.J.E.: *Data Mining Primer – Overview of Applications and Methods*. Cary, SAS Institute, 1998) This result could only be derived using free (goalless) data analysis using data mining. Possible business consequences could be to place a pallet of beer next to the diaper department on Fridays, or perhaps to keep the beer as far from the diapers as possible, in order to lead young fathers past as many attractive offers as possible.

is supported by tools that control the procurement and integration of data. The data warehouse manager shown in Figure 12.1 can also consist of multiple components. It uses and generates metadata that describe both data sources and the data warehouse.

12.1.3 Extraction, Transformation, Loading

The typical process when operating a data warehouse consists of the steps of extraction, transformation, and loading (ETL). This process is performed cyclically based on metadata such as modeling and transaction information, in such a way that the data warehouse is kept close to the state of the operational systems. The process of importing current data can be done periodically, triggered by an event or a query. The structure of the metadata for transformation is part of the design of a data warehouse, which we will briefly examine in the next section.

12.1.3.1 Extraction

The first step consists of the extraction of data from the source systems. In general, not all of the data is exported from a source system, but rather only the segment categorized during design as important for the data warehouse. How greatly this area can be limited depends on the context, because, after all, an enterprise never has completely decoupled processes or data.

From the point of view of a data warehouse landscape in production, the extraction largely concerns *delta data*, that is, data that has originated since the last export.

12.1.3.2 Transformation

During transformation, the extracted data is converted from the starting format to the target format. Two types of heterogeneity must be overcome. On the one hand, different data models (in the sense of data description techniques; see Chapter 3) can be used, for instance, relationally formatted data or data in files (see Figure 12.2). The files may be very different and individually formatted. In the example, we have listed the widespread formats XML and CSV, which can only be transformed with difficulty.

The second form of heterogeneity is found at the schema level and is therefore related to the way in which an object in the real world is modeled in different source systems. For instance, the price for a product may be stored in one system as an attribute in a table. In another system, one that supports price scales, for instance, the price may be stored in a separate table.

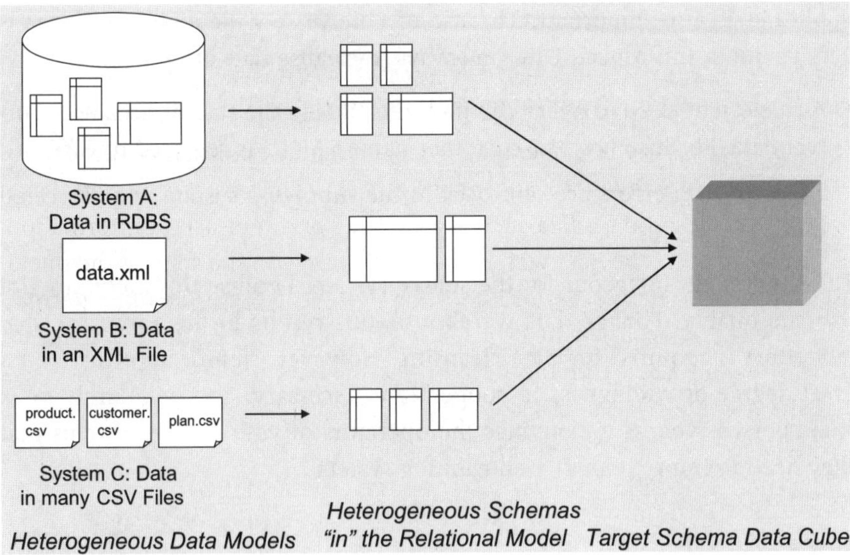

Figure 12.2 Schema Transformation and Integration

Detecting these contradictions and specifying solutions is one task of data warehouse design. Not every contradiction can be solved cleanly. A simplification in comparison with federated databases, however, results from the fact that no data is written to the source system and that the target schema in the data warehouse is already defined. Thus, the question isn't:

- "What does the database structure look like that models all existing source data correctly?", but rather:
- "How can we best force the existing data into the data warehouse? This pragmatic approach can be seen in the success of numerous data warehouse projects?"

During transformation, the data can also be cleaned up (*data cleansing*). It is an illusion to assume that databases are "clean." The spectrum of errors ranges from switched letters in names of customers, to unassigned data fragments, to modeling errors and contradictions. It may be that the statement that 70% of the cost of an OLAP project is spent on consolidation is only a rule of thumb. However, the costs that actually arise here shouldn't be underestimated, even though they're lower in the context of a well-maintained SAP system.

The integration of the data is done in the *staging area*. To integrate data from different sources, data cleansing is equally important. Identical objects must be detected and their data merged. The detection and possible correction of duplicates is also important. The use of enterprise-wide coding systems is very useful in this aspect. Different ways to cleanse data are possible:

- A rule can be used to overwrite incorrect data in the staging area with correct data. For instance, the customer name SAP IG is replaced by SAP AG.
- Detected data errors are sent back to the supplying system and corrected there.

The latter is advantageous for the source system, because this increases global data quality. For the data warehouse, this results in the advantage that less effort is required for data cleansing. However, significant effort and a great degree of willingness to cooperate is necessary. You will surely need some persuasiveness to convince the operators of your source systems that they need to improve their well-running system.

12.1.3.3 Loading

The third step consists of loading the database. The data are loaded from the staging area into the data warehouse. After logical integration during design and in the transformation step, this is where the physical integration takes place. The loading also includes the aggregation of the data corresponding to the data warehouse model.

12.1.4 Data Structures and Design of a Data Warehouse

In the design phase of the data warehouse, you must determine which data types will be stored for OLAP and data mining applications. Multidimensional data models are well suited to this task and can be represented as cubes.[2] In a next step, an attempt is made to model the cube using relational databases.

The data cube (or *OLAP cube*) models a descriptive property in every dimension. The cell of the cube is a key figure. In Figure 12.3, these are the dimensions product, time, and customer. A cell might then contain the value of the sales proceeds received:

2 A few remarks on the term *cube*: We can only directly imagine three-dimensional (or two-dimensional) cubes. From the point of view of the data warehouse, of course, more than three dimensions are possible and even required. Another remark for the mathematician: These are not actually cubes, because their edges may have different lengths.

- With a certain customer
- In a particular timeframe
- For a particular product group

As the fourth dimension, we could imagine the salesperson, in order to identify successful salespeople with respect to product, customers, and perhaps time.

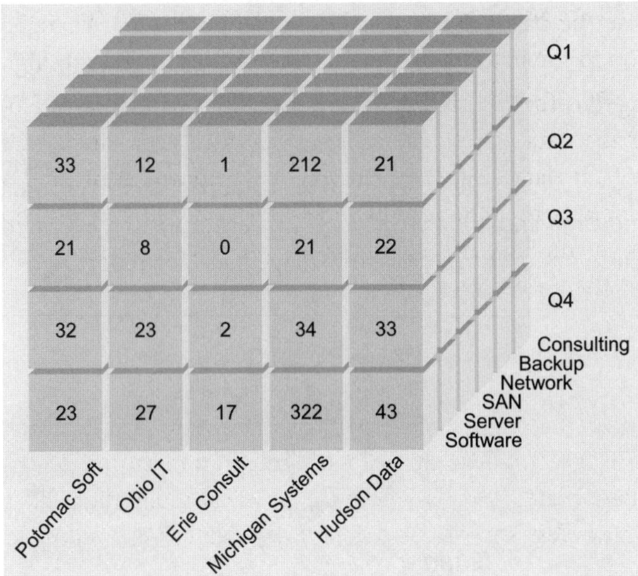

Figure 12.3 Example of Data Cubes

For instance, 21,000 Dollars were received from customer Havel Data in the first quarter. However, Figure 12.3 shows another dilemma in the presentation. The edges of the cube don't consist of four, five, or six parts, but generally of several thousand. This leads to the question: How detailed should the resolution be in each dimension? In the example, we were very specific about the customer, even though it might have made sense to provide more detail, for instance, that they are a large company. In the product dimension, too, detail is necessary, because the details of what software was sold when and how are all interesting. The time dimension should also be examined more closely to identify short-term trends and perhaps to correct for them.

However, if there is a great deal of precision in all dimensions, the following problems arise:

- The data cube becomes very large and needs a lot of storage space.
- The data cube is very large, so queries take a long time.
- The data cube is too unmanageable to be immediately useful.

The first problem is solved by the storage technique of modern database systems. To solve the second problem, aggregation can be used in the loading phase, because both the key figures of the individual products and the redundant key figures of the product groups can be stored. This redundancy is not critical, because the base data in the data warehouse is not changed anymore. Aggregation in the loading phase must be implemented with high performance. When loading deltas, however, the aggregation results must be adapted.

The third problem is solved by the concept of *data marts*. *Subcubes*, data cubes of a lower dimension and a higher level of aggregation, are generated and partly stored. These represent an easy-to-manage basis for reporting.

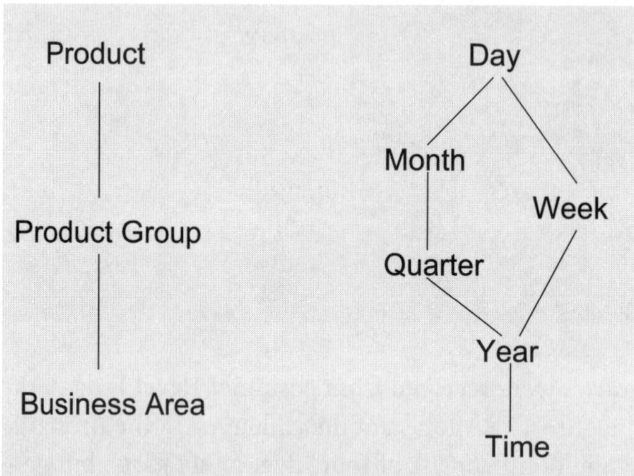

Figure 12.4 Hierarchical Dimensioning

During aggregation, care must be taken that these are not always simple hierarchies, as shown in Figure 12.4 for the product dimension. An example is the time dimension, where a view by calendar week overlaps with months or quarters.

The modeling of a data cube in a relational database is done using a central fact table (see Figure 12.5). This is called ROLAP (*Relational OLAP*). The following approaches are used:

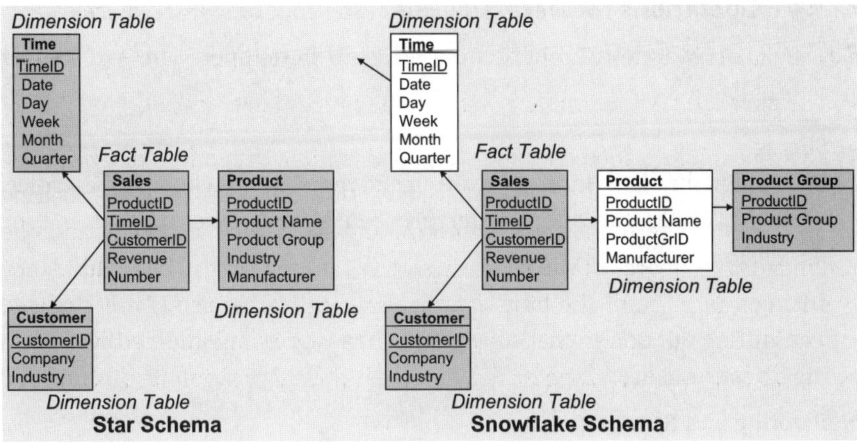

Figure 12.5 Star Configuration and Snowflake Configuration

- **Star schema**
  A central fact table contains the figures and the keys to the associated dimension tables. The third normal form (see Chapter 3) is violated. However, there are performance advantages.
- **Snowflake schema**
  The star configuration is refined to achieve third normal form. In Figure 12.5, this is diagrammed for the product dimensions, in which the partially dependent part for product groups is moved into its own table.
- **Galaxy schema**
  Multiple fact tables are connected to the dimension tables so that different key figures can be stored.

Note that the data in the dimension tables have a reference to the data in the fact tables over a very long period of time. Thus, the keys should be seen as identities that do not change. The reuse of IDs must be ruled out. Data is never deleted, even if a product is no longer produced, for instance.

As an alternative to ROLAP, true multidimensional storage is discussed under the heading of MOLAP (*Multidimensional OLAP*). MOLAP was initially outpaced by ROLAP, because only relational databases were capable of managing the large quantities of data needed for production data warehouses. In the meantime, however, MOLAP concepts have been available in the important database management systems.

The concepts named are also used in SAP NetWeaver BI.

12.1.5 Operations for Data Analysis

To use a data warehouse, there are a series of basic operations we'll cover here briefly:

- **Slicing**
  Dimensionality is reduced by cutting slices out of the cube. For instance, only the values for one quarter are considered, eliminating the time dimension.
- **Dicing**
  The cutting out of a partial cube results in a type of selection while retaining dimensionality.
- **Pivoting and Rotating**
  By exchanging dimensions or rotating the cube, an analysis from different points of view is possible.
- **Roll-up**
  Aggregation along the hierarchy is used to generate new information. The dimensionality is retained.
- **Drill-down**
  Aggregated information can be examined in more detail by drilling down.
- **Drill-across**
  By switching from one cube to another, you can examine differently produced cubes (for instance by drill-down, slicing, and dicing).

These operations found their counterparts in SQL relational databases. However, they are also supported by GUIs.

12.1.6 Data Mining

Data mining has the goal of discovering hidden relationships in the data warehouse. Statistical methods are used to do this. Typical data mining tasks are:

- **Description**
  Description presents data in an understandable and summarized form. OLAP is used for this task.
- **Deviation analysis**
  This determines any deviations from statistical norms.
- **Dependency analysis**
  Dependency analysis is intended to discover dependencies between objects and attributes. One of the best-known examples of this is shopping cart analysis.

- **Clustering**
  The goal here is to find groups of similar objects. This might be customer groups, for instance, who have similar properties and from whom similar behavior can be expected.
- **Classification**
  This is the categorization of an object into a class and the prediction of its behavior based on certain properties.
- **Effects forecast**
  An effects forecast predicts quantitative target values.

A series of highly specialized tools exists for data mining, including those from DBMS manufacturers. Data mining is an interactive process that is controlled by a data mining specialist together with users trained in economics.

12.1.7 Benefits

The construction and operation of a data warehouse are costly processes, but they promise extensive benefits if successful.

The data warehouse improves data integration. Decentralized data checks are no longer necessary. The data warehouse allows fast queries and extensive analyses while relieving operational applications from that burden. Using special operations, techniques, and user interfaces, the data warehouse provides flexible access options for the enterprise's data inventory.

Management profits from the ability to provide better information. Trends are recognized early, and a rapid reaction to change is possible. This can improve customer satisfaction, for instance. A successful data warehouse project also leads to the harmonization of terms in the enterprise. This supports cooperation and mutual understanding. However, in areas that must deviate from the usual terms and nomenclature, additional measures will be necessary for employee motivation and training, as well as for the adaptation of application systems.

12.2 Data Warehousing with Oracle

The Oracle database offers a variety of concepts and techniques for the realization and use of a data warehouse. Moreover, Oracle is one of the leading manufacturers of OLAP and data mining tools. We will give you a brief overview in this section of Oracle data warehousing.

12.2.1 Technology and Architecture

One goal Oracle has pursued during continued development of its database management system was particular suitability for OLAP. Oracle thus presents itself as a DBMS with extensive data warehouse functionality in its core. This include, among others:

- Support for the ETL process through the DBMS
- The ability to administrate very large databases (ultra large databases, ULDB) in the petabyte or even exabyte range
- Special storage and access structures for the multidimensional data of the data cube
- An embedded OLAP engine
- Special data models and SQL constructs

Note that data warehouse support has been enriched from version to version with improved and new concepts. In the following text, we primarily focus on Oracle 10g.

The sqlplus login to an Oracle system gives your first information about the components available for data warehousing:

```
Connected to:
Oracle Database 10g Enterprise Edition Release 10.2.0.1.0 - Production
With the Partitioning, OLAP and Data Mining options
```

To support the ETL process, since Oracle 8i there have been *transportable tablespaces*. In Oracle 9, different block sizes were overcome, and as of Oracle 10, even operating system boundaries are no obstacle (meaning bit and byte orders). The following SQL query can be used to display the platforms supported by your Oracle system:

```
select platform_name from v$transportable_platform
```

The cross-platform capability enables the transport of data from the OLTP system into the OLAP system without export and import operations, and largely regardless of the data volume. In the data warehouse, it can also be used for the supply of data marts that have their own DBMS systems. In connection with Oracle streams, tablespaces from running Oracle systems can be transported, achieving higher speeds than with FTP. Oracle streams are used to effect the automatic transport of blocks that are changed during transport.

During transport, the RMAN discussed in Chapter 9, *System Operation and Monitoring*, is used, which also performs any necessary conversions.

For the export and import of data, Oracle provides the tools `exp` and `imp`. They connect to Oracle as clients, using a special format. These tools allow both command-line-controlled operation and interactive operation, as shown in Figure 12.6 for the export of the *spfli* table.

The *data pump* introduced in Oracle 10g represents a powerful solution for server-based loading of data and metadata. The unloading of data and metadata is done simultaneously. The data pump should be faster than Oracle 9i tools, by a factor of 2 when exporting and a factor of 15 when importing. Figure 12.7 shows a diagram of the components and processes of the data pump. The client process is only a trigger for the process, which then runs entirely inside Oracle. The *master controller process* (MCP) manages everything and writes the current status to the status queue, on the basis of which the individual export instructions for the command queue are derived.

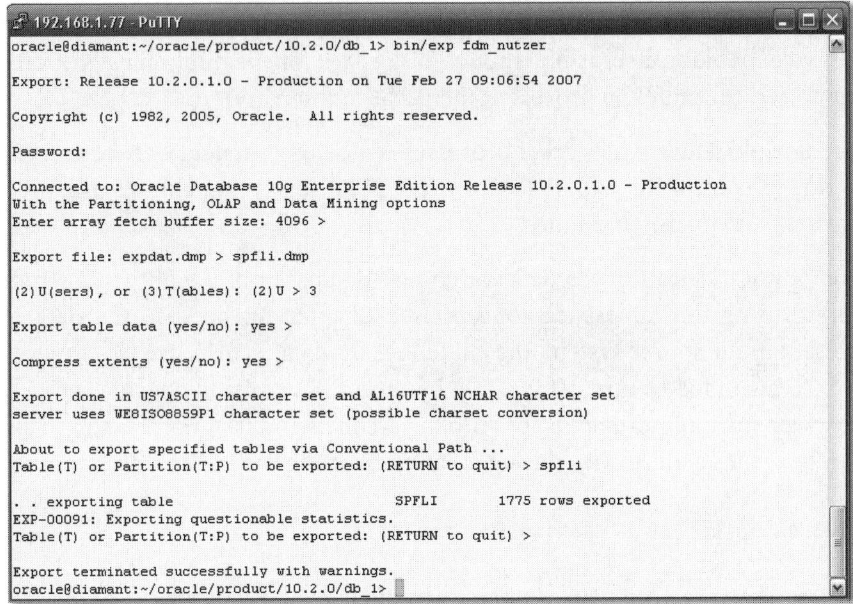

Figure 12.6 Export with exp

The metadata is collected by MCP in the master table, which is then appended to the dump files at the conclusion of the export process. The MCP also starts a flexibly adjustable number of parallel worker processes, which load the data from the database into the dump files for the individual export steps.

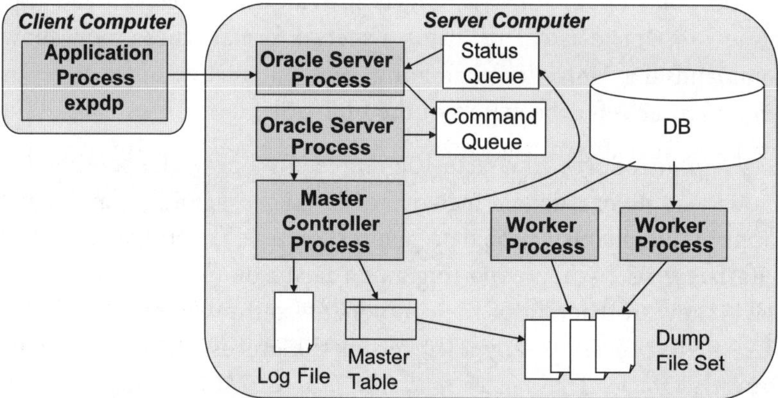

Figure 12.7 Export with Data Pump

One advantage of this new concept is not just that the parallelization improves speed, but that it also improves reliability. If an export crashes, for instance, because there is not enough disk space for the dump files, the data pump can continue the process at the point of interruption.

The flexible number of worker processes can be used in data warehouse scenarios to control the export load on the OLTP source system, allowing for daytime and overnight modes.

The physical design of the data warehouse database can benefit from structuring using the tablespace concept (see Chapter 3). because the data is present in the source system, the guidelines for data security are less strict. It is recommended to turn off logging, because this results in advantages such as lower space requirements for redo log archives and faster processing. This can be set for a tablespace during creation by using the `nologging` clause:

```
create tablespace dimension_a … nologging
```

Due to the very large data volumes and their continual growth, *Automatic Storage Management* (ASM) has particular significance. The limits on the file system are removed. The Oracle system accesses the disk drives directly and can use ASM to implement striping and mirroring. These optimize according to physical points of view and perform an automatic I/O tuning. The self-tuning of main memory additionally simplifies administration.

Another important concept is *partitioning*, introduced in Version 8. Partitions support special search operations and are easy to distribute over different files (media), processors, and computers. The following partitioning types are possible in Oracle:

- **Range partitioning**
  The data in a table is distributed to different partitions based on certain value ranges. This allows range queries to be processed more quickly. Partitions can be created in the table definitions or can be split off during running operation.
- **Hash partitioning**
  The data is scattered over the partitions. A record is assigned to a partition based on a hash function on an attribute. Hash partitioning allows a very fast hash join.
- **Composite partitioning**
  For very large tables, the advantages of range and hash partitioning can be used together.
- **List partitioning**
  Lists of particular values are assigned to a partition. This is especially useful for data warehouse databases, which are often not normalized.

Partitioning represents a tradeoff between ease of administration and ease of use. High performance due to refined partitioning results in additional requirements for administration.

The indexing of data in the data warehouse is different from that in OLTP systems. Indices used exclusively for maintaining uniqueness constraints are overhead, because they require space and slow the loading process. Uniqueness should already be ensured by the source system and the ETL process itself. It is deactivated with `disable validate` for the uniqueness constraint, but because this makes the checking of foreign keys slower, checking should also be disabled for foreign keys by using `disable novalidate`.

Bitmapped indices and *bitmapped join indices* are particularly well-suited for data warehouses.[3] These store values in a more compact form as a bitmap, which can also be more quickly selected by logical operations. As shown in Figure 12.8, in the bitmapped join index, bitmaps are formed from the key attributes of the dimension table and collected in the fact table. If we now want to see all of the figures from the customer Havel Data, we mask the bit-

3 Alternatively, these can also be called *bitmap indices or bitmap join indices.*

map with AND 11000 (suppression the product ID) and then with XOR 10000. If the result is 0, the record is a hit. These operations are very fast, because they are implemented close to the hardware.

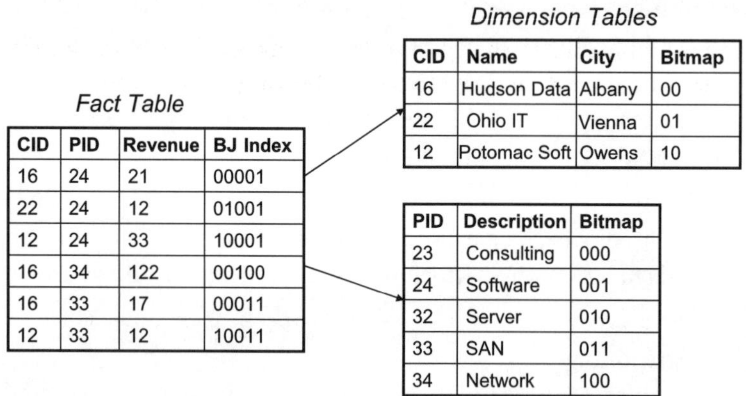

CID	PID	Revenue	BJ Index
16	24	21	00001
22	24	12	01001
12	24	33	10001
16	34	122	00100
16	33	17	00011
12	33	12	10011

CID	Name	City	Bitmap
16	Hudson Data	Albany	00
22	Ohio IT	Vienna	01
12	Potomac Soft	Owens	10

PID	Description	Bitmap
23	Consulting	000
24	Software	001
32	Server	010
33	SAN	011
34	Network	100

Figure 12.8 Bitmapped Join Index in Oracle System

In Oracle 10, all queries are stored in the *statistic workload repository*. For each query, the runtime and resources used can be determined. Based on that information, self-tuning of SQL queries is possible. Moreover, statistics are generated on an ongoing basis, meaning old statistics are no longer used.

The concept of the *analytic workspace* is Oracle's way of providing a MOLAP data type. The data is organized by subject. An analytic workspace contains multidimensional basis data, aggregation results, hierarchical information, and dynamic calculation rules; these result in performance advantages.

The administration of analytic workspaces can be done with a GUI. The *Analytic Workspace Manager* is available for this purpose. The construction of analytic workspaces is supported directly by the Oracle Warehouse Builder. Oracle allows the alternating combination of ROLAP and MOLAP.

12.2.2 Concepts and Language Extensions in Oracle

We already mentioned the idea of the data mart in Section 12.1, *Basics and Concepts of Data Warehousing*. Data marts represent physical data structures that store a segment of the data warehouse as special application-oriented views. Oracle also offers the concept of the *materialized view* in a similar way. Of course, this generates redundancy, which is not critical as long as you don't write to the views.

Using a fast refresh mechanism, the materialized views can be adapted for high performance when the basis tables (here, the data warehouse during a delta update) change. Whether it makes sense or not to use a fast refresh can be determined using the `dbms_mview` package. Materialized views also allow the definition of indices.

The following example illustrates the creation of a materialized view for the SBOOK table (see Chapter 3), which aggregates by airline and month:

```
create materialized view sbook_mv
build immediate
refresh complete on demand
enable query rewrite
as select carrid,  to_char(fldate,'MM') as month, max(to_
char(fldate,'Q')) as quarter, count(*) as passno, avg(luggweight)
as averageweight
from sbook
group by carrid, to_char(fldate,'MM')
```

In combination with materialized views, Oracle offers the *query rewrite* function since Version 8i. The Oracle optimizer can rewrite a query in such a way that it no longer accesses the basis tables, but accesses the materialized view instead. The performance advantage is significant.

An important step in building a data warehouse is the physical integration of data from different sources. Oracle DML (Data Manipulation Language) offers the `merge` statement for this purpose, which combines the `insert` and `update` statements.

```
merge into product_dw pn
using product_sys_b pa
on pn.p_id = pa.prod_nr
when matched then update set pn.weight = pa.weight,
       pn.sales = pn.sales + po.sales
when not matched insert (pn.p_id, pn.sales, pn.weight)
       values (po.prod_nr, po.sales, po.weight)
```

The product table in the data warehouse, for instance, is already filled with product data from source system A, which includes a product ID, the sales received, and the external dimensions of the product. The statement shown in the example now inserts the product data into the data warehouse table. If the product already exists, the weight is filled in and sales are totaled up. If there is no entry, a new record is created. As a result, we now have records with weights and external dimensions, some without weight, and some without external dimensions.

Another construct that supports the construction of a data warehouse with Oracle is *multitable insert*. This conditional `insert all` statement allows:

- The conditional insertion of multiple source columns into a target column
- The conditional insertion of records from one table into multiple target tables

As described in Section 12.1, schema heterogeneity often makes such restructuring necessary.

On the query side, Oracle provides the SQL statements needed for OLAP. The following instruction demonstrates the use of the `rollup` clause on the materialized view `sbook_mv`:

```
select month, quarter, sum(passno)
from sbook_mv
where carrid='LH'
group by rollup ( quarter, month)
```

The individual monthly results and totals are given as quarterly results.

The `cube` clause can be used to generate all possible aggregation levels, which is needed for drilling down:

```
select month, quarter, sum(passno)
from sbook_mv
group by cube ( quarter, month)
```

Using the `grouping` clause, you can generate a Boolean value that indicates the aggregation level to which a row belongs:

```
select month, quarter, sum(passno), grouping (quarter) q,
grouping (month) m
from sbook_mv
group by cube ( quarter, month)
```

Oracle 10g introduces a few new SQL constructs for data warehousing. The *model concept* allows the display of relational data on the Oracle side as a spreadsheet, with convenient multidimensional calculations. Simple addressing of rows is supported, along with sequences, wildcards, loops, and a lookup on other worksheets. This provides the data warehouse developer with an extension that can be seen as an "Excel killer" in terms of understandability, flexibility, performance, and power.[4] Another novelty in Oracle 10g is frequent itemsets that can be used for the data mining task of shopping cart analysis, for instance. This is the determination of the most commonly occurring combination in a list. The new Oracle algorithm saves huge joins using a multiple counter.

12.2.3 Tools

Besides the structures and applications implemented in the DBMS, Oracle also provides a series of tools to support data warehousing.

The role of the data warehouse manager is taken by the *Oracle Warehouse Builder*. It supports the design of the data warehouse and controls the ETL process and the construction of data marts or analytic workspaces. The management of the production data warehouse is supported by metadata. Components and analysis functions allow continual auditing to improve data quality. This builds on internal Oracle mechanisms.

The ETL process is supported by an internal debugger for data flows and integrated functions for data cleansing, for instance, for checking of names and addresses, as well as match and merge. The Oracle Warehouse Builder offers an interactive graphical interface for the design phase that generates PL/SQL packages as an output. These then perform the extraction, transformation, and loading during ongoing operation *in* the Oracle server.

The *Oracle Business Intelligence Discoverer* (OracleBI Discoverer) is used to examine the data warehouse. It enables the interactive creation of reports or the design of report formats. A web interface provides access to both relational structures and analytic workspaces. Special portlets are used to offer numerous display options that support an intuitive understanding of the data.

The *OracleBI Spreadsheet* add-in supports the direct use of data warehouse data in Excel. When accessing Oracle, the Excel user is supported by wizards.

---

4 See Kennel, A., Trivadis AG: *www.trivadis.com/Images/kennel_model_klausel2_tcm16-12136.pdf*

OracleBI Beans allow the use of OLAP functionality corresponding to the component model. They support the design of queries as well as numerous calculation and visualization methods important for OLAP applications.

With Oracle Data Miner, Oracle provides a power tool that can perform classical data mining tasks. Powerful algorithms are implemented for that purpose, which achieve high performance when executed near the system's core. According to SAP Note 990955, the Oracle Data Miner should be used in SAP Business Information Warehouse (BW) 3.5 or in SAP NetWeaver BI 7.0. This allows embedding of the Oracle data mining processes into the SAP Data Mining Framework.

12.3 SAP NetWeaver BI: An Overview

In this section, we'll take a closer look at the concepts, methods, functions, and objects of SAP NetWeaver BI. As required by Inmon in his definition of the data warehouse (see Section 12.1), SAP NetWeaver BI provides all of the functions for the specialized, integrated, stable, and historical collection of data for the support of management decisions.

SAP NetWeaver BI is a stand-along data warehouse solution. It is now integrated into all SAP products through the NetWeaver stack. For instance, if you call the Support Package Manager in an SAP ERP system based on NetWeaver Release 2004 or even 7.0 (2004s), you will always find the component Business Intelligence (BI). That means you can use integrated BI in these systems (after corresponding configuration and the display of the technical and business content) for reporting purposes. From the point of view of performance, this doesn't make much sense, because especially in the area of the Oracle database a completely different parameterization is configured for OLTP systems (such as ECC) and OLAP systems. It might be better to use a stand-alone system with well-defined parameters for the actual application and the database. The parameterization of Oracle for SAP NetWeaver BI will be discussed in Section 12.4, *SAP NetWeaver BI on Oracle*.

Figure 12.9 shows an overview of the individual parts of SAP NetWeaver BI. The functions of the ETL process are modeled on the lowest level. This makes it clear that SAP applications and non-SAP applications can be integrated with SAP NetWeaver BI.

A variety of interfaces are available to load data into the data targets using the staging engine. Data targets, or *InfoProviders*, are master data objects,

InfoCubes, Operational Data Store (ODS) objects, and the Persistent Staging Area (PSA), all available as buffers. An open hub service can be used to transmit data from one SAP NetWeaver BI system into other SAP NetWeaver BI systems (such as data marts), or to supply SAP applications and non-SAP applications.

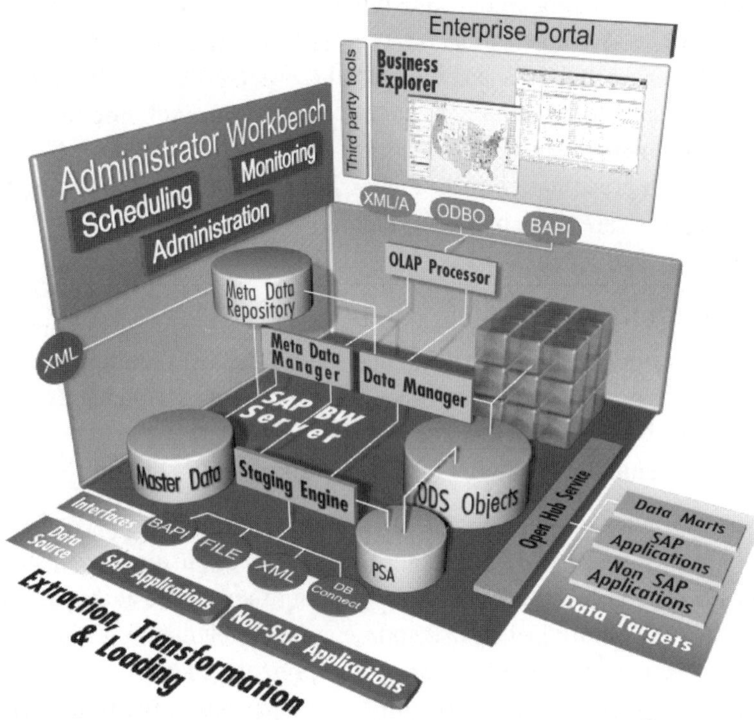

Figure 12.9 SAP NetWeaver BI Components (Source: SAP)

The user models the individual data warehousing objects and data flow using the *Data Warehousing Workbench* (DWB), previously called the *Administrator Workbench* (AWB). The execution and monitoring of the ETL process are also performed using this tool. The AWB can be reached through the SAP GUI. Reporting requests to the InfoProviders, however, are sent through the Business Explorer (BEx), a tool that requires Microsoft Excel, or through web applications to the OLAP processor. The processor reads the data from the desired InfoProvider and evaluates it.

The main feature of data stored in a data warehouse is its *multidimensionality*. Multidimensionality means data is not shown in tables, but is determined by any other arbitrary analysis-relevant criteria. This has the effect that it can be described as precisely as possible. To illustrate this, a cube in three dimensions is often taken, but this happens only because only three dimensions can be shown in a picture. In reality, a data cube isn't subject to such limitations, from a purely logical standpoint. Restrictions are only due to the data warehouse system itself.

SAP NetWeaver BI allows the use of up to 16 dimensions. Of those, three are already specified and cannot be reassigned by users. If you look at other data warehouse products, 13 dimensions don't seem to be many. However, this is only due to the difference in terms used. In the SAP NetWeaver BI system, each dimension can contain up to 248 characteristics. Many other providers call these characteristics dimensions. The features in SAP NetWeaver BI can contain navigation attributes in turn. For each InfoCube, therefore, at least 3,224 characteristics are available for modeling.

12.3.1 Business Content

The modeling of information models that should satisfy requirements is often a lengthy and highly complex task. The effort required increases, the more individual the requirements, and the less developers can rely on templates. But many enterprises always model the same sets of content.

This is where the idea of *business content comes in*. SAP provides predefined SAP NetWeaver BI information modes for the analysis of business processes. The business content objects are preconfigured, but they can be adapted. The models include extractors in the SAP source systems, elements of the data model such as InfoObjects and InfoCubes, components for the data loading process such as InfoSources and forwarding rules, reporting, and other basis components.

SAP provides business content through an add-on that is updated during regular updates using support packages. From release to release, even from one support package to another, more and more content objects are provided in the SAP NetWeaver BI system.

Business content can be used in the following ways:

- With no modifications
- With refinements or broadening
- As a template for your own business content

Three different object versions are distinguished in SAP NetWeaver BI. Objects that are present in a so-called *D-version* are SAP delivery objects. The

A-version includes objects that are active and can be used. Objects that are marked as modified are in their *M-version*. The basic rule is that you can only work with objects from business content if they are available in their A-version. You must activate these objects in the AWB. This activation process is often very lengthy. When loading new business content in support packages, you should ensure that you don't overwrite or even delete your own content which is in use.

The business content can be searched in the Metadata Repository of SAP NetWeaver BI. The Metadata Repository Browser is available for this purpose. Using this browser, you can search for either active or inactive objects, show dependencies between objects, and show the data flow in the SAP NetWeaver BI system and the multidimensional structures of the InfoCubes. If needed, a search machine can be added to the Metadata Repository Browser in the form of a TREX server. This provides a convenient, fast search option.

12.3.2 Data Modeling

Data models are an important tool. They are primarily used in development requiring a data-oriented view. They are useful for the designer of a database and are a useful basis for discussions with decision makers.

When designing databases for OLTP systems, the ARIS model is the most popular, making a distinction between the *technical concept* (semantic level), the *data processing concept* (DP concept, logical level), and the *implementation* (physical level). At the technical concept level, we use an entity-relationship model (ERM), at the DP concept level, we use the relational model, and at the lowest level, we use a description of relational database systems. This subdivision can also be made in the area of OLAP systems.

For instance, for the semantic data modeling in the SAP NetWeaver BI system, there is the *multidimensional entity relationship model* (MERM). The MERM is a derivation of the ERM mentioned above and is extended with objects. Using three layers, ERM models are converted into MERM models, which can then be used for multidimensional data modeling:

- Identification of relevant data
- Generation of fact relations
- Creation of the dimensions

The model generated in this way can be implemented as a logical design, that is, in the CP concept. To do this, SAP NetWeaver BI uses the extended SAP star configuration, which is a further development of the classical star configuration.

In a classical star configuration, relational database systems (such as Oracle) are used to model facts and dimensions in tables. The individual rows in a dimension table are identified by a minimum attribute combination — the primary key. This primary key is stored as a foreign key in the fact table and represents the primary key there. Using this primary and foreign key relationship, the connection between the fact table and the dimension tables results. This results in a star-shaped arrangement of tables, with the fact table as the center and the dimension tables as the points. In addition to the foreign keys, the fact table contains the key figures. In the example shown in Figure 12.10, the figures in the fact table are costs, quantity, and sales. The dimension tables Product, Time, and Customer contain the dimensional attributes product and industry, customer, headquarters, ABC classification, and region, as well as calendar day and calendar year. The fact table should be built as thin as possible for performance reasons, that is, with few columns, but due to the number of records, it can become very long. The dimension tables, on the other hand, are very broad, but the number of records is significantly smaller than in the fact tables.

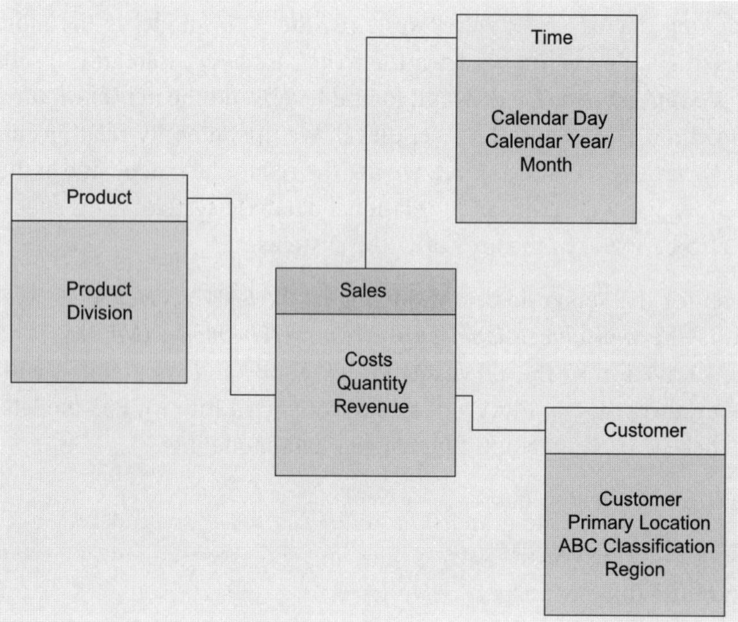

Figure 12.10 Classical Star Configuration

The problems with the classical star configuration are significant:

- No support for multiple languages
- Alphanumeric foreign keys, which reduce performance
- No support for time-dependent master data
- Hierarchical relationships modeled using attributes in the dimension table

These points led SAP to extend the classical star configuration. The fact table remains unchanged from the way it was introduced. The characteristics in the dimensions consist of the data field and three additional optional segments:

- **Texts**
  Descriptions (short, medium, and long text) for a characteristic can be defined in text tables. Time- and language-dependent storage is possible.
- **Hierarchies**
  Characteristics can be assigned an arbitrary number of external hierarchies for structured data access using drill-down.
- **Master data**
  The property fields of a characteristic (attributes) can be stored in a separate master data table on a time- and language-dependent basis.

Attributes, texts, and hierarchies are all optional. They can be activated when the characteristic is created. An important property is that these three segments are created separately from the actual InfoCube, whose fact tables, along with the dimension tables, form the *solution-dependent* part. This is where the combinations of figures and characteristics are stored. The connection between the tables is carried out using the *dimension ID* (DIM-ID). This is an artificial key with a size of four bytes. The solution-dependent part is based on a very specific area of information.

The characteristics, with their master data, text, and hierarchy tables, form the *solution-independent* area. They are independent of the fact and dimension tables of a particular InfoCube and are available to the entire SAP NetWeaver BI system. This separation can also be seen in the different modeling areas within the Data Warehousing Workbench (see Figure 12.11).

The connection between the dimension tables and the characteristic tables, as well as between the characteristic tables and the associated master data, text, and hierarchy tables, is implemented using *surrogate IDs* (SID) in the extended SAP star configuration. Every characteristic variant is assigned a unique four-byte integer. This takes on the role of an artificial primary key. Thus, the natural primary key, that is, the data element itself, is extended with the high-performance SID. In the dimension table, the SID is entered as the foreign key and represents the connection between the dimension table and the characteristic table. The relationship between a characteristic and its master data, text, and hierarchy tables is also implemented using the SID.

The use of surrogate IDs also solves a problem in the cooperation between OLTP and OLAP systems. If an attribute of the primary key of a table from the OLTP is used as a unique key, we speak of a *production key*. The use of such a key, however, would fail because a characteristic is often loaded from multiple operational systems with different primary keys. Artificial keys can be optimized for minimum storage requirements, they can be used throughout the warehouse due to their generalized structure, and they are inherently unique. An operational system, on the other hand, can always reassign a primary key.

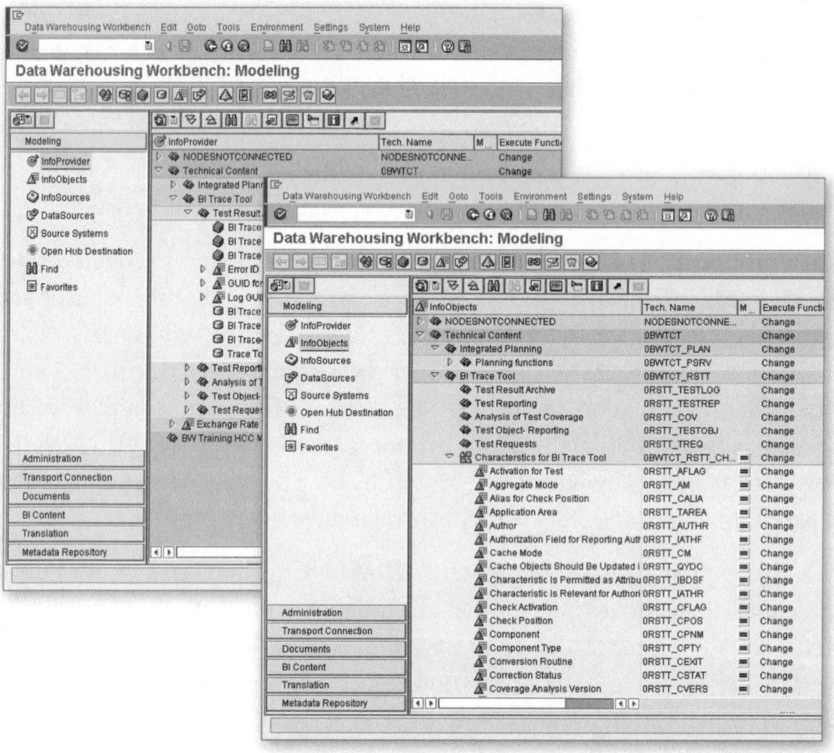

Figure 12.11 Areas in the Data Warehousing Workbench

Figure 12.12 shows the extended SAP star configuration based on our example of sales. In this case, no hierarchies were used. In the upper part of the figure, you can see the solution-dependent part, with the fact table of the

InfoCube and the dimension tables Time, Product, and Customer. The fact tables and dimension tables are connected through the dimension IDs. In the solution-independent part, the characteristics are shown. The industry and product are characteristics that have no text and no master data. The data elements are connected to the dimension table directly by means of the SID. The Region characteristic was created with text, but not with master data, so an additional text table was created with medium-length text as a data element. This uses an SID to point to the SID table of the Region characteristic. The Customer characteristic, finally, contains texts, master data, and additional attributes. A master data table exists with the data element "customer," and with the attributes ABC classification and headquarters, which use SIDs to point to the SID tables with the data elements of the characteristics. Due to the encoding and thus existence of the master data table, it is possible to enter master data and explicitly load the characteristics through the ETL process.

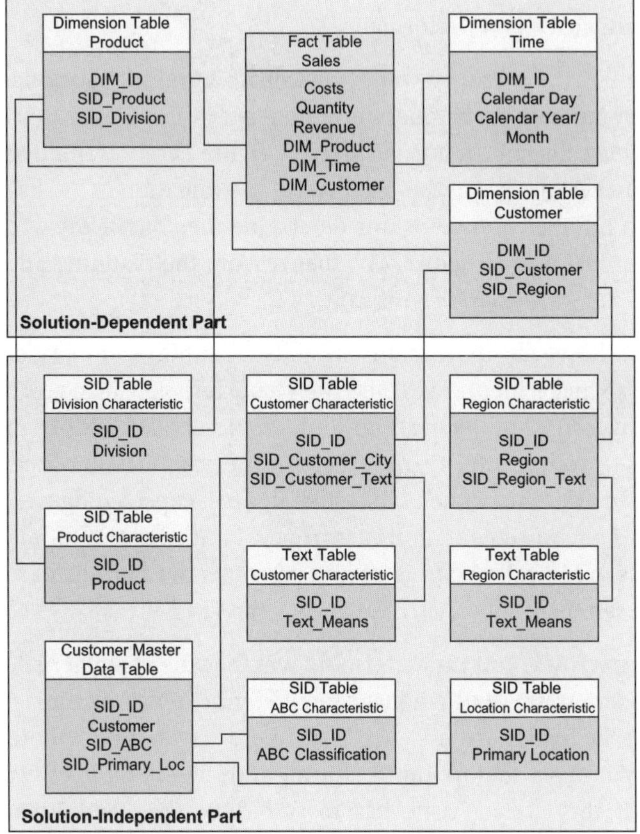

Figure 12.12 Example of Extended SAP Star Configuration (without Hierarchies)

12.3.3 Modeling of Business Intelligence Objects

From the description of the multidimensional data model, you already know the difference between key figures and characteristics. In SAP NetWeaver BI, both objects are called *InfoObjects*.

InfoObjects are the basic information carriers in an SAP NetWeaver BI system. Using key figures and characteristics, the data needed to build data targets such as InfoCubes is modeled in a structured form. InfoObjects are assigned to catalogs, and catalogs are assigned to InfoAreas. SAP NetWeaver BI differentiates InfoObject catalogs for characteristics and for key figures. The assignment is used to categorize all objects in SAP NetWeaver BI.

The central element is the key figure, which we found in the fact table of our InfoCube. *Key figures* are measurable figures from the real world. Their semantics are determined by the type of dimensions used. Many key figures are numeric. Text key figures are not supported by the SAP NetWeaver BI system, but they are theoretically possible. Examples of key figures from the business field are sales, costs, and performance.

From the point of view of the user who wants to evaluate a multidimensional database, the direct components of a query are modeled in the dimensions. Every influencing value relevant for a particular key figure is represented as a dimension and is to a certain extent the "entryway" to evaluation of the key figures. The type and number of dimensions determine the complexity and evaluation options for the data structure. For that reason, the planning and layout of dimensions are particularly significant.

In SAP NetWeaver BI, however, dimensions are only a content summary of the characteristics that make them up. Thus, the characteristics in the SAP NetWeaver BI area cover most of the meaning and function of dimensions in other data warehouse products. In nearly every business application area, the characteristics used are time, value type (actual figures, expected figures, planned figures), and measurement units (currency, unit). Just as often, characteristics such as organizational unit, region customer, and product are used. Characteristics can be of type `Char`, `Numc`, `Dats`, or `Tims`.

When creating characteristics, you can determine whether the characteristic should have master data (time- and language-dependent) , texts, or hierarchies. Hierarchies can be loaded from a source system or created directly in SAP NetWeaver BI. You have the option of storing multiple hierarchies for each characteristic. If the characteristic has master data, then additional attributes can be assigned to the characteristic. Attributes themselves also represent InfoObjects, but they don't need to be characteristics, because a key figure can also be stored as an attribute.

You also have the option of *grouping* attributes. Grouped attributes are a special case. In some cases, a characteristic is not uniquely determined by its own data element. Thus, a second attribute is needed to generate a unique primary key. A cost center, for instance, is only uniquely addressed in combination with its controlling area. Thus, the characteristic "cost center" has a grouped attribute "controlling area."

The process of creating and activating an InfoObject is carried out in four steps:

1. Creation of the InfoObjects
2. Checking for syntactic correctness
3. Saving the definition
4. Activation of the InfoObject and associated generation of the database tables needed

The InfoCube, the central data storage for all evaluations and reports, is also stored in InfoAreas, just like InfoObjects. The InfoCubes are built of key figures and characteristics, and the characteristics are assigned to dimensions. Three of those dimensions are predetermined to be time, unit, and InfoPackage. Due to its exceedingly high significance, the time dimension is essential in a database with large amounts of historical data, and the unit dimension labels the key figures stored in the InfoCube with their units (currency, dimensional units, etc.). In the InfoPackage dimension, a unique request ID is stored during the ETL process for the loaded data packages.

To create an InfoCube, the following steps are required:

1. Create the InfoCube
2. Add key figures
3. Add characteristics
4. Generate dimensions
5. Assign characteristics in dimensions
6. Test, save, and activate

In addition to the InfoCubes, *Operational Data Stores* (ODS) can also be created as data targets. An ODS object can be used as an alternative to a relatively detailed InfoCube. In these objects, consolidated and cleansed transaction data is stored at the document level. This data is stored, however, in transparent, flat database tables. Fact and dimension tables are not created here.

When defining the dimensions, you can set two additional options: *line item* and *high cardinality*. Ideally, dimensions have a small cardinality — in comparison with fact tables, at any rate. However, if an InfoCube is built, for instance, which uses the characteristic "document," then there will have to be a entry in the dimension table for nearly every entry in the fact table. That makes the fact table nearly as large as the dimension table. Relational and multidimensional database systems in general have problems with handling such dimensions efficiently.

If you define dimensions of that nature, line item and high cardinality options give you two ways to optimize:

- Line item means the dimension contains exactly one characteristic. The result is that no dimension table is created. The SID table of the characteristic takes on the role of the dimension table. By omitting the dimension table, we don't need to generate IDs for entries in the dimension table. One very large table in the star configuration is the eliminated, so SQL-based queries are simpler. However, a dimension marked as a line item cannot be assigned characteristics later.
- High cardinality means the dimension will have many variants. Depending on the database platform, this information is used to perform physical optimizations. For instance, index types other than the default may be used. In general, a dimension has a high cardinality when the number of dimension entries corresponds to 20% (or more) of the number of fact table entries. In case of doubt, however, you can simply not mark the dimension as higher cardinality.

SAP recommends that for line times, if possible, ODS objects should be used instead of InfoCubes, because the data is stored in flat, relational tables.

Always keep in mind that the granularity you choose for the data you keep in your InfoProviders has the greatest effect on drive space and performance. If you reduce the granularity, you gain the option of running more detailed reports. Reduction means data loss — but a performance win. Extensive dimension tables always have an effect on performance. If you define a lot of time- and language-dependent characteristics with master data, texts, and other attributes, a report will take more time to generate.

12.3.4 Basics of Data Extraction

This section is concerned with the ETL process in the SAP NetWeaver BI system. In the first step, we come to the staging scenarios. For the provision of data in the SAP NetWeaver BI system, there are two different processes:

- Staging without persistent data storage, meaning data is always obtained again and is only available for the duration of a transaction in SAP NetWeaver BI.
- Staging with persistent data storage, meaning data loaded from the source systems remains stored in SAP NetWeaver BI for the duration of a transaction.

The staging scenario without persistent data storage is implemented in SAP NetWeaver BI using the concept of *RemoteCubes*. A RemoteCube is an InfoProvider whose data is not administered or stored in SAP NetWeaver BI, but in the source system. In SAP NetWeaver BI, only the structure of the RemoteCube is defined. The data is read from another system through an interface during runtime for reporting. This variant is recommended when up-to-date availability of data from the source system is needed, or when only small amounts of data must be accessed on a sporadic basis. Moreover, in comparison, a replication of the data into the SAP NetWeaver BI system is too costly, and only a very small and restricted group runs simultaneous queries on the needed data inventory in the source system. The decisive disadvantage of this scenario is that the source system feels the load of the reporting queries.

In persistent data storage, you store the data in the SAP NetWeaver BI system. The data is extracted from the source system, stored unchanged in a buffer called the Persistent Staging Area (PSA), and then written directly to the InfoProvider using transformations. InfoProviders that can be loaded with data include the InfoCube, ODS objects, and characteristics with master data tables.

Systems that provide data for extraction into the SAP NetWeaver BI system are called *source systems*. Data can be obtained from systems other than SAP, too. The integration of flat files (ASCII or CSV format), foreign systems (that is, non-SAP systems), and other SAP NetWeaver BI systems are all possible as source systems in SAP NetWeaver BI. The SAP NetWeaver BI system is limited to the storage of structured data. You have no access to unstructured data such as Internet, video, or music files.

In the source system, logically associated data is provided in the form of DataSources. These are always source system-specific. They contain a set of fields that are provided in a flat structure, the extraction structure, for data transmission to SAP NetWeaver BI. In the form of a selection from those fields, the transfer structure, the data is transmitted from the source system to SAP NetWeaver BI. To display the DataSources in the SAP NetWeaver BI system, a replication is performed. Here, a replica of the DataSource is stored in SAP NetWeaver BI.

An InfoSource is a unit of logically grouped InfoObjects. It describes the set of all available data for a business case or a type of business case. The InfoSource draws data from one or more DataSources using a transmission rule. The structure in the InfoSource is the communication structure, and in contrast to the transfer structure, it is source-system-independent. There are two basic types of InfoSources:

1. InfoSources with flexible forwarding
2. InfoSources with direct forwarding

In both types, data is transformed using a transmission rule. A data target can be supplied by multiple InfoSources, which can in turn receive data from multiple DataSources.

The transmission rule determines which fields of the transfer structure are transmitted into which fields of the communication structure and how. The transmission rule can include transformation rules. The following alternatives are available:

1. The fields of the transfer structure are written to the communication structure without any modification.
2. A constant is assigned to the field of the communication structure. The transfer structure is ignored in this case.
3. ABAP routines are stored to perform the modification of field contents and assigned to particular fields in the communication structure. All of the capabilities of the ABAP programming language are available in this case.
4. Formulas provided by SAP NetWeaver BI are stored in the transmission rule, modifying field content or filling fields in the communication structure with content not provided by the transfer structure.

The last element of the data loading process is the forwarding rule. It specifies how the data (key figures, time characteristics, characteristics) are written from the communication structure of an InfoSource to the InfoProvider. You connect an InfoSource to an InfoCube, an ODS object, or a characteristic with a master data table. For InfoCubes, there are two different possibilities for definition of the forwarding rule for a key figure:

- No forwarding
- Addition, minimum, or maximum

For ODS objects, the *overwrite* variant is also available. Forwarding of data into characteristics with master data tables can draw on the following rules:

- Overwrite
- No forwarding

The PSA provides an initial storage for master and transaction data loaded from the attached source systems into SAP NetWeaver BI. In the PSA, data is loaded into transparent relational database tables corresponding to the transfer structure. The data may contain errors if it already contained errors in the source system. They are therefore a snapshot of the source with identical compression. The logical data packets (requests) can be checked in the PSA for quality, order, and completeness and manually changed if necessary.

An InfoPackage, finally, defines the conditions for the data request from any source system. This includes both selection conditions and the starting conditions for data requests, options for posting of data, and the types of error correction.

Using the starting conditions mentioned, the load due to the extraction process can be minimized. This must be started when resources are not entirely needed for production operations. For instance, this might be at night or on the weekend. If particular data is absolutely necessary for reporting, such as during monthly reporting, the process can also be started on an event-triggered basis.

12.3.5 Loading of Master and Transaction Data

In SAP NetWeaver BI, there are two different types of application data:

1. Transaction data
2. Master data

Transaction data is loaded into the fact table of an InfoCube. Master data, on the other hand, can be found in the segments of characteristics, that is, the attributes, texts, and hierarchies. Let's first take a look at the loading master data into the segments of the characteristics.

As already explained, master data, as a solution-independent part, is stored separately from the solution-dependent data in the InfoCube. The master data, unlike transaction data, is not forwarded to the InfoCube, but rather to the appropriate master data table of the characteristic. The master data tables of a characteristic are supplied from an InfoSource of that characteristic. If an InfoSource with direct forwarding is used, it is assigned to a fixed data target, and the definition of a forwarding rule is omitted when loading master data. If an InfoSource with flexible forwarding is used, a forwarding rule must be created.

Before SAP BW Release 3.0A, only transaction data could be forwarded flexibly, whereas master data was only forwarded directly, so that there was a distinction between master and transaction data InfoSources. This distinction no longer exists as of SAP BW 3.0A. Transaction and master data alike can be flexibly forwarded. Thus, it is not immediately obvious in the system whether an InfoSource with flexible forwarding concerns transaction data or master data. We therefore recommend that you specify that in the name of the InfoSource.

The procedure for loading master data looks like this:

1. Insert the characteristic as a data target.
2. Define the InfoSource (flexible or direct).
3. Assign the source system and DataSources.
4. Edit the transfer structure and the transmission rules.
5. Create the forwarding rule (for a flexible InfoSource).
6. Create the InfoPackage and schedule it for execution using start options.

In what order should the application data be loaded into the SAP NetWeaver BI system? In principle, a fixed sequence can't be specified for this procedure. However, the general approach is to start with master data and then load transaction data. The following points support this approach:

- When loading the transaction data, referential integrity with the master data can be ensured. This means transaction records can be rejected that refer to characteristic values that don't exist, but this is only possible if the master data records are already available.
- It may be necessary within the forwarding rules to write master data attributes from the characteristics directly into the fact table. For that to be possible, the master data must already be available during the loading of the transaction data.

Loading of transaction data is nearly identical to the loading of master data. Only the InfoSource, however, can be used with flexible forwarding. The procedure looks like this:

1. Define a flexible InfoSource.
2. Assign the source system and DataSources.
3. Edit the transfer structure and the transmission rules.

4. Create the fowarding rule.
5. Create the InfoPackage and schedule it for execution using start options.

Whereas the definition of InfoPackages in the *scheduler* provides the options of distributing extraction requests with selection criteria over background processes with job scheduling, thus automating the procurement of data, the *monitor* is a tool for the monitoring of data requests. A list of all data requests to be analyzed gives you information about the success or failure of an action.

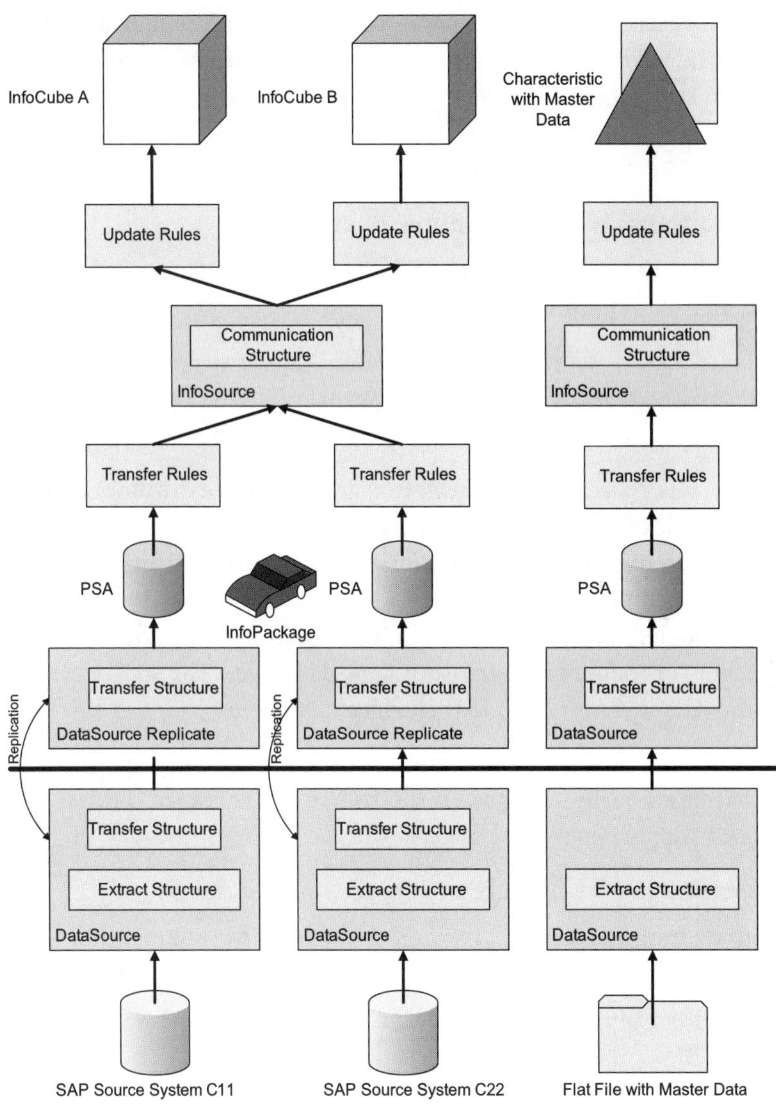

Figure 12.13 Data Flow in SAP NetWeaver BI Systems

Administration of InfoCube gives you an overview of the requests loaded into an InfoCube. Each request has a unique number that is stored in the system for all InfoCubes of a specific dimension InfoPackage. Individual records cannot be deleted from the fact table — only complete requests.

Figure 12.13 shows the described data flow in a SAP NetWeaver BI system and the objects that participate in it. The car symbolizes the InfoPackage responsible for the data request, driving along a path to extract the data, transform it, and load it. The characteristics with master data are loaded from a flat file in this example. For this special case, there is no replication of the DataSource. The InfoSource responsible for the transaction data receives the data from two DataSources from different source systems and passes the data on to two cubes.

12.3.6 Delta Extraction from Source Systems

The decision between a full extraction or an incremental one can have a decisive influence on performance.

Full extraction, called *full upload*, is equivalent to a snapshot of the entire data inventory and can involve a very large data volume. A full upload is always used in the case of initial filling of an InfoProvider.

To reduce the data volume to be transmitted, incremental extraction, or *delta uploads*, are used. In a very simple type of delta upload, only the changes between the current snapshot and the previous one are transmitted. However, snapshots run the risk that the sequence of changes may no longer be completely modeled. A more involved solution that includes the capability of later tracking of changes is to transmit logged changes. The source system monitors the data inventory and logs changes in a queue.

A delta upload then makes it possible to load into SAP NetWeaver BI only the data that has actually changed in the source system since the last ETL process. Delta support enables:

- The fast exchange of changed records in the source system
- A reduced transmission of records between the source and SAP NetWeaver BI systems
- A lower number of records through data preparation in SAP NetWeaver BI
- Faster calculation of aggregate values and faster compression

For SAP source systems, different *delta procedures* are available. A delta procedure is a basic property of the extractor in the source system and specifies the way in which data will be transmitted. If an extractor isn't delta-capable, data cannot be transmitted by delta upload.

The delta procedure is an attribute of the DataSource. It specifies how the data from the DataSource will be transmitted to the data target. For instance, you can use it to determine the data targets for which a DataSource is suitable, how it is to be forwarded, and how it is serialized. Depending on the delta procedure, the system itself decides whether a serialization per request or per data packet is necessary.

The following delta procedures exist for SAP source systems:

1. Deltas are formed with after, before, and reverse images, which are forwarded directly to the delta queue. The technical name of the delta procedure in the system is *ABR*. A reverse image sends the record with a negative sign and simultaneously marks it for deletion. The data packages are serialized. With this delta procedure, both overwriting and addition are allowed. This procedure thus permits forwarding both into an ODS object or into an InfoCube.
2. For the delta procedure with the technical name *ADD*, the extractor provides additive deltas serialized by request. This serialization is needed because the extractor provides each key once within a request, and changes to the nonkey fields would otherwise not be correctly transmitted. It allows only the addition of fields and can be forwarded into either an ODS object or an InfoCube.
3. Another procedure forms the deltas with after-images and writes them directly into the delta queue. Here, the data is serialized by packet, because the same key may be transmitted multiple times within a request. The procedure doesn't allow direct forwarding into an InfoCube, meaning there must always be an intermediate ODS object. The technical name of this delta procedure in the system is *AIM/AIMD*.

When loading from flat files, the user must select a suitable delta procedure when editing the transfer structure. This controls the correct type of forwarding.

The delta queue represents a data buffer in the source system. Records are automatically written into it, either through a posting transaction in the source system or during extraction through a functional component according to a data request from the BI. The records are transmitted from the scheduler into SAP NetWeaver BI in the case of a delta request. The delta queue stores the data in a compressed form and is repeatable. That means the data from the last extraction procedure is kept in the delta queue. This repeat mode for the delta queue is target-system-specific.

12.3.7 Reporting

For reporting on the different InfoProviders, various analysis tools are available that take the requirements of a wide range of user types into consideration.

Three groups of end users are differentiated:

- Consumers are users of SAP NetWeaver BI who use the analytical functions of the system to a small degree. They work with predefined queries that report on fixed sets of data. Consumers need an easy-to-use user interface.
- Analysts, on the other hand, navigate within reports and perform analyses from very different perspectives. For their work, they need a tool with plenty of analytical possibilities.
- The group of authors is very small. They must have complete access to predefined queries and data collections, as well as having the option of creating new queries.

In SAP NetWeaver BI, the requirements of the end users named are taken into consideration, because different functionality and reporting possibilities are provided that can be restricted to the appropriate groups using the SAP NetWeaver BI permission system.

Data stored in SAP NetWeaver BI can be presented and processed using different tools:

- **Transaction LISTSCHEMA**
  Data access for database administrators is possible using Transaction LISTSCHEMA, among others. They can use this tool to display the fact table, the dimension tables, and the master tables of characteristics. The integrated data browser functionality allows examination of the structure and content of the tables. It should be noted that Transaction LISTSCHEMA does not display hierarchy and text tables and lists inactive or nonexistent tables (for instance, segments of characteristics that weren't created).
- **BEx Browser and BEx Analyzer**
  The Business Explorer includes two tools: the BEx Browser and the BEx Analyzer. The BEx Browser makes it possible to select reports. The BEx

Analyzer, on the other hand, is used for the display and generation of reports and the interactive analysis of data. The Query Designer is available for the definition of queries. SAP provides the Business Explorer as an Excel add-in.

- **Web reporting**
  Web reporting presents OLAP functionality, such as that offered by the Business Explorer, in a web interface. As of Basis release 6.40, no separate software installation is required, because the generation of BSPs is carried out by SAP NetWeaver Application Server. Moreover, custom web applications can be created using the Web Application Designer. These applications can be integrated into the portal, for instance, and display current reports on data.
- **Other tools**
  Evaluation tools by third-party providers can also be integrated through certain interfaces.

We'll limit our discussion of the topic of reporting tools to Business Explorer at this point, because the functionality of web reporting is basically identical to it. Using Query Designer in the BEx Analyzer, you can create query definitions. These are based on exactly one InfoProvider. If a query definition is stored to a working folder as a query and executed, the OLAP processor ensures that the request is sent to the SAP NetWeaver BI server. It takes existing aggregates into consideration on its own. The query definition and the working folder are stored on the SAP NetWeaver BI server. In the folder, the query can be modified independently of the query definition, navigation states can be changed, and functionality can be executed by Excel.

Besides the InfoCubes, ODS objects, and characteristics with master data already named, which can also be loaded with data by the ETL process, InfoProviders are available for reporting that have no physical data in SAP NetWeaver BI. These are:

- **RemoteCube**
  Receives the data at runtime from a source system.
- **MultiCube**
  Combines several InfoCubes.
- **InfoSet**
  Combines flat tables through a join, summarizing ODS objects or characteristics with master data.

Using Query Designer, you create a query definition on an InfoProvider you selected previously. In the Query Designer, the key figures from the fact table and the characteristics from the dimension table are available.

If the key figures from the underlying InfoCube don't give the desired result, you can build calculated figures into the query definition. The definition can be entered on either the query definition level or the InfoCube level. Keep in mind that calculated figures on the query level are only valid for the query definition you are creating. Calculated figures on the InfoCube level can be used for any query definitions based on that cube. To calculate figures, you can use basic, percentage, date, mathematical, and trigonometric functions, as well as Boolean operators.

Using variables, you can design queries more flexibly, because variables are filled with values dynamically when the query is updated. Depending on the variable type and processing type selected, you can enter them manually before executing the query or automatically process them.

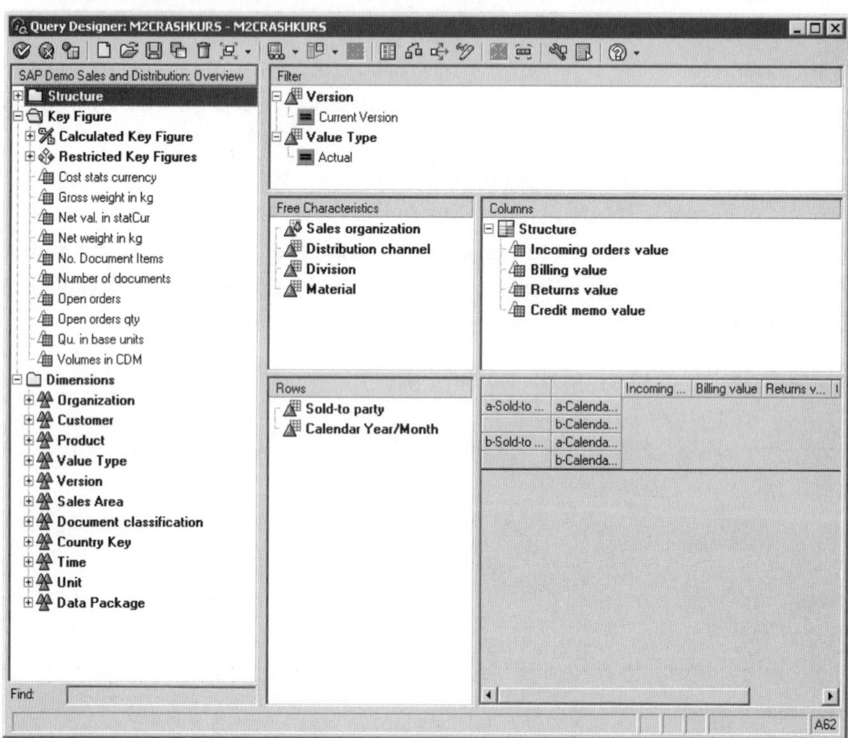

Figure 12.14 Query Designer in the BEx Analyzer

Figure 12.14 shows the global view of the Query Designer. On the left side are all of the key figures and characteristics available in the underlying InfoCube. You can use drag-and-drop to insert these into the rows and columns of the query definition or into the free characteristics available to the user for later executions of the query.

Queries are defined by:

1. Selecting an InfoProvider on which the query is defined
2. Using reusable structures that already contain characteristic or key figure combinations (if they already exist)
3. Selecting characteristics from the InfoProvider and if necessary restricting them to certain values, ranges, or hierarchical nodes
4. Using variables for values, hierarchies, hierarchical nodes, formulas, and texts (if already available) or defining new variables as needed
5. Selecting key figures from the InfoProvider
6. Formulating calculated figures and possibly limiting them by combination with characteristics
7. Defining exception cells
8. Performing an assignment of characteristics and key figures to rows or columns and thus determining a starting view for query analysis

For more detailed questions, the multidimensional data model provides you with various operations for manipulation of the data cube. These primarily exchange dimensions and aggregation levels. The BEx Analyzer's context menu in the result area for a query, for instance, provides you with different analytical options, which are then passed to the OLAP processor, interpreted, and then used on the data inventory. The analytical operations introduced in Section 12.1.5, *Operations for Data Analysis*, can also be used in SAP NetWeaver BI.

So that problems in an enterprise can be detected and corrected as early as possible, *exception reporting* can be set up. This allows you to detect, mark, highlight, and notify about exceptional deviations from previously determined values of key figures in the results of a query. This notification is carried out by defined sequential processing. Thus, notification can use a short message service (SMS) or an email.

The definition of georelevant characteristics and the creation of shape files allows you to display data on maps using *BEx Map*. BEx Map (an example is shown in Figure 12.15) is the geographical information system of SAP

NetWeaver BI built into the Business Explorer. It evaluates geographical information together with business-relevant key figures.

The map on which you can display statistical geocharacteristics is provided in the form of *shape files*. You need three different but associated files:

1. ***.shp**
   Contains the actual geodata that form the map.
2. ***.shx**
   Contains an index that improves the access time to the map.
3. ***.dbf**
   Contains the attributes of the individual geoelements.

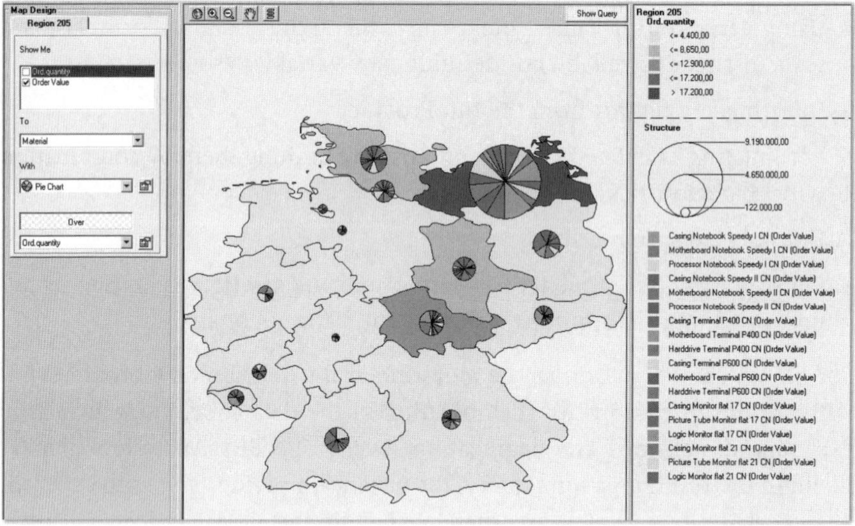

Figure 12.15 Geovisualization with BEx Map

To visualize data using BEx Map, the following steps are required:

1. Encoding of georelevant characteristics (for instance, the state) during InfoObject entry as a geofeature
2. Loading of the shape files into the SAP NetWeaver BI system
3. Definition of a query with geocharacteristics and integration of a map

Using a variety of graphical customization options, you can display and evaluate the different figures in the BEx Map however you like. The functionality of BEx Map has been a part of the SAP NetWeaver Enterprise Portal since Release 7.0.

Besides the objects and functions presented so far, which are also valid in BW Releases 3.x, a few new features were included in SAP NetWeaver BI 7.0. For instance, on the backend, in the SAP NetWeaver BI 7.0 server, a new data loading process was implemented. InfoProviders can now be changed using remodeling tools, and the user has new objects available for data storage. Most changes are found on the frontend side. The operation of the BEx Analyzer was extended with drag-and-drop functionality, the overall appearance is more modern, and the user can develop custom templates for reporting much more easily. Web reporting has been entirely included in SAP Enterprise Portal 7.0 as of this release, and now nearly all functions from the BEx Analyzer are also available there. To be able to use them, the installation of the J2EE part of the SAP NetWeaver Application Server Java is mandatory.

12.4 SAP NetWeaver BI on Oracle

The SAP Business Information Warehouse (SAP BW) was originally a standalone package based on the SAP kernel and SAP ABAP. From a technical point of view, that is still the case today, but it is no longer considered a separate product but has become a part of the SAP NetWeaver stack along with the component's SEM (Strategic Enterprise Management) under the name of SAP NetWeaver Business Intelligence (SAP NetWeaver BI). Thus, every SAP software system with an ABAP Basis release of 6.40 or higher, also includes SAP NetWeaver BI. Only the SAP package APO (Advanced Planner and Optimizer) — also more recently called SCM (Supply Chain Management) — already had an "internal" SAP NetWeaver BI in earlier versions, because it needed data warehouse functionality for certain asks, for instance, sales planning (DP).

SAP NetWeaver BI may now be included in the NetWeaver stack and thus in nearly all SAP installations, but for the administration of such a system, it makes a big difference whether the system is used as a data warehouse, that is, a classical business intelligence solution, as an ERP system, or as another type of system such as CRM. Nobody will, or should, consider combining an OLTP and an OLAP system in one database. In the following examples, we'll assume a data warehouse system, or a system in which this functionality is used primarily. According to SAP definitions, this is true of the following installations:

- SAP NetWeaver BI systems in classical data warehouse use
- APO with primarily DP use
- SAP NetWeaver BI-based SEM BCS (Strategic Enterprise Management Business Consolidation Services)

Furthermore, we'll assume SAP BW release 3.5 (NetWeaver 04) and SAP NetWeaver BI 7.0 (NetWeaver 04s or 7.0). However, it should be noted that at least for the configuration of the Oracle database, as of SAP BW 2.0 there are no differences. On the other hand, the procedure to create Oracle table statistics, for instance, is very different.

A particularly critical point in all data warehouse systems, and thus for SAP NetWeaver BI as well, is performance. Here, most of your attention should go to Oracle configuration. However, one general restriction is necessary in this regard: The most important criterion for the performance of an SAP NetWeaver BI system is the design of the InfoCubes. Errors made here can't be compensated for by even the most optimum configuration.

In this context, we should also note that SAP provides *performance fixes* for SAP NetWeaver BI when errors are discovered in the SAP standard that have a negative influence on performance. Thus, if you find problems, you should search for corresponding notes on SAP errors in the SAP Service Marketplace.

12.4.1 SAP NetWeaver BI Tables and Indices in the Oracle Database

The SAP NetWeaver BI data is stored in the database in different tables according to a defined naming schema. The basic structure of the namespaces or naming convention according to the SAP standard is: */BI[0|C]/<code for meaning><object>*. Besides the prefix BI[0\C] there are additional prefixes for partner and customer namespaces, for instance, for the Bank Analyzer. The definition of the individual prefixes is in the control tables RSNSPACE (SAP NetWeaver BI default namespaces) and RSPSPACE (SAP NetWeaver BI partner or customer namespaces), whose maintenance is done in Transaction RSNSPACE.

The SAP-internal namespace is BI0, with the customer's objects located by default in namespace BIC. The codes, or keys, for the meanings of SAP NetWeaver BI tables are alphabetically listed in Table 12.2.

<table>
<tr><th>Key</th><th>Meaning</th><th>Template table</th></tr>
<tr><td>/BI[0|C]/D*</td><td>Dimension tables</td><td>RSDMDIMTAB</td></tr>
<tr><td>/BI[0|C]/E*</td><td>E-fact tables (consolidated)</td><td>RSDMFACTAB</td></tr>
<tr><td>/BI[0|C]/F*</td><td>F-fact tables</td><td>RSDMFACTAB</td></tr>
<tr><td>/BI[0|C]/H*</td><td>Hierarchy tables</td><td>RSDMHIETAB</td></tr>
<tr><td>/BI[0|C]/I*</td><td>Hierarchical structure of the SID tables</td><td>RSDMINCTAB</td></tr>
<tr><td>/BI[0|C]/J*</td><td>Hierarchical interval tables</td><td>RSDMHINTAB</td></tr>
<tr><td>/BI[0|C]/K*</td><td>Hierarchy of the SID tables</td><td>RSDMHSITAB</td></tr>
<tr><td>/BI[0|C]/M*</td><td>View of master data tables</td><td>RSDMCHKTAB</td></tr>
<tr><td>/BI[0|C]/P*</td><td>Master data table (time-independent)</td><td>RSDMCHNTAB</td></tr>
<tr><td>/BI[0|C]/Q*</td><td>Master data table (time-dependent)</td><td>RSDMCHTTAB</td></tr>
<tr><td>/BI[0|C]/R*</td><td>SID views</td><td>RSDMSIDVIEW</td></tr>
<tr><td>/BI[0|C]/S*</td><td>SID tables</td><td>RSDMSIDTAB</td></tr>
<tr><td>/BI[0|C]/T*</td><td>Text tables</td><td>RSDMTXTTAB</td></tr>
<tr><td>/BI[0|C]/X*</td><td>SID tables for time-independent navigation attributes</td><td>RSDMASITAB</td></tr>
<tr><td>/BI[0|C]/Y*</td><td>SID tables for time-dependent navigation attributes</td><td>RSDMASTTAB</td></tr>
<tr><td>/BI[0|C]/Z*</td><td>Hierarchy of SID views</td><td>RSDMHSIVIEW</td></tr>
</table>

Table 12.2 Keys for the Meanings of the SAP NetWeaver BI Tables

For every table or view type there is a template table that is used as the blueprint when creating a corresponding SAP NetWeaver BI table. This template primarily determines the technical properties of a table, for instance, the category for size or the settings for use of the SAP table buffers. By default, in SAP NetWeaver BI, all SID and master data tables are single-record buffered, which can have negative impact on performance at a size of over 100,000 records. Deactivation of SAP table buffering can help somewhat here (see SAP Note 550784).

A particular feature is the namespace for SCM- or APO-specific objects, which are in the "internal" SAP NetWeaver BI system of SCM/APO. It is */BI[0|C]/9A<meaning code><object>*, and in pure SAP NetWeaver BI systems it is deactivated. There is also an area for temporary SAP NetWeaver BI objects defined as follows: */BI0/0<code for object type><object>*. Table 12.3 lists the keys for temporary objects.

Key	Object type
/BI0/01*	Tables with intermediate query results
/BI0/02*	Heirarchy of intermediate results
/BI0/03*	Query views generated during query processing
/BI0/04*	Stored procedures used for the compression and condensing of InfoCubes
/BI0/05*	Contains the names of triggers needed
/BI0/06*	Corresponds to type 01*, but it can be reused
/BI0/0D*	Contains results of BI open-hub processes
/BI0/0P*	Materialized partial results of complex queries, if more than 50 tables participate in a JOIN (a special form of /BI0/01).

Table 12.3 Keys for the Meanings of Temporary SAP NetWeaver BI Tables

The temporary objects can be deleted with no consequences, unless, of course, they are in use, in which case the query or transaction will be cancelled. All or some of the temporary object types listed in Table 12.3 can be deleted with the ABAP program `SAP_DROP_TMPTABLES`.

Besides the actual SAP NetWeaver BI tables, the associated indices are also of interest. Depending on the type of table, both B-tree indices and bitmap indices are used. The following provides a brief overview of the indices of the most important (most frequent) SAP NetWeaver BI table types:

- **F-fact tables**
  For normal InfoCubes, a bitmap index (naming convention: <tablename>.~010, 020, etc.) is created on each dimension, unless the corresponding column has high cardinality, in which case a B-tree index is generated instead. For transactional InfoCubes, on the other hand, only B-tree indices are used.
- **E-fact tables**
  In these tables, both index types are always used. There is a bitmap index (naming convention: <tablename>.~010, 020, etc.) on each dimension and an additional B-tree index (naming convention: <tablename>.~P) over all of the dimensions together.
- **Dimension tables**
  These always have two B-tree indices (0 and 010): a primary index (0) on the column for the dimension ID, and a secondary index over all columns together.

- **SID tables**
  Here there are also always two B-tree indices (0 and 001): the primary index (0) on the characteristic column and the secondary index over the SID column.

You can use Transaction RSRV for an analysis of the SAP NetWeaver BI tables. Under menu item **All elementary tests • Database**, you can find various tests to check, for instance, all of the indices for all tables in an InfoCube. For example, you might also check whether the type of index matches the rules above.

The *bitmap indices* on the fact tables are of particular importance, because they are very important for the performance of the SAP NetWeaver BI system, because only with bitmap index is a STAR transformation possible. Using this transformation, very fast bitmap operations can be used to test conditions on dimension tables with corresponding records from the fact tables. Bitmap indices especially make sense for columns with low cardinality, that is, with a small number of different values in a table column. During the design, ensure that the fact tables, that is, the dimensions, don't have high cardinality if possible, in order to be able to use the speed advantages of bitmap indices.

To determine the type of an index, you can either use Transaction RSRV mentioned above, or submit the following SQL command:

```
SQL> select INDEX_NAME, INDEX_TYPE from DBA_INDEXES where TABLE_
NAME = '<table name>';
```

Manual maintenance of SAP NetWeaver BI tables and their indices is done through **ABAP Dictionary • Database Utility** (Transaction SE14). Figure 12.16 shows this transaction after opening an E-fact table.

The administrator can use the Storage parameters button for both indices or the table itself to change the storage parameters. It is particularly interesting to be able to administrate the individual indices, for instance, to delete them in order to replace them with new indices with different parameters.

Warning

If you delete an index without additional settings and then create it again, then regardless of the type of table, you will always be creating a B-tree index. During manual maintenance, always note the type of table and if necessary check the flag for a bitmap index in the storage parameters.

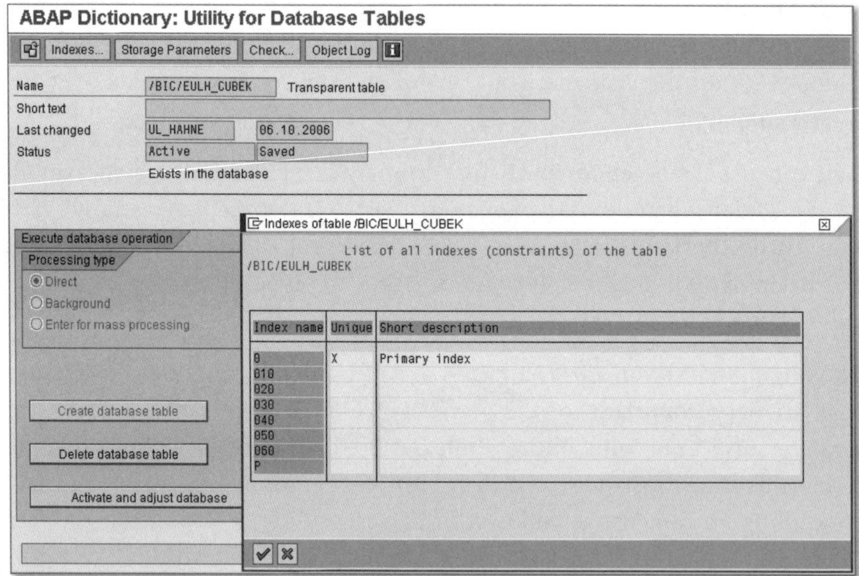

Figure 12.16 Manual Maintenance of a SAP NetWeaver BI Table

12.4.2 Configurations of the Oracle Database

Due to the different characteristics of SAP ERP and SAP NetWeaver BI systems already discussed (OLTP versus OLAP), the two systems have different parameterizations for the Oracle database. At this point, we should state that SAP, with Oracle database 10g, is moving away from that different parameterization, only giving one recommendation for all SAP systems, with a few exceptions. There are two reasons for this: First, the SAP-internal Oracle standard parameterization covers nearly all points of OLTP and OLAP systems, and second, SAP NetWeaver BI is a part of the NetWeaver stack, which since SAP basis 6.40 is found "underneath" every SAP ERP system.

In the following text, we still want to cover the different topics in Oracle parameterization for SAP NetWeaver BI and also show some of the differences between Oracle releases. Because the list of all relevant Oracle parameters would far exceed the scope of this book, we will limit our discussion to the most important parameters for the individual points of focus. At the end of this section, you'll find a reference to the SAP Notes for Oracle parameterization for SAP NetWeaver BI, in which all parameters are listed. The following points must be noted when configuring an Oracle system:

- **Tablespaces**
  The temporary tablespace PSAPTEMP is particularly relevant for SAP NetWeaver BI.
- **Memory**
  Both the SGA areas and the PGAs as well are relevant.
- **I/O**
  Configuration for particular consideration of the heavy read activities and the configuration of Oracle-internal data processing are critical.

The configuration of the PGAs and the temporary tablespace will be covered separately in Section 12.4.3. All of the other points are covered here.

Because SAP NetWeaver BI databases generally grow very quickly, the configuration of tablespaces is important. The use of *dictionary-managed tablespaces* (DMTSs) is particularly critical, because here the administrator must ensure that the right choice of the extent parameters `INITIAL` and `NEXT` doesn't lead to a critical number of extents due to the growth of the corresponding InfoCube tables. The template tables for the E- and F-fact tables in Table 12.2, due to their technical parameters, are already labeled as large tables, but in an SAP NetWeaver BI system in the terabyte range, this is often insufficient. The prerequisite for correct settings, however, is knowledge of the content and growth of the individual InfoCubes. This knowledge is generally not possessed by the Oracle or SAP Basis administrator, so cooperation with the people responsible for the SAP NetWeaver BI application is necessary.

By using LMTS, these problems are largely blunted — hence SAP's recommendation to use LMTS whenever possible. Moreover, there is also the question of whether in very large SAP NetWeaver BI systems (>1 TB) it makes sense to keep all of the data in one tablespace. This is the case if the SAP standard configuration is retained, because then all SAP NetWeaver BI tables are created in the "main tablespace" PSAP<SID>. Whether this distribution makes sense or is even needed depends on many factors, so a single statement is impossible, but be aware of this possibility.

Configuration of the Oracle storage areas for a SAP NetWeaver BI system is carried out according to the following rules of thumb:

1. The SGA areas are configured as for an SAP ERP system, but...
2. ...The PGAs are more important.

The point of this is that the storage of an Oracle database server for an SAP NetWeaver BI system should be distributed to the benefit of the PGAs (more on PGAs in the following section). Of course, that doesn't mean the SGA is unimportant, but, in particular, the data buffer can't take the strain in large SAP NetWeaver BI systems when gigabyte-scale InfoCubes are loaded. Automatic displacement effects occur that cannot be prevented and that reduces the hit ratio correspondingly, unless, of course, there is a corresponding additional storage space for the data buffer.

The recommendations for sizes of individual buffers in the Oracle SGA correspond to those of an R/3 or SAP ERP system for all Oracle releases (8.1.7 or higher). That means that for JAVA_POOL_SIZE, LARGE_POOL_SIZE, and LOG_BUFFER, the values described in the SAP Notes listed below apply. For the two large SGA areas DB_BLOCK_BUFFERS, or DB_CACHE_SIZE and SHARED_POOL_SIZE, the tips in Section 8.2.2, *Analyzing the Database*, apply. These values depend on both the storage available and on the load expected. Sizing by SAP and hardware experts is absolutely required here.

The last part of our list of points concerns the configuration of database I/O and internal data processing. In an SAP NetWeaver BI system, read I/O is of primary importance. This allows a higher degree of parallel data processing, because read operations are easier to parallelize, which improves performance. This is why the following Oracle parameters are particularly relevant:

- **DB_FILE_MULTIBLOCK_READ_COUNT (I/O)**
  This parameter specifies the number of blocks read while reading from the hard drive. In Oracle 8.1.7 the parameters HASH_MULTIBLOCK_IO_COUNT and SORT_MULTIBLOCK_READ_COUNT still existed for the number of blocks in HASH and SORT operations. However, these were set to the same value as DB_FILE_MULTIBLOCK_READ_COUNT.
- **FILESYSTEMIO_OPTIONS (I/O)**
  This parameter activates the possible modes for I/O operations. Under Oracle 8.1.7, this parameter was still hidden as a "_" parameter, and officially it was only possible to activate asynchronous I/O using DISK_ASYNCH_IO.
- **PARALLEL_EXECUTION_MESSAGE_SIZE (parallel)**
  This parameter specifies the size of the Oracle-internal messages for parallel processing.
- **PARALLEL_MAX_SERVER (parallel)**
  This parameter determines the maximum number of parallel query processes that Oracle may start.

Table 12.4 gives some information about the values SAP recommends for the parameters listed and shows the development between Oracle releases. For additional comparison, the last column shows the recommendations for an SAP ERP system.

Parameters	8.1.7	9i	10g	SAP ERP with Oracle 9i
DB_FILE_MULTIBLOCK_READ_COUNT (I/O)	32	32	128	8
FILESYSTEMIO_OPTIONS (I/O)	DISK_ASYNCH_IO=TRUE	SETALL	SETALL	SETALL (9i) DISK_ASYNCH_IO=TRUE (<9i)
PARALLEL_EXECUTION_MESSAGE_SIZE (parallel)	16384	16384	16384	2148
PARALLEL_MAX_SERVER (parallel)	#CPUs x 8	#CPUs x 10	#CPUs x 10	5

Table 12.4 SAP Recommendation for Selected Oracle Parameters

As of Oracle 10g, with a few exceptions, the same recommendations apply for both SAP NetWeaver BI and SAP ERP systems. The Oracle parameters listed for the three points are, of course, not even close to being all of the parameters you must set as an administrator. In the following SAP Notes, you'll find SAP's recommendations for the operation of SAP NetWeaver BI systems on an Oracle database:

- SAP Note 632424: *Oracle 8.1.7* Database Parameterization for SAP NetWeaver BI*
- SAP Note 632556: *Oracle 9.2.0* Database Parameterization for SAP NetWeaver BI*
- SAP Note 830576: *Parameter Recommendations for Oracle 10g*

These notes are especially important for the administrator because they are always updated, especially with regard to parameters that must be set as workarounds for bugs discovered, for instance. Thus, you'll find different Oracle event and "_" parameters there that must be set for certain Oracle patch levels to avoid errors.

12.4.3 PGA and Temporary Tablespace

The most frequent performance-relevant database operations in SAP NetWeaver BI are JOIN, SORT, and bitmap operations. These especially burden the PGAs of the individual Oracle shadow processes, or if they are insufficient, the temporary tablespace. Thus, in the following text, we'll take a look at these two parts of the Oracle database.

The PGA was introduced in Chapter 3 and Chapter 8. As an administrator of Oracle 9i or higher, you have the option of using automatic PGA administration. If you do, then PGA administration for Oracle 9i and Oracle 10g Release behaves according to the following rules:

- The entire memory an Oracle instance can use for the PGAs is determined by the PGA_AGGREGATE_TARGET parameter.
- The size of one work area is limited to 5% of PGA_AGGREGATE_TARGET or a maximum of 100 MB. An Oracle shadow process, however, can have a number of work areas. The "_" parameter _SMM_MAX_SIZE can change that limitation. Warning: Under no circumstances should you set this parameter. If you do, you will not get support from SAP or Oracle. This is mentioned here only for the sake of completeness.
- The sizes of all work areas in a process are limited to at most 200 MB. The "_" parameter _PGA_MAX_SIZE can change that limitation, however. The parameter is used according to the SAP recommendation for each Oracle release.

In Oracle 10g Release 2, numerous improvements were made internally in all aspects of PGA administration. For instance, the fixed upper limits for work areas and PGAs of a process have been removed. These are now determined automatically according to the value of PGA_AGGREGATE_TARGET.

Note

To activate automatic PGA administration under Oracle 9i, you must set the parameter WORKAREA_SIZE_POLICY to AUTO:

```
SQL> alter system set WORKAREA_SIZE_POLICY=AUTO;
```

For Oracle 10g, this is automatic once the parameter PGA_AGGREGATE_TARGET has been set to a value other than 0.

Figure 12.17 shows the relationships between the Oracle shadow processes, the PGAs, and the work areas when using automatic PGA administration. It also shows the parameters that determine the size of the individual areas.

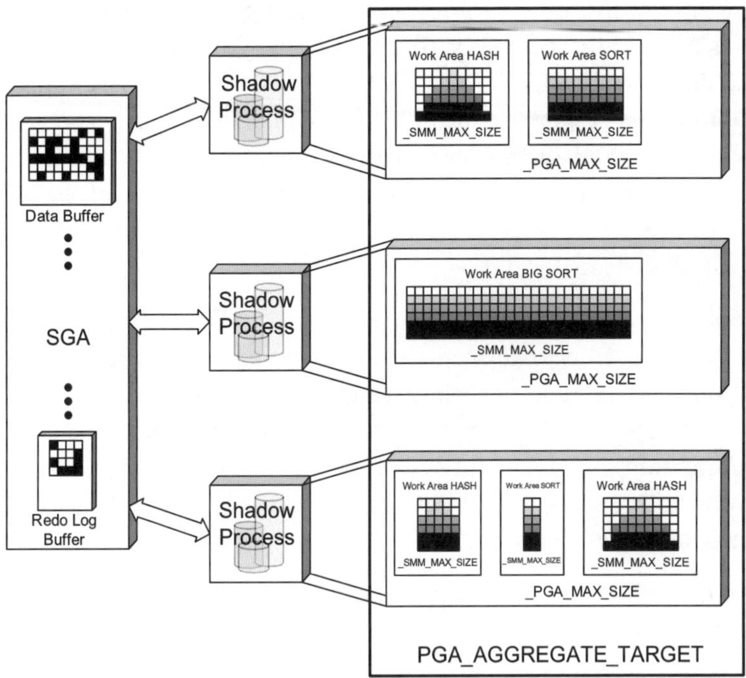

Figure 12.17 Oracle PGAs and their Parameters

During PGA configuration for an SAP NetWeaver BI system, you should set the following parameters with the SAP recommendations for the specific Oracle release:

- **Oracle 10gR2 (with automatic PGA)**
  - `PGA_AGGREGATE_TARGET` to 40% of the memory available on the database server.
- **Oracle 9i and 10gR1 (with automatic PGA)**
  - `PGA_AGGREGATE_TARGET (P_A_T)` to 40% of the memory available on the database server.
  - `_PGA_MAX_SIZE` to 400 MB if `P_A_T` > 4 GB, 600 MB if `P_A_T` > 8 GB, or 800 MB if `P_A_T` > 12 GB.
- **Oracle 8.1.7, 9i, and 10g (without automatic PGA)**
  - `BITMAP_MERGE_SIZE` = 33554432
  - `CREATE_BITMAP_AREA_SIZE` = 33554432
  - `HASH_AREA_SIZE` = 2 × `SORT_AREA_SIZE`
  - `SORT_AREA_SIZE` ≥ 10 MB

In Section 8.2.2, *Analyzing the Database*, we described how you can tell whether your PGA configuration is sufficient. Use the V$PGASTAT, V$PGA_TARGET_ADVICE, and V$SQL_WORKAREA_HISTOGRAM views introduced there to optimize the size of the entire memory for PGAs. The SAP recommendation of 40% of available memory for PGA_AGGREGATE_TARGET should be considered a starting point and adjusted after analysis of the V$ views listed. Oracle, for instance, recommends using 70% of the memory for the PGA in OLAP systems.

If, despite optimum PGA configuration or due to a lack of memory, the database operation cannot be performed in RAM, that is, *optimal execution* is impossible, then the temporary tablespace (generally PSAPTEMP) is used. Not only for the operations listed, but also for typical SAP NetWeaver BI STAR transformations, the temporary tablespace is needed to a high degree. If access to hard drive storage can't be avoided, it should at least be carried out at the maximum possible speed.

There are two basic possibilities for using the temporary tablespace: as DMTS with permanent content or as LMTS with temporary content. These are the two tablespace types supported by SAP for PSAPTEMP (see also Section 4.4.2, *Tablespace Types*). The express recommendation is to create the temporary tablespace as LMTS; this is the default setting for all SAP installations from SAP Basis 6.40 on. This provides two great advantages over use of a DMTS:

1. Optimization of storage parameters (INITIAL, NEXT, etc.) is eliminated. Only the UNIFORM clause must be taken into consideration under some circumstances.
2. The LMTS with temporary content is created with the option NOLOGGING, meaning no redo logs are written when writing temporary objects. This yields a significant performance advantage.

When creating the temporary tablespace, regardless of whether DMTS or LMTS is used, the question of whether to use automatic PGA administration or not is of crucial importance. If it is not used, the parameter HASH_AREA_SIZE must be found in the parameterization for PSAPTEMP. If you create the temporary tablespace as DMTS without using automatic PGA administration, that is, for instance, under Oracle 8.1.7, the storage parameterization looks like this:

- INITIAL = HASH_AREA_SIZE
- NEXT = HASH_AREA_SIZE

- MINEXTENTS = Default value
- MAXEXTENTS = UNLIMITED
- PTCINREASE = 0

If you create the temporary tablespace as LMTABLESPACE as recommended, but also work without automatic PGA administration, then automatic segment administration must be deactivated by setting the UNIFORM SIZE parameter to the value HASH_AREA_SIZE when creating PSAPTEMP.

If, on the other hand, automatic PGA administration is used, for a temporary tablespace created as LMTS, the automatic segment administration must be activated with the AUTOALLOCATE parameter. Determination of the extent size with UNIFORM SIZE doesn't make sense in this context, because PGA administration will determine the size of the work areas dynamically. You should avoid use of automatic PGA administration in combination with a temporary tablespace created as DMTS.

The second and equally important way to influence the performance of PSAPTEMP is in configuration of the I/O. We already looked at the different alternatives in Chapter 8. Because the temporary tablespace is particularly important in an SAP NetWeaver BI system, it should at least be located on a fast RAID system and thus be distributed over as many drives as possible. If I/O performance is still a problem, don't be afraid of the increased overhead for the use of raw devices. Move your temporary tablespace accordingly.

The size of the temporary tablespace in an SAP NetWeaver BI system depends primarily on the scope of the data. Thus, PSAPTEMP should be at least twice as large as the largest fact table, but at least 10 gigabytes in size. Depending on the size of the SAP NetWeaver BI system, there are no upper limits. In general, the administrator shouldn't try to save on temporary tablespace, because needs will rise with the degree of parallelism in Oracle use. While an SAP OLTP system generally doesn't use parallel queries in Oracle, they are used in some places in SAP NetWeaver BI, for instance, when building InfoCubes.

SAP Note 544521 provides instructions on how to use the ORA_PARALLEL_DEGREE parameter to control the use of Oracle parallel queries in SAP NetWeaver BI.

12.4.4 Statistics for SAP NetWeaver BI Tables

For the SAP NetWeaver BI tables, Oracle statistics are just as important as for all other SAP tables. When generating these statistics for the SAP NetWeaver BI tables, however, there are a few differences.

First, the SAP NetWeaver BI statistics must always be created with *histograms*. In principle, histograms are statistics about the contents of a column that give information about the distribution of values in that column. For instance, if the values 1 through 20 appear in column S1 of a table T1, then the histogram of column S1 tells us how often value 1 appears, how often 2 appears, and so on. Histograms especially make sense when the appearance of the individual values are distributed very unevenly, for instance, when the value 8 occupies 60% of column S1 and the other values are evenly distributed. Exactly that phenomenon is often observed in InfoCube tables. Normal statistics for table T1 would ensure that for a `SELECT` with a `WHERE` clause on a value from column S1, an index scan would be performed, which in the case of `WHERE S1='8'` would result in a very poor response time. A histogram on S1 allows the Oracle Optimizer to detect this uneven distribution, and for `WHERE S1='8'` it performs a full table scan for access. For further information on Oracle histograms, see SAP FAQ Note 797629.

The second difference lies in the time of generation of statistics. The statistics for the non-SAP NetWeaver BI tables are created by the administrator by scheduling a corresponding `BRCONNECT` run at a certain time. This applies initially to the SAP NetWeaver BI tables as well, but not exclusively, because there are also statistics run that are initiated by SAP NetWeaver BI itself. That means that after certain procedures, for instance, an aggregate roll-up or after change runs, the SAP NetWeaver BI system updates the affects statistics on its own. This is done to keep the statistics up to date without waiting for the next scheduled statistics run, which is especially important when queries are running on the data involved during those operations. If it can be absolutely ensured that no queries or few queries will be running during the operations, for instance, at night or on the weekend, then for performance reasons the SAP NetWeaver BI initiation of statistics updating can be deactivated (see SAP Note 555030). After the end of the operations, the statistics update should be handled all at once.

The third difference, at least up until Oracle 9i, is the method of creation of Oracle statistics. From Oracle 8 on, there are two methods of creating statistics for the Cost-Based Optimizer (CBO): the classical SQL command `ANALYZE`, and the PL/SQL package DBMS_STATS. The tool `BRCONNECT` uses the command ANALYSE to create statistics up to and including Oracle 9i. As of Oracle 10g, DBMS_STATS is used exclusively. The administrator can also force the use of DBMS_STATS for releases earlier than Oracle 10g as well, by setting the stats_dbms_stats parameter in the BR*Tools parameter file init<DBSID>.ora (SAP Note 424239). Exactly that procedure is recommended for SAP NetWeaver BI systems under Oracle releases lower than 10g, because for a SAP NetWeaver BI system, the statistics should always be generated with DBMS_STATS. For DBMS_STATS to be used for statistics runs initiated by the SAP NetWeaver BI system itself, the control table RSADMIN must be maintained. The exact procedure for this is described in SAP Note 351163.

The scheduled creation of Oracle statistics as of BW 3.0B and BRCONNECT 6.20 is carried out with the standard call:

```
brconnect -c -u / -f stats -t all
```

BRCONNECT uses the namespace entered in the RSNSPACE table to detect SAP NetWeaver BI tables automatically and handle them accordingly. Previously, this wasn't so easy, which is why statistics creation for the SAP NetWeaver BI tables is handled by the ABAP report SAP_ANALYSE_ALL_INFOCUBES. This report was made obsolete by the conversion from the old SAPDBA to BRCONNECT.

The parameter stats_info_cubes in the file init<DBSID>.ora still gives the administrator the ability to influence the working of BRCONNECT on SAP NetWeaver BI tables today, however, and can also process tables other than just SAP NetWeaver BI tables, for instance. For more information on this parameter, see SAP Note 424239.

12.4.5 Oracle Data Miner and the SAP BI Accelerator

In this last section, we'll give you a few more tips about performance and the additional options when using SAP NetWeaver BI.

If you want to perform data mining on your SAP NetWeaver BI data inventories, SAP NetWeaver BI provides the Data Mining Framework. Besides SAP-specific functionality, you can also integrate external tools here, such as the *Oracle Data Miner* (ODM). SAP certifies an ODM connector that is installed on SAP NetWeaver Application Server Java. In Figure 12.18, you can see the interaction of the components when ODM is used.

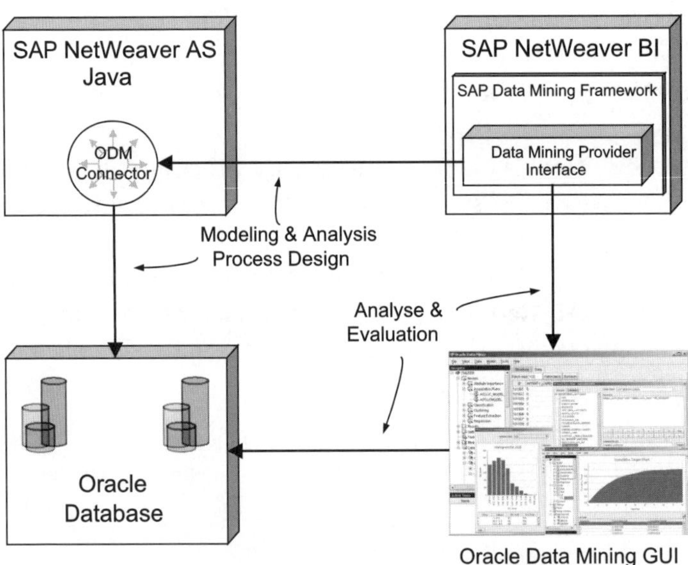

Figure 12.18 Integration of Oracle Data Mining into SAP NetWeaver BI

Table 12.5 shows the available components and their versions and how they must be combined, that is, their compatibility.

Component	Version	
SAP BW/SAP NetWeaver BI	3.50	7.00
SAP Web/NetWeaver AS Java	6.40	7.00
Oracle database	9i	10g
ODM Connector	1.1	2.1

Table 12.5 Compatibility of Components when Using ODM

ODM, in comparison with other external data mining solutions, has the advantage that the data can remain unchanged in the Oracle database and examined there. A transformation to another format or a different database is not required. Moreover, the ODM Connector for data mining uses Oracle-specific specialized techniques provided by the Oracle database itself.

Furthermore, we'd like to refer you to a relatively new product by SAP in the area of business intelligence. For any OLAP application, there is always the risk that despite modern hardware, optimum configuration, and a "perfect" design, certain queries and reports can no longer be run in an acceptable timeframe, simply due to the amounts of data. To extend that limit upward,

SAP has worked with Intel and HP to develop the *SAP NetWeaver Business Intelligence Accelerator* (BI Accelerator).

This product is a combination of hardware and software that accelerates the response time to a query by a factor of 10–200 depending on the application. This acceleration is achieved using separate handling of the data involved according to the procedure shown in Figure 12.19.

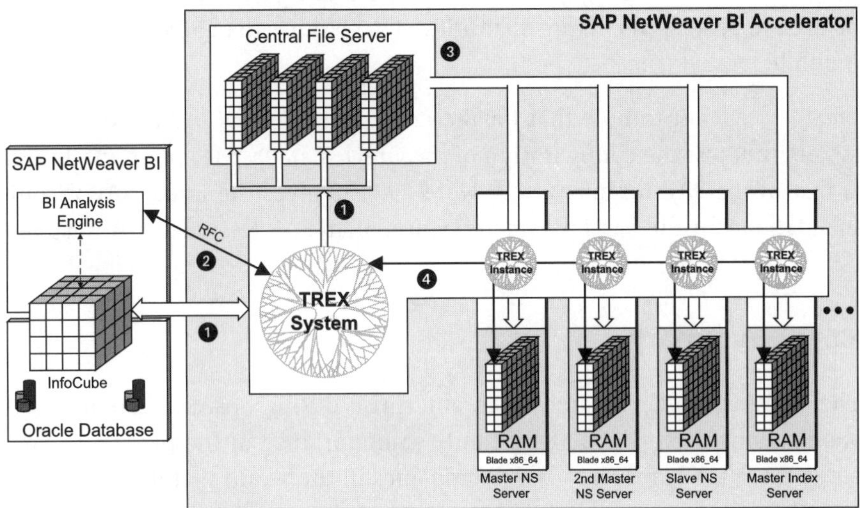

Figure 12.19 Structure of the SAP NetWeaver BI Accelerator

The process when using the SAP NetWeaver BI Accelerator is as follows:

❶ The data in an InfoCube is completely, that is, not in aggregation, replicated to the file system. There, the data is indexed and compressed by the TREX system, which forms the core of the SAP NetWeaver BI Accelerator. This compression, which stores data by column instead of by row, enables reduction in the amount of data by up to a factor of 10. The resulting index is divided into multiple parts, so that it can be searched in parallel by multiple TREX instances. For changes to the original InfoCube, there are delta replications and indexing mechanisms.

❷ A query from the SAP NetWeaver BI Analyze engine normally goes to an InfoCube in the database. However, if the SAP NetWeaver BI Accelerator is in used, the query goes to the TREX system by RFC connection.

❸ On the first access to the index of an InfoCube, the parts needed are loaded into memory in the TREX instances. They remain there for later requests, even after the first query.

❹ All TREX instances process the query in their memory in parallel and aggregate the data dynamically if necessary. The results return to the SAP NetWeaver BI system by RFC.

The principle of the SAP NetWeaver BI Accelerator is easy to understand: massive parallelization and acceleration by means of the use of many cheap CPUs (X86_64) and RAM. In a BI Accelerator Box there are at least four blades, each with eight gigabytes of RAM. Naturally, many more blades can be used to process very large quantities of data (more than 50 gigabytes up to multiple terabytes).

Finally, we want to note that for the performance of an SAP NetWeaver BI system, not just the configuration of the Oracle database is important, but so is that of the SAP instances. SAP Note 192658 gives the initial SAP recommendations for the basis parameterization of an SAP NetWeaver BI system.

12.5 Summary

The analysis of data created in an enterprise during business activity, data warehousing, has gained significantly in importance in the past few years. Now, there are hardly any large companies in the world that don't perform this type of business analysis.

With its SAP NetWeaver Business Intelligence solution, SAP offers a mature, complete product for this market, which utilizes its capabilities primarily in combination with other SAP solutions. However, the flexible SAP NetWeaver architecture also enables the connection of a variety of third-party software, both as data source and for support of data mining functions.

By using an Oracle database under SAP NetWeaver BI, all of the advantages of this combination can be used for the analysis of business data, including the capability of using the Oracle data mining described here. By using trusted SAP Basis technology and its tools, the administration of this combination is essentially no different than that of an SAP ERP system, for instance. However, the administrator must pay particular attention to the increased requirements relative to performance and the special SAP NetWeaver BI-specific tables and indices.

Oracle's current version is a power OLAP system. Besides internal improvements for the administration of ultralarge databases and performance increases, we can also see continued conceptual development of the data warehouse functionality. While the first approaches in Oracle 8 supported the ROLAP concept and offered initial SQL extensions for it, Oracle 10g, with its Analytic Workspaces provides true MOLAP, whose structure (design, ETL) and use (metadata, operation, reporting, data mining) is supported by a wide variety of tools.

"Understanding is love; that which we do not love, we do not understand; what we do not understand, is not there for us."
Bettina von Arnim

13 Afterword and Outlook

The high percentage of production SAP systems running on Oracle databases shows the significance of the cooperation of SAP and Oracle. From the technical point of view, SAP and Oracle are an ideal team.

In the first chapters, we presented both systems individually and together. In many areas, we went into some depth and gave tips and instructions for the solution of important problems. Of course, even an 800-page book can only cover part of the great many possible problems. An understanding of the relationships and processes can help you solve your own problems.

Furthermore, in the administration of Oracle-based SAP systems, a comprehensive view of your system landscape helps. By careful planning of the system landscape and transport system, as well as systematic examination of installation and maintenance activities in a system lifecycle, long-term stable, high-performance, and reliably running SAP installations result. Many Oracle problems can be avoided in advance by such solution management, and many problems that might have been attributed to the overall system can be corrected using Oracle tools.

This view of technical management was elaborated in the three major areas of system operation, data security, and performance. We offered you a conceptual and thorough look that can help you in the management and optimization of your daily work.

Furthermore, we looked at Oracle administration with respect to the areas of Java and SAP NetWeaver BI. Both have already gained widespread acceptance and present particular challenges to the organization and administration of the Oracle database.

We think that in the chapters presented we have described the important areas of administration of SAP on Oracle databases in both a technical and easily understood manner.[1] Of course, many topics and future trends were not covered, or only to an unsatisfactory extent, for example, adaptive computing, the Solution Manager, and the integration with SAP NetWeaver Exchange Infrastructure.

In summary, it must be said that the success of SAP systems on Oracle databases promises a long system lifetime and thus a long period of usability of the knowledge presented here. Even though SAP and Oracle are competitors in the market for enterprise software, both know how important cooperation is for their customers:

- At *www.oracle.com/sap*, Oracle maintains a special website for SAP customers.
- SAP doesn't provide a specific administration tool like BR*Tools for any other supported database.
- For Oracle, there are over 5,000 Notes in the SAP Service Marketplace. That's nearly as many as for all other databases combined.

Even though SAP only introduces new Oracle features conservatively, this is only due to the enterprise-critical use of SAP software. SAP and Oracle are powerful partners from a technical point of view who are successful together. With R/3, SAP set a new standard in the area of standard business software, and the Oracle database was a similar achievement for Oracle in the area of relational database systems. Both systems can be called market leaders and innovation drivers, and for this reason, too, there is a notable dependency.[2] Each system profits from the continued development of the other. In that sense, Oracle-based SAP systems will probably enjoy a long and interesting future.

Magdeburg, in May, 2007
André Faustmann, Michael Höding,
Gunnar Klein, and Ronny Zimmermann

1 We would really have liked to buy this book — unfortunately, it has only just now become available.

2 Comparable to the soccer stars in a top team, where competition promotes performance but team play is the most important thing in the final analysis.

Appendix

A Flight Data Model

A.1 SQL Script for Creating the Database

```
drop table scarr;
drop table spfli;
drop table sflight;
drop table sbook;

create table scarr (
  carrid char(3),
  carrname varchar(20),
  ulr varchar(255)
);

create table spfli (
  carrid char(3),
  connid number(8),
  countryfr char(3),
  cityfrom varchar(20),
  airpfrom varchar(3),
  countryto char(3),
  cityto varchar(20),
  airpto varchar(3),
  fltime number(10),
  deptime char(4),
  arrtime char(4),
  distance number(9)
);

create table sflight (
  carrid char(3),
  connid number(8),
  fldate date,
  price number(15,2),
  planetype varchar(10),
  seatsmax number(4)
);
```

```
create table sbook (
  carrid char(3),
  connid number(8),
  fldate date,
  bookid number(8),
  customid number(8),
  custtype char(1),
  smoker char(1),
  luggweight number(8),
  order_date date,
  passname varchar(25)
);

create sequence fli_seq;
create sequence book_seq;
quit
```

A.2 Perl Script for Generating the Database Content

```
#use strict;
use CGI::Carp qw(fatalsToBrowser);
use DBI;
$ENV{ORACLE_SID}="orcl";
$ENV{ORACLE_HOME}="/oracle/oracle/product/10.2.0/db_1";
my $connection=DBI->connect("DBI:Oracle:orcl",'fdmuser',"fdmfdm");
and so on
```

B General Options of the BR*Tools

B.1 Functions of BRSPACE

Table B.1 lists options for all functions of BRSPACE including the associated file extensions (.<ext>) for the session logs. All of these functions are started from the command prompt in the following manner:

```
brspace -f <option for the function> <options>
```

Option	Function	.<ext>
dbalter	ALTER function for the Oracle database, for example, to change the archive log mode or to trigger a log file switch.	*.dba*
dbcreate	Creation of a complete Oracle database.	*.dbc*
dbparam	Changes the parameters of the Oracle database.	*.dbp*
dbstart	Starts the database.	.dbr
dbshut	Stops the database.	.dbs
dbshow	Displays many different pieces of information about the database, such as redo log files, segments, free extents, and so on, depending on the suboption used.	.dbw
dfalter	ALTER function for data files, such as enlarging, changing the autoextend, and so on.	.dfa
dfmove	Moves data files.	.dfm
idrebuild	Carries out an index rebuild for individual or several tables.	.idr
idalter	ALTER function for indexes.	.ida
tbalter	ALTER function for tables, for instance, to change the monitoring process or to decrease the size of table segments (segment shrinking as of Oracle 10g).	.tba
tbexport	Exports individual tables or a complete tablespace into files in the file system in the context of an offline reorganization, for example.	.tbe
tbimport	Imports individual tables or a complete tablespace.	.tbi
tbreorg	Reorganizes single or multiple tables and requires various options for that purpose.	.tbr

Table B.1 Functions of BRSPACE

Option	Function	.<ext>
tsalter	ALTER function for tablespaces, for example, setting tablespaces online and offline or renaming tablespaces (as of 10g).	.tsa
tscreate	Creates a new tablespace and requires several options.	.tsc
tsdrop	Deletes a tablespace.	.tsd
tsextend	Extends a tablespace and requires a number of options, such as TS-Name, the size of the extension, and so on.	.tse

Table B.1 Functions of BRSPACE (Cont.)

B.2 Functions of BRARCHIVE

Table B.2 lists options for all functions of `BRARCHIVE` including the associated file extensions (.<ext>) for the session logs. All of these functions are started from the command prompt in the following manner:

```
brarchive <options>
```

Options	Function	.<ext>
-copy_delete_save -cds	Creates a second copy of the online redo log files that have already been archived. This triggers the archiving process and deletes the file.	.cds
- compress -k	Sets the compression mode.	.cma
-second_copy_delete -scd	Creates a second copy of the offline redo log files that have already been archived. After that, the files are deleted.	.cpd
-copy_save -cs	Creates a second copy of the offline redo log files that have already been archived. The newly created copy is archived after that.	.cps
-second_copy -sc	Creates a second copy of the offline redo log files that have already been archived.	.cpy
-delete_copied -dc	Deletes the offline redo log files that were copied twice.	.dcp
-delete_saved -ds	Deletes the offline redo log files that were archived.	.dsv
-fill -f	Fills a backup tape while the system waits for the next offline redo log file.	.fst

Table B.2 Functions of BRARCHIVE

Options	Function	.<ext>
-query -q	Sets the query mode.	.qua
-save -s	Archives the offline redo log files.	.sve
-save_delete -sc	Archives the offline redo log files and then deletes the files.	.svd
-double_save -ss	Archives the offline redo log files simultaneously on two backup devices.	.ssv
-double_save_ delete -ssd	Archives the offline redo log files simultaneously on two backup devices and deletes the files afterward.	.ssd
-initialize -i	Initializes the tapes.	.tia

Table B.2 Functions of BRARCHIVE (Cont.)

B.3 Functions of BRCONNECT

Table B.3 lists options for all functions of BRCONNECT including the associated file extensions (.<ext>) for the session logs. All of these functions are started from the command prompt in the following manner:

```
brconnect -f <option for the function> <options>
```

Option	Function	.<ext>
stats -f nocheck	Does not check the statistics.	.aly
check	Checks the database system.	.chk
chpass	Changes the database user password.	
cleanup	Deletes the database logs.	.cln
stats -d	Deletes corrupted statistics.	.dst
crsyn	Creates public synonyms for SAP tools.	
dbshut	Shuts down the database immediately.	
next	Adjusts the next extension to the table size.	.nxt

Table B.3 Functions of BRCONNECT

Option	Function	.<ext>
`stats -f nocoll`	Checks the statistics only by analyzing the primary indexes. The statistics are renewed for tables that would need new ones the next time BRCONNECT is called.	.opt
`-q` `-query`	Defines the query mode.	.quc
`stats`	Renews the Optimizer statistics.	.sta
`stats -v`	Confirms the table and index structures.	.vst

Table B.3 Functions of BRCONNECT (Cont.)

B.4 Functions of BRBACKUP

Tables B.4 and B.5 list options for all functions of BRBACKUP including the associated file extensions (.<xyz> or .<ext>) for the session logs. All of these functions are started from the command prompt in the following manner:

```
bbackup -f <option for the function> <options>
```

Option	Function	.<ext>
`-k only`	Defines the compression mode.	.cmb
`-w only_dbv`	Checks the backup upon completion.	.dbv
`-db`	Deletes a backup.	.ddb
`-q`	Fixes the query mode.	.qub
`-d`	Defines the BACKINT and mount parameters.	.rmp

`-i`
`-i force`
`-i show`
	Initializes tape drives.	.tib

Table B.4 Functions of BRBACKUP

Possible Variants of the x Component of the Ending	
The entire database was backed up.	a
Full (Level-0) backup (`backup_mode = full`)	f
Extended (Level-1) backup (`backup_mode = incr`)	i
One or several tables or files were backed up (partial backup)	p

Table B.5 Log File Endings and their Meaning

Possible Variants of the y Component of the Ending	
The backup process was carried out offline. (backup_type = offline | offline_force | offline_standbye | offline_split | offline_mirror | offline_stop)	f
The backup process was carried out online. (backup_type = online | online_cons | online_split | online_mirror)	n
Possible Variants of the z Component of the Ending	
Local disk (backup_device_type = disk | disk_copy | disk_standby)	d
External backup program used; backup performed file by file (backup_device_type = util_file | util_file_online)	f
Tape device on a remote system (backup_device_type = pipe|pipe_auto|pipe_box)	p
Backup using RMAN (backup_dev_type = rman_util | rman_disk | rman_stage)	r
Remote disk (backup_dev_type = stage|stage_copy|stage_standby)	
Tape device (backup_dev_type = tape|tape_auto|tape_box)	t

Table B.5 Log File Endings and their Meaning (Cont.)

B.5 Functions of BRRESTORE

Table B.6 lists options for all functions of BRRESTORE including the associated file extensions (.<ext>) for the session logs. All of these functions are started from the command prompt in the following manner:

```
brrestore <option>
```

Option	Function	.<ext>
-a -archive -a1	Restores offline redo log files from the first copy.	.rsa
-a2 -archive2	Restores offline redo log files from the second copy.	

Table B.6 Functions of BRRESTORE

Option	Function	.<ext>
-b -backup	Restores database files that were saved using brbackup.	.rsb
-b2 -backup2	Restores files by calling the backup tools via the BACKINT interface.	
-n -number	Enables the restoration of a file directly from a backup drive without having to enter the name of the backup log or the sequential number.	.rsf
-n2	Enables the restoration of a file from a backup drive into a specific target directory.	
-q -query	Defines the query mode.	.qur

Table B.6 Functions of BRRESTORE (Cont.)

B.6 Functions of BRRECOVER

Table B.7 lists options for all functions of BRRECOVER including the associated file extensions (.<ext>) for the session logs. All of these functions are started from the command prompt in the following manner:

```
brrecover <options>
```

Option	Function	.<ext>
dbshow	Recovers and executes the offline redo log files.	.alf
dbstart	Recovers the entire database.	.crv
dbshut	Database point-in-time recovery.	.dpt
dbparam	Resets the entire database.	.drs
tsextend	Disaster recovery.	.drv
dbcreate	Recovers individual backup files.	.rif
dbalter	Tablespace point-in-time recovery.	.tpt

Table B.7 Functions of BRRECOVER

C References

Ahrends, J., Lenz, D., Schwanke, P. und Unbescheid, G.: *Oracle 10g für den DBA*, Addison-Wesley, 2006.

ANSI/ISO/IEC 9075 – 2:2003: *ISO International Standard: Database Language SQL – Part 2: Foundation (SQL/Foundation)*, Dezember 2003.

Bauer, A. und Günzel, H.: *Data-Warehouse-Systeme. Architektur, Entwicklung, Anwendung*, Dpunkt, 2004.

Burke, B. und Monson-Haefel, R.: *Enterprise Java Beans 3.0*, O'Reilly, 2006.

Burke, B. und Monson-Haefel, R.: *Enterprise Java Beans 3.0*, O'Reilly, 2006.

Christiansen, A., Höding, M., Rautenstrauch, C. und Saake, G.: *Oracle 8 effizent einsetzen*, Addsion-Wesley, 1998.

Conrad, S.: *Föderierte Datenbanken Konzepte der Datenintegration*, Springer, 1997.

Gamma, E., Helm, R., und Johnson, R.: *Entwurfsmuster*, Addison-Wesley, 2004.

Hagemann, S. und Will., L.: *SAP R/3-Systemadministration – Basiswissen für das R/3-Systemmangement*, Galileo Press, 2003.

Heuer, A. und Saake, G.: *Datenbanken: Konzepte und Sprachen*, Mitp, 2000.

Inmon, W. H.: *The Data Warehouse and Data Mining*. In: Commun. ACM 39 (11): 49 – 50, 1996.

Kalosi, D.: *Vimming with SQL*Plus, http://www.oracle.com/technology/pub/articles/kalosi_vim.html*, Oracle Technology Network, 2007.

Kecher, C.: *UML 2.0 – Das umfassende Handbuch*, Galileo Press, 2006.

Keller, H. und Krüger, S.: *ABAP Objects. ABAP-Programmierung mit SAP NetWeaver*, SAP PRESS, 2006.

Linkies, M. und Off, F.: *Sicherheit und Berechtigungen in SAP-Systemen*, SAP PRESS, 2007.

Potts, W. J. E.: *Data Mining Primer – Overview of Applications and Methods.* SAS Institut, Cary, 1998.

Saake, G., Heuer, A. und Sattler, K.-U.: *Datenbanken – Implementierungstechniken*, Mitp, 2005.

Schneider, T.: *SAP-Performanceoptimierung*, SAP PRESS, 2005.

Sippel, S.: *Oracle Packages Teil IX: Locally Managed Tablespaces DBMS_SPACE_ADMIN* in *Ordix News* 1/2003, Ordix AG, 2003.

Skulschus, M., Michaelis, S. und Wiederstein, M.: *Oracle 10g. Programmierhandbuch*, Galileo Press, 2006.

Stahlknecht, P. und Hasenkamp, U.: *Einführung in die Wirtschaftsinformatik*, Springer, 2004.

Stürner, G.: *Oracle 7 – die verteilte semantische Datenbank*, dbms, 1992.

Tanebaum, A.-S.: *Computernetzwerke*, Pearson Studium, 2003.

Throll, M. und Bartosch, O.: *Einstieg in SQL.* Galileo Press, 2004.

Türker, C.: *SQL 1999 und SQL 2003. Objektrelationales SQL, SQLJ und SQL/XML*, Dpunkt, 2003.

D Authors

André Faustmann studied information management at the Otto von Guericke University in Magdeburg, Germany. Since 2000, he has been working at the SAP University Competence Center (SAP UCC) in Magdeburg, where he is responsible for hosting a wide range of SAP solutions for universities, third-level colleges, universities of cooperative education, and vocational schools throughout Germany. His many years of experience with SAP systems range from Release 4.6 to NetWeaver 7.0 (2004s). He is also a certified technology consultant for SAP NetWeaver AS and Enterprise Portal and Knowledge Management.

Michael Höding is professor of information management at the Brandenburg University of Applied Sciences. He strives to give students an understanding of the interaction between SAP and Oracle to prepare them as much as possible for the workplace. After completing his studies in information technology in Magdeburg and Braunschweig, and being awarded a PhD degree at Otto von Guericke University, he was involved in setting up the SAP University Competence Center (SAP UCC) in Magdeburg. He is a certified consultant for SAP UNIX/ORACLE. Michael Höding devotes his free time to his family and amateur radio contesting. He also spends time running (up to marathon level) to get himself away from the keyboard.

Gunnar Klein works for T-Systems in Magdeburg, where he is part of the SAP Basis team. He studied information management at Otto von Guericke University in Magdeburg and worked for six years as an SAP Basis administrator in the SAP University Competence Center. His experience with SAP systems ranges from Release 4.6 to NetWeaver 7.0 (2004s). He is also a certified consultant for SAP NetWeaver AS and SAP Enterprise Portal and Knowledge Management.

Ronny Zimmermann works at the SAP University Competence Center at Otto von Guericke University in Magdeburg, where he is responsible for a wide range of SAP systems using Oracle databases. He has been a certified consultant for SAP NetWeaver and SAP NetWeaver Portal for many years. When he is not busy pursuing his passion for soccer and passing this on to his son Aron, he spends his time motorcycling with his wife Urte and watching his daughter Laura dancing.

Index

C

D

E

F

M

N

O

P

Q

R

S

T

U

V

W

X

Z

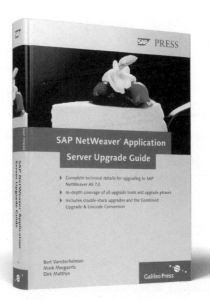

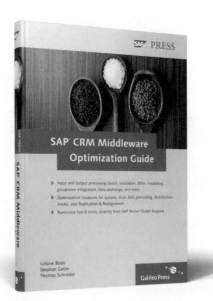

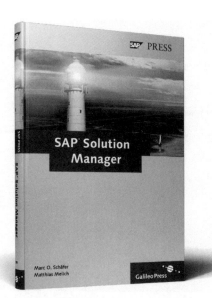

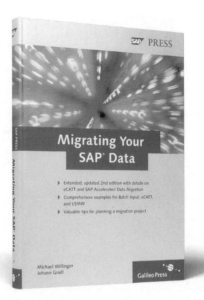

Understand the principles of administration and development

Gain insights on KM, collaboration, unification, application management, and the transport system

462 pp., 2008, 69,95 Euro / US$ 69.95
ISBN 978-1-59229-145-8

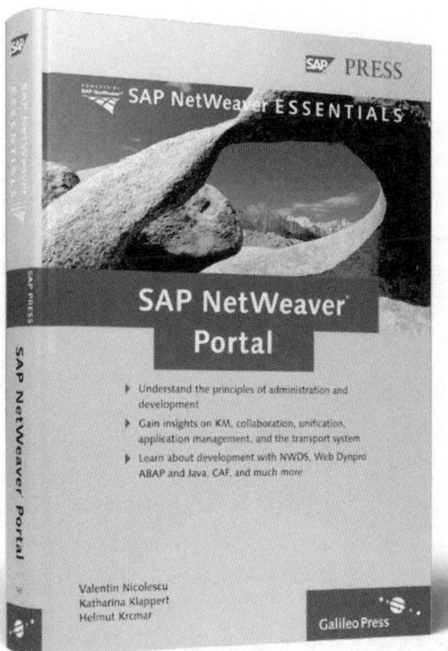

SAP NetWeaver Portal

www.sap-press.com

Valentin Nicolescu, Katharina Klappert, Helmut Krcmar

SAP NetWeaver Portal

This book introduces IT managers, portal administrators and consultants to the structure and application areas of SAP NetWeaver Portal (Release 7.0). A main focus is to describe key portal functions and the underlying architecture — all from the technical viewpoint. Topics covered include role management, authentication mechanisms, knowledge and content management, developing and administrating applications, application and system integration, as well as many more. Readers gain a solid technical grounding in all the relevant aspects of the SAP NetWeaver Portal, and the skills needed to effectively implement them in practice.

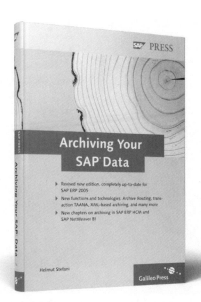

Expert insights on local SAP scheduling facilities such as CCMS, BI and Mass Activities

Techniques to maximize the full capabilities of SAP central job scheduling by Redwood

312 pp., 2006, 69,95 Euro / US$ 69.95
ISBN 1-59229-093-0

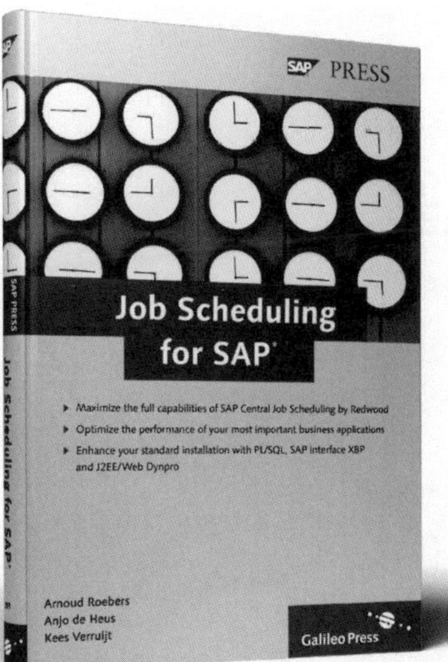

Job Scheduling for SAP

www.sap-press.com

K. Verruijt, A. Roebers, A. de Heus

Job Scheduling for SAP

With this book, you'll learn the ins and outs of job scheduling with "SAP Central Job Scheduling by Redwood" and "Redwood Cronacle." Uncover critical details on the architecture, plus exclusive technical insights that cannot be found elsewhere. The authors cover both decentralized and centralized SAP job scheduling and provide you with practical advice to drastically bolster standard installation and configuration guides. Special attention is paid to both individual CCMS and SAP BI jobs as well as to integration methods for these enterprise-level job chains. Best Practices from real-world case studies ensure that this book leaves no stone unturned.

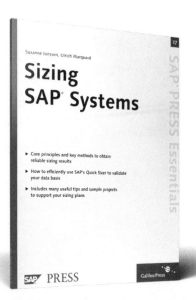

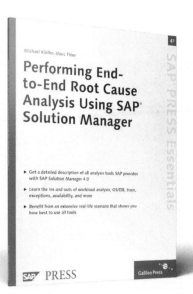